ENVIRONMENTAL LAW FOR SUSTAINABILITY

This volume of new essays presents critical new scholarship on law for sustainable development. Its contributors provide international and comparative perspectives on the current state of environmental law and its future directions. Aimed at both students and scholars in law and other social sciences, it goes beyond conventional descriptions of environmental law and policy to a theoretical and interdisciplinary analysis of the role of law in sustainable development. Starting from the premise that ecological sustainability requires environmental law systems to be sensitive to a wide array of institutional, social and economic issues and to emerging forms of environmental governance beyond conventional legal regulation, the book explores: future directions in command regulation; changing forms of public administration; risk assessment and precautionary regulation; ecological justice; public participation in environmental decision-making; indigenous peoples and the environment; industry self-regulation; economic instruments; sustainable finance; the state of international environmental law; and environmental law in developing countries.

Series: Osgoode Readers
Volume 1

The Osgoode Readers offer interdisciplinary and cosmopolitan treatments of the essential elements of a variety of legal fields. Each chapter in an Osgoode Reader takes the form of a critical synthesis providing a succinct, engaging overview and analysis of contemporary issues and problems that are both shaping and being shaped by the law. The core of each Osgoode Reader consists of newly written chapters that build on each contributor's recent field-leading work, alongside chapters that are revised versions of recently published articles that have been thoroughly reworked to suit the focus and flow of the reader.

Osgoode Readers are distinguished by their attention to fresh perspectives dealing not only with traditional legal concerns but also with newer challenges posed by changes in social, ethical, economic and political environments. Osgoode Readers are organized and their analysis framed in ways that are alert to comparative-law insights and are intended to be relevant across legal jurisdictions.

Each Osgoode Reader is primarily aimed at upper-year LLB and JD, as well as graduate law, courses as either companion volumes or core prescribed readings. Most readers will also appeal to law scholars interested in keeping abreast of current developments in their own field, as well as researchers new to the field in question.

Environmental Law for Sustainability: A Reader

Edited by

Benjamin J. Richardson
Professor at Osgoode Hall Law School of
York University in Toronto

and

Stepan Wood
Professor at Osgoode Hall Law School of
York University in Toronto

•HART•
PUBLISHING

HART PUBLISHING
OXFORD AND PORTLAND, OREGON
2006

Published in North America (US and Canada) by
Hart Publishing
c/o International Specialized Book Services
920 NE 58th Avenue, Suite 300
Portland, OR 97213-3786
USA
Tel: +1 503 287 3093 or toll-free: (1) 800 944 6190
Fax: +1 503 280 8832
E-mail: orders@isbs.com
Web Site: www.isbs.com

Hart Publishing, Salter's Boatyard, Folly Bridge, Abingdon Rd, Oxford, OX1 4LB
Telephone: +44 (0)1865 245533 Fax: +44 (0)1865 794882
email: mail@hartpub.co.uk
WEBSITE: http//:www.hartpub.co.uk

British Library Cataloguing in Publication Data
Data Available

ISBN-13: 978-1-84113-544-1 (paperback)
ISBN-10: 1-84113-544-5 (paperback)

Typeset by Compuscript Ltd, Shannon
Printed and bound in Great Britain by
Biddles Ltd, Norfolk

Environmental Law for Sustainability: A Reader

Edited by

Benjamin J. Richardson
Professor at Osgoode Hall Law School of
York University in Toronto

and

Stepan Wood
Professor at Osgoode Hall Law School of
York University in Toronto

•HART•
PUBLISHING

HART PUBLISHING
OXFORD AND PORTLAND, OREGON
2006

Published in North America (US and Canada) by
Hart Publishing
c/o International Specialized Book Services
920 NE 58th Avenue, Suite 300
Portland, OR 97213-3786
USA
Tel: +1 503 287 3093 or toll-free: (1) 800 944 6190
Fax: +1 503 280 8832
E-mail: orders@isbs.com
Web Site: www.isbs.com

Hart Publishing, Salter's Boatyard, Folly Bridge, Abingdon Rd, Oxford, OX1 4LB
Telephone: +44 (0)1865 245533 Fax: +44 (0)1865 794882
email: mail@hartpub.co.uk
WEBSITE: http//:www.hartpub.co.uk

British Library Cataloguing in Publication Data
Data Available

ISBN-13: 978-1-84113-544-1 (paperback)
ISBN-10: 1-84113-544-5 (paperback)

Typeset by Compuscript Ltd, Shannon
Printed and bound in Great Britain by
Biddles Ltd, Norfolk

CONTENTS

LIST OF CONTRIBUTORS

Carolyn Abbot is a Lecturer in Law at the University of Manchester. Before coming to Manchester, she lecturered at the Lancashire Law School. Her main research interests are environmental law and regulation, with a particular interest in the theory and practice of environmental law enforcement. She participated in a consultancy project for the European Commission that investigated criminal sanctions for environmental offences.

Klaus Bosselmann is an Associate Professor of Law at the University of Auckland and Director of its New Zealand Centre for Environmental Law. Previously, he was a judge and a law professor in Berlin. He is a member of the IUCN Commission on Environmental Law and the IUCN Academy of Environmental Law. His research interests include international and comparative environmental law, legal theory and environmental philosophy. He has been a consultant to the OECD, UNEP, the EU Commission and the governments of Germany and New Zealand.

Francis Botchway is a Reader in Law at the University of Hull and a Visiting Professor in Energy and Environmental Law at Leuven University. He was previously a Lecturer at Warwick Law School. He holds law degrees from Ghana, Dalhousie, Harvard and Manchester. His main interests are environmental law and international economic law. Francis has published widely in these areas and recently won the Willoughby Prize for his contribution to the IBA Journal of Energy and Natural Resources Law.

Robin Connor is a Senior Policy Analyst with the Ministry of Fisheries in Wellington, where he contributes to the development of the institutional framework for New Zealand's ground-breaking fisheries management system. Robin continues to work on independent collaborative research and publication projects in the areas of fisheries management and the institutional dimensions of sustainability and economic development.

Donna Craig is a Professor of Desert Knowledge at Charles Darwin University, working on Indigenous and arid lands research with the Desert Knowledge Co-operative Research Centre in Australia. She holds a joint appointment as Professor at the Centre for Environmental Law at Macquarie University. Donna has also participated in the IUCN's Specialist Group in Environmental Law and Indigenous Peoples, and is a member of the IUCN Academy of Environmental Law.

Stephen Dovers is a Professor at the Centre for Resource and Environmental Studies, at the Australian National University. He undertakes research and education in the areas of policy and institutional dimensions of sustainability, science–policy linkages, decision-making in the face of uncertainty, adaptive management and environmental history.

David Driesen is the Angela R Cooney Professor at Syracuse University College of Law. He holds a JD from the Yale Law School and served as an attorney in the Natural Resources Defense Council's air and energy programme prior to entering academia. His first book, *The Economic Dynamics of Environmental Law* (MIT Press, 2003) won the Lynton Keith Caldwell award for the best book of the year in science, technology and environmental studies.

Jaye Ellis is an Assistant Professor in the Faculty of Law and School of Environment at McGill University. She teaches and conducts research in the fields of international environmental law, public international law and global environmental politics. Research projects include principles of international environmental law, high seas fisheries, environmental protection in the high seas and Antarctica, and the international climate change regime.

Elizabeth Fisher is Fellow and Lecturer in Law, Corpus Christi College and the Faculty of Law, University of Oxford. She has written widely on issues of public law, risk and the precautionary principle in numerous different jurisdictions.

Ikechi Mgbeoji is an Assistant Professor at Osgoode Hall Law School. He teaches and researches in the areas of intellectual property law, with emphasis on patents, comparative intellectual property law and the legal regulation of biotechnology; torts; use of force in international relations; and international environmental law. Prior to joining Osgoode, he taught at the University of British Columbia. He holds graduate degrees in law from Dalhousie University, Canada.

Oren Perez is an Associate Professor at the Faculty of Law, Bar-Ilan University, Israel. He wrote his doctoral dissertation at the London School of Economics and Political Science (1997–2000) and won the Marie Curie Fellowship. His main fields of interest are environmental law, international economic law and legal theory. His recent publications include *Ecological Sensitivity and Global Legal Pluralism: Rethinking the Trade and Environment Conflict* (Hart Publishing, 2004).

Jona Razzaque is a Senior Lecturer with the University of the West of England, teaching EU law and environmental law at undergraduate and postgraduate levels. She previously worked for the Foundation for International Environmental

Law and Development (FIELD). Jona has also held academic positions at the University of London's Queen Mary College and University College London. She has published widely on access to environmental justice.

Benjamin Richardson is an Associate Professor at Osgoode Hall Law School. His principal teaching and research interests are Aboriginal law, environmental law and financial regulation. Previously, he lectured at the Universities of Auckland and Manchester. Also, he was a policy advisor in an Australian government nature conservation agency and a consultant to the IUCN on projects in Kenya and Nepal.

Stepan Wood is an Associate Professor at Osgoode Hall Law School, where he co-ordinates the joint LLB/Master in Environmental Studies programme. His principal teaching and research interests are environmental law, corporate social responsibility and voluntary codes. He is vice-chair of the Standards Council of Canada's advisory committee on EMS standards and a frequent Canadian delegate to ISO meetings. He worked previously as a lawyer in New York and a law clerk to the Supreme Court of Canada.

Law and Development (FIELD). Jona has also held academic positions at the University of London's Queen Mary College and University College London. She has published widely on access to environmental justice.

Benjamin Richardson is an Associate Professor at Osgoode Hall Law School. His principal teaching and research interests are Aboriginal law, environmental law and financial regulation. Previously, he lectured at the Universities of Auckland and Manchester. Also, he was a policy advisor in an Australian government nature conservation agency and a consultant to the IUCN on projects in Kenya and Nepal.

Stepan Wood is an Associate Professor at Osgoode Hall Law School, where he coordinates the joint LLB/Master in Environmental Studies programme. His principal teaching and research interests are environmental law, corporate social responsibility and voluntary codes. He is vice-chair of the Standards Council of Canada's advisory committee on EMS standards and a frequent Canadian delegate to ISO meetings. He worked previously as a lawyer in New York and a law clerk to the Supreme Court of Canada.

1

Environmental Law for Sustainability

BENJAMIN J. RICHARDSON* AND STEPAN WOOD**

A. Introduction

Some 40 years into the 'modern' environmental era, how much closer is humankind to an ecologically and socially sustainable relationship with its environment, and what role can environmental law, in all its various forms, play in securing such a relationship? These are the central questions addressed by this book. The answer to the first question remains sobering despite several decades of efforts at environmental regulation. There have been notable successes, especially in the advanced industrialised countries, but in the past five decades environmental change has been more rapid than at any other time.[1] Virtually all of Earth's ecosystems have been significantly transformed through human actions, causing widespread degradation of ecosystem services.[2] Far from improving since the 1992 Rio Earth Summit made 'sustainable development' the centrepiece of international and domestic environmental policy, most indicators of environmental quality have continued to deteriorate in most parts of the world.[3] As the governments assembled at the 'Rio+10' conference in Johannesburg recognised:

> The global environment continues to suffer. Loss of biodiversity continues, fish stocks continue to be depleted, desertification claims more and more fertile land, the adverse effects of climate change are already evident, natural disasters are more frequent and more devastating, and developing countries more

* Professor, Osgoode Hall Law School, York University.
** Professor, Osgoode Hall Law School, York University.

1 Millennium Ecosystem Assessment, *Ecosystems and Human Well-Being: Synthesis* (Island Press, 2005), at www.millenniumassessment.org.

2 *Ibid.*

3 UNEP, *10 Years After Rio: The UNEP Assessment* (UNEP, 2002).

> vulnerable, and air, water and marine pollution continue to rob millions of a decent life.[4]

Even in Western Europe, often considered to have the most sophisticated environmental laws, 'state of the environment' reports document little improvement in regional environmental quality.[5] As China, India and other large developing economies expand further and modernise, the planet will surely be placed under even greater ecological stress. The result of all this, as the board of the Millennium Ecosystem Assessment warned recently, is that 'human activity is putting such strain on the natural functions of Earth that the ability of the planet's ecosystems to sustain future generations can no longer be taken for granted'.[6]

What role has environmental law played in relation to these sobering trends, and what role might it play in reversing them? This is much more difficult to answer, and the goal of this volume is more to stimulate critical reflection on this question than to provide definitive answers. Law—understood in the conventional sense of official state law—has come to be widely accepted as a central vehicle for environmental protection, because of its ability to create authoritative standards and decision-making procedures for land use planning, pollution control and nature conservation, among many other elements of modern environmental governance. Yet debate rages over the existing and future contributions of law to sustainability, including the choice of legal instruments (eg Abbot, chapter 3, Driesen, chapter 9), the design of legal institutions (eg Dovers and Connor, chapter 2), the appropriate ethical foundations for environmental law (eg Bosselman, chapter 5), the role for public deliberation in law-making (eg Razzaque and Richardson, chapter 6), the relation between environmental protection and indigenous and other human rights (eg Richardson and Craig, chapter 7), the appropriate legal response to pervasive uncertainty and risk (eg Fisher, chapter 4), the choice of targets for legal intervention (eg Richardson, chapter 10), the prospects for environmental law in developing countries (eg Richardson, Mgbeoji and Botchway, chapter 13), and the role of various forms of legal ordering 'beyond' state law, from international law to corporate voluntary initiatives (eg Ellis and Wood, chapter 11, Perez, chapter 12, Wood, chapter 8).

[4] Johannesburg Declaration on Sustainable Development (2002), UN Doc A/CONF.199/20, at 1, para 13.

[5] See the reports of the European Environment Agency at www.eea.eu.int.

[6] Millennium Ecosystem Assessment, *Living Beyond Our Means: Natural Assets and Human Well-Being (Statement from the Board)* (pre-publication draft, Millennium Ecosystem Assessment, 2005) 2.

B. The Continuing Chronicle of Environmental Law

While 'modern' environmental law has its immediate origins in nineteenth century legislation[7] and antecedents in antiquity,[8] the so-called 'modern era' of environmental law dates from the 1960s, when a liberal political climate in Western nations, coupled with changing economic conditions and improved scientific understanding of humanity's ecological impacts, created the conditions for heightened public awareness and willingness to speak out about environmental deterioration. During the early 1960s the first signs of widespread concern emerged in the wake of the best-sellers *Silent Spring* (1962) by Rachel Carson[9] and *The Quiet Crisis* (1963)[10] by US Secretary of the Interior, Stewart Udall. They challenged the notion that maximisation of economic benefits to industry and commerce equated unequivocally with the social good.

Throughout the industrialised world a new model of environmental law emerged, entailing the creation of detailed pollution and planning statutes and new specialist agencies equipped with wide-ranging controls on the economy.[11] In the US, the Nixon administration founded the Environmental Protection Agency in 1970 to administer the National Environmental Policy Act 1969. In Europe, for instance, the Netherlands established a Department for Public Health and Environmental Hygiene in 1971, and in West Germany a Federal Environmental Agency and the Council of Environmental Advisors were established as a bridge towards a new administrative system for environmental policy.[12] These initiatives were often complemented by medium-specific pollution control legislation, following the precedents of the Water Pollution Control Act 1948[13] (in the US) or

[7] The UK was the first industrialising nation to introduce public environmental regulation, in the form of sanitation and town planning statutes in the mid-19th century: D Hughes, *Environmental Law* (Butterworths, 1996) ch 1. Other industrialising countries followed later: DAR Williams (ed), *Environmental and Resource Management Law* (Butterworths, 1997) 10–11. The trend was not restricted to the industrialising world. Practically all of India's forests, eg, were governed by forest management legislation by 1900: N Desai, 'Sustainable Development: A Brief Introduction' (2003) 15 *Georgetown International Environmental L Rev* 812, 813.

[8] Eg *Case Concerning the Gabcíkovo-Nagymaros Dam (Hungary v Slovakia)* [1997] ICJ Rep 7 (separate opinion of Weeramantry J).

[9] R Carson, *Silent Spring* (Fawcett Crest, 1962).

[10] SL Udall, *The Quiet Crisis* (Holt, Rinehart and Winston, 1963).

[11] The first specialist pollution control body, however, was Britain's Alkali Inspectorate, established in 1863, to address certain factory emissions: S Bell, *Bell and Ball on Environmental Law* (4th ed, Blackstone Press, 1997) 300. In relation to the US, see RF Blomquist, 'Clean "New World": Toward an Intellectual History of American Environmental Law, 1961–1990' (1990) 25 *Valparaiso University L Rev* 1.

[12] D Wallace, *Environmental Policy and Industrial Innovation. Strategies in Europe, the USA and Japan* (Earthscan, 1995) 63–4.

[13] Ch 758, 62 Stat 1155 (1948), codified as amended in various sections of 33 USC.

the Clean Air Act 1956[14] (in the UK). By the late 1960s, Japan had become one of the most polluted nations in the world, but a turn-around began with the famous 'Pollution Diet' of 1970, which passed a raft of comprehensive environmental protection measures.[15] The speed of these changes in the industrial economies was astonishing—Plater describing them as 'a massive upwelling of layer upon layer of substantial public and private law doctrines, almost volcanic in the power and mass of its eruption since the early 1960s'.[16]

Environmental regulation in this era was built upon the assumption that law can effect social change through direct and purposive intervention in the minute detail of social relations. In this instrumentalist model, which Teubner calls 'substantive' law,[17] the province of environmental law was to enunciate general environmental goals, such as clean air or water, or more specific targets for environmental quality, and prescribe in detail the behaviour required to achieve these goals. In this book, Abbot (chapter 3) traces the main contours of environmental regulation in this 'substantive law' model. By enacting environmental statutes and establishing specialised administrative agencies with delegated rule-making and enforcement authority, governments created complex, finely detailed regulatory regimes to intervene directly in environmentally harmful processes.[18] The dominant regulatory technique was 'command-and-control' regulation, involving essentially the prohibition of defined behaviour, often with licensed exceptions, and enforcement through a mix of civil and criminal law processes.[19] The theory was that governments would 'command' (often in minute detail) what polluters must do and how they must do it, and then 'control' the observance of these prescriptions through monitoring, inspection and enforcement.

Command regulation became the basis of a plethora of environmental law processes, including planning, environmental impact assessment, conservation area management, and pollution and waste licensing. Environmental regulation was predominantly sector-based and medium-specific, organised around industry-by-industry regulation of emissions of specific pollutants into particular media (air, water or soil). National environmental planning mechanisms and risk management procedures were also developed in this period, as Dovers and Connor (chapter 2) and Fisher (chapter 4) discuss.

[14] S Bell and D McGillivray, *Environmental Law* (5th edn, Blackstone, 2000) 411.

[15] See S Kawashima, 'A Survey of Environmental Law and Policy in Japan' (1995) 20 *North Carolina Journal of International Law and Commercial Regulation* 231.

[16] ZJB Plater, 'From the Beginning, A Fundamental Shift of Paradigms: A Theory and Short History of Environmental Law?' (1994) 27 *Loyola of Los Angeles L Rev* 981, 1003.

[17] Eg G Teubner, 'Substantive and Reflexive Elements in Modern Law' (1983) 17 *L & Society Rev* 239, 240, 253–4; Abbot, ch 3, this vol.

[18] E Orts, 'Reflexive Environmental Law' (1995) 89 *Northwestern University L Rev* 1227, 1257.

[19] Bell and McGillivray, above n 14, 177–89 (discussing the nature of environmental regulation from a UK perspective).

This growing edifice of command regulation was accompanied in many jurisdictions by state ownership of natural resources and nationalisation of—or at least a leading role for state enterprises in—some of the most environmentally harmful industry sectors such as energy, oil and gas and transportation.[20] The implication for environmental regulation was that in such jurisdictions some forms of resource exploitation and pollution were within states' direct control rather than in the hands of third parties that the state would regulate at a distance. In general, the 'command' model of regulation was extended only partially, if at all, into these state-controlled economic domains.

This model of environmental governance came under pressure even before it was fully developed in the industrialised democracies. While pressures came from many directions throughout the 1980s and 1990s, three developments were particularly influential: a reconfiguration of the state in the governance of society and economy, a change in the character of the environmental crisis, and the emergence of a global consensus around an agenda for corporate social responsibility.

First, the 1980s and 1990s witnessed widespread reconsideration and reconfiguration of the role of the state in the regulation of business, society and environment. Since the late 1970s the 'command' model of regulation has come under sustained attack, as Abbot (chapter 3) and Driesen (chapter 9) indicate. The assumption that law can transform society for the better by intervening directly and authoritatively in the substance of social relations was questioned on both empirical and normative grounds. Many commentators began to argue that command environmental regulation, whatever its early successes, had become too cumbersome, costly and rigid, and was nearing the limits of its technical capacity.[21] Some warned that it was at risk of 'break[ing] down under its own weight'.[22] Others warned that the proliferation of detailed legal regimes was leading to the 'juridification' of social spheres—a sort of socio-political sclerosis in which the state threatened to overwhelm the social relations it purported to regulate.[23] Yet others pointed to the new dynamics of globalisation, arguing that contemporary global transformations—from global financial markets and production networks to global environmental change—increasingly escape or overwhelm the regulatory capacity of territorially bounded nation states.[24]

[20] In many developing countries, this 'nationalisation' model of resource management was adopted without the corresponding edifice of command regulation or the redistributive institutions of the welfare state. See Richardson, Mgbeoji and Botchway, ch 13, this vol.

[21] N Gunningham and P Grabosky, *Smart Regulation* (Clarendon Press, 1998).

[22] Orts, above n 18, 1241.

[23] Eg G Teubner (ed), *Juridification of Social Spheres* (Walter de Gruyter, 1987).

[24] Eg D Cohen, 'The Role of the State in a Privatized Regulatory Environment' in K Webb (ed), *Voluntary Codes* (Carleton Research Unit for Innovation, Science and Environment, 2004) 35; S Strange, *The Retreat of the State* (Cambridge UP, 1996).

The idea of the 'limits of law', which had been around since Plato's time,[25] was vigorously reasserted by commentators from various locations on the political spectrum.[26] Analysts on the left argued that the ability of the liberal-democratic state to regulate economic activity is constrained by the requirements of the capitalist market economy.[27] The state is caught between demands to intervene and restrict the mechanism of capitalist accumulation in order to contain its social and environmental impacts, and the imperative to allow these mechanisms to operate relatively freely to produce the economic goods considered necessary to satisfy social welfare.[28] From a somewhat different perspective, critical legal scholars argued that the seeming neutrality of the rule of law reinforced existing power relations at the expense of vulnerable groups in society.[29] They also demonstrated the indeterminacy of law, associated with the rise of the regulatory state and the enhanced reliance on discretionary administrative powers.[30] Finally, as Abbot notes (chapter 3), scholars of 'reflexive law', drawing on critical traditions in Continental social theory, argued for a new form of law which, rather than dictating the details of regulated behaviour, would stimulate self-reflection and self-correction by regulated actors in line with regulators' goals.[31]

During the same period, but with more political success, neoconservatives launched a withering attack on the interventionist state from the perspective of both individual liberty and the superiority of free markets, enlisting neoclassical economics to argue that command regulation and the welfare state were inefficient, anti-innovative and ineffective.[32] Public choice and market liberalist theorists asserted the case of 'government failure', attacking the growth of bureaucracy and distortion of public policy by rent-seeking interest groups, and the consequential losses for the economy.

In this critical atmosphere, substantial changes were made to existing regimes for environmental regulation. Early neoconservative political successes in the US and Western Europe gave rise to a 'regulatory reform' agenda that was soon picked up and championed by the OECD and later the World Bank, the latter in the form

[25] Plato, 'Statesman' in RM Hutchins (ed), *Great Books of the Western World, vol 7: Plato* (trans B Jowett, Encyclopedia Brittanica, 1952) 580.

[26] Eg C Stone, *Where the Law Ends: The Social Control of Corporate Behavior* (Harper and Row, 1975); P Nonet and P Selznick, *Law and Society in Transition: Toward Responsive Law* (Harper Colophon, 1978).

[27] B Jessop, *State Theory: Putting Capitalist Societies in their Place* (Pennsylvania State UP, 1990) 356.

[28] See KJ Walker, 'The State in Environmental Management: The Ecological Dimension' (1989) 37 *Political Studies* 25; CE Lindblom, 'The Market as Prison' (1979) 44 *Journal of Politics* 324.

[29] See generally RM Unger, *Law in Modern Society: Towards A Criticism of Social Theory* (Free Press, 1976).

[30] See G Frug, 'The Ideology of Bureaucracy in American Law' (1984) 97 *Harvard Law Review* 1276.

[31] Teubner, above n 17, 254–6; Orts, above n 18; G Teubner, L Farmer and D Murphy (eds), *Environmental Law and Ecological Responsibility* (John Wiley, 1994) .

[32] For the principal economic arguments see Abbot, ch 3, and Driesen, ch 9, both this vol.

of 'good governance' prescriptions for developing countries.[33] In the hands of neoconservative governments such as those of Reagan and Thatcher, 'regulatory reform' appeared to consist mainly of deregulation and government downsizing. But deregulation was often accompanied by a growth of new regulation, as governments shifted from public ownership and direct service provision to arm's-length regulation of the provision of services by others in markets created by the retreating state. The paradoxical result was that the rise of neoconservatism, with its deregulatory rhetoric, was in practice accompanied by substantial increases in the number of regulatory agencies, the volume of official regulation and the domains of activity subject to official regulation.[34]

By the early 1990s, the debate over deregulation had been largely superseded by an agenda for 'responsive' or 'smart' regulation.[35] This was presented as a more nuanced alternative to the excesses of neoconservatism, which would see the state employ a sophisticated menu of regulatory instruments to 'steer' rather than 'row' the ship of state.[36] Social democratic political parties recouped much of the ground they had lost to neoconservatism in the 1970s and 1980s by building their political platforms around this new version of the regulatory reform agenda, most notably in Germany (Schroeder's Social Democrats), the UK (Blair's New Labour) and the US (Clinton's Democrats).[37] Under banners such as 'government reinvention', centrist governments throughout the industrialised world presided over a transformation of environmental regulation that was often more radical than that effected by neoconservative governments.

Several key themes characterise this contemporary transformation of environmental regulation. First, state regulation is increasingly concerned with setting overall directions, goals and environmental performance requirements, leaving details of implementation to be sorted out through inter alia co-regulation, negotiated agreements, and informed consumer choice. Secondly, governments increasingly employ private sector managerial methods and entrepreneurial ethics, and use markets and competition in the provision of public services.[38] Thirdly, there has been a substantial move toward public transparency and

33 Eg E Bardach and RA Kagan, *Going by the Book: The Problem of Regulatory Unreasonableness* (Temple UP, 1982); OECD, *Regulatory Reform and International Market Openness* (OECD, 1996); World Bank, *Governance and Development* (World Bank, 1992).

34 J Jordana and D Levi-Faur, 'The Politics of Regulation in the Age of Governance' in J Jordana and D Levi-Faur (eds), *The Politics of Regulation* (Edward Elgar, 2004) 1.

35 I Ayres and J Braithwaite, *Responsive Regulation: Transcending the Deregulation Debate* (OUP, 1992); Gunningham and Grabosky, above n 21; C Sunstein, 'Paradoxes of the Regulatory State' (1990) 57 *University of Chicago Law Review* 407.

36 D Osborne and T Gaebler, *Reinventing Government* (Addison-Wesley, 1992).

37 Eg US White House, *Reinventing Environmental Regulation* (USGPO, 1995); T Blair, *New Britain* (Fourth Estate, 1996); A Giddens, *The Third Way and its Critics* (Polity, 2000).

38 Eg K McLaughlin, SP Osborne and E Ferlie, *New Public Management: Current Trends and Future Prospects* (Routledge, 2002).

accountability since the late 1980s. With respect to private sector polluters this is evidenced, for example, by the proliferation of mandatory 'right to know' pollution disclosure regimes and voluntary corporate environmental reports (see Abbot, chapter 3, and Wood, chapter 8). In the public sector, as Richardson and Razzaque (chapter 6) relate, it is seen in the creation of increasingly robust mechanisms for public disclosure and participation (eg environmental impact assessment processes, environmental bills of rights), as well as an increase in citizen enforcement of environmental laws against governments themselves. Respect for human rights is a fourth theme in the contemporary transformation of environmental law. More attention began to be given to the rights and interests of minorities affected by development decisions, notably indigenous peoples (see Richardson and Craig, chapter 7).

Finally, the contemporary period is marked by experimentation with a more sophisticated mix of regulatory tools that seek to enlist, to the greatest extent possible, non-state actors and resources in the task of environmental regulation.[39] This includes experimentation with economic instruments such as taxes and tradable entitlements (Driesen, chapter 9), and voluntary instruments (Wood, chapter 8).[40] It also involves a new emphasis on 'meta-regulation', including state regulation of industry self-regulation, private actors' regulation of state activity, the state's regulation of its own regulation (eg regulatory impact analysis, creation of auditors-general), and international regulation of national regulation.[41] There is also increasingly a focus on new targets of regulation including 'gatekeepers' such as financial institutions and third-party-certification bodies (eg Richardson, chapter 10), along with an increasing reliance on information-based instruments, the public purse and capacity-building instead of formal legal authority.[42]

The second major source of pressure on the 'conventional' model of environmental governance prevailing in the industrialised democracies in the 1970s and 1980s was a transformation in the character of the environmental crisis facing contemporary society, or at least a transformation in the way this crisis was perceived. The environmental problems that commanded political attention in the industrialised democracies and in global environmental policy circles changed in important ways during this period, as problems such as acid rain, ozone depletion, climate change, persistent toxic substances and hormone-disrupting chemicals came to the front of

[39] Eg P Grabosky, 'Using Non-Governmental Resources to Foster Regulatory Compliance' (1995) 8 *Governance* 527.

[40] See G Bándi, 'Financial Instruments in Environmental Protection' in G Winter (ed), *European Environmental Law: A Comparative Perspective* (Dartmouth, 1996); OECD, *Environmental Policy: How to Apply Economic Instruments* (OECD, 1991).

[41] Eg Jordana and Levi-Faur, above n 34; C Scott, 'Private Regulation of the Public Sector: A Neglected Facet of Contemporary Governance' (2002) 29 *Journal of Law and Society* 56; GB Doern *et al* (eds), *Changing the Rules: Canadian Regulatory Regimes and Institutions* (U Toronto Press, 1999).

[42] C Scott, 'Regulation in the Age of Governance: The Rise of the Post-Regulatory State' in Jordana and Levi-Faur, above n 34, 145.

the political agenda. In the earlier period the most prominent environmental problems were immediately accessible to sensory perception and common sense: belching smokestacks, effluent-filled waterways, dead fish and birds, smog, oil spills, etc.[43] Many of them involved easily identified stationary sources and could be dealt with through simple end-of-pipe controls. Now, however, many of the most prominent environmental problems are more or less invisible, involve insidious processes that are not directly accessible to the senses and are the cumulative products of the activities of innumerable, highly dispersed, often mobile actors, most of which are operating within existing legal pollution limits.[44] Causal relationships are often unclear, and causes and effects are often separated across substantial spans of space or time, as Ellis and Wood (chapter 11) point out.

The new forms of ecological degradation differ from those faced by regulators in the 1960s and 1970s in several ways: they entail greater reliance on scientific expertise; the consequences of some problems, notably climate change, are latent and highly uncertain; and many problems are transnational or global in scale. In turn, many ecological dilemmas such as greenhouse gas emissions can only be effectively addressed, not through end-of-pipe solutions, but through strategies that fundamentally target economic growth and resource consumption patterns.

As the dominant understanding of environmental problems has changed, environmental regulation has changed too, in at least four directions: first, a shift in emphasis from 'local' to 'global'; secondly, a shift from end-of-pipe control to integrated pollution prevention; thirdly, an increasing tendency to rely on scientific expertise; fourthly, a shift in the characterisation of environmental protection from 'zero-sum' to a 'win-win' opportunity; and, finally, a shift in rhetoric from 'environmental protection' to 'sustainable development'.

First, increasing awareness of global ecological interdependence has posed major challenges to the state-centred world where environmental management responsibilities are largely territorially organised.[45] Environmental law has been influenced by the increasingly apparent transboundary character of ecological problems. Acid rain, ozone depletion and global warming, among other threats, cut to the core of our economic systems.[46] The primary response, show Ellis and Wood (chapter 11), has been the rapid development of a new body of international environmental law and institutions, overlying national legal systems.[47] This new

43 M Hajer, *The Politics of Environmental Discourse* (OUP, 1995).

44 *Ibid.*

45 See especially K Conca, 'Environmental Change and the Deep Structure of World Politics' in RD Lipschutz and K Conca (eds), *The State and Social Power in Global Environmental Politics* (Columbia UP, 1993) 306.

46 See eg F Pearce, *Acid Rain* (Penguin, 1987); P Read, *Responding to Global Warming: The Technology, Economics and Politics of Sustainable Energy* (Zed Books, 1993); RE Benedick, *Ozone Diplomacy: New Directions in Safeguarding the Planet* (Harvard UP, 1991).

47 PW Birnie and AE Boyle, *International Law and the Environment* (Oxford UP, 2000); A Kiss and D Shelton, *International Environmental Law* (Graham and Trotman, 1991).

emphasis on transboundary and global environmental problems and on regional or global management of such problems tends, however, to marginalise some of the environmental problems that are most pressing in developing countries, such as sanitation, clean water, soil quality and desertification, unless they can be linked to the global policy agenda (eg deforestation or toxic waste dumping).

Secondly, the conventional model of linear, reactive, end-of-pipe pollution control regulation may work reasonably well for basic local pollution abatement, but it probably cannot stop 'pesticides from reaching the poles, carbon dioxide from building up in the atmosphere, or hormonal imbalances from damaging fish'.[48] The new environmental problems call for integrated approaches to environmental regulation that seek to prevent environmental damage throughout the entire product life cycle, from initial conception, through raw materials extraction and industrial feedstock formulation, to ultimate end-of-life disposal. This was reflected in moves away from functional compartmentalisation toward holistic, cross-media environmental management, along with integration of environmental concerns into non-environmental agencies. It was also reflected in partial displacement of hierarchical command regulation by mechanisms designed to allow industry to integrate environmental concerns into its own cost and risk calculations (eg through economic instruments and the 'polluter pays' principle). Governments and other actors around the world have begun to experiment with such approaches, from the US Pollution Prevention Act of 1990 to the European Union's Integrated Product Policy of the early 2000s.[49]

Thirdly, because of the invisibility, complexity and uncertainty of the new environmental crises, governments are under increasing pressure to rely on scientific expertise to define the problems, prioritise them, and often conceptualise the appropriate solutions.[50] At the same time they are under increasing pressure to open environmental regulatory processes to public scrutiny and participation, as Richardson and Razzaque discuss (chapter 6). These two contending pressures pull environmental law in different directions, exacerbating a tension that has always been inherent in environmental regulation.

Fourthly, these tendencies in environmental regulation have been accompanied by a reconceptualisation of the environmental challenge as a 'win-win' proposition rather than a zero-sum game.[51] In the earlier period environmental protection was generally regarded as an unproductive cost that had to be imposed by regulation and absorbed by industry. The assumption that 'environmental protection is costly' was gradually displaced in public policy and business discourses by

48 B Wylynko, 'Beyond Command and Control' in RB Gibson (ed), *Voluntary Initiatives: the New Politics of Corporate Greening* (Broadview, 1999) 161, 161.

49 European Commission, *Communication on Integrated Product Policy*, COM(2003)302 final.

50 Hajer, above n 43.

51 *Ibid*; P Christoff, 'Ecological Modernisation, Ecological Modernities' (1996) 5 *Environmental Politics* 476.

the proposition that 'pollution prevention pays'. Environmental improvement was increasingly seen as an opportunity for business, opening up new markets, enhancing competitiveness and stimulating innovation.[52] As Hajer argues, what was previously seen as a fundamental threat to the system of industrial capitalism is now an opportunity for its renewal.[53]

This emerging consensus around the 'win-win' character of environmental problems was closely associated with a transformation in the central goal of environmental regulation, from environmental protection to 'sustainable development'. The idea of sustainable development as the animating goal of environmental policy began to emerge as early as the IUCN's 1980 World Conservation Strategy, and has dominated legal and policy discourse since the 1987 Brundtland Report[54] and the 1992 Earth Summit in Rio.[55] Based on conceiving economic prosperity as dependent on maintenance of environmental health, sustainable development is perhaps the most significant normative influence on environmental regulation today. It has 'reinvigorat[ed] governance' through the reformulation of environmental plans and new institutions and regulatory techniques.[56] At a regional level, it has been enshrined in the European Union (EU) Treaty as a fundamental objective,[57] and is a goal of the NAFTA Side Agreement on Environmental Cooperation.[58]

This brings us to the third and final development that has put pressure on the conventional model of environmental regulation, namely the emergence of a remarkably broad consensus around the notion of corporate social responsibility ('CSR'). The notion of CSR has been around for many years. For most of the twentieth century there was widespread disagreement whether it was possible or desirable at all.[59] While this debate continues,[60] it has been overshadowed since the late 1980s by a growing acknowledgement of corporations as partners in the

[52] M Porter and C Van der Linde, 'Green and Competitive: Ending the Stalemate', *Harvard Business Review*, Sept–Oct 1995, 120.

[53] Hajer, above n 43.

[54] WCED, *Our Common Future* (Oxford UP, 1987).

[55] By way of background, see V Koester, 'From Stockholm to Brundtland' (1990) 20 *Environmental Policy and Law* 14; P Sands, *Principles of International Environmental Law* (Manchester UP, 1995) 52–8.

[56] JC Dernbach, 'Sustainable Development as a Framework for National Governance' (1998) 49 *Case Western Reserve L Rev* 1, 7; see further NA Robinson, 'Legal Structures and Sustainable Development: Comparative Environmental Law Perspectives on Legal Regimes for Sustainable Development' (1998) 3 *Widener Law Symposium Journal* 247.

[57] Art 2, Consolidated version of the Treaty establishing the European Community [1997] OJ C/340/173.

[58] Art 1, North American Free Trade Agreement, Side Agreement on Environmental Cooperation (1993) 32 ILM 1480.

[59] Eg M Friedman, *Capitalism and Freedom* (U Chicago Press, 1962); J Wiener 'The Berle–Dodd Dialogue on the Concept of the Corporation' (1964) 64 *Colorado L Rev* 1458; DL Engel 'An Approach to Corporate Social Responsibility' (1979) 32 *Stanford L Rev* 1.

[60] Eg J Bakan, *The Corporation* (Penguin Canada, 2004).

quest for a sustainable future.[61] In this view, it is not only possible but desirable and profitable for business firms to take responsibility for their social and environmental impacts, respond to the interests and demands of a wide range of internal and external stakeholders and pursue the 'triple bottom line' of economic, social and environmental performance.[62] Rather than being (only) a part of the problem of environmental degradation, business is now seen by many governments, intergovernmental organisations and environmental non-governmental organisations as a part of the solution, a crucial partner whose participation, resources, knowledge and innovation are essential to achieve ecological and social sustainability. This reconceptualisation of the business–environment–society relationship works in synergy with both the realignment of the state and the redefinition of the environmental crisis discussed above, leading inter alia to more co-operative and flexible styles of environmental regulation and increased reliance on economic instruments and voluntary initiatives of the kinds discussed by Driesen (chapter 9) and Wood (chapter 8).

Despite these general trends in environmental law, one should recognise that the history of environmental law is not interchangeable across countries, and there are salient differences in styles of regulation, policy priorities and pace of reforms. Even within countries different approaches are evident, notably the special environmental governance arrangements that exist for indigenous communities, as discussed by Richardson and Craig (chapter 7). Vogel has documented differences in the national regulatory cultures of North American and European states,[63] though in recent years a combination of environmental and trade-related pressures has contributed to a certain harmonisation of environmental regulations.[64] But stark differences remain between the industrial, developed nations of Europe, North America, Australia and New Zealand, on the one hand, and the emerging economies of the South, on the other. In this volume, Richardson, Mgbeoji and Botchway (chapter 13) among other contributors discuss trends in environmental law affecting developing countries. Although they have often looked to the West for ideas and precedents, or adapted colonial-era laws, the nature of their regulatory law and policy often differs greatly from the experience of the North. In many parts of Asia, Africa and Latin America, environmental law

[61] Eg TN Gladwin, *Building the Sustainable Corporation* (National Wildlife Federation, 1992); M Hopkins, *The Planetary Bargain: Corporate Social Responsibility Comes of Age* (St. Martin's Press, 1999).

[62] J Elkington, *Cannibals With Forks: The Triple Bottom Line of 21st Century Business* (New Society, 1998).

[63] D Vogel, *National Styles of Regulation: Environmental Policy in Great Britain and the United States* (Cornell UP, 1986).

[64] See generally OECD, *Economic Globalisation and the Environment* (OECD, 1997); R Revesz, 'Federalism and Environmental Regulation: An Overview' in RL Revesz, P Sands and RB Stewart (eds), *Environmental Law, the Economy and Sustainable Development* (Cambridge UP, 2000) 37 (focusing on Europe).

has ostensibly begun to reach maturity, manifested by extensive legislative initiatives, the founding of environmental management agencies, judicial activism and the environmental jurisprudence created thereon.[65] But these achievements can be misleading. In reality, much legislation draws on Western models insufficiently tailored to local circumstances, and is poorly implemented due to insufficient institutional resources and broader problems of weak public governance.[66]

C. Law for Sustainability

This book is about environmental law *for sustainability.* The relationship between environmental law and sustainability operates in at least two directions. First, environmental law may have an impact on sustainability, in terms of whether it helps to move societies toward ecologically sustainable patterns of production and consumption. Secondly, sustainability—both as an idea and as a set of practices—may have an impact on environmental law, for instance leading to a preference for some legal doctrines, institutions or instruments over others. It is easier to trace the latter kind of effects than the former, but, given the complexity of socio-legal phenomena, it is difficult to assess either with any certainty. The contributions to this book nonetheless explore both of these dimensions in fruitful and imaginative ways.

No single conception of sustainability is shared by the contributors to this book, let alone the wider environmental law community, and no attempt is made here to impose one. In recent years, as indicated above, 'sustainable development' has emerged as the principal expression of the idea of sustainability in contemporary environmental law. As Dovers and Connor point out (chapter 2), 'sustainability' and 'sustainable development' are not synonymous. 'Sustainability' is a higher-order social goal or a fundamental property of natural or human systems, whereas 'sustainable development' is the variable (and we would add contestable) policy manifestation of society's attempts to address that goal and enhance that property.[67] Beyond this, sustainability remains essentially a contested discourse rather than a set of reified policy concepts and management procedures.[68] Many

[65] See B Boer, 'The Rise of Environmental Law in the Asian Region' (1999) 32 *University of Richmond L Rev* 1503; B Richardson, 'Environmental Law in Postcolonial Societies: Straddling the Local – Global Institutional Spectrum' (2000) 11 *Colorado Journal of International Environmental Law and Policy* 1.

[66] See U Desai (ed), *Ecological Policy and Politics in Developing Countries.* (SUNY Press, 1998); ED McCutcheon, 'Think Globally, (En)Act Locally, Promoting Effective National Environmental Regulatory Infrastructure in Developing Nations' (1998) 31 *Cornell International Law Journal* 395.

[67] Dovers and Connor, ch 2, this vol, at n 1.

[68] See T O'Riordan, 'The Politics of Sustainability' in K Turner (ed), *Sustainable Management: Principles and Practice* (Westview Press, 1988) 31 *et seq*, which includes a brief history of the concept of sustainability.

see sustainable development as riddled with ambiguity and contradictions that undermine its usefulness.[69] Some see it as a fundamentally flawed agenda for technocratic global management and continued depredation of the global majority and planetary life support systems.[70] The most publicised definition of the concept, that of the WCED, explains it as: 'development which meets the needs of the present without compromising the ability of future generations to meet their own needs'.[71] Among the many rival views in the sustainability discourse a broad distinction can be made between 'weak' and 'strong' sustainability. The former aims essentially to make our political and economic systems more 'environmentally sensitive', but without any fundamental institutional change. Strong sustainability, by contrast, demands radical institutional and policy changes in order to maintain the total stock of natural capital including biological diversity, as well as ethical and cultural change as against mere technological and managerial solutions.[72] Accordingly, some commentators prefer to speak of 'sustainability' rather than 'sustainable development', in order to eschew the exploitative connotation in the uncritical use of the word 'development'.[73]

So far, the sustainability discourse has coalesced into a set of fairly general normative principles, rather than a precise formula for environmental policy, as Wood and Ellis set out in the international context (chapter 11).[74] The *integration principle* suggests that development decisions should take into account their environmental sequelae.[75] The principle may be implemented for example through environmental impact assessment of project proposals, explains Abbot (chapter 3). The principle of *equity* has two major components. *Intergenerational equity* requires that the present generation ensure that the health and productivity of the biosphere is maintained or enhanced for the benefit of posterity.[76] Strategic environmental planning is one legal tool for this goal. *Intragenerational equity,* on the other hand, addresses justice between contemporary communities and nations.[77]

[69] M Redclift, *Sustainable Development: Exploring the Contradictions* (Routledge, 1989); SR Dovers and JW Handmer, 'Contradictions in Sustainability' (1993) 20 *Environmental Conservation* 217.

[70] Eg W Sachs, 'Environment' in W Sachs (ed), *The Development Dictionary* (Zed Books, 1992) 26; W Sachs (ed), *Global Ecology* (Zed Books, 1993).

[71] WCED, above n 8.

[72] See HE Daly and JB Cobb, *For the Common Good: Redirecting the Economy toward Community, the Environment and a Sustainable Future* (Beacon, 1989).

[73] See D Pearce, E Barbier and A Markandya, *Sustainable Development: Economics and Environment in the Third World* (Earthscan, 1990) (discussing a 'vector of development').

[74] See R Harding, M Young and E Fisher, *Sustainability – Principles to Practice* (Fenner Conference on the Environment, 1994).

[75] See RD Margerum and SM Born 'Integrated Environmental Management: Moving from Theory to Practice' (1995) 38 *Journal of Environmental Planning & Management* 371; P Bartelmus, 'Accounting for Sustainable Growth and Development' (1992) 3 *Structural Change & Economic Dynamics* 241.

[76] See EB Weiss, *In Fairness to Future Generations: International Law, Common Patrimony, and Intergenerational Equity* (Transnational Publishers, 1989).

[77] See I Voinovic, 'Intergenerational and Intragenerational Equity Requirements for Sustainability' (1995) 22 *Environmental Conservation* 223.

Protection of human rights and enhanced opportunities for public participation, as discussed by Richardson and Razzaque (chapter 6), provide one means to promote intragenerational equity. Legal protections for indigenous peoples' lands and environmental resources, suggest Richardson and Craig (chapter 7), is another way by which environmental law is becoming more sensitive to cultural and social justice issues. Finally, addressing inequities between the global 'North' and 'South' is an indispensable requirement of intragenerational equity, yet one of the most intractable problems in environmental affairs, as both Richardson, Mgbeoji and Botchway (chapter 13) and Ellis and Wood (chapter 11) demonstrate.

The sustainability principle that has attracted the greatest fervour is the *precautionary principle*, gaining recognition in EU and international law.[78] Given uncertainty about the long-term effects of human activities, the precautionary principle recommends taking preventive action before risks are conclusively established, since delay may prove to be more costly to society and nature.[79] In this volume, Fisher (chapter 4) looks at how environmental law systems have evolved to manage risk and to develop precautionary approaches to environmental policy-making. The question of costs is central to the principle of *internalisation of environmental costs*, which addresses the environmental externalities of market transactions and the degradation of public goods that are undervalued by markets.[80] The principle requires that economic decision-makers 'internalise' these values and costs, through eco-taxes and tradable emission permits for instance.[81] Driesen (chapter 9) examines this aspect of sustainability and highlights the array of economic instruments now being deployed by governments.

During the 1990s, states began to revamp their legal systems to provide a more strategic framework for sustainability. Many adopted grand environmental plans, complemented by specialist agencies with wide-ranging powers.[82] New Zealand was the first country to enshrine sustainable management as the guiding principle for its environmental decision-makers, through its foundational Resource Management Act 1991.[83] In Australia, a National Strategy for Ecologically

[78] E Hey, 'The Precautionary Principle in Environmental Law and Policy: Institutionalising Precaution' (1994) 4 *Georgetown International Environmental L Rev* 303, 307; Ellis and Wood, ch 11, this vol.

[79] See J Cameron and J Abouchar, 'The Precautionary Principle' (1991) 14 *Boston College International & Comparative L Rev* 1; D Bodansky, 'Scientific Uncertainty and the Precautionary Principle' (1991) 33 *Environment* 4.

[80] See M Massarrat, 'Sustainability through Cost Internalisation' (1997) 22(1) *Ecological Economics* 29.

[81] A variation on the principle is the 'polluter pays' principle: OECD, *The Polluter Pays Principle: Definition, Analysis, Implementation* (OECD, 1975).

[82] See generally K Ginther *et al* (eds), *Sustainable Development and Good Governance* (Nijhoff, 1995); K Hausker, 'Reinventing Environmental Regulation: The Only Path to a Sustainable Future' (1999) 29 *Environmental Law Reporter* 10,148.

[83] Resource Management Act 1991, s 5; see further O Furuseth and C Cocklin, 'Institutional Framework for Sustainable Resource Management: The New Zealand Model' (1996) 35 *Natural Resources Journal* 243.

Sustainable Development was enacted in 1992,[84] and the sustainability principles were codified as the statutory objects of various environmental agencies.[85] Sustainability concepts also appeared in Japan, featuring in the government's Basic Environment Plan of 1994.[86] In the US, an advisory President's Council on Sustainable Development (PCSD) was established in 1993, which later published *Towards a Sustainable America*.[87] Sustainability has featured strongly in Europe under the influence of the EC's landmark Fifth Environmental Action Programme and EU directives.[88] In May 2001 the European Commission issued a European Union Strategy on Sustainable Development.[89] Yet, while governments have generally been prompt to create a new layer of institutions, real progress in transforming their economies has lagged considerably.

Dovers and Connor (chapter 2) show that sustainability presents formidable policy and legal problems for governments. The likelihood of absolute ecological limits to human activity, the existence of irreversible environmental impacts and concomitant sense of policy urgency, and the systemic problem sources located in patterns of production and consumption are some of the challenges that demand greater innovations in policy instruments and management institutions.[90] More radical possibilities of reform have yet to be seriously advanced. These could include an emphasis on the promotion of ethical change, as argued by Bosselmann (chapter 5), to unseat the dominant anthropocentric and instrumental policies of environmental management. Alternatively, we could reform the underlying mechanisms of capital allocation that shape growth and investment. In this respect, Richardson (chapter 10) argues that the financial services sector (eg banks and mutual funds) must be reformed and harnessed as a means for promoting improved corporate environmental performance. Internationally, some such as Perez (chapter 12) stress the need for overhauling trade law and other international economic institutions that presently tend to sacrifice environmental considerations that clash with free trade and investment.

[84] Department of the Environment, Sport and Territories, *National Strategy for Ecologically Sustainable Development* (AGPS, 1992).

[85] Eg the Protection of the Environment Administration Act 1991 (NSW) s 6(1)(a) provides that the objectives of the Environmental Protection Authority include: 'to protect, restore and enhance the quality of the environment in New South Wales, having regard to the need to maintain ecologically sustainable development'.

[86] See Japan Environment Agency, *Basic Environment Plan*, at: www.eic.or.jp/eanet/en/pol/landp.html.

[87] President's Council on Sustainable Development (PCSD), *Towards a Sustainable America: Advancing Prosperity, Opportunity, and a Healthy Environment for the 21st Century* (PCSD, 1999).

[88] See eg N Haigh and C Lanigan, 'Impact of the European Union on UK Environmental Policy Making' in TS Gray (ed), *UK Environmental Policy in the 1990s* (Macmillan, 1995) 18.

[89] European Commission, *A Sustainable Future for a Better World: European Union Strategy for Sustainable Development*, COM(2001)264 final.

[90] See also S Dovers, 'Sustainability: Demands on Policy' (1997) 16 *Journal of Public Policy* 303.

Without a new wave of institutional reforms along these lines, it is doubtful that the current menu of environmental law instruments and policies will steer society away from its still largely negative trajectory. Is there hope of radical change for the better soon? Not necessarily. The sustainability discourse is in danger of being—indeed many would say it already has been—co-opted and tamed by interests opposed to fundamental economic and social policy change for the sake of the health and survival of the planet. It is dangerous to assume that human society will 'inevitably' progress towards more effective systems of environmental law. Crucial to the achievement of sustainable development is the need for institutional frameworks that can assist people to transcend the tension between short-term, individual self-interest and broader, long-term social welfare. To Goodwin, the core task is to reorient social and economic systems 'as if the future mattered'.[91]

D. Approach of The Book

Many of these aspects of environmental law and sustainability are explored in this volume. But the vast and complex nature of these topics makes it impossible to discuss them all intelligently within a single volume of essays. Thus, *Environmental Law for Sustainability* does not capture all facets of modern environmental law. For instance, it touches only briefly on property law instruments. The property rights movement, particularly influential in the US, has promoted controversial solutions like privatisation of publicly-held resources and reliance on common law tort remedies to ensure internalisation of environmental costs.[92] Nor does the book have the space to consider in detail many of the innovations in environmental law, including informational policy mechanisms (eg eco-labelling and corporate environmental reporting), nature conservation legislation or integrated pollution control. Nor does the book fully capture the diversity of national experiences. Many of the contributors focus on environmental law in Western economies, primarily because arguably the most comprehensive and diverse reforms have been pioneered here. Some chapters also canvass environmental law in the context of indigenous peoples, developing countries and international-level reforms. Nonetheless, all of the contributors have canvassed the relevant literature to give readers a gateway for further exploration in detail of these and other important topics of environmental law.

91 NR Goodwin, 'Economic Meanings of Trust and Responsibility' in NR Goodwin (ed), *As If the Future Mattered: Translating Social and Economic Theory into Human Behaviour* (U Michigan P, 1994) 45.

92 See B Yandle (ed), *Land Rights: The 1990s Property Rights Rebellion* (Rowan and Littlefield, 1995); TL Anderson and DR Leal, *Free Market Environmentalism* (Pacific Research Institute for Public Policy, 1991).

Environmental Law for Sustainability takes the form of a 'reader'—a collection of essays each providing a pithy perspective on some of the key roles of contemporary environmental law in promoting sustainability. The essays are not intended merely to survey and report on developments, but critically to appraise achievements, deficiencies and outstanding problems to be resolved. The edited collection is not, however, a reader in the traditional format. Rather than reproduce extracts from the 'classic' published works on the subject, this volume contains fresh writings that build on recent research undertaken by the contributors. Although anchored in contributions from Osgoode Hall faculty (Richardson, Wood and Mgbeoji), the reader provides views from a range of scholars based in Europe, North America, Australasia and Israel.

The volume is structured in four parts. Part I examines the state of 'command' regulation (Abbot, chapter 3)—the traditional mainstay of environmental law—and new directions in such regulation, involving risk management and precaution (Fisher, chapter 4). The institutional challenge of sustainable development, along with some of the prominent responses to this challenge, is also canvassed (Dovers and Conner, chapter 2). The social and human rights dimensions of environmental law for sustainability are considered in Part II. The chapters approach these issues from the perspectives of 'ecological justice' and ethical change (Bosselmann, chapter 5), public participation reforms to environmental law (Richardson and Razzaque, chapter 6), and indigenous environmental rights (Richardson and Craig, chapter 7). These chapters illustrate that sustainability is just as much about social justice and protection of cultural diversity as it is concerned with plants, animals and ecosystems.

In Part III of the reader, Wood (chapter 8), Driesen (chapter 9) and Richardson (chapter 10) review the growing reliance on economic methods and tools in environmental law. They include market incentives for improved environmental performance (eg eco-taxes and tradable emission permits), the role of the financial services sector (eg ethical investment and green lending), and the emergence of self-regulation and voluntary approaches to environmental governance.

The final Part of the volume canvasses some of the global and comparative law dimensions to the topic. These chapters highlight the current state of international law-making on the environment (Wood and Ellis, chapter 11), the interaction between international economic law and environmental policy (Perez, chapter 12) and the experiences of developing countries in building environmental law regimes (Richardson, Mgbeoji and Botchway, chapter 13).

Part 1

Environmental Regulation and Administration

2

Institutional and Policy Change for Sustainability

STEPHEN DOVERS* AND ROBIN CONNOR**

A. Introduction

This book deals with environmental law and the modern agenda of sustainable development.[1] The environment as a focus for law is a familiar domain in theory and practice, and legal responses to specific environmental issues in the past have tended to be straightforward regulatory measures. The policy agenda of sustainability is deeper and broader, highly contested and still evolving, and legal responses less confined to the regulatory category. Promoting sustainability requires changes to the way policy is made and to underlying institutional settings. It is increasingly appreciated that human institutions determining policy processes, legal regimes and the organisation of government are often causes of unsustainability and barriers to implementing plans for sustainable development. The paradox is that, while a major part of the problem, it is only through institutions that humans achieve social goals such as sustainability.

This chapter explores the requirements for serious policy and institutional change for sustainability, with reference to the role of law. This reflects the emerging understanding that the causes of sustainability problems are *systemic*, located deep in patterns of production and consumption, settlement and governance, and hence that policy and institutional responses must comprise multiple, co-ordinated strategies that attend these underlying causes.

In the face of worsening environmental and often human welfare conditions, traditional reliance on regulatory policy instruments for environmental protection, where individuals, households and firms are instructed how to act, has been

* Professor, Centre for Resource and Environmental Studies, The Australian National University.

** Senior Policy Analyst, Ministry of Fisheries Wellington, New Zealand.

[1] In this chapter, *sustainability* is defined as a higher-order social goal or as a fundamental property of natural or human systems, whereas *sustainable development* is the variable policy manifestation of society's attempts to address that goal and enhance that property.

strongly questioned. A common statement is that 'regulation doesn't work' and other policy approaches should be used, especially self-regulation, economic instruments and community empowerment.[2] Lawyers and others have been tardy in making two obvious rejoinders to this criticism. First, such claims are often unsupported by empirical analysis of the efficacy of regulatory programmes to establish whether regulation is a deficient policy response or whether the issue is poor regulatory design and/or implementation. Nonetheless, reliance on any one policy instrument is inadvisable, and regulation alone is unlikely satisfactorily to address complex problems.

Secondly, insufficient attention is paid to other roles of law and legal change as a component of policy and institutional change. Law offers more than regulation—defining agency objectives, mandating information gathering and other functions, structuring societal debate, guaranteeing public participation, ensuring transparency or creating new institutional forms. For policy and institutional change for sustainability such roles are crucial, and many are explored in other chapters of this book. This chapter aims to connect law to the larger arena of policy and institutional change, constructed in several parts:

—Section 1 introduces key concepts in the fields of public policy and institutional design.
—Section 2 discusses the nature of sustainability as a policy and institutional challenge, and why existing policy processes and the disciplines and professions that underpin such processes may have difficulty gaining purchase on sustainability problems.
—Section 3 uses examples of policy and institutional change to develop principles to inform policy and institutional change, under the broad categories of (re)framing problems and (re)organising government.
—Section 4 comments on the role of law in broader policy and institutional responses to four core sustainability principles: precaution, policy integration, multi-scale governance, and public participation.
—Section 5 discusses the need for adaptive approaches to policy and institutional change in the face of uncertainty.

The chapter describes the nature of policy and institutional change for sustainability and provides frameworks for analyzing and prescribing directions for

[2] Regulation in this sense is often referred to as 'command-and-control', a characterisation that is politically pointed in alluding to repressive centralised economies. There is also an assumption that environmental 'commands' have been enforced, which is often not the case. Officials in regulatory agencies might characterise the policy style, rather, as command-then-compromise. See generally, Abbot's chapter, this vol.

change—it does not present a menu of policy or institutional options. To do that would require significantly more space, and moreover the choice of policy approach or institutional form will depend on the political, legal, economic, social and environmental context.[3]

B. Defining Policy and Institutions

1. Key Terms

Analysing and prescribing policy and institutional responses to sustainability requires a consistent understanding of the terms 'policy' and 'institution', which are used variably across disciplines and in everyday life. This section provides a basis for consistent use and for applying these terms to the sustainability problems. Another requirement is for an appreciation of the nature of sustainability as a policy domain, the subject of Section 3.

Thinking about how policy is made and implemented has shifted over time.[4] Early characterisations of policy as a linear, rational process producing optimal responses to well-defined problems (the 'rational-comprehensive' approach) have given way to a recognition of complexity, political realities and imperfect information—policy problems are not 'solved' but rather addressed, re-formulated and revisited. A common approach is the 'policy cycle' model, recognising multiple policy systems and sub-systems nested within complex institutional settings.[5] So, rather than just governments making and implementing policy in a linear fashion, we must account for many policies, players, organisations and institutions interacting in multiple ways—policy processes operating within complex institutional systems. The following definitions provide clarity and recognise considerable complexity around core terms:

[3] This chapter draws on empirical work by the author and colleagues: S Marsden and S Dovers (eds), *Strategic Environmental Assessment in Australasia* (Federation Press, 2002); S Dovers and S Wild River (eds), *Managing Australia's Environment* (Federation Press, 2003); and especially R Connor and S Dovers, *Institutional Change for Sustainable Development* (Edward Elgar, 2004); S Dovers, *Environment and Sustainability Policy: Creation, Implementation, Evaluation* (Federation Press, 2005).

[4] A thorough introduction to past and current thinking in public policy is provided by M Howlett and M Ramesh, *Studying Public Policy: Policy Cycles and Policy Subsystems* (2nd edn, Oxford UP, 2003). For comprehensive treatments of government and public administration, see SE Finer *The History of Government from the Earliest Times* (Oxford UP, 1997); BG Peters and J Pierre, *Handbook of Public Administration* (Sage Publishing, 2003).

[5] Institutions in the sense discussed here are discussed in more detail by DC North, *Institutions Institutional Change, and Economic Performance* (Cambridge UP, 1990). For further perspectives, see RE Goodin (ed), *The Theory of Institutional Design* (Cambridge UP, 1996).

—*Institutions* are persistent, predictable arrangements, rules, norms, laws, processes or customs serving to structure and co-ordinate the political, social, cultural or economic transactions and relationships between individuals and groups in a society. They may be formal (eg, legal doctrines, rules of parliamentary function) or informal (eg, social norms). Although persistent, institutions evolve constantly. The role of institutions is to render transactions and relationships more predictable, thus reducing uncertainty in the way in which members of society interact, whether in resolving difference or working toward mutual goals. Institutions are embedded in complex, interactive systems of many institutions, organisations and actors (or *institutional systems*), and in understanding social and policy change this interdependency must be taken into account.

—*Organisations* such as departments, associations, agencies, etc, are manifestations of deeper institutions. Some may be persistent, recognisable and influential enough to be considered institutions, but generally organisations can be more quickly dissolved or radically changed (eg, a government department is an organisational manifestation of the rules produced by the institutional system of parliamentary democracy).[6]

—*Public policies* are positions taken and communicated by governments—'avowals of intent' that recognise and frame a problem in a particular way, and state what will be done about it. Policies are produced through multi-component and variable *policy processes* involving government and non-government players. The framework presented in Figure 1 and Table 1 is one representation of policy processes. Because of their cyclical, reiterative character, policy processes may also be referred to as *policy cycles*.

—*Policy programmes* are more specific and substantial manifestations of a policy, comprising elements of implementation as well as of intent. Beneath this level, for an applied policy, there will be a variable number of on-ground projects in particular places. For example, a *policy* on river conservation may include a *programme* of community-based water monitoring and remedial works, through which are funded discrete *projects*.

—Policy is influenced and formulated by multiple *policy actors*, as individuals and in organised groups. Around any particular issue there will be a discernible *policy community*, comprising all those actively involved in the policy

[6] It may be difficult to distinguish between institutions and organisations. For example, within an organisation, there will be internal 'institutions', rules, norms, reporting hierarchies, etc, and laws may be institutions in their own right but also policy instruments applied by a government in a specific context.

discussion. A smaller *policy network* will have responsibility for or power within actual policy formulation and implementation.

—The concept of *policy sub-systems* refers to the fact that, within the broader landscape of public policy in a jurisdiction, separate structures and processes exist for specific sectors or issues. That is, one can delineate the policy sub-system concerned with environmental policy as opposed to public health policy or between pollution policy and nature conservation policy.

—Within a policy network or sub-system, there are individuals or organisations often referred to as 'policy or decision makers'—those with the mandate and power to make policy. The concept of 'policy network' captures this, but there is an important further distinction—the *responsible authority*, with the legal competence and responsibility within the jurisdiction (nation, state or province, local government area, etc) to make formal policy decisions. The responsible authority may be an individual (eg, Minister or Secretary, senior official with *delegated authority* from government, or a court), or an organisation such as a government department or an industry association or firm. While policies are influenced by multiple decisions by different actors, someone is responsible and this may be defined by law or custom.

—*Policy instruments* are the 'tools' used by governments in partnership with other players to implement policies and achieve policy goals, for example a regulation, education campaign, tax or intergovernmental agreement.

—*Management* describes 'on-the-ground' actions both in implementing a policy instrument and the more tangible physical actions required. Policy sets the direction and management does things to achieve that direction.[7] Managers and policy-makers may be the same or separate individuals or organisations.

The term 'policy' is often used interchangeably to refer to all the above or to a specific policy statement issued by government (the policy statement) that may or may not define a problem well or detail actions to be taken. A policy statement is usually an 'avowal of intent', and may not describe crucial elements of a policy

[7] It is worth noting that while a distinction between policy and administration, or 'steering' and 'rowing', is at the heart of contemporary public administration theory, many critics argue that the two are indivisible and that the policy–administration dichotomy may be employed to mask and legitimise the delegation of critical political decisions to unaccountable executive agencies or private firms: eg D Beetham, *Bureaucracy* (2nd edn, U Minnesota Press, 1996) 94; Canadian Institute for Environmental Law and Policy (CIELAP), *The 'New Public Management' Comes to Ontario* (CIELAP, 2000) 31–2.

process that come *before and after* deciding a policy. Policy cycle models are often used to summarise this larger process. Such models should not be mistaken for what happens in reality or as strict guides to what may happen, but are devices to inform policy analysis and prescription.[8] With that in mind, Figure 1 presents a framework in the style of a policy cycle model, identifying stages within the policy process, and Table 1 details the constituent elements within those stages.

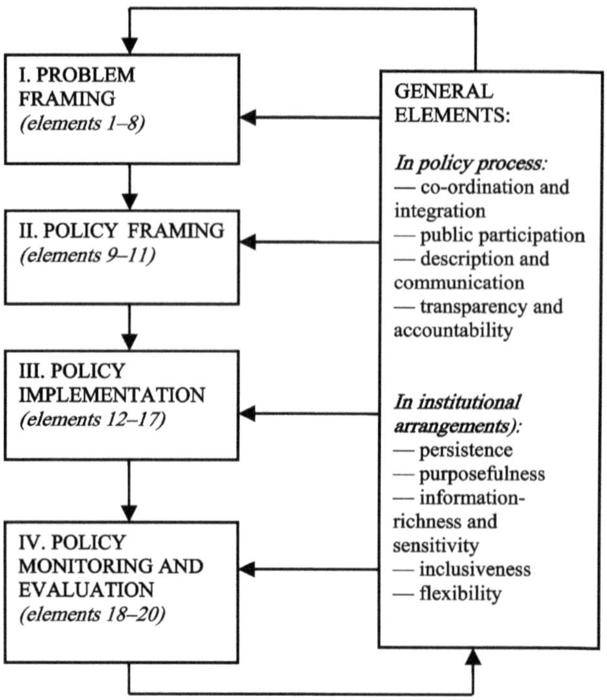

FIGURE 1: *Summary framework for analysis and prescription of environment and sustainability policy (for detail, see Table 1)*

[8] Many writers now tend toward interpretive rather than prescriptive characterisations of policy—eg. F Fischer, *Reframing Public Policy* (Oxford UP, 2003); M Hajer and H Wagenaar (eds), *Deliberative Policy Analysis: Understanding Governance in the Network Society* (Cambridge UP, 2003). However, a qualified prescriptive model is used here for clarity and brevity.

TABLE 1: *Detail of framework for analysis and prescription of environmental and sustainability policy (see Figure 1 for summary framework)*

Stage I: Problem framing:

1 Discussion and identification of relevant social goals
2 Identification and monitoring of topicality (public concern)
4 Identification of problematic environmental or human change or degradation
5 Isolation of proximate and underlying causes of change or degradation
6 Assessment of risk, uncertainty and ignorance
7 Assessment of existing policy and institutional settings
8 Definition (framing and scaling) of policy problems

Stage II: Policy framing:

9 Development of guiding policy principles
10 Construction of general policy statement (avowal of intent)
11 Definition of (measurable) policy goals

Stage III: Policy implementation:

12 Selection of policy instruments/options
13 Planning of implementation
14 Planning of communication, education, information strategies
15 Provision of statutory, institutional and resource requirements
16 Establishment of enforcement/compliance mechanisms
17 Establishment of policy monitoring mechanisms

Stage IV: Policy monitoring and evaluation:

18 Ongoing policy monitoring and routine data capture
19 Mandated evaluation and review process
20 Extension, adaptation or cessation of policy and/or goals

General elements, applicable throughout policy and institutional systems:

In policy processes:

—policy co-ordination and integration (across and within policy fields)
—public participation and stakeholder involvement
—transparency, accountability and openness
—adequate communication mechanisms (multi-directional, democratically structured).

In institutional arrangements:

—persistence over time
—purposefulness via widely recognised mandate and goals
—information-richness and -sensitivity, including gathering, use and ownership
—inclusiveness in policy formulation and implementation
—flexibility, through evaluation, experimentation and learning.

Again, this is not a model of how the policy world works but an analytical and prescriptive framework—a *checklist* of things best not forgotten. Although many elements appear obvious, frequent policy failure suggests that obvious elements of good policy are sometimes forgotten. In reality, the implied sequence may not be followed, with policy actors entering the process at various stages, and specific elements not so relevant as they have been fulfilled already. A key point is the emphasis on what comes *before and after* element 10 (policy statement)—the need for information, discussion, analysis and problem framing, and the critical demands of implementation, monitoring, evaluation and adaptation.

It is apparent from Table 1 that many disciplines, professions and knowledge systems and interests are relevant. Natural and social sciences and the humanities, indigenous knowledge, and community, NGO and industry perspectives are required in different parts of the process. Law can serve as an example. In stage I (problem framing), legal perspectives are required in elements 5–7 in Table 1, as statutory and related policy and institutional settings will influence underlying causes of unsustainable behaviours, sources of and responses to risk and uncertainty, and the assessment of existing policy. In stage II legal analysis can be critical to establishing principles and goals. In stage III, law plays a central role in policy instrument choice and implementation, providing institutional capacity, and enforcement. A legal basis for policy monitoring and review may also be required. Law is important also to embedding the general elements in Table 1—defining transparency and accountability, enabling public participation, and underpinning suitable institutional arrangements.

Although detailed, each element shown in Figure 1 and Table 1 conceals a complex area of theory and practice beyond this short chapter—the public policy literature offers more insights into such matters.[9] To indicate the detail beneath one important element, we can discuss policy instrument choice (element 12), recalling debates over the merit of regulatory versus other policy approaches.

2. Policy Instrument Choice

Policy instrument choice is a crucial matter, but is often based on convenience, disciplinary bias or familiarity rather than informed judgement, and debates over instrument choice tend to be simplistic arguments about which instrument is 'best'.[10] This is unsatisfactory, as no one instrument will always be the best, many options exist, and within general classes there are many specific instruments. Rarely is a single instrument used in implementing a policy, rather a mix of instruments is typically used, although perhaps with one instrument representing the chief strategy. For example, a price mechanism such as a tax will require a legislative base and some form of communication or education. In fact, there is

[9] See Howlett and Ramesh, above n 4; Fischer, above n 8;

[10] This tendency is beginning to change with the emergence of numerous more subtle, sophisticated analyses of the problem of instrument choice, eg N Gunningham and P Grabosky, *Smart Regulation* (Clarendon Press, 1998).

significant overlap among instruments—for example, a law may be an educative device or an institutional strategy, or be used to create messages (economic incentives) through penalties or price controls. With these considerations in mind, the main instrument classes include:

—*Research and development* (eg, atmospheric research, monitoring of environmental quality);
—*Information and education,* including publicity campaigns, formal education in schools, training programmes, award schemes, public reporting (eg, official 'state of the environment' reports, pollution inventories, corporate environmental reports), product certification (eg, ecolabels) and assessment procedures (eg, environmental impact assessment);
—*Economic instruments* designed to provide positive or negative incentives for specified behaviour, including property rights (eg, tradeable pollution or resource rights), taxes (eg, carbon taxes), charges (eg, effluent charges), user fees, fines, grants, subsidies (eg, tax breaks for wind power), liability rules and deposit-refund schemes;
—*Self-regulation and voluntarism,* including industry codes of conduct (eg, the chemical industry's Responsible Care), mandatory self-regulation, co-regulation, 'challenge' programmes (eg, greenhouse gas reduction challenges), industry–community agreements, voluntary government–industry agreements and voluntary covenants on property title (eg, conservation covenants);
—*Direct or 'command' regulation,* including government-mandated standards and targets, permits and licences, inspections, prosecutions and orders;
—*Legislation and quasi-legislation,* including statutes, delegated legislation (eg, administrative regulations), intergovernmental agreements (eg, the Kyoto Protocol) and internal or non-binding rules, policies or guidelines issued by administrative authorities;
—*Institutional and organisational reform,* including removal of conflicting policies; and
—*Deliberate inaction* ('doing nothing').

Faced with such a rich and potentially confusing menu of policy instruments, policy-makers may apply selection criteria so that the instrument(s) chosen suits the problem at hand. While selection criteria can be categorised in a variety of ways, it is useful to divide them into three groups.[11] First, *effectiveness criteria* address

[11] Useful sources on instrument selection criteria include Gunningham and Grabosky, above n 10, 387ff; L Pal, '"There Ought to Be a Law!" Instrument Choice: An Overview of the Issues', Research and Statistics Division Strategic Issues Series (Canadian Department of Justice, 2000).

instruments' effectiveness in achieving the policy-maker's goals and include efficiency (cost-benefit analysis), cost-effectiveness, information requirements, dependability (to achieve goals), corrective vs. antidotal focus (address symptoms or causes), flexibility (across contexts, time), influence on other policy sectors and impacts on equity. *Procedural criteria* address the processes by which instruments are chosen and include transparency, accountability, inter-agency co-ordination and stakeholder participation. Finally, *implementation criteria* address obstacles to implementation of the chosen instrument(s) and include costs over time, political and social acceptability, legal and constitutional constraints, institutional feasibility, monitoring requirements, ease of enforcement or evasion, and ease of communication to those affected.

That informed instrument choice is complicated should not surprise, as policy interventions to enhance sustainability are intended to change the behaviour of individuals and groups operating in complex social systems, interacting with complex natural systems. Neither should it surprise that a common reaction to complexity, in the face of demands for quick policy responses, is reliance on simplifying strategies such as ideology or recourse to the familiar. However, rarely is a single instrument used, but rather a mix of instruments even when one represents the dominant strategy.

One way to make sense of the complexity of instrument choice is to think of *instruments as information* intended to change the behaviour of individuals and groups. The task then is selecting the best media for the message. Three classes of instrument, though, will always be required, even if as minor elements. These are *legal*, in societies subject to the rule of law where policy interventions without legal basis can be challenged; *institutional*, because humans achieve social goals only through institutions and implementation requires a suitable institutional setting; and *educational*, because people expected to implement or comply with a policy intervention must understand its logic and implications.

'Policy intervention' is a strong term, but reflects the reality that policy and institutional change for sustainability aims to change individual and/or group behaviours. This is true whether a policy instrument is applied by government alone, in partnership with other actors, or by non-government actors such as community groups or industry associations. All policy is social engineering, aiming to change the way people produce and consume and interact with the environment and other people. Considering policies as messages conveyed through institutional systems prompts us to approach the question of instrument choice as a problem of selecting the best media for the message. Understanding institutions as the arrangements which structure material, financial or informational *transactions* between individuals and groups reinforces this. In terms of policy and institutional change for sustainability, it also prompts us to reflect on the nature of sustainability problems.

C. Sustainability as Policy and Institutional Challenge

1. The Nature of Sustainability

It is important to recognise the complexity of the sustainability idea, where the crucial shift has been to place on a single research and policy agenda three categories of issues—traditional resource and environmental issues (nature conservation, pollution, resource use, etc), higher-order issues concerning the integrity of entire natural systems (nutrient cycles, global climate, evolutionary viability of ecosystems, etc), and societal, economic and human development issues (poverty, production and consumption, urbanisation, health, human rights, security, etc). To comprehend and deal with such issues as interdependent rather than separate is a massive task.

Sustainability is not a simple or achievable goal and sustainable development a policy challenge not achievable in the short term. One author describes sustainable development as the universally agreed goal of human progress.[12] While this claim remains controversial, sustainability is best understood as a *higher order social goal* akin to other goals widely supported in a given society, such as democracy, equity, religious conformity, rule of law or justice. Such goals are contested and not quickly achieved, but are generational tasks to be pursued persistently over decades, through concerted learning and policy and institutional change.[13]

2. The Sustainability Policy Agenda

(a) Key Principles

While the sustainability policy agenda is often traced to the 1992 UN Conference on Environment and Development, concern over the long-term sustainability of human societies goes back further.[14] The modern idea of sustainability can be dated from the classic 'Spaceship Earth' essay by economist Kenneth Boulding in 1966, and the modern sustainability debate from 1972 and the first international meeting on environment held at Stockholm and the publication of the controversial *Limits to*

[12] P Harrison, *The Third Revolution: Population, Environment, and a Sustainable World* (Penguin, 1992).

[13] Connor and Dovers, above n 3.

[14] United Nations (UN), *Agenda 21: The Programmeme of Action From Rio* (UN, 1992); and see SV Boyden, *Western Civilisation in Biological Perspective: Patterns in Biohistory* (Clarendon Press, 1987); C Ponting, *A Green History of the World* (Penguin, 1990); JR McNeil, *Something New Under the Sun: An Environmental History of the Twentieth Century* (Penguin, 2001), and a number of articles in vol 1(1) of the *Journal of Ecological Economics*.

Growth.[15] The 1980 World Conservation Strategy and subsequent national strategies evidenced evolution of understanding of the problems and challenges. These concerns were focused by the World Commission on Environment and Development in 1987, building upon previous United Nations processes on environment, human development and security.[16] Further back, concern over resource depletion is very old, from Ancient Greece through to the eighteenth to nineteenth-century classical economists, and traditional societies that incorporated concern for natural systems in customary law.[17]

The sustainability policy agenda is not static or uncontested, but international agreements and much national policy have the following central elements, stated as principles or instructions to those involved in making policy:[18]

—An overall objective of a pattern of economic and human development that does not damage the opportunities for future generations to use natural resources and enjoy a healthy environment, while allowing for human development goals, especially for the world's poor, to be met in the near term.
—Recognition that all mainstream social and policy goals must include concern for:
  —the importance of biodiversity and ecological life support systems;
  —the need to treat environment and development in an integrated way rather than as competing considerations.
—Guiding principles for policy-and decision-making:
  —factoring in both short and long term considerations;
  —integrating environmental, social and economic concerns;
  —taking precautionary measures in the face of possible serious environmental degradation (Precautionary Principle);
  —considering global implications of domestic policy directions;
  —utilising innovative policy approaches, such as participation, institutional change and market mechanisms; and
  —involving communities in decision-making.

These are general in nature, and many international and national policy statements and interest group manifestoes detail targets and actions. Such *principles*

[15] K Boulding, 'The Economics of the Coming Spaceship Earth' in H Jarrett (ed), *Environmental Quality in a Growing Economy* (Johns Hopkins UP, 1966) 3; DH Meadows *et al*, *The Limits to Growth: A Report For the Club of Rome's Project on the Predicament of Mankind* (Universal Books, 1972); Declaration of the United Nations Conference on the Human Environment (Stockholm Declaration) 1972, 11 ILM 1416.

[16] UN, above n 14.

[17] For a survey of such historical antecedents, see eg *Case Concerning the Gabcikovo-Nagymaros Project (Hungary/Slovakia)*, [1997] ICJ Rep 3, Separate Opinion of Judge Weeramantry.

[18] This draws on international documents such as the 1992 Rio Declaration, and the way in which such statements have been translated into domestic policy in various countries: see also L Elliott, *Global Politics of the Environment* (Palgrave Macmillan, 2004); WM Lafferty and J Meadowcroft (eds), *Implementing Sustainable Development* (Oxford UP, 2000).

are to be applied in policy processes dealing with any of the suite of substantive *issues*, so a large number of issues and principles will be on a policy agenda. This creates a potentially confusing situation, but one that can be clarified by the hierarchy illustrated in Table 2, which uses two examples to identify the elements of a policy agenda, one under the social goal of sustainability and the other under the goal of public health.

An important distinction in Table 2 is that between a *substantive issue* (observed or predicted situation perceived as either undesirable or as offering positive opportunity) and the restatement of this issue as one or more *policy problems* (tractable and amenable to a policy response). Governments and other policy actors not only address problems confronting them, but invent and reframe them.[19]

(b) Issues versus Problems

From a policy perspective, recognising substantive issues is only the start of the process of identifying and clarifying policy problems that can be addressed through policy and institutional change (Figure 1). To give a further example,

TABLE 2: *Hierarchy of elements of a policy agenda*

	Example 1	*Example 2*
Social goal	***Public health***	***Sustainability***
Substantive issue (example)	Sub-standard health outcomes in disadvantaged households.	Climate change/global warming.
Policy problem (selected)	Increase access/use of medical services by poor households.	Reduce energy-related greenhouse gas emissions.
Policy principles (selected)	Equity of access; efficiency in public expenditure.	Polluter/beneficiary pays; precaution; equity; regional economic considerations.
Policy (selected)	Universal health scheme.	Prices in energy sector to reflect environmental costs.
Policy actions/ instruments (selected)	Income-tested health services card entitling holder to reduced cost services; subsidies to doctors information campaign.	Carbon tax at 'well-head'; enabling legislation; tax revenue funds adjustment grants to energy producing regions and rebates for poor households.

[19] On this, see M Hajer, *The Politics of Environmental Discourse* (Clarendon Press, 1995); N Rose, *Powers of Freedom: Reframing Political Thought* (Cambridge UP, 1999).

'biodiversity' is a scientific idea conveying the diversity of life at genetic, species and ecosystem scales, and the notion that maintenance of such diversity is necessary for the functioning of natural systems and of services they supply to society. 'Protecting biodiversity' is a social goal, associated with which are a large number of actual policy problems, such as regulating illegal wildlife harvests or providing incentives for the retention of native vegetation on private land.

It is widely believed that sustainability problems are particularly difficult to understand and resolve, but it is important to consider carefully what makes them so. Table 3 summarises the key attributes of policy problems in sustainability. It

TABLE 3: *Attributes of policy problems in sustainability*

1. Broadened and variable spatial scales, and broadened and deepened temporal scales, very different from the scales typifying political, social and economic systems and processes.
2. Possible absolute ecological limits to human activities, and possible sudden changes (threshold effects) in natural systems.
3. Often cumulative rather than discrete environmental impacts of human activities.
4. Irreversible impacts, and related policy urgency and high stakes.
5. Complexity within and connectivity between problems, both within and across the three arenas of environment, society and economy.
6. Pervasive risk and uncertainty, and lack of information on the state of the environment, human impacts, implications of these impacts and efficacy of policy and management interventions.
7. New moral dimensions, concerning non-human species and future human generations, and multiple interests and values.
8. Systemic rather than simple problem causes, embedded in patterns of production, consumption, settlement and governance.
9. Lack of uncontested research methods, policy instruments and management approaches, and need for new, integratative or interdisciplinary approaches
10. Key environmental assets not traded in formal markets and thus not assigned economic value.
11. Poorly defined roles and responsibilities for resource and environmental policy and management, and poorly defined property rights over environmental resources.
12. A mixture of public and private costs and benefits arising from use of the environment.
13. Strong demands and justification for community participation in policy formulation and on-ground environmental management.
14. Sheer novelty as a suite of policy problems, stated only recently as a formal policy agenda.

is important to note that not all are evident for any one issue or problem and many are interrelated.[20]

Some attributes in Table 3 are particular to sustainability and large-scale environmental problems, such as concern for other species, ecological thresholds and temporal scale. Others are encountered in other policy domains, such as uncertainty, public–private costs and benefits, or demands for participation. However, taken together, they lead to two critical suggestions.

First, significant sustainability issues such as climate change, biodiversity or integrated land and water management evidence these attributes more often, and more often in combination, than is the case with many other policy issues such as service delivery or economic development. This implies that *sustainability problems are different in kind* from many problems in other policy domains. Existing policy processes, institutions, professional skills and research and analytical approaches have evolved against problems that do not display these attributes so often, so there is a prima facie case that existing policy approaches, institutional arrangements and knowledge systems may have difficulty handling sustainability problems. Other policy problems are not 'easy', nor are related disciplines deficient, but sustainability is a different problem set that requires different approaches and knowledge.

Secondly, identification of such attributes focuses attention on the adequacy of policy responses *across a range of issues and problems* rather than separately. An example can illustrate. Tradable resource rights are increasingly proposed in water management and have been implemented widely in fisheries management.[21] The policy communities and research bodies concerned with these two sectors are largely unconnected, and the argument that rights markets in water might be informed by empirical analysis of the fisheries experience with individual transferable quota is often met with the comment 'that's fish, this is water'. However, recognising common problem attributes (Table 3, 10–12) rather than isolating the problems in separate sectors, invites joint policy analysis and learning.

The recognition of the common attributes of sustainability problems suggests the need for whole-of-field understanding, capacities and institutional and policy settings.[22] Table 4 attempts to give a sense of what such a whole-of-field approach might involve, summarising the core policy and institutional challenges in sustainability.

The sustainability agenda and the more specific challenges defined in Table 4 have been responded to in various ways by governments and policy communities.

[20] S Dovers, 'Sustainability: Demands on Policy' (1997) 16 *Journal of Public Policy* 303.

[21] OECD, *Tradeable Permits: Policy Evaluation, Design, and Reform* (OECD, 2004).

[22] Intellectual and practical responses to the nature of sustainability problems are the subject of an active and expanding literature. For reviews see F Berkhout, M Leach and I Scoones (eds), *Negotiating Environmental Change: New Perspectives from the Social Sciences* (Edward Elgar, 2002); E Page and J Proops (eds), *Environmental Thought* (Edward Elgar, 2003).

TABLE 4: *Environment and sustainability: policy and institutional challenges*

Challenge	*Explanation: Sustainability requires policy and institutional settings that. . . .*
1. Long term policy	Emphasise longer term ('supra-electoral') considerations alongside nearer term imperatives.
2. Inter- and intra-generational equity	Require and/or enable explicit balancing and/or integration of equity considerations across generational time spans.
3. Global dimensions	(a) Recognise and act upon global dimensions of sustainability problems, and (b) connect domestic and international information strategies, understanding, policy processes and institutions.
4. Policy integration	Allow and/or enforce integration and joint analysis of environmental, social and economic factors and policy.
5. Biodiversity and ecological processes	Place higher priority on protection and management of biodiversity and underlying ecological processes.
6. Resource use	Ensure sustainable extraction of renewable resources, and manage the use of non-renewable resources to ensure longer term satisfaction of human development needs.
7. Information focus	Encourage and/or demand high priority on information gathering, dissemination and use, and connections between information systems and policy processes.
8. Precaution	Mandate pro-environment and -sustainability decisions in the face of uncertainty (proactive rather than reactive policy).
9. Inter-jurisdictional	Where necessary due to the spatial scale of problems, allow and/or enforce management, policy and institutional responses across political, geographic and administrative boundaries.
10. Participation	Encourage and enable the participation of interested and affected members of the public in higher-order policy and in on-ground management.
11. Innovative policy approaches	Enable and experiment with innovative policy approaches, such as information-based strategies, institutional reform, community-based management or market-based instruments

(c) Policy and Institutional Responses

Existing policy and institutional responses to sustainability vary significantly across jurisdictions, issues and sectors. Conveying that detail is impossible, but an overall characterisation can be sketched.[23] A significant number of international policies and agreements on environment and sustainability have been developed, although the implementation and strength of these agreements have attracted criticism.[24] These range from general ones on sustainability (eg, emerging from Rio in 1992 and Johannesburg in 2002)[25], through global agreements on issues such as fisheries, forests, biodiversity and climate change,[26] to countless more specific regional or bilateral agreements. Less impressive but still positive and noticeable has been implementation of such agreements at national level.

Most national and sub-national (state, provincial) governments have a sustainable development policy, implemented to a greater or lesser degree.[27] Sectoral or issue-defined policies exist in abundance—greenhouse, biodiversity, fisheries, pollution, energy, wastes, water resources, etc—and again the effectiveness of implementation varies widely. In terms of the policy styles and instruments used to give effect to policies, the traditional mainstays of environmental policy, regulation and public education, have increased in application even as they have come under question.[28] This questioning recognises the complexity of the causes of unsustainable behaviours, and seeks to address the incentive structures and other determinants of behaviour rather than simply issuing instructions. What are termed 'new environmental policy instruments' are increasingly advocated and used, especially market mechanisms, self-regulation by industry and partnership approaches involving multiple interest groups.[29] The involvement of communities in on-ground management activities, and to a lesser extent of stakeholder groups in policy formulation, has also become more popular.[30]

There has been much experimentation with new organisational forms, such as 'mega-departments' that cover multiple sectors, integrated catchment management bodies, inclusive national councils for sustainable development (NCSD), and

[23] Country reports to various UN agencies, and particularly to the Commission for Sustainable Development, are a source of detail on national scale responses, as are the series of Performance Reviews published by the Organisation for Economic Cooperation and Development (OECD).

[24] See G Speth (ed), *Worlds Apart: Globalisation and the Environment* (Island Press, 2003); Elliott, above n 18.

[25] Rio Declaration on Environment and Development 1992, 31 ILM 874; Johannesburg Declaration on Sustainable Development (2002), at www.johannesburgsummit.org.

[26] Eg Agreement for the Implementation of the Provisions of the United Nations Convention on the Law of the Sea of 10 Dec 1982 relating to the Conservation and Management of Straddling Fish Stocks and Highly Migratory Fish Stocks 1995, 34 ILM 1542; UN Framework Convention on Climate Change 1992, 31 ILM 849.

[27] For an analysis of selected strategies, see D Swanson *et al*, *National Strategies for Sustainable Development: Challenges, Approaches and Innovations in Strategic and Co-ordinated Action* (International Institute for Sustainable Development, 2004).

[28] See eg Abbot's ch, this vol.

[29] See Gunningham and Grabosky, above n 10; T Sterner, *Policy Instruments for Environmental and Natural Resource Management* (Resources for the Future Press, 2002); H Pellikaan and RJ van der Veen, *Environmental Dilemmas and Policy Design* (Cambridge UP, 2002). See also Part III of this book.

[30] See Richardson and Razzaque, this vol.

whole-of-government mechanisms including commissioners for environment or offices of sustainability within central agencies.[31] 'Multi-stakeholder partnerships' or processes (MSP) have become a strong trend, especially in developing countries where institutional capital may be otherwise in short supply. However, the institutionalisation of such partnerships in terms of mandate, resources and permanence has not progressed far: few governments willingly give up legal and decision-making power. Overall, sustainability has yet to become a widespread core principle in policy or governance, and lacks the institutional underpinnings to raise it to supplant economic and social considerations as the primary policy drivers and criteria by which success in governance is judged.

Responses thus far are widely viewed as insufficient, with even official national and international policies recognising this.[32] But precisely 'how much' policy and institutional reform is needed is inherently contestable and impossible to define in the face of uncertainty and complexity. The degree of change required to embark on a transition to sustainability is certainly not trivial, definitely significant, and perhaps profound. For the purposes of the next part of this chapter, which is to distil lessons from experiences in institutional change, it is more tractable to ask not what degree of change, but rather what *kind*.

The five general elements regarding institutions identified in Table 1 are broad characteristics of institutions, organisations, management regimes and policy processes that define an 'adaptive' approach: that is, an approach which engages in positive change, but in a closely monitored fashion allowing ongoing learning and improvement:

—persistence over time;
—purposefulness via widely recognised mandate and goals;
—information-richness and -sensitivity, including gathering, use and ownership;
—inclusiveness in policy formulation and implementation; and
—flexibility, through evaluation, experimentation and learning.

It is difficult to identify clearly 'successful' policy and institutional responses in these terms, but we can look for believable cases of reform reflecting these five principles and learn from them.

[31] There is the broader issue of what are known as whole-of-government or 'connected' arrangements in public policy and administration in many jurisdictions better to implement cross-sectoral policy, including often at new organisational or spatial scales (especially regional and local): see H Sullivan and C Skelcher, *Working Across Boundaries: Collaboration in Public Services* (Palgrave, 2002). This is associated with larger forces of change in public administration, eg T Christensen and P Lægreid (eds), *New Public Management: the Transformation of Ideas and Practice* (Ashgate, 2002); K McLaughlin, SP Osborne and E Ferlie (eds), *New Public Management: Current Trends and Future Prospects* (Routledge, 2002).

[32] Eg UN, *Plan of Implementation of the World Summit on Sustainable Development* (UN, 2002).

D. Cases and Principles for Policy and Institutional Change

1. Overview

This section draws a set of principles to inform policy and institutional change from five case studies that represent leading international examples of institutional and policy reform for sustainability, analysed through a conceptual framework developed from the fields of institutional economics and policy learning. More detailed descriptions, analyses and sources are given elsewhere.[33] The aim is better to understand the key elements of institutional change for sustainability, through identification and analysis of the main variables that shaped the following:

—Several decades of *environmental policy in the European Union*, as the world's leading example of inter-jurisdictional policy and institutional development in the environmental domain. This allows tracing earlier environmental concerns through to the modern sustainability agenda in a multi-jurisdictional setting. It illuminates both impressive progress and deficits in implementation.

—New Zealand's Resource Management Act 1991 (RMA), including the process leading to it and subsequent implementation, as the world's most significant example of national-scale legislative, organisational and policy reform driven by sustainability concerns, where environmental responsibilities were allocated across national, regional and local scales. The RMA case allows analysis of a pro-sustainability reform from the level of national legislation and society-wide debate down to district level implementation.

—Progress with the definition and implementation of *strategic environmental assessment* (SEA), as a prominent option for integrating environmental, social and economic considerations at higher levels of policy formulation. Although reasonably well understood, subject to many legislative provisions and pertinent to sustainability, SEA has rarely been implemented or practiced in a purposeful fashion.

—*National Councils for Sustainable Development* (NCSD) and equivalent bodies established since 1992 in 70+ countries, representing cross-sectoral and inclusive mechanisms for national policy discourse and co-ordination. NCSD represent experiments in national-scale partnerships between

[33] Connor and Dovers, above n 3.

government and civil society, but vary from impressive and influential to very marginal.

—*Property rights instruments* (PRIs), drawing particularly on the most intensively analysed of these, individual transferable quota in fisheries. Property rights are a fundamental social institution, and the increasing advocacy and use of property rights instruments, driven largely by economic arguments, allows consideration of a 'transformative' policy instruments that expose the nature of policy change that is embedded in and has the potential deeply to affect institutional and cultural systems. This case emphasises that an important *institution* (ie, property rights) can also be viewed in a more specific problem context as a possible policy *instrument* (eg, tradeable water rights, requiring redefinition of the property rights regime in water).[34]

Detailed analyses of these cases, which we have reported elsewhere, allowed the identification of a set of general principles to inform discussions of and prescriptions for ongoing institutional change. These principles are broad enough to be considered across different contexts, but sufficiently operational to be applied in concrete cases. The following discussion summarises these principles, with reference to the fives cases, under two categories: (re)framing the problem, and (re)organising government.

2. (Re)Framing the Problem

The importance of problem framing was emphasised earlier (Figure 1), as a precondition for designing a policy or institutional response. Indeed, framing provides the characterisation of a problem that will predetermine the range of potential responses. Sustainability represents a complex suite of significant problems, pervaded by uncertainty, which do not fit with existing knowledge systems and intellectual and practical capacities. It will take significant time and effort to 'get our heads round' the problem set, especially in parts of the institutional system that have not previously thought much about interconnected environmental, social and economic phenomena. Coming to see problems in new ways and admitting new approaches to policy will involve changes in values among members of policy communities, and making policies for sustainability really work will require generalised changes in social values. Therefore, space and opportunity for discourse and reflection on the sustainability idea is needed in institutional systems, so that familiarity and understanding can be developed as a prerequisite for operational responses. Under

[34] On property rights in resource management, see N Dolšak and E Ostrom (eds), *The Commons in the New Millennium: Challenges and Adaptations* (MIT Press, 2003); E Ostrom, *Governing the Commons* (Cambridge UP, 1990).

(re)framing the problem, we consider the need to provide institutional space for the sustainability discourse, the interdependence of normative and institutional change, and the role of legal change.

Principle 1: Accommodating a Discourse on Sustainability in Institutional Systems

The sustainability idea results from convergence of three concerns, each with its own values, problem definition and language—ecological integrity, economic efficiency, and social justice. It is increasingly realised in these traditionally separate discourses that their central concerns are tied to use of the environment and this has drawn them into the sustainable development debate.

One precondition for institutional change for sustainable development is therefore the provision of a discursive space where these concerns can be brought together.[35] Reconciliation of the three is not simple conceptually or practically and there is no agreed vision of a sustainable future. This makes it vital to provide for ongoing discursive exploration of the sustainability idea and its implications, and development of agreement on principles for moving forward. Such exploration is undertaken in a range of locations throughout civil society (universities, NGOs, business and political think tanks) and in some government agencies. However, it appears that providing state sanctioned forums for consensus formation is a precursor to formal institutional change.

National Councils for Sustainable Development (NCSD) are an obvious mechanism, allowing ongoing discussion of sustainability, input into government processes, and a site for the seeding of related research effort. The effectiveness of the Councils in maintaining a productive discourse cannot yet be judged, given their recent emergence. A key is the flow of discussion out into other parts of the institutional system and community, and to do that the Councils must be well connected within the institutional system in a jurisdiction. Variations in function and form of existing NCSDs indicate flexibility within the core idea of such a body to allow such fit. However, a central location and good political support in government will enhance the ability of an NCSD to promote discourse and the likelihood of longevity. A small number of 'second generation' NCSDs (UK, Belgium, Canada) illustrate the possibility of more deeply embedding such mechanisms following experience with a less permanent version.[36]

[35] The creation of discursive, deliberative or inclusive modes of policy and governance is the subject of a growing literature. See A Fung and EO Wright (eds), *Deepening Democracy: Institutional Innovation in Empowered Participatory Governance* (Verso, 2003); J Dryzek, *Deliberative Democracy and Beyond: Liberals, Critics, Contestations* (Oxford UP, 2000); WM Lafferty (ed), *Governance for Sustainable Development: The Challenge of Adapting Form to Function* (Edward Elgar, 2004); A Dobson, *Citizenship and the Environment* (Oxford UP, 2003). For a cautionary view, see B Cooke and U Kothari (eds), *Participation: The New Tyranny?* (Zed Books, 2001).

[36] C Maurer, *Rio +8: An Assessment of National Councils for Sustainable Development* (World Resources Institute, 1999).

Environmental policy in the European Union (EU) highlights several types of locality within an institutional system where productive discourses can occur. The reiterative process for development of Environmental Action Programmes (EAPs) provides a continual discussion.[37] Many now commonly accepted principles of sustainable development appeared in EAPs from the 1970s, indicating that this process was an incubator for the development of sustainability ideas. Other sites in Europe included the Green Forum and Policy Co-ordination Groups, and processes for development of the Sustainable Development Strategy.[38]

New Zealand's Resource Management Act (RMA) resulted from a resource management law reform (RMLR) process set up to integrate resource management legislation and administration. This process was well resourced and consultative, creating a wide debate over conceptual and practical aspects of sustainability. However, the RMA's provisions for ongoing dicussion and policy development through the preparation of national policy statements were largely neglected. Instead, debate over policy values was left largely to the courts. There are other spaces in the framework for ongoing debate at the regional and local levels, but those discussions are generally uninformed because of the failure to utilise the higher level opportunities to articulate sustainability values. The result of the neglect of this element of the sustainability puzzle is widespread discontent with the framework.[39] There is a tendency to blame either the drafting of the Act as ambiguous or a lack of initiative by local government, but rather the discontent stems from the lack of elaboration of agreed national values in policy statements, and the empty core of the system where discourse over values could have continued.

Strategic environmental assessment (SEA) refers to assessment of the environmental costs and benefits of proposed public policies, plans and programmes, as against discrete projects.[40] It allows environmental, social and economic considerations to be integrated at a high level of policy formation before any specific development projects are considered. SEA is capable of providing a substantial discursive space, but the focus of SEA is mostly on the implications of policy for the biophysical environment. However, SEA has the integrating function of forcing consideration of how environmental concerns can be incorporated in high level policy, and this requires confrontation of conceptual and values issues at the core of sustainability.

[37] Eg European Commission, *Environment 2010: Our Future, Our Choice. The Sixth Environmental Action Programmeme of the European Community*[2002] OJ L/242/1.

[38] European Consultative Forum on the Environment and Sustainable Development, *EU Sustainable Development Strategy* (European Community, May 2001).

[39] BJ Richardson and K Palmer, 'The Future of the New Zealand Resource Management Act' (1998) 3 *Asia Pacific Journal of Environmental Law* 376.

[40] R Therivel and MR Partidario (eds), *The Practice of Strategic Environmental Assessment* (Earthscan, 1996).

Examination of the use of tradeable quota in fisheries has shown that these property rights instruments (PRIs) are often perceived and applied as *just another tool in the toolbox*, rather than a potentially transformative instrumentality with deep institutional implications. Although PRIs can address sustainability, lack of discussion, especially of potential equity impacts, has contributed to social and institutional resistance. The portrayal of PRIs as policy instruments with universal application and predetermined natural characteristics tends to set them apart from the normative discussion. By not being included in the sustainability discourse, where value preferences can be negotiated, their application and consequent transformative impacts can be, or can be perceived as, hostile to sustainability principles.

Principle 2: Recognising and Utilising the Interdependence of Normative and Institutional Change

Normative change refers to change in group-held values. To be effective, institutional systems embody values consistent with those of a sufficient proportion of the affected populace—that is, institutional change must seek some congruence with publicly held values. This interdependence of normative and institutional change is a crucial consideration. In the case of institutional change in complex policy areas, the development of such congruence proceeds in an iterative manner, led from the top by political figures or perhaps driven by the population, but either way public debate is vital.[41]

The magnitude of the value shift to secure sustainable development is significant, and the timeframe required to achieve alignment of social values with sustainability can be expected to span decades. For some the value change may come only after long experience of an institutional framework that embodies sustainability principles; others will embrace change more quickly, adjusting behaviour ahead of formal rules. The difficulty with sustainability lies in the articulation and adoption of a different value set challenging some currently strongly held values, including the ideology of economic progress. What a sustainable world will be like, how we will get there, and how we will learn to be content with it are unclear. Yet normative change and institutional change for sustainability have commenced, and can progress only incrementally.

EU environment policy evidences the development of expressions of sustainability principles, institutional arrangements encouraging policy integration, the eventual application of legal rules, and the explicit inclusion of sustainability commitments in constitutional documents.[42] This unfolded over three decades in a process that gradually built commitment while applying 'soft' rules to change behaviour.

[41] See LJ Alston *et al* (eds), *Empirical Studies in Institutional Change* (Cambridge UP, 1996).
[42] M Lee, *EU Environmental Law: Challenges, Change and Decision-Making* (Hart Publishing, 2005).

The RMA attempted to push normative change through major reform to governance and procedures in resource management, requiring observation of the embodied sustainability values in all actions under its influence.[43] This is seemingly a top-down approach to normative change, but the development of the RMA included an open consultative process, and it allows for similarly open development of a range of subordinate instruments that embody, articulate and refine principles at increasingly local levels. Prior to the RMLR process, a small group of people in New Zealand had developed value positions that supported sustainability and contributed to the adoption of a strong normative content and implied normative change in the Act. The failure of central government to implement the national policy statement process to extend the values debate was a crucial choice seriously disabling the development and take-up of a sustainability values set. The strategy was to embed sustainability principles in the Act at a level of generality that made agreement possible within the constraints of time and politics afforded by the electoral system. The NPS and other public processes were intended to involve the community in debates and consensual agreements on values and policies. The lack of articulation of these contextualised sustainability values has required those implementing the policy and planning system at the local level to reinvent the wheel many times and left the public confused and disappointed.

Mechanisms such as NCSDs have a role to play in connecting institutional and normative change by engaging key groups in sustained interaction around the sustainability idea, likely leading to normative change within individuals and beyond. They can also serve to sensitise the policy community to the practical implications of the values associated with sustainability.

In a more prescriptive manner, SEA as a procedural requirement embeds regard to environment and sustainability into a range of policy making contexts. This will, quickly or slowly, influence members of policy communities who have never had to think routinely about the environmental or sustainability implications of decisions. Importantly, an educative process is established that may contribute to both practical sustainability problem-solving and normative change.

PRIs change the basis of access to and allocation of resources, imposing a different set of value priorities privileging economic and ecological considerations over social ones.[44] This shift can have a range of impacts on the economy of resource use, ecological integrity and social cohesion. The state of these factors at the time change is proposed will influence the reaction of stakeholders. However, length of cultural tradition under the existing regime is also significant—societies with deeper traditions of resource access will generally find the transformation of

[43] BV Harris, 'Sustainable Management as an Express Purpose of Environmental Legislation: The New Zealand Attempt' (1993) 8 *Otago Law Review* 51.

[44] D Grinlinton, 'Property Rights and the Environment' (1996) 4 *Australian Property Law Journal* 41.

values under PRIs more challenging. The explanation for this lies in the implied normative change for these individualised rights to operate. The new incentive structures created that deliver economic and conservation results are generally focused on individuals, but disrupt trust and reciprocity relationships important to social cohesion. Property rights impose a different set of value priorities, by privileging economic and ecological considerations over social ones. PRI regimes can be modified to make concessions to social values by trading off some efficiency gains without compromising ecological objectives. At the same time, consultative and educative processes may facilitate enough normative change for the adoption of PRIs with a greater understanding and willingness by stakeholders.

Principle 3: Recognising and Utilising the Interdependence of Legal and Institutional Change

Law provides a means for more profound change to institutions, as the national institutional systems of a modern state are based in the codification of rules to establish order. Law may also represent barriers to innovative policy and institutional change. Statute law is the most common route for dealing with public good issues such as sustainability, but examples of strong statutory expression of sustainability principles are rare.

In the EU, there has been a slow process of building the legal underpinnings following negotiated advances in environmental policy. Attempts to regulate to control the impacts of activities on the environment were weak at first due to the need to justify this within the constitutional setting of the European Community. This involved identification of distortions in markets in Member States caused by differentiated environmental laws. Combined with establishment of the right of states with stricter national environmental regulation to retain high levels of protection, the system worked to improve the performance of other states. Since the constitutional basis for environmental policy was established in the 1987 Single European Act and upgraded in the 1992 Maastricht Treaty utilising sustainability language, EU regulations and directives have had more force, such as enshrining a requirement for a 'high level of protection' for the environment and mandating the Precautionary Principle as a fundamental tenet.[45] This is a strongly regulatory approach, although market-based instruments are encouraged in later EAPs.

The use of PRIs to manage common pool resources is usually authorised by statute, in part because existing legal doctrines supporting unrestricted use of these resources have generally resulted in overuse and economic waste under conditions of scarcity. Legislation allows the government to define the right, particularly as representing a proportional share of available resources rather than a fixed

[45] Lee, above n 42.

quantity, and potentially allows the cancellation of the right by further legislative change.[46] PRIs represent an attractive strategy, but their use to change allocation patterns confronts equity norms. Where normative debate has not occurred or has been polarised and misdirected, the introduction of PRIs by legislation may cause unnecessary social dislocation, reduce citizens' commitment to the institutional system, and invite legal challenge.

Provisions for both SEA and NCSD exist in both law and non-binding policy. Legal requirement for SEA seeks to force policy integration to happen, whereas legal provision for an NCSD creates a process to encourage integration. However, statutory provision for SEA has been largely discretionary and this has led to poor implementation. This emphasises that the nature of statutory expression is as crucial as its mere existence. There is more chance of persistence for an initiative such as an NCSD when it has a legislative base. The clarity of mandate and organisational design in legislation is also crucial. Importantly, the process of legislative drafting in a parliamentary system with transparent legislative review mechanisms will be subject to greater scrutiny and debate than a simple policy decision.

The RMA as integrated legislation operates at general and specific levels, combining a traditional planning and regulatory approach with the broad expression of sustainability. At local scales law is needed to bind decisions, whereas at the highest level the most interesting lesson from section 5 of the RMA, which states broad objectives and principles, has been to enable ongoing discussion of what sustainability means. At the same time, this section does an intricate job of providing a values framework in legislation, particularly through the 'environmental bottom line'—that is, emphasising ecological integrity over both economic efficiency and social equity. In defining *sustainable management of natural and physical resources* as the purpose of the Act and making all action under the Act subordinate to this, the RMA sets up a dynamic that seeks to define the detail of the implicit values set. The resulting discourse has been inevitable and useful, given the influence of the Act, and the central yet contestable location of the sustainability idea in it.

Recourse to the courts to argue over the meaning and application of sustainability principles may be viewed as regrettable, yet the RMA case suggests that contestation is inevitable, given uncertainty and multiple values.[47] The most clearly stated sustainability principle—the precautionary principle (PP)—has yet to attract consensus over its meaning or implementation, despite a significant literature and emerging jurisprudence.[48] The law and courts are part of what should

[46] Eg, in relation to New Zealand's individual transferable fish quotas: CJ Batstone and BMH Sharp, 'New Zealand's Quota Management System: the First Ten Years' (1999) 23(2) *Marine Policy* 177.

[47] K Grundy, 'Purpose and Principles: Interpreting Section 5 of the Resource Management Act' in PA Memon and HC Perkins (eds), *Environmental Planning and Management in New Zealand* (Dunmore Press, 2000) 64.

[48] See J Cameron and T O'Riordan (eds), *Interpreting the Precautionary Principle* (Earthscan, 1994).

be an explicitly multiple strategy for learning the meaning of sustainability, along with enabling and maintaining inclusive policy debate, and technical development of methods and techniques to operationalise such principles.

Principle 4: Recognising and Utilising International Law and Policy as Drivers of Policy and Institutional Change

Sustainability has been most strongly expressed internationally, and domestic policy is influenced by international discussions, law and policy processes in a number of ways, and international processes are in turn shaped by countries that are influential leaders or powerful laggards. While this may appear obvious, the role of international law and policy as drivers of domestic normative, institutional and policy change may be less well appreciated at finer resolutions.[49]

Our five examples evidence varying relationships with the international level. EU environmental policy is an international process in its own right, as well as a formative influence on emerging, global discourse on sustainable development. The RMA represents an early response to sustainability, while NCSDs are more recent and explicit responses, often portrayed as national-scale extensions of the UN Commission on Sustainable Development. This linkage is strengthened by the focus of some NCSDs on synergies possible through co-ordinated implementation of international treaties. Future prospects for SEA are substantially tied to implementation of the EU's SEA Directive[50] and the SEA protocol to the Espoo Convention.[51]

Beyond the generality that institutional and policy change at the national level is connected to international processes, we can identify more specific connections. International processes—summits, conferences of parties, protocols to existing treaties, etc—establish minimum and often vague standards for policy response, such as Agenda 21's exhortation to states to develop national sustainable development strategies. Further, reporting and negotiation processes under international instruments provide visible opportunities for reconsideration of the adequacy of domestic policy settings, and international debates guarantee that accessible discussion of sustainability is maintained even if is limited in a particular country. Finally, international processes make visible a variety of ideas

[49] For discussions, see OR Young, *The Institutional Dimensions of Environmental Change: Fit, Interplay, and Scale* (MIT Press, 2002); SA Ebbin (ed), 'Institutions and the Production of Knowledge for Environmental Governance: Empirical Evidence from Marine and Terrestrial Systems' (Special Issue) (2004) 4(2) *International Environmental Agreement: Politics, Law and Economics*; Lafferty and Meadowcroft, above n 18.

[50] Directive 2001/42/EC on the assessment of the effects of certain plans and programmes on the environment, [2001] OJ L/197/30.

[51] Protocol on Strategic Environmental Assessment to the Convention on Environmental Impact Assessment in a Transboundary Context, 21 May 2003, available at www.unece.org/env/eia/documents/protocolenglish.pdf.

about policy and institutional responses and thereby expand potential sources of policy learning.

3. (Re)Organising Government

Our second set of principles concerns the structure and function of government, which is widely understood to require substantial change properly to comprehend and respond to sustainability. While many comment on the decline of the power of the state, governments remain crucial to pursuing sustainability for two reasons. First, even in countries where 'neoliberal' policy prescriptions have been most influential, government is not so diminished as to have to let go of the power to regulate, create institutions, engage citizens, and shape individual and collective behaviours. Secondly, sustainability is a long-term social goal, and such goals invite collective endeavours, or at the least many individual and group efforts aided (most often) through state institutions. To inform consideration of the organisation of government for sustainability, the following discussion highlights three principles: policy integration; subsidiarity and scale; and the need for reiterative processes.

Principle 5: Placing Priority on the Integration of Environmental, Social and Economic Concerns in Policy and Practice

Policy integration is key to sustainability and the convergence of concerns for ecological integrity, economic efficiency, and social justice (equity) in relation to human use of the environment, and acknowledgment of their interdependence.[52] This presents a series and hierarchy of challenges. The initial challenge is to integrate these concerns conceptually into the sustainability idea—to understand the interpenetration of ecology, economy and society, knowing that action in one domain affects the whole. Then comes the task of articulating general principles to guide action, and from that the development of strategies and policies by sector or issue, and then plans for action. Integration at each level, carried out inside or outside government, involves the agreement of a coherent set of values and priorities covering relevant social, economic and ecological concerns, reconciliation of differing views, priorities and interests. All interests cannot be maximised at once, hence trade-offs and collective value judgements are involved.

Yet the 'environmental-social-economic' construction is only shorthand for something more complicated, and our examples evidence multiple dimensions of policy integration—across those broad policy arenas, but also within each of them, and across administrative/political and spatial/geographical scales. The challenge is clearly a multi-faceted one. Given the recent emergence of the sustainability

[52] See further A Lenschow (ed), *Environmental Policy Integration* (Earthscan, 2002).

problem, lowly status of environment in institutional systems, and compartmentalised structures of government and policy-making, difficulty in implementation and institutional resistance should be expected.

There are two preconditions for policy integration: on the one hand, policy processes and organisational structures; and on the other, techniques and methods. This chapter is more concerned with the former, but the split may hide the close relationship between process and technique, a blurred differentiation under conditions of complexity and uncertainty where processes should be also viewed as operational pathways to further evolution of understanding and capacity.

SEA represents an integration strategy inserting environmental considerations into other policy processes. As the longest standing proposed integration strategy, the history of SEA practice illustrates the difficulties of implementing even a reasonably well understood procedure with available application techniques. Factors include resistance in central agencies, lack of widespread understanding of SEA, discretionary rather than mandatory provisions, and uncertainty as to the appropriate location and head of power for SEA. Against that, the idea of SEA has been revived since the articulation of the sustainability idea.

The history of integrating environmental policy in the European Union offers important insights.[53] Initially the EU relied primarily on a 'bottom up' approach to integration, seeking to educate and influence the process of cultural change in agencies and communities. Following the establishment of a legal basis for action and some normative change reflected in the values of members of the European Parliament (EP), the Directorate General (DG) Environment forged a political alliance with the EP Environment Committee to force integration of environmental considerations in development planning. This imposed SEA/EIA functions on the application of some €30 billion of the annual EU budget. Within one budget cycle the powerful Directorate General controlling these resources restructured to accommodate the new emphasis, made commitments to environmental considerations and began what appears to be a culture change. Such accommodation can work in two ways. First, having been forced to change, individuals or organisations over time embrace the logic of environmental concern. Alternatively, officials who already accept sustainability as important are provided with a mechanism whereby that concern could be incorporated into procedures and practices.[54] Other attempts to inject environmental considerations into EU policy have not been so effective. The use of 'integration correspondents'

[53] See T Malek *et al* (eds), *European Union Environmental Policy and New Forms of Governance* (Ashgate, 2001).

[54] The phenomenon of an enforced procedure leading to a change in outlook within an organisation has been termed the 'worm in the brain' effect: see RV Bartlett, 'Ecological Reason in Administration: Environmental Impact Assessment and Administrative Theory' in R Paelke and D Torgerson (eds), *Managing Leviathan: Environmental Politics and the Administrative State* (Behaven Press, 1990) 81–96.

in each sectoral DG as a contact point for the Environment DG merely lead to defence of business as usual. Reports regularly highlighted no-regrets policies and actions, but not the basis upon which decisions were made.

New Zealand's RMA attempted to embed policy integration across natural resource management and land use planning, spatial and administrative scales, and government and civil society, made possible through the concurrent reform of resource management legislation and local government.[55] In the system, integration is driven by a singular purpose embedded in the institutional framework that expresses the logic of sustainable development. It includes social and economic imperatives, but makes protection of the environment the over-riding value priority.

Many NCSDs seek policy integration through linking different parts of the institutional system, generally as a subsidiary aim behind the goal of creating government–civil society partnerships. However, the existence of an inclusive dialogue space for the various policy communities relevant to sustainability is certainly a significant advance on not having such a mechanism. While there is little empirical evidence of the effectiveness of NCSD in promoting policy integration, proponents and participants claim some impact.[56] It may be that the primary integrative impact is at the conceptual level, for the membership but also for government and civil society through influence of NCSD statements and reports that articulate integration. The NCSD experience has also helped to identify familiar issues critical to policy integration—strength of political support, clarity of mandate, resources and appropriate institutional home.

PRIs expose different aspects of the integration challenge. A reframing of the problem is implicit with PRIs, where efficiency and ecological imperatives gain primacy over the previously dominant distributional equity goal. This indicates the delicacy and importance of balance within the integration task, and the need explicitly to recognise competing value sets. PRIs as an implementation instrument show the ease with which the balance of integration can change even when not intended, such as through unforeseen but arguably predictable social equity and local economic impacts. This highlights that policy integration is not simply a challenge to be implemented, but one that must be catered for in the design of a policy regime, creation of organisational capacity and processes of implementation, and ongoing maintenance of the policy regime.

Many other integration strategies exist, including commissioners for environment or centrally located sustainability policy units, the use of tax instruments, cross-sectoral policy development, joint management of policy programmes

[55] D Grinlinton, 'Integrated Environmental Management in New Zealand' (2000) 17 *Aoyama Law Review* 85.

[56] M Janicke and H Jorgens, 'National Environmental Policy Planning in OECD Countries' (1998) 7(2) *Environmental Politics* 27.

across portfolios and the application of multi-criteria techniques in policy analysis.

Principle 6: Implementing Subsidiarity—The Institutional Politics of Scale and Power

The principle of subsidiarity instructs that decisions should be taken at the most effective level.[57] This is for *political* reasons (representation of affected parties in decision-making, gaining constituency support, political accountability), *administrative* reasons (economies of scale in decision-making, reducing unnecessary consideration of issue detail at higher levels) and *substantive* reasons (information availability, nature of the problem and the values at stake). However, in the structuring and organisation of governance and allocation of rights and responsibilities, power and control of resources and influence are being contested. Hence subsidiarity is an important but controversial issue in the reorganisation of government.

In structural change for sustainable development the issue is especially critical due to pervasive uncertainty in interactions with environmental systems. Information distance in feedback loops between decision-makers and their impacts on the environment, economy and society should be minimised to reduce response times in the event of surprise. This dictates that decisions should be made at the lowest level consistent with the scope of the issue. However, as most issues have multiple dimensions that operate at different scales (eg, management of surface water within one property, a sub-catchment, or a larger river basin), there will always be tensions over the appropriate level for the allocation of decision-making power, and the need for some sharing of responsibility through oversight of decision-making at higher levels.

In the EU there is significant political tension over devolution of power. The situation is clouded by the nature of the EU as a confederation of sovereign states, the political utility of governments being seen to be a defender of national sovereignty, as well as the actual issue of control of policy spheres. However, the adoption of subsidiarity as an agreed principle of EU governance forces debate to focus on longer term policy effectiveness and appropriateness, as opposed to short-term political considerations. This re-emphasises the importance of promoting debate and agreement on, and adoption of, sustainability principles into the formal institutional system. A feature of the EU system related to subsidiarity is the existence of shared central capacity. This is expressed throughout the EU system of governance, but has been significant to the institutionalisation of sustainability particularly through the Directorate General for Environment and its sub-directorate

[57] This principle has been most prominent in EU policy-making: AE de Noriega, *The EU Principle of Subsidiarity and Its Critique* (Oxford UP, 2003).

predecessor and the establishment of the European Environment Agency.[58] Together with the cycle of EAPs over an average span of six years, such central capacity provides persistence and flexibility through supra-electoral continuity.

Another key expression of subsidiarity occurs with New Zealand's RMA. The system of environmental governance set out in the Act and the co-ordinated local government legislation allocates competences throughout the system. It specifies roles for government, national level processes for development and expression of consensus on values, policy and environmental standards, and responsibilities of regional and territorial authorities for policies and plans to control the effects of activity on the environment. The schema is such that activities that have purely local effects are regulated locally, but matters deemed to be of national importance are dealt with, at least in principle, at national level. Again, though, the lack of development of NPS has crippled this to an extent, indicating the interdependence of the principles discussed here.

Although most relevant to inserting environmental considerations horizontally across other policy sectors, establishment of an SEA process reflects similar issues as the RMA of placement of rights and responsibilities vertically in hierarchical policy systems. The attention to tiering of SEA through policies, plans and programmes (PPPs) in confederate Europe illustrates this, given that different levels in the policy system (local, provincial, national, supra-national) have differentiated responsibilities for these.[59] This forces cognisance of the influence of broader policy directions on subsidiary activities, in keeping with a more sophisticated understanding of complex institutional and policy systems. Negotiating rules of subsidiarity within a jurisdiction will be easier than within, say, a federal or confederate system.

Principle 7: Allowing for Reiteration and Learning

Sustainability is a long-term project, where the necessary shift in values and institutional arrangements to integrate social, economic and ecological concerns may itself be an intergenerational issue. Significant structural change will take decades—recognition of this makes institutional provision for long-term reiterative processes a logical step. The uncertainties about the best pathway dictate periodic reassessment, adjustment and recommitment to principles, policies and actions. As values adjust under new environmental and institutional conditions, new options and trade-offs will emerge as desirable and viable—any process of institutional change for sustainable development should consider reiterative processes as fundamental building blocks for an adaptive system. Although

[58] U Collier, 'Sustainability, Subsidiarity and Deregulation: New Directions in EU Environmental Policy' (1997) 6(2) *Environmental Politics* 1.

[59] See eg TB Fischer, *Strategic Environmental Assessment in Transport and Land Use Planning* (Earthscan, 2002).

incrementalism is commonplace in policy processes, over time scales relevant for sustainability, normal processes appear ad hoc and disjointed. The challenge is to maintain efforts and learning processes over time.

The EU evidences some aspects of a reiterative process. The process backbone of Europe's leading role in developing institutionalised capacity for sustainability has been the EAP. These have sufficient longevity to span electoral and appointment cycles in Member States and the central EU polity. They have gradually built a basis for policy through successive iterations and have locked in commitments to protect the environment and advance the sustainability agenda. Part of the force of the EAP is to remind successive generations of politicians and bureaucrats of what has already been agreed. The peak opportunity to do this is at the point where a new EAP is proposed for adoption. By this stage, those engaged in reviewing progress under the existing plan and generating agreement among states on the new one have spent years developing a revised and strengthened agenda. The process is thus continuous, with sufficient tenure of each plan and continuity between plans to provide for relative certainty while also pursuing progressive change.

E. Policy, Institutions and the Law

The preceding section advanced principles to inform policy and institutional change, derived from empirical analyses of existing, credible cases of reform. The role of law was touched upon several times, and explicitly as a principle itself. This section considers further the role of law in underpinning significant policy change, recalling the earlier argument that (usually statute) law is a 'universal policy instrument', necessary to any substantial policy intervention. To consider this further, four central imperatives in sustainability are discussed: the precautionary principle; policy integration; multiple scales of policy and governance; and public participation. The discussion is not detailed and other chapters in this book explore issues further: the aim here is to evidence the role of law in supporting and enabling broader policy efforts.

The precautionary principle (PP). The focus of discussion of the precautionary principle has been on (i) its incorporation into legislation and interpretation of statutory expressions in the courts, and (ii) the broader, political meaning of the PP in terms of the degree of action required to attend environmental degradation. The first is a largely legal issue, while the second is in the domain of discussion of social goals. Statutory expression is necessary to adopting the changed social value that the principle represents—society wishes to be more careful with the environment, and decision-makers are instructed to act accordingly. However, to operationalise the principle, its statutory expression is only the first step. Instructions for decision-makers on how to implement precaution in varying contexts are often missing. These would include frameworks such as adaptive management or risk management procedures, processes such as SEA or strategic planning, and decision support techniques such as multi-criteria analyses or deliberative designs. This indicates again that significant and effective policy interventions are complex packages relying on the interdependence of multiple elements. The legal aspect of the PP is crucial, but fully effective only when linked to organisational and management processes, and to operational techniques making it more than a vague instruction in enabling legislation.[60]

Policy integration (environmental, social, economic). This tenet of sustainability is obvious, necessary, and above all supremely difficult. It requires traditionally separate and even hostile rationalities and actors to be brought into proximity, and moreover to understand and incorporate each other's modes of knowledge construction, analytical methods and problem definitions. There are no widely accepted means for integration, and available strategies include procedures such as SEA, institutional measures such as NCSDs, interdepartmental committees and commissioners for sustainability and/or environment, and techniques such as natural resource accounting and sustainability indicators. As discussed in Section 3, provision for such strategies in legislation can make them less discretionary and ensure transparency, persistence and methodological consistency. Three decades after the first statutory provisions for SEA, and after very little implementation, policy-makers still struggle to articulate clearly the values and goals of SEAs.[61] Policy integration as a principle is expressed in law often as the PP, as part of the increasingly regular listing of sustainability principles for decision-makers to take into account, however it has received far less implementation and discussion in legal practice and analysis. Policy informers have still fully to work out how legislation can best promote the integration of environmental policies, especially the relation to procedures for implementation.

Non-traditional and multiple scales of policy and governance. A central difficulty with sustainability is the lack of fit between traditional political, jurisdictional and administrative boundaries, and the characteristics of natural-human system processes. The latter show little respect for the former, making policy and institutional responses to sustainability based around existing demarcations of information, law and policy making difficult (this is defined by attributes 1, 5 and 11 in Table 3). Examples are biodiversity management over landscape scales, key processes such as climate and nutrient cycles, and catchment scale hydrological phenomena.[62] One

[60] A Trouwborst, *Evolution and Status of the Precautionary Principle in International Law* (Kluwer, 2002); C Raffensberger and J Tickner, *Protecting Public Health and the Environment: Implementing the Precautionary Principle* (Island Press, 1999).

[61] Therivel and Partidario, above n 40.

[62] See examples in F Berkes, C Folke and J Colding (eds), *Linking Social and Ecological Systems: Management Practices and Social Mechanisms for Building Resilience.* (Cambridge UP, 1998).

aspect of this is intergovernmental co-operation and delineation of responsibilities to different levels of government, discussed above through the concept of subsidiarity. While challenging, that is only part of the necessary response. Increasingly, governments and stakeholders are constructing policy and management regimes defined by non-traditional scales—locality, sub-national region, bioregion, catchment and so on. An important 'non-spatial' scale is where policy is focused on issues or sectors (eg, energy, biodiversity, transport, water quality, etc), which also typically defy administrative boundaries. While these scales may fit better with the problems being addressed or with underlying biophysical or social processes, it is rare that initiatives such as catchment management bodies, bioregional plans or sectoral policy are well-supported by institutional or legal provision.[63] Both intergovernmental co-ordination and non-traditional scales of policy and management require legal underpinning, and present challenges for law.

Public participation. Virtually all sustainability policy promotes inclusion of stakeholders and the community in policy and management. In environmental law, the major focus on public participation is provision for citizens' rights to know about, comment on and/or object to policy and development proposals. Yet this is only a small part of the scope of participation in modern sustainability discussions. A major trend in resource and environmental management and in human development has been community-based programmes and activities, and the issue of participation is particularly important at emerging, non-traditional scale activities such as catchment and regional management, and in emerging institutional experiments such as NCSDs.[64] While governments have embraced community-based management as a programme delivery mechanism, citizen participation in higher order policy process has not expanded notably. Concurrently with the rise of the sustainability idea, there has been increasing advocacy of participatory and deliberative forms of policy and politics, and these proposals have found strong reception in the non-government policy community concerned with sustainability.[65] There is a discernable transition in the environment and sustainability domains from public participation in environmental protection and development control, toward participatory modes of governance. That transition requires different service from law, as all the participatory forms mentioned above, and many others that exist, require appropriate institutional settings and

[63] See eg the legal reforms for watershed management discussed in M Bond and M Comino, 'Environmental Justice and the Water Market in Australia' in K Bosselmann and BJ Richardson (eds), *Environmental Justice and Market Mechanisms* (Kluwer, 1998) 232.

[64] See S Chamala and KJ Keith, *Participative Approaches for Landcare: Perspectives, Policies, Programmes* (Australian Academic Press, 1995).

[65] For a summary of deliberative democracy and designs, see R Munton, 'Deliberative Democracy and Environmental Decision-Making' in F Berkhout, M Leach and I Scoones (eds), *Negotiating Environmental Change: New Perspectives from the Social Sciences* (Edward Elgar, 2002). For longer treatments, see Dryzek, above n 35; Hajer and Wagenaar, above n 8.

processes. These can be enabled, enhanced and maintained through legal provision that extends well beyond the 'command-and-control' epithet so often used to characterise the role of law.

F. Learning Policy and Institutional Change

Sustainability represents an immense policy and institutional challenge to be attended over a period of decades. This is captured in the five principles proposed in Figure 1 and Table 1 to inform analysis and prescription of policy processes and institutional settings—persistence, purposefulness, information-richness, inclusiveness and flexibility—a directed yet adaptable approach demanding recognition that we are experimenting and (hopefully) learning. Thus, consideration of what policy and institutional learning entail, and when opportunities for policy and institutional change may arise, is warranted. Policy learning is a complex and surprisingly rare phenomenon.[66] At minimum, it is useful to detail what policy learning entails. Table 6 identifies major forms of learning, who engages in learning, and to what effect.

Across contexts the nature of learning will vary, and these categories can structure thinking about how to maximise learning opportunities to accommodate different interests and needs. In an exercise of policy analysis or experimentation, multiple forms of learning may occur within an individual or group and across groups. Instrumental and government learning focus on how to achieve *existing goals* defined in line with prevailing constructions of problems, within existing institutional forms. Social and political learning seek new ways to define goals and problems, and new institutional forms. Sustainability demands that attention be paid to both.

In actively embedding learning in the policy system, the question of *where to learn from* is an important one. Given that sustainability is a recent agenda and notable policy and institutional interventions are few and scattered, it makes sense to cast widely for insights into what may and may not work. This is a complex arena, and here we can recognise two issues: the need for greater detail in identifying sources of insights and lessons; and the transferability of policy lessons across jurisdictions and sectors. On the first, policy is composed of many parts, and learning from a policy experience can be focused on three levels:

[66] Adaptive management refers to the framing of management and policy interventions as 'experiments', which are explicitly tested and learnt from: see KN Lee, *Compass and Gyroscope: Integrating Science and Politics for the Environment* (Island Press, 1993); LH Gunderson *et al* (eds), *Barriers and Bridges to the Renewal of Ecosystems and Institutions* (Columbia UP, 1995).

TABLE 6: *Policy learning: forms and purposes*[67]

Form	*What is learned?*	*Who learns?*	*To what effect?*
Instrumental learning	How well policy instruments have achieved goals	Members of policy networks, esp. government officials engaged in policy formulation and implementation	Better design and implementation of policy instruments to achieve predetermined goals
Government learning	How well administrative arrangements and processes for implementation have worked	Members of policy networks, esp.senior officials responsible for design and maintenance of policy process	Better designed administrative structures and processes within the bureaucratic systems
Social learning	How useful are our constructions of policies and goals	Broader policy communities, incl. both more and less closely engaged actors within and outside government	Reframed problems and related goals, via changed understanding of cause-effect relationships, or altered social preferences
Political learning	How to best engage with and influence political and policy processes	Policy actors wishing to (i) change policy agendas and outcomes or (ii) defend the status quo	Changed problem definition, policy goals, membership of the policy network, and/or understanding of desirable institutional forms.

1. *Sub-programme detail*: adaptation of lessons at the detail of specific elements of the policy process and programme (eg, aspects of the monitoring programme, statutory framework, participatory process or communication strategy from one context that can inform policy design and implementation in another).
2. *Policy programme*: searching for a complete policy package (all the elements in Table 1) or an institutional or organisational model that can be transferred to another situation.

[67] Adapted from P May, 'Policy Learning and Policy Failure' (1992) 12 *Journal of Public Policy* 33; CJ Bennett and M Howlett, 'The Lessons of Learning: Reconciling Theories of Policy Learning and Policy Change' (1992) 25 *Policy Sciences* 275; Dovers and Connor, above n 3.

3. *Policy style*: different broad policy ideas that can be explored and tried elsewhere (eg, from another country which has tried self-regulatory rather than regulatory pollution control, or tradeable rights rather than licensing).

Simple mimicry is a crude form of policy and institutional learning. Moreover, 'lessons' imposed by higher authorities or powerful interests may well be unsuitable to the context in which they are applied. Across contexts, direct transfer is rarely appropriate, and it is proposed that levels 1 and 3 are where policy learning and the transfer of lessons are best pursued—one size does not fit all. Very often, for reasons of haste and lack of resources or analytical capacity it is at the programme or organisational model level (2) where transferable lessons are often sought—grab a package of components from one context and transplant it elsewhere. Conceptualisation, design and implementation of new and innovative policies are more likely to arise from the exploration of different policy styles (level 3), matched with the selection and adaptation of a range of more specific insights and lessons from a range of sources (level 1). This reflects an important but at times overlooked rule: there is no such thing as a completely successful or unsuccessful policy intervention or institutional design. All exist on a continuum and few cannot offer either positive or cautionary lessons—most can provide both.

The second consideration is the transferability of lessons from one jurisdiction or sector to another. It makes clear sense to seek lessons widely, but care must be taken to ensure that the lessons are appropriate to the home problem context. The basis of comparative policy and institutional analysis and lesson drawing can include commonalities or contrasts in political/legal system, the types of substantive issues faced, policy instruments or institutional strategies used, or similarity in underlying problem attributes (Table 3).

Locating and translating lessons for policy and institutional change is one thing—having these designs implemented in a possibly unsympathetic political and institutional environment is another. How opportunities for policy change occur has been much discussed in the policy literature, and includes considerations such as who sets agendas, implementation costs, institutional constraints, urgency, and especially the idea of 'policy windows'.[68] Policy windows are periods of opportunity or imperative for policy change, often after a period of reasonable stability in policy style and instruments used. Policy windows vary in kind and degree—why and how they open and how big a change in policy is possible. We

[68] In this area, particularly influential has been the work of JW Kingdon, *Agendas, Alternatives and Public Policy* (Little and Brown, 1984).

can identify two types, *predictable and unpredictable*, and illustrate with examples of the kinds of situations where policy windows may open:

- *Predictable* policy windows open in situations such as: the lead-in period to a government budget; after review of a policy programme or where problems with an existing policy are recognised; publication and consideration of a major review such as a regular state of environment report; finalisation or ratification of an international agreement that will require domestic implementation; or an election whether that returns the old government or a new administration.
- Unpredictable policy windows result from events such as: scientific discoveries; unforeseen environmental changes like drought, wild fires or pollution episodes; sudden realisation of policy failure; an unexpected rise in the influence of a particular interest group; and quick changes to international settings such as may occur after a disease or pest outbreak or an important environmental policy decision within an influential country that affects trade.

Different interests will be positioned to recognise and engage with different policy windows, depending on the transparency of the policy process and its responsiveness to non-government actors. The above is a summary classification, but provides a basis for understanding diverse opportunities for policy change. Some policy windows allow the prospect of big shifts in policy, such as the election of a new government or a large scale and sudden environmental change. In other cases, the magnitude of possible change will be much less. Caught in the moment, policy-makers and stakeholders may see little evidence of change, despite an abundance of rhetoric and evident policy ad hocery and amnesia. However, taking a longer view of adaptive policy and institutional systems, 'apparent [policy] volatility can become, in retrospect, the stately march of consistent underlying change'.[69] Whether the change is sufficient relative to the problems being addressed is another matter, and opinions differ on this in the case of sustainability.

G. Concluding Comment

Policy and institutional change for sustainability has proceeded far more slowly than would seem to be demanded by the magnitude and urgency of the problem

[69] G Davis, 'Introduction: Public Policy in the 1990s' in A Hede and S Prasser (eds), *Policy-making in Volatile Times* (Hale and Iremonger, 1993) 15.

set. However, the process of significant institutional accommodation of new and complex social goals is rarely swift. Nor is it evenly paced, as opportunities for institutional change may arise suddenly. The ability to respond to windows of opportunity depends on building familiarity and capacity in policy communities and the public, development of a suite of policy options that have been well-thought through and communicated, and maintaining a sophisticated understanding of the various elements that must be utilised, including the multiple roles of law in complex policy interventions and institutional reform. The aim of this chapter has been to connect the unfolding policy and institutional agenda of sustainability more closely to that of environmental law. This defines a broader appreciation of the role of law, away from a regulatory instrument to conceptualising law as a fundamental underpinning of policy and institutional systems as they evolve slowly toward being tools for enhancing rather than barriers to sustainability.

3

Environmental Command Regulation

CAROLYN ABBOT*

A. Introduction

The need to minimise environmental degradation and preserve the rich diversity of the world's natural resources is an important feature of sustainability and is, in fact, one of the most challenging problems facing governments locally, nationally and globally. In pursuing the sustainability agenda, environmental regulation can play an important role by influencing the behaviour of those individuals and companies whose actions have a negative impact on the environment. The term 'environmental regulation' is often used in its widest sense to include not only forms of direct regulation but also indirect and flexible forms of control, including self-regulation and voluntary initiatives such as environmental management systems and economic instruments. However, this chapter will consider one particular regulatory technique, so-called 'command and control' regulation.

Put simply, the term 'command and control' refers to the prescriptive nature of regulation, the command, supported by the imposition of some negative sanction, the control.[1] In other words, it involves the 'command' of the law, backed by the authority of the State.[2] Command and control can take numerous forms. It is *generally* characterised by centrally set environmental standards or targets (for example, limits on the emission of a certain pollutant into a watercourse) which are underpinned by the use of sanctions in the event of non-compliance. In many instances, these standards are implemented through an environmental licence or permit. Command regulation has also traditionally encompassed environmental planning instruments such as parks and protected areas regulation and environmental impact assessment (EIA),[3] all of which have an important function in regulating land use.

* Lecturer, University of Manchester School of Law.

[1] N Gunningham and P Grabosky, *Smart Regulation: Designing Environmental Policy* (Clarendon Press, 1998) 4.

[2] B Hutter (ed), *A Reader in Environmental Law* (Oxford UP, 1999) 5.

[3] As these instruments have a gatekeeping function, they should arguably be classified separately.

In this chapter, we examine environmental command and control regulation, with a view to considering its future role within a sustainable development policy framework. In Section B we briefly consider stages in the development of command and control regulation, with reference to political economy and ideology. Sections C, D and E give a critical account of three traditional command techniques: environmental standards, environmental licences and environmental planning tools. In Section F, we analyse the command model with reference to five criteria: effectiveness, cost efficiency, administrative flexibility, accessibility and dependability. Although there is evidence to suggest that the system has achieved some success in reducing environmental damage, critics assert that there are more effective and efficient methods of attaining environmental goals. This has led to a discernable shift away from reliance on command and control to the use of a broader mix of instruments such as emissions trading and environmental management systems. However, regulators have also responded to these criticisms by introducing innovative ways of improving upon traditional forms of command and control regulation by, for example incorporating load-based and accredited licensing techniques. In Section G, we investigate some of these developments.

B. Stages in the Development of Command and Control Regulation

Command regulation in the form of standards implemented through licences has been the cornerstone of government efforts (particularly in the industrialised world) to prohibit or restrict environmentally damaging activities.[4] Although regulations for dealing with urban and environmental issues emerged largely in response to the problems of industrialisation and urbanisation posed in the nineteenth century, these laws were not concerned with environmental protection per se but were designed to deal with housing, public health and town planning.[5] Government intervention in the form of pollution control laws designed to promote environmental improvement has its origins in the late 1960s and early

[4] See generally on command regulation and its development in an environmental context, E Rubin, 'Law and Legislation in the Administrative States' (1989) 89 *Columbia Law* Review 369; D Vogel, *National Styles of Regulation: Environmental Policy in Great Britain and the United States* (Cornell UP, 1986).

[5] M Grant, *Urban Planning Law* (Sweet and Maxwell, 1982).

1970s, when governments began to recognise the importance of controlling pollution other than where human health was directly threatened.[6]

In investigating the growth of environmental regulation, Albert Weale traced the responses of seven European and North American governments to the problem of pollution.[7] He found that in the early 1970s most governments set up independent expert panels to provide advice on environmental matters. This led to the establishment of administrative bodies and the enactment of pollution control legislation dealing with air, water and land.[8] This legislation typically required regulated entities to hold a licence to discharge pollutants to air or water and, generally speaking, these licences were medium-specific. In the US, for example, 500 different industries were subject to uniform water effluent limits based on the best available control technology (BAT) so long as the costs did not shut down the plant. In contrast, in the UK, far fewer substances were made the subject of quantitative emission controls, and pollution had to be controlled using the 'best practicable means' (BPM). Although some attempts were made to establish ambient and receptor standards, they were noticeably absent from command and control at this time. As Robinson writes, 'the systems imposed immediate limits on particular, widespread pollutants emitted from the most obviously polluting industries'.[9]

This combination of prohibitions, licences and standards represented the 'command' aspect of pollution regulation. The 'control' aspect usually took the form of the threat of criminal or quasi-criminal liability, supported by legal regimes for monitoring, reporting, inspection, prosecution and sanctions.

The philosophy behind pollution control during this period was pragmatic and striving not to eliminate pollution but to employ the 'dilute and disperse' concept to achieve an 'optimal' level of pollution.[10] For example, standards required (a) the use of abatement measures such as end-of-pipe filters and scrubbers; (b) better pollution diffusion through taller chimneys; and (c) in the case of highly toxic chemicals such as nuclear wastes, the typical approach was product containment

[6] So what aroused the interest of governments at this time? During the post-Second World War period, the industrialised world witnessed large economic and population growth. This, combined with advances in new technologies, meant that pollution was, at least in terms of scale, a relatively new problem. Rising educational standards and the maturing of a generation concerned with quality of life stimulated public interest. In addition media coverage, pressure group campaigns and popular interest increased dramatically in a relatively short period of time. These factors, amongst others, go some way to explaining the upsurge of political activism relating to environmental protection. See further SP Hays, 'The Structure of Environmental Politics Since World War II' (1981) 14(4) *Social History* 719.

[7] A Weale, *The New Politics of Pollution* (Manchester UP, 1992).

[8] NA Robinson, 'Legal Structures and Sustainable Development: Comparative Environmental Law Perspectives on Legal Regimes for Sustainable Development' (1998) 3 *Widener Law Symposium Journal* 247.

[9] D Robinson, 'Regulatory Evolution in Pollution Control' in T Jewell and J Steele (eds), *Law in Environmental Decision-Making - National, European and International Perspectives* (Clarendon Press, 1998) 35.

[10] WF Baxter, *People or Pengiuns: The Case for Optimal Pollution Control* (Columbia UP, 1974).

and isolation. In the event of non-compliance, the command and control systems were usually underpinned by criminal liability. In countries such as the US and Germany, criminal laws were complemented by civil liabilities and procedures, whereas in other jurisdictions such as the UK and Sweden, administrative penalties and procedures could also be invoked.

This model of pollution control regulation is an example of an ideal type of law that has been called 'substantive law'.[11] Substantive law is characterised by detailed, particularised policies, programmes and rules through which governments seek to mould social behaviour in pursuit of specific social goals.[12] Legal rules in this model tend to be purposive, open-textured and result-oriented rather than value-neutral and universal. Environmental command regulation, with its substantive goals for pollution emissions or environmental quality and its detailed administrative arrangements, is a good example of substantive law.

Substantive law can be contrasted with two other ideal types of law. 'Formal law' is characterised by neutral, universal rules and procedures that leave substantive value judgements to private actors.[13] Formal law predominated in the liberal democracies before the emergence of the welfare state, but was increasingly displaced by substantive law in the second half of the twentieth century. Traditional private law doctrines of nuisance, trespass and negligence are often identified as examples of 'formal law' in the environmental field. According to some observers, both formal and substantive law are now ceding ground to a third type of law. This type is called 'reflexive law' because, rather than dictating the details of regulated behaviour, it provokes self-reflection and self-correction by regulated actors in line with regulators' goals.[14]

The displacement of 'formal law' by detailed, substantive government intervention constitutes an important development in the evolution of environmental law and still provides the framework for current environmental command systems. These systems have however become more sophisticated in recognition of the sustainable development agenda. As we shall see, regulatory obligations and liabilities now reflect concepts such as pollution prevention and the taking of precautionary action, both of which incorporate a preventive dimension into policy-making. End-of-pipe solutions to environmental problems are being replaced by pollution prevention measures for sustainable development, which can be advanced most effectively if ecological problems are anticipated before they appear.[15] The

[11] Eg G Teubner, 'Substantive and Reflexive Elements in Modern Law' (1983) 17 *Law and Review* 239. See also P Nonet and P Selznick *Law and Society in Transition: Toward Responsive Law* (Harper Colophon, 1978).

[12] *Ibid*, 253–4.

[13] *Ibid*, 252–3.

[14] *Ibid*, 254–6.

[15] See further N de Sadeleer, *Environmental Principles: from Political Slogans to Legal Rules* (Oxford UP, 2002) ch 2.

precautionary principle takes prevention one step further and represents an important milestone in risk reduction.[16]

Some contemporary changes to the traditional command model are introducing 'reflexive' elements into environmental law, which reflect a so-called 'third stage' in the evolution of modern legal systems.[17] In contrast with the heavy hand of command regulation, which aims to control behaviour directly, a system based on reflexive law 'attempts to create incentives and procedures that induce entities to act in certain ways and to engage in internal reflection about what form that behaviour should take . . . the state sets goals, but shares more of the responsibility for achieving them with regulated entities'.[18] In the command and control arena, a reflexive legal strategy is reflected in initiatives such as creating compliance incentives through leadership programmes. But policy instruments such as environmental management systems and economic incentives, both of which are arguably replacing the traditional command approach, are also representative of reflexive law.

C. Environmental Standards

1. Background

The word 'standard' in the context of pollution regulation means the precise limits imposed by law on the amount of permissible pollution in the environment. The Royal Commission on Environmental Pollution (UK) provides a more detailed definition:

> We understand an environmental standard to be any judgement about the acceptability of environmental modifications resulting from human activities which fulfils both the following conditions:
>
> (a) it is formally stated after some consideration and intended to apply generally to a defined class of cases;
> (b) because of its relationship to certain sanctions, rewards or values, it can be expected to exert an influence, direct or indirect, on activities that affect the environment.[19]

16 *Ibid*, ch 3; see also Fisher's ch, this vol.

17 Teubner, above n 11; EW Orts, 'Reflexive Environmental Law' (1995) 89 *Northwestern University Law Review* 1227.

18 DJ Fiorino, 'Rethinking Environmental Regulation: Perspectives on Law and Governance' (1999) 23 *Harvard Environmental Law Review* 441, 448.

19 Royal Commission on Environmental Pollution, *21st Report: Setting Environmental Standards* (Cm 4053, 1998) 1.16.

There are a number of different types of environmental standard that can be used to achieve positive social and environmental change.[20] Although there is some difference in the terminology used in different statutes in different jurisdictions, environmental standards can be divided into two categories, each of which serves quite different purposes in environmental policy. On the one hand, some standards are set by reference to the target being protected, for example the aquatic environment. Ambient and receptor standards, the two most important target standards, set levels on the maximum pollutant concentration permitted in the environment at any one place and are used by enforcing authorities to ensure that standards on discharges do not cumulatively infringe the level set in the ambient standard. On the other hand, source-related standards are set by reference to the pollution source. These standards may be further divided into performance or emission standards, specification or process standards and product standards. Conformity with performance standards is measured by reference to what is emitted rather than the effect of the pollutant on the receiving environment whilst specification standards control the activities which produce pollution rather than the actual quality or quantity of the discharge. Product standards control the characteristics of a manufactured product, with the aim of protecting against possible environmental damage resulting from its use, disposal or even manufacture. All these standards perform different roles and have different strengths and weaknesses. For example, from a cost-effectiveness perspective, target standards are preferred over performance standards and performance standards are more cost-effective than specification standards. But specification standards are arguably easier (and therefore less costly) to enforce.

Before considering the types of standards in more detail it is useful to consider one current area of contention: should the law fix specific, uniform standards of emission or leave it to the regulatory authority to determine standards appropriate to particular circumstances? This has been (and remains) an intensely debated question. Arguments both for and against uniform standards are persuasive. Some academic writers such as Ackerman and Stewart argue that uniform standards do not necessarily lead to the most socially efficient form of pollution control, for the harm arising from a given activity and the cost of preventing that harm may vary considerably according to the circumstances of the regulated company. In their analysis of uniform standards in the US, they posit that '[t]he present regulatory system wastes tens of billions of dollars every year, misdirects resources, stifles innovation, and spawns massive and often counterproductive litigation'.[21] Uniform

[20] See C Hilson, *Regulating Pollution—A UK and EC Perspective* (Hart Publishing, 2000); D Wilkinson, *Environment and Law* (Routledge, 2002) 134–44; M Ochsner, 'Pollution Prevention: An Overview of Regulatory Incentives and Barriers' (1998) 6 *New York University Environmental Law Journal* 586.

[21] BA Ackerman and RB Stewart, 'Reforming Environmental Law' (1985) 37 *Stanford Law Review* 1333, 1333.

standards, they say, ignore both variations in the cost of reducing pollution amongst plants and geographic variations in pollution effects. In contrast, Latin, a staunch defender of uniform environmental standards, recognises a number of advantages over differentiated standards including:

> decreased information collection and evaluation costs, greater consistency and predictability of results, greater accessibility of decisions to public scrutiny and participation, increased likelihood that regulations will withstand judicial review, reduced opportunities for manipulative behavior by agencies in response to political or bureaucratic pressures, reduced opportunities for obstructive behavior of regulated parties . . .[22]

Differentiated standards do however pose difficulties of their own. Whilst differentiated standards can have due regard to factors such as variations in plant location and operating costs, Latin argues that critics of uniform standards fail to consider the practical, economic and political constraints that would prevent the introduction of alternative instruments or would hamper their performance.

2. Target Standards

Target standards reflect some of the very first environmental regulatory techniques adopted by governments. By attempting to limit the effects of discharges on the environment (the target) they are concerned with the amount of harm to or the deterioration of a particular environmental medium such as air or water, and not directly with the activities of the polluter.[23] There are two types of target standards: ambient and receptor standards. Receptor standards are applied directly to the individual discharger, and render him or her liable for causing perceptible harm to the environment. For example, the Canadian Fisheries Act 1985 makes it an offence to carry on any works or undertakings that result in the harmful alteration, disruption, or destruction of fish habitat.[24] Ambient standards, on the other hand, establish concentration ceilings for a given pollutant in a given environmental medium. For example, countries such as Australia have established ambient air quality standards for air pollutants such as carbon dioxide and lead.[25] By focusing on what requires protection, target standards are able in theory to deal with inputs to the environment from all sources and via all potential pathways. They are thus able to address the effects of potentially harmful combinations of substances on the

[22] H Latin, "Ideal Versus Real Regulatory Efficiency: Implementation of Uniform Standards and 'Fine-Tuning' Regulatory Reforms" (1985) 37 *Stanford Law Review* 1267, 1271.

[23] Eg a standard requiring that a discharge of a pollutant to water is not harmful to fish or other aquatic animals would be defined as a target standard.

[24] RS 1985, c F-14, s 35.

[25] See further the National Environmental Protection Measure for Ambient Air Quality, established by the federal government of Australia in 1998.

environment. However, constant monitoring of the environment can prove to be impractical and expensive, and in areas where a target standard is already being met there is little incentive for polluters to improve their performance.

3. Source-based Standards

There are three main types of source-based standards: performance or emission standards, specification or process standards and product standards. Performance or emission standards, in the form of prohibitions on the discharge of certain substances or maximum emission limits, focus on the amount or concentration of a pollutant that may be discharged from a particular point-source. For example, in order to combat pollution caused by increasing car usage, governments are setting vehicle emission standards. Unlike specification standards, the individual or company subjected to the standard is free to achieve the desired level by whatever technique it prefers. In many countries, emission standards are the most widely used pollution control mechanism. But why? Unlike target standards, they are relatively easy to control and monitor by sampling at the point of emission. Enforcement is aided because of the simplicity of the causation requirements where there is a point of discharge.[26] And in contrast with specification standards, they can be tightened progressively to encourage dischargers to improve the process whilst still retaining choice as to how this is done. In this way tough emission standards can have 'technology-forcing' properties, inducing technological innovation to reduce compliance costs. Performance standards do, however, have one main drawback in that they are not suited to controlling non-point emissions such as pesticide run-off.

Specification or process standards are concerned with controlling the industrial activities that produce the pollutants themselves and constitute a direct interference with the manufacturer's behaviour.[27] They are therefore very different from performance standards because, as long as the manufacturer complies with the standard, the quality or quantity of the discharge is of no concern unless, of course, it is the subject of an independent performance standard. Specification standards can exist in either a positive or a negative form. For example, they may lay down prescriptions as to the construction of the plant, directives may be given as to how a plant is to be used, and they may specify the abatement methods to be adopted. Increasingly, governments are having recourse to 'benefits-based' specification standards such as BATNEEC (Best Available Techniques Not Entailing Excessive Cost), or more, recently, BAT (Best Available Techniques).[28] The principal strength

[26] It should be noted, however, that point-source emission limits sometimes involve very complicated mathematical dispersion models that are anything but simple to apply.

[27] G Richardson, AI Ogus and P Burrows, *Policing Pollution: A Study of Regulation and Enforcement* (Clarendon Press, 1992) 38.

[28] S Bell and D McGillivray, *Environmental Law* (5th edn, Blackstone, 2000) 384, 396–8.

of specification standards is that, in contrast with target and performance standards, they are proactive and can prevent a pollution incident from occurring. In addition, the administrative costs of enforcement compared, for example, with performance standards are far less than the additional operating costs imposed on industry for, to monitor compliance with a specification standard, the enforcing authority need only ensure that the prescribed directives have been followed.[29] However, it could be argued that they act as a disincentive for producers to find more effective ways of reducing pollution unless the standards are made progressively stricter. The technique also implies that central government is in the best position to determine the relationship between environmental harm and polluting activities. Consequently, not only is the process of maintaining specification standards in line with technological advances cumbersome, but it undoubtedly leads to a loss of flexibility at site level.

Finally product standards specify permitted or prohibited product characteristics, for example, requiring vehicle manufacturers to fit catalytic converters on all new cars. They may also take the form of outright bans or phase-outs of particular products such as chlorofluorocarbons or leaded gasoline. In recent years some governments have pushed product standards in a new direction with the emergence of the concept of extended producer responsibility, also known as product stewardship. This is a matter to which we shall return in Section G.

4. Conclusion

Despite the increasing use of alternative instruments such as market-based mechanisms and informational measures, the dominant approach to regulation remains the setting of standards by a central regulatory authority. Regulatory systems undoubtedly rely on a combination of target and source standards to achieve their aims, but choosing the most effective and efficient combination is far from easy as pollution poses problems for standard setting which are significantly more complex than those experienced in other policy areas. First, as account must be taken of future generations, and the benefits of environmental protection comprise not only health considerations but also a range of social amenities, any valuation is highly speculative. Secondly, high abatement costs and uncertainty about the impact of pollutants leads to a difficulty in deciding the appropriate trade-off between environmental protection and industrial production. And due to the variations in the environmental characteristics of different regions, it is difficult to translate goals into standards tailored to suit individual firms.

[29] Richardson, Ogus and Burrows, above n 27, 39–40.

A final important factor for consideration is the role of science in environmental standards-setting.[30] Environmental law relies heavily on science for its legitimacy. Scientific and technical knowledge underpins decisions relating, for example, to the establishment of maximum emission limits of a particular pollutant from an industrial process. Scientific expertise plays a key role in identifying environmental problems, determining their severity, prioritising them and conceptualising appropriate solutions.[31] The centrality of scientific expertise has increased as the leading environmental problems of the day have shifted from phenomena accessible to direct sensory perception and common sense (eg, belching smokestacks, effluent-filled waterways, dead fish and birds) to ones that are increasingly invisible, diffuse, cumulative and inaccessible to immediate sensory perception (eg, climate change, persistent organic pollutants).[32]

This central role for science is qualified, however, by several factors. First, in most environmental regulation regimes, scientific findings and recommendations are only advisory, and actual decisions on environmental standards and other regulatory matters often depart substantially from scientific advice. This may be appropriate in view of the fact that environmental standards-setting is never a 'purely technical' matter, but it also opens many regulators to criticism for ignoring scientific 'realities' or bowing to industry pressure.

Secondly, recent crises, such as the outbreak of mad cow disease, have however invoked large-scale public distrust in scientific expertise and advice. This has prompted calls for broader participation and greater accountability in technical, environmental rule-making.[33] Thirdly, many governments depend heavily on regulated industries themselves for the scientific and technical knowledge on which environmental regulation is based, which may compromise the legitimacy and credibility of such regulation. Further, recent years have seen an increasing emphasis on the validity of indigenous, traditional and local knowledge as inputs into environmental regulation, displacing scientific expertise somewhat from its central perch.[34] There have also been considerable advances in our understanding of the natural environment in which we live, making it more likely that scientific certainty in a number of important areas such as climate change will not be achieved. This not only necessitates a precautionary approach to decision-making but also means that whoever is given the task of legal intervention cannot therefore rely solely on objective scientific evidence. Those entrusted with this task

[30] Eg AF Chalmers, *What is this Thing Called Science? An Assessment of the Nature and Status of Science and its Methods* (U Queensland Press, 1976); SE Gaines, 'Science, Politics, and the Management of Toxic Risks Through Law' (1990) 30 *Jurimetrics Journal* 271.This theme is also explored in Fisher's ch, this vol.

[31] Eg M Hajer, *The Politics of Environmental Discourse* (Clarendon Press, 1995).

[32] *Ibid.*

[33] See further Richardson and Razzaque, this vol.

[34] GM Morin-Labatut and S Akhtar, 'Traditional Environmental Knowledge: A Resource to Manage and Share' (1992) 4 *Journal of the Society for International Development* 24.

must also have regard to a wider variety of fundamentally divided interests, thereby making political choices as to the correct stance to adopt. Institutional and procedural frameworks must therefore be adapted to meet these new challenges.

D. Environmental Licensing

A licence can be defined as an instrument created under government authority that requires all businesses or individuals with specified characteristics to gain prior approval. Under a licensing system, regulated conduct is authorised when the relevant authority has approved the application. Non-compliance with any specified standards given effect to in the licence may result in enforcement action.[35] It is therefore an ex ante enforcement mechanism that is designed primarily to prevent, or at least minimise, a particular type of harm.

Environmental licences or permits are an important part of the command and control system, for they are the primary 'instruments through which state environmental protection agencies specify how individual facilities must comply with environmental regulations and laws'.[36] This is achieved through the use of licence conditions. In establishing these conditions, the regulatory authority can have regard inter alia to the local environment including the physical, geographical and geological peculiarities of the surrounding land, thereby allowing for the creation of control regimes that are tailored to each individual applicant. And in accordance with the polluter pays principle, the regulatory authority will normally be able to recoup the administrative costs associated with the licence approval system through a fee charging system.

Generally speaking, environmental licences can be divided into two categories. Some licences authorise the discharge of pollutants into the environment; for example, under the Resource Management Act 1991 (New Zealand) a resource consent can entitle the holder to discharge a contaminant from any industrial or trade premises into the air.[37] In contrast, other licences authorise the operational activities of the licence holder; for example, in the UK, it is unlawful to carry out a process listed as polluting or potentially harmful without an authorisation from the enforcing authority.[38]

[35] Bureau of Industry Economics Report 96/10, *Business Licences and Regulation Reform* (Australian Government Publishing, 1996) 6.

[36] KB Heller, SJ Kelly and LJ Bloch, 'Flexible Permitting Promotes Operating Flexibility and Facilitates Environmental Protection' (May 1999) Environmental Management Online, www.awma.org/em/99/May99/contents.asp, 1, 1.

[37] S 15.

[38] This is a reference to the concept of Integrated Pollution Control introduced in the Environmental Protection Act 1990. In most cases the regulatory body is the Environment Agency, established by the Environment Act 1995.

In many respects, the key features of an environmental licence are that it facilitates the application of environmental standards to individual entities and provides ex ante control of polluting activities. Licences are also valuable for a number of other reasons. One such reason relates to the fact that licences can be used to correct information failures which arise because consumers, other businesses or the regulatory authority have less than perfect information. As business must seek prior approval from the regulatory authority before a licence is granted, it is necessary that the authority has sufficient information to make an informed decision on the licence application. There is therefore a requirement that, when applying for either a licence or any sort of modification to that licence, the business or individual will have to provide certain specified information. The provision of this information also enables the regulatory authority to set the appropriate standards, thereby ensuring that pollution is minimised or prevented. In addition, as the regulatory authority is notified of any source of potentially polluting activity, enforcement costs may be reduced through the efficient inspection of businesses. Consumers and other businesses are also usually given access to much of this information through a scheme of public environmental registers. A licensing system can also be used to ensure that only those businesses or individuals who satisfy certain criteria can obtain a licence. Coupled with the use of individual licence conditions, this allows the regulator to exert considerable control over licensed operations. For example, in the UK, those applicants who apply for a licence to treat, keep or dispose of waste must be deemed 'fit and proper persons'.[39] The licence applicant must not have been convicted of a relevant offence, must satisfy technical competence provisions and must have adequate financial provision to discharge her obligations under the licence.

Permit-based regimes do, of course, have their disadvantages. By their nature, they are not as suited to situations where the environment is affected by non-point-source pollution, for example where a river picks up contaminants from several different factories situated on a riverbank. And compared with other more flexible regulatory instruments, they tend to be relatively expensive to administer and enforce. Moreover, licensing schemes are generally inflexible, so they are unable to respond when there is a sudden change in economic or environmental conditions.

The above appraisal of licensing as a regulatory technique illustrates the numerous goals and objectives which can be incorporated into a licensing regime. It can internalise pollution externalities, ensure the polluter pays for the environmental damage, remain flexible to allow for tailor-made decision-making, and encourage a proactive approach to pollution prevention. It has become and remains the standard technique used by governments seeking to regulate, in particular, point-source pollution emanating from a definite location. But modern

[39] Environmental Protection Act 1990 s 74(3).

strategies to address environmental degradation make use of both a combination of regulatory techniques and a broader range of regulatory actors. Licences play in important role in designing this 'smart' regulation.[40] They can be and are used to underpin more flexible instruments such as trading schemes and voluntary agreements by ensuring that participants at least meet minimum performance levels.

E. Environmental Planning Instruments

The instruments we have discussed so far, namely environmental standards and licences, are generally used when dealing with traditional forms of pollution such as the emission of pollutants to air, water or land. Many other kinds of activities, however, also have impacts on the environment and have become the subjects of command regulation. Some activities, such as the development of a wind farm or a residential subdivision, may affect the environment in a different way by, for example, destroying valuable wildlife habitat or affecting the visual amenity of land. One of the main threats to sustainable development is, in fact, the loss of biodiversity: the World Wildlife Fund has estimated that we have lost 30 per cent of the world's natural wealth in a period of just 25 years.[41] To minimise further environmental damage, the law utilises another very different form of command and control in the form of environmental planning instruments such as environmental impact assessment (EIA), strategic environmental assessment (SEA), and parks and protected areas regulation. Other prominent examples, discussion of which is beyond the scope of this chapter, include official plans, zoning bylaws, subdivision controls and building codes.[42] All these legal techniques can be used in efforts to safeguard sustainability.

1. Environmental Impact Assessment and Strategic Environmental Assessment

Environmental impact assessment is an evaluation of the impact of a proposed development project on the natural and human-made environment. Historically, EIA can be traced to the US National Environmental Policy Act of 1969.[43] EIA

[40] This is a reference to Gunningham and Grabosky's work (above n 1) on designing environmental policy.
[41] World Wildlife Fund *Living Planet Report* (WWF, 1998).
[42] See further JB Cullingworth, *Town and Country Planning in Britain* (Unwin Hyman, 1988); P McAuslan, 'Planning Law's Contribution to the Problems of an Urban Society' (1974) 37 *MLR* 134.
[43] 42 USC 4321–4347, 1 Jan, 1970, 83 Stat 852.

requirements were soon introduced in countries such as Japan, Canada, Australia and China. France and Germany were the first European countries to introduce EIA procedures and an EC Directive passed in 1985[44] made EIA procedures mandatory in all European Member States. At present, almost all developed countries have mandatory EIA procedures and a number of developing and transitional countries are embracing the EIA philosophy, the main driver of which is the use of EIA by international development banks and aid agencies.[45]

The theory of EIA is that better information about the environmental impacts of proposed projects will produce better-informed public debates and better decisions about whether and under what conditions projects will be allowed to proceed.[46] It is a process which, at the direction of a public authority, involves the presentation, collection, publication and assessment of information and is ideally, although not always in practice, 'a systematic, integrative and iterative process in which consultation and participation are integral to any project evaluation'.[47] The main product of an EIA is an environmental statement which usually contains a description of the proposed development, the data necessary to identify and assess its environmental effects, a description of proposed mitigation measures and a summary of information which is accessible to lay persons. In some cases this statement is produced by a public authority, in others by the project proponent itself. A public authority then usually evaluates the significance of the environmental impacts of the project and decides whether and under what conditions to allow the project to proceed.

Secondly, the legal effect of EIAs varies across jurisdictions. Most EIA regimes are focussed on producing information rather than dictating any particular course of action. While critics often argue that the findings of public EIA panels should be binding on governments, public authorities usually retain the discretion to decide whether and in what form projects will go ahead. EIA legislation is thus an odd variety of command regulation. It is command regulation in the sense that it makes EIA mandatory for certain projects, but, unlike environmental standards and licences, it usually produces only recommendations as to the measures to be taken to protect the environment against the harmful impacts of proposed projects. It is usually up to public authorities to translate these into binding requirements, which they do through other regulatory tools such as licences.

[44] Council Directive 85/33/EEC of 16 Sept 1985[1985] OJ L/175/40, as amended by Council Directive 97/11/EC of 3 Mar 1997[1997] OJ L/73/5.

[45] G Handl, *Multilateral Development Banks: Environmental Principles and Concepts Reflecting General International Law and Public Policy* (Kluwer, 2001).

[46] US Council on Environmental Quality, *The National Environmental Policy Act: A Study of Its Effectiveness After Twenty-Five Years* (Executive Office of the President, 1997); LW Canter, *Environmental Impact Assessment.* (McGraw-Hill, 1977); WR Sheate, *Making an Impact: A Guide to EIA Law and Policy* (Cameron May, 1994); N Robinsion, 'International Trends in Environmental Impact Assessment' (1992) 19 *Boston College Environmental Affairs Law Review* 591.

[47] Royal Commission on Environmental Pollution, *23rd Report—Environmental Planning* (Cm 5459, 2002) 7.22.

An ongoing controversy is how to define the scope of an EIA. Should an EIA consider the need for or alternatives to the proposed project? Should an EIA consider the cumulative effects of future projects alongside the current project?[48] This last point requires elaboration because it has spawned a massive debate of its own. Project-based EIA is not able to consider the cumulative effects of small projects, cannot deal adequately with induced impacts where a project stimulates further development, is not suited to tackling global environmental impacts such as greenhouse gas emissions and is therefore limited in its ability to contribute to sustainable development. Another kind of assessment, known as Strategic Environmental Assessment (SEA), addresses such integrative issues by assessing environmental impacts at the broad level of the public policies, plans and programmes within which discrete projects are proposed and implemented.[49] A recent development within the European Community is the Strategic Environmental Assessment Directive,[50] which requires certain plans and programmes on the environment to be subjected to environmental assessment procedures. According to the Director General of the Commission's Environment Directorate, this plugs the 'gap by requiring the environmental effects of a broad range of plans and programmes to be assessed, so that they can be taken into account while plans are actually being developed'.[51] The SEA Directive can therefore be seen as a progressive step forward from project-level environmental assessments.

Finally, unlike pollution control licensing systems, it should be noted that a key component of EIAs and SEAs is that they provide access to information and public participation, the importance of which has recently been acknowledged in, and potentially strengthened by, the Aarhus Convention.[52] At their most basic level, they provide developers, planning authorities and members of the public with information relating to development proposals, thereby ensuring that projects are open to scrutiny by all stakeholders. This may not only restore faith in public authority decision-making, which has been lost following incidents such as the BSE crisis, but may also improve the quality of the decision and reduce opposition.

48 RK Burris and LW Canter, 'Cumulative Impacts are Not Properly Addressed in Environmental Assessment' (1997) 17 *Environmental Assessment Review* 5.

49 C Wood and N Djeddour, 'Strategic Environmental Assessment: EA of Policies, Plans and Programmes' (1992) 10 *Impact Assessment Bulletin* 3.

50 Directive 2001/42/EC on the assessment of the effects of certain plans and programmes on the environment OJ L/197/30. For a detailed discussion of the Directive and the UK's implementation of its requirements see *J Robinson*, 'The Environmental Assessment of Plans and Programmes' [2004] *Journal of Planning Law* 1028.

51 European Commission's Guidance on the Implementation of Directive 2001/42 (2003), available at http://europa.eu.int/comm/environment/eia/sea-support.htm, foreword.

52 Convention on Access to Information, Public Participation in Decision-making and Access to Justice in Environmental Matters (Aarhus, 25 June 1998). For a discussion of the Convention, see M Lee and C Abbot, 'The Usual Suspects? Public Participation Under the Aarhus Convention' (2003) 66 *MLR* 80.

2. Parks and Protected Areas Regulation

Since Victorian times, governments have created control systems to protect certain areas of land which are under threat.[53] But the twentieth century has made more diverse and contradictory demands of the environment, where the 'scientific and preservationist goals of nature conservation and landscape protection have been pursued at the same time as economic and social demand or need, for the provision of food, raw materials, amenity, recreation, employment and housing'.[54] Whilst traditional planning and development control systems (including EIAs) can be used to regulate development in the public interest, it is commonly accepted that certain areas of land merit greater protection. Command and control techniques have been used to respond to these challenges. In countries such as Australia, Canada and the UK, a large proportion of land is formally 'designated' as protected from certain activities. Some forms of designation such as national parks are intended, primarily, to create and maximise opportunities for human recreation and enjoyment. The main purpose of other areas such as nature reserves is to preserve flora and fauna by limiting the rights of both landowners and members of the public.[55] Another vital purpose served by parks and protected areas legislation is to regulate, and in some cases facilitate, resource exploitation including forestry and mining.

Balancing the varying and often diverse interests of stakeholders is a far from easy task. While doing so in the case of publicly owned land is daunting enough, it becomes even more difficult when dealing with privately owned land. The extent to which the rights of a landowner to use his land as he wishes (as the common law has traditionally allowed) should be compromised in the name of ecology has been the focus of much debate. In balancing these interests, few formal and absolute restrictions are generally imposed. Instead, sites are identified as being of value and are given official government recognition by means of formal designation. The conservation value of the land is taken into account through consultation and other procedural requirements.

F. An Assessment of Command and Control

The ability of command and control regulation to minimise the environmental impact of potentially polluting activities has been the subject of much debate.

[53] BH Hibbard, *A History of the Public Land Policies* (U Wisconsin Press, 1965); C Reid, *Nature Conservation Law* (U Dundee Press, 2002).

[54] N Herbert-Young (ed), *Law, Policy and Development in the Rural Environment* (U Wales Press, 1999) introduction.

[55] For an overview of protected areas in Canada see S Elgie, 'Protected Spaces and Endangered Species' in EL Hughes, AR Lucas and WA Tilleman, *Environmental Law and Policy* (3rd edn, Edmond Montgomery, 2004).

Whilst on the one hand it has indisputably contributed to the abatement of environmental damage particularly in terms of reducing air and water pollution, on the other it has been widely criticised by lawyers, economists and policy-makers for being inflexible and inefficient. In this section, we will assess the command and control technique, giving specific examples to illustrate stories of success and failure.[56]

1. Effectiveness

As stated above, in many respects, command and control regulation has been successful in curbing pollution.[57] Recently, the Environment Agency (England and Wales) reported that command and control has clearly contributed to some striking environmental improvements:

—since 1990, sulphur dioxide emissions to air have fallen by 75 per cent, nitrogen oxides by 52 per cent;
—water pollution (measured by biochemical oxygen demand) fell by 65 per cent in the five years to 2001;
—environmental incidents fell by 30 per cent between 1997 and 2000.[58]

Similarly in the US, many of the dramatic improvements made to the natural environment since the 1970s have been attributed to end-of-pipe, command and control approaches. The first pollution control Act in the US in the 1970s, the Clean Air Act,[59] is commonly stated to have achieved its objectives:

> [T]he EPA, in its 1988 Report to Congress, reported that air pollution had been reduced in the past decade. Sulfur oxides and VOCs were down seventeen percent, carbon monoxide decreased twenty-five percent, total suspended particles were reduced twenty-one percent, and lead emissions were cut ninety-four percent. Moreover, this occurred

[56] Many different lists of the strengths and weaknesses of command regulation can be found in the literature, but space constraints prevent us from considering them exhaustively in this chapter. See E Bardach and R Kagan, *Going by the Book—The Problem of Regulatory Unreasonableness* (Temple UP, 1982), I Ayres and J Braithwaite, *Responsive Regulation: Transcending the Deregulation Debate* (Oxford UP, 1992).

[57] For defences of substantive law solutions to contemporary environmental and social problems, see M Galanter, 'Law Abounding: Legislation Across the North Atlantic' (1992) 55 *MLR* 1; Latin, above n 22. However, as noted by Hilson, above n 20, 127, command and control cannot take full responsibility for improvements in environmental quality in the past 25 years. Society's shift away from coal to less polluting fuels such as gas and a general decline in heavy industry are also likely to have had a significant effect.

[58] Environment Agency, *Delivering for the Environment: A 21st* Century Approach to Regulation (Environment Agency, 2004) 6.

[59] 42 USC §§ 7401–7661.

> while the US population grew an estimated twenty percent between 1970 and 1988, and the gross national product increased fifty-nine percent in constant dollars.[60]

Improvements to US water quality have also been accredited to command and control. Twenty-five years ago, only one third of waters in the US were safe for fishing and swimming. The US Clean Water Act,[61] by requiring major industries to meet performance standards and employing a permit system to ensure compliance, has succeeded in improving water quality throughout the country, and now two thirds of waters are suitable for these activities.[62] Similar successes are mirrored in other jurisdictions.[63]

Most of the successes attributed to command techniques relate to pollution emanating from single, point sources such as industrial plants and domestic chimneys. Problems remain, however, 'with more risk-related, invisible pollution from such sources, with visible and invisible pollution from mobile and diffuse sources, and with pollution from product use and disposal'.[64] Command and control is therefore not as effective in dealing with matters such as diffuse air and water pollution from agriculture and air pollution from vehicles. Moreover, newly emerging environmental problems including climate change and indoor air pollution are ill-suited to command systems. In addition, many of the pollution programmes originating from the early 1970s, by focusing on single environmental media, merely shifted pollution from one medium to another, rather than actually reducing it.[65] A pollution shift, as opposed to reduction, is illustrated by the attempts of the New South Wales government in the 1970s and 1980s to reduce the emission of toxic substances into waterways. Rather than stipulate that emissions should be reduced, the regulator encouraged businesses to discharge the substances into the sewage system. As a result, the problem was merely shifted from one water source to another.[66]

2. Cost-efficiency and Compliance Incentives

Pollution is often the by-product of a socially desirable and beneficial activity, but government intervention to tackle pollution imposes significant costs (both direct and indirect) on the regulated community. Some critics argue that the high direct

60 AW Reitze, 'A Century of Pollution Control Law: What Worked; What's Failed: What Might Work' (1991) 221 *Environmental Law* 1549, 1615.

61 33 USC §§1251–1376.

62 See US EPA achievements, at www.epa.gov/water.

63 Japan is a notable success story: H Nishimura, *How to Conquer Air Pollution: A Japanese Experience* (Elsevier, 1989).

64 Hilson, above n 20, 127.

65 Ochsner, above n 20, 601.

66 See S Beder, *Toxic Fish and Sewer Surfing—How Deceit and Collusion are Destroying Our Great Beaches* (Allen and Unwin, 1989).

and indirect costs associated with command and control are often attributed to the fact that standards are set and enforced, not by the regulated community, but by governments or their representatives which, to its critics:

> puts government in the position of making the business and operating decisions that the regulated industry should make . . . while government is better able to determine what society's goals should be and build the necessary incentives and accountability mechanisms to get companies to achieve them, the private sector is in a better position to determine what mix of technologies, process changes, or management practices would achieve the regulatory goals.[67]

Ultimately, safeguarding the environment can be expensive in the short term whatever the longer term benefits.[68] It is therefore paramount that policy-makers, when designing a regulatory system, use the most cost-effective instruments (ie, those that produce the desired results at the lowest aggregate cost). However, the direct costs of command and control, such as administrative and compliance costs, can be high.[69] As previously noted, command and control (at least in the form of uniform standards) is arguably an inefficient regulatory technique as it fails to recognise the fact that, due to the heterogeneity of regulated firms and industries and geographical variations in pollution effects, the costs of reducing pollution will vary. The only way to minimise the overall cost of pollution control is to have facilities control pollution at the same marginal abatement cost (ie, the cost to abate one more unit of pollution), not the same emission level or control technology.[70] Uniform standards are incapable of achieving this.[71] Take, for example, a standard which requires the metal processing industry to reduce lead emissions by 10 per cent. It is presumed that for any two companies (X and Y) the cost of meeting this standard is the same, when, in fact, marginal abatement costs differ between firms. It would rarely be cost-effective to make both companies reduce emissions by 10 per cent. Company X may find it cheaper to reduce emissions than Company Y, and so the lowest cost solution would be to require

[67] DJ Fiorino, 'Toward a New System of Environmental Regulation: The Case for an Industry Sector Approach' (1996) 26 *Environmental Law* 457.

[68] Eg, it was estimated that total pollution control expenditures in the mid-1990s in the US ran to approximately 2% of GDP. National Council for Science and the Environment Congressional Research Service Reports 95-147ENR, *Environmental Policy and the Economy: Conflicts and Concordances* (National Council for Science and the Environment, 1995) abstract.

[69] Administrative costs are those associated with the permit application procedure, record keeping, acquiring relevant information and perhaps negotiating with the enforcement agency. Compliance costs comprise the capital expenditure on new equipment and the adaptation of old plant, any additional annual operating costs and any productivity losses.

[70] RW Hahn and RN Stavins, 'Incentive-Based Regulation: A New Era for an Old Idea?' (1991) 18 *Ecology Law Quarterly* 1.

[71] On the other hand, market based incentives such as trading schemes can ensure that emissions reductions are achieved at the lowest cost.

Company X to cut back more than Company Y. In his analysis of UK pollution control regulation, Hilson accepts that with the introduction of concepts such as BATNEEC (Best Available Techniques Not Entailing Excessive Costs), some regimes consider such costs on an ad hoc basis, but 'none appears to consider marginal abatement costs systematically'.[72]

In addition to these direct costs, there are also often indirect or unintended consequences of regulation that may have a huge impact over and above direct costs. These indirect costs, which include the distortion of competition within a market, productive inefficiency and the inhibition of technical change, can be substantial.[73] When regulations make it more difficult for new firms to enter the market, this creates a barrier to entry and enables those firms in the market to maximise profits by selling at a greater price. Regulation may also force production costs up, thus creating productive inefficiency. And it can potentially inhibit market innovation.[74] For example, by forcing firms to spend resources on complying with regulatory requirements, regulators may cause capital resources to be diverted from investment in market innovation. And in the case of the manufacturing industry, standards may restrict the manufacturers' freedom to adopt new products and processes that would enjoy market success.

Although it is often maintained that the cost of complying with environmental regulations unduly restricts business profitability and competitiveness, reduces economic growth and stifles innovation, this is not a view shared by all. Michael Porter argues that stringent business regulation can, in fact, enhance competitive advantage and stimulate firms to discover hidden opportunities.[75] In terms of direct costs, pollution prevention measures can result in cost savings through, for example, improved energy and raw material usage. Indeed, evidence suggests that firms are increasingly making the link between good environmental practice and commercial benefits. For example, in a UK benchmarking survey of environmental awareness, 78 per cent of businesses with 50 to 250 employees cite reduced operating costs as a benefit of compliance.[76] By subjecting industry to tough standards, firms are put under pressure to improve quality and upgrade technology. Where regulations anticipate standards that will spread internationally, the industry is given a head start in developing products and services that will be valued

[72] Hilson, above n 20, 112.

[73] RB Stewart, 'A New Generation of Environmental Regulation?' (2001) 29 *Capital University Law Review* 21, 30–2.

[74] See further RB Stewart, 'Regulation, Innovation and Administrative Law: A Conceptual Framework' (1981) 69 *California Law Review* 1256.

[75] ME Porter, *The Competitive Advantage of Nations* (Macmillan Press, 1990); see also ME Porter and C van der Linde, 'Green and Competitive: Ending the Stalemate' [1995] *Harvard Business Review* 397; G Haq *et al*, 'Determining the Costs to Industry of Environmental Regulation' (2001) 11 *European Environment* 125.

[76] The percentage (49%) is lower for companies with fewer than 50 employees. See further Environment Agency *et al*, *2002 Netregs Benchmarking Survey: How Green are Small Businesses?* (Environment Agency, 2002).

elsewhere. Examples of this sort of a regulatory 'race to the top' include 'Sweden's tough standards for product safety and environmental protection . . . [which] have been a significant source of competitive advantage in a variety of industries'.[77] Furthermore, environmental standards may create a new market in pollution control equipment and services.

Command and control techniques also arguably fail to provide adequate incentives to go beyond the minimum standards. This is especially the case where the regulated entity has incurred costs in installing pollution control technology in order to meet the standard. As put by Gunningham and Graboksy, '[t]he inability to encourage firms to go "beyond compliance", through a process of continuous improvement and cultural change, is one of the most serious failings of command and control in its traditional forms'.[78] Although the government can, of course, create incentives by making standards stricter, this can be difficult and ideally requires the government to have detailed knowledge of what standards would be most appropriate for different industries. The counter-argument is that firms may go beyond compliance in anticipation of any future tightening of standards, thereby giving them a competitive advantage.

3. Administrative Flexibility

A key component of any environmental command and control system is that considerable administrative flexibility or discretion is afforded to public regulators in setting, applying and enforcing the laws. Some critics argue that there needs to be more administrative flexibility in command regulation, while others argue that there is already too much.

The main drawbacks of administrative flexibility relate to predictability, fairness, simplicity, cost, transparency and the risk of 'regulatory capture'. A system in which legal requirements and penalties are prescribed in detail and applied uniformly does have its benefits. Settled and precise rules are advantageous to both regulated enterprises and enforcement officials. Precise rules may limit the exposure of business to unpredictable and expensive *post hoc* changes and may also provide them with some assurance that they will be regulated no more stringently than their competitors. For enforcement officials, rules that specify standards in

[77] Porter, above n 75, 648. It is important also to note the flip-side of the competitive advantage thesis. Many analysts argue that tougher environmental regulations put jurisdictions at a competitive disadvantage, leading to a regulatory 'race to the bottom' (or at least a 'regulatory chill') in which governments adopt lax environmental standards in response to industry threats to relocate to jurisdictions with lower regulatory costs: see RL Revesz, "Rehabilitating Interstate Competition: Rethinking the 'Race to the Bottom' Rationale for Federal Environmental Regulation" (1992) 67 *New York University Law Review* 1210; KH Engel, "State Environmental Standard-Setting: Is There a 'Race' and is it 'To the Bottom'?" (1997) 48 *Hastings Law Journal* 271.

[78] Gunningham and Grabosky, above n 1, 45.

objective numerical terms facilitate proof of violations. This makes the enforcement of precise regulation faster and more efficient: inspectors can carry out more inspections each week, and decisions can be made mechanically. Too much administrative discretion, on the other hand, tends to foster 'back-room' decision-making in which regulated industries have more opportunities to participate and more influence than environmental groups and ordinary citizens, in some cases allowing industry to 'capture' regulatory processes.[79] It also tends to hinder public scrutiny of environmental standard-setting.

On the other hand, administrative discretion does have advantages, the principal of which is the ability to take into account the characteristics of specific pollutants, receiving environments, industrial processes or individual polluters' costs and location without having to turn to legislatures for approval in every case. Administrative flexibility may allow for more effective and efficient regulation. Enforcement officials *must* be given broadly worded grants of discretion that allow them to order regulated enterprises to do whatever seems necessary in the particular circumstances, as well as discretion to relax the rules and tailor their enforcement procedures to the situation. The drive for detailed rules, by contrast, raises the spectre of excessive rigidity. Bardach and Kagan warn of the dangers of equal treatment. They argue that strict, uniform laws can lead to both regulatory 'unreasonableness (the imposition of uniform regulatory requirements in situations where they do not make sense) and unresponsiveness (the failure to consider arguments by regulated enterprises that exceptions should be made)'.[80]

4. Complexity

Another criticism of command and control relates to its legal complexity. This is especially the case where licensing regimes are refined and amended to include new substances or facilities which did not originally fall within the regulatory net. This results in voluminous, complex laws and the creeping 'juridification' of more and more social spheres.[81] In many countries, such as Canada and Australia, firms have to grapple with a large number of both federal and state environmental laws. And for members of the EU, according to a recent report produced by the Confederation of British Industry, environmental regulations account for nearly one third of the 700 directives passed by the Union.[82] For large companies, keeping

[79] Eg R Revesz, *Foundations of Environmental Law and Policy* (Oxford UP, 1997) 183–220; for the seminal 'regulatory capture' theory literature, see RA Posner, 'Theories of Economic Regulation' (1975) 5 *Bell Journal of Economics and Management Science* 335; G Tullock, *The Politics of Bureaucracy* (Public Affairs Press, 1965).

[80] Bardach and Kagan, above n 56, 58.

[81] G Teubner, *Juridification of Social Spheres* (De Gruyter, 1987); Orts, above n 17, 1315.

[82] Confederation of British Industry (CBI), *The UK As a Place to Do Business: UK Environmental Regulation* (CBI, 2004).

track of and complying with hundreds or thousands of complex and confusing legal requirements consumes massive financial and human resources. For many small and medium-sized enterprises (SMEs), knowing and understanding the legal requirements to which they are subject, let alone complying with them, is an insurmountable obstacle. The fact that there are vast volumes of scientifically and technically complex regulations undoubtedly has an impact on the effectiveness of these laws, for, if the regulated community can neither understand nor keep up to date with new regulations, the ability of the rules to minimise environmental impacts is severely hampered.[83]

It is perhaps not surprising that the level of environmental regulation has, in the opinion of many, reached saturation point. Bardach and Kagan explain this by focusing on how the demand for protective measures arises.[84] Much regulation is fuelled by a series of accidents which highlight to the public the need for legal intervention. Although the harmful effects are typically traced to the actions of the firms that evaded the law, legislators, however, are not concerned with punishing those firms by passing *ex post facto* laws, but do need to reshape future legislation in light of the accidents. This 'transforms individual acts of malfeasance into social problems requiring society-wide solutions'.[85] As a consequence, regulation is cast in general terms and is applicable to all classes of individuals and organisations who are creating both major and minor risks.

5. Dependability

Assuming adequate monitoring and enforcement, command and control can also be seen as a dependable mode of regulation: 'the behaviour expected of regulatees can be specified with considerable clarity (for example, through the provision of national minimum standards), making it relatively straightforward to identify breaches of the legal standard and enforce the law'.[86] This also makes it attractive as a political tool. With its emphasis on standard-setting and penalties in the event of non-compliance, it sends a clear message to the public that polluting behaviour will not be tolerated.

However, in the absence of voluntary compliance, environmental regulations are successful and dependable only if they are effectively enforced. This is a key weakness of command and control systems which generally rely on public enforcement by regulatory authorities or, in some, cases, government departments. In order to be effective they must have sufficient resources to monitor compliance and take appropriate action in the event of a breach. This, however, is often not the case with most environmental regulators working within tight operational

[83] Environment Agency, above n 76, 9.
[84] Bardach and Kagan, above n 56, 66–71.
[85] *Ibid*, 67.
[86] Gunningham and Grabosky, above n 1, 41.

budgets. Federal and provincial environmental regulators in Canada (like many other jurisdictions), for example, experienced dramatic budget cuts in the 1980s and 1990s. At the federal level, over a period of 10 years from 1988 to 1998 the budget for Environment Canada fell by 30 per cent, from CAN$800 million to $550 million, more than $200 million of which was set aside for weather forecasting.[87] Similar cutbacks were made in provincial environmental ministries. This led to an unprecedented reduction in inspection and enforcement activities and attracted much criticism from government auditors and environmental pressure groups.[88]

The ease with which regulations can be enforced also depends on the nature of the regulated community. Enforcement is least problematic when the regulated community is comprised of easily identifiable and accessible firms, as this assists regulators in monitoring compliance. Problems are, however, accentuated where the regulated community (as is the case in areas such as waste management) is comprised of a multitude of small, transient firms or individuals, as monitoring their activities and subsequently enforcing the laws is all the more difficult. This has been compounded by the fact that in many countries the vast majority of businesses are small companies. In the UK for example, SMEs (that is companies with fewer than 200 employees) are responsible for approximately 70 per cent of total environmental pollution.[89]

Even where regulators do have adequate financial and staff resources, much recent criticism (and, as we shall see, reform) has been directed at expanding the range of enforcement options. Environmental offences are committed for a multitude of reasons. Some firms deliberately breach the controls in an attempt to save on the costs of compliance, whilst others commit offences due to organisational failure and poor working practices.[90] It is therefore essential that regulators have a large enough range of enforcement tools to enable them to target their enforcement response to the individual offender. These tools must punish the offender, ensure future compliance and deter others from committing similar offences. Traditionally, in countries like Canada and the UK, reliance has been placed on the use of fines, but, as they are generally low compared with factors such as the environmental harm caused by the offence, their ability to achieve

[87] G Toner, 'Environment Canada's Continuing Roller Coaster Ride' in G Swimmer (ed), *How Ottawa Spends 1996–97: Life Under the Knife* (Carleton UP, 1996) 99.

[88] See eg CIELAP, *Ontario's Environment and the Common Sense Revolution—A Fifth Year Report* (Canadian Institute of Environmental Law and Policy, 2000); Third Report of the Standing Committee on Environment and Sustainable Development, *Enforcing Canada's Pollution Laws: The Public Interest Must Come First!* (House of Commons, May 1998).

[89] Groundwork, *Small Firms and the Environment: A Groundwork Status Report* (Groundwork Foundation, 1998).

[90] RA Kagan and JT Scholz, 'The Criminology of the Corporation and Regulatory Enforcement Strategies' in K Hawkins and J Thomas (eds), *Enforcing Regulation* (Kluwer-Nijhoff Publishing, 1984).

these objectives is hampered.[91] This is particularly so in the case of corporate offenders which have no body to incarcerate and which perceive fines as part of an everyday business loss. For example, when Esso Australia Pty Ltd was found guilty of 11 offences under the Occupational Health and Safety Act 1985 (Victoria), which led to the deaths of two people and seriously injured seven, the AUS$2 million fine was initially considered to be substantial.[92] But considering that the company earns approximately AUS$2 million per day from its Bass Strait operations,[93] the fine could be described as derisory. Furthermore, fines and other traditional criminal penalties do not compel a company to review its management procedures and practices, and therefore may not prevent future breaches.

G. Recent Innovations in Command and Control

Despite the success of command and control at abating certain types of pollution, we have seen that it has a number of weaknesses. Legislators, policy-makers and regulators have recognised this and, by building on the strengths of the traditional command and control model, have adopted a broader, more comprehensive approach to environmental regulation. In this section, we will consider some of these recent developments. We begin by examining the concepts of extended producer responsibility and product stewardship, both of which have emerged in recent years as important guiding principles in the design of regulatory policy and standard-setting. Secondly, we briefly consider the shift from pollution control to pollution prevention in command regulation. We then discuss a range of initiatives designed to promote beyond compliance outcomes and enable cost-effective pollution control methods. Finally, we consider the introduction of improved compliance and enforcement mechanisms.[94]

The general thrust of these innovations in command and control have been, first, to expand the scope of regulated firms' environmental responsibility beyond their immediate surroundings to encompass other stages in production and consumption cycles; and, secondly, to increase the 'responsiveness' of command regulation by introducing flexibility and elements of reflexivity. There is tension between these two trends, the first tending to increase the scope and demands of command regulation, the second tending to relax them.

[91] See eg UK House of Commons Environmental Audit Committee Sixth Report, *Environmental Crime and the Courts* (12 May 2004) HC 126.

[92] *Director of Public Prosecutions v Esso Australia Pty Ltd* [2001] VSC 263.

[93] P Gregory and M Shaw, 'Esso Fined a Record $2M', *The Age*, 31 July 2001, 1.

[94] Because of space constraints, this chapter cannot consider other significant recent innovations in command regulation, pollution release and transfer registries, ecosystem management, bioregional planning and other forms of integrated planning.

1. Extended Producer Responsibility and Product Stewardship

The concept of extended producer responsibility (EPR) is emerging as an important development in the design of regulatory strategy. Defined by the OECD as a strategy which suggests that 'the use and post-consumer phase of a product's life cycle are important aspects of the 'pollution' for which responsibility must be assumed under the polluter-pays principle', the principle represents a broader approach to traditional product standards.[95] Although these standards imposed responsibilities and liabilities on producers, thereby producing incentives for safe production, the post-consumer phase of a product's life-cycle was often described as the weakest link in the producer responsibility chain, with the responsibility for the product transferred to the consumer at the point of sale.[96] Instead, EPR initiatives emphasise that responsibility is shared between all parties in the product's life cycle from manufacturer to retailer to consumer.

The greatest 'mover' in this area is the European Community, which has been active in introducing laws and policies which embrace the EPR principle. One of the most recent examples is the Waste Electrical and Electronic Equipment (WEEE) Directive which is holistic in nature and addresses product design, collection, treatment, recovery/reuse/recycling, financing and information.[97] Most importantly, it makes producers responsible for financing most of these activities (producer responsibility) and ensures that private householders are able to return WEEE without charge. Its 'sister' directive on the Restriction of the Use of Certain Hazardous Substances in Electrical and Electronic Equipment (RoHS), aims to limit the environmental impact of such equipment when it reaches the end of its life by minimising the use of hazardous substances in its manufacture.[98]

Other countries such as the US have lagged behind Europe on this matter, perhaps reflecting a reluctance on the part of government to embrace the polluter pays principle in a traditional manufacturing context. The EPR concept has been most widely accepted by certain industry sectors in the US, which have moved independently towards EPR by introducing their own initiatives. A good example of this is the carpet industry. Not only have several major companies embraced EPR, but this has led to a public–private partnership administered through a third party organisation called CARE (Carpet America Recovery Effort).[99]

[95] OECD Environment Monographs no 114 on Pollution Prevention and Control, *Extended Producer Responsibility in the OECD Area, Phase 1 Report, Legal and Administrative Approaches in Member Countries and Policy Options for EPR Programmes*, OECD/GD (96) 48 (OECD, 1996) 6.

[96] See KF Kroepelien, 'Extended Producer Responsibility—New Legal Structures for Improved Ecological Self-Organization in Europe?' (2000) 9 *Review of European Community and International Environmental Law* 165, 166.

[97] Directive 2002/96/EC [2002] OJ L/37/24.

[98] Directive 2002/95/EC [2002] OJ L/37/19.

[99] See further NC Kibert, 'Extended Producer Responsibility: A Tool for Achieving Sustainable Development' (2004) 19 *Journal of Land Use and Environmental Law* 503, 517–20.

Product Stewardship, on the other hand, is an established environmental policy objective in the US. It is related to the concept of EPR although it is, in many senses, a watered-down version, as it distributes responsibility for waste management among government, manufacturers, consumers and retailers, rather than imposing it primarily on manufacturers. For example, the National Electronics Product Stewardship Initiative (NEPSI) in the US brings together federal, state and local governments, manufacturers, retailers, recyclers and environmental groups to develop solutions to the issue of electronic product management.[100]

2. Pollution Prevention

As mentioned in the introduction, the philosophy of environmental command regulation has shifted recently from end-of-pipe control to pollution prevention. Pollution prevention (P2) involves efforts to reduce or avoid the creation of pollutants or generation of waste at source, rather than trying to control them later. P2 originated as a legal principle in the US. The federal Pollution Prevention Act of 1990[101] made P2 a national policy, requiring the US EPA to develop and implement a P2 strategy and establishing a hierarchy in which reduction or prevention of pollution at the source is the first priority in all US EPA activity. While the focus of P2 policy is on grants, education and voluntary action, the EPA is increasingly integrating P2 into its mainstream regulatory activities, including rule-making, licensing and enforcement.[102] Other jurisdictions quickly followed suit, enshrining P2 as a guiding principle for environmental policy. While most make P2 voluntary, a few explicitly mandate it as part of a command and control regime. The EU's Integrated Pollution Prevention and Control Directive of 1996, for example, operationalises P2 via a mandatory pollution licensing scheme.[103]

Like EPR and product stewardship, P2 programmes may have substantive law or reflexive law characteristics depending on how they are designed. Those that require firms to develop and implement P2 plans and provide support or incentives for doing so are the clearest examples of reflexive regulation, stimulating firms to identify and pursue opportunities to reduce and avoid pollution without dictating in detail how they should do so.

3. Promoting Regulatory Flexibility

As we have seen, one of the major failings of the traditional system of command and control was that it did not encourage the regulated community to achieve

[100] National Electronics Product Stewardship Initiative, available at www.nepsi.org.
[101] 42 USC §§13101–13109.
[102] US EPA 'P2 Policy', available at www.epa.gov/p2/p2policy/index.htm.
[103] Council Directive 96/61/EC of 24 Sept 1996 concerning integrated pollution prevention and control (IPPC Directive) [1996] OJ L/257/26.

greater pollution reduction than that required by the law, but was designed merely to bring companies up to a minimum legal standard. Whilst it is obviously still important to ensure that companies, especially environmental 'laggards', achieve the minimum standard of compliance, the system failed to facilitate and reward environmental 'leaders' who have the ability, the resources and the desire to go beyond compliance.[104] Attempts have been made in various jurisdictions to encourage regulatory flexibility, a term 'applied to a range of policy initiatives that seek to address these challenges by providing incentives for individual enterprises to achieve beyond-compliance outcomes building on an existing regulatory framework'.[105] In many instances, these initiatives will also empower companies to choose the most cost-effective pollution control methods, removing much of the decision-making from government bodies. Measures which promote regulatory flexibility are designed to integrate with the existing regulatory framework and in this sense can be distinguished from other voluntary approaches. Examples of flexible programmes are taken from the US and Canada, where the focus is on improving the performance of environmental leaders, and Australia, where initiatives are designed to provide incentives for both leaders and laggards.

These regulatory flexibility initiatives differ from traditional command and control regulation in two important ways. First, they tend to have a strongly reflexive character, taking a systematic, process-based approach to regulation which is concerned not merely with achieving goals but with influencing managerial strategy and encouraging self-management. By empowering the regulated firm to think about solutions to environmental problems, they recognise that those directly involved in, for example, running a plant may achieve better results than externally set standards. Secondly, in contrast to traditional command and control regulation, where, as we have already noted, the scope for community participation is often limited,[106] many regulatory flexibility programmes require the disclosure of information and consultation with local communities. In this respect, they represent a move towards 'facilitative regulation whereby stakeholders are involved in the development and implementation of co-operative strategies to improve environmental quality'.[107] This can, amongst other things, improve relationships between industry and the community and assist in enforcement by creating a third party oversight mechanism.

[104] The distinction between environmental 'laggards' and 'leaders' has been adopted by N Gunningham and D Sinclair, *Leaders and Laggards: Next-generation Environmental Regulation* (Greenleaf Publishing, 2002).

[105] *Ibid*, 110.

[106] But see Richardson and Razzaque, this vol, who trace the increasing move toward public transparency and participation in environmental regulation.

[107] Gunningham and Sinclair, above n 104, 158.

One of the first examples of a regulatory flexibility initiative was Project XL (for eXcellence and Leadership) in the US.[108] Developed under the Clinton–Gore Administration's Reinventing Environmental Regulation initiative, Project XL substituted government-designed and -mandated controls with a control mechanism designed by the regulated entity and other stakeholders.[109] Under the initiative, an applicant committed to more stringent emission limits than required by law. In return, the Environmental Protection Authority altered regulatory requirements to reduce compliance costs. Those companies wishing to participate in Project XL had to satisfy eight criteria, the most important of which was that the results would be better than those that would have been achieved had the company complied with the command and control scheme.[110]

Building on the experience of Project XL and other related initiatives, regulators in the US and Canada are providing incentives for improved environmental performance through a two-track system of regulation. In many instances, a company (with certain environmental credentials) can opt either to continue with traditional forms of regulation or can utilise a more flexible approach. The leading example of this approach is the US EPA's National Environmental Performance Track programme, launched in 2000, under which companies that satisfy certain basic criteria (eg, environmental audit and public disclosure) can go beyond compliance in return for incentives such as technical assistance, use of logos for public relations and marketing, regulatory flexibility and streamlining.[111] More recently, in September 2004, the Ministry of the Environment (Ontario) officially launched its Environmental Leader's Program.[112] To be accepted onto the programme, applicants have to demonstrate, inter alia, a good record of environmental compliance and a commitment to long-term pollution reduction. In return, the Ministry offers incentives such as technical assistance, faster decisions on applications and greater regulatory certainty.

But the success of initiatives like Project XL and the Environmental Leader's Program is debatable. According to Crow, many of them 'seem to operate more or less at the margins of the existing regulatory system, tinkering with incremental changes'[113] with Project XL, in particular, being the subject of substantial and

[108] As of Jan 2003, the US Environmental Protection Agency was no longer accepting proposals for new XL projects.

[109] WJ Clinton and A Gore, *Reinventing Environmental Regulation* (Environmental Protection Agency, 1995).

[110] Regulatory Reinvention XL Pilot Projects, 60 Fed Reg (1995) 27,282, 27,287.

[111] US EPA, *National Environmental Performance Track*, available at www.epa.gov/performancetrack/about.htm. See too Wisconsin's Green Tier Program, available at www.dnr.state.wi.us/org/caer/cea/environmental/background/history/factsheet1.htm.

[112] See generally www.ene.gov.on.ca/envision/general/leadership/index.htm. For a more detailed description of the programme, see 'A Framework for Ontario's Environmental Leaders Program' (Ministry of the Environment, Environmental Innovations Branch, July 2004).

[113] M Crow, 'Beyond Experiments' (May/June 2000) *The Environmental Forum* 19, 29.

ongoing criticism.[114] Many have attracted very low participation by industry. Furthermore, these initiatives are only targeted at improving the performance of environmental leaders and are not directed at tackling environmental laggards. But, as suggested by Gunningham and Sinclair, 'it will be some time before it emerges whether the sceptics are correct in questioning why so many resources are being devoted to making the top 20% (or perhaps only the top 5%) even better, rather than concentrating on the most serious problems or under-performers'.[115]

Another approach to regulatory flexibility is represented by corporate environmental plans and alternative licensing schemes. The Victorian Environmental Protection Authority (VEPA) in Australia was one of the first regulators to promote regulatory flexibility by using Environmental Improvement Plans (EIPs) in its bid to reduce polluting emissions from major industrial sites.[116] According to VEPA:

> An EIP is an effective tool to guide a company's environmental management through a process of continuous improvement . . . An EIP enables an organisation to improve environmental performance through a comprehensive approach to environmental management. It includes an action plan with goals and timelines, together with provision for ongoing monitoring and reporting of environmental performance. An EIP is a company's public commitment to improve performance. Progress against the plan is regularly reviewed and reported to the public.[117]

Where appropriate, EIPs should be developed with community input, often through the setting up of Community Liaison Committees which bring together stakeholders in the project including local residents, key company representatives and EPA officers.[118] Unlike initiatives such as Project XL, EIPs are targeted at both environmental leaders and laggards. Laggards either can be compelled to develop an EIP under section 31C(6) of the Environment Protection Act 1970 (Vic) or can be 'persuaded' to adopt a plan. Other companies with good environmental performance records (ie, environmental leaders) can volunteer to implement an EIP. One year later, the EPA extended the scheme by offering accredited licences, an

[114] For general critiques of Project XL see R Steinzor, 'Regulating Reinvention: Does the Emperor Have Any Clothes?' (1996) 26 *Environmental Law Reporter, News and Analysis* 10,527; L Susskind and J Seconda, 'The Risks and Advantages of Agency Discretion: Evidence from the EPA's Project XL' (1998) 17 *UCLA Journal of Environmental Law Policy* 67.

[115] Gunningham and Sinclair, above n 104, 115.

[116] A number of other Australian states have also progressed down this regulatory path including Queensland, South Australia and Tasmania. However, Victoria remains the pioneer of this approach in Australia.

[117] EPA Victoria Information Bulletin 739, *Guidelines for the Preparation of Environmental Improvement Plans* (Environment Protection Agency, June 2002) 1.

[118] See further EPA Victoria Information Bulletin 740 *Guidelines for Running Community Liaison Committees* (Environment Protection Agency, Nov 2001).

alternative to the standard prescriptive approach to works approval and licensing. Applicants for an accredited licence must have implemented or established an EIP, an environmental management system and an environmental audit programme. Providing the licensee can also 'demonstrate a high level of environmental performance and an ongoing capacity to maintain and improve that performance',[119] she will be issued with an accredited licence which provides her with a high degree of operational freedom and autonomy. Therefore, unlike EIPs, accredited licences are available only to the higher echelon of environmental leaders—the best of the best. Governments in other jurisdictions have also experimented with corporate environmental plans and alternative licensing schemes, with European countries such as the Netherlands taking a leading role.[120]

Gunningham and Sinclair have recently evaluated the effectiveness of EIPs and accredited licences.[121] In interviews with industry, VEPA and community representatives they found that EIPs had, in general, been successful, although the level of success was far more pronounced in the case of environmental leaders who had commonly achieved beyond-compliance outcomes. In contrast, the success of accredited licences was somewhat limited. After nearly eight years, only 17 companies (out of 1,200 'scheduled premises') have enrolled in the accredited licence programme. According to interviewees, the system did not provide adequate incentives and the costs of taking up an accredited licence did not, in most instances, outweigh the benefits.

Another innovation directed at encouraging companies to go 'beyond compliance' and deliver ongoing pollution reduction is the concept of load-based licensing. Licence fee structures have traditionally been based on the scale of the licensed operation, and as such have not directly reflected the environmental impact of the operation. However, under a load-based licensing scheme, licence fees are linked to pollutant emissions. As and when such emissions are reduced, so the licence fee will drop, thereby producing an incentive to reduce discharges of pollutants. This initiative has been adopted in many jurisdictions, including Australian states such as New South Wales.[122]

4. Improving Enforcement

Unfortunately, not all companies (or indeed individuals) will voluntarily comply with their environmental obligations. An effective command and control system

[119] EPA Victoria Information Bulletin 424C *Accredited Licensee System Guideline for Applicants* (Environment Protection Agency, July 2004) 1.

[120] Eg Netherlands Ministry of Housing, Spatial Planning and the Environment, *Environmental Policy for Industry in the Netherlands* (Ministry of Housing, Spatial Planning and the Environment, 2000).

[121] Gunningham and Sinclair, above n 104, 166–77.

[122] BJ Richardson, 'Economic Instruments in Australian Pollution Control Law' in G Bates and Z Lipman (eds), *Pollution Law in Australia* (Butterworths, 2002) 49.

must therefore be underpinned by credible enforcement but, as we have already seen, this is not the case. This section will discuss various innovations targeted at improving enforcement, including targeted enforcement, self-reporting of violations, on-the-spot fines, creative sentencing and adverse publicity orders. One of the key problems faced by contemporary environmental agencies is how to achieve credible enforcement when the number of regulatory officials is far outweighed by the number of firms (especially SMEs) that need regulating, especially in an atmosphere of continuing budgetary and staffing constraints. Although there is no ready solution to this problem, a number of strategies have been developed that at least serve to mitigate its effects. For example, the Environment Agency in England and Wales has recognised that it is not possible to inspect and assess compliance across the entire regulated community. It therefore has, as one of its four principles of enforcement, the 'targeting' of enforcement action. By this, it makes sure that:

> [R]egulatory effort is directed primarily towards those whose activities give rise to or risk of serious environmental damage, where the risks are least well controlled or against deliberate or organised crime. Action will be primarily focused on lawbreakers or those directly responsible for the risk and who are best placed to control it.[123]

As is implicit from the definition of 'targeting' above, compliance assessment will be allocated on the basis of risk, which includes an assessment of management and operating performance, complexity of the activity, environmental impact and location. In order to assist in achieving this goal, the Agency has developed a number of compliance strategies. For example, eight years ago, the Agency established an operator and pollution risk appraisal (OPRA) scheme, whereby companies are scored on the effectiveness of their environmental management and the level of pollution hazard at individual sites.[124] Processes that score poorly will receive more attention from the Agency in terms of inspections and general regulation.

In Ontario, Canada, the Ministry of the Environment has gone one step further by establishing an Environmental SWAT team dedicated to inspecting and monitoring those sectors with high non-compliance rates and/or sectors which may have a significant impact on public health and the environment due to their operations. The sectors are identified using risk assessment techniques, and unannounced inspections have been carried out in sectors such as pesticide applicators, electro-metal platers and industrial recycling plants.[125]

[123] Environment Agency, *Enforcement and Prosecution Policy* (Environment Agency, Nov 1998) para 16.

[124] Environment Agency, *Environmental Protection Operator and Risk Pollution Risk Appraisal* (Environment Agency, April 2004). In addition to using this information to target enforcement action, the Agency publishes companies' scores under its OPRA scheme. Access to such information will also enable financial institutions, investors and competitors to measure companies' environmental performance.

[125] Ontario Ministry of the Environment, 'The Environmental SWAT Team', available at www.ene.gov.on.ca/envision/swat.

It is also possible to compensate for grossly inadequate resources by encouraging regulated firms to report their own violations. Some academic commentators argue that it is generally socially desirable for the structure of enforcement to be such as to encourage self-reporting. Self reporting reduces enforcement costs because, when an incident occurs, the regulator does not have to expend time and money in detecting the pollution and establishing its source. One way of encouraging self reporting is to lower the sanction for those individuals who disclose their own infractions. For example, the EPA in Western Australia can encourage self-reporting by virtue of the fact that it has the power to modify penalties if certain conditions are satisfied. In order for an individual or corporation to take advantage of the reduced penalties, it must meet a number of conditions. The company must inter alia provide the regulator with details of the offence as soon as is reasonably practicable, and it must take all reasonable and practicable steps to minimise and remedy any adverse environmental effects of the offence. [126]

As discussed previously, it is imperative that regulators use the most efficient and effective enforcement tools in the event of a breach. Command and control regimes have traditionally been underpinned by the criminal law, a particularly crude and expensive method of tackling environmental deviants. In response to this, and the fact that criminal penalties (in the form of fines and imprisonment) are not always conducive to compliance and deterrence goals, the enforcement 'toolbox' has been expanded significantly, and regulators now have recourse to administrative powers and civil procedures when dealing with non-compliant individuals or companies. We shall focus on two of these relatively new enforcement tools: on-the-spot fines (also known as infringement notices) and adverse publicity orders.[127]

In a number of jurisdictions including the US, Canada, Germany and Australia, environmental regulators have the power to serve an on-the-spot fine in the case of certain offences.[128] These fines are therefore classed as administrative as opposed to judicial penalties. Under most systems, regulators give the offending party the opportunity to discharge or compensate for the breach by paying a specified sum of money. Alternatively, the recipient of the fine can elect to have the matter dealt with by a court where the penalty payable on a finding of guilt will

[126] See P Spillman, 'The Western Australian Environment Protection Amendment Act 1998' (1998) *Journal Environmental Law and Policy* 287, for further details. Broadly similar policies are in place in the US to encourage self-auditing, self-reporting and self-correction of environmental violations: US Environmental Protection Agency, *Audit Policy: Incentives for Self-Policing* (1995), 60 Fed Reg 66706 (Dec 22).

[127] For a more detailed discussion of environmental enforcement mechanisms see C Abbot, 'The Enforcement of Pollution Control Laws in England and Wales: A Case for Reform?' (2005) 22(1) *Environmental and Planning Law Journal* 68.

[128] Eg R Edwards, 'Spot Fines to Target Green Crime', *Sunday Herald*, 16 Mar 2003 (referring to Scotland); Queensland Environmental Protection Agency (QEPA), 'Queensland's New Environmental Nuisance Laws—Fact Sheet No. 1' (QEPA, 2001).

be considerably higher than the maximum available under an infringement notice. There are several advantages to this administrative sanction, the main one relating to the fact that 'the use of the infringement notice provides relief from the high number of prosecutions that would otherwise have to be conducted to enforce the law . . . and it reduces the costs of criminal justice'.[129] As the fines are less costly to impose, a regulatory official will be more inclined to exercise his power. These fines are also attractive to regulators because they ensure that offences are 'officially' recognised (and penalised) without the need to prove any elements of the offence. Although critics of on-the-spot fines voice concerns about the lack of judicial scrutiny, their potential to trivialise crimes and their 'one-size fits all' approach, there have been calls for their introduction by governments, regulators and academic scholars in, for example, the UK.[130]

There have also been numerous initiatives aimed at improving the deterrent value of the criminal law. In many jurisdictions, a director or senior officer of a company can be held personally liable for the acts of the company, and there is evidence to suggest that regulators are increasingly having recourse to such powers. In addition, creative or alternative sentencing options such as mandatory EMS adoption, mandatory environmental auditing and the funding of community environmental projects have been embraced by courts in Australia, Canada and the US, and are being explored by countries such as the UK.[131]

Another enforcement tool which, unlike on-the-spot fines, is more suitable when dealing with larger business entities as opposed to SMEs or individuals, is the use of adverse publicity or corporate shaming. In recent years, an increasing number of legislative bodies are conferring on the courts, as opposed to the regulators, the power to impose adverse publicity orders on those offenders convicted of a criminal offence. By conferring such powers, authorities presume that negative publicity is effective as a corporate sanction and will have a greater deterrent value than criminal fines. The extent to which negative publicity has a stigmatising effect on corporations has been the subject of academic debate for many years. Empirical studies suggest that companies are sensitive about prestige as an interest over and above profits.[132] This, coupled with the fact that, unlike that of fines, the impact of adverse publicity is not limited by the amount of money which a company can afford to pay makes adverse publicity a potentially successful weapon in the fight against corporate environmental crime.

[129] R Fox, 'Infringement Notices: Time for Reform' (1995) 50 *Trends and Issues in Criminal Justice* 1, 4.

[130] See eg *Environmental Crime,* above n 91 para 43; AI Ogus and C Abbot, 'Sanctions for Pollution: Do We have the Right Regime?' (2002) 14(3) *Journal of Environmental Law* 2.

[131] See further C Abbot, 'The Regulatory Enforcement of Pollution Control Laws: The Australian Experience' (2005) 17(2) *Jounal of Environmental Law* 161.

[132] B Fisse and J Braithwaite, *The Impact of Publicity on Corporate Offenders* (State UNY Press, 1983); K Hawkins, *Environment and Enforcement: Regulation and the Social Definition of Pollution* (Clarendon Press, 1984).

There are, of course, concerns about adverse publicity orders. Unlike fines, their impact on turnover is unknown and there are clearly situations which would not warrant their use. Moreover corporate shaming tactics will be useful only where the company has a public profile to damage. Nevertheless, they have been widely adopted in countries such as Australia and there are calls for their introduction in the UK.[133] The shaming of poor environmental performers is not, of course, limited to the enforcement context. Schemes that require companies both to disclose information to the public and to involve the community in environmental planning clearly recognise, albeit indirectly, the importance of corporate prestige and image.

5. Innovations in Command and Control: Conclusion

Principle 10 of the Rio Declaration on Environment and Development declares that 'states shall enact effective environmental legislation'.[134] Governments, by reformulating traditional command and control approaches, have endeavoured to improve the effectiveness and efficiency of their regulatory models in achieving sustainable development objectives. There are other important developments which operate on the periphery of command and control. Take, for example, access to environmental information. It is clearly important that public authorities, when setting standards, awarding licences or even formulating overall policy objectives, act on the basis of accurate and up-to-date information. But the principle of environmental justice entails the sharing of information amongst *all* stakeholders including members of the public generally, environmental interest groups and the press. The implementation of environmental databases known generically as Pollutant Release and Transfer Registries provides a baseline of information and data on, inter alia, potentially harmful releases to air, water and soil from industrial facilities, with countries such as the US and the UK developing their own registries. Access to information also supports rights of public participation, an issue which shall be revisited in Chapter 5.

H. Conclusion

Command and control regulation, in its many guises, has formed the hub of government efforts to curb industrial pollution for at least three decades. Although an examination of the literature could lead readers to conclude that its merits as a regulatory technique are outweighed by its defects, this would be unfair, as it has

133 Eg UK House of Commons Environmental Audit Committee, above n 91.
134 Rio Declaration on Environment and Development 1992, 31 ILM 874.

achieved some considerable success in eliminating certain forms of pollution. But policy-makers and regulators have been relatively quick to recognise many of the problems associated with the command and control model, all of which hinder the sustainability agenda. In response, they have found innovative and interesting ways of building on the traditional command framework, with a view to promoting further the sustainability agenda. Legislative initiatives are increasingly reflecting principles of sustainable development such as public participation, access to information, pollution prevention, producer responsibility and the taking of a precautionary approach. And substantive and procedural initiatives encourage regulatory flexibility and promote compliance and enforcement. Although many of these latter initiatives are in their infancy, and it is therefore difficult to determine their relative success or failure, their introduction does suggest that command and control will remain, a fundamental part of any modern environmental law framework. Authorities reliance on just direct regulation is, however, waning. Governments are increasingly recognising that alternative mechanisms such as market-based incentives and voluntary instruments may be able to achieve the same outcomes as direct regulation but in a more cost-effective way. This is not to say that command and control is redundant. But what we are witnessing is the design of a new regulatory framework: 'one which still involves government intervention, but selectively, and in combination with a range of market and non-market solutions, and of public and private orderings'.[135]

[135] Gunningham and Graboksy, above n 1, 10.

4

Risk and Environmental Law: A Beginner's Guide

ELIZABETH FISHER*

A. Introduction

For the intrepid environmental law scholar and practitioner the concept of 'risk' appears impossible to ignore. The term 'risk' and its accompanying language are not only common inclusions in legislation, policy, case law and academic commentary, but are also increasingly framing environmental law discourse. Indeed it is now common for environmental problems to be characterised in terms of risk and the bulk of environmental regulatory law to be thought of as 'risk regulation'.

This chapter provides readers with a starting point for thinking critically about the relationship between risk and environmental law. The chapter is subtitled 'a beginner's guide' because to think critically about these concepts there is a need to think about the area afresh and in terms of first principles. Consequently, and ironically, a sophisticated analysis of risk and its implications for environmental law requires that one first understands the basic terms. This is because, as will become clear, those terms are not as basic as they seem. The chapter's major purpose is to show that, while risk in all its various dimensions is an important feature of environmental law, it must also be treated with care, for three reasons. First, 'risk' has come to dominate environmental law because of the promotion of a tool for decision-making—risk assessment. This has most obviously occurred in the United States (US) but is also the case in other jurisdictions. Moreover, risk assessment has been promoted due to a range of socio-political factors to do with the role of public administration. Secondly, the terms 'risk' and 'risk assessment' can be defined in many different ways depending on context. The way in which these terms are defined will influence what is understood to be a particular environmental problem and what are acceptable solutions to that problem. Thirdly,

* Tutor and Fellow in Law, Corpus Christi College, Oxford. I would like to thank the editors and Lucia Zedner for their comments on previous drafts of this chapter. Any errors or omissions are my own.

neither of the above two points means that risk as a concept should be ignored. Rather, scholars and lawyers must critically analyse how risk is being defined and deployed in any particular context.

This chapter is structured as follows. The first section gives a brief overview of some of the key features of environmental law and regulation. The second section presents a brief history of the use of risk assessment in environmental law with a focus on the US, where risk has most obviously come to dominate environmental law. The third section examines the second point highlighted above—that there is no single definition of, or discourse about, risk, and different definitions will result in environmental problems being characterised in divergent ways. The fourth section examines the final point—that scholars and lawyers must take a critical approach to examining risk in environmental law. This is illustrated by an analysis of how the precautionary principle has been interpreted in the European Union (EU) by the European Commission in their Communication on the Precautionary Principle.[1]

A number of preliminary points should be made. First, while this chapter refers to the literature on risk it does not attempt to be an exhaustive interdisciplinary overview of the many risk discourses that exist.[2] In particular, the concept of risk has a long and complex history which is quite separate from its use in either law or environmental policy.[3] Nor is this chapter an analysis of the methodological problems inherent in risk assessment, although it should be stressed that there are many.[4] Secondly, this chapter concentrates on how risk is deployed in legal reasoning and doctrine, and this requires an analysis of case law, policy and legislation. The focus is thus neither on legal theory[5] nor on regulatory theory.[6] Thirdly, and following on from this, legal culture is a major determinant of how risk is defined and deployed in any jurisdiction.[7] This chapter very much focuses upon risk and environmental law within Western democracies, and in particular the US and the EU, and care must be taken with making generalisations across jurisdictions. Fourthly, the term 'environmental law' is used quite loosely in this chapter

[1] Commission of the European Communities (European Commission), *Communication from the Commission on the Precautionary Principle,* COM(2000)1 final.

[2] D Lupton, *Risk* (Routledge, 1999); C Jaeger *et al*, *Risk, Uncertainty, and Rational Action* (Earthscan, 2001); R Boyne, *Risk* (Open UP, 2003).

[3] P Bernstein, *Against the Gods: The Remarkable Story of Risk* (John Wiley, 1996) and V Covello and J Mumpower, 'Risk Analysis and Risk Management: An Historical Perspective' (1985) 5 *Risk Analysis* 103.

[4] K Shrader-Frechette, *Burying Uncertainty: Risk and the Case Against the Geological Disposal of Nuclear Waste* (U California P, 1993); A Stirling, 'Risk, Uncertainty and Precaution: Some Instrumental Implications from the Social Sciences' in F Berkhout *et al* (eds), *Negotiating Environmental Change: New Perspectives From Social Science* (Edward Elgar, 2003).

[5] J Steele, *Risks and Legal Theory* (Hart Publishing, 2004).

[6] C Hood *et al, The Government of Risk: Understanding Risk Regulation Regimes* (Oxford UP, 2001).

[7] D Nelken, 'Disclosing/Invoking Legal Culture' (1995) 4 *Social & Legal Studies* 437.

to refer not only to laws concerned with protecting the environment but also those concerned with protecting human health. This reflects the fact that contemporary discussions about risk have tended to merge these two areas of law.

B. Basic Features of Environmental Problems and Environmental Law

Sustainability has become one of the most talked about concepts in contemporary environmental law. This is not surprising as the emphasis on sustainability is a reflection of the fact that the most fundamental feature of environmental decision-making is the need to make decisions about future environmental quality. A necessary aspect of that decision-making process is for decision-makers to think about whether laws will actually deliver 'sustainable' outcomes, and this in turn depends on our knowledge about the future and the likely consequences of our actions. In essence this raises issues of risk, and thus it is not surprising that a reader on environmental law for sustainability would include a chapter on the topic. With that said, however, the symbolism of risk transcends that of sustainability, and while they are closely related topics, risk is a concept in its own right. Before exploring that concept in more detail it is useful to chart briefly some of the key features of environmental problems and environmental law which are often forgotten in examining different areas of environmental law and in thinking about the concept of sustainability.

The first thing to note is that, as Dryzek states, environmental problems 'are found at the intersection of ecosystems and human social systems'[8] and are thus complex. Environmental problems are a messy mix of physical phenomena and of socio-political conflicts over those phenomena. Understandings of those physical phenomena are often extremely limited due to a series of methodological, epistemological and ontological problems with science that are commonly described as scientific uncertainties.[9] That said, science remains the main means by which those problems are understood.[10] From a socio-political perspective, environmental problems also tend to be highly polycentric,[11] in that they are not easily reducible to a dispute between two parties, but rather involve a range of parties who have directly or indirectly caused an environmental problem or are interested in how it is resolved. As the activities and actors contributing to environmental problems are many, this also makes the assignation of responsibility for environmental harm

[8] J Dryzek, *The Politics of the Earth: Environmental Discourses* (Oxford UP, 1997) 8.

[9] B Wynne, 'Uncertainty and Environmental Learning' (1992) 2 *Global Environmental Change* 111; M Smithson, 'Ignorance and Science' [1993] *Knowledge: Creation, Diffusion & Utilization* 133.

[10] B Latour, *Politics of Nature: How to Bring the Sciences into Democracy* (Harvard UP, 2004) 4.

[11] L Fuller, 'The Forms and Limits of Adjudication' (1978) 92 *Harvard Law Review* 353, 395–7.

difficult. Moreover, as different actors involved in an environmental dispute have different understandings about the value of environmental protection[12] and how a community should develop,[13] there are also divergent understandings of what the actual problem is. While some may understand the problem as a discrete physical problem that requires a technological fix, others may understand it as being due to widespread cultural practices and that a solution will be achieved only through radical social adjustment. As a consequence of all of this environmental law tends to consist of a variety of ad hoc legislative schemes that reflect divergent policy goals and disparate understandings of environmental problems.[14]

The second important feature of environmental problems and environmental law is the central role of the state. From a legal and regulatory perspective, discussions of the state have grown highly unfashionable in light of the state's changing nature[15] and the proliferation of new regulatory techniques.[16] The reality is, however, that the state is still the major actor in environmental law—it initiates and shapes environmental law regimes as well as being held to account for them.[17] Its role is controversial, however, for two interrelated reasons. First, in light of the many different understandings of environmental problems it becomes very difficult for the state to provide a 'commonly accepted and legitimate meta-rationality' to frame those problems.[18] In constructing and promoting environmental regulatory regimes, the state must privilege one view of environmental problems over another.[19] Secondly, environmental law, and in particular its crucial standard setting aspects, is primarily the province of administrative governance due to the fact it is only public administration that can provide the forum for bringing together the necessary information, expertise and relevant parties, as well as ensuring the application of legislated prescriptions to the facts—all necessary elements of standard setting.[20] The problem is that public administration is the 'awkward family heirloom' of the democratic state,[21] and few can agree on what makes it legitimate,

[12] T O'Riordan, *Environmentalism* (2nd edn, Pion, 1983); D Pepper, *Modern Environmentalism: An Introduction* (Routledge, 1996).

[13] See the work of cultural theory: M Schwarz and M Thompson, *Divided We Stand: Redefining Politics, Technology and Social Choice* (Harvester Wheatsheaf, 1990).

[14] T McGarity, 'The Goals of Environmental Legislation' (2004) 31 *Boston College Environmental Affairs Law Review* 529.

[15] C Foster and C Plowden, *The State Under Stress* (Open UP, 1996).

[16] I Ayres and J Braithwaite, *Responsive Regulation—Transcending the Deregulation Debate* (Oxford UP, 1992).

[17] E Fisher, 'Unpacking the Toolbox: Or Why the Public/Private Divide Is Important in EC Environmental Law' in J-B Auby and M Freedland (eds), *The Public Law/Private Law Divide: Une Entente Assez Cordiale?* (LGDJ Diffuseur, 2004) 205.

[18] Jaeger *et al*, above n 2, 251.

[19] M Douglas and A Wildasky, *Risk and Culture* (U California Press, 1982).

[20] E Fisher, *Risk Regulation and Administrative Constitutionalism* (Hart Publishing, forthcoming) ch 1.

[21] C Farina, 'The Consent of the Governed: Against Simple Rules for a Complex World' (1997) 72 *Chicago Kent Law Review* 987; B Cook, *Bureaucracy and Self Government: Reconsidering the Role of Public Administration in American Government* (Johns Hopkins UP, 1996).

or if it is legitimate at all.[22] Thus many environmental disputes are really disputes over the proper role of public administration.[23]

The final feature of environmental law to note is that there is a constant tension between viewing environmental law as a product of particular legal cultures and viewing it as an expression of universal legal norms. With regard to the former, the highly socio-political nature of environmental problems, as well as the central role for nation states in its promotion, might lead one to conclude that any environmental law regime is a product of a particular jurisdiction and that any comparative analysis must pay careful attention to comparative law methodology.[24] Thus, ideas, principles and regulatory techniques cannot simply be transplanted from one jurisdiction to another.[25] From another perspective, however, national environmental law is increasingly being driven forward by international developments. Principles such as sustainable development, prevention and precaution are now common to most jurisdictions.[26] In light of this, some commentators have pointed to the need to rethink understandings of legal systems and legal reasoning.[27]

The implications of the above discussion for thinking about environmental law and risk can be summed up in two points. The first is that the formidable complexity of environmental law is not superficial, but rather a product of socio-political conflict and the nature of environmental problems. If we think about risk and environmental law we must think about these issues. Secondly, environmental problems and environmental law are deeply embedded in political, social and legal culture. A study of risk and environmental law cannot only concentrate on the law but must also take into account the forces behind it.

C. A Brief History of Risk Assessment in Environmental Law

A common statement now found in environmental law literature is that people are concerned about environmental and public health risks and that the role of

[22] G Frug, 'The Ideology of Bureaucracy in American Law' (1984) 97 *Harvard Law Review* 1276; C Harlow and R Rawlings, *Law and Administration* (2nd edn, Butterworths, 1997) ch 1–3.

[23] Fisher, above n 20.

[24] O Kahn Freund, 'On Uses and Misuses of Comparative Law' (1974) 37 *MLR* 1.

[25] P Legrand, 'The Impossibility of Legal Transplants' (1997) 4 *Maastricht Journal of European and Comparative Law* 111.

[26] J Wiener, 'Something Borrowed For Something Blue: Legal Transplants and the Evolution of Global Environmental Law' (2001) 27 *Ecology Law Quarterly* 1295.

[27] N De Sadeleer, *Environmental Principles: From Political Slogans to Legal Rules* (Oxford UP, 2002).

environmental regulatory law is to reduce such risks.[28] Take, for example, this recent statement by two US environmental lawyers:

> The tort system promotes safety by requiring a person who has injured someone else to pay compensation if the defendant has violated applicable tort rules that define when compensation is due. Risk regulation, by comparison, seeks to reduce personal and environmental injuries before they occur by addressing the potential causes of such injuries—that is, the 'risk' of such injuries. Because risk regulation operates before injuries occur, it does not require that people die or be injured, or that the environment be harmed, before it goes into effect.[29]

At first sight such a statement seems rather commonsensical and a concise way of summing up the goals of environmental protection legislation. It identifies a subject matter for environmental regulation—risk—and the purpose of environmental regulation—the reduction of such risk. In doing so it also seemingly highlights a feature of environmental decision-making noted above—scientific uncertainty. Of course, the relationship between risk and uncertainty is not a very straightforward one, nor is it obvious what these terms mean. These issues will be explored later in this chapter, but here the focus is upon how this characterisation came to be.

What is clear from the literature is that describing environmental law in terms of risk is a relatively recent fashion. Thirty years ago the concept of risk was virtually never discussed in environmental law, and while the term was used in some legislation it carried with it little conceptual significance.[30] Moreover, an analysis of the history of how risk has come to play such an important role in environmental law reveals that this development has been driven less by discussions about risk and more by the promotion of a decision-making tool—risk assessment.

Much of that history has taken place in the US where the concept of risk perhaps most dominates environmental law and policy. To understand why this is the case one must start with the founding of contemporary environmental regulatory law in the late 1960s and early 1970s.[31] In a flurry of bipartisan legislative hyperactivity many different pieces of environmental legislation were passed and a number of different administrative agencies were set up including the Consumer Protection Safety Commission (CPSC), Environmental Protection Agency (EPA) and the Occupational Safety and Health Administration (OSHA).

[28] M Adler, 'Risk, Death, and Harm: The Normative Foundations of Risk Regulation' (2003) 87 *Minnesota Law Review* 1293; H Chang, 'Risk Regulation, Endogenous Public Concerns, and the Hormones Dispute: Nothing to Fear But Fear Itself' (2004) 77 *Southern California Law Review* 743.

[29] S Shapiro and R Glicksman, *Risk Regulation at Risk: Restoring a Pragmatic Approach* (Stanford Law and Politics, 2003) 1–2.

[30] S 3(1) of the Health and Safety at Work Act 1974 (UK) and Toxic Substances Control Act 1976 15 USC § 2605(a) (USA).

[31] C Sunstein, *After the Rights Revolution* (Harvard UP, 1990).

As well, the powers of older agencies such as the Food and Drug Administration (FDA) were strengthened. These agencies all had quite different institutional structures, legislative powers, and were all required to make regulations in a range of different ways.[32] The creation of these agencies gave rise to a debate about their legitimacy and in particular what their role and nature should be.[33] On the one hand, there were those who understood environmental law to be a similar agenda to civil rights and an extension of the 'Great Society' programme of the early 1960s.[34] On this view, the role of these new agencies was to promote environmental protection even in the face of scientific uncertainty.[35] Debate and the exploration of complex problems were seen as a particularly important aspect of an agency's role. Such a perspective tended to encourage an expansive approach to construing these agencies' legislative mandates.[36] On the other hand, some viewed the task of these agencies in far more discrete terms as addressing particular technical issues or problems, and thus agency decision-makers needed to be restrained in exercising their powers.[37] Those holding this perspective often pointed to the failures of the New Deal agencies brought about by bureaucratic inertia and agency capture.[38] Legal frameworks and rules needed to ensure that the new agencies retained their 'proper role as the servant[s] of government' so as not to become 'monsters' with 'no practical limitations on [their] discretion'.[39]

The development of risk assessment techniques was part of this debate, although to begin with few of these techniques actually existed. While mathematical concepts of risk and probability were in regular use in other fields[40] they had little role to play in environmental decision-making. Furthermore, the general study of the relationship between adverse consequences and particular activities was in a relatively basic form in the environmental and public health area, and such studies were routinely hampered by a range of scientific uncertainties including the epistemological limits of science and a lack of experimental data.[41]

32 For further details see Fisher, above n 20, chapter 2.

33 Cook, above n 21.

34 J Morone, *The Democratic Wish: Popular Participation and the Limits of American Government* (revised edn, Yale UP, 1998).

35 D Bazelon, 'Science and Uncertainty: A Jurist's View' (1981) 5 *Harvard Environmental Law Review* 209.

36 W Ruckelshaus, 'The Role of the Environmental Protection Agency' (1971–72) 1 *Environmental Affairs* 528.

37 T Lowi, *The End of Liberalism: The Second Republic of the United States* (2nd edn, WW Norton and Co, 1979).

38 H Friendly, *The Federal Administrative Agencies: The Need for Better Definition of Standards* (Harvard UP, 1962).

39 *Greater Boston Television Corp v FCC*, 444 F 2d 841 (DC Cir, 1970) 850. Also see H Leventhal, 'Environmental Decision Making and the Role of the Courts' (1974) 122 *University of Pennsylvania Law Review* 509, 511.

40 F Knight, *Risk, Uncertainty, and Profit* (Century Press, 1964) and T Porter, *The Rise of Statistical Thinking 1820–1900* (Princeton UP, 1986).

41 K Shrader-Frechette and E McCoy, *Method in Ecology: Strategies for Conservation* (Cambridge UP, 1993); J Adams, *Risk* (UCL Press, 1995) 45.

This is not to say that these new administrative agencies did not utilise scientific information. All were given open-ended scientific research legislative powers, which they used.[42] What they did not do regularly however, was carry out quantitative assessments of the risks arising from particular activities or products.

From the 1950s onwards quantitative risk assessment techniques were being developed in specific fields such as engineering (particularly atomic energy) and the assessment of the health effects of carcinogens, but these were not immediately translatable into the regulatory field and often depended on a number of value assumptions about how carcinogens and complex systems worked.[43] With that said, risk assessment was promoted within these new agencies due to it being viewed as a means of making decision-making more objective and 'rational' and thus more accountable and effective, particularly important issues in an era of budget cutbacks and increasing concern with over-regulation.[44]

By 1976, several crude mathematical models for risk assessment had been developed by the new agencies, but there were differing views on their utility. While the EPA used risk assessment on a regular basis, the FDA used it less often, and OSHA used it only for priority setting.[45] In 1977 these three agencies and the CPSC formed an Interagency Regulatory Liaison Group which developed common guidelines on risk assessment.[46] While the guidelines set out risk assessment methodologies and stressed the importance of regulatory decision-making being based on the 'best judgements of scientists',[47] they did not definitively state what should be the actual role of risk assessment in regulatory decision-making. Moreover, in 1980, OSHA published a generic carcinogenic policy in which it recognised the limits of science and set out a more policy-based approach to standard setting.[48]

The impetus for resolving what role risk assessment should play in standard setting came from the courts. Since the early 1970s the courts had regularly been engaged in judicial review of the rule-making decisions of these agencies and there was an ongoing debate about what form such review should take.[49] The doctrinal and legislative complexity of that case law should not be underestimated,[50] but by

[42] S Jasanoff, *The Fifth Branch: Science Advisers as Policy Makers* (Harvard UP, 1990) 39.

[43] National Research Council (NRC), *Science and Judgement in Risk Assessment* (National Academy Press, 1994) 31–2 and Jaeger *et al*, n 2, 89–95.

[44] P Yeager, *The Limits of Law: The Public Regulation of Private Pollution* (Cambridge UP, 1991) 182–5.

[45] For a history of this period see NRC, above n 43, 32.

[46] M Landy *et al*, *The EPA: Asking the Wrong Questions: From Nixon to Clinton* (Oxford UP, 1994) ch 6.

[47] 44 Fed Reg 38858, 6 July 1979.

[48] Classification and Regulation of Potential Occupational Carcinogens, 45 Fed Reg 5002, 22 Jan 1980.

[49] The most obvious example of this is the debate between Chief Judge Bazelon and Judge Leventhal in the DC Circuit of the Federal Court of Appeals over 'hard look' review. See *NRDC v Nuclear Regulatory Commission*, 547 F 2d 633 (DC Cir, 1976) and *Ethyl Corp v EPA*, 541 F 2d 1 (DC Cir, 1976).

[50] Fisher, above n 20, ch 3.

the late 1970s there was a growing consensus that agencies must ensure that their regulations had a factual basis shaped by a rational methodology if such a regulation was to withstand judicial review.[51] The Supreme Court in *Industrial Union Department, AFL-CIO v American Petroleum Institute*[52] (the *Benzene* decision) confirmed this by stating, among other things, that OSHA must establish a 'significant risk' before it could regulate. This effectively nullified OSHA's generic carcinogenic policy in which risk assessment had very little role to play,[53] and also promoted the concept of risk to the top of the regulatory agenda.

One of the direct consequences of the *Benzene* decision was that Congress commissioned the National Research Council (NRC) to write a report on whether risk assessment should be separated from policy-making and whether there should be uniform guidelines for risk assessment across the regulatory agencies. The NRC concluded that while no separate organisation should undertake risk assessment, (either institutionally or otherwise), a 'clear conceptual distinction' should be made between risk assessment and risk management.[54] In other words, decision-making about risk should be divided into a 'scientific process' of risk assessment, in which the scientific information about risk was collected and evaluated and a 'political' process of risk management in which a policy decision was made about what regulatory action should be taken in relation to that risk. Such a division would appear to guarantee the objectivity of decision-making. The NRC also concluded that uniform guidelines should be promoted across the agencies.[55] The NRC's report, also known as the Red Book, has become the authoritative statement on the role of risk assessment in environmental regulation not only in the US but also, more recently, in other jurisdictions.[56] This is despite the fact that the NRC itself was critical about the utility of the risk assessment/risk management distinction in its later reports.

What the NRC report, reforms in Presidential oversight[57] and the accompanying judicial developments[58] did was to prompt Federal regulatory agencies in this area to think in terms of risk. Thus the EPA produced reports on priority setting and comparative risk assessment,[59] and the courts continued to scrutinise decisions on

[51] *American Petroleum Institute v OSHA*, 581 F 2d 493 (5th Cir, 1978) and *National Lime Association v EPA*, 627 F 2d 416 (DC Cir, 1980).

[52] *Industrial Union Dept AFL-CIO v American Petroleum Institute,* 448 US 607 (1980).

[53] S Jasanoff, 'Science and the Limits of Administrative Rule Making: Lessons from the OSHA Cancer Policy' (1982) 20 *Osgoode Hall Law Journal* 536.

[54] NRC, *Risk Assessment in the Federal Government: Managing the Process* (National Academy Press, 1983) 151.

[55] *Ibid*, 153–65.

[56] See eg the risk assessment and risk management distinction in European Commission, above n 1.

[57] R Plides and C Sunstein, 'Reinventing the Regulatory State' (1995) 62 *University of Chicago Law Review* 1, 39.

[58] Fisher, above n 20, ch 2.

[59] Science Advisory Board, *Reducing Risk: Setting Priorities and Strategies for Environmental Protection* (US Environmental Protection Agency, 1990) and United States Environmental Protection Agency, *Unfinished Business: A Comparative Assessment of Environmental Problems* (US Environmental Protection Agency, 1987).

the basis of how rigorously decision-makers adhered to risk assessment and other analytical methodologies.[60] Moreover, Congress attempted to legislate for risk assessment methodologies.[61]

By the late 1990s environmental law in the US was increasingly being labelled and conceptualised as 'risk regulation' by many commentators.[62] This became the generic term for health and environmental law.[63] The significance of this re-branding of environmental law should not be underestimated. Not only was environmental law being described in terms of risk, but the problems with it were also being diagnosed in such terms. From this perspective environmental law was hampered by poor risk assessment techniques, inconsistency, the regulatory creation of substitute risks and problems of tunnel vision.[64] More difficult debates about the legitimacy of regulatory agencies tended to be ignored and the challenges for environmental law were understood in terms of a 'pragmatic' search for the right risk assessment methodology.[65]

What is striking about this transformation of environmental law into risk regulation is that it was almost solely a product of the utilisation of risk assessment as a decision-making methodology. Until the 1990s the concept of risk itself was virtually ignored. The NRC in its first two reports did not even define risk[66] and the Supreme Court in the *Benzene* decision was rather ambiguous about what the term 'significant risk' meant.[67] Moreover, while there were many critiques of the dominance of 'risk' thinking, they focused more on the limits of risk assessment as a decision-making tool than on the concept of risk itself. Thus risk assessment was criticised for ousting non-scientific values;[68] ignoring the socio-political nature of risk conflicts;[69] giving a false façade of certainty;[70] and creating inefficiencies and ossification.[71] By the 1990s there was a sharp polarisation between those who promoted risk assessment as a 'sound science' for good regulatory

[60] *AFL-CIO v OSHA*, 965 F 2d 962 (11th Cir, 1992); *Corrosion Proof Fittings v EPA*, 947 F 2d 1201 (5th Cir, 1991); *Competitive Enterprise Institute v NHTSA*, 956 F 2d 321 (DC Cir, 1992).

[61] C Sunstein, *Free Markets and Social Justice* (Oxford UP, 1997) ch 14.

[62] S Breyer, *Breaking the Vicious Circle: Towards Effective Risk Regulation* (Harvard UP, 1993); Shapiro and Glicksman, above n 29.

[63] Eg www.riskworld.com.

[64] Breyer, above n 62, ch 1.

[65] C Sunstein, *Risk and Reason: Safety, Law and the Environment* (Cambridge UP, 2002) 26.

[66] NRC, above n 54, 18–9 and NRC, above n 43, 25–6.

[67] While the term was not meant to be a 'mathematical straitjacket' it did appear from Justice Steven's plurality opinion to have a quantitative aspect to it: *Benzene*, above n 52, 655.

[68] K Shrader-Frechette, *Risk and Rationality: Philosophical Foundations for Populist Reforms* (U California Press, 1991).

[69] S Rayner and R Cantor, 'How Fair is Safe Enough?: The Cultural Approach to Societal Technology Choice' (1987) 7 *Risk Analysis* 39.

[70] W Wagner, 'The Science Charade in Toxic Risk Regulation' (1995) 95 *Columbia Law Review* 1613.

[71] T McGarity, "Some Thoughts on 'DeOssifying' the Rulemaking Process" (1992) *41 Duke Law Journal* 1385.

decision-making[72] and those who viewed risk assessment as a profound distortion of environmental regulatory regimes.[73]

This focus on risk assessment as opposed to risk is significant because it also gives us a clue about what forces were driving these developments. Risk assessment was promoted by many actors because it was perceived as ensuring more rational decision-making and thus more 'legitimate' public administration, or at least more 'legitimate' according to one group of actors. Writing in 1983 shortly after the publication of the Red Book, EPA Administrator, Ruckelshaus noted that:

> Risk assessment at [the] EPA must be based only on scientific evidence and scientific consensus. Nothing will erode. . . . public confidence faster than the suspicion that policy considerations have been allowed to influence the assessment of risk.[74]

Risk assessment legitimised the unelected power of public administration and ensured that agencies such as the EPA remained 'instrument[s] of policy'[75] due to the fact that they could act only if they could establish a risk. It was heavily promoted alongside other analytical tools such as cost/benefit analysis and regulatory impact analysis.[76]

In other words, the transformation of environmental law into risk regulation in the US had less to do with the identification of risk as a physical 'reality' and more with anxieties about the nature and role of the administrative state.[77] Commentators talk in terms of risk because they believe that characterising environmental law in such terms will lead to better public administration. This preoccupation with legitimate administrative governance has not been limited to the US. By the late 1990s the concepts of risk and risk assessment were becoming popular in other jurisdictions[78] such as Canada,[79] Australasia[80] and the EU.[81] Thus, for example, risk assessment began to be promoted in the United Kingdom (UK) in the early 1980s[82] in a radical departure from the previous regulatory paradigm

[72] J Graham and J Wiener, *Risk Versus Risk: Tradeoffs in Protecting Health and the Environment* (Harvard UP, 1995).

[73] T McGarity, 'A Cost Benefit State' (1998) 50 *Administrative Law Review* 7.

[74] W Ruckelshaus, 'Science, Risk and Public Policy' (1983) 221 *Science* 1026, 1027.

[75] *Ibid*, 1026.

[76] Sunstein, above n 61, ch 14.

[77] Fisher, above n 20, ch 3.

[78] For an overview of different methodologies being developed in different jurisdictions see the OECD/IPCS's database on chemical risk assessment methodologies, available at http://webdomino1.oecd.org/ehs/ipcs.nsf.

[79] Canadian Environmental Protection Act 1999 and Government of Canada, *A Framework for the Application of Precaution in Science-based Decision Making about Risk* (Government of Canada, 2002).

[80] S 50 of the Gene Technology Act 2001 (Australia) and Standards Australia, *AS/NZS 4360: 2004 Risk Management* (Standards Australia, 2004).

[81] Commission of the European Communities *First Report on the Harmonisation of Risk Assessment Procedures* (Health and Consumer Protection Directorate-General, 2000).

[82] Royal Society, *Risk Assessment—A Group Study Report* (Royal Society, 1983).

in which the emphasis had been on interpersonal negotiation between regulatory inspectors and the regulated.[83] A number of different executive and advisory bodies produced reports on risk assessment and risk management, and risk assessment began to dominate environmental decision-making.[84] In all cases the promotion of risk assessment was designed to ensure 'better' public administration. This was viewed as particularly important in the wake of a number of regulatory crises such as that over BSE[85] and was also consistent with deregulatory agendas.[86]

Risk assessment was not just promoted within national jurisdictions. It also began to play a role in trade law. In particular, the World Trade Organisation's (WTO) 1994 Agreement on Sanitary and Phyto-Sanitary Measures (the SPS Agreement) requires Members to base their sanitary and phytosanitary measures on a risk assessment.[87] There are a number of reasons for the promotion of risk assessment in this context, but it is manly due to a belief that risk assessment ensures that signatories to trade agreements do not act in a discriminatory and arbitrary manner.[88] While the WTO SPS regime is distinct from national regimes it has acted as a conduit for transferring ideas about risk assessment from one jurisdiction to another,[89] as well as drawing on national understandings of good risk regulation.[90]

Alongside these developments in environmental law, risk assessment and risk management techniques have also been promoted in other regulatory areas such as criminal justice[91] and public finance,[92] as well as being used as overarching frameworks for governance.[93] These other developments are not of direct concern in this chapter, although it is interesting to note that this has led some to characterise the role of the state as one of 'handling risk'.[94]

[83] K Hawkins, *Environment and Enforcement* (Oxford UP, 1984).

[84] E Fisher, 'Drowning by Numbers: Standard Setting in Risk Regulation and the Pursuit of Accountable Public Administration' (2000) 20 *Oxford Journal of Legal Studies* 109.

[85] UK Government, *The Food Standards Agency: A Force for Change* (Cm 3830, TSO, 1998).

[86] Regulatory Impact, Unit *Better Policy Making: A Guide to Regulatory Impact Assessment* (Cabinet Office, 2003).

[87] Art 5(1).

[88] W Maruyama, 'A New Pillar of the WTO: Sound Science' (1998) 32 *International Lawyer* 651.

[89] D Wirth, 'International Trade Agreements: Vehicles for Regulatory Reforms?' (1997) *University of Chicago Legal Forum,* 331.

[90] A Sykes, 'Regulatory Protectionism and the Law of International Trade' (1999) 66 *University of Chicago Law Review* 1 and Fisher, above n 20, ch 5.

[91] M Feeley and J Simon, 'Actuarial Justice: The New Criminal Law' in D Nelken (ed), *Actuarial Justice: The New Criminal Law* (Sage Publications, 1994).

[92] Treasury Taskforce, *Partnerships for Prosperity* (HM Treasury, 1997).

[93] E Fisher, 'The Rise of the Risk Commonwealth and the Challenge for Administrative Law' [2003] *Public Law* 455.

[94] *Ibid*; Standards Australia, above n 80; Strategy Unit of the Cabinet Office, *Risk: Improving Government's Capability to Handle Risk and Uncertainty, Full Report: A Source Document* (TSO, 2002).

D. The Many Definitions of Risk and Risk Assessment

The previous section has shown that the conceptualisation of environmental regulatory law as risk regulation has a far more complex history than such a label suggests. Risk has tended to take on an almost iconic and timeless status in contemporary environmental law discourse, but looking at the historical development of risk and environmental law such status seems dubious. Risk, like most regulatory concepts, is the product of political and social forces. What is also clear from closer scrutiny is that, while there tends to be a presumption that there are settled understandings of the definitions of 'risk' and 'risk assessment', this is not the case. This is perhaps best shown by returning to the US context.

As already noted, risk assessment techniques were developed out of a number of different disciplines and in particular engineering and toxicology. With regard to the former, probabilistic risk assessment was developed as a way of assessing the probabilities of failure of complex technological systems. This technique rests on the assumption that such systems can be comprehensively understood and that probabilities can be assigned to various types of systems failure.[95] In contrast, techniques developed in relation to toxicology and the related field of epidemiology are concerned with assessing the causal effects of particular substances using animal bioassays and epidemiological studies.[96] Those carrying out risk assessments in this area are dealing with open ended systems, and often studies are not only concerned with assessing probabilities but also determining the nature of a risk.

Thus, even at the outset, the term 'risk assessment' could mean different things. Developments in the US have not led to a universal understanding of what is a risk assessment. Most obviously, different techniques have been developed in relation to different types of risk although the determinative factor is not so much whether what are at risk are humans or the environment, but more what is the state of existing scientific knowledge about those risks. Thus, for example, the NRC has defined human health risk assessment as:

> the evaluation of scientific information on the hazardous properties of environmental agents and on the extent of human exposure to those agents. The product of the evaluation is a statement regarding the probability that populations so exposed will be harmed, and to what degree.[97]

This definition tends to characterise risk assessment as a process in which the hazardous properties of an agent and the nature of exposure can be identified. Thus,

[95] Jaeger *et al*, above n 2, 89–91.
[96] *Ibid*, 91–3, and NRC, above n 43, 29–33.
[97] NRC, above n 54, 25–6.

in their 1983 report the NRC identified risk assessment as a four-step process—hazard identification, dose-response assessment, exposure assessment and risk characterisation.[98] In contrast, the EPA has defined ecological risk assessment as:

> A process that evaluates the likelihood that adverse ecological effects may occur or are occurring as a result of exposure to one or more stressors. The process is used to systematically evaluate and organise data, information, assumptions, and uncertainties in order to help understand and predict the relationships between stressors and ecological effects in a way that is useful for environmental decision making.[99]

Here, there is more an expectation that a risk assessment will provide some insight into what is actually occurring in a particular environment as opposed to generating a probability. This broader approach to risk assessment is not surprising considering the often limited understandings about how ecosystems work.

The variations in risk assessment do not end there, however. Thus, for example, Rhomberg in 1997 wrote a 173-page survey of the different chemical risk assessment methodologies used by US Federal administrative agencies. The variations were enormous, often within the same organisation. He noted that these variations can be:

> attributed to the different questions being asked of the risk assessment process in different regulatory contexts by different environmental statutes. In part it reflects different institutional judgments about the most appropriate methods and different scientific judgments about matters with high scientific uncertainty. And in part it reflects a simple policy choice made for the sake of consistency within each organisation (which, owing to independent histories, become inconsistent among organisations).[100]

In other words, how risk assessment is defined is not just due to scientific factors but also institutional and socio-political ones as well. Thus we saw above that the distinction between risk assessment and risk management made by the NRC in its Red Book was in part due to its terms of reference which were a direct product of the *Benzene* decision.

Moreover, the highly objective understanding of risk assessment as promoted in the 1983 Report has been severely criticised by a number of official bodies including the NRC itself. In 1994 the NRC published a substantive report in which it explored the problems of scientific uncertainty and discretion in risk assessment.[101] In 1996 it published *Understanding Risk*, in which it concluded that the

[98] *Ibid*, 3.

[99] US Environmental Protection Agency, *Guidelines for Ecological Risk Assessment* (EPA/630/R-95/002F Final 1998) 1.

[100] L Rhomberg, *A Survey of Methods for Chemical Risk Assessment Among Federal Regulatory Agencies* (National Commission for Risk Assessment and Management, 1997) 2.

[101] NRC, above n 43.

assessment/management distinction, while useful for insulating scientific activity from political pressure, was problematic, in that it ignored the close interrelationship between the evaluation of scientific information and policy discussion.[102] It argued that the focus should be on risk characterisation which it described in the following manner:

> Risk characterization is the outcome of an analytic-deliberative process. Its success depends critically on systematic analysis that is appropriate to the problem, responds to the needs of the interested and affected parties, and treats uncertainties of importance to the decision problem in a comprehensible way. Success also depends on deliberations that formulate the decision problem, guide analysis to improve decision participants' understanding, seek the meaning of analytic findings and uncertainties, and improve the ability of interested and affected parties to participate effectively in the risk decision process. The process must have an appropriately diverse participation or representation of the spectrum of interested and affected parties, of decision makers, and of specialists in risk analysis, at each step.[103]

This is a radical departure from the approach seen in the Red Book and it grants considerable discretion to public administration. A year later the Presidential/ Congressional Commission on Risk Assessment and Risk Management also concluded that the assessment/management distinction was not a helpful one, although the approach it outlined was less radical than that above.[104] These divergent characterisations of risk assessment can be partly explained as due to different terms of reference and different subject matters. Thus, for example, *Understanding Risk* was not a direct response to a court case as the Red Book was, and thus was not posited as a solution to a problem of accountability as that report was. Likewise, *Understanding Risk* was concerned with ecological risk assessment where, compared to human health risk assessment, there has been less focus on the development of a strict methodology due to the significant scientific uncertainties involved and the dynamic nature of scientific knowledge.

The variations in definitions of risk assessment become even more obvious when one turns to other jurisdictions. Thus a survey conducted by the UK Interdepartmental Liaison Group on Risk Assessment (ILGRA) revealed a wide variation in how government departments made decisions about risk.[105] Indeed in many cases the term 'risk assessment' was avoided altogether.[106] When the term was used it often took on different meanings. Thus while ILGRA broadly defined

[102] NRC, *Understanding Risk: Informing Decisions in a Democratic Society* (National Academy Press, 1996) 36–6.

[103] *Ibid*, 3.

[104] Presidential/Congressional Commission on Risk Assessment and Risk Management (CRARM), *Framework for Environmental Health Risk Management—Volume One* (CRARM, 1997).

[105] ILGRA, *Use of Risk Assessment Within Government Departments* (Health and Safety Executive, 1996).

[106] Health and Safety Executive, *Reducing Risks, Protecting People* (Health and Safety Executive, 1999).

it as a 'tool for extrapolating from statistical and scientific data' the UK Parliamentary Office of Science and Technology defined 'risk assessment' in 1996 to include not only the scientific evaluation of risks but their management as well.[107] This latter definition is consistent with the Australian definition,[108] although the Australians define the 'scientific' part of decision-making about risk as risk analysis while the Parliamentary Office described it as risk evaluation. In contrast, risk analysis is defined under the EU Regulation on principles of food law and establishing the European Food Safety Authority (EFSA) as consisting of risk assessment, risk management, and risk communication.[109] The term 'risk assessment' is defined as 'a scientifically based process consisting of four steps: hazard identification, hazard characterisation, exposure assessment and risk characterisation', a definition similar to that seen in the Red Book.[110]

In contrast again, risk assessment is defined in the WTO SPS Agreement very broadly as:

> The evaluation of the likelihood of entry, establishment or spread of a pest or disease within the territory of an importing Member according to the sanitary or phytosanitary measures which might be applied, and of the associated potential biological and economic consequences; or the evaluation of the potential for adverse effects on human or animal health arising from the presence of additives, contaminants, toxins or disease-causing organisms in food, beverages or feedstuffs.[111]

What is understood by this is open to question. The WTO Dispute Settlement Panel in the *EC-Hormones* case, one of the first disputes in relation to the SPS Agreement, defined risk assessment in terms of the risk assessment/risk management distinction seen in the Red Book. The Panel stated that risk assessment must be understood as a 'scientific examination of data and factual studies' that required Members to evaluate the 'potential or probability' of an adverse event occurring.[112] The Appellate Body, however, in the same dispute settlement proceeding argued there was no authority for making the risk assessment/risk management distinction and that the danger of the Panel's approach was that it excluded from the scope of assessment 'all matters not susceptible of quantitative analysis'.[113] In other

[107] Parliamentary Office of Science and Technology, *Safety In Numbers* (TSO, 1996) 10.

[108] T Beer and F Ziolkowski, *Environmental Risk Assessment: An Australian Perspective* (Supervising Scientist Report No 102, 1995).

[109] Art 3(10) of Regulation 178/2002 laying down the general principles and requirements of food law, establishing the European Food Safety Authority and laying down procedures in matters of food safety [2002] OJ L/31/1.

[110] Art 3(11).

[111] Annex A.4.

[112] Panel Report, *EC Measures Concerning Meat and Meat Products (Hormones)—Complaint by the United States*, WT/DS26/R/USA, 13 Feb 1998, paras 8.91–98.

[113] Appellate Body Report, *European Communities—Measures Concerning Meat and Meat Products (Hormones)*, WT/DS26/AB, 16 Jan 1998, paras 181, 187.

words, they acknowledged that risk assessment may be qualitative in nature. To make matters more complicated the SPS Agreement encourages harmonisation on the basis of standards set by such international bodies as the Codex Alimentarius Commission.[114] Over the last couple of years that body has been developing a set of working principles for risk analysis that is more consistent with the framework regulating the EFSA.[115]

The discussion so far has not concentrated upon how the term 'risk' is defined. This is because, while there is an ongoing focus on risk assessment, 'risk' as a concept has been ignored.[116] Likewise, while scientific uncertainty is noted to be a feature of decision-making in this area, its meaning is rarely elaborated.[117] When there is some fleshing out of what these terms mean, it quickly becomes clear that different actors hold divergent views about how these terms should be defined.

Compare the definition of risk contained in two official US reports published within a year of each other. The 1996 NRC report, discussed above, defined risk as a:

> [c]oncept used to give meaning to things, forces or circumstances that pose danger to people or to what they value. Descriptions of risk are typically stated in terms of the likelihood of harm or loss from a hazard and usually include: an identification of what is 'at risk' and may be harmed or lost (eg health of human beings or an ecosystem, personal property, quality of life, ability to carry on an economic activity); the hazard that may occasion this loss; and a judgment about the likelihood that harm will occur.[118]

Such a definition is clearly consistent with their description of risk assessment in that it acknowledges the context-bound notion of characterising risk and conceptualising it in non-quantitative terms. In contrast the Presidential/Congressional Commission on Risk Assessment and Risk Management that reported in 1997 defined risk in more quantitative terms as a:

> probability that a substance or situation will produce harm under specified conditions. Risk is a combination of two factors:
>
> —The probability that an adverse event will occur (such as a specific disease or type of injury).
> —The consequences of the adverse event.
>
> Risk encompasses impacts on public health and on the environment, and arises from exposure and hazard. Risk does not exist if exposure to a harmful substance or situation

[114] Art 3(1).
[115] Codex Alimentarius Commission, *Report of the Twentieth Session of the Codex Committee on General Principles*, ALINORM 04/27/33A, Paris, 3–7 May 2004, paras 37–43.
[116] An exception to this is Art 3(9) of Regulation (EC) No 178/2002, above n 109.
[117] For an exception to this see NRC, above n 43.
[118] NRC, above n 102, 215–6.

> does not or will not occur. Hazard is determined by whether a particular substance or situation has the potential to cause harmful effects.[119]

This is the more conventional definition of risk used by those carrying out risk assessment in the environmental protection field, and the distinction between hazard and risk is a particularly important one.[120] It originated from risk assessment in the engineering context and is quite distinct from how risk is defined in other areas such as economics.[121]

Another example of the problem of finding a uniform definition of risk can be seen in the 1992 report of the UK Royal Society on *Risk: Analysis, Perception and Management.*[122] The Report was meant to be an official report of the Royal Society and a follow up to its 1983 Report that promoted risk assessment.[123] There was, however, no agreement among those writing the report over how risk should be defined, so that the report was recast as a contribution to an ongoing discussion rather than as an official report of the Royal Society.[124]

The lack of a coherent definition can also be seen in the variations in how scientific uncertainty is discussed in policy reports. Problems of quantification,[125] lack of research,[126] limits of methodology[127] and ignorance[128] may all be noted, but rarely in the same document. In part this is not surprising; the types of scientific uncertainty in relation to different environmental problems vary considerably. Thus, for example, while in toxicological risk assessment there is a rich discussion about the relative uncertainties involved in animal bioassays as opposed to epidemiological studies, the uncertainties facing those doing ecological risk assessment are far more about whether any particularly ecological system can be properly understood. Moreover, the language of uncertainty varies considerably from discipline to discipline.[129]

There are many different scientific ways of understanding risk and risk assessment. The same is also true of social scientific understandings of risk. While many social science commentators criticise mainstream risk policy they do so on diverse

[119] Presidential/Congressional Commission on Risk Assessment and Risk Management, above n 104, 1.

[120] Royal Society, *Risk, Analysis, Perception and Management* (Royal Society, 1992) 4.

[121] Royal Commission on Environmental Pollution, *Setting Environmental Standards, 21st Report* (TSO, 1998) 51 and Fisher, above n 93, 466–70.

[122] Royal Society, above n 120.

[123] Royal Society, above n 83.

[124] Royal Society, above n 120, 12. For a discussion of this see Adams, above n 41, 7–9.

[125] Royal Commission on Environmental Pollution, above n 121, 55–6.

[126] Independent Expert Group on Mobile Phones, *Mobile Phones and Health* (IEGMP Secretariat, 2000).

[127] NRC, above n 43, ch 9.

[128] NRC, above n 102, 5.

[129] Compare NRC, above n 43, and R Carpenter, 'Limitations in Measuring Ecological Sustainability' in T Trzyna (ed), *A Sustainable World: Defining and Measuring Sustainable Development* (IUCN- World Conservation Union, 1995) 175.

grounds and from fundamentally different starting points.[130] Thus, for example, there are those who criticise risk assessment because it ignores the psychological aspects of risk perception. From this perspective 'risk acceptability' must take into account the psychological reasons why individuals place divergent values on different types of risks.[131] This group of commentators are quite distinct from those that seek to show that risk assessment is a flawed methodology and not the 'sound science' it claims to be.[132] Distinct again are those commentators who use cultural theory to show that within different institutional cultures divergent approaches to risk acceptability will emerge.[133] Others conceptualise technological risks as part of modernisation and think that the development of a politics of risk amounts to a reflexive process by which a citizenry seeks to question both governing and modernisation processes.[134] Then there are those that characterise the development of risk assessment as part of a technology of control and domination.[135] Moreover, among these different commentators are quite profound divisions about the nature of risk and risk assessment. Some see risk as socially constructed, and some do not.[136] Some view risk assessment as fundamentally flawed while others merely view it as a limited tool.[137] Some see science as necessary and others see it as technocratic domination.[138] Just as with mainstream policy no single discourse about risk can be found among the social scientists.

Matters are complicated by the fact that the use of risk is not neutral, and understanding environmental problems in terms of risk has a powerful impact on how those problems are characterised and 'solved'. If risk is understood primarily in quantitative terms then only those aspects of an environmental problem that can be measured will be subject to analysis.[139] If, however, a broader definition such as the NRC's 1996 definition is used, other forms of information will be utilised in the decision-making process. However, if the deployment of risk is understood to be a means of domination and control then even the legitimacy of this more inclusive approach is to be doubted.[140] If risk is understood as a touchstone for debates

[130] For an overview see Lupton, above n 2, and Jaeger *et al*, above n 2.

[131] B Fischoff *et al*, *Acceptable Risk* (Cambridge UP, 1981).

[132] Shrader-Frechette, above n 4.

[133] M Douglas, *Risk Acceptability According to the Social Sciences* (Routledge and Kegan Paul, 1985) ; Schwarz and Thompson, above n 13.

[134] U Beck, *Risk Society: Towards A New Modernity* (Sage Publications, 1992).

[135] M Dean, *Governmentality: Power and Rule in Modern Society* (Sage Publications, 1999) ch 9.

[136] B Szerszynski *et al*, 'Introduction: Ecology, Realism and the Social Sciences' in S Lash *et al* (eds), *Introduction: Ecology, Realism and the Social Sciences* (Sage Publications, 1996) 10–12.

[137] Compare Shrader-Frechette, above n 4, and AJ Brown, 'Prayers of Sense and Reason: Mining, Environmental Risk Assessment and the Politics of Objectivity' (1992) 9 *Environmental Planning & Assessment Journal* 387.

[138] Compare Latour, above n 10, and F Fischer, *Technocracy and the Politics of Expertise* (Sage, 1990).

[139] T Porter, *Trust in Numbers: The Pursuit of Objectivity in Science and Public Life* (Princeton UP, 1995).

[140] P O'Malley, 'Uncertain Subjects: Risks, Liberalism, and Contract' (2000) 29 *Economics and Society* 460.

about modernity, however, then a more inclusive response to environmental decision-making is needed, but one that extends beyond the collection of scientific information to include normative debate.[141]

The same is true of risk assessment. A risk assessment methodology will define how a problem is understood. Thus, for example, the NRC's definition of human health risk assessment above rests on the assumption that hazardous properties of agents can be identified and that exposure to those agents can be adequately assessed. This is even though our knowledge of carcinogens and other toxins is often very poor. The same is true of probabilistic risk assessment developed in the engineering field, which rests on the assumption that all forms of system failure can be identified before they occur, even when accidents such as that at Three Mile Island showed that this is not the case.[142] What this amounts to is that the use of risk and risk assessment in any particular context privileges a particular meta-rationality.[143] As is clear from the above, however, it is difficult to conclude what meta-rationality is being privileged without looking at the legislative and policy context governing any particular environmental law issue.

E. Moving Forward: a Constructive Approach to Thinking about Risk and Environmental Law

The discussion so far has largely been concerned with deconstructing the present discourse about risk and environmental law. In doing so it has highlighted two points. First, thinking of environmental regulatory law as risk regulation is a relatively new phenomenon, and one that has been primarily driven by the promotion of risk assessment as a means of ensuring legitimate public administration. Moreover, these developments have mainly occurred in the US although they can be seen in other jurisdictions. Secondly, there are actually many different definitions of risk and risk assessment being used in environmental regulation. These variations cannot only be seen between different jurisdictions but also within jurisdictions and even within regulatory agencies. The same is true in social science commentary. Moreover, how 'risk' and 'risk assessment' are defined will have a powerful influence on how environmental problems and acceptable solutions are characterised.

All this would seem to be rather sobering for those who were expecting this chapter to provide a clear framework for thinking about risk and environmental

[141] Stirling, above n 4.
[142] President's Commission on the Accident at Three Mile Island, *Final Report* (Government Printing Office, 1980).
[143] Jaeger *et al*, above n 2, 251.

law. Rather than providing a firm foundation for the student or practitioner to build on, the above analysis appears to do the opposite. Not only do conventional 'objective' concepts of risk and risk assessment prove problematic, there also appears no single social scientific explanation of why this is the case. The strong temptation in such circumstances is to embrace post-modern relativism and either to ignore risk altogether or argue there is no 'right' answer. This however is neither a desirable nor a realistic option.

It is not desirable because what is striking about the issues highlighted above is that they are entirely consistent with the features of environmental law seen in the first section of this chapter. Environmental problems are physically and socio-politically complex and different environmental law regimes will define environmental problems and their solutions in divergent ways. Moreover, those problems are not simply about the physical state of the environment but also encompass issues about how we are governed and how communities should develop. Describing environmental regulatory law as risk regulation does not eradicate these features, but rather draws our attention to them. In thinking about risk we actually can begin to see more clearly some of the real issues shaping environmental law. It is perhaps not surprising that Ewald has noted that risk has become the 'single point upon which contemporary societies question themselves, analyse themselves, seek their values and, perhaps, recognise their limits'.[144]

Post-modern relativism is also not realistic, because the reality in most jurisdictions is that risk is an entrenched feature of environmental law which cannot be ignored in decision-making. Moreover, it is becoming the fundamental issue at the heart of a number of legal disputes.[145] Cases must be resolved, and crucial to their resolution is for some decision to be made about the role and nature of risk and risk assessment.

In this last section it will be shown that the conclusions above need not lead to post-modern angst and self-pity. Rather, an appreciation of these points requires environmental lawyers to take a more careful and critical approach to analysing how risk and risk assessment are deployed in environmental decision-making. In particular, it requires scholars and lawyers to appreciate that risk and risk assessment do not have fixed definitions and different definitions are due to divergent legal cultures, socio-political forces and decision-making contexts. The utility of such an approach for thinking about risk is best illustrated by an example, and this last section focuses on a legal principle closely related to both risk and sustainability—the precautionary principle—and how it has been interpreted by the European Commission.[146]

[144] F Ewald, 'Risk in Contemporary Society' (2000) 6 *Connecticut Insurance Law Journal* 365, 366.

[145] *American Dental Association v Martin*, 984 F 2d 823 (7th Cir, 1993); *T Mobile (UK) Ltd v First Secretary of State* [2004] EWCA Civ 1763; and Appellate Body Report, *European Communities—Measures Concerning Meat and Meat Products (Hormones)*, WT/DS26/AB/R; WT/DS48/AB/R (World Trade Organisation, 16 Jan 1998).

[146] European Commission, above n 1.

The precautionary principle has been a controversial and high-profile principle due to its inclusion in national and international regulatory regimes since the 1980s.[147] This is not surprising as it is concerned with one of the most intractable aspects of environmental decision-making—scientific uncertainty.[148] Broadly speaking, and acknowledging that there is no settled view on the matter,[149] the principle requires decision-makers to take seriously the problems that scientific uncertainty creates for regulatory decision-making in both the environmental and public health field.[150] A common formulation of the principle states that:

> Where there are threats of serious or irreversible damage, lack of full scientific certainty shall not be used as a reason for postponing cost-effective measures to prevent environmental degradation.[151]

The problems created by scientific uncertainty are multitudinous and include: the fact that 'no evidence of harm' does not mean 'no harm', that scientific assessments are limited in predicting the consequences of actions, that there is often no way of collecting the information to assess future impacts, and that there are ontological limitations on the capacity to predict future outcomes.[152] Indeed, the precautionary principle prompts us to reflect on the fact that, while sustainability requires us to think about the future impacts of present actions, this is a complex process because we cannot, with any accuracy, gauge what those impacts will be.

Following on from this, a fundamental feature of the precautionary principle is that it is not concerned with guaranteeing particular outcomes, but rather with the *process* by which a decision is made.[153] This is not only logical in light of the inability to predict outcomes in cases of scientific uncertainty, it is also consistent with the principle's status as a *legal* principle.[154] Identifying the principle as being concerned with the process by which decisions are made does not, however, provide any clear guidance in relation to what that process may be, and what is clear

[147] R Harding and E Fisher (eds), *Perspectives on the Precautionary Principle* (Federation Press, 1999); T O'Riordan *et al* (eds), *Reinterpreting the Precautionary Principle* (Cameron May, 2001); A Trouwborst, *Evolution and Status of the Precautionary Principle in International Law* (Kluwer, 2002); and C Sunstein, *The Laws of Fear: Beyond the Precautionary Principle* (Cambridge UP, 2005).

[148] See S Jasanoff and B Wynne, 'Science and Decision Making' in S Rayner and E Malone (eds), *Human Choice and Climate Change—Volume One* (Battelle Press, 1998).

[149] For discussions of differing definitions see R Stewart, 'Environmental Regulation Under Uncertainty' (2002) 10 *Research in Law and Economic,* 71; Sunstein, n 147, ch 1.

[150] C Raffensberger and J Tickner, *Protecting Public Health and the Environment: Implementing the Precautionary Principle* (Island Press, 1999).

[151] Principle 15, Rio Declaration on Environment and Development, (1992) 31 ILM 874.

[152] Wynne, above n 9; A Klinke and O Renn, 'Precautionary Principle and Discursive Strategies: Classifying and Managing Risks' (2001) 4 *Journal Risk Research* 159.

[153] E Fisher and R Harding, 'The Precautionary Principle: Towards a Deliberative, Transdisciplinary, Problem-Solving Process' in Harding and Fisher, above n 147, 290.

[154] E Fisher, 'Precaution, Precaution Everywhere: Developing a 'Common Understanding' of the Precautionary Principle in the European Community' (2002) 9 *Maastricht Journal of European and Comparative Law* 7.

from a study of the operation of the principle in different contexts and legal cultures is that the process might take on many different forms.[155] Thus it is very difficult to talk about the operation of a single precautionary principle and, as with environmental law generally, scholars and lawyers must be aware that definitions cannot be transplanted from one regime to another.[156]

With that said, a few generalisations can be made. Not surprisingly the principle has been advocated by those who see a heavy reliance on risk assessment as problematic, and who argue the need for a more broadly based approach to decision-making which takes into account both the physical and socio-political complexities of environmental decision-making.[157] In other words, the precautionary principle requires a more flexible, discursive process in which there is a greater role for administrative discretion. In contrast, those who oppose the precautionary principle tend to characterise it as a mandate for arbitrary decision-making or as a 'trump' card that hides ulterior motives because it allows decision-makers to make decisions without a factual basis.[158] This same group tend to be ardent supporters of risk assessment.[159] Again, as with risk, the reason for this division is driven by a number of different factors. In the national/supranational setting opinions about precaution tend to be shaped by different understandings about the legitimate role of public administration, while in the international setting they tend to be influenced by understandings about the autonomy sovereign states have, or should have, under international agreements.[160] In relation to this latter point, a quite significant issue of the last decade has been whether, and when, the precautionary principle allows states to derogate from their obligations under international trade agreements.[161]

From the brief discussion above it can be seen that the precautionary principle raises many of the same issues that we saw above in relation to risk and risk assessment, and in particular those in relation to how 'rational' regulatory action is defined. Moreover, in some legal cultures[162] such as the EU risk assessment, risk and the precautionary principle have become intertwined.

[155] *Ibid.*

[156] See Section B.

[157] Stirling, above n 4, and A Klinke and O Renn, 'A New Approach to Risk Evaluation and Management: Risk-Based, Precaution Based, and Discourse Based Strategies' (2002) 22 *Risk Analysis* 1071.

[158] G Majone, 'What Price Safety? The Precautionary Principle and its Policy Implications' (2002) 40 *Journal of Common Market Studies* 89 and C Sunstein, 'Beyond the Precautionary Principle' (2003) 151 *University of Pennsylvania Review* 1003.

[159] Graham and Wiener, above n 72; Sunstein, above n 65.

[160] Fisher, above n 154, 20–23.

[161] J Scott and E Vos, 'The Juridification of Uncertainty: Observations on the Ambivalence of the Precautionary Principle within in the EU and WTO' in C Joerges and R Dehousse (eds), *Good Governance in Europe's Integrated Market* (Oxford UP, 2002).

[162] Although this is not the case in all jurisdictions. See eg the Australian debate in Harding and Fisher, above n 147, where risk has not played such a significant role.

In terms of its history and application in the EU, the precautionary principle was enshrined in the 1992 Treaty of Rome as a basis for Community policy although it was not defined.[163] Within the EU context, the principle has a number of overlapping spheres of operation,[164] including its deployment by Member States in non-EU areas;[165] its application by Member States in the application of EU law;[166] its application by Member States to derogate from EU law;[167] its application by Community institutions in law- and policy-making;[168] and the EU's reliance on it to derogate from international obligations.[169] When one considers that each of these different spheres of operation raises distinct issues concerning the reasonableness and acceptability of Member State and Community action across a series of overlapping legal cultures then one can see there is a very real challenge in developing a 'common understanding' of the principle within the EU.[170] This is further complicated by the fact that within the EU context the principle applies to a range of environmental protection, health protection and consumer protection activities, each of which involve different forms of uncertainty and risk.[171]

Despite the diversity of situations to which the principle applies there have been attempts to identify a common definition of it within the EU context.[172] The most high-profile and significant example of this was the publication in 2000 of the European Commission's Communication on the Precautionary Principle. Strictly speaking that document is meant only to set out how the Commission applies or intends to apply the precautionary principle,[173] but the guidelines contained in the Communication are now commonly used to assess the validity of Member State action as well.[174] This is not surprising, considering the Commission's explicit statement in the Communication that they also wish to promote a 'common understanding' of how to assess and manage risk within the Community.[175] Moreover, regulatory regimes such as the EU's food safety regime have been clearly influenced by the guidelines.[176]

[163] Art 174(2).
[164] Fisher, above n 154.
[165] One example is mainstream town planning.
[166] Case C–236/01 *Monsanto Agricoltura Italia SpA* [2003] ECR I–8105.
[167] Case C–95/01 *Criminal Proceedings Against Greenham and Abel* [2004] 3 CMLR 33.
[168] Case T–13/99 *Pfizer Animal Health SA* [2002] ECR II–3305.
[169] Appellate Body Report, above n 113.
[170] Fisher, above n 154.
[171] Case T–74/00 *Artegodan GmbH* [2002] ECR II–4965.
[172] De Sadeleer, above n 27, ch 3.
[173] European Commission, above n 1, 3, 9.
[174] Case E–3/00 *EFTA Surveillance Authority* [2001] 2 CMLR 47; *Monsanto*, above n 166; and Case C–192/01 *Commission v Denmark* [2003] ECR I–9693.
[175] European Commission, above n 1, 3, 9.
[176] Regulation 178/2002 laying down the general principles and requirements of food law, establishing the European Food Safety Authority and laying down procedures in matters of food safety [2002] OJ L/31/1.

The starting point for the guidelines is to characterise standard setting and risk appraisal in terms of risk analysis, and thus as a three-step process involving risk assessment, risk management, and risk communication.[177] The Communication states that the principle applies to risks only where a risk assessment has identified a 'potential risk' and the uncertainties surrounding it.[178] An assessment of the risk requires:

> reliable scientific data and logical reasoning, leading to a conclusion which expresses the possibility of occurrence and the severity of a hazard's impact on the environment, or health of a given population including the extent of possible damage, persistency, reversibility, and delayed effect.[179]

Risk assessment is then defined as having the four components set out in the Red Book.[180] Putting these two statements together, it is not obvious what form a risk assessment should take. The latter statement suggests a specific procedure while the former is more general. Moreover, the Communication also stresses that any 'prudential' approach to taking into account scientific uncertainty as part of the risk assessment process should be seen as quite distinct from the application of the precautionary principle.[181] Such a prudential approach, however, would seem to take into account many of the uncertainties that are normally understood as the subjects of the precautionary principle.[182] The second step of applying the precautionary principle is that there must be a decision to act or not to act, and this, the Commission stresses, is a political decision directly concerned with 'acceptable risk', and as such is part of risk management.[183]

As well as these two steps the Commission states that there must be a transparent and inclusive process assessing the consequences of different forms of action and inaction.[184] This process is primarily an analytical one and presumably could be carried out with the first step in some cases. How it relates to risk management is not discussed, nor are the mechanisms for transparency and inclusiveness expanded upon. Finally, there must be a decision in relation to what measures should be taken, and the Commission stresses that such measures must be consistent with the principles of risk management and must be proportional, non-discriminatory, consistent, based on an examination of potential costs and benefits, subject to revision in light of new data and capable of assigning responsibility for the production of more scientific evidence.[185] This list broadly reflects requirements in WTO and EU law.

[177] European Commission, above n 1, 3.
[178] *Ibid*, 13.
[179] *Ibid*.
[180] *Ibid*, 13 and Annex III.
[181] *Ibid*, 12.
[182] *Ibid*, 13–14. Wynne, above n 9.
[183] *Ibid*, 14.
[184] *Ibid*, 16.
[185] *Ibid*, 17–20.

In terms of providing a set of guidelines for applying the precautionary principle the Communication is far from being a clear or logical document. First, as already noted, there seem to be no fixed understandings of risk assessment or uncertainty informing the document. This has clearly created problems for its legal interpretation.[186] Moreover, although the Communication would appear to relate to all areas where the precautionary principle may apply, the discussion of risk assessment in Annex III is directed at the health field. Secondly, it is not clear how each of the steps identified by the Commission in the Communication relate to each other. The Communication divides up its guidelines into 'the constituent parts of the precautionary principle' and 'guidelines for applying the precautionary principle' but it is ambiguous when and how each step in the decision-making process must occur. Thirdly, the Communication seems to be odds with conventional understandings of the precautionary principle, in that it appears to place great weight on risk assessment in circumstances of scientific uncertainty where any risk assessment is likely to be unreliable. Moreover, the list of requirements in relation to what measures can be applied ignores the problems of scientific uncertainty. There also appears to be no appreciation that the risk assessment/management divide is a problematic one.

Yet the Communication makes more sense when one understands it less as a set of guidelines drafted in isolation and more as a product of its context and surrounding legal culture. In particular, the Communication has been shaped by two distinct agendas—a concern to ensure that EU decision-making is consistent with the WTO SPS regime and anxieties over the validity of Community regulation. When seen from this perspective both the disjunctions in the Communication and the reasons for them can be identified more clearly.

The first major catalyst for the Communication was the WTO dispute settlement proceeding in relation to the EU's ban on beef derived from cattle treated with growth hormones.[187] In the Communication the Commission makes constant reference to the WTO SPS Agreement which regulated such bans.[188] The result of that dispute settlement process was that the EU's ban was found to be inconsistent with the SPS Agreement because the EU had not established that its ban was based on a risk assessment.[189] As already noted above, however, there were quite dramatic differences between the Panel and the Appellate Body about what type of risk assessment was required.[190] The Appellate Body also concluded (as did the Panel) that the precautionary principle could not override the provisions of the SPS Agreement. The Appellate Body further noted, however, that the

[186] See Fisher, above n 20, ch 6. For the case law see *Pfizer, above* n 168, and Case T–70/99 *Alpharma* [2002] ECR II–3495.

[187] For an overview of the dispute settlement process see J Paulwelyn, 'The WTO Agreement on Sanitary and PhtyoSanitary (SPS) Measures as Applied in the First Three Disputes: EC-Hormones, Australia-Salmon and Japan-Varietals' (1999) 2 *Journal of International Economic Law* 641.

[188] European Commission, above n 1, 3, 11, 12, 20, 21, 27, 28.

[189] Art 5(1). See para 208.

[190] Fisher, above n 20, ch 5.

principle was reflected in the right under the Agreement for Member States to establish their 'own level of protection'[191] and that:

> a panel charged with determining, for instance, whether 'sufficient scientific evidence' exists to warrant the maintenance by a Member State of a particular SPS measure may, of course, and should, bear in mind that responsible, representative governments commonly act from perspectives of prudence and precaution where risks of irreversible, e.g. life-terminating, damage to human health are concerned.[192]

These two decisions shaped the Communication in three ways. First, the Commission uses the decisions for its definition of risk assessment although there appears to be no appreciation that there is a disparity between the Panel and the Appellate Body on this point. Secondly, the Commission's strong statement that the principle is part of risk management and risk assessment, as well its reference to the 'prudential' treatment of scientific uncertainty in risk assessment, is derived from these decisions. Thirdly, the Communication is very much focused on SPS measures when in fact it applies to all Community action in relation to the precautionary principle.

The second catalyst for the Communication is an increased concern about the accountability of EU institutions,[193] and the Communication stresses throughout that the precautionary principle should never be used as a justification for arbitrary decision-making.[194] What little commentary there has been on the Communication has tended to focus on this issue and whether the principle as elaborated in the Communication provides an appropriate standard for assessing the legitimacy of administrative action.[195] Thus, Sunstein has stated that the Communication is 'partly sensible' because of its emphasis on risk assessment and proportionality but also 'frequently vague' because it does not set down clear guidelines.[196] In contrast, those who construe the precautionary principle as requiring a more deliberative and broadly based approach to regulation would clearly see the Communication's guidelines as placing too great a reliance on risk assessment.[197] The problem is that, as seen above, what is understood as 'arbitrary' will depend on what is understood to be the role and nature of legitimate public administration, and this will vary considerably.

[191] Paras 124–5.

[192] Para 124.

[193] G Majone, 'The Credibility Crisis of Community Regulation' (2000) 38 *Journal of Common Market Studies* 273; C Harlow, *Accountability in the European Union* (Oxford UP, 2002).

[194] European Commission, above n 1, 12, 15 and 21.

[195] K Lenaerts, ''In the Union We Trust': Trust Enhancing Principles of Community Law' (2004) 41 *CML Rev* 317; S Wolf, 'Risk Regulation, Higher Rationality and the Death of Judicial Self Restraint: A Comment on Ladeur' (2004) 41 *CML Rev* 1175.

[196] Sunstein, above n 147, 121. See also G Marchant and K Mossman, *Arbitrary and Capricious: The Precautionary Principle in the European Union Courts* (AEI Press, 2004) 23.

[197] Compare the guidelines with P Harremoës *et al* (eds), *The Precautionary Principle in the Twentieth Century: Late Lessons From Early Warnings* (Earthscan, 2002) ch 16. It is interesting to note that there have been few criticisms of the Communication in the literature from this perspective.

In particular, the principle tends to require a more flexible, discretionary administrative regime than is promoted by a heavy use of risk assessment. Yet the guidelines in the Communication attempt to reconcile the precautionary principle with risk assessment, and arguably this leads to a paradoxical situation where decision-makers are both required to take into account scientific uncertainty and act only on the basis of objective evidence.[198] This paradox can be seen in the way in which the European Court of Justice and Court of First Instance have struggled in their interpretation of the principle as elaborated in the Communication.[199] As one Advocate General has noted, the guidelines as interpreted by the courts exhibit:

> all the tension inherent in applying the precautionary principle; on the one hand, a measure cannot be based on a purely hypothetical risk, yet on the other hand, one cannot wait until the risk has been established with certainty.[200]

Commentators have tended to be critical of the courts' reasoning in these decisions because of these tensions,[201] but the paradox is not so much the judiciary's fault but a result of the fact that the Communication actually provides no coherent model of legitimate regulatory action. Furthermore, while anxiety over the legitimacy of Community action was a catalyst for the Communication, the guidelines are also increasingly being applied to and by Member States.[202] This raises a fundamental question over whether the legitimacy issues raised by Community institutions are the same as those raised by Member State actions.[203]

This brief example illustrates how in practice an understanding of the different ways in which risk and risk assessment are defined is vitally important for understanding what law and policy actually says, as well as understanding what conceptual problems such law and policy raise. The Communication begins to make far more sense when concepts of risk and risk assessment are understood to be products of their surrounding contexts and cultures. Thus we can see how definitions of these two terms have been awkwardly translated across different legal cultures, and we can also see how guidelines have been shaped by a concern to be consistent with a range of legal frameworks and legitimacy concerns. Such an analysis, however, does more than provide insight. It also paves the way for an analytical agenda. Thus, for example, in relation to the Communication there is, among other things, a need to: assess whether the Commission's interpretation of the

[198] Fisher, above n 20, ch 6.

[199] Most notably in *Pfizer,* above n 168, paras 109–173.

[200] *Commission v Denmark,* above n 174, para 101 of the AG's opinion.

[201] R Lofstedt, 'The Swing of the Regulatory Pendulum in Europe: From Precautionary Principle to (Regulatory) Impact Analysis' (2004) 28 *Journal of Risk & Uncertainty* 237; C MacMaolain, 'Using the Precautionary Principle to Protect Public Health: Pfizer v Council' (2003) 28 EL Rev 723.

[202] *Monsanto,* above n 166, and ILGRA, *The Precautionary Principle: Policy and Application* (ILGRA, 2002).

[203] Fisher, above n 20, chapter 6.

WTO Dispute Settlement Panel's and Appellate Body's decisions is legally correct; determine whether the definition of risk assessment provided in the Communication is relevant to every situation to which the precautionary principle applies; and determine whether the same guidelines should apply to both Community institutions and Member States.

Each of these is a significant question which has implications for both the theory and practice of risk and environmental law. Moreover, this mode of analysis leads us back to the three key features of environmental law highlighted at the start of this chapter. Environmental problems are socio-politically and physically complex, and this limits the ability to have universal concepts of risk, risk assessment and the precautionary principle. The role of the state is profoundly important, and an understanding of risk, risk assessment and the precautionary principle will be shaped by understandings of legitimate state action.[204] Finally, legal culture does matter. In thinking about risk environmental lawyers need to pay careful attention to legal context and legal reasoning.

F. Conclusion

This chapter has provided an introduction to risk and environmental law for environmental lawyers and environmental law scholars. It has highlighted three points. First, the increasing tendency to conceptualise environmental regulatory law in terms of risk regulation is the product of a long and complicated history in which risk assessment has had a significant role to play. We cannot think of either risk or risk assessment in isolation but must look at the many different social, political and legal forces that have led to these developments. Secondly, there are no agreed definitions of risk and risk assessment in environmental law, and these terms mean many different things. Accordingly, care must be taken in using these terms, particularly when such terms have a powerful impact on how environmental problems are conceptualised. Thirdly, not only do the two preceding points reflect the nature of environmental problems and environmental law, but understanding them helps environmental lawyers make sense of environmental law and policy, and this was illustrated in the last section by the analysis of the European Commission's Communication on the Precautionary Principle. In conclusion, then, risk does not provide a neat formula for understanding and conceptualising environmental law. What it does, however, is to provide a means of understanding the many complexities that are a very real part of the subject. Consequently, thinking about risk is a necessary part of being an environmental lawyer and a necessary element of environmental law for sustainability.

[204] *Ibid.*

Part 2

Ethical and Human Rights Dimensions

5

Ecological Justice and Law

KLAUS BOSSELMANN*

A. Introduction

The notion of ecological justice (or 'eco-justice') is fairly new[1] and not widely known among lawyers. This is in stark contrast to environmental justice, one of the most commonly used terms in the general environmental debate.[2] What is the difference between these aspects of justice and why is ecological justice important for environmental law?

This chapter argues that environmental law should be informed by ecological justice in much the same way as law in general is informed by justice. Generally understood conceptions of 'justice' are concerned with fair distribution of social goods and burdens. Distributional concerns are in the centre of most theories of justice. They are also in the centre of justice theories with respect to environmental protection. However, there are two different relational aspects to be considered here: the justice of the distribution of the environment among people, and the justice of the relationship between humans and the rest of the natural world.

The former is usually captured by the term 'environmental justice'. What about the latter? Whether or not the relationship between humans and the rest of the natural world has anything to do with 'justice' is controversial. Those who agree speak of 'ecological justice' as a concept to include both relational aspects. Those who disagree insist that our relationship with the rest of the natural world is a matter of ethics and morality, but not justice. For them, 'environmental justice' is the only term available to describe distributional problems with respect to environmental protection.

* Associate Professor, University of Auckland, Faculty of Law. The assistance of Meredith Webb, Chapman Tripp Research Fellow, is gratefully acknowledged.

[1] First termed by N Low and B Gleeson Justice, *Society and Nature* (Routledge, 1998) 2; K Bosselmann, 'Justice and the Environment: Building Blocks for a Theory on Ecological Justice' in K Bosselmann and B Richardson (eds), *Environmental Justice and Market Mechanisms: Key Challenges for Environmental Law and Policy* (Kluwer, 1999) 30.

[2] The Google Internet search brings up nearly 500,000 references for environmental justice compared to 6,000 for 'ecological justice'.

Traditionally, legal relationships—including those of justice—are perceived as relationships purely between people: people have no legal obligations towards nature, and nature has no rights towards people. Environmental law has been moulded in this anthropocentric perception of law. However, since the early 1970s this anthropocentric perception has been challenged from an environmental ethical point of view. The dichotomy between anthropocentric and ecocentric positions continues to influence theoretical conceptions of environmental law.

More recently, environmental ethics has taken an interest in theories of justice. As mentioned—and in line with the general environmental law debate—there are two broad approaches. One is to keep ethics and justice strictly separate, the other is to reconceptualise justice in the light of environmental ethics. While each approach can be associated with either an anthropocentric or ecocentric perspective, it is important to note that the eco-justice debate does not entirely follow this divide. There have been serious attempts to accommodate some form of ecocentrism within the liberal, Rawlsian[3] conception of justice, which considers justice to apply to relations only among people, not between humans and non-humans. One of the key issues in the current eco-justice debate is whether our responsibilities towards the future and the rest of the natural world can be fully addressed by extending the liberal idea of justice.

The first section of this chapter explores how liberal positions and ecological positions have tried to accommodate environmental ethics in the idea of justice. Although there is some common ground between them, liberal extensionism cannot explain why individual freedoms such as property rights should be restrained for ecological reasons. Rather than adding duties to rights, ecological realities urge us to consider re-definitions of rights themselves.

For a theory of eco-justice it is not enough to call upon environmental ethics. Unless we see all the various conceptions of justice as reflections of ethics, we will not be able to transform them. But even if we agree that 'all claims of justice are rooted in certain values other than justice itself',[4] the problem of reaching sufficient commonality of values remains. Can a commonality of values simply be assumed or would it merely be the result of a public discourse? This question leads us to the problem of how ecocentric norms can be institutionalised in ways that are consistent with democratic process. As will be shown in Part B, ecocentrism neither can be imposed nor will it emerge naturally from a discoursive democracy. Ecocentrism needs to be reasoned to make sense, although making sense does not necessarily emerge from reasoning in a pretext of liberal democracy.

An important argument in favour of eco-justice is the notion of sustainability. Despite the ongoing confusion surrounding the meaning of 'sustainable development', a good argument can be made that sustainability is an ethical concept rooted

[3] Named after its main proponent, John Rawls: J Rawls, *A Theory of Justice* (Oxford UP, 1993).
[4] A Heller, *Beyond Justice* (Basil Blackwell, 1987) 120.

in ecocentrism. Ecological sustainability implies acknowledgement of the intrinsic values of 'non-human others', and the need to express such intrinsic value in political and legal concepts, not the least of which is the idea of justice. Part C will, therefore, explore the intersections between sustainability and justice.

The core argument in favour of eco-justice is that it best expresses the ethics of ecological sustainability. Its key elements can help to define environmental law for sustainability. The final part of the chapter will show how eco-justice has informed recent trends in environmental and sustainable development law and how it can help to guide future trends.

The following section presents some theoretical approaches to ecological justice. They reflect differing political ideologies depending on how individuals are placed in their social and ecological context. The various positions will then be evaluated. As we will see, the defining criterion for a theory of ecological justice is the degree to which ecological concerns inform justice rather than ethics. The relationship between justice and ethics is at the heart of the eco-justice debate.

B. Liberal and Ecologist Approaches to Eco-Justice

1. Emergence of Environmental Justice Theories and Practices

Environmental policy and ethical debates around the world have increasingly been informed by various concepts of justice.[5] The term 'environmental justice' first rose to prominence through the environmental justice movement in the United States, which began in the 1970s.[6] It focused mainly on the unjust distribution of benefits and burdens in the context of environmental use and protection. Hofrichter's *Toxic Struggles* book publicised the inequities of siting locally undesirable land uses such as landfills and hazardous industries in the poor, often non-white communities.[7]

The growing political salience of environmental justice was reflected in President Clinton's famous Executive Order 12898, requiring government agencies to identify and address health and environmental effects on minority and low-income populations.[8] In Australia, environmental justice concerns first materialised in the

[5] See, by way of introduction, ZJB Plater, 'From the Beginning, A Fundamental Shift of Paradigms: A Theory and Short History of Environmental Law?' (1994) 27 *Loyola of Los Angeles L Rev* 981.

[6] D Faber (ed), *The Struggle for Ecological Democracy: Environmental Justice Movements in the United States* (Guilford Press, 1998).

[7] R Hofrichter, *Toxic Struggles: The Theory and Practice of Environmental Justice* (New Society Publishers, 1993); RD Bullard, *Dumping in Dixie: Race, Class, and Environmental Quality* (Westview Press, 1999)).

[8] Federal Actions to Address Environmental Justice in Minority Populations and Low-Income Populations (11 Feb 1994).

'Green Ban' movement in Sydney. Trade unions and community groups allied to halt environmentally and socially harmful developments, eventually winning rights of public participation in development decisions that might disproportionately harm certain localities or communities.[9]

A large literature on the subject emerged in the 1970s and 1980s, as academics, environmental activists and community groups demanded greater attention to environmental justice in government, economy, society and personal life. In general, this scholarship and activism did not address the question of the role of law or reform of environmental law. The 'deep ecology' movement attempted to construct a comprehensive ecocentric world view and way of life based on the equality of all forms of life and the rejection of all forms of domination, especially human domination of nature.[10] The 'social ecologists' emphasised the impacts of social hierarchy, ie domination over other humans on environmental health.[11] The animal rights movement contributed to the debates by pushing to extend the notion of justice beyond human beings.[12] 'Ecofeminists' highlighted the connections between patriarchy, environmental degradation and social injustice.[13] Not all commentators agreed, however, that it would be possible to forge shared conceptions of environmental justice in a 'postmodern' world comprised of heterogeneous and discordant societies.[14]

These were largely Western debates. The connections between human rights, environmental protection and justice were also taken up during the 1980s and 1990s by indigenous peoples' movements and environmental community groups in developing countries. A vast potpourri of environmental philosophies and practices relevant to environmental justice has been documented around the planet.[15] Of acute concern are the inequities of access to land, which have been commonly linked to deforestation and environmental mismanagement as the landless etch out a meagre living in environmentally marginal areas.[16] Environmental justice concerns were thus central to the 1993 rebellion of the

[9] M Burgmann and V Burgmann, *Green Bans, Red Union: Environmental Activism and the New South Wales Builders Labourers' Federation* (UNSW Press, 1998).

[10] See A Naess, *Ecology, Community and Lifestyle* (Cambridge UP, 1989); B Devall and G Sessions, *Deep Ecology: Living as if Nature Mattered* (Peregrine Smith Books, 1985).

[11] M Bookchin, *The Ecology of Freedom: The Emergence and Dissolution of Hierarchy* (Cheshire Books, 1982); C Spretnak and F Capra, *Green Politics* (Bear and Company, 1986).

[12] See P Singer, *Animal Liberation* (Random House, 1965); T Regan and P Singer (eds), *Animal Rights and Human Obligations* (Prentice-Hall, 1989); E Hargrove, *The Animal Rights—Environmental Ethics Debate* (SUNY Press, 1992).

[13] See V Plumwood, *Feminism and the Mastery of Nature* (Routledge, 1994); CJ Cuomo, *Feminism and Ecological Communities* (Routledge, 1998); K Warren (ed), *Ecofeminism: Women, Culture, Nature* (Indiana UP, 1997).

[14] AE Gare, *Postmodernism and the Environmental Crisis* (Routledge, 1995).

[15] JB Callicott, *Earth's Insights: A Multicultural Survey of Ecological Ethics from the Mediterranean Basin to the Australian Outback* (U California P, 1994).

[16] N Myers, 'World's Forests: Problems and Potentials' (1996) 23 *Environmental Conservation* 156.

Chiapas peoples of Mexico deprived of access to their traditional lands,[17] as well as to India's Chipko village movement of the 1970s that sought to reclaim community control of local forests.[18] The well-being of indigenous peoples worldwide from Sarawak to Siberia has also increasingly been framed in terms of the relationships between environmental protection and social justice.[19]

All of these disparate arguments and concerns form the background to the particular philosophical debate that is the focus of this chapter: namely, the possibility of a truly ecological conception of justice. Much of this debate has centred around the distinction between what Rawls termed 'public reason arguments' and 'comprehensive ideals'.[20] The former refer to the construction of a framework of basic constitutional principles that might be seen as neutral, allowing all reasonable people to agree to them. The latter refer to competing conceptions of the substantive 'good' drawn from moral, religious or philosophical doctrines that might be argued out in a process of democratic deliberation or discursive democracy. Developments in the eco-justice debate can be considered broadly under two heads: the liberal approach and the ecological. Liberals tend to be satisfied with liberalism's conventional definition of environmental issues as comprehensive ideals that may compete democratically. Ecologists, by contrast, attempt to introduce non-humans into the community of justice, the body charged with the construction of society's institutional and constitutional framework, thereby guaranteeing the consideration of nature's concerns.

2. The Liberal Approach to Eco-justice

Democratic liberals attempt to extend a liberal theory of justice to include environmental concerns. They reject the contention that ecologism and democratic liberalism are incompatible. The central concern of the liberals is to reconcile liberalism's preoccupation with the individual, self-interest and state neutrality with a commitment to good environmental practice. The aim is to further environmental goals through the paradigm of liberalism in preference to a replacement. This tends to result in contingently green policy, reliant on democratic majorities, rather than a strong state commitment to ecologism.

17 N Harvey, *The Chiapas Rebellion: The Struggle for Land and Democracy* (Duke UP, 1998).

18 H Rangan, 'From Chipko to Uttaranchal: Development, Environment, and Social Protest in the Garhwal Himalayas' in R Peet and M Watts (eds), *Liberation Ecologies* (Routledge, 1996); R Guha, *The Unquiet Woods: Ecological Change and Peasant Resistance in Himalaya* (U California P, 1989).

19 See D Hyndman, *Ancestral Forests and the Mountain of Gold: Indigenous Peoples and Mining in Indonesia* (Westview Press, 1994); LE Sponsel, *Indigenous Peoples and the Future of Amazonia: An Ecological Anthropology of an Endangered World* (U Arizona P, 1995).

20 Rawls, above n 3.

(a) Bell

Derek Bell focuses upon the Rawlsian distinction between public reason arguments and the separate concept of comprehensive ideals, seeking to demonstrate that environmentally friendly policies may be justified under both heads. He notes that a weak form of sustainability and a conception of environmental justice may be justified by two of the public reason arguments Rawls identifies; life-sustaining properties and human health.[21] More however can be achieved through comprehensive arguments where majority support can be found. Thus, according to Bell, Rawls's approach permits adherence to ecocentric arguments where constitutional essentials and questions of basic justice are not at issue.[22]

Bell mounts a defence of this 'environmentally friendly' liberalism by responding to objections that Rawls's theory precludes a liberal state from adhering to environmental policies even under comprehensive ideals. The objections relate to Rawls's 'difference' principle and commitment to neutrality. In relation to the former it has been argued that the difference principle, as a pre-eminent political value, requires that any action taken by the state benefit the worst-off in society. This would rule out environmental policies in circumstances where they are not of direct benefit to the impecunious in terms of income and wealth enhancement. In Bell's opinion, this is inaccurate, as the principle is concerned not with growth but with the distribution of income between social groups. A fair distribution of resources is more important than overall wealth maximisation.[23] Because distribution is not offended by state commitment to environmental goods, neither is Rawls's difference principle.

The neutrality objection claims that the advancement of comprehensive arguments through democracy conflicts with Rawls's commitment to neutrality. It is argued that the market is a more impartial regulator than a democracy, where a minority may have their options curtailed by the majority.[24] In response Bell argues that market regulation, unlike democratic liberalism, is not fundamentally neutral. A market-based approach erroneously assumes that all resources are from personal income and private wealth, ignoring the existence of collectively owned resources.[25] A market approach can be defended only through a liberal individualistic comprehensive ideal and therefore, unlike democratic liberalism, is not fundamentally neutral.[26]

Bell's thesis illustrates that liberalism and environmentalism are not incompatible. It is not clear, though, that beyond basic environmental goods, provided

[21] D Bell, 'How can Political Liberals be Environmentalists?' (2002) 50 *Political Studies* 703, 707–8.
[22] *Ibid*, 707.
[23] *Ibid*, 715–6.
[24] *Ibid*, 716.
[25] *Ibid*, 719.
[26] *Ibid*, 719–20.

through public reason arguments, a liberal state in practice will embrace environmentalism. As Bell notes, Rawlsian liberalism is a 'contingently' rather than an 'intrinsically' green liberalism. The adoption of green policies by the state is dependent on majority support.[27]

(b) Barry

John Barry has also considered the compatibility of a state's embracement of environmental goods with Rawls's commitment to neutrality. Barry separates out classical and social liberalism, noting that whilst the former is inconsistent with a sustainable society the latter is not. He writes that, provided the political institutions and values of a liberal democracy can be divorced from the capitalist market-based economy, a greened liberalism is feasible.[28] In his view social liberalism contains many of the requisite tools for a commitment to environmentalism. Specifically, Barry contemplates a role for the precautionary principle in relation to irreplaceable natural resources, providing environmental protection in the face of scientific uncertainty.[29] Employment of the precautionary principle is, he asserts, consistent with Rawls's insistence on neutrality. Claims to the contrary reflect too narrow a view of neutrality, ignoring the way environmental protection can enhance liberty through protecting options.[30] He argues that because his conception of the precautionary principle does not prescribe avenues of action, but rather rules out certain decisions and uses, the requirement of neutrality is not offended.[31]

The harm principle is also central to Barry's exposition. He sees it as redefining the notion of private property in land.[32] This involves recognition that the impact of individuals' decisions relating to their private property can affect in such a way that those decisions cannot be considered to be of a private nature.[33] The growth of regulations relating to land use is seen as an example of the state's perception of land as common not private property.[34] Barry, though, is careful to emphasise that strict justification is required for the invocation of state intervention to avoid impinging upon the liberty of individuals.[35] The tools Barry identifies as offered by liberalism do little more than place loose limits on the destructiveness of 'progress'.

[27] *Ibid*, 721.
[28] J Barry, 'Greening Liberal Democracy: Practice, Theory and Political Economy' in J Barry and M Wissenburg (eds), *Sustaining Liberal Democracy: Ecological Challenges and Opportunities* (Palgrave, 2001) 67.
[29] *Ibid*.
[30] *Ibid*, 68.
[31] *Ibid*, 71.
[32] *Ibid*, 72.
[33] *Ibid*, 75.
[34] *Ibid*, 74.
[35] *Ibid*, 78.

(c) Wissenburg

Marcel Wissenburg also identifies tools that might serve to make liberalism capable of responding to environmental needs. He focuses his argument for a greener democratic liberalism on Rawls's 'savings principle'. The savings principle developed by Rawls aims at creating intergenerational justice through an acknowledgement by those in the original position (ie, the first generation) that it is in their mutual interest to require the protection of primary goods for the next generation. Wissenburg seeks to demonstrate that the savings principle is applicable to all liberal theories, not just Rawlsian or contractarian ones.[36] This is accomplished, in his view, first by recognising that generations do not exist in linear formation but contemporaneously.[37] At any one time up to six generations may be interacting. Secondly, Wissenburg notes a new condition added by Rawls in *Political Liberalism* to those in the original position; all generations must have followed a similar principle aimed at 'savings'.[38] In light of these two conditions, Wissenburg asserts that the savings principle must be accepted as the only rational option, because it leads to mutual advantage, is in the self-interest and supports individual liberty. The savings principle is to the advantage of every next generation. This makes its rejection it irrational; therefore it is a necessary condition for a just society. Conversely if the savings principle were absent from a given society that would render the society unjust, as there would be a bias in favour of previous generations.[39]

Wissenburg then expands the conditions implicit in Rawls's original position that are needed to reach an agreement around the savings principle. In doing so he moves beyond the veil of ignorance, demonstrating that a savings principle is applicable to all liberal theories because it appeals to the bedrocks of liberalism; mutual advantage, self-interest and individual liberties.[40] In this way the savings principle is presented as a precursor to the existence of a just liberal society.

Having demonstrated the necessity of the 'savings principle' to democratic liberalism Wissenberg considers what form the 'savings principle' might take in practice. He develops a principle of 'Restraint', entailing a commitment to avoid destroying goods in cases where they are irreplaceable.[41] Such a stance is defended through appeal to liberal aims of benefit maximisation; options are better left open on the ground that the present generation cannot foresee whether a resource might be put to better use at a future time.[42] In situations where necessity

[36] M Wissenburg, 'An Extension of the Rawlsian Savings Principle to Liberal Theories of Justice in General' in A Dobson (ed), *Fairness and Futurity: Essays on Environmental Sustainability and Environmental Justice* (Oxford UP, 1999) 174.
[37] *Ibid*, 177.
[38] *Ibid*, 175–6.
[39] *Ibid*, 180–1.
[40] *Ibid*, 183–90.
[41] *Ibid*, 193.
[42] *Ibid*, 194.

demands the destruction of a resource and an equivalent is unavailable, 'proper' compensation should be paid.

Acceptance of the restraint principle in Wissenburg's view would have significant implications for liberalism. The principle would operate to challenge the absoluteness of private property rights.[43] There would be a shift in the burden of proof to those destroying elements of the natural world to justify their destruction and provide a replacement or compensation. Wissenburg contends that a principle of restraint would solve many of the debates around the conflict between intra- and intergenerational justice by ensuring that all attempts are made to protect the environment without sacrificing the needs of the present generation.[44] Finally Wissenburg sees the principle as responding to concerns relating to non-human nature, because the principle protects the natural world insofar as where it is unavoidable no ecological being should be damaged.[45]

3. Ecologists

What is referred to here as 'ecologists' stands for a group of theorists with ecological thinking as their base. Rather than seeking to fit environmental concerns into existing social systems, such as law and justice, ecological theorists aim for transforming social systems themselves. The ecological crisis is seen as a profound challenge to human perceptions and social institutions.

The concern of most theorists in this group is for an ecological ethic that penetrates social and legal norms. The inclusiveness of such an ethic is widely shared among indigenous people, Non-Western cultures and environmental philosophers, yet attempts specifically to relate ecological ethics to justice are rare. Philosophers tend to focus on issues of ethics, while lawyers tend to focus on issues of justice with little common ground between them.

However, the following social and political theorists have aimed for common ground. They do not accept the traditional boundaries between ethics and justice, nor do they see the Rawlsian concept of justice as adequate for our time. Ecological positions are characterised by their attempt to reconceptualise justice altogether.

(a) Low and Gleeson

Nicholas Low and Brendan Gleeson argue that limiting morality to the human species is no longer defensible in light of scientific developments and the growing awareness of the interdependence between humankind and nature.[46] In response

[43] *Ibid*, 197.
[44] *Ibid.*
[45] *Ibid.*
[46] Low and Gleeson, above n 1, 155.

they posit two overarching principles of ecological justice to guide decision-making. First, 'ecological justice is that every natural entity is entitled to enjoy the fullness of it's own form of life'. Secondly, 'all life forms are mutually dependent and dependent on non-life forms'.[47] Noting that the principles may operate in practice to create conflict in decision-making they are qualified by three distinctions.[48] The first is that life has moral precedence over non-life, the second is that individualised life forms take moral precedence over life forms that exist only as communities and, finally, humans take precedence over other life forms.[49] These conditions are aimed at resolving competing values and ensuring a moral distinction between human and non-human life remains. Accepting these moral rules of thumb, Low and Gleeson consider the institutional and constitutional processes for putting ecological justice into place. Rejecting the present system as incapable of delivering ecological justice in this form they consider new models of governance.[50]

It is important to note that Low and Gleeson view justice not as absolute, but dialectic. Thus there are no universal principles but an evolving debate about the bases of justice.[51] Conflicts are conceived of as a matter for human moral judgement as resolved by the institutions developed for such a purpose.[52]

(b) Baxter

In preference to requiring ecologists to develop their own theory of distributive justice, Brian Baxter attempts to extend Brian Barry's theory of distributive justice, justice as impartiality,[53] to meet ecological concerns. This approach is chosen on the grounds, that it is the most defensible of distributive justice theories.[54] Barry takes his starting point from Scanlon's modification of Rawls's original position. Scanlon's position operates not by mutual consensus but by the veto of members of the community of justice. In his conception a liberal democratic framework is among the basic constitutional rules reasonable people will not object to. Through this democratic framework conceptions of the 'good' compete for acceptance. Where a majority accept ecological justice as a 'good' worthy of support the state may legitimately apply it. However, conversely, this means that were a majority to support the extermination of whole species this would not constitute an injustice.[55] Baxter finds such a position untenable and attempts to extend Barry's theory to ensure that such an outcome is not possible.[56] He

[47] *Ibid*, 156.
[48] *Ibid*, 156–7.
[49] *Ibid*, 157.
[50] *Ibid*, 189–93.
[51] *Ibid*, 197.
[52] *Ibid*, 200.
[53] B Barry, *Justice as Impartiality* (Clarendon Press, 1995).
[54] BH Baxter, 'Ecological Justice and Justice as Impartiality' (2000) 9 *Environmental Politics* 43, 45.
[55] *Ibid*, 49.
[56] *Ibid*, 50.

achieves this through an expansion of those involved in the formulation of the basic structure of impartial justice to include non-humans. Baxter contends that Barry has largely neglected the issue of who should comprise the community of justice, incorrectly defining members. Barry describes his theory as solving the concerns of 'how people with competing conceptions of the good may be brought freely to live on terms which all can accept as reasonable'.[57] This conception mandates that those belonging to the community of justice must have competing conceptions of the good, thereby ruling out non-humans. Baxter objects, noting that the inarticulate in the form of children and the disabled have interests that must be protected by the community of justice without ever having competing conceptions of the good.[58] The possession of a competing conception of the good is not therefore a necessary requirement.

Introducing the inarticulate into the community of justice, however, does not solve the question of representation. Baxter asserts that a solution could lie in allowing the inarticulate, whether human or non-human, to have their interests protected through the use of proxies.[59] Members of the community of justice may act as guardians, speaking on behalf of non-human nature and future generations.[60] Including non-humans within the community does not impede Barry's notion of neutrality. This is because the act is independent of notions of the 'good' and is concerned instead with criteria of admission into the community.[61] This position, Baxter emphasises, does not require an equality of consideration between human and non-human interests; instead it merely requires that the interests of the non-human world be considered prior to decisions being made.[62]

(c) Eckersley

Robyn Eckersley, noting the failure of Rawls's theory of democratic liberalism to respond to green concerns, takes her starting point from Habermas.[63] The latter advances a dialogical approach to developing a theory of justice whereby the focus is on the debate through which principles of justice are constructed. This contrasts with the monological approach employed by Rawls where the fundamental principles that govern the basic structure of society are developed in advance of the discourse. Dialogical theories aim to reach mutual agreement around the superior argument insisting that all those affected by decisions should be active participants in the dialogue leading up to those decisions.[64] The central issue for

[57] *Ibid*, 52.
[58] *Ibid*, 53–4.
[59] *Ibid*, 55.
[60] *Ibid*.
[61] *Ibid*, 57.
[62] *Ibid*, 60. See also BH Baxter, A Theory of Ecological Justice (Routledge, 2004).
[63] R Eckersley, *The Green State: Rethinking Democracy and Sovereignty* (MIT Press, 2004) 141.
[64] *Ibid*, 116.

dialogical theorists is the limits on the discourse. Central to the successful workings of discursive democracy is free and open communication.[65]

Eckersley identifies ecological interests as 'generalisable' interests; these are by definition not sectional, private or selfish.[66] Generalisable interests, she notes, are protected by the mode of communication presupposed by the discourse ethic where political communication is not distorted by power imbalances. In such an environment, generalisable interests may be successfully defended publicly against narrower sectional interests. Although more likely to deliver green policies, Eckersley believes that this is not guaranteed and is in fact contingent upon the superiority of ecological arguments.[67] In light of this, her key concern is to bring non-human and future generations into the speech community. This requires tackling the hurdle of the discourse ethic's resistance to allowing individuals to speak on behalf of others. In the context of nature Eckersley responds to the criticism that humans are incapable of speaking for non-humans because of the risk that humans are unable to move beyond their inherent anthropocentricism.[68] This obstacle is overcome by an acknowledgement that the human view of nature is incomplete, culturally filtered and provisional, and therefore care must be taken in relations with nature.[69] Once she achieves a place for non-humans in the speech community she turns to the more difficult issue of how their speech can be represented.[70] Eckersley advances a form of trusteeship held by humans for nature. She also introduces another option, a basic rule of thumb to guide human decision-makers away from damaging the environment that cannot speak for itself. She suggests the precautionary principle as such a norm that would achieve the goal of protecting those incapable of participating actively in the discourse.[71] The principle, she argues, could be entrenched constitutionally to ensure systematic consideration is granted to ecological concerns.

(d) Schlosberg

David Schlosberg focuses on the meaning of justice, seeking to have it expanded from issues of distribution to encompass notions of recognition and participation.[72] This wider conception of justice flows from an acceptance of Iris Young's view of injustice as institutionalised domination and oppression.[73] Injustice can only be

[65] *Ibid.*
[66] *Ibid*, 117.
[67] *Ibid*, 119.
[68] *Ibid*, 123.
[69] *Ibid*, 125.
[70] *Ibid*, 127–38.
[71] *Ibid*, 135.
[72] D Schlosberg, 'The Justice of Environmental Justice: Reconciling Equity, Recognition, and Participation in a Political Movement' in A Light and A De-Shalit (eds), *Moral and Political Reasoning in Environmental Practice* (MIT Press, 2003) 79.
[73] *Ibid*, 81.

solved through this tripartite notion of justice rather than, as has been traditionally assumed, through questions of distribution alone. Recognition is central to human dignity and involves acknowledgement that some communities are unfairly affected by environmental degradation.[74] Political participation through inclusive decision-making is seen as achieving more just outcomes for communities in question.[75] Schlosberg is hopeful that a tripartite view of justice might help to forge links between the environmental justice movement and other social justice movements.[76]

Schlosberg has also recently extended his argument to encapsulate elements of ecological justice. He sees a lack of recognition of the natural world as a central cause of humankind's oppression and domination of nature.[77] The application of recognition to nature is defended against the objection that the self-worth of nature cannot be adversely affected by non-recognition because of an inability to suffer psychological harm. He rejects the objection on the ground that the central element of injustice on the due to non-recognition is not the psychological harm suffered by the subject but rather the lack of recognition by a society.[78]

Schlosberg then identifies two directions that might be taken in constructing a framework for recognition of nature. The first would respond to nature's intrinsic worth. The second would focus on the importance of nature for humans.[79] Recognition of nature can, according to Schlosberg, be defended under both criteria. Physical abuse, he notes, is a key element of disrespect that in turn is an aspect of non-recognition.[80] The further ground of human self-interest in the face of environmental catastrophe also supports respect for nature.[81] Schlosberg further considers whether recognition of nature is a violation of the central principles of liberalism. He contends that including the natural world into the community of justice through recognition does not devolve into a notion of the good. It is the procedural conditions for justice that are affected, rather than any particular definition of the good. Certain notions of the good may no longer be available, for example, destruction of species.

After defending the expansion of recognition to nature, Schlosberg turns to considering how participation of nature might be achieved. For this to occur he asserts it is necessary to consider the institutional biases against nature that lead to unequal distributions.[82] These can be overcome through more open and

[74] *Ibid.*
[75] *Ibid*, 92.
[76] D Schlosberg, 'Three Dimensions of Ecological Justice' (paper prepared for *Political Research Annual Joint Sessions*, Grenoble, France, 6–11 Apr 2001), available at www.essex.ac.uk/ecpr/jointsessions/grenoble/papers/ws6/schlosberg.pdf (draft), forthcoming in R Eckersley and J Barry (eds), *Environmental and Ecological Justice: Theory and Practice in the US* (MIT Press, 2005) 20.
[77] *Ibid*, 12.
[78] *Ibid*, 14.
[79] *Ibid.*
[80] *Ibid*, 15.
[81] *Ibid.*
[82] *Ibid.*

participatory structures of environmental decision-making that encourage greater political engagement and a diversity of viewpoints to be expressed. An increase in diverse human participation is thus central. Thus, widening public standing to the courts, greater access to environmental information and more rights for public consultation in environmental decision-making (eg, environmental impact assessment submissions and public hearings) are the kind of reforms that Schlosberg would applaud.[83] Nature itself has a more direct role to play through signals that may be interpreted by humans. Similarly, in this connection, Christopher Stone earlier argued that trees and other components of nature should have 'standing' in our legal systems, to be articulated through democratically chosen environmental guardians.[84] Schlosberg also picks up on Dryzek's call for a consideration of nature's signals expressed through disruptions to nature's integrity. Examples include global warming, droughts, floods, species extinction and other physical occurrences.[85] Schlosberg thus places emphasis on involving both the human and the non-human world in the democratic discourse.

4. Evaluation

The various approaches to eco-justice all aim for integrating the non-human world in environmental decision-making. Principally, the integration can be pursued either through the ethical discourse or through the justice discourse. It would not matter if both discourses would equally lead to better decision-making. But do they? According to Rawls, justice is based on a commonly agreed discourse and, therefore, facilitated by institutions (law and governance). Ethics, on the other hand, reflect comprehensive ideals that cannot per se be communicated through institutions. Ethics may inform justice, but cannot guide decision-making in ways that the institutions of justice are offering.

The categorical distinction between justice and morality determines all liberal conceptions of justice. The inherent assumption is that issues of justice are different from, and superior to, moral values. Justice represents the values of an assumed public rationality (individual freedom and rights) that disassociates itself from a morality of compassion and empathy. No matter how importantly the non-human world may be regarded by humanity, it stays outside its *justitia communis*.

Rawls has always been clear about this exclusion: 'the status of the natural world and our proper relation to it is not a constitutional essential or a basic question of justice'.[86] While he acknowledged 'duties' in this regard, he described them as

[83] See NP Spyke, 'Public Participation in Environmental Decisionmaking at the New Millennium: Structuring New Spheres of Public Influence' (1999) 26 *Boston College Environmental Affairs Law Review* 263; J Steele, 'Participation and Deliberation in Environmental Law: Exploring a Problem-solving Approach' (2001) 21 *Oxford Journal of Legal Studies* 415.

[84] C Stone, 'Should Trees Have Standing?' (1972) 45 *Southern California L Rev* 450.

[85] Schlosberg, above n 76, 17.

[86] J Rawls, *Political Liberalism* (Oxford UP, 1993) 246.

'duties of compassion and humanity' rather than duties of justice. Any 'considered beliefs' morally to include the non-human world 'are outside the scope of the theory of justice'.[87] Rawls' 'original position' cannot assume a morality without a moral agent. An agent can be a person living today or a fictitious person living tomorrow, but has to be a 'person'. Interestingly, non-human entities can qualify as persons—a corporation for example—but non-human living entities cannot.

Liberal approaches to justice are bound to exclude the non-human world. Attempts for an extension of justice can be made, of course, but they can hardly be marginalised as a 'green twist' (Wissenburg) of Rawls' original position. Why should Rawls or any liberal throw the baby out with the bath water? Their anthropocentric bias prevents them from expanding inter-human justice to include 'inter-species' justice.

Legal theories of justice traditionally suffer from avoiding the moral debate. That is why no legal theory has ever embraced an eco-ethical concept of justice.[88] Ethics, in whatever form, ought to be understood as informing *any* idea of justice. There is no justice without some underpinning morality, just as there are no human rights without ethical assumptions. For example, whether or not property rights should be defined to include obligations is not a matter of the 'law', but of ethical reasoning underpinning it. Most constitutions define private property as a combination of guaranteed individual freedom and limiting social responsibility. Property cannot be protected in abstract, but only in a social context.

It can, therefore, be reasoned that human rights are limited, not solely by their social context, but also by their ecological context. Individual freedom is determined not just by laws of society, but also by laws of nature. The ecological approach to human rights has influenced human rights theory, constitutional development in Germany[89] and international law.[90]

It is worth comparing the justice debate to the rights debate. Fundamentally, the objections against a concept of ecological justice are the same as those against ecological rights. Central to the liberal idea of justice has been the liberal conception of rights. And even though neither Rawls nor Ronald Dworkin nor any other leading liberal theorist of justice has argued for the possibility of extending rights to animals and plants,[91] it would be possible to do so, at least

[87] J Rawls, *A Theory of Justice* (Oxford UP, 1993) 448.

[88] To my knowledge, apart from myself and other members of the IUCN's Environmental Law Commission Specialist Group on Ethics, there is no lawyer among ecologically minded theorists of justice.

[89] K Bosselmann, 'Human Rights and the Environment: Redefining Fundamental Principles?' in B Gleeson and N Low (eds), *Governance for the Environment* (Palgrave, 2001) 118.

[90] P Taylor, 'From Environmental to Ecological Human Rights: A New Dynamic in International Law' (1998) 10 *Georgetown Environmental L Rev* 309; K Bosselmann, *Ökologische Grundrechte* (Nomos, 1999).

[91] With the possible exception of Joseph Raz who writes: 'Rights ground requirements for action in the interest of other beings': J Raz, *The Morality of Freedom* (Oxford UP, 1986).

structurally. Whether or not non-human entities like animals or plants can have rights is a matter, not so much for lawyers, but for philosophers to decide. From a legal perspective rights can be attributed to all sorts of entities like, for example, companies and states. From a philosophical perspective, on the other hand, the issue becomes more complex and many have written about nature's rights. There is, in fact, a tradition of rights for nature since ancient times (Stoic School) including such names as Spinoza, Leipnitz, Goethe, Schopenhauer, Bentham and, in our days, Jonas, Meyer-Abich or Singer. All of these are philosophers, but it was Christopher Stone[92] who triggered a broad public debate on rights and social change. After 30 years of debate it can be concluded today that nature's rights are acceptable only to liberal theorists, but not to those of an ecocentric persuasion.

At a closer look, rights and ecocentric ethics are ultimately opposed to one another. Take, for example, Giagnocavo and Goldstein,[93] who have argued that the concept of nature's rights is tantamount to a 'quick legal fix', which, like many other legal solutions, precludes the deep questions necessary for genuine world change.[94] Giagnovcavo and Goldstein reject rights theory as a 'false claim' as they give the holder some advantages, but this amounts to valuing only by legal institutions, not society at large.[95] This and other criticisms of the political weakness of rights are often directed against Stone. Ironically, Stone himself explicitly recognised the limitations of his 'rights' theory and has repeatedly stressed the crucial importance of a changed environmental consciousness. An ecological reform of environmental policy and law will not happen without 'a radical shift in our feelings about 'our' place in the rest of Nature'.[96]

The importance of the rights debate was that, for the first time, modern legal theory was forced into a discussion on fundamental ethical issues. Without Stone and like-minded lawyers we would not today be in a situation where it becomes possible to contemplate a theory of ecological justice.

If a mere extension of rights is not delivering ecological decision-making, why should an extension of justice help us? Applying liberal principles more widely only reinforces individualism and anthropocentrism. Instead, we need to examine the principles themselves. If they are 'blind' of the ecological context of human existence, they need to be reconsidered.[97]

[92] C Stone, 'Should Trees Have Standing?' (1972) 45 *Southern California L Rev* 450; see also C Stone, *Earth and Other Ethics: The Case for Moral Pluralism* (Harper and Row, 1987).

[93] C Giagnocavo and H Goldstein, 'Law Reform or World Re-form' (1990) 35 *McGill L J* 346.

[94] *Ibid.*

[95] *Ibid*, 357.

[96] Stone, above n 92, 495 ; see generally 489–501.

[97] It should be conceded, though, that we need more debate on whether a liberal approach to eco-justice is a step in the right direction or further way from it. See B Almond, 'Rights and Justice in the Environmental Debate' in D Cooper and J Palmer (eds), *Just Environments—Intergenerational, International and Inter-Species Issues* (Routledge, 1995) 6; Bosselmann, above n 1, 39.

C. Incorporating Environmental Ethics in Justice

Relating the environmental ethical discourse to the justice discourse automatically raises a few important questions. One is: can the ecocentric approach be reconciled with the anthropocentric approach, or are they mutually exclusive? A second question concerns the ethical discourse itself. How could ecocentrism be accepted as a basis for eco-justice? Can it be 'assumed' in a similar way as anthropocentrism and individual autonomy are assumed for the liberal approach to eco-justice? Or can ecocentrism only be achieved through a public dialogue, ie promoted as discourse ethic?

1. Anthropocentrism or Ecocentrism?

As indicated above, the relationship between anthropocentrism and ecocentrism is not one of gradual difference, but one of paradigmatic dichotomy.[98] This does not mean, however, that they cannot co-exist in law. As we will see later, there are many examples in domestic and international environmental law where traditional anthropocentric instruments of 'natural resource' management co-exist with modern ecocentric instruments of ecosystem management. Environmental law can accommodate ethical pluralism in much the same way as it can reflect political pluralism.

There are limits however. In law, 'moral pluralism'[99] can work only as long as there are no irreconcilable positions at the same 'conflict level'.[100] An example is the protection of endangered species and biodiversity. The panda bear can well be protected for anthropocentric reasons, while biodiversity requires an ecocentric approach, at least, potentially. Ecosystem protection, including that of humans and the non-human world, is a lot more complex, ultimately requiring us to think ecocentrically. As J Baird Callicott observed, you cannot follow a 'happy-go-lucky moral pluralism' switching from Bentham's utilitarianism to Schweitzer's reference for life on to Leopold's land ethic and back to Kant's categorical imperative without reflecting on what might be at stake.[101]

What, then, is at stake when considering 'ecological' rather than 'environmental' justice? The complexities of the 'environment' are best captured by the term

[98] The dichotomy is, of course, not total. There are many shades of anthropocentric ethical positions as well as a variety of non-anthropocentric, ie ecocentric positions. For a comprehensive discussion of the various positions and their importance for environmental law, see K Bosselmann, *When Two Worlds Collide: Ecology and Society* (RSVP, 1995) 317–40; K Bosselmann, 'The Concept of Sustainable Development' in K Bosselmann and D Grinlinton (eds), *Environmental Law for a Sustainable Society* (NZCEL, 2002) 89–96.

[99] Stone, above n 92.

[100] *Ibid*, 205.

[101] JB Callicott, 'The Case Against Moral Pluralism' (1990) 12 *Environmental Ethics* 99, 115.

'ecological integrity'. It reflects the view that there are natural processes necessary to maintain the Earth's life support systems that humans and all life depend on. In other words, it is not the environment, but the interactions between the various life forms—including human beings—with which we should be concerned. This view is not 'objective', but reflective of observations made. Those observations include ecological systems, evolutionary and other processes. But no observation can be made without some form of reflection or interpretation. We could ask, for example, why is there scientific interest in the environment at all? Quite obviously, environmental research followed the realisation that there are problems with the environment (pollution, degradation, etc). There is a close nexus between perceptions, observations and reflections. Our knowledge will never be 'objective', ie purely based on 'facts'.[102]

We can conclude, therefore, that notions such as 'ecological integrity' or 'ecological sustainability' express perceptions of ecological realities, not ecological reality itself. But so does the notion 'environment'! It expresses the perception of something surrounding us: here are we, the environment is the 'other'. The adjective 'environmental' does not connect both spheres in the way the adjective 'ecological' does. This term acknowledges not only the complexities of the natural world, but also the fact that humans are part of it.

Such terminological differences are not only of linguistic interest, they are also reflective of an ethical dilemma. The Western anthropocentric tradition, in which the term 'environment' was moulded, is reinforced if we continue to perceive human-nature complexities as merely 'environmental' relationships. Closer to the—scientific—truth would be to speak of ecological relationships. The former favours ethical anthropocentrism, the latter ethical ecocentrism.

The conceptual differences between environmental and ecological terminologies may well disappear over time. For many, 'environmental' relationships are already perceived as holistic, ecological relationships. It is important, though, to avoid confusion. As long as there is no generally accepted view that the 'environment' includes the communality of humans and the natural world, it is better to distinguish between environmental (anthropocentric, liberal) and ecological (ecocentric) approaches to justice.

The ecological approach to justice is based on ecocentrism. But how can this basis be communicated? Why should it have more validity than the anthropocentric basis?

2. Ontological or Discourse Ethic?

All theories of justice claim validity for modern democratic societies. In fact, the justice discourse has, for a long time, assumed that justice and democracy are

[102] B Mackey, 'The Earth Charter and Ecological Integrity' (2004) 8(1) *Worldviews* 76; Bosselmann, above n 98, 291–315.

mutually reinforcing. A democratic society is more 'just' than an undemocratic society and will strive for justice as a key objective. Likewise, justice can flourish only in a democratic society and will encourage ever more democratic forms of decision-making.

The assumption has been that the members of society are equipped with individual freedoms and equal rights. Each member has the same right of access to justice and decision-making. The members of society alone are entitled to organise their political system. Consequently, the system of justice results from a—hypothetical—dialogue between free individuals.

This liberal approach to justice found its best expression in Rawls's theory. Its central constructs of 'original position' and 'veil of ignorance' allow for a justice concept without presupposed ethics. The appropriate rules of justice will emerge from this hypothetical dialogue. As no-one is to know their individual future fate, each member will aim for rules that are acceptable for everyone. The individual fear of ending up as one of the worst-off members of society ultimately shapes the rules and values of justice.

The geniality of Rawls's theory lies in guaranteeing basic equal rights (the 'first principle of justice') without attempting further to define what these rights may entail. Such non-ethical, 'secular' approach reinforces the pluralism of modern liberal, democratic society. The only 'problem' is that only liberal, democratic society benefits from Rawls's theory of justice. Effectively, Rawls's theory locks society into a permanent liberal future: any move towards a more communitarian or collectively organised society ends at the barrier of individual rights.

The 'hidden' liberal ideology in Rawls is widely criticised. The question is, however, how far this critique needs to be taken to accommodate the concern for the environment. Is it sufficient to add some basic concerns such as a 'no harm' principle or 'savings principle' to an otherwise untouched veil of ignorance? Or is it necessary to unveil the assumed ignorance?

Structurally, these questions can be answered by examining the means under which socially binding norms are identified. They can be identified either through reasoning (monological or ontological approach) or through public debate (dialogical or discourse approach). Monological approaches to justice presuppose some idea of how society ought to be organised. Presupposed basic individual rights and democratic principles are examples of monological approaches. These rights and principles can also be part of dialogical approaches; however, the assumption here is that they result from a public dialogue free of tyranny (Habermas) and not from any political ideology. The difference that discourse ethic is trying to make is the rejection of liberal theory as the only valid basis of society.

Politically, the discourse principle aims for emancipation from the liberal state. In doing so it emphasises the role of procedure. Nothing can be accepted unless being derived from rational, free discourse. In Habermas' words: '[a]ccording to the discourse principle, just those norms deserve to be valid that could meet with the approval of those potentially affected, in so far as the latter participate in rational discourses'.[103] The limitation of this discourse approach to norms is its fixation with 'rational' discourse. Does rationality necessary exclude the non-human world from the discourse?

Habermas shares the basic assumption of Rawls and his environmentally minded followers that norms can be derived only from rationality. They all stand in the tradition of Modernity that accepts rationality as the sole guide for ethics. It can be found in utilitarianism, Kant's imperative and contemporary contractual theory. In this tradition, the ethical discourse will always follow the rational discourse, for example, of justice.

The argument against ethical rationalism is that it has not stopped us from fundamentally changing the conditions that make human life possible. The development of modern civilisation and technology has altered human behaviour in such a way that traditional ethics can no longer provide necessary orientation. In Einstein's famous words, '[t]he means for solving a problem cannot be the same as the ones that brought about the problem in the first place'.

Nobody has formulated the ecological challenge towards ethics and justice more precisely than Hans Jonas. In his seminal text on the imperative of responsibility,[104] Jonas showed that the key assumptions made by traditional ethics are no longer valid, namely that the *conditio humana* is unchangeable, that human behaviour can be calculated on the basis of rational analysis and that human responsibility is limited to social context (ethics and justice). These assumptions expressed themselves in a rigid anthropocentrism that entirely excluded the non-human world from ethical and moral categories.[105]

If we assume, therefore, that the current ecological crisis has its roots in the *conditio humana* of European civilisation,[106] we need to re-visit both the procedural and normative aspects of ethics and justice. Neither monological nor dialogical approaches are in themselves sufficient; the former tend to be too presumptuous, the latter too unambitious.

Following the concepts of self-reflective discourses on justice proposed by Young,[107] Tully[108] and Kingwell,[109] we need a justice discourse that allows for both

[103] J Habermas, *Between Facts and Norms: Contributions to a Discourse Theory of Law and Democracy* (trans W Rehg, Polity Press, 1996) 127.

[104] H Jonas, *The Imperative of Responsibility: In Search of an Ethics for the Technological Age* (trans H Jonas, U Chicago P, 1984).

[105] *Ibid*, foreword.

[106] R Bahro, *Avoiding Social and Ecological Disaster: The Politics of World Transformation* (Gateway books, 1994), Part II, ch 6; Bosselmann, above n 98, 71.

[107] I Young, *Justice and the Politics of Difference* (Princeton UP, 1990).

[108] J Tully, *Strange Multiplicity: Constitutionalism in an Age of Diversity* (Cambridge UP, 1995).

[109] M Kingwell, *A Civil Tongue: Justice, Dialogue and the Politics of Pluralism* (Pennsylvania State UP, 1995).

openness and transformation. Considering the systemic character of the crisis that we are in we should be able to incorporate ecocentric values when thinking about justice without assuming that they can be inscribed, like individual rights have been inscribed in modern theories of justice. I call this the ecological justice discourse.

Eckersley's concept of 'green justice'[110] adequately describes this discourse. She argues that the transformation of notions of justice to accommodate nature must be undertaken within the broader context of our system of democracy and public government. Justice is an inherent part of the modern democratic state, and yet in urgent need of revising. Liberal justice theories ignore the close nexus between liberalism, anthropocentrism and environmental degradation. They cannot capture the ecocentric concept of justice. Equally, we cannot rely on mere discourse ethic. No matter how 'free of tyranny' this discourse is, it will not itself produce the required ecological discourse.

The main limitation of discourse ethic is its own anthropcentric tradition. If this tradition behind the rational discourse goes unquestioned we will not be able to move beyond the Kantian and contractualist framework. In this framework, only moral agents count. From a non-anthropocentric perspective the limitation of moral theory to *agents* is unacceptable; rather it is enough that a being receives recognition as a moral *subject*. That such beings may not have the capacity to communicate (directly) or reciprocate moral favours should not matter.

What should matter, instead, is the capacity of humans to act not only for themselves, but also for those who cannot act for themselves. In this way potentially all beings affected by environmental decisions, but not actively participating in the moral dialogue, would have their voices heard. Whether this concern for 'the others' requires institutional representation—for example, through agencies of guardianship[111] or trusteeship[112]—or whether it can be internalised in some other way[113] is an interesting subject of debate. For the acceptance of ecocentrism and eco-justice, however, it is necessary only to internalise what has remained externalised in theories of justice todate.

[110] R Eckersley, 'Green, Justice, the State and Democracy' 2001, available at www.arbid.unimelb.edu.au/envjust/papers/allpapers/eckersley. See also Eckersley, above n 63.

[111] On guardianship models used or proposed in several countries see K Bosselmann, 'A Legal Framework for Sustainable Development' in K Bosselmann and D Grinlinton (eds), *Environmental Law for a Sustainable Society* (NZCEL, 2002) 145, 151–2.

[112] On trusteeship models in international law, see P Taylor, *An Ecological Approach to International Law* (Routledge, 1999) 283–5; P Sand, 'Trusteeship for Common Pool Resources: Zur Renaissance des Treuhandbegriffs im Umweltvölkerrecht' in S von Schorlemer (ed), *Praxishandbuch UNO* (Springer Verlag, 2002) 201.

[113] On the importance of the precautionary principle in this regard see Eckersley, above n 63, 136–7; Bosselmann, above n 111, 153.

D. The Three Principles of Ecological Justice

Having seen how environmental ethics can influence and shape the justice discourse, we can now focus on contents. What does the concept of ecological justice entail? Can it be sufficiently defined to provide guidance for the development of environmental law?

The proximity of ecocentrism to ecological sustainability provides the most promising basis for a workable theory of ecological justice. Environmental law is increasingly influenced by the concept of sustainable development. And despite the never-ending debate on how this concept could be defined, there is a worldwide consensus on some of its core ideas. These ideas form part of the concept of ecological justice. To become a truly ecological concept, justice needs to reach out into the non-human world. As we will see, the 'missing link' in both the sustainable development debate and the justice debate is the recognition of ecological integrity. It is not enough to care for humans living today and those living tomorrow when the natural processes that sustain life are at risk. There is a need to identify and recognise the ethical and legal importance of ecological integrity.

The famous Brundtland definition[114] contains two ethical elements that are widely accepted as being essential to the idea of sustainable development: concern for the poor (intragenerational justice or equity); and concern for the future (intergenerational justice or equity). *The concern for the poor* includes all social and minority groups discriminated against by the social and economic system. Conflicts between rich and poor, white and non-white, Western lifestyle and indigenous cultures and North and South belong here. The environmental justice movement in the United States has its origins in those conflicts. The concern for the poor (social justice) represents the social dimension of ecological justice and can usefully be termed *intragenerational justice*. The importance for a theory of ecological justice is to determine the relationship between intragenerational and intergenerational issues as there are competing claims and priorities.

The concern for future generations is a familiar feature in international and environmental law. Since Edith Brown Weiss' influential classic text,[115] rights and interests of future generations have been incorporated in international agreements and national legislation. The notions of 'justice for future generations' and *intergenerational justice* may be less familiar, but both have become increasingly popular in recent years, obviously reflecting a broader acceptance of the idea that justice spans past, present and the future. One of the issues to be discussed here is

[114] Sustainable development is 'development that meets the needs of the present without compromising the ability of future generations to meet their own needs': World Commission on Environment and Development (WCED), *Our Common Future* (WCED, 1987) 8.

[115] E Brown Weiss, *In Fairness to Future Generations* (Transnational Publishers, 1989).

whether intergenerational justice is to be seen as an anthropocentric concept or whether it has ecocentric implications.[116]

However, these two elements leave us with a crucial question. What do they mean with respect to the environment? If we are to share environmental goods and burdens fairly among us living today and also leave something for the future, what exactly do we preserve? The integrity of the planetary ecosystem (the 'natural stock') or our current knowledge about natural resources and ways to use them (the 'capital stock')?

For reasons of principle we are unable to determine the needs of future generations. Only more or less informed guesses are possible about the options that future generations may justifiably expect. The reasonable choice, therefore, is for a duty to pass on the integrity of the planetary ecosystem as we have inherited it (ecological integrity). Uncertainty requires precaution, and there seems no better precautionary measure than assuming that future generations would like the planetary ecosystem as bountiful as we have found it.

And yet, such an obvious duty is neither suggested by the Brundtland definition nor favoured by governments or big business. As their morality is confined to traditional social ethics, they do not consider the importance of an environmental ethic to incorporate nature or the planetary ecosystem. Instead, the standard view is that society, economy and environment are somehow of equal importance. As a result, sustainable development is perceived as a balancing act between economic, social and environmental goals, with trade-offs as a necessary outcome. There is no guidance that could ensure, for example, a preference for ecological sustainability or the needs of future generations. Without such guidance, policies may become more integrated, but they will make little difference to existing unsustainable patterns of production and consumption.

This business-as-usual approach is commonly known as 'weak sustainability'. If associated with moral obligations to the future, weak sustainability policies consider it our sovereign decision what kind of assets, 'stock' or legacy we wish to leave for future generations. It could be the 'natural stock', but it also could be its substitute, for example, the knowledge to alter the natural stock (eg, through genetic engineering). Such 'capital stock' gift to the future implies the very possibility of destroying the planet's conditions of life. We simply do not know and possibly never will.

To preserve the integrity of the planetary ecosystem is the only reliable alternative and may, in fact, be a desirable goal for most people. However, this goal needs moral and legal recognition in order to become 'internalised'. Only then will the

[116] See eg D Tladi, 'Of Course for Humans: A Contextual Defence of Intergenerational Equity' (2002) 9 *South African Journal of Environmental Law & Policy* 177, on the one hand, and K Bosselmann, 'Strong and Weak Sustainable Development: Making the Difference in the Design of Law' in M Kidd (ed), *Environmental Law Foundations for Sustainable Development* (MCN, forthcoming 2005), on the other.

'weak' become the 'strong'; and thereby resolve the weaknesses of the Brundtland report's definition of sustainable development. A third element, therefore, needs to be added to the two mentioned above:[117] concern for the non-human natural world (interspecies justice or equality).

The concern for the non-human natural world is in the centre of environmental ethics. The question here is which idea of justice could accommodate such concerns best. As we have seen, from a liberal, anthropocentric point of view the non-human world is outside the *justitia communis*. From an ecocentric point of view *justia communis* includes both the human and non-human world. It may already be seen as an important step that, today, there is vivid discussion of 'justice for the non-human world'[118] and *interspecies justice.*[119] This term resembles affinities with intra- and intergenerational justice. The inclusion of an elaborate concept of interspecies issues is certainly crucial for a theory on ecological justice as distinct from mere social justice.

Interspecies justice (or concern for the non-human natural world) is not mentioned in the standard definitions of sustainable development of any of the international agreements related to sustainable development (eg, 1992 Rio Declaration, Agenda 21, 2002 Johannesburg Declaration). However, this may be due to the fact that the anthropocentric notion of sustainable development has dominated the political debate. In literature, environmental or ecological sustainabilty has emerged as an ecocentric conception that includes the recognition of intrinsic values. This ecocentric conception stands against a technocentric conception of sustainability[120] promoted by the UNCED process and most governments. As Andrew Dobson has observed, the ecocentric approach marks the point at which economists leave the sustainability debate.[121]

At the heart of the conflict between the technocentric and the ecocentric approach lies the ambivalence of the word sustainability[122] which—not unlike the word 'love' or 'justice'—causes uniform agreement, yet great confusion as to what it actually means. It is widely accepted, though, that ultimately there are just two possible meanings. One starts from the argument that 'sustainability is not

[117] Bosselmann, above n 111, 145, 147–56.

[118] Almond, above n 97, 18.

[119] *Ibid*, 15; see also J Palmer, 'Just Ecological Principles?' in Cooper and Palmer, above n 97, 31–2; A Johnson, 'Barriers to Fair Treatment of Nonhuman Life' in *Ibid*, 165; and T Hayword, 'Interspecies Solidarity: Care Operated Upon by Justice' in T Hayword and T O'Neill (eds), *Justice, Property and the Environment* (Ashgate, 1997).

[120] See D Pearce, *Blueprint 3: Measuring Sustainable Development* (Earthscan, 1993) 18–19.

[121] A Dobson, 'Environmental Sustainability: An Analysis and Typology' (1996) 5 *Environmental Politics* 401, 416.

[122] C Mitchum, 'The Sustainability Question' in R Gottlieb (ed), *The Ecological Community* (Routledge, 1997) 359; also W Beckerman, 'Sustainable Development: Is it a Useful Concept?' (1994) 3 *Environmental Values* 191; J Pezzey 'Sustainability: An Interdisciplinary Guide' (1992) 1 *Environmental Values* 321.

enough'.[123] The concern here is that sustainability too readily denotes stasis and equilibrium whereas life is about change and growth. From this perspective development is the important dynamic element, making sustainable development a concept which ensures lasting economic growth and energy production or—in the words of the World Bank—simply a 'development that lasts'.[124] Opposed to this philosophy of more-is-better lies the philosophy of different-not-more. It asks the question 'sustainability of what?'. The concern here is that sustainable development simply means to sustain the Western way of life at the expense of the poor and of future generations. To be sustained are not the economic, but the ecological conditions requiring substantial changes in economy and society. From this perspective the central issue is environmental sustainability[125] and not development, making a concept of a sustainable society preferable, perhaps, to sustainable development.[126]

The (anthropocentric) market-based approach and the (ecocentric) equity approach to sustainable development represent different political agendas.[127] It is, therefore, not possible *a priori* to define the relationship between sustainable development and ecological justice. However, an analogy can be drawn between both concepts. 'Ecological' can be understood as modifying 'justice' in much the same way as 'sustainable' can be understood as modifying 'development'. On this basis, the only permissive paths to development are those that are ecologically sustainable. Likewise, the only permissive paths to justice are those that recognise ecological sustainability.

The importance of ecological sustainability cannot be overestimated. For example, it gives further guidance on the meaning of intragenerational justice. Concern for the poor, essentially, the support for development in the Third World, is a high priority. In fact, since the 2000 UN Millennium Goals and the 2002 Johannesburg Summit there has been an agreed consensus among states that eradication of poverty and economic development in poor countries should have priority over other goals associated with sustainable development. Such priority can, however, not mean to allow unsustainable development. Ecological sustainability requires discouraging of unsustainable energy sources, for example, as opposed to sustainable, ie renewable energy sources. The ecological integrity of planetary systems should be a benchmark for any form of development. Similarly,

[123] V Ruttan, 'Sustainability is Not Enough' (1988) 3 *American Journal of Alternative Agriculture* 607.

[124] World Development Report 1992 (World Bank, 1992) 34.

[125] E Brown Weiss, 'Introductory Note' (1992) 31 ILM 814. See also Art 1 of the Draft International Covenant on Environment and Development, prepared by the Commission of the World Conservation Union (IUCN) on Environmental Law (Mar 1995): 'The objective of this Covenant is to achieve environmental conservation and sustainable development by establishing integrated rights and obligations'.

[126] See L Brown, *Building a Sustainable Society* (Norton, 1981) and the annual *State of the World* reports of the Worldwatch Institute on progress toward a 'sustainable society'.

[127] Dobson, above n 121, 423.

interspecies justice should be a benchmark for any form of ecological justice. As it implies the recognition of the intrinsic value of the non-human natural world, interspecies justice can be very effective in law.

The example of the law related to biotechnology can illustrate this. At the international level, biotechnology became the subject of international law through the 1992 Convention on Biological Diversity.[128] Along with a general trend in recent international environmental law, the Biodiversity Convention takes the approach of ecosystem protection (ie protecting entire habitats rather than individual species as such).[129] It does so by introducing (in its Preamble) an 'intrinsic value of biological diversity', in addition to 'the ecological, genetic, social, economic, scientific, educational, cultural, recreational and aesthetic values of biological diversity and its components'. This is recognition of the distinction between (ecocentric) intrinsic values and (anthropocentric) instrumental values of the environment. Article 19 of the Biodiversity Convention calls for the Contracting States to take legislative measures towards controlling biotechnological research activities. The problem is that the Convention, like most treaties, leaves the means of implementation totally to the discretion of states.

At the municipal level, several countries have introduced such controlling legislation, among them Germany with its Gene Technology Law (*Gentechnikgesetz*) of 1990. Such legislation regulates details of notification and licensing of genetically modified products (like, eg, the release of those products into the environment), but it always does so on the basis that there is a fundamental right to conduct genetic engineering in the first place. The principle of free production and sale is the rule; any restrictions are the exception. The burden of proof, therefore, is not with the producer introducing a new risk potential (eg, for biological diversity), but with the general public represented, for example by expert commissions such as the Environmental Risk Management Authority in New Zealand or various ethical commissions in the UK. Whether or not activities of genetic engineering are acceptable is determined by weighing up social costs and benefits. The problem is that such social costs and benefits are exclusively determined by values of human utility. As there are no intrinsic values of ecosystems and their components to be considered, the only relevant counterweight comes from possible infringements on rights of health protection, ie human health risks associated with genetically modified products. Once these concerns are met nothing could stop genetic engineering from fundamentally altering the natural genetic structures. The recognition of nature's intrinsic values would have, at least, the potential to rectify such grave imbalances and provide the counterweight necessary for more balanced decisions.

Apart from those reasons of improving the *results* of decision-making there are reasons of improving the *basis* for decision-making. Before today's complete

[128] UN Doc 6.10. 31 IL 818 (1992).
[129] A Kiss and D Shelton, *International Environmental Law* (Transnational Publishers, 1991) 11.

breakdown of ethical agreement—the 'moral catastrophe' (Alasdair MacIntyre) modernity has witnessed[130]—there was once a well-established ethical basis for decision-making. We could go back to the beginning of modern civilisation and remind ourselves of the close links between ethics, justice and law. In Aristotle's quest for justice,[131] for example, we find the directive of 'the good life' and some of the virtues associated with such a life: imagination, openness, empathy. The life of someone who is unimaginative, closed-up and rigid *may* be 'good', of course, but it is reasonable to suggest that such a person is indifferent towards fellow humans and non-human life around him/her. Being alienated and cut off from the natural world has become a dominant feature of modernity. So, following the precepts of Aristotle's 'good life' and its virtues may help to rediscover, for example, what empathy is all about.[132] It seems to me that there is no contradiction between empathy for the natural world and the good life of humans. There is a lot to suggest that the tragedy of modernity has been to create a dichotomy between autonomy and dependence; we badly need a more sophisticated sense of human interdependence.[133] A sense of interconnectedness may well be the key for future decision-making.

Ultimately, there are no 'reasons' why we should adopt intrinsic values of nature. Ethical reasoning can only help in clarifying some arguments. Ultimately, we have to rely on our ability to learn from past experience and see things differently. Interspecies justice is a new concept which cannot simply be attached to the idea of justice. The 'barriers to fair treatment of non-human life'[134] are deeply embedded in the psyche of modernity and can be removed only by re-visiting both the idea of justice and our place in the world.

The elements of ecological justice are now before us, and we may have enough building blocks for a possible theory. However, since the building blocks sit on ecocentric foundations they cannot claim to be universally acceptable. They may be useful, though, to facilitate further discussion. The aim should, in any case, be to work on a conception which does justice to humans and nature alike. The idea of eco-justice is, however, far from being speculative. Recent developments in international and municipal law give an indication how eco-justice is being implemented in environmental policy and legislation.

[130] A MacIntyre, *After Virtue; A Study in Moral Theory* (Duckworth, 1981).

[131] See J Urmson, *Aristotle's Ethics* (Oxford UP, 1988); W Hardie, *Aristotle's Ethical Theory* (Oxford UP, 1980).

[132] A connection between ecocentric awareness and 'the good life' is made by D Cooper, 'Other Species and Moral Reason' in Cooper and Palmer, above n 97, 137, 145–7.

[133] See J Tronto, *Moral Boundaries* (Routledge, 1993) 101.

[134] Johnson, above n 119, 165–79.

E. Ecological Justice as a Guide for Environmental Law

There is no example of a conscious, deliberate attempt to implement ecological justice in legislation. This should not be surprising, however, considering not only the novelty of this idea, but also the function of justice as a fundamental concern. Law will always reflect some sense of justice, but not in a direct manner as it would, for example, implement a specific principle. What is 'fair' and 'just' depends on the subject matter of the law, its ideological and political context and the importance that may be given to specific aspects of justice.

The practical use of eco-justice is its focus on the wider ecological context that legislation, administration and judicial review operate in. If we are conscious of the three principles of eco-justice, we have a more informed view of how environmental law should be designed and interpreted.

Some examples in the area of domestic and international environmental law can illustrate how eco-justice has already influenced legislative developments.

1. New Zealand Resource Management Act 1991

New Zealand's environmental legislation is often hailed as one of the world's most advanced,[135] although this may be true for its ambition rather than its current operation. The Environment Act 1986 and the Conservation Act 1987 espouse an ecocentric approach by providing holistic definitions for the 'environment' (including humans and nature) and recognition of 'intrinsic values of ecosystems'. The actual implementation of this approach occurred during a reform period between 1984 and 1991 when the Resource Management Act (RMA) was adopted. The RMA is the legal framework for integrated and sustainable management of natural and physical resources, and has the 'ethic of sustainable management'[136] at its core. The RMA is a remarkable example of efforts to incorporate sustainable development into law as it integrates socio-economic and environmental issues.[137] It is also a good example of applied ecological justice as it provides for a definition

[135] One political historian described the reforms as 'the greatest changes anywhere, anytime, in any democracy' quoted in P May *et al* (eds), *Environmental Management and Governance* (Routledge, 1996) 43; see also M Kloepfer and E Mast, *Das Umweltrecht des Auslandes* (Duncker and Humblot, 1995) 301–10.

[136] S Upton (Minister for the Environment), 'The Resource Management Act, Section 5: Sustainable Management of Natural and Physical Resources' (Second Annual Conference of the Resource Management Law Association 1994); see also K Grundy, 'Sustainable Management: A Sustainable Ethic?' (Third Annual Conference of the Resource Management Law Association, 1995).

[137] The overall objective of Agenda 21 (and elaborated in 8 chapters) is to restructure decision-making so that consideration of socio-economic and environmental issues is fully integrated. Apart from this, the Brundtland definition of sustainable development (see, above n 114) was considered by the legislators, but the term 'management' was preferred to 'development' because of a lesser degree of social equity and global distribution issues inherent in the RMA.

of sustainable management that espouses aspects of the three principles of eco-justice. Also relevant is the RMA's affirmation as a policy matter of 'national importance' the 'relationship of Maori and their culture and traditions with their ancestral lands, waters, sites',[138] as well as the Maori stewardship principle of 'Kaitiakitanga',[139] to which government decision-makers must have regard, when implementing the legislation.

The RMA identifies two major functions of 'sustainable management', the *management* function and the *ecological* function. The object of the management function is the use, development and protection of resources, which includes social, economic and cultural well-being and the health and safety of people and communities. The object of the ecological function is sustaining the potential of resources, safeguarding the life-supporting capacity and avoiding adverse environmental effects as described in paragraphs (a), (b) and (c) of subsection 5(2) of the RMA.

The word 'management' is a neutral term and sets no particular values and priorities. However, use, development and protection of resources are equally important and to be managed simultaneously. It is in this context that both intragenerational and intergenerational justice appear. Under section 5(2) decisions regarding the distribution of resources must sustain the needs of future generations. Distribution does not follow a quantification of such needs, but rather the criterion of absolute equality. Despite the reference to 'the reasonably foreseeable needs', resource distribution is determined by sustaining the potential of resources *in view* of future needs, rather than by those needs themselves. This would be consistent with the ethical approach to intergenerational equity as defined above, thus *potentially* consistent with an ecocentric interpretation of future generations.[140] The proper reading of future generations—whether reduced to humans or life as a whole—depends very much on the reading of the overall ethics shaping sustainable management.

While the management functions are essentially anthropocentric in character, the ecological functions are not. Paragraphs (b) and (c)—and arguably even (a) (concerning future generations)—of section 5(2) of the RMA express long-term considerations on the basis of ecocentrism. However, crucial for this interpretation is the proper meaning of the little word 'while' between management and ecological functions[141] and the proper linking of the remaining sections (6 to 8).

[138] RMA s 6(e).

[139] *Ibid*, s 7(a).

[140] K Bosselmann and P Taylor, 'The New Zealand Law and Conservation' (1995) 2 *Pacific Conservation Biology* 113, 119–20.

[141] The relevant passage of s 5(2) reads: 'Managing the use . . . of . . . resources in a way . . . which enables people and communities to provide for their . . . well-being . . . *while* (a) sustaining the potential of . . . resources [for] . . . future generations; and (b) safeguarding the life-supporting capacity . . .; and (c) avoiding, remedying, or mitigating any adverse effects' (emphasis added).

There has been a lot of debate whether 'while' introduces the ecological functions as being superior or as being subordinate to the management functions.[142] The former is referred to as 'ecological bottom-lines', the latter as an 'overall judgement approach'.[143]

A grammatically correct interpretation would suggest 'while' to mean 'by way of' rather than a non-committed 'and' or 'also'. Consequently, all management functions are to be conducted in an ecologically sound way as defined in paragraphs (a) to (c).[144] Interspecies equity can be seen as being addressed in these paragraphs and further defined in the 'other matters' of section 7 for which decision-makers are to 'have particular regard'. Among theses matters are the 'intrinsic values of ecosystems' (paragraph (d)) and the 'concept of katiakitanga' (paragraph (a)) which, in relation to a resource, includes the 'ethic of stewardship based on the nature of the resource itself'. Recognition of intrinsic values and reference to guardianship clearly espouse an ecocentric understanding of interspecies equity.

Leaving aside the number of difficulties that have occurred in practice,[145] the RMA is by no means value-free. The ethics and values expressed in the definition of sustainable management carry the elements of eco-justice.[146] Intragenerational, intergenerational and interspecies equity are all being addressed, albeit not always in a language clear enough to define the interrelations between them and ethical principles underlying them. Yet, ecocentrism clearly defines the ecological functions, thereby helping us to understand that environmental justice is, essentially, justice for those who cannot speak for themselves.

2. Ecosystem Regimes and Management

In a broader sense, environmental law has been increasingly informed by ecology and ecosystem approaches. The science of ecology is concerned with a number of

[142] See B Pardy, 'Planning for Serfdom: Resource Management and the Rule of Law' [1997] *New Zealand LJ* 69; DAR Williams, *Environmental and Resource Management Law* (Butterworths, 1997) 75.

[143] In relation to the former see *New Zealand Rail Ltd v Marlborough District Council* [1993] 2 NZRMA 449 470; *Marlborough District Council v Southern Ocean Seafood Ltd* [1995] NZRMA 220 227. In relation to the latter see *North Shore City Council v Auckland Regional Council* [1997] NZRMA 59 93–4; *RFBPS of NZ Inc v Manawatu-Wanganui Regional Council* [1996] NZRMA 241 269; *Transit NZ v Auckland Regional Council* Environment Court (A/100/2000) Aug 2000, not yet reported, 36.

[144] Bosselmann and Taylor, above n 140, 117. It should be noted that various policy papers seem to favour more of a 'balance' between management and ecological functions; on the other hand, Environment Court Judge S. Kenderdine speaks of 'cumulative safeguards' supporting the view expressed here; *Foxley Engineering Ltd. v Wellington* CC [1994] W 12/94.

[145] These led, in Nov 1998, to proposals by the government to remove some of the procedural obstacles within the RMA.

[146] See also A Gunn and C McCallig, 'Environmental and Social Justice in an Urban Setting—Sustainable Management and the New Zealand Resource Management Act 1991' ('Environmental Justice' conference, University of Melbourne, Oct 1997).

levels of relationships between organisms and their environment.[147] These levels include genes, individuals, populations, communities, ecosystems, landscapes to, ultimately, the entire Earth. Historically, ecologists confined their work to one ecological level and very few forms of interaction with other levels. However, there has been a growing trend of ecologists to look at more complex interactions among a number of levels. This trend is increasingly reflected in environmental laws becoming more integrated and wider in their approach.

Generally speaking, environmental laws and regulations seek to control human interactions with ecosystems. If these interactions are seen from the viewpoint of an autonomy of human life, then both the scientific explanation through ecology and the control mechanisms through law will be comparatively simple: the environment appears separate from humans and will be protected insofar as necessary to maintain quality of human life. Essentially, the autonomous self is retained intact and affected by only certain impacts (pollution, water scarcity, etc).

If, by contrast, the interactions are seen from the viewpoint of relationships between humans and nature, then the environment appears as more fundamental to human life. The more the complexities of these relationships are understood, the more emphasis will be given on interdependences between humans and nature. This second viewpoint of humans regards the self as a momentary concretisation of components and processes of a large ecosystem. In other words, the boundaries between the human and the natural sphere disappear.

Currently the development of environmental law is somewhere between the first and the second viewpoint. Recent trends towards ecosystem regimes suggest that environmental law may reach this second viewpoint at some point in the future. The ecosystem approach to legal regimes[148] is visible in the use of terms such as 'carrying capacity', 'biodiversity' or 'ecosystems', but also in the increased use of normative principles such as integrated environmental management, the precautionary principle or the concept (ecologically) sustainable development. Ecosystem regimes have an inherent tendency towards greater comprehensiveness and higher complexity. Along with this tendency the interdependences between

[147] For good overall discussions of ecology and its various subdivisions see R McIntosh, *The Background of Ecology: Concept and Theory* (Cambridge UP, 1985); M Begon *et al*, *Ecology: Individuals, Populations and Communities* (Blackwell Science, 1996) and M Bush, *Ecology of a Changing Planet* (Prentice Hall, 2000).

[148] See eg O Young, *Resource Regimes: Natural Resources and Social Institutions* (U California P, 1982); E Ostrom, *Governing the Commons: The Evolution of Institutions for Collective Action* (Cambridge UP, 1990). See also B Pardy, 'Changing Nature: The Myth of the Inevitability of Ecosystem Management' (2003) 20 *Pace Environmental L Rev* 675 (arguing that all present ecosystem management regimes are of an instrumental, rational and anthropocentric nature). But see also the rejoinder by JB Ruhl, 'The Myth of What is Inevitable under Ecosystem Management: A Response to Pardy' (2004) 21 *Pace Environmental L Rev* 315.

humans and nature will be more obvious, and with them the need for ecological justice.

The rise of ecosystem regimes[149] has been gradual, but steady. Early examples of legal regimes mandating an ecosystem approach to environmental protection include the 1978 Great Lakes Water Quality Agreement between Canada and the United States,[150] and the 1980 Convention on Antarctic Marine Living Resources.[151] During the 1990s, ecosystem management reached a certain stage of maturity. The New Zealand RMA is one prominent example, but most OECD countries concerned themselves with similar integrated and ecosystemic environmental law regimes. Typically, ecosystems such as marine and coastal areas, regional areas (eg, water catchments, forestry), biodiversity, even climate systems lead to more comprehensive statues and regulations involving broader concepts ('sustainability'), integrated management plans and new institutions. Several countries including the Netherlands, Scandinavia, Germany and Australia adopted new general environmental codes informed by sustainable development.[152] In addition, most European countries created institutional frameworks for sustainability in the form of Green Plans (Netherlands, Sweden, France) and National Strategies (UK, Germany, etc).[153] Similar strategies were adopted in Canada, USA, Australia and New Zealand.[154]

Exactly what principles the various ecosystem regimes follow is not always clear. There is certainly no consistent set or hierarchy of guiding principles. Sometimes the emphasis is on procedural management issues, sometimes on substantive goals of ecological integrity; one law may emphasise resource use, another precaution and a third the needs of future generations.[155] It is obvious, however, that all the various principles touch upon eco-justice issues. In some way or other they are all concerned with issues of intragenerational, intergenerational and interspecies justice. The further development of ecosystem laws—and environmental law in

[149] R Brooks *et al*, *Law and Ecology: The Rise of the Ecosystem Regime* (Ashgate, 2002) 2.

[150] Agreement between Canada and the United States of America on Great Lakes Quality, 1978: US Environmental Protection Agency Great Lakes Water Quality Agreement, available at www.epa.gov/glnpo/glwqa/1978/.

[151] (1980) 19 ILM 841.

[152] See JC Dernbach, 'Sustainable Development as a Framework for National Governance' (1998) 49 *Case Western Reserve L Rev* 1; NA Robinson, 'Legal Structures and Sustainable Development: Comparative Environmental Law Perspectives on Legal Regimes for Sustainable Development' (1998) 3 *Widener Law Symposium* J 247.

[153] See M Jänicke and H Jörgens, 'National Environmental Policy Planning in OECD Countries' (1998) 7(2) *Envtl Politics* 27; HD Johnson and DR Brower, *Green Plans: Greenprint for Sustainability* (U Nebraska P, 1997).

[154] Eg Environment Canada, *Canada's Green Plan* (Ministry of Supply and Services, 1990).

[155] Some regimes combine several of these competing tendencies simultaneously, eg Conference of the Parties to the Convention on Biological Diversity, Decision V/6, 'Ecosystem Approach' in Report of the Fifth Meeting of the Conference of the Parties to the Convention on Biological Diversity, UN Doc UNEP/CBD/COP/5/23, Annex III (22 June 2000).

general—would greatly benefit from a new jurisprudence with eco-justice at its core.[156]

3. International Sustainable Development Law

Ecosystemic approaches to law-making are also known in international law. Treaty law recognises intrinsic values of the natural world, for example, with respect to biological diversity.[157] To some extent the Convention on Biological Diversity[158] has pushed the frontiers of international environmental law further than ever before, expressly incorporating the precautionary principle,[159] common concern of humankind[160] and common but differentiated responsibilities,[161] and including reference to intrinsic values.[162]

Apart from the Biodiversity Convention many environmental agreements have recognised the intrinsic value of the biosphere. Examples include the 1991 Protocol on Environmental Protection amending the 1959 Antarctic Treaty,[163] the 1982 World Charter for Nature[164] and a number of treaties related to the preservation of ecosystems[165] and endangered species.[166] Mention should also be made of the 32 so-called 'Alternative Treaties', which several hundred non-governmental organisations negotiated at the 1992 Earth Summit in Rio de Janeiro. For example, in response to the failed UN Earth Charter—substituted by the anthropocentric Rio Declaration—the non-governmental organisation (NGO) delegates

156 Such new, ecological jurisprudence suggests that legal rules should be closely tied to scientific findings ('ecology') and ethical norms ('justice'): M Fondacaro, 'Toward an Ecological Jurisprudence Rooted in Concepts of Justice and Empirical Research' (2000) 69 *University of Missouri at Kansas City Law Review* 179. Another promising approach focuses on the relationship between ecological integrity and justice: D Pimentel, L Westra and R Noss (eds), *Ecological Integrity: Integrating Environment, Conservation and Health* (Island Press, 2000); P Miller and L Westra (eds), *Just Ecological Integrity: The Ethics of Maintaining Planetary Life* (Rowman and Littlefield, 2002).

157 Bosselmann, above n 1, 50.

158 Convention on Biological Diversity (1992) 31 ILM 851.

159 Note that reference to the precautionary principle is in the Preamble only, an express article included in the fifth negotiating draft was removed: see A Boyle, 'The Rio Convention on Biological Diversity' in M Bowman and C Redgwell (eds), *International Law and the Conservation of Biological Diversity* (Kluwer, 1996) 37.

160 Preamble.

161 Eg Art 6.

162 Preamble.

163 (1991) 30 ILM 1455, recognising the intrinsic value of the Antarctic ecosystem,

164 (1983) 22 ILM 455, stating, in its preamble, that '[e]very form of life is unique, warranting respect regardless of its worth to man and, to accord other organisms such recognition, man must be guided by a moral code of action. . .'.

165 Eg Convention on Wetlands of International Importance Especially as Waterfowl Habitat (1971) 996 UNTS 245; Berne Convention on the Conservation of European Wildlife and Natural Habitats [1983] BGBL 372, recognising intrinsic value of wild fauna and flora.

166 Examples include the Convention on International Trade in Endangered Species and the recently amended regime on whaling: D'Amatao and SK Chopra, 'Whales: Their Emerging Right to Life' (1991) 85 *American Journal of International Law* 21.

adopted an 'Earth Charter' based on an ecocentrically defined responsibility for the earth.[167] The 1995/2001 IUCN Draft International Covenant on Environment and Development follows a similar approach.[168]

Since the mid-1990s the Earth Charter had been negotiated by many hundreds of civil society groups representing the world's cultural, ethnic and religious diversity. Through the various Earth Charter Community Summits, individuals and NGOs have been working towards an agreement on a comprehensive ethical framework for sustainable development, unlike that offered by any existing state-based treaty regime.[169] In 2000, the Charter was adopted in The Hague and has since been endorsed by a number of international organisations and states.[170] The Charter takes a systemic view on peace, security, social and ecological justice, human rights and democracy. None of these can be achieved without the others, and they all need to be developed to reflect the Charter's idea of sustainable development. Its principles are, therefore, guidelines for the entire way nations and people ought to conduct their affairs. This makes the Earth Charter a suitable constitution for a new world order.

The Charter provides the 'values and principles for a sustainable future'.[171] It assumes the validity of the Brundtland definition for sustainable development, but clearly identifies the 'missing link' of ecological sustainability mentioned above. Principle I(1) ('Respect Earth and life in all its diversity') reflects the core of ecological justice 'Recognise that all beings are interdependent and every form of life has value regardless of its worth to human beings'. The first set of principles I(1) to (4) on ('respect and care for the community of life') and principles II(5) to (8) ('ecological integrity') further describe interspecies justice that have been missing in the general discourse on sustainable development. Principles III(9) to (12) ('social and economic justice') and IV(13) to (16) ('democracy, non-violence, and peace') then describe intragenerational and intergenerational justice.

The Earth Charter thus illustrates the potential of the NGO sector to step ahead of states and forge new environmental norms to guide future international environmental law. International environmental law is increasingly recognising aspects of interspecies justice. It is timely, therefore, to adopt a systemic approach and shape future sustainable development law along the lines of ecological justice.

[167] Published in Pacific Institute of Resource Management (ed), *Commitment for the Future: The Earth Charter and Treaties agreed to by the International NGOs and Social Movements* (Pacific Institute of Resource Management, 1992).

[168] Eg Art 2 establishes the principle of respect for all forms of life, available at www.iucn.org/themes/law/pdfdocuments/EPLP31ENsecond.pdf.

[169] See Earth Charter Community Summits, at www.earthchartersummits.org.

[170] See eg UNESCO Resolution 32 C/COM.III/Dr.1 (adopted 16 Oct 2003) and IUCN Resolution CGR.REC003 (adopted 24 Nov 2004).

[171] Earth Charter Commission, Earth Charter: Values and Principles for a Sustainable Future 2002, available at www.earthcharter.org.

F. Conclusion

This chapter has examined the notion of 'ecological justice', and its differences from the more widely known concept of 'environmental justice'. It has argued that environmental law should be informed by ecological justice, in much the same way as law in general is informed by justice. It has shown how traditional liberal and anthropocentric conceptions of justice are wholly inadequate as a basis for justice in an environmental law context. Some developments in international environmental policy (eg, the Earth Charter) or national law (eg, New Zealand's Resource Management Act) suggest some ways by which ecological justice is beginning to be embodied in environmental law.

6

Public Participation in Environmental Decision-making

BENJAMIN J. RICHARDSON* AND JONA RAZZAQUE**

A. Introduction: The Importance of Participation

Public participation in environmental decision-making has become an indelible feature of many environmental regulatory systems world-wide over the past few decades. Individuals and organisations affected by development approvals, pollution licences, land use plans and other types of regulatory processes have increasingly demanded greater consultation, and more transparent and accountable decisions. Parliamentary democracy ratified through periodic electoral contests is widely viewed as insufficient to provide meaningful public input into day-to-day environmental decision-making. Governing elites' hostility to independent protest and community self-expression has encouraged the creation of 'surrogate political processes',[1] wherein citizens' views are channelled into and considered in alternate administrative and judicial structures.[2]

In these structures, public participation assumes a variety of forms. It can occur through education, information dissemination, advisory or review boards, public advocacy, public hearings and submissions, and even litigation.[3] By these means, public participation may assist decision-makers to understand and identify public interest concerns while formulating environmental policies.[4] Greater citizen

* Professor, Osgoode Hall Law School, York University.

** Senior Lecturer, University of the West of England, and recently Staff Lawyer, Foundation for International Environmental Law and Development (FIELD).

1 RB Stewart, 'The Reformation of American Administrative Law' (1975) 88 *Harvard L Rev* 1660, 1712.

2 See generally C Offe, 'New Social Movements: Challenging the Boundaries of Institutional Politics' (1985) 52 *Social Research* 817.

3 S Stec and S Casey-Lefkowitz, *The Aarhus Convention: An Implementation Guide* (UNECE, 2000) 85. On definition of the 'public', see DN Zillman, 'Introduction to Public Participation in the 21st Century' in D. Zillman *et al*, *Human Rights in Natural Resource Development: Public Participation in the Sustainable Development of Mining and Energy Resources* (Oxford UP, 2002).

4 E Petkova, C Maurer, N Henninger and F Irwin, *Closing the Gap: Information, Participation, and Justice in Decision-making for the Environment* (World Resources Institute, 2002) 66–67.

input may promote environmental justice and help integrate ecological and social considerations in governmental decisions.[5] Further, participation may enhance the accountability, and thus acceptability, of environmental decisions.[6] This may lead to less litigation, fewer delays and generally better implementation of decisions.[7] Thus, as Lawrence Tribe once warned, the *way* policy decisions are made has important implications for the outcomes of those decisions.[8]

Public participation is particularly significant in the context of sustainable development. Sustainability depends largely on the way economic, social and environmental considerations have been integrated in decision-making. The principles of inter- and intra-generational equity in sustainable development discourse reflect the centrality of public involvement and social justice.[9] Implementation of the precautionary principle, another part of the sustainability discourse, also depends on public input into the assessment of acceptable risks. Environmental threats, such as climate change or genetically modified organisms, are often characterised by scientific and technical uncertainties and risks for which people often hold very different and competing preferences.[10] Public participation can help assess these uncertainties and risks, and weigh them against perceived benefits.[11]

Several interrelated factors have fuelled the growth of participatory processes in decision-making. The first is increased public awareness and concern about the relationships between ecological health and human well-being.[12] Secondly, the growth of human rights in legal and political systems has heightened people's expectations of participation in policy-making.[13] Thirdly, the prevailing concerns of the international community for 'good governance' and the strengthening of civil societies have contributed to increasing interest in the use of participatory mechanisms.[14] Also, weaknesses in the legitimacy of the state and lack of trust in

[5] M Lee and C Abbot, 'The Usual Suspects? Public Participation under the Aarhus Convention' (2003) 66 *MLR* 80, 82–85.

[6] NP Spyke, 'Public Participation in Environmental Decision-making at the New Millennium: Structuring New Spheres of Public Influence' (1999) 26 *Boston College Envtl Affairs L Rev* 263, 269–70; see also J Habermas, *Communication and the Evolution of Society* (Beacon Press, 1991).

[7] DA Wirth, 'Public Participation in International Processes: Environmental Case Studies at the National and International Levels' (1996) 7 *Colorado Journal of International Law & Policy* 1.

[8] L Tribe, 'Technology Assessment and the Fourth Discontinuity: The Limits of Instrumental Rationality' (1972) 46 *Southern California L Rev* 617.

[9] I Voinovic, 'Intergenerational and Intragenerational Equity Requirements for Sustainability' (1995) 22(3) *Environmental Conservation* 223.

[10] J. Ebbesson, 'The Notion of Public Participation in International Environmental Law' (1997) 8 *Yearbook of International Environmental Law* 59.

[11] J Steele, 'Participation and Deliberation in Environmental Law: Exploring a Problem Solving Approach' (2001) 21 *Oxford Journal of Legal Studies* 426. B Doherty and M de Geus, *Democracy and Green Political Thought: Sustainability, Rights and Citizenship* (Routledge, 1996).

[12] B Barton, 'Underlying Concepts and Theoretical Issues in Public Participation in Resource Development' in Zillman, above n 3, at 81–3.

[13] *Ibid.*

[14] M Pimbert and T Wakeford, 'Overview-Deliberative Democracy and Citizen Empowerment' (2001) PLA Notes, available at www.iied.org/docs/pla/pla_fs_5.pdf.

governments have fuelled popular demands for more grass-roots, direct involvement in decisions.[15]

Different models have been proffered to analyse the range of forms of public participation. One model, known as Arnstein's 'ladder', shows the spectrum of participation opportunities, beginning with mere notification, and extending to consultation and even joint decision-making power.[16] The lowest levels of participation may effectively amount to non-participation.[17] The highest level of participation, says Arnstein, is where the public has the power to negotiate with decision-makers and to veto proposed decisions. Another model of participation distinguishes between 'top-down' and 'bottom-up' approaches. The former is where the government initiates participation, the latter where communities do so.[18] Thirdly, some commentators distinguish between *substantive* and *procedural* dimensions of participation.[19] Participatory rights may derive from substantive human rights, such as a right to live in a healthy, unpolluted environment, and may be enshrined in a constitution or statutory bill of rights.[20] By contrast, procedural rights concern the methods of decision-making, and typically encompass public consultation, information provision and access to the courts.[21] Substantive and procedural rights are often intertwined: for instance, a substantive right to a healthy environment usually requires procedural rights to be heard in decisions that might affect those substantive rights.[22]

Law plays a crucial role in all these approaches. Open-ended discursive experiences based on custom or current controversy may be too fragile and insufficient to sustain the desired policy and political transformation. Law can provide two remedial functions in this respect. First, through decision rules and procedures it can enable democratic will to emerge. Secondly, through its ability to codify norms and structure institutions, it can effectively channel this political power throughout society, as a force for social coordination. In other words, law creates a structure for participation that helps crystallise and protect society's environmental goals.

This chapter is divided into five parts. Section B traces briefly the historical evolution of public participation reforms. Section C considers their theoretical context. Sections D and E survey legal reforms for participation, including the seminal Aarhus Convention. The final part canvasses some problems commonly associated with the democratisation of environmental decision-making.

15 *Ibid*, 24–5; see also A Dobson, *Justice and the Environment* (Oxford UP, 1998).

16 SR Arnstein, 'A Ladder of Citizen Participation' (1969) 35(4) *Journal of the American Institute of Planning* 216.

17 *Ibid*, 217.

18 S Langton (ed), *Citizen Participation in America* (Lexington Books, 1978).

19 Steele, above n 11, 415–6.

20 *Ibid*.

21 Ebbesson, above n 10, 70–5; P Birnie and A Boyle, *International Law and the Environment* (Oxford UP, 2002) 261.

22 Ebbesson, above n 10, 63–9.

B. Historical Perspectives on Participation

Public participation provisions began to appear in the planning and environmental regulations of some states during the late 1960s and 1970s,[23] coinciding with the political upheavals of these times when publics agitated for more democratic governance and stronger environmental protection.[24] During the 1970s and early 1980s, commentators increasingly emphasised the value of a 'bottom-up', people-centred approach to economic development.[25] Economists such as Schumacher stressed the value of grass-roots, small-scale decision-making to promote social welfare.[26] By the 1990s, consultation and participation became the buzzwords of successful environmental decision-making, feeding into broader discourses on 'good governance', 'environmental justice' and 'environmental citizenship'.

In developing countries, the participation agenda often manifested in calls for greater local community involvement in development planning and poverty alleviation projects, especially in the context of development aid schemes.[27] Post-colonial commentators argued that the post-War decolonisation process was 'prematurely celebratory', given the persistence of widespread oppression and poverty in many developing countries.[28] They advocated further reforms to recently-independent states to widen community participation in government to ensure social and economic policies addressed people's primary needs.[29] Recent development policies have sought to decentralise decision-making and enhance local institutional capacities (eg, through strengthening local government and NGOs) to create a more participatory milieu.[30] These trends have been accentuated by recent global policy initiatives, such as the 'Local Agenda 21' movement for sustainable development.[31]

In developed nations, the public participation agenda achieved similar prominence, though it has tended to take a more legal form than in many developing

[23] Eg, in the UK, in its planning legislation of the 1960s. The creation of the Royal Commission on Environmental Pollution (1969) and the Department of the Environment (1970) was the governmental response to these public pressures: see generally J McCormick, *The Global Environment Movement* (Wiley, 1995). In the US, the National Environmental Policy Act of 1969 provided for participation by the general public: see S Kuhn, 'Expanding Public Participation is Essential to Environmental Justice and the Democratic Decision Making Process' (1999) 25(4) *Ecology Law Quarterly* 647.

[24] Barton, above n 12, 81.

[25] Spyke, above n 6, 269;

[26] EF Schumacher, *Small is Beautiful: Economics as if People Mattered* (Harper and Row, 1973).

[27] M Aycrigg, *Participation and the World Bank: Successes, Constraints and Responses* (World Bank, 1998).

[28] A McClintock, *Imperial Leather* (Routledge, 1995) 12–13.

[29] A Memmi, *The Colonizer and the Colonized* (Beacon Press, 1991); G Rajan and R Mohanram (eds), *Postcolonial Discourse and Changing Cultural Contexts* (Greenwood Press, 1995).

[30] BJ Richardson, 'Environmental Law in Postcolonial Societies: Straddling the Local—Global Institutional Spectrum' (2000) 11(1) *Colorado Journal of Environmental Law & Policy* 1, 45–7.

[31] J Agyeman and B Evans, 'Sustainability and Democracy: Community Participation in Local Agenda 21' (1995) 22(2) *Local Goverment Policy Making* 35.

countries where it has typically been confined to policy mechanisms.[32] Some eco-activists saw the best prospects for change in parliamentary electoral contests through the formation of green political parties. Although green parties have survived in several Western polities, notably Germany and Australia, they have yet seriously to challenge the electoral dominance of the mainstream parties.[33] Most public participation has thus occurred not through legislative fora but in the proliferation of administrative-based consultation, information and review mechanisms established pursuant to environmental and planning laws.[34]

Numerous societal conflicts over development choices in the 1970s and 1980s fuelled popular demands for more participation in decision-making. For example, in Australia, a series of protracted and often violent conflicts over logging in World Heritage forests caused governments to look for more peaceful means by which citizens could be involved in resource management policy.[35] In the urban areas of many countries, community groups mobilised for more say in decisions about brownfield redevelopment and urban amenity planning.[36] Public participation reforms in Canada, New Zealand, the US and other countries with indigenous minorities were also influenced by the Aboriginal self-determination movement.[37] The emergence of Aboriginal land claims and demands for self-governance provided another lever for legal reforms to enhance community involvement in environment and development decision-making.

Internationally, the rhetoric of good governance has received considerable attention. Empowerment of civil societies has been identified as one of the best means to promote good environmental governance.[38] Major international environmental policy statements in the 1980s and 1990s routinely called for increased community involvement in environmental decision-making.[39] International financial institutions,

32 O Renn, T Webler and P Wiedemann (eds), *Fairness and Competence in Citizen Participation: Evaluating Models for Environmental Discourse* (Kluwer, 1995).

33 SP Hays, 'The Structure of Environmental Politics Since World War II' (1981) 14 *Journal of Social History* 719; E Bomberg, *Green Parties and Politics in the European Union* (Routledge, 1998).

34 Stewart, above n 1.

35 BJ Richardson, 'A Study of Australian Practice Pursuant to the World Heritage Convention' (1990) 20(4) *Environmental Policy & Law* 143.

36 See eg A Jakuhowicz, 'The Green Ban Movement: Urban Struggle and Class Politics' in J Halligan and C Pairs (eds), *Australian Urban Politics* (Longman, 1984) 143.

37 PG McHugh, *Aboriginal Societies and the Common Law: A History of Sovereignty, Status and Self-determination* (Oxford UP, 2005) 315–65.

38 J Steffek and P Nanz, 'Deliberation and Democracy in Global Governance: The Role of Civil Society' in S Thoyer and B Martimort-Asso (eds), *Participation for Sustainability in Trade* (Ashgate, 2005).

39 See eg World Commission on Environment and Development, *Our Common Future* (Oxford UP, 1987); World Conservation Union, *Caring for the Earth* (IUCN, 1990). This realisation is also evident in a growing body of international legal instruments: eg Stockholm Declaration (1972) 11 ILM 1416, Rio Declaration on Environment and Development (1992) 31 ILM 874, Declaration of the World Summit for Sustainable Development (2002), and UNECE Convention on Access to Information, Public Participation in Decision Making and Access to Justice in Environmental Matters (Aarhus Convention) (1999) 38 ILM 517, discussed below.

like the World Bank and its 'sister' regional banks, also reformulated their lending procedures to require more information disclosure and consultation with affected parties.[40] These initiatives acknowledge that civil society can also play an important role in making the decision-making processes of international organisations more transparent.[41]

C. Theoretical Approaches to Public Participation

There has been a plethora of academic writings on the virtues of public participation in policy-making, especially in relation to environmental policy.[42] Not all environmentalists however have always championed democracy: for example, during the 1970s, several commentators such as Ophuls and Hardin believed that the intensification of societal conflict over an ever-decreasing pool of natural resources could be dampened only through the enlightened despotism of an authoritarian state.[43] Today, the complex and multi-faceted nature of sustainability, involving various social objectives flanking and supporting environmental protection, suggests that no single institution can be expected to hold all of the expertise and knowledge needed for good decision-making.[44] Popular involvement in environmental decision-making has been rationalised from two main perspectives, a *process* perspective and a *substantive* perspective. The latter is based on arguments that public participation improves the substantive outcomes of decision-making processes; the former that it bolsters the democratic legitimacy of those decisions. Across these two perspectives, several schools of thought on the rationale and role of public participation have arisen.

First, there is the 'rational elitism' school, which treats environmental policy as complex and technical, requiring primarily technical and administrative expertise. This doctrine emphasises decision-making by experts, and concedes limited participation to the general public when they hold information that may assist experts.[45] Technical environmental risk assessments and economic cost-benefit analyses of development proposals are situations in which governments often

40 Barton, above n 12, 84.

41 S Oberthür *et al*, *Participation of NGOs in International Environmental Governance: Legal Basis and Practical Experience* (FIELD and Ecologic, 2001); see also J Razzaque, 'Transparency and Participation of Civil Society in International Institutions Related to Biotechnology: A Brief Study of the Bio-safety Protocol, WTO and Codex Alimentarius' in Thoyer and Martimort-Asso (eds), above n 38.

42 See discussion in Barton, above n 12, 84–98.

43 W Ophuls, 'Leviathan or Oblivion?' in HE Daly (ed), *Toward a Steady-State Economy* (WH Freeman, 1973); G Hardin, *Exploring New Ethics for Survival* (Viking Press, 1972).

44 See generally K Ginther *et al* (eds), *Sustainable Development and Good Governance* (Nijhoff, 1995).

45 Barton, above n 12, 86–7.

favour 'expert' participation.[46] But this approach, which pretends that science is 'objective' and 'apolitical', obfuscates the fundamental way in which social values influence decision-making. For example, even if the scientific information about a hazard and its likelihood is relatively clear, the acceptable level of environmental risk is arguably a political question.[47] Another strand of the rational elitism model is known as 'corporatism'. Corporatist modes of interest group intermediation, for instance, have been widely used in round-table negotiations of economic policy-making in Scandinavia and Germany.[48] Corporatist styles of participation have also been used in the environmental policy round-tables adopted in Australia and Canada.[49] However, corporatism offers only a 'functional representation' to representatives of large strategic groups such as trade unions, industry and business councils, and sometimes renowned environmental NGOs.[50]

A second approach to participation is the 'liberal democratic' one, which stresses procedural rights for individuals and NGOs to be consulted and heard in decision-making. When electoral legitimacy is weak, procedural legitimacy assumes greater salience. The traditional polyarchal mechanisms (eg, elections and political parties) of liberal-democratic systems have been criticised as unable to manage the demands of competing interest groups in modern societies. To Offe, the 'conflict-generating potential of the institutions of the democratic polity by far outweighs their conflict-resolving capacity'.[51] Consequently, most liberal-democratic states have sought to create supplementary public consultation and information processes in administrative and legislative decision-making.[52] Thus, the propensity of modern environmental legislation is to identify the factors relevant to agency decision-making, one of which is the input made by the public consulted. Through procedural reforms, concerned persons have rights of access to relevant information, to make submissions on environmental decisions, and to use courts to enforce environmental laws.

Apart from bolstering the legitimacy and public acceptability of policy decisions, the procedural reforms of liberal-democratic systems may also shape substantive policy outcomes. For example, simple obligations of openness may illuminate the uncertainties and value judgements inherent in experts' advice, allowing *political* decision-makers to reach conclusions on the basis of a wider array of evidence. Public involvement can also facilitate community co-operation

[46] See S Jasanoff, *The Fifth Branch: Science Advisors as Policymakers* (Harvard UP, 1990); S Breyer and V Heyvaert, 'Institutions for Regulating Risk' in RL Revesz, R Sands and RB Stewart (eds), *Environmental Law, the Economy and Sustainable Development* (Cambridge UP, 2000).

[47] P Slovic, *The Perception of Risk* (Earthscan, 2000); M Douglas and A Wildavsky, *Risk and Culture* (U California P, 1983).

[48] PC Schmitter and G Lehmbruch (eds), *Trends Toward Corporatist Intermediation* (Sage, 1979).

[49] M Howlett, 'The Round Table Experience: Representation and Legitimacy in Canadian Environmental Policy-making' (1990) 97 *Queen's Quarterly* 580.

[50] C Offe, *Contradictions of the Welfare State* (MIT Press, 1987) 167.

[51] *Ibid*, 164.

[52] See J Habermas, *Legitimation Crisis* (Beacon Press, 1973), Offe, above n 50.

in implementing environmental decisions, such as anti-littering and recycling campaigns. The sense of ownership and responsibility for decisions that comes from being part of decision-making can encourage more thoughtful environmental behaviour. Regulation theorists often see third party involvement and transparency as a way to keep regulators accountable, again a means of improving outcomes.[53] Opening decision-making processes can reduce the risk of agency 'capture' by their industry clientele.[54] However, not all commentators share such a sanguine view of participatory proceduralism. Liberal-democratic procedural reforms may hardly challenge the structure of governing elites' power: citizens may be heard, but their views are given weight in discretionary decision-making only insofar as they are seen as consistent with the 'seamless web of bureaucratic control and coordination'.[55] Further, liberal-democratic methods hardly provide an institutional framework for active citizen interaction, learning and ethical transformation.

These limitations have engendered a third model of participation, known as deliberative democracy, which seeks to empower citizens in the actual making of decisions and to reorient decision processes to fundamental ethical and social values.[56] While sustainable development cannot be guaranteed, wide participation in political debate is seen as essential to allow for the pedagogic cultivation and exchange of environmental values.[57] Deliberative models of decision-making dovetail closely with the deep and radical ecological schools of thought. For the self-styled 'eco-anarchist' Murray Bookchin, the human domination and exploitation of nature are largely a consequence of hierarchical social relations, being a reflection of the domination of human by human.[58] Deep ecologists thus often stress the value of egalitarian, community-based means of decision-making.[59]

Whether citizen participation is 'deliberative' depends on many factors, including whether the participants represent all sectors of the community.[60] Touraine has identified popular social movements as the most creative source of new norms to regenerate dialogue in public institutions.[61] But, because the complexity of

[53] I Ayres and J Braithwaite, *Responsive Regulation* (Oxford UP, 1992); N Gunningham and P Grabosky, *Smart Regulation: Designing Environmental Policy* (Oxford UP, 1998).

[54] M Levine and J Forrence, 'Regulatory Capture, Public Interest and the Public Agenda: Toward a Synthesis' (1990) 6 *Journal of Law, Economics and Organisation* 167.

[55] A Fraser, 'Legal Theory and Legal Practice' (1976) 44–45 *Arena* 123, 147.

[56] J Bohman and W Rehg (eds), *Deliberative Democracy: Essays on Reason and Politics* (MIT Press, 1997).

[57] See B Doherty and M de Geus (eds), *Democracy and Green Political Thought—Sustainability, Rights and Citizenship* (Routledge, 1996); G Smith, *Deliberative Democracy and the Environment* (Routledge, 2003).

[58] M Bookchin, *The Ecology of Freedom: The Emergence and Dissolution of Hierarchy* (Cheshire Books, 1982).

[59] B Boer, 'Social Ecology and Environmental Law' (1984) 1(3) *Environmental & Planning LJ* 233.

[60] J Elster (ed), *Deliberative Democracy* (Cambridge UP, 1998); B Barber, *Strong Democracy: Participatory Politics for a New Age* (U California P, 1984); J Dryzek, *Deliberative Democracy and Beyond: Liberals, Critics, Contestations* (Oxford UP, 2000).

[61] A Touraine, *The Voice and the Eye: An Analysis of Social Movements* (Cambridge UP, 1982).

modern life probably makes it impossible to assume or develop shared social values on many environmental and economic issues, some commentators argue that at best we can hope to agree on the institutional processes by which we can deliberate policy. Habermas has posited an 'ideal speech situation', or a set of rules for communication and discourse, by which rational decision-making is most likely to flourish.[62] Dryzek has argued that mediation and negotiation are institutional means to achieve such a rational discourse in an environmental policy setting.[63] Other methods are some forms of social impact assessment and public environmental inquiries.[64]

The foregoing approaches to public participation are not necessarily mutually exclusive, and elements of each have featured in the related 'environmental citizenship' and 'environmental justice' movements. The former sees public participation as a means of nurturing a new ethos of environmental responsibility,[65] while the latter champions democratic decision-making as a way to ensure social equity in the distribution of the environmental costs and benefits of policy decisions.[66] The complex, normative and political nature of environmental decisions means that public involvement is necessary at many levels. Active citizen involvement in environmental decisions would be hampered, for instance, without the presence of basic rights to access information and to receive notice of pending development proposals. Most examples of public participation canvassed in this chapter are of the liberal-democratic variety. They emphasise public access to environmental information, participation in administrative decision-making (eg, environmental assessments and development applications) and access to justice (eg, standing in courts to enforce regulations). While these participatory reforms have improved the quality of many environmental decisions, they have hardly engendered a major paradigm shift to ecologically sustainable development. Most participatory techniques so far hardly seem to threaten existing political institutions, since they operate within those institutions, and leave power and authority mostly unfettered.

Apart from the theoretical debates about participation in public government, it should be noted that numerous commentators also advocate more openness and public involvement in corporate governance. The ethical investment movement

[62] J Habermas, *The Theory of Communicative Action 1: Reason and the Rationalization of Society* (Beacon Press, 1984); see also K Popper, *The Open Society and Its Enemies* (Routledge, 1986).

[63] JS Dryzek, *Rational Ecology, Environment and Political Economy* (Basil Blackwell, 1987).

[64] See LM Lake (ed), *Environmental Mediation: The Search for Consensus* (Westview Press, 1980); D Craig, 'Social Impact Assessment: Politically Oriented Approaches and Applications' (1999) 10 *Environmental Impact Assessment Review* 37; see also Bosselmann, this vol, on the philosophical dimensions of this debate.

[65] R Engel 'The Faith of Democratic Ecological Citizenship,' (Nov 1998) *Nature, Polis, Ethics* S31.

[66] KS Shrader-Frechette, *Environmental Justice: Creating Equality, Reclaiming Democracy* (Oxford UP, 2002); E Gauna, 'The Environmental Justice Misfit: Public Participation and the Paradigm Paradox' (1998) 17 *Stanford Envtl L J* 3.

has long championed greater shareholder activism in business decision-making to give more attention to the social and environmental effects of corporate policies.[67] This can be applied through corporate–shareholder dialogue and submission of shareholder proposals. Further, many company law theorists advocate a 'stakeholder' approach to corporate management, whereby a wider range of social interests including workers, consumers and local communities are given a voice in company policy, alongside shareholders.[68] The German system of corporate governance, guaranteeing representation of employees on company governing boards, comes closest to this model.[69] Apart from these major structural reforms, public participation in corporate governance may also be advanced by modest initiatives such as corporate social and environmental reporting obligations.[70]

D. The Aarhus Convention and its Implementation

1. Public Participation Provisions of the Aarhus Convention

One of the unique developments in the public participation arena is the 1998 Aarhus Convention.[71] While there are other international environmental treaties that contain public participation clauses,[72] only the Aarhus Convention is dedicated exclusively to participation. Although the Convention is a product of the United Nations (UN) Economic Commission for Europe, it is open to accession by any UN member state (with the approval of the parties). The Convention is a globally significant example of the legal consolidation of measures to enhance public participation in relation to administrative decision-making, freedom of information and access to justice.

The Aarhus Convention imposes participation standards for decision-making by public authorities. They relate to activities that may significantly affect the environment (eg, construction of a power plant), or policies, programmes and

[67] R Sparkes, *The Ethical Investor* (HarperCollins, 1995); R Sparkes, *Socially Responsible Investment. A Global Revolution* (John Wiley and Sons, 2002)

[68] JE Parkinson, *Corporate Power and Responsibility: Issues in the Theory of Company Law* (Clarendon Press, 1995); D Campbell, "Towards a Less Irrelevant Socialism: Stakeholding as a 'Reform' of the Capitalist Economy" (1997) 24 *Journal of Law & Society* 65.

[69] D Charny, 'The German Corporate Governance System' [1998] *Columbia Business L Rev* 145.

[70] Mandatory environmental reporting has been introduced in Australia, Britain, France and the US, among many countries: see KMPG Environmental Consulting, *International Survey of Environmental Reporting* (KPMG, 1999).

[71] Convention on Access to Information, Public Participation in Decision Making and Access to Justice in Environmental Matters (Aarhus Convention), (1999) 38 ILM 515.

[72] Eg Convention on Environmental Impact Assessment in a Transboundary Context (1991) 30 ILM 800, Art 16; North American Agreement on Environmental Cooperation (1993) 32 ILM 1480, Arts 13–14.

plans relating to the environment.[73] The procedural rights are to be applied without discrimination as to citizenship, nationality or domicile.[74]

The first pillar of the Convention is participation in administrative decision-making. Article 6 requires public notice of environmental decision-making to be given when 'all options are open', to allow public comment and input into the process.[75] Public authorities[76] must also take public feedback into account in their final decisions.

Secondly, governments must make relevant information available to the public when requested, and the Convention stipulates time-frames for responding to these requests.[77] Article 4 creates a presumption in favour of information disclosure and public authorities may deny a request for information only on the basis of the list of specific grounds for refusal.[78] Further, public authorities may refuse to disclose information that would impair the ability of a person to receive a fair trial, or would adversely affect national defence or public security.[79]

The third pillar of the Convention is 'access to justice'. These provisions are closely tied to the other two pillars of the treaty. Article 9(1) provides for review of a refusal or failure to respond to a request for access to information. Article 9(2) provides for the challenge of substantive or procedural legality of decisions subject to Article 6 (above) and also 'where so provided for under national law'. Finally, Article 9(3) mandates access to administrative or judicial procedures to challenge acts and omissions by private and public bodies that contravene national law relating to the environment. The Convention also requires proceedings to be 'fair', 'equitable' and 'not prohibitively expensive', and that there be 'adequate and effective remedies'.[80]

Overall, the Aarhus Convention provides a useful framework for public participation along the lines of the liberal-democratic model. Its participatory rights are linked to various legislative, administrative and judicial decision-making points. Implementation of these provisions however depends on strong political support by state parties.

2. Implementation of the Convention

The Aarhus Convention signalled the culmination, rather than the beginning, of public participation reforms made since the 1970s. States' enthusiasm to ratify the

73 Arts 6–7. Annex I lists those activities that must be subject to the requirements under Art 6.
74 Art 3(9).
75 Art 6.
76 Public authority is defined in Art 2(2) and covers any body or any natural or legal persons performing public administrative functions, and may include privatised companies providing public services: Stec and Casey-Lefkowitz, above n 3, 44.
77 Arts 4 and 5.
78 Art 4(3).
79 Art 4(4).
80 Art 9(4).

treaty reflects the fact that many governments already provide for similar kinds of public involvement in environmental decision-making. Within the European Union (EU), virtually all Member States have either signed or ratified the Aarhus Convention. However, scope for public participation at the EU level itself is less developed, making the EU's ratification of Aarhus especially significant.[81]

The European Commission has undertaken necessary measures to implement the Convention by adopting regulations to align EU legislation to the Convention.[82] The EC's enthusiasm for the Aarhus Convention partly reflects a desire to shore up its own democratic legitimacy. The Convention is of particular importance to the EU institutions (eg, the Commission, the Parliament and the Council) as they are covered by its definition of 'public authorities'.[83] The EU has adopted a directive concerning public access to environmental information, reflecting the first pillar of Aarhus.[84] In addition, two important pieces of EU environmental legislation[85] have been amended to take account of the public participation in certain environmental decision-making procedures. Directive 2003/35/EC[86] updates provisions on public participation in national procedures on environmental impact assessment and integrated pollution prevention and control, and introduces rules on access to justice. In addition, provisions related to access to justice are introduced in the Directive on environmental liability.[87] However, the latter provisions fail to specify that access be fair, timely and not prohibitively expensive. The European Commission has also adopted a proposal for a directive to address the requirements of access to justice in environmental matters.[88]

[81] See list of parties to the Convention, at www.unece.org/env/pp/ctreaty.htm.

[82] Proposal for a Council Decision on the conclusion, on behalf of the European Community, of the Convention on access to information, public participation in decision-making and access to justice regarding environmental matters, COM(2003)625 final.

[83] See the proposed Regulation of the European Parliament and of the Council on the application of the provisions of the Aarhus Convention on Access to Information, Public Participation in Decision-making and Access to Justice in Environmental Matters to EC institutions and bodies, COM (2003) 622 final.

[84] Directive 2003/4/EC on public access to environmental information and repealing Council Directive 90/313/EEC [2003] OJ L/41/26.

[85] Directive 85/337/EEC concerning the environmental impact assessment for certain public and private projects (EIA Directive [1985] OJ L/175/40); and Council Directive 96/61/EC concerning integrated pollution prevention and control (IPPC Directive) [1996] OJ L/257/26.

[86] Directive 2003/35/EC providing for public participation in respect of the drawing up of certain plans and programmes relating to the environment and amending with regard to public participation and access to justice Council Directives 85/337/EEC and 96/61/EC [2003] OJ L/156/17.

[87] See Arts 12 (Request for Action) and 13 (Review Procedures) of Directive 2004/35/EC on environmental liability with regard to the prevention and remedying of environmental damage [2004] OJ L/143/56.

[88] Commission proposal for a Directive on access to justice (COM(2003)624); see further J Razzaque, 'Access to Justice in Environmental Matters at EU Member State Level' (2005) 5 *Yearbook of European Environmental Law*, 63.

At the EU Member State level, all 25 parties have national laws to enable some participation in their decision-making processes. However, the contexts in which these procedural rights operate are diverse, and reflect differences of legal and democratic traditions. Mindful of this, the European Commission's proposed directive on access to justice on environmental matters addresses only the acts and omissions of public authorities, and does not extend to private entities. On the ground of the 'subsidiarity' principle (ie, that decisions should be made at the lowest level of government where feasible), the Commission believes that administrative or judicial review of the environmental behaviour of private entities is best left to individual Member States to determine. Even in relation to the public sector, 'standing' rules vary considerably among EU Member States.[89] Similar variations in national practice have been documented in relation to the other limbs of Aarhus concerning participation in administrative decisions and access to information.[90]

E. Legal Mechanisms for Public Participation

1. Constitutional Provisions and Environmental Rights

National constitutions often lay down fundamental human rights, sometimes known as a bill of rights. Increasingly, constitutions also incorporate fundamental environmental rights.[91] These rights can support public interest litigation or judicial review for environmental protection.[92] Constitutional norms that oblige governments to protect the environment or give citizens enforceable rights to a clean and healthy environment may be more secure than statutory rights, which are more vulnerable to change or repeal by the government of the day. On the other hand, constitutions do not provide a suitable framework for prescribing in detail environmental standards and rules including participation provisions, which are better elaborated through legislation. Thus, because of their generality, the effectiveness of constitutional norms in shaping environmental law hinges considerably on the willingness of the courts to interpret and elaborate on their application.[93]

[89] J Ebbesson, 'Comparative Introduction' in J Ebbesson (ed), *Access to Justice in the Environmental Matters in the EU* (Kluwer, 2002) 20, 23.

[90] United Nations Economic Commission for Europe, *Synthesis Report on the Status of Implementation of the Convention* ECE/MP.PP/2005/18 (ECOSOC, Apr 2005).

[91] Numerous examples are contained in C Bruch, W Coker and C Van Arsdale, 'Constitutional Environmental Law: Giving Force to Fundamental Principles in Africa' (2001) 26 *Columbia Journal of Environmental Law* 131; EF Brown, 'In Defense of Environmental Rights in East European Constitutions' (1993) *University of Chicago Law School Roundtable* 191.

[92] J Razzaque, *Public Interest Environmental Litigation in India, Pakistan and Bangladesh* (Kluwer, 2004) ch 2.

[93] Eg the role of Canadian courts in developing Aboriginal rights, which are merely 'recognised and affirmed' by s 35(1) of the Constitution Act 1982.

In many Asian and African countries, constitutions incorporate a panoply of human rights, including rights to life, free expression and assembly, along with specific environmental protection clauses.[94] But often these rights tend to be merely rhetorical and consequently are ignored by policy-makers. For example, the Constitution of South Korea was amended in 1980 to provide its citizens with the right to live in a healthy and clean environment,[95] but the Supreme Court of Korea has construed this provision as not self-executing and enforceable in its own right.[96] By contrast, constitutional norms play a much greater role in the legal systems of Western countries such as the US, Canada and Australia.[97] Even nations without a written constitution, such as Britain, have acquired an extensive body of human rights through the common law and from international treaties such as the European Convention on Human Rights,[98] which the UK incorporated domestically via the Human Rights Act 1998.

Apart from constitutional entrenchment, participatory rights can be articulated through a statutory environmental bill of rights (EBR), as seen in Ontario and Michigan, for instance.[99] To illustrate, the Ontario EBR of 1994 established an Environmental Registry as part of a framework for notifying and consulting the public with regard to proposed legislation, policies, regulations and other legal instruments that may significantly affect the environment.[100] Although the EBR does not provide a substantive right to a healthy environment, it does expand procedural rights.[101] While it is a significant precedent, it remains difficult to assess whether the improved participation has per se changed the quality of authorities' environmental decisions.[102]

[94] B Ajibola, 'Individual Human Rights in African Context' in A Anghie and G Sturgess (eds), *Legal Visions of the 21st Century: Essays in Honour of Judge Christopher Weeramantry* (Kluwer, 1998); L Beer (ed), *Constitutionalism in Asia* (U California P, 1979).

[95] Constitution of the Republic of Korea, Art 35, available at: www.oefre.unibe.ch/law/icl/ks00000_.html.

[96] Eg *Dae-bup-won* [DBW] [Supreme Court] 94 ma 2218 (23 May 1995) (S Korea).

[97] DP Kommers, JE Finn and GJ Jacobson, *American Constitutional Law* (2nd edn, Rowman, 2004) 425, 432–5.

[98] (1950) ETS 5/213, UNTS 222.

[99] DK Slone, 'The Michigan Environmental Protection Act: Bringing Citizen-initiated Environmental Suits into the 1980's' [1985] *Ecology Law Quarterly* 271; P Muldoon 'Ontario Environmental Bill of Rights' (1992) 3(1) *Earthkeeper* 44; C Miller, *Environmental Rights: Critical Perspectives* (Routledge, 1998).

[100] MA Schofield and DS Thompson, 'Access to Justice and the Right to a Healthful Environment in Canada: Public Participation in Environmental Decision Making' (1994) 3/4 *Review of European Community and International Environmental Law* 232.

[101] DP Emond, 'An Environmental Bill of Rights—Ontario Style' (1994) 1 *Government Information in Canada/Information Gouvernementale au Canada* 1(2–3) (1994), available at www.usask.ca/library/gic/v1n2/emond/emond.html.

[102] RD Lindgren, 'The Environmental Bill of Rights Turns 10 Years-old: Congratulations or Condolences?', Environmental Commissioner's EBR Law Reform Workshop (16 June 2004).

2. Participation in Administrative Decision-making

One of the pillars of the Aarhus Convention is public participation in administrative decision-making. Such participation can arise in a variety of contexts, including in decisions concerning specific development proposals, plans and policies, and in regulation-making processes.[103] Most public participation reforms adopted in this field entail rights to make written submissions and to be involved in public inquiries, with concomitant obligations on decision-makers to take into account public opinion. The oldest and most basic of these reforms are simple 'notice and comment' provisions, in place since the 1960s in most US environmental regulatory regimes and subsequently adopted in many other jurisdictions. Modern environmental legislation, delegating powers to administrative agencies, often makes participation a central agency function.[104] These participation mechanisms can be illustrated by environmental impact assessment (EIA) regulation.

Public participation in the EIA process can assist the integration of economic, social and ecological objectives in decision-making.[105] Although historically expert specialists dominated EIA procedures, in many jurisdictions these procedures have evolved to allow for extensive public input in the assessment process.[106] At the 'screening stage', which is an initial consideration of whether a proposal may have significant impacts on the environment, people may help identify potential impacts of the proposal. If the proposal is deemed to require an EIA, the 'scoping stage' serves to identify the range of significant impacts that need to be evaluated. This stage provides an opportunity to identify public interest and priorities for assessment.[107] Although most jurisdictions have legislated public rights to access information and to make submissions during these stages, in some cases such as Canada the scoping phase remains entirely up to the responsible authority.[108] The weight given to public comments in the environmental assessment is also usually a matter of agency discretion in many jurisdictions. A major analysis of the Canadian, US and European EIA processes concluded that the degree of public participation affects the quality of the assessment process, which in turn affects the quality of the decision.[109] Although it is argued that public participation slows down the EIA process, one underlying rationale of EIA is to ensure socially acceptable environmental results.[110]

[103] See A Boyle and MR Anderson (eds), *Human Rights Approaches to Environmental Protection* (Clarendon Press, 1996).

[104] Eg Australia's Environmental Planning and Assessment Act 1979 (NSW) s 5.

[105] See also the discussion of EIA regulation in Abbot's ch, this vol.

[106] See J Holder, *Environmental Assessment: The Regulation of Decision Making* (Oxford UP, 2004).

[107] See CM Wood, *Environmental Impact Assessment: A Comparative Review* (Prentice Hall, 2002); J Glasson, R Therivel and A Chadwick, *Introduction to Environmental Impact Assessment* (UCL Press, 1999).

[108] Canadian Environmental Assessment Act, SC 1992, c 37, *as amended* SC 2003, c 9.

[109] Wood, above n 107, chs 2, 3 and 5.

[110] WA Tilleman, 'Public Participation in the Environmental Impact Assessment Process: A Comparative Study of Impact Assessment in Canada, the United States and the European Community' (1995) 33 *Columbia Journal of Transnational Law* 337.

The public environmental inquiry is another means for concerned citizens to be heard.[111] It provides an opportunity for direct community dialogue in the spirit of deliberative democracy. The public inquiry technique was pioneered in the UK and is used in much of its planning legislation. For instance, once a planning application is submitted to a Local Planning Authority (LPA), community groups can submit comments on the environmental statement. In addition, if there is a public inquiry against the decision taken by the LPA, the local community can send written comments or present its views in person.[112] Moreover, the Secretary of State has the discretion to 'call in' for a public inquiry any application for his or her own determination if the proposal involves planning issues of more than local importance.[113] However, these processes can be time consuming and expensive: the public inquiry on Heathrow Terminal 5 lasted almost four years and cost over £80 million.[114] Public environmental inquiries have been used extensively in several other jurisdictions as an adjunct to EIA processes. Australia's Industry Commission and Resource Assessment Commission each conducted numerous public inquiries into contentious resource management proposals during the 1990s.[115] Some major environmental assessment inquiries have also been established under New Zealand's Resource Management Act 1991.[116]

An EIA may come too late to result in major changes in proposed activities that can protect the environment. In those cases, a strategic environmental assessment (SEA) process may be more beneficial as it allows people to participate at the policy- (or plans or programmes) making level, which in turn shape future, specific development projects. SEA is a procedure integrated in the political decision-making process that is intended to ensure that the long-term environmental sequelae of various plans and programmes are identified and assessed before being adopted.[117] In the EU, the SEA Directive[118] stipulates that prior to the adoption of a plan or programme, or its submission to the legislative process, the competent national authority must carry out an environmental report. The public are to be given an opportunity to comment on the draft plan or programme and the

[111] G Hart, 'The Value of Inquiries System' (1997) 25 *Journal of Planning and Environmental Law* 8.

[112] Town and Country Planning Act 1990 s 78.

[113] *Ibid*, s 77.

[114] K Thorpe, 'The Heathrow Terminal 5 Inquiry: An Inquiry Secretary's Perspective' (1999) 15 *Planning Inspectorate Journal* 8.

[115] TL Hundloe, 'The Role of the Industry Commission in Relation to the Environment and Sustainable Development' (1992) 51 *Australian Journal of Public Administration* 476; BJ Richardson and BW Boer, 'Federal Public Inquiries and Environmental Assessment' (1995) 2(2) *Australian Journal of Envtl Management* 90, 92.

[116] BJ Richardson, 'Public Environmental Inquiries: Lessons for New Zealand' (1996) 1 *Butterworths Resource Management Bulletin* 252.

[117] R Therivel and MR Partidario (eds), *The Practice of Strategic Environmental Assessment* (Earthscan, 1996).

[118] Directive 2001/42/EC on the assessment of the effects of certain plans and programmes on the environment [2001] OJ L/197/30.

accompanying environmental report. The relevant public authority has a duty to inform the parties concerned and all consultees of the result of the consultation, and the reasons for choosing the final plan or programme.

3. Access to Information

Liberal access to environmental information has many advantages. It makes it easier for the public to participate in administrative and judicial processes; it helps promote more rational, informed decision-making; and it fosters transparent and accountable decision-making.[119] Apart from ensuring access to a broad range of information, effective access to information laws should include obligations on agencies to collect and maintain relevant information, to meet information requests in a timely manner, and to keep information application fees low and within the means of all people.[120]

So far, most environmental information reforms have targeted the public sector, and few address disclosure of information by the private sector. The relevant Aarhus Convention provisions deal only with government information. Nonetheless, the right of citizens to access information is becoming widespread and even recognised in constitutional law. For example, the constitutions of Uganda, South Africa and Thailand guarantee the right of the public to information.[121] In addition, as of 2004 over 50 countries worldwide passed access to information legislation, of which many included provisions related to environmental information.[122] In some countries (eg, South Africa, Thailand) environmental protection laws provide specific provisions for environmental information[123] complementing access to information laws. There are also examples of countries having specific legislation on access to environmental information.[124] In addition, some countries have constitutional provisions, specific freedom of information legislation and environmental protection laws with specific provisions on information.[125]

Omnibus access to information legislation is often complemented by sector-specific information regulations and business self-regulation initiatives. The corporate social responsibility movement has fuelled increased public disclosure of

[119] JR Robinson, *et al*, 'Public Access to Environmental Information: A Means to What End?' (1996) 8(1) *Journal of Environmental Law* 19, 20.

[120] Petkova *et al*, above n 4, 37–40.

[121] D Banisar, 'Global Survey: Freedom of Information and Access to Government Record Laws Around the World' (May 2004), available at: www.freedominfo.org/survey/global_survey2004.pdf.

[122] *Ibid.*

[123] World Resources Institute (WRI), *World Resources 2002–2004—Decisions for the Earth: Balance, Voice and Power* (WRI, 2004) ch 3.

[124] In Britain, the Environmental Information Regulations 2004 implement the EU Directive on Access to Environmental Information, SI 2004 No 3391.

[125] Eg, Mexico, South Africa and Thailand: Petkova *et al*, above n 4, ch 3.

corporate environmental policy and performance information.[126] Some of this disclosure is voluntary, while some is associated with regulation. There are several ways in which environmental disclosure is occurring, principally:[127] (i) public inventories of uses and releases of toxic chemicals;[128] (ii) environmental auditing of business operations;[129] and (iii) eco-labelling programmes that identify products with preferable environmental characteristics.[130] For instance, in order to enhance public accountability by industry, the US enacted the Emergency Planning and Community Right to Know Act 1986[131] to require certain industries publicly to disclose their annual emissions, recycling of chemicals, accidental releases and source reduction measures. Mandating disclosure of environmental information can help regulators, consumers, financial sponsors, as well as the companies themselves, better to understand the environmental impacts. Through education and awareness, pressure can be exerted on companies to improve their environmental behaviour.

2. Access to Justice

(a) Judicial review

A traditional means by which environmentally concerned persons can participate is through court action to challenge the legality of administrative decisions made pursuant to legislation. Judicial review is a procedure by which decisions of public bodies exercising environmental responsibilities can be challenged in court and a means by which the courts can supervise public bodies' exercise of their statutory authority. Judicial review is usually concerned with the decision-making process rather than the decision itself.[132] The basic principle is that it is not for the judges to interfere in the decision as this is within the remit of the decision-maker, unless the decision is 'manifestly unreasonable' or the way in which the decision

[126] See further ch 7, this vol.

[127] F Irwin and MF Repko, 'From Public Disclosure to Public Accountability: What Impact will it have on Compliance?' (1999), available at www.inece.org/2ndvol1/irwin.htm.

[128] SM Wolf, 'Fear and Loathing About the Public Right to Know: The Surprising Success of the Emergency Planning and Community Right to Know Act' (1996) 11 *Journal of Land Use & Environmental Law* 217.

[129] Environmental auditing describes a technique for allowing a company or a regulator to assess the impact of its activities on the environment, which includes procedures beyond the scope of a traditional financial audit: see N Gunningham and J Prest, 'Environmental Audit as a Regulatory Strategy: Prospects and Reform' (1993) 15 *Sydney L Rev* 492.

[130] In the EU, companies are using product labelling to make environmental claims. Eco-labels are used to communicate that the environmental impacts are reduced over the entire life-cycle of a product without specifying the production practices. See FIELD, 'Legal and Policy Issues in the Market Access Implications of Labelling for Environmental Purposes', Briefing paper (FIELD, 2003).

[131] Pub L 99–499, Title III, 17 Oct 1986, 100 Stat. 1729, codified at 42 USC §§ 11001–11050.

[132] Lord Woolf, J Jowell and AP Le Sueur, *De Smith, Woolf and Jowell's Principles of Judicial Review* (Sweet and Maxwell, 1999) part I.

was arrived at is flawed.[133] But the success of a judicial review application may not secure the desired outcome. A court may find the agency's decision to be unlawful and, while reconsidering the matter, the public body may come to the same conclusion in a lawful way.[134] In judicial review proceedings in common law systems, such as in the UK, courts do not directly consider the merits of any public decision, act or omission.[135] However, in some cases they will indirectly consider the merits through the doctrine of 'manifest unreasonableness'.[136] Judicial review proceedings do not therefore usually examine whether the decision taken was good or bad from a broad policy or ethical perspective, but merely check to see whether the public body has acted within its statutory powers.

Apart from the narrow focus of judicial review on procedural and jurisdictional issues, the judicial forum is not conducive to the deliberative model of democratic decision-making. The rigidly structured format for the presentation of evidence and cross-examination of participants is far removed from the communicative discourse championed by theorists.[137] Argument transpires through the language of 'rights', 'duties' and 'procedures', which tends to squeeze out less precise ethical and policy considerations to the dispute.[138] The wider policy significance of a case can be lost, as judges tend to decide cases on as narrow grounds as possible.

(b) Public Interest Litigation

Public interest litigation (PIL) is a legal mechanism allowing individuals and NGOs to vindicate a 'public interest', and it has been widely used to uphold environmental law.[139] It is a form of legal proceeding in which redress is sought in respect of injury to the public in general. In a PIL, the collective rights of the public are affected and there may be no direct injury to any individual member of the public.[140] Although PIL for environmental causes originated in the US,[141] the concept of PIL has arisen in numerous jurisdictions and today is most widely practised in India.[142] The growth of PIL in India was facilitated by the inclusion

[133] M Supperstone and J Goudie, *Judicial Review* (Butterworths, 1997) ch 3.
[134] *Ibid.*
[135] H Southey and A Fulford, *Judicial Review* (Jordan, 2004) ch 1.
[136] Supperstone and Goudie, above n 133, ch 3.
[137] AR Lucas, 'Legal Foundations for Public Participation in Environmental Decision-making' (1976) 16(1) *Natural Resources Journal* 73, 100.
[138] Dryzek, above n 63, 146–7.
[139] Cassels identified four characteristics of PIL: liberalisation of *locus standi;* procedural and remedial flexibility; ongoing judicial participation and supervision; and creative and active interpretation of legal and fundamental rights: J Cassels, 'Judicial Activism and Public Interest Litigation: Attempting the Impossible?' (1989) 37 *American Journal of Comparative Law* 498.
[140] SJ Sorabjee, 'Introduction to Judicial Review in India' [1999] *Judicial Review* 128.
[141] J Sax, *Defending the Environment: A Handbook for Citizen Action* (Vintage Books, 1970).
[142] CD Cunningham, 'Public Interest Litigation in Indian Supreme Court: A Study in the Light of American Experience' (1987) 29 *Journal of the Indian Law Institute* 495.

of fundamental duties in the Constitution, the promotion of legal aid at the national level and the adoption of various social-justice related laws.[143] The historical development of PIL in India shows that the judiciary has been very active in relaxing the standing rules giving access to marginalised communities to the court and interpreting the constitutional rights in a liberal manner in order to enhance the rule of law.[144] The judiciary has also taken an inquisitorial role and appointed commissions of enquiry, monitored its own directions, initiated *suo motu* proceedings,[145] accepted *amicus curiae* briefs, supervised implementation of its orders and awarded compensation to the aggrieved.[146] Over the years, the subject matter of PIL in environmental matters has become more complex. The Indian case studies of the 1980s on PIL related to the environment show that they were mainly covering various sectoral issues, eg, air, water, mining or forest conservation.[147] In the 1990s, the categories have become more sophisticated and dealt with complex areas of waste management, protection of bio-diversity, access to environmental information, and groundwater management.[148]

Among the various types of civil suits or actions that can be brought through PIL, the class action can be one of the most empowering. A class action may be allowed in some tort claims that have an impact on a large number of people (eg, tobacco litigation in the US).[149] Separate adjudication of common questions of law or fact could give rise to inconsistent decisions. Moreover, an action brought by an individual member of the class may achieve a result affecting the interests of other members and may substantially impede their ability to protect their interests. Therefore, class actions can be cost-effective, easier to finance, may reduce courts' time and delay, and may spread the cost of litigation among the litigants. The courts, however, are also required to consider whether the class action overrides any question affecting an individual member and whether it would bring a fair and efficient result to the controversy. In recent years in the US there has been an increase in the number of class actions and the size of damages

[143] S Ahuja, *Public Interest Litigation in India: A Socio-legal Study* (PhD thesis, University of London, 1996) 115.

[144] R Dhavan, 'Whose Law? Whose Interest?' in J Cooper and R Dhavan (eds), *Public Interest Law* (Blackwell, 1986) 21.

[145] In order to provide complete justice, the Constitution of India allows the Supreme Court (Art 142) and the High Court (Art 226) to take account of letter and petition from individuals or groups and move the matter as PIL.

[146] Razzaque, above n 92, ch 5.

[147] A Rosencranz and S Divan, *Environmental Law and Policy in India* (Oxford UP, 2001).

[148] Razzaque, above n 92, ch 1.

[149] Eg, Federal Rules of Civil Procedure, Rule 23 (US); Federal Court of Australia Act 1976, Part IVA, enacted by Federal Court of Australia Amendment Act of 1991; Class Proceedings Act 1992 (Ontario). For a useful discussion of class actions, see C Loveday, 'Multi-Party Rules: US, Canada, Australia and the UK' *International Business Lawyer*, (Feb 1998) 77.

awards.[150] The US recently enacted legislation to alleviate the impact of class actions against the corporate sector.[151]

(c) Standing

Public interest litigation, along with other types of litigation, is possible only if the court gives the applicant standing to argue its case. The traditional rule of standing suggests that judicial redress is available only to persons who have suffered a direct injury by reason of a violation or threatened violation of his or her right or interest.[152] For instance, in the Australian case of *Australian Conservation Foundation v Commonwealth*, the NGO applicant was expected to demonstrate a 'special interest' in the proceedings, rather than a mere 'intellectual' or 'emotional' concern.[153] Often rights to seek judicial review or other appeal mechanisms are limited to parties directly involved in the initial administrative decision and do not extend to so-called 'third parties'. Thus, in the UK, for instance, there are no third party rights of appeal against some decisions made under planning legislation.[154] It is frustrating for affected communities as they, unlike the developers, cannot appeal against the planning decision. Though the Royal Commission on Environmental Pollution has recommended expanding third party rights of appeal,[155] the UK government has rejected its proposals.[156]

In recent years, courts in many jurisdictions have become willing to hear arguments from environmental groups and concerned individuals who have no direct economic or other ostensibly concrete interests at stake.[157] Often, the increased

[150] AH Barnett and TD Terrell, 'Economic Observations on Citizen Suits Provisions of Environmental Legislation' (2001) 12 *Duke Environmental Law Policy Forum* 1.

[151] The Class Action Fairness Act of 2005, Pub L 109–2 (17 Feb 2005), 118 Stat 4, seeks to keep large class actions out of state courts (where awards tend to be higher and defendants are often faced with multiple court actions) and to limit what its proponents see as exorbitant settlements and attorneys' fees.

[152] P Cane, 'The Function of Standing Rules in Administrative Law' [1980] *Public Law* 303; C Hilson and I Cram, 'Judicial Review and Environmental Law: Is there a Coherent View of Standing?' (1996) 16 *Legal Studies* 1.

[153] (1980) 54 ALJR 176.

[154] In a planning decision, local communities are the third party; the first party is the developer and the second party is the Local Authority. *Report by the Environmental Justice Project* (WWF, Leigh Day and Co and the Environmental Law Foundation, 2004) 33; Green Balance *et al, Third Party Rights of Appeal in Planning* (Friends of the Earth, 2002).

[155] Royal Commission on Environmental Protection (RCEP), *23rd Report on Environmental Planning* (RCEP, 2002) ch 5, paras 30–47.

[156] *The Government's Response to the Royal Commission on Environmental Pollution's Twenty-Third Report Environmental Planning (England)* (Cm 5888, TSO, July 2003). The UK government argued that the public has the opportunity to participate in the land-use plan-making process. Secondly, the majority of the decisions are made by elected local authority members who are directly accountable to the local electorate: Department for Transport, Local Government and the Regions (DTLR), *Planning: Delivering a Fundamental Change* (DTLR, 2001) paras 6:21 and 6:22. At present, Scotland is considering whether to widen third party right of appeal in planning applications.

[157] Eg, *R v Inspectorate of Pollution and Another, ex parte Greenpeace (No 2)* [1994] 4 All ER 329; *R v Secretary of State for Foreign Affairs* [1995] 1All ER 611; *Algonquin Wildlands League v Ontario (Min. of Natural Resources* [1996] 21 *Canadian Environmental Law Reports* (New Series) 102 (Ontario Divisional Ct); *Sierra Club of Canada v Canada (Min. of Finance)* [1999] 2 FC 211 (Fed Ct Trial Div).

flexibility is a direct result of statutory reforms. For example, the Environmental Planning and Assessment Act 1979 (NSW) in Australia gave open standing to 'any person' to challenge a decision made under the legislation.[158] New Zealand's Resource Management Act 1991 provides that 'any person' may participate in any of the planning and development decision-making processes and the enforcement provisions of the Act.[159] In Britain, however, reforms to the rules of standing made in 1977 still left the judiciary with considerable discretion.[160] Civil Procedure Rules made under the Supreme Court Act 1981 provide that any applicant for judicial review should have a 'sufficient interest' in the matter to which the application relates.[161] No test or formula is provided as to how the court should determine the sufficiency of interest.[162]

In the US, citizens bringing suit over environmental laws in federal court must satisfy a three part test to survive a standing challenge: 'injury in fact' (concrete, particularised injury that is actual or imminent, not conjectural), causation (causal connection between the injury and the conduct complained of) and redressability (likelihood that the injury will be redressed by a favourable ruling).[163] Injury suffered by individuals may be redressed by litigation brought on their behalf by organisations representing them.[164] An organisation must allege and prove that its individual members have suffered injury and would themselves satisfy the requirements of standing, and that the general purpose of the organisation is consistent with the interest the group is pursuing in the suit.[165] 'Injury in fact' requires harm to the recreational, aesthetic or economic interests of the plaintiffs themselves, rather than harm to the environment per se,[166] and a series of Supreme Court decisions in the 1990s took a particularly narrow view of this requirement.[167] However,

[158] S 123.

[159] S 86, 311, 316.

[160] For a discussion on the reform: R Gordon, *Judicial Review and Crown Office Practice* (Sweet and Maxwell, 1999) Part 3. For changes in 2000, see the *Crown Office Digest* (2000) 382.

[161] For a discussion on cases where the standing issue has been examined: S Grosz, 'Access to Environmental Justice in Environmental Law' in D Robinson and J Dunkley (eds), *Public Interest Perspectives in Environmental Law* (Wiley Chancery, 1995) 194; C Harlow, 'Public Interest Litigation in England: The State of the Art' in J Cooper and R Dhavan (eds), *Public Interest Law* (Basil Blackwell, 1986) 107.

[162] Sufficiency of interest is described as 'a mixed question of fact and law; a question of fact and degree and the relationship between the applicant and the matter to which the application relates, having regard to all the circumstances of the case': Supreme Court Practice 1993, vol 1, para 53/1–14/11.

[163] *Lujan v Defenders of Wildlife,* 504 US 555, 112 S Ct 2130 (1992).

[164] *Sierra Club v Morton,* 405 US 727, 2 ELR 20192 (1972).

[165] For a discussion on standing in the USA, see DH Robbins, 'Public Interest Environmental Litigation in US' in Robinson and Dunkley (eds), above n 161.

[166] Eg *Sierra Club v Morton,* 405 US 727, 92 S Ct 1361 (1972).

[167] *Lujan v National Wildlife Federation,* 497 US 871, 110 SCt 3177 (1990); *Lujan v Defenders of Wildlife,* 504 US 555, 112 S Ct 2130 (1992).

evidence of a recent more liberal approach to standing may assist public interest groups to bring environmental cases in the US courts.[168]

The reasons for such restrictions on a standing test relate in one way or another to the 'flood-gates' argument.[169] A relaxed standing rule may mean a flood of applications to the courts, requiring public bodies to spend more time preparing their defences. Moreover, an increase in cases could result in further delays in determining cases. In addition, an increase in the number of applications would put pressure on the already constrained time of existing judges or require extra judges experienced to deal with environmental matters. This may detract from the quality of judgments. Lastly, there is another fear that the judiciary will engage in settling the disputes better resolved through political process.[170]

(d) Environmental courts and ADR processes

Environmental courts and alternative dispute resolution (ADR) mechanisms provide a means for facilitating public access to justice. They are institutions that have significant public participation implications. The rationale for special environment courts is that, because many environmental issues are assumed to be highly complex and technical problems, they require specialised institutions for evaluation of the claims and evidence.[171] It would also enhance the role of specialist judges in developing a consistent environmental jurisprudence.[172] However, the appropriate jurisdiction and structure of a separate environmental forum has been the subject of much debate.[173] Arguments for environmental courts based on the need for specialist judicial and technical expertise sit uncomfortably with some theories of public participation that are critical of expert, elite decision-making bodies that work to exclude lay people. Therefore, environmental courts may be more congruent with the rational elitist models of participation rather than those championing active, community involvement in decision-making. At

[168] See *Friends of the Earth Incorporated v Laidlaw Environmental Services*, 528 US 167, 120 S Ct 693 (2000). Here, the aesthetic and recreational interests of members of the plaintiff organisation were injured by the defendant's discharge of mercury into the North Tyger River in North Carolina in violation of a permit issued under the Clean Water Act. The Supreme Court held that the plaintiff had standing under the Clean Water Act's citizen suit provisions to seek the assessment of civil penalties for the violations.

[169] GR Nicol, 'Rethinking Standing' (1984) 72 *California L Rev* 68.

[170] B Hough, "'Standing' for Pressure Groups and the Representative Plaintiff" [1991] *Denning LJ* 77.

[171] R Carnwarth, 'Environmental Enforcement: The Need for a Specialist Court' [1992] *Journal of Environment & Planning Law* 798.

[172] Lord Woolf spoke of a specialist tribunal with a general responsibility for overseeing and enforcing safeguards provided for the protection of the environment. According to him, 'It would be a "one stop shop" which should lead to faster, cheaper and more effective resolution of dispute in the environmental area': 'Are the Judiciary Environmentally Myopic?' (1991) 4(1) *Journal of Environmental Law* 1.

[173] Eg, in the UK, the debate has continued on for more than 15 years: Lord Justice Carnwarth, 'Judicial Protection of the Environment: At Home and Abroad' (2004) 16 *Journal of Environmental Law* 315.

present, only a few countries have successfully established environmental courts with a liberal approach to standing.[174]

An alternative to the formality of environmental courts are informal ADR[175] measures, including negotiation, arbitration and mediation. All of these measures potentially offer less costly and less adversarial means of dispute resolution, and in theory create a decision-making milieu more accommodating of policy, ethical and other non-legal arguments. Negotiation is a process by which the parties voluntarily seek a mutually acceptable agreement to resolve their common dispute. Arbitration is an adjudicative process in which one or more arbitrators issue a judgment on the merits (which may be binding or non-binding) after an expedited, adversarial hearing in which each party has the opportunity to present evidence and arguments.

Mediation, in particular, has been praised for its potential to offer a participatory, informal and amicable setting whereby a wide variety of parties can be involved.[176] Essentially, mediation is a process under which an impartial person, the. mediator, facilitates communication between the parties to promote reconciliation or settlement.[177] Mediation has been successfully used to deal with a wide variety of environmental disputes related to local planning and development, participatory forest management, and community fisheries.[178] Drzyek sees mediation as a potential 'discursive forum' that can institutionalise the promise of deliberative democracy.[179] In contrast to the hearing of cases in courts, mediation procedures emphasise win-win solutions for all. This helps to create a stronger commitment among participants to respect decisions.

There are however some drawbacks to the effectiveness of ADR as a participatory tool. For example, regulatory agencies overseeing the ADR processes could

[174] Eg, the Land and Environmental Court of New South Wales, the Planning and Environment Court in Queensland, and the Environment Court in New Zealand. Malcolm Grant, in his report, commented that 'the performance of Australasian model is impressive in terms of assembling and deploying appropriate expertise, operating advanced case management techniques with rapid turnaround of business, incorporating systems of alternative dispute resolution (ADR) and in providing and effective mechanism for enforcement': M Grant, *Environment Court Project: Final Report* (DETR, 2000) 4–11.

[175] HT Edwards, 'Alternative Dispute Resolution: Panacea or Anathema?' (1986) 99 *Harvard L Rev* 668.

[176] See further J Harrison, 'Environmental Mediation: The Ethical and Constitutional Dimension' (1997) 9(1) *Journal of Environmental Law* 79.

[177] R Lyster, 'Should We Mediate Environmental Conflict: A Justification for Negotiated Rulemaking' (1998) 20 *Sydney L Rev* 579.

[178] D Shapiro, 'ADR and the Environment' (2001) 1(3) *Journal of ADR, Mediation and Negotiation* 16, discussing examples of environmental mediation, including two from the USA (cleaning up of Hanford Nuclear Military base and Cape Cod endangered species conservation) and the UK (Brent spar floating oil storage buoy and dead fish River Eden), and Canada (Winnipeg Bridges Dispute). In all these examples, many public interest groups, tribal groups, or low-income communities were involved in the mediation.

[179] Dryzek, above n 63, 212–4.

become less accountable if judicial oversight were removed from the dispute settlement process. Some parties might be omitted from the process, or the mediator might be unable to balance the unequal power of the disputants.[180] Even though mediation and other ADR processes are usually less expensive options to litigation, the equal participation of all groups may still be hampered by financial constraints. A corporate developer is more likely than a community group to have the resources to hire a lawyer, scientific consultant or mediator in the ADR process.[181] Secondly, because the decisions of ADR are often unenforceable in court, developers might use ADR processes for tactical reasons to waste time while pushing ahead with their project.[182] The lack of monitoring afterwards to ensure that an ADR-derived settlement is complied with can also undermine the value of these mechanisms.

(e) Legal Aid and Intervenor Funding

Public participation in environmental decision-making often hinges upon financial resources. Financial constraints are particularly acute for those seeking remedies through the courts, where the costs of hiring counsel and researching evidence can be exorbitant, in addition to the risk of an adverse costs award should the case be lost. Therefore, government provision of legal aid and intervenor funding are vital complements to participation reforms.

Most developed countries have legal aid schemes, where assistance depends on various criteria including: (i) the applicant's disposable income and capital; (ii) the subject matter and merits of the case, including the presence of public interest considerations; and (iii) the lack of other funding. Some developing countries such as India have also established legal aid schemes.[183] Through the Legal Services Authorities Act 1987, the Indian government has sought to provide free and competent legal services to the weaker sections of the society.[184] Only a few jurisdictions offer legal aid specifically for environmental litigation. In Australia, for instance, the New South Wales government offers legal aid for public interest environmental litigation.[185] In Britain, the Legal Services Commission provides

[180] J Harrison, 'Environmental Mediation: The Ethical and Constitutional Dimension' (1997) 9(1) *Journal of Environmental Law* 85.

[181] M Doyle, *Advising on ADR: The Essential Guide to Appropriate Dispute Resolution* (Advice Service Alliance, 2000).

[182] *Ibid.*

[183] For the history of legal aid in India, see S Singh, *Legal Aid: Human Rights to Equality* (Deep and Deep, 1996); SL Whitson, '"Neither Fish, Nor Flesh, Nor Good Red Herring" *Lok Adalats:* An Experiment in Informal Dispute Resolution in India' (1992) 15 *Hastings International and Comparative Law Rev* 391.

[184] The Act establishes a National Legal Aid Fund (ss 15–17), and specifically targets legal aid to scheduled castes and tribes and persons of particular social placement (s 12).

[185] Legal Aid Commission Act 1979 (NSW) s 47l; see B Boer, 'Legal Aid in Environmental Disputes' (1986) 3(1) *Environmental & Planning LJ* 22.

legal aid that can also extend to environmental cases.[186] In both jurisdictions, if the case is lost, legal aid offers some measures of protection against adverse costs awards.

As a system, legal aid can be criticised for its bias towards expensive, court-based solutions. Under most legal aid schemes, where claims vastly exceed available funds, it is difficult to target resources to the priority areas.[187] Often, legal aid does not cover the whole cost of the litigation and fails to attract experienced lawyers to take on environmental cases.[188] Moreover, almost all legal aid schemes have some form of means testing, which may arbitrarily exclude certain deserving sections of the community. Most fundamentally, legal aid is not particularly effective as an instrument for systemic social change: it does challenge the basic cost and accessibility of the judicial system.

Intervenor or participant funding also aims to increase public participation in judicial and administrative processes, such as EIA procedures. It provides funds to people who otherwise could not afford the necessary legal or expert consultant fees and who have no alternative funding sources. Canada has pioneered the intervenor funding model,[189] at both a provincial level with Ontario's Intervenor Funding Project Act 1988 and federally through the Canadian Environmental Assessment Act 1992. These schemes channel public funds to individuals, NGOs or Aboriginal organisations seeking to contribute to environmental assessments.[190] However, their budget is limited and those eligible for participant funding are parties with a direct local interest, community knowledge or Aboriginal traditional knowledge, or expert information relevant to the likely environmental effects of the project.[191] The Canadian Environmental Assessment Act (CEEA) has designated eight distinct areas to which participant funding may apply, including professional fees and the purchase of information materials.[192] The CEEA gives higher priority to measures increasing local participation and the dissemination of third-party expertise.[193] In some jurisdictions including Canada, intervenor funding and concomitant environmental legal aid

[186] J Dunkley, 'Legal Aid Rules for Environmental Cases', *ELFline*, 10 Jan 2004, available at www.elflaw.org/news/showarticle.php?action=display&id=36&type=elfline.

[187] For criticisms RK Gordon and JM Lindsay, 'Law and the Poor in Rural India: The Prospects for Legal Aid' (1990) 5 *American University Journal of International Law and Policy* 658.

[188] MI Jeffrey, 'Intervenor Funding as Key to Effective Citizen Participation in Environmental Decision-Making' (2002) 19 *Arizona Journal of International and Comparative Law* 643.

[189] This innovative legislation was repealed in 1996.

[190] AR Lucas, 'Canadian Participatory Rights in Energy Resource Development: The Bridges to Empowerment?' (2004) 24 *Journal of Land Resources & Environmental Law* 195, 200.

[191] Canadian Environmental Assessment Agency (CEAA), *Canadian Environmental Assessment Act, Participant Funding Program* (CEAA, Apr 2004); Jeffrey, above n 188, 674–5.

[192] *Guide on Participant Funding Program* (Apr 2004) 11, available at www.ceaa-acee.gc.ca/012/013/Participant-Funding_e.pdf.

[193] *Ibid.*

programmes have been drastically slashed or withdrawn altogether owing to government fiscal constraints.[194] Both initiatives are very sensitive to fluctuations in fiscal policy.

F. Conclusion: Constraints to Public Participation and Future Reforms

The actual practice of public participation in environmental decision-making often differs markedly from theoretical models. The legal provision of opportunities for participation in environmental decision-making does not itself ensure that participation will occur or be meaningful. There are numerous barriers to effective public participation.

For a start, the classical vision of an Aristoleian-style deliberative democracy has been criticised as unrealistic in contemporary mass societies.[195] Collective decisions may reflect conformity rather than genuine unanimity. Janis argues that groups of people who deliberate together 'tend to maintain esprit de corps by unconsciously developing a number of shared illusions and related norms that interfere with critical thinking and reality testing'.[196] Another concern is that individuals or groups do not have an equal chance to use participation reforms. If the best arguments are to prevail, participants must have an equal ability to participate. This is rarely, if ever, true. Marxist theory posits that the ability to participate in policy-making is closely tied to one's economic and political power.[197] Feminist theory also shows that participation is tied to gender; for instance, Agarwal shows that the exclusion of women from public institutions is a widespread problem in many countries.[198] The environmental movement itself has been criticised for its social elitism, supposedly dominated by the better educated and wealthier segments of society with little representation from blue-collar workers or the poorest.[199] It is no coincidence that many of the most polluted and unattractive places to live are occupied by the most disadvantaged groups of society, victims of the NIMBY ('not in my backyard') attitude and power of privileged classes.[200] Thus, many of the benefits from increased opportunities in environmental policy-making may, without additional corrective action, accrue to those who already

[194] Eg R Lindgren, 'Harris Government Kills Intervenor Funding Law', *Intervenor* Mar/Apr 1996 (describing cuts to Ontario's intervenor funding regime).

[195] J Elster, *Sour Grapes: Studies in the Subversion of Rationality* (Cambridge UP, 1983) 35–42.

[196] I Janis, *Groupthink* (Houghton Miffin, 1982) 35.

[197] See N Poulantzas, *State, Power, Socialism* (New Left Books, 1978).

[198] Eg B Agarwal, *A Field of One's Own: Gender and Land Rights in South Asia* (Cambridge UP, 1994).

[199] DE Morrison and RE Dunlop, 'Environmentalism and Elitism: A Conceptual and Empirical Analysis' (1986) 10 *Environmental Management* 581.

[200] RD Bullard, *Dumping in Dixie: Race, Class, and Environmental Quality* (Westview Press, 1999).

enjoy considerable advantage in society. Consequently, strategies to promote public participation should be linked to a broader strategy of social change.[201]

The notion that *what* is to be represented in decision-making has priority over *who* is to do the representing has been criticised by post-colonial theorists who ascribe pre-eminence to questions of identity such as race, gender and ethnicity.[202] Rationalist conceptions of discussion may distort and constrict both what is counted as legitimate speech and who is regarded as qualified to be a speaker. When Spivak asks, 'Can the subaltern speak?', she raises the question whether oppressed minorities are able truly to represent and speak for themselves when they are constituted as subjects only through the positions that have been permitted by their colonisers.[203] Their voice, argues Spivak, is invariably modulated through some colonising discourse or narrative. There is also the enduring problem of how to give a voice to nature per se, a problem first raised by Stone in his polemic on 'Should Trees Have Standing?'.[204] Since Western deliberative norms, argues Young, are dominant and agnostic, different 'voices' and styles of communication need to be recognised and accorded equal legitimacy in policy-making processes.[205] The problems of cross-cultural dialogue and representation of minority interests most obviously occurs in relation to Aboriginal peoples. The Berger Inquiry of the 1970s into a proposed natural gas pipeline in Canada is a rare example of a participation process sensitive to these concerns.[206] The case for a politics of identity thus provides a crucial supplement to the communicative politics of ideas.

Many deficiencies with public participation can be traced to flaws in the enabling legal and institutional frameworks. For example, the terms of reference of an EIA or an environmental inquiry may be drafted narrowly by authorities to exclude certain contentious issues. More seriously, participation exercises can be a charade, to legitimate government policies already approved. For example, during the famous environmental inquiry into the Ranger uranium mine in Australia, the federal government was surreptitiously searching for potential buyers of uranium from the would-be mine.[207] If inputs from people are not integrated into final decisions, ultimately people will become disillusioned with the process as a whole, harming the quality of environmental decisions and of the environment itself.

[201] K Graham, *The Battle for Democracy* (Wheatsheaf Books, 1986) 150.

[202] S Benhabib (ed), *Democracy and Difference: Contesting the Boundaries of the Political* (Princeton UP, 1996).

[203] GC Spivak, 'Can the Subaltern Speak?' in P Williams and L Chrisman (eds), *Colonial Discourse and Post-colonial Theory* (Harvester Wheatsheaf, 1994) 66, 103.

[204] C Stone, 'Should Trees Have Standing?' (1972) 45 *Southern California L Rev* 450.

[205] I Young, *Justice and the Politics of Difference* (Princeton UP, 1990).

[206] TR Berger, *Northern Frontier, Northern Homeland: The Report of the Mackenzie Valley Pipeline Inquiry* (Minister of Supply and Services, 1978).

[207] Richardson and Boer, above n 115.

The costs and procedural technicalities of participation procedures are a related concern. Excessively technical and bureaucratic procedures for public involvement can be a major hurdle for fruitful consultation. Complex, encyclopaedic-size EIA reports, for instance, tend to hinder rather than facilitate public scrutiny of proposed developments. Lack of technical support and difficulties in gaining access to clear information can diminish the public's ability to provide a meaningful voice in decisions. There are also financial costs of widening public participation in decision-making. These are costs to the participants themselves (eg, gaining access to information, preparing submissions, attending hearings and litigating), costs to governments faced with slower and more complex decision-making, and costs to developers concerned about stalled investments. The most expensive participation institution is the public environmental inquiry.[208] Access to the courts is also prohibitively expensive for most individuals, and therefore public interest litigation is unlikely in the absence of generous state legal aid and intervenor funding schemes.

One way to overcome some of these barriers would be to shift the onus from people to governments to initiate and ensure participation. Agencies should be obliged to initiate consultation with persons or organisations identified by some fair means as having a stake in a proposed decision. This already occurs to a limited extent in some environmental legislation.[209] Further, governments should establish public participation watchdogs, to monitor and verify that environmental decision-making processes are in fact transparent, participatory and accountable. The creation in Canada and New Zealand of environmental ombudsman-type positions, answerable to parliament, illustrates this approach.[210] Negotiation and real power-sharing processes should also be more widely used, as already demonstrated by Canada's comprehensive land claims agreements negotiated with Aboriginal peoples.[211] These are only a few of many possible reforms.[212]

For the long term, the theory and practice of public participation in environmental law need to pay more attention to the hollowing out of the state, as more and more public assets are privatised, policy functions delegated to the market and other deregulation reforms sweep the world. To focus on participation 'in the state' may become less relevant when market institutions increasingly call the tune. We need to consider how corporate governance, financial institutions and

[208] *Ibid*, 101.

[209] Eg New Zealand's Fisheries Act 1996, s 12, requires the Minister to initiate consultations with certain groups including Maori when making resource management plans.

[210] Canada has a Commissioner of the Environment and Sustainable Development, www.oag-bvg.gc.ca; and New Zealand a Parliamentary Commissioner for the Environment, www.pce.govt.nz.

[211] BJ Richardson, D Craig and BW Boer, *Regional Agreements for Indigenous Lands and Cultures in Canada* (Australian National University, 1995).

[212] For further examples, see WM Lafferty and J Meadowcroft (eds), *Democracy and the Environment: Problems and Prospects* (Edward Elgar, 1996).

other features of modern markets can be made more transparent and open to participation and control by civil society. The values we hold as consumers participating in markets are arguably quite different from the values we would express as citizens participating in political processes.[213]

The encroachment of capitalist market systems into nearly all spheres of life poses a related, very serious challenge. Global capitalism has eroded the normative-generating capacities of civil society. Apathy over social values and public policy is an endemic feature of politics today. We live in a world of more information but less meaning. This is an abstract world Baudrillard characterises as 'hyper-reality', where a decentralised consumer society floods us with images and information but little normative guidance.[214] The moral indeterminacy and nihilism of our so-called 'post-modern' consumer society may emasculate attempts to motivate citizens to participate in their public governance.

[213] M Sagoff, 'Economic Theory and Environmental Law' (1991) 79 *Michigan L Rev* 1393.

[214] J Baudrillard, 'The Hyper-realism of Simulation' in C Harrison and P Wood (eds), *Art in Theory 1900–1990: An Anthology of Changing Ideas* (Blackwell, 1993) 1043.

7

Indigenous Peoples, Law and the Environment

BENJAMIN J. RICHARDSON* AND DONNA CRAIG**

A. Introduction

Sustainable development and environmental law are often understood as Western concepts and institutions. But, in fact, the oldest examples of environmentally sustainable cultures are found among indigenous peoples. Lacking the myth of superabundance, aboriginal peoples traditionally saw themselves as part of the community of nature, and were aware that persistent violation of its ecological functions would inevitably reverberate and harm their own culture.[1] Their customary laws and traditions helped ensure that they lived by the laws of nature.

Indigenous peoples are not only relevant to the general goal of sustainable development and environmental protection, but they themselves embody a culture and way of life that deserves to be sustained. Sustainability is not just about how we manage plants, animals and ecosystems, but extends to sustaining the myriad of human cultures.[2] Indigenous peoples are believed to comprise about three-quarters of the world's cultural diversity, based on indicators of language.[3] It would seem odd to be preoccupied with sustaining biological diversity but not

* Professor, Osgoode Hall Law School, York University.
** Professor, Macquarie University and Charles Darwin University.

[1] See D Craig, 'Implications of Indigenous Rights and Customary Laws on the Development of Environmental Law for Sustainable Development' in L Sun and L Kurukulasuriya (eds), *UNEP's New Way Forward: Environmental Law and Sustainable Development* (UNEP, 1995); GA Klee (ed), *World Systems of Traditional Resource Management* (VH Winston and Sons, 1980); A Durning, *Guardians of the Land: Indigenous Peoples and the Health of the Earth* (Worldwatch Institute, 1992).

[2] For instance, the IUCN's environmental strategies have increasingly emphasised the social and cultural aspects of sustainability: World Conseravtion Union (IUCN), *Caring for the Earth: A Strategy for Sustainable Living* (IUCN, 1990).

[3] DA Posey, 'Culture and Nature: The Inextricable Link' in UNEP, *Cultural and Spiritual Values of Biodiversity* (UNEP, 2000) 1, 3 (estimating that 5,000 or more of the world's 7,000 languages are spoken by tribal peoples).

the cultural diversity of humankind. Indigenous peoples' distinct livelihoods add considerably to the cultural wealth of humanity.

Today, in many corners of the world, resurgent indigenous communities which survived colonial policies of genocide and assimilation are pushing for a greater role in environmental management. Their quest for self-government is increasingly intertwined with demand for more voice in environmental management.[4] In numerous ways, the authority to determine use of a property's natural resources is as significant as title to the land itself. Rights to hunt, fish and harvest timber are usually crucial to the economic and cultural vitality of indigenous peoples.

Not only does the environment underpin indigenous culture; indigenous peoples often are centrally implicated in the protection of nature. They are usually physically closest to nature, and economically they are most likely to be affected by environmental and resource management policies and practices. Indigenous peoples hold extensive ecological knowledge and wisdom, emphasising food self-sufficiency and local resource conservation.[5] While cultural, demographic and technological changes have considerably altered the relationships and impacts indigenous peoples have on their surroundings, many communities continue to use the environment in a relatively benign way that can provide lessons for wider society on how to develop sustainably.

The aim of this chapter is to illuminate the environmental practices of indigenous peoples, and to assess the legal structures and relationships that have emerged to promote their involvement in contemporary environmental decision-making. The approach is to sample pertinent developments from a range of jurisdictions and regions, with some emphasis on developments in Australia, Canada, New Zealand/Aotearoa and the United States, where some of the most substantial reforms for indigenous participation in or control of environmental governance have arisen. While indigenous peoples' struggles have been tied largely to their conflicts with specific nation-states, it is important to recognise that some indigenous peoples' initiatives do not fit within the dominant statist framework of national and international law. For example, the Inuit Circumpolar Conference

[4] An extensive literature on the interaction between aboriginal law and environmental law is growing: see eg M Blumm, 'Retracing the Discovery Doctrine: Aboriginal Title, Tribal Sovereignty, and their Significance to Treaty-making and Modern Natural Resources Policy in Indian Country' (2004) 28 *Vermont L Rev* 713; E Goodman, 'Protecting Habitat for Off-Reservation Tribal Hunting and Fishing Rights: Tribal Co-Management as a Reserved Right' (2000) 30 *Environmental Law* 279; GD Meyers, 'Different Sides of the Same Coin: A Comparative View of Indian Hunting and Fishing Rights in the United States and Canada' (1991) 10 *UCLA Journal of Environmental Law & Policy* 67; D Curran and M M'Gonigle, 'Aboriginal Forestry: Community Management as Opportunity and Imperative' (1999) *37 Osgoode Hall LJ* 711.

[5] See MA Altieri and LC Merrick, 'In Situ Conservation of Crop Genetic Resources through Maintenance of Traditional Farming Systems' (1987) 41(1) Economic Botany 98; GM Morin-Labatut and S Akhtar, 'Traditional Environmental Knowledge: A Resource to Manage and Share' (1992) 4 *Development Journal of the Society for International Development* 24.

has brought together indigenous peoples from across the Arctic regions of several jurisdictions to develop common policies.[6]

B. Indigenous Sustainable Livelihoods

A central feature of nearly all indigenous peoples' cultures is their close affinity with nature. Without wishing to rehearse the lengthy debates regarding the definition of indigenous peoples—also known as aboriginal or native peoples—they tend to be understood as culturally distinct groups traditionally regarded, and self-defined, as descendants of the original inhabitants of areas to which they share a strong, often spiritual, attachment.[7] The cultural distinctiveness of indigenous peoples includes the aspects of language, social organisation, religion and spiritual values, modes of production, laws and institutions.[8] They generally share an experience of subjugation, dispossession, exclusion or discrimination, whether or not these conditions persist.[9] There are estimated to be over 300 million aboriginal peoples worldwide, dispersed over more than 70 countries.[10] In developed countries, they include the Maori of New Zealand, the Australian Aborigines, the Indians and Inuit of North America and the Sámi peoples in Scandinavia. There are also substantial indigenous communities in Latin America (eg, Ache (Paraguay), Mapuche (Chile), Miskito (Nicaragua)), Africa (eg, Batwa (central Africa), Bushmen (southern Africa)) and Asia (eg, Cordillera (the Philippines), Ami (Taiwan)).

Their legal claims are invariably tied to the cultural and economic relationships they hold with the environment. Indigenous peoples seek ownership of land and other resources traditionally utilised; control over, or at least effective participation in, resource management; and an equitable share of the benefits arising from the use of environmental resources. A United Nations (UN) report summarised that they are at one and the same time 'victims of environmental degradation and protectors of vulnerable ecosystems'.[11] Moreover, a UN workshop on Traditional Knowledge and Biological Diversity reasoned that: 'there was a direct relation

[6] Inuit Circumpolar Conference: www.inuitcircumpolar.com.

[7] See further UN's Working Group on Indigenous Peoples, *Preliminary Report on the Study of the Problem of Discrimination Against Indigenous Populations*, UN Doc E/CN.4/Sub.2/L.566 (1982).

[8] EI Daes, 'Standard-Setting Activities: Evolution of Standards Concerning the Rights of Indigenous People', UN ESCOR Sub-Commission on Prevention of Discrimination and Protection of Minorities, UN Doc E/CN.4/Sub.2/AC.4/1996/2, P 26 (1996), 69.

[9] *Ibid.*

[10] J Burger, *The Gaia Atlas of First Peoples: A Future for the Indigenous World* (Doubleday, 1990) 18–19, 180–85.

[11] UN, *Human Rights and the Environment*, Preliminary Report submitted to the Sub-Commission on Prevention of Discrimination and Protection of Minorities, UN Doc E/CN.4/Sub.2/1991/8, para 23.

between cultural diversity, linguistic diversity and biological diversity and that the quickening pace of loss of traditional knowledge was having a corresponding devastating impact on all biological diversity'.[12] One manifestation of this link is 'cultural landscapes'—natural areas that have evolved and been shaped by human use over thousands of years, and hold spiritual significance to indigenous peoples. The concept of cultural landscapes is recognised under the World Heritage Convention: New Zealand's Tongariro National Park, a sacred region to Maori, was the first cultural landscape listed under the convention for international protection.[13]

A burgeoning literature has praised the environmental knowledge and practices of indigenous peoples.[14] Posey highlights seminal features of indigenous livelihood systems as including: co-operation, concern for the well-being of future generations, local-scale self-sufficiency, and restraint in resource exploitation.[15] There is also commonly a strong spiritual base to traditional livelihood systems, and indigenous peoples often view themselves as guardians and stewards of nature.[16] Knowledge of flora and fauna and their uses may be transferred through elders, rituals, initiation and story telling. Thus, a 1997 study by the World Conservation Union's (IUCN) Inter-Commission Task Force on Indigenous Peoples declared that 'they are the sole guardian of vast habitats critical to modern societies . . . [and] their ecological knowledge is an asset of incalculable value'.[17] But while these and like studies illuminate general traits of aboriginal societies relevant to sustainability, they tend to be less helpful in guiding decision-making in specific communities or particular environmental contexts. Such highly essentialised depictions of indigenous cultures may also problematically equate cultural change with loss.

Indigenous knowledge is not simply a relic of ancient hunter-gatherer societies, but continues to be relevant and adapted to contemporary resource management challenges.[18] For example, Aborigines' traditional fire management techniques

[12] This was noted in the Workshop on Traditional Knowledge and Biological Diversity, *Report of the Workshop,* UNEP/CBD/TKBD/1/3 (1997) 2.

[13] S Forbes, '*Tongariro National Park World Heritage Cultural List: He Koha Tapu—A Sacred Gift*' (Government of New Zealand, 1993).

[14] See D Brokensha, DM Warren and O Werner, *Indigenous Knowledge Systems and Development* (UP of America, 1980); JD Hughes, *American Indian Ecology* (Texas Western Press, 1983); H Brody, *Maps and Dreams: Indians and the British Columbia Frontier* (Douglas and McIntyre, 1988); B DeWalt, 'Using Indigenous Knowledge to Improve Agricultural and Natural Resource Management' (1994) 53 *Human Organization* 123.

[15] Posey, above n 3, 4; see also F Berkes, 'Traditional Ecological Knowledge in Perspective' in JT Inglis (ed), *Traditional Ecological Knowledge: Concepts and Cases* (International Development Research Centre, 1993) 1, 4; RE Johannes (ed), *Traditional Ecological Knowledge: A Collection of Essays.*(IUCN, 1989).

[16] *Ibid.*

[17] IUCN Inter-Commission Task Force on Indigenous Peoples, *Indigenous Peoples and Sustainability: Cases and Actions* (IUCN, 1997) 35.

[18] AL Booth and HM Jacobs, 'Ties That Bind: Native American Beliefs as a Foundation for Environmental Consciousness' (1990) 12 *Environmental Ethics* 27.

have been reintroduced in some outback national parks in Australia to restore biological diversity that co-evolved in response to periodic burning of the spinifex landscapes.[19] In the Amazon, Indian tribes continue to practise traditional and sustainable uses of forest resources.[20] The Ye'kuana people of the Venezuelan Amazon fashion plants into building materials, baskets, kitchenware and other household effects.[21] Many indigenous knowledge systems are rooted in traditional agricultural production, such as the techniques for the farming of maize in central Chiapas, Mexico,[22] and the production of potatoes among the Boliche people of Ecuador's highlands.[23] For African hunter-gather communities, harvesting may be tempered by declarations of closed and superstitious beliefs such as animal totems and taboo species.[24] For example, Ghana's Ashanti people treat their lakes as sacred, restricting fishing and waste deposition.[25] Kenya's Bukusu protect wetlands for their role in holding cultural rites such as male circumcision ceremonies.[26] These and other customary practices may be based on peer-group pressure, social custom, and can oscillate to harder legal norms depending on environmental conditions and resource scarcity.

Though there is clearly a strong nexus between nature and indigenous culture,[27] commentators sometimes romanticise about that 'nexus' in a way that is ultimately unhelpful to understanding the complex relationships between aboriginal peoples and their environment.[28] For instance, because they are often seen as environmental guardians, it is reasoned 'commercial consumption, exploitation of natural resources, and notions of enrichment are not part of indigenous cultures'.[29] While indigenous peoples' rights to self-determination should not be crudely dependent upon some functional relevance to modern environmental

[19] R Kimber, 'Black Lightning: Aborigines and Fire in Central Australia and the Western Desert' (1983) 18 *Archaeology in Oceania* 38.

[20] See eg DA Posey, 'Indigenous Management of Tropical Forest Ecosystems: The Case of the Kayapó Indians of the Brazilian Amazon' (1985) 3 *Agroforestry Systems* 189.

[21] N Arvelo-Jiménez, 'The Use of Natural Resources by the Ye'kuana People of Amazonia (Venezuela)' in IUCN, above n 17, 266, 271–2.

[22] MR Bellon and SB Brush, 'Keepers of Maize in Chiapas, Mexico' (1994) 48(2) *Economic Botany* 196.

[23] A Benzing, 'Andean Potato Peasants are Seed Bankers (1989) 5(4) *ILEIA Newsletter* 12.

[24] CK Omari, 'Traditional African Land Ethics' in JR Engel and JG Engel (eds), *Ethics of Environment and Development: Global Challenge, International Response* (U Arizona Press, 1990) 167, 169.

[25] S Appiah-Opoku and B Hyma, 'Indigenous Institutions and Resource Management in Ghana', *Indigenous Knowledge and Development Monitor* Nov 1999, 1, 3.

[26] RW Kareri, 'The Sociological and Economic Values of Kenya's Wetlands' in SA Crafter *et al* (eds), *Wetlands of Kenya: Proceedings of a Seminar an Wetlands of Kenya* (IUCN, 1992) 99, 102.

[27] See further RV Aruradha, 'In Search of Knowledge and Resources: Who Sows, Who Reaps?' (1997) 6 *Review of European Community and International Environmental Law* 263.

[28] Eg AT Durning, *Guardians of the Land: Indigenous Peoples and the Health of the Earth* (Worldwater Institute, 1992).

[29] JP Kastrup, 'The Internationalization of Indigenous Rights from the Environmental and Human Rights Perspective' (1997) 32 *Texas International LJ* 97, 114.

management, it should be acknowledged that not all indigenous lifestyles are always compatible with contemporary environmental challenges.[30]

It would seem naïve to construe all traditional indigenous cultures as reflecting some kind of golden age, devoid of environmental degradation.[31] The environmental practices of indigenous peoples are diverse and we should be cautious of nostalgic generalisations. Notably, their environmental credentials have been questioned on the basis of historical evidence of ecological transformation of areas they traditionally inhabited,[32] and contemporary environmental pressures stemming from modern technologies and population change.[33] For example, Alaskan natives have been implicated in the degradation of their forest resources.[34] Economic and social changes have severely disturbed many traditional, local resource management systems through the expropriation of land, displacement of communities and incorporation of subsistence economies into capitalist markets. John Borrows argues that recent environmental problems associated with indigenous peoples have arisen largely because they 'themselves have become colonized' and come to perpetuate the environmentally destructive habits of the dominant non-aboriginal society.[35] The integrity and relevance of indigenous communities' environmental values is affected when their members live increasingly in urban areas outside tribal structures and their traditional, subsistence economy. Thus, because indigenous self-determination and environmental protection may not always be mutually reinforcing, institutions are needed to reconcile aboriginal rights with overarching collective responsibilities for environmental protection to ensure development is sustainable.

But often a greater threat to the traditional territories of indigenous peoples is external development pressures. All too often indigenous peoples' environmental needs have been sacrificed for the development greed of others. Presently, the most serious assaults are occurring in Latin America, where indigenous territories

[30] Eg, hunting can conflict with nature conservation policies: M Colchester, *Salvaging Nature: Indigenous Peoples, Protected Areas and Biodiversity Conservation* (World Rainforest Movement, 1994); JS Akama, 'The Evolution of Wildlife Conservation Policies in Kenya' (1998) 15 *Journal of Third World Studies* 103.

[31] LM Shields, 'Are Conservation Goals and Aboriginal Rights Incompatible?' (2000) 10 *Journal of Environmental Law & Practice* 187.

[32] See T Flannery, *The Future Eaters* (Reed Books, 1995); T Flannery, *The Eternal Frontier* (Atlantic Monthly Press, 2001); J Diamond, *The Rise and Fall of the Third Chimpanzee* (Vintage, 1992); R Edgerton, *Sick Societies: Challenging The Myth of Primitive Harmony* (Maxwell MacMillan, 1992); KH Redford and AM Stearman, 'Forest-Dwelling Native Amazonians and the Conservation of Biodiversity: Interests in Common or in Collision?' (1993) 7(2) *Conservation Biology* 248.

[33] See eg SW Lawry, 'Tenure Policy Toward Common Property Natural Resources in Sub-Saharan Africa' (1990) 30(2) *Natural Resources Policy* 403.

[34] F Cassidy and N Dale, *After Native Claims: The Implications of Comprehensive Claims Settlements for Natural Resources in British Columbia* (Oolichan Books, 1988) 104–7.

[35] J Borrows, 'Living between Water and Rocks: First Nations, Environmental Planning and Democracy' (1997) 47(4) *U Toronto LJ* 417, 424.

are under multiple pressures from commercial agribusiness, mining, plantation forestry, industrial logging, oil and gas pipelines and government-sponsored resettlement of landless peasants.[36]

One of the most incendiary points of conflict has been mining.[37] When governments first set aside reserves for aboriginal peoples in Australia, Canada and other colonised lands, they often attempted to select land believed to contain no valuable minerals. In spite of this conscious effort to withhold the benefits of rich natural resources, minerals, oil and natural gas have been discovered on reserve lands. Often indigenous peoples have fiercely resisted mining, especially when their living areas, hunting grounds or religious sites are affected. In recent years indigenous peoples in Guatemala and Honduras have battled against transnational mining companies working in cohort with governments unsympathetic to native land rights.[38] But in some other cases mining has been welcomed. For example, a 1991 public inquiry into mining on aboriginal traditional lands in a conservation zone in northern Australia found:

> The Jawoyn do not oppose mining per se. . . . A number of Jawoyn people are in favour of mining . . . They do not consider [the affected lands] as significant culturally or religiously, although they express concerns about disturbance to certain sites outside the Zone. These pro-mining Jawoyn people appear to be motivated by a desire for personal and community advancement in a context of limited alternative employment opportunities and welfare dependency.[39]

Dams have been another ubiquitous threat to indigenous peoples worldwide. Notorious examples include the Quebec government's damming of rivers following into James Bay[40] and the Indian government's Narmada River dam.[41] The flooding of traditional hunting grounds and the physical displacement of whole communities were a high price to pay in the name of national economic development in both cases. According to the World Dams Commission, large dams in India displaced between 16 and 38 million people from 1950 to 1990

[36] Arvelo-Jiménez, above n 21, 266; VC Arthaud, 'Environmental Destruction in the Amazon' (1994) 7 *Georgetown International Environmental L Rev* 195, 201ff.

[37] See L Starke (ed), *Breaking New Ground: Mining, Minerals, and Sustainable Development. The Report of the MMSD Project* (Earthscan, 2002); RT Libby, *Hawke's Law: The Politics of Mining and Aboriginal Land Rights in Austrailia* (U Western Australia Press, 1989).

[38] S Cuffe, *Global Actors, Mining and Community-Based Resistance in Honduras and Guatemala* (Rights Action, 2005).

[39] Resource Assessment Commission, *Kakadu Conservation Zone Inquiry: Final Report* (AGPS, 1991). Indigenous organizations in the Canadian North have also welcomed and participated in numerous mining, oil and gas ventures: eg R Boychuk, 'The Road from Bathurst Inlet' 124(2) *Canadian Geographic* 40; Inuvialuit Corporate Group, *Annual Report 2002* (Inuvialuit Regional Corporation, 2003).

[40] R Niezen, 'Power and Dignity: The Social Consequences of Hydro-electric Development for the James Bay Cree' (1993) 30 *Canadian Review Sociology & Anthropology* 510.

[41] T Nachowitz, 'Repression in the Narmada Valley, India' (1988) 12(3) *Cultural Survival* 23; C Alvares and R Billorey, *Damming the Narmada: India's Greatest Planned Environmental Disaster* (Third World Network, 1988).

and about 40 per cent of those displaced were tribal people.[42] Many other people, while not physically displaced, experience severe disruption to their traditional livelihoods. For instance, the Urrá 1 dam on the Upper Sinú River in Colombia physically displaced 12,000 people but also adversely affected more than 60,000 fishermen.[43] The World Dams Commission also cautions that dams tend to have a wide range of more subtle adverse effects associated with the increased exposure of indigenous peoples to the national economy, and thus to market forces beyond their control.[44]

Dams and mines are only some of the most obvious threats to indigenous livelihoods. Commercial forestry operations also frequently threaten traditional knowledge and local communities.[45] Apart from direct logging of their territories, commercial forestry and government policies often give little recognition to non-timber forest values and non-domesticated species, to the detriment of indigenous peoples.[46] Even the creation of nature conservation parks can hurt indigenous peoples, by removing them from their traditional hunting and foraging grounds.[47] Government regulation of natural resources management too frequently ignores or displaces customary environmental management traditions, yet often without offering a viable alternative owing to institutional deficiencies in distant central state regulation.[48]

Recently, the long-range environmental impacts of 'dominant' societies upon indigenous peoples, especially toxic contamination in the Arctic food chain, have become a cause for great concern.[49] Such problems really illustrate the cruel irony of indigenous peoples' situation: not only are those closest to nature the worst affected by environmental degradation, but Western societies impose environmental harms on indigenous societies from a great distance away. In the case of toxic contamination these effects are even worse on indigenous peoples than on people in the industrialised areas where the toxins are emitted.

The following sections canvass the legal standards and rights developed in international and domestic law pertaining to indigenous peoples and their environments. Legal rights and institutions are important, because most commentators

[42] World Dams Commission (WDC), *Dams and Development* (WDC, 2000) 104, 110.

[43] *Ibid*, 105.

[44] *Ibid*, 100.

[45] P Utting, *Trees, People and Power. Social Dimensions of Deforestation and Forest Protection in Central America* (Earthscan, 1993).

[46] UN Food and Agriculture Organization (FAO), *Non-wood Forest Products for Rural Income and Sustainable Forestry* (FAO, 1995).

[47] See examples detailed in World Rainforest Movement (WRM), *Protected Areas: Protected Against Whom?* (WRM, Jan 2004); E Kemf (ed), *Indigenous Peoples and Protected Areas. The Law of Mother Earth* (Earthscan, 1993).

[48] For a perspicacious study on these themes in Pakistan, see A Bilal, H Haque and P Moore, *Customary Laws: Governing Natural Resource Management in the Northern Areas* (IUCN Law Programme, 2003).

[49] DL Brown, 'Toxic-tainted Arctic Animals Passing Poisons on to Inuit', *Seattle Times*, 22 May 2001, 7.

agree that indigenous communities are more likely to continue environmentally sustainable practices and to maintain their cultural integrity when they enjoy territorial security and autonomy.[50]

C. The International Dimension of Indigenous Peoples' Environmental Rights

1. General International Law Developments

International law has become increasingly influential in shaping legal standards for indigenous peoples, particularly in demanding greater 'state accountability for its management of aboriginal affairs'.[51] The emergence of indigenous peoples as a subject of international law, and the concomitant acknowledgement of their land, environmental and cultural rights, has helped to attenuate the old absolutist notions of state sovereignty inimical to a resuscitation of the indigenous polity.[52]

The first treaty to address the plight of indigenous peoples was the International Labour Organisation (ILO) Convention 107 of 1957,[53] which 'gave indigenous peoples a foothold in the international system through the conceptual and institutional medium of human rights'.[54] Eventually condemned for its assimilationist philosophy, the 1957 treaty was superseded by the ILO's 1989 Convention Concerning Indigenous and Tribal Peoples in Independent Countries.[55] During the 1990s, a UN working group circulated a draft Declaration on the Rights of Indigenous Peoples,[56] which purported to codify and develop the international law of human rights for indigenous peoples, stressing political rights to self-determination.[57] In 2002 the UN created a Permanent Forum on

[50] JB Alcorn, 'Noble Savage or Noble State? Northern Myths and Southern Realities in Biodiversity Conservation' (1994) 2(3) *Ethnoecologica* 7; Posey, above n 3.

[51] PG McHugh, *Aboriginal Societies and the Common Law. A History of Sovereignty, Status and Self-Determination* (Oxford UP, 2005) 289.

[52] See generally SJ Anaya, 'Divergent Discourses about International Law, Indigenous Peoples, and Rights Over Lands and Natural Resources: Toward a Realist Trend' (2005) 16(2) *Colorado Journal of International Law and Policy* 237; WJ van der Wolf, 'Indigenous Peoples Rights in International Law' (1999) 3 *Global Journal of Human Rights Law* 45.

[53] International Labour Organisation Convention concerning the Protection and Integration of Indigenous and Other Tribal and Semi-Tribal Populations in Independent Countries, No 107 (1957) 328 UNTS 247.

[54] McHugh, above n 51, 298.

[55] ILO Convention No 169 1989, 28 ILM 1382; see further RL Brash, 'An Advocate's Guide to the Convention on Indigenous and Tribal Peoples' (1990) 15 *Oklahoma L Rev* 209.

[56] UN Doc E/CN4/Sub2/1994/2/Add1 ('UN Draft Declaration').

[57] For an introduction, see CA Gourd, 'Making a Name for Ourselves: The United Nations Draft Statement on the Rights of Indigenous Peoples' (1999) 7(1) *Tulsa Journal of Comparative and International Law* 121.

Indigenous Issues to provide a means for more direct consultation.[58] Further international statements on the rights of indigenous peoples are under preparation. Regionally, for instance, the Inter-American Commission on Human Rights in 1995 drafted an Inter-American Declaration on the Rights of Indigenous Peoples.[59] As a result of these developments, indigenous peoples are increasingly viewed as separate from the states they reside in, with their own voice in the international decision-making process.

Both the revised ILO Convention and the UN Draft Declaration address rights to territory and natural resources. The Declaration proclaims indigenous peoples' rights to own, develop and control the use of their traditional lands;[60] the right to restitution of traditional lands unlawfully confiscated or damaged;[61] and the need for indigenous peoples' consent for the approval of any development project affecting their lands.[62] The Declaration has failed so far to attract sufficient interest from governments to achieve endorsement in the UN General Assembly. The ILO Convention requests states parties to 'respect the special importance for the cultures and spiritual values of the peoples concerned of their relationship with the lands or territories . . . and in particular the collective aspects of this relationship'.[63] It requires states to respect indigenous 'rights of ownership and possession' of the lands 'which they traditionally occupy', as well as those to 'which they have traditionally had access for their subsistence and traditional activities'.[64] In order to secure those rights, Article 15(1) declares that indigenous peoples have the right to 'participate in the use, management and conservation' of their natural resources. Although governments' obligations under the ILO Convention are potentially far-reaching, the effectiveness of the Convention can be questioned because fewer than 20 states have ratified it.[65] Moreover, ratification of the ILO Convention (like other treaties) does not guarantee that it will be properly implemented. For instance, although in 1991 Bolivia legislated to incorporate the ILO Convention into its domestic law, and amended its constitution, the government has opened up 'protected' tribal lands to foreign oil companies.[66]

But there are few international forums for hearing complaints from aggrieved indigenous persons or tribes.[67] One is the so-called '1235 procedure' established by

[58] UN, 'Establishment of a Permanent Forum on Indigenous Issues', E/RES/2000/22.

[59] Inter-American Commission on Human Rights, Draft Declaration on the Rights of Indigenous Peoples, 2 Sept 1995, OEA/Ser/L/V/II.90 Doc 9, Rev 1.

[60] UN Draft Declaration, above n 56, Art 26.

[61] *Ibid*, Art 27.

[62] *Ibid*, Art 30.

[63] ILO Convention 169, above n 55, Art 13.

[64] *Ibid*, Art 14.

[65] The ratifying states are drawn mainly from Latin America and Scandinavia, and do not include Australia, Canada or the US.

[66] L Sargent, 'The Indigenous Peoples of Bolivia's Amazon Basin Region and ILO Convention 169: Real Rights or Rhetoric' (1998) 29 *Inter-American L Rev* 451.

[67] MM de Bolívar, 'A Comparison of Protecting the Environmental Interests of Latin-American Indigenous Communities from Transnational Corporations Under International Human Rights and Environmental Law' (1998) 8(1) *Journal of Transnational Law & Policy* 105, 136–8.

the UN Economic and Social Council to investigate human rights violations, which operates under the Optional Protocol to the 1966 International Covenant on Civil and Political Rights.[68] Another procedure is available under the Inter-American human rights regime. For instance, in 2001 the Inter-American Court of Human Rights found against the Nicaraguan government, and ordered compensation, for breaching international human rights when it failed to protect the traditional lands of the Awas Tingni community by allowing a foreign company to log forests on the community's traditional lands.[69] Because the Inter-American Court held that Nicaragua's laws were ineffective in addressing lands held communally and its remedies were illusory, given the delays in demarcating and titling the lands, the Court required Nicaragua to adopt 'legislative, administrative and other measures . . . to create an effective mechanism' to carry out those activities within 15 months 'with full participation by the community'.[70] This case is far-reaching as it is the 'first legally binding decision by an international tribunal to uphold the collective land and resource rights of indigenous peoples in the face of a state's failure to do so'.[71]

2. International Environmental Law

According to one recent scholarly article on the subject, 'a fundamental change is occurring in the way indigenous peoples' rights, aspirations, and knowledge influence international environmental law'.[72] While there is certainly legal change, states remain wary of conceding indigenous rights in international environmental law, which may restrict national economic options. States have tended to confine their support to general and often vague policy statements rather than specific legal standards.

Certainly, it is now commonplace to find references to indigenous peoples in international environmental declarations, resolutions and policies.[73] The Rio Declaration on Environment and Development declared:

> indigenous people . . . have a vital role in environmental management and development because of their knowledge and traditional practices. States should recognize and duly

[68] 999 UNTS 302; see eg *Lovelace v Canada*, GAOR Supp (No. 40) (36th Session), UN Doc A4/36/40, Annex XVIII (1981); *Kitok v Sweden*, GAOR Supp (No. 40) (43rd Session), UN Doc A/43/40/197/1985 (10 Aug 1988).

[69] *Mayagna (Sumo) Awas Tingni Community v Nicaragua*, Inter-Am CHR 79(2001).

[70] *Ibid.*

[71] SJ Anaya and C Grossman, 'The Case of Awas Tingni v. Nicaragua: A New Step in the International Law of Indigenous Peoples' (2002) 19 *Arizona Journal of International and Comparative Law* (2002) 1, 2.

[72] J Firestone, J Lilley and IT de Noronha, 'Cultural Diversity, Human Rights, and the Emergence of Indigenous Peoples in International and Comparative Environmental Law' (2005) 20 *American University International Law Review* 219, 220.

[73] See BJ Richardson, 'Indigenous Peoples, International Law and Sustainability' (2001) 10(1) *Review of European Community and International Environmental Law* 1; RK Hitchcock, 'International Human Rights, the Environment and Indigenous Peoples' (1994) 5 *Colorado Journal of Environmental Law and Policy* 1.

> support their identity, culture and interests and enable their effective participation in the achievement of sustainable development.[74]

Likewise, Agenda 21 called for the empowerment of indigenous peoples through, among other means, 'recognition of their values, traditional knowledge and resource management practices' as well as 'traditional and direct dependence on renewable resources and ecosystems'; strengthening their active participation in the national formulation of policies and laws; and involving them in 'resource management and conservation strategies'.[75] The Barbados Programme of Action in 1994 was perhaps the first realisation at the global level of this post-Agenda 21 plan for indigenous peoples, with a particular focus on use and protection of their traditional environmental knowledge.[76] Ten years after Agenda 21, the international community reaffirmed these sentiments at the World Summit on Sustainable Development in Johannesburg.[77]

Among international environmental treaties, there are scattered, minor references to indigenous peoples. Under the International Convention for the Regulation of Whaling,[78] in 1989 the International Whaling Commission approved a small aboriginal subsistence whaling quota.[79] The prohibition on hunting polar bears imposed by the Agreement on Polar Bears of 1973 does not apply in relation to hunting 'by local people when using traditional methods in the exercise of their traditional rights'.[80] The Convention on Conservation of North Pacific Fur Seals of 1976 exempts indigenous groups inhabiting certain coastal areas from the ban on sealing when not using specified modern technologies.[81] Despite their seemingly positive intention, the traditional hunting method prescriptions are viewed by some indigenous peoples as patronising and discriminatory, denying them a right to technological and economic development.[82]

The Convention on Biological Diversity of 1992 (CBD) contains the most broadly based provision for advancing indigenous peoples' environmental claims.[83] Article 8(j) obliges state parties to:

[74] (1992) 31 ILM 876, Principle 22.

[75] UN Conference on Environment and Development (UNCED), *Agenda 21* (UNCED, 1993) ch 26.

[76] *Report of the Global Conference on Sustainable Development of Small Island Developing States*, Barbados, 25 Apr–6 May 1994, UN Doc A/CONF.167/9 (1994).

[77] Report of the World Summit on Sustainable Development, *Plan of Implementation* (2002) UN Doc A/CONF.199/20.

[78] (1946) 161 UNTS 72.

[79] The Commission has established a sub-committee to deal with aboriginal subsistence whaling: see NC Doubleday, 'Aboriginal Subsistence Whaling: The Right of Inuit to Hunt Whales and Implications for International Environmental Law' (1989) 17 *Denver Journal of International Law & Policy* 373.

[80] Art III(d), Agreement on Polar Bears 1973, 13 ILM 13.

[81] Art VII, Convention on Conservation of North Pacific Fur Seals 1976, 27 UST 3371.

[82] *Indigenous Peoples and Sustainability*, above n 17, 64–65.

[83] (1992), 31 ILM 818.

> respect, preserve and maintain knowledge, innovations and practices of indigenous and local communities embodying traditional lifestyles relevant for the conservation and sustainable use of biological diversity and promote their wider application with the approval and involvement of the holders of such knowledge, innovations and practices and encourage the equitable sharing of benefits arising from the utilization of such knowledge, innovations and practices.

But Article 8(j) refrains from using more specific language such as 'rights' and 'peoples', and it is quite soft, in that it leaves states tremendous discretion, using the phrases 'as far as possible and appropriate' and 'subject to its national legislation'.

Indigenous peoples and other local resource user groups have also articulated their own agenda for control and management of their lands and environment. Important statements include the Kari-Oca Declaration[84] adopted at the indigenous tribes' parallel forum to the 1992 Earth Summit, and the Charter of the Indigenous and Tribal Peoples of the Tropical Forests adopted at an international meeting in Malaysia.[85] Indigenous peoples also have campaigned for stronger international controls on long-range toxic chemicals, which have been devastating the Arctic food chain. In this respect, the recent Stockholm Convention on Persistent Organic Pollutants could be of particular benefit to the Inuit peoples of the Arctic.[86]

Policy changes have also occurred in some multilateral development banks (MDBs). The World Bank was the first to introduce a special policy for the treatment of indigenous or tribal peoples in development projects.[87] Until the 1980s, MDB practice assumed that all rural communities in developing countries were basically alike (ie, economically underdeveloped and indigent) and that consequently project designs did not need to contain special provisions for ethnically or culturally distinct populations. Setting the tone for policy changes among the MDBs in 1991 was the World Bank's Operational Directive 4.20. Its stated aim was 'to ensure that indigenous peoples do not suffer adverse effects during the development process, particularly from Bank-financed projects, and that they receive culturally compatible social and economic benefits'.[88] Despite the World Bank's progressive moves, its classification of indigenous peoples is controversial. The Directive identifies indigenous peoples according to a set of criteria that excludes individuals who migrate and adopt a different lifestyle from that of their communities.

[84] Reproduced in M Terena, 'The Kari-Oca Conference in Rio' in L van de Fliert (ed), *Indigenous Peoples and International Organisations* (Spokesman, 1994) 181.

[85] Charter of the Indigenous-Tribal Peoples of the Tropical Forests, Feb 1992, Malaysia, available at homepage of the International Alliance of the Indigenous-Tribal Peoples of the Tropical Forests, available at: www.gn.apc.org/iaip/chart/char1.html.

[86] (2001) 40 ILM 531.

[87] GA Sarfaty, 'The World Bank and the Internalization of Indigenous Rights Norms (2005) 114 *Yale LJ* 1791.

[88] World Bank, *Operational Directive (OD 4.20): Indigenous Peoples* (World Bank, 1991) 6.

3. Intellectual Property Rights and Aboriginal Culture

In addition to land- and natural resource-based claims, some indigenous peoples have turned to intellectual property (IP) law to protect their environmental knowledge and practices, and to benefit from any commercial exploitation.[89] The emergence of IP law as a new frontier of indigenous rights is perhaps best illustrated by the sweeping claim filed by the Maori to the Waitangi Tribunal for control of knowledge-based uses of New Zealand's entire panoply of indigenous flora and fauna.[90] Traditional knowledge informs indigenous environmental activities in many ways, including for medicine, foodstuffs and construction materials.[91] Native cultural and intellectual property is also being recognised for its commercial value, such as for biotechnology and popular art. But indigenous peoples remain vigilant about such uses without their consent.

The importance of consent or agreement of indigenous peoples when dealing with biodiversity within their control was reiterated by the 1992 Report of the UN Secretary General on the Intellectual Property of Indigenous Peoples.[92] The UN's Draft Declaration on the Rights of Indigenous Peoples also affirmed their right 'to special measures to control and develop their sciences, technologies, seeds, medicines, knowledge of flora and fauna, oral traditions, designs, art and performances'.[93] The Biodiversity Convention did not address how indigenous traditional knowledge would be protected, but did suggest that its application be 'with the approval and involvement of the holders of such knowledge, innovations and practice'.[94]

Standard intellectual property rights (IPRs) such as copyright, trade marks and patents are not easily adapted to indigenous knowledge.[95] They are designed to promote innovation and commercialisation of knowledge, whereas indigenous communities tend to be more interested in preserving the integrity of existing, traditional knowledge. As marketable, portable commodities, IPRs do not sit easily with indigenous knowledge tied to a specific cultural milieu.[96] The IPR requirement of authorship also poses difficulties for indigenous communities

[89] See eg T Janke, *Our Culture, Our Future: Proposals for the Recognition and Protection of Indigenous Cultural and Intellectual Property* (Michael Frankel and Co, 1997).

[90] See Waitangi Tribunal, at www.knowledge-basket.co.nz/waitangi/welcome.html.

[91] See M Gadgil, F Berkes and C Folke, 'Indigenous Knowledge for Biodiversity Conservation' (1993) 22(2/3) *Ambio* 1151; Inglis, above n 15.

[92] UN Economic and Social Council, EICN.41Sub.2/1992/30 of 6 July 1992.

[93] Above n 56, Art 29.

[94] Above n 83 Art 8(j).

[95] Canadian Department of Indian and Northern Affairs, *Intellectual Property and Aboriginal People: A Working Paper* (Department of Indian and Northern Affairs, 1999); S Patel, 'Can the Intellectual Property Rights System Serve the Interests of Indigenous Knowledge?' in S Brush and D Stabinsky (eds), *Valuing Local Knowledge* (Island Press, 1996).

[96] S Gudeman, 'Sketches, Qualms, and Other Thoughts on Intellectual Property Rights' in Brush and Stabinsky, above n 95, 103.

where traditional knowledge has evolved from generation to generation and is owned collectively.[97] Indigenous knowledge, processes and products are commonly perceived as part of an existing body of knowledge and practice and do not, consequently, qualify as 'new' in terms of the novelty criteria of IP laws. Further, the cap on the duration of some forms of IP (eg, 20 years for a patent) makes the model unsuitable for protecting indigenous knowledge indefinitely.

Currently, there are no international legal instruments that create specific IP standards tailored to indigenous knowledge or cultural practices.[98] Nationally, some governments have adopted measures to protect indigenous intellectual property, including constitutional protection (eg, Venezuela[99] and Brazil[100]) and the model law on community rights and access to biological resources drawn up by the Organisation of African Union.[101] Also, a new community-integrated IP rights model, building on the work of the UNESCO's proposed Model Provisions for the Protection of Folklore,[102] is being developed.

Supporters of IP systems argue that these rights can 'create effective incentives for innovative use of biodiversity, which in turn creates profits on which innovators can draw in negotiating benefit-sharing arrangements with the holders of traditional knowledge and biodiversity'.[103] But even if indigenous knowledge can be protected in this way, some people remain suspicious that IPR may amount to a 'new form of colonization',[104] linked to indigenous knowledge 'piracy'.[105] Existing legal protections tailored for indigenous IP may be of little value, as the recent example of Brazil suggests. A 1999 Presidential Decree created the Brazilian

[97] Some indigenous communities are reported to recognise individual or family authorship and creation rights concerning certain forms of knowledge and practice: see DA Cleveland and SC Murray, 'The World's Crop Genetic Resources and the Rights of Indigenous Farmers' (1997) 38 *Current Anthropology* 477, 483–85.

[98] See Brush and Stabinsky, above n 95; F Yamin and D Possey, 'Indigenous Peoples, Biotechnology and Intellectual Property Rights' (1997) 2(2) *Review of European Community and International Environmental Law* 141.

[99] Republic of Venezuela Constitución de 1999, Art 124.

[100] Constitution of the Federative Republic of Brazil 1988, Art 231.

[101] African Model Legislation for the Protection of Rights of Local Communities, Farmers, Breeders and for the Regulation of Access to Biological Resources of 1998, published by the Organisation of African Unity, Scientific, Technical and Research Commission.

[102] Model Provisions for National Laws on the Protection of Expressions of Folklore Against Illicit Exploitation and Other Prejudicial Actions (1982), published by the Unesco Committee of Governmental Expects on the Intellectual Property Aspects of the Protection of Expressions of Folklore; D Craig, 'Global Sustainable Development: Human Rights, Environmental Rights and Indigenous Peoples', Working Paper 2003/03 (Australian Human Rights Centre, 2003).

[103] DR Downes, 'How Intellectual Property Could Be a Tool to Protect Traditional Knowledge' (2000) 25 *Columbia Journal of Environmental Law* 253, 257; R Dobhal, 'Recognizing Biodiversity and Indigenous Knowledge System Under New Intellectual Property Regime' (1999) 76 *Current Science* 1063.

[104] D Possey and G Dutfield, *Beyond Intellectual Property: Toward Traditional Resource Rights for Indigenous Peoples and Local Communities* (International Development and Research Centre, 1996) 219.

[105] V Shiva, *Biopiracy* (Between the Lines, 1997).

Association for the Sustainable Use of Biodiversity in the Amazon (Bioamazonia) to manage the region's genetic resources on behalf of the federal government. Its bio-prospecting agreement with the Swiss multinational company has been criticised for 'its failure to obtain the permission of the indigenous Amazon people and its . . . failure to provide them with direct compensation'.[106]

D. Indigenous Environmental Governance in a National Context

1. Introduction

The increased involvement of indigenous peoples in environmental decision-making has arisen in multiple ways, including through government legislation, customary rights recognised by courts, treaties and, more recently, negotiated political settlements. International experience indicates that indigenous peoples are in a much stronger position to manage their resources when they have ownership of the land involved.[107]

This involvement of indigenous peoples in the wider environmental law system and policy-making process of the state reflects a broader shift towards a more pluralistic legal order.[108] Legal pluralism, in its simplist form, refers to 'a situation in which two or more legal systems coexists in the same social field'.[109] In reality, virtually all societies contain both formal state and informal, non-state forms of normative ordering (eg, those generated by the market and civil society).[110] Often legal pluralism is associated with reforms formally to acknowledge a separate space in state law for an alternate legal order. This already exists in Britain (eg, the separate legal system in Scotland) and Canada (a civil law system in Quebec). Several legal systems such as in Australia and the South Pacific have also sought to accommodate aboriginal customary laws in relation to family law, land tenure, criminal justice.[111]

[106] RL Scott, 'Bio-Conservation or Bio-Exploitation: An Analysis of the Active Ingredients Discovery Agreement Between the Brazilian Institution Bioamazonia and the Swiss Pharmaceutical Company Novartis' (2002) 35 *George Washington International L Rev* 977, 993.

[107] See L Burton, 'Indigenous Peoples and Environmental Policy in the Common Law Nation-States of the Pacific Rim: Sovereignty, Survival, and Sustainability' [1998] *Colorado Journal of International Environmental Law Yearbook* 136; JM Glenn and AC Drost 'Aboriginal Rights and Sustainable Development in Canada' (1999) 48 *ICLQ* 176.

[108] See generally MB Hooker, *Legal Pluralism: An Introduction To Colonial and Neo-Colonial Laws* (Clarendon Press, 1975).

[109] S Merry, 'Legal Pluralism' [1988] *Law and Society Rev* 869, 871.

[110] J Griffiths, 'What is Legal Pluralism?' (1986) 24 *Journal of Legal Pluralism* 1.

[111] Eg Australian Law Reform Commission (ALRC), *Recognition of Aboriginal Customary Law* (ALRC, 1986).

Environmental law marks another part of the legal system that is being pried open to aboriginal values, customs and practices. Sack has emphasised that legal pluralism 'is more than the acceptance of a plurality of law; it sees this plurality as a positive force to be utilised-and controlled-rather than eliminated'.[112] Similarly, the greater involvement of indigenous peoples in resource management offers possibilities to strengthen aboriginal culture and to promote sustainable development.

Nonetheless, some legal pluralist theorists would see such accommodation into the formal system of state law as potentially antagonistic to a truly pluralistic normative order because law reform of this sort perpetuates 'legal centrism'.[113] In other words, it may simply reinforce the existing hierarchy of normative ordering, with nation-state regulation at the apex. Sinha contends that this problem requires 'discovering modes of allocation of decision-making authority that would maximise the coexistence of these normative orders'.[114] In the field of environmental law, despite recent important reforms to recognise aboriginal customary law, such an allocation of decision-making authority has not occurred in most jurisdictions.

Historically, indigenous peoples secured toe-hold acknowledgement of their hunting and related subsistence activities in treaties imposed by colonial overlords. In North America, the eighteenth century treaties were negotiated to maintain peace, trade alliance and military support.[115] The Canadian Supreme Court in the *Marshall* case interpreted a 1760 treaty between Nova Scotia's Mi'kmaq people and the British Crown as guaranteeing their rights to fish for a moderate livelihood in return for their allegiance to the Crown in its war against France.[116]

As the European colonisers became more numerous and settled during the nineteenth century, treaties served primarily to obtain indigenous lands and resources. Only the better organised indigenous peoples such as New Zealand's Maori were able to negotiate reasonable terms. Their Treaty of Waitangi of 1840 provided that the Crown:

> guarantees to the Chiefs and Tribes of New Zealand . . . the full exclusive and undisturbed possession of their Lands and Estates Forests Fisheries and other properties which they may collectively or individually possess so long as it is their wish and desire to retain the same in their possession.[117]

[112] P Sack, 'Legal Pluralism: Introductory Comments' in P Sack and E Minchin (eds), *Legal Pluralism: Proceedings of the Canberra Law Workshop VII* (Australian National University, 1988) 1.

[113] W Tie, *Legal Pluralism: Toward a Multicultural Conception of Law* (Ashgate, 1999) 162, 167.

[114] SP Sinha, 'Legal Polycentricity' in H Petsersen and H Zahle (eds) *Legal Polycentricity: Consequences of Pluralism in Law* (Dartmouth, 1995) 47, 48.

[115] See LG Robertson, *Conquest by Law: How the Discovery of America Dispossessed Indigenous Peoples of their Land* (Oxford UP, 2005).

[116] *R v Marshall* [1999] 3 SCR 456; see, further, LI Rotman "'My Hovercraft Is Full of Eels': Smoking Out the Message of *R. v. Marshall*" (2000) 63 *Saskatchewan L Rev* 617.

[117] Art 2.

But the differences in cultural understandings, intentions and assumptions underpinning the treaties often made them very soon irrelevant. Notoriously, for instance, the *Wi Parata* judgement of 1877 dismissed the Treaty of Waitangi 'as a simple nullity. No body politic existed capable of making a cession of sovereignty ... So far as the proprietary rights of the natives are concerned, the so-called treaty merely affirms the rights and obligations which, *jure gentium*, vested in and devolved upon the Crown'.[118] Consequently, many disputes about treaties persist, particularly because many agreements assert the loss of lands and resources to which indigenous peoples say their forebears never consented. Modern treaty negotiations, such as the comprehensive land claims agreements in Canada, have been pursued with expectations of greater equity and a guaranteed land and natural resources base for indigenous participants.

Substantial advances in the recognition of indigenous traditional hunting and fishing rights have been made in most countries since the 1970s. These advances have come about through government legislation, court cases and new treaty negotiations. Although most reforms have arisen in those Western countries with indigenous minorities (eg, Canada and New Zealand), indigenous peoples in other regions have also benefited from reforms. The following sections survey progress, beginning with Latin America and Asia to illustrate some trends in developing countries.

2. Latin America

Since the colonial era, indigenous peoples have always been the poorest and most disadvantaged group in Latin American societies. They represent 10 per cent of the region's population.[119] Even in countries where they comprise a majority or considerable ethnic minority of the total population—as in Bolivia, Guatemala or Peru—they have been largely excluded from overall economic development, social services and legal protection.[120] The operations of international companies—like Texaco and British Petroleum in Ecuador and Colombia—have produced severe threats to the environment of the indigenous peoples. Similar problems have also arisen in the Brazilian Amazon due to the influx of gold miners, logging companies and landless peasants. But it is not a region without legal reform for indigenous peoples.

A distinctive feature of the 'Latin American model' is the constitutional law recognition in most nations of multi-ethnicity and pluriculturalism.[121] Latin American states have renewed their constitutions to acknowledge the status of

[118] *Wi Parata v Bishop of Wellington* [1877] 3 NZ Jur (OS) SC 72, 78.

[119] G Hall and H Patrinos, *Indigenous Peoples, Poverty and Human Development in Latin America: 1994–2004* (World Bank, 2005) 1.

[120] *Ibid*, 3–8.

[121] See DL Van Cott, *Indigenous Peoples and Democracy in Latin America* (St Martin's Press, 1984).

indigenous populations as distinct peoples. Their constitutions have also established norms that recognise the indigenous communal mode of land tenure, which involves jurisdiction over the management of natural resources. Thus, the Constitution of Guatemala establishes the right to cultural identity[122] and includes provisions aimed at protecting the lands of indigenous peoples.[123] The Paraguayan Constitution recognises the right of indigenous peoples to preserve and develop their ethnic identity; the right freely to apply their system of political, social, economic, cultural and religious organization, and their right to enforce customary indigenous law.[124] The Constitution of Peru inter alia allows indigenous communities' institutions to exercise judicial functions pursuant to their customary law within their territory.[125] The Bolivian Constitution contains a similar provision, and a guarantee of indigenous peoples' use and sustainable exploitation of their traditional natural resources.[126]

Other constitutional reforms, such as those in Brazil, still fail to recognise the ownership rights of indigenous peoples, although possession rights are acknowledged.[127] The Constitution also provides that 'hydric resources, including energetic potentials, may only be exploited, and mineral riches in Indian land may only be prospected and mined with the authorization of the National Congress, after hearing the communities involved, and the participation in the results of such mining shall be ensured to them, as set forth by law'.[128]

In addition to normative changes giving improved recognition of indigenous land rights, some countries have made practical progress in demarcation and titling of indigenous lands.[129] In Colombia, large areas of indigenous peoples' land have been titled as integral *resguardo* territories covering hundreds of thousands or several million hectares.[130] The Amazon's Huaorani people received from the Ecudorian government some 676,000 hectares of Amazon land in 1990, dedicated as a Huaorani ethnic reserve.[131] Government agencies and environmental scientists in the region are starting to acknowledge that large indigenous territories and communal land tenure regimes are compatible with nature conservation goals.[132]

[122] República de Guatemala Constitución de 1985 con las reforma de 1993, Art 59.
[123] *Ibid*, Art 67.
[124] Constitución de la República de Paraguay 1992, Art 63.
[125] Constitución Política del Perú de 1993, Art 149.
[126] República de Bolivia Constitución Política con Texto Acordado en 1995, Art 171.
[127] Constituição da República Federativa do Brasil 1988, Art 231(1).
[128] *Ibid*, Art 231(3).
[129] R Plant and H Soren, 'Land Titling and Indigenous Peoples', *Sustainable Development Department Technical Papers Series* (Inter-American Development Bank, 2001).
[130] P Bunyard, *The Colombian Amazon: Policies for the Protection of Its Indigenous Peoples and their Environment* (Ecological Press, 1990).
[131] JE Brady, 'The Huaorani Tribe of Ecuador: A Study in Self-Determination for Indigenous Peoples' (1997) 10 *Harvard Human Rights Journal* 302.
[132] T Walschburger, 'Delimitación y Manejo de Territorios Indígenas Ecológicamente Equilibrados en Áreas de Selva Húmeda Tropical' in M Cárdenas, HD Correa and M Gómez (eds), *Derechos Territoriales Indígenas y Ecología* (Cerec-Fundación Gaia, 1992) 261.

Sometimes, however, government legislation does not properly give effect to constitutional norms. Constitutional law provisions can be too vague and general to provide a basis for meaningful legal regulation. In several cases, national legal frameworks still rest on inappropriate Western property concepts and land-use models incongruous with indigenous concepts of territory and the spatial resource needs of indigenous livelihoods. In Peru, for example, ownership rights and title are still awarded only on land dedicated to agriculture near human settlements. But the wider indigenous territories remain the property of the state.[133] Both Peru's Law of Native Communities and the Law of *Campesino* Communities give local communities exclusive rights to use the natural resources on their lands and a certain amount of decision-making power over those resources, but they are severely constrained within the limits of their traditional use patterns.[134]

Furthermore, even laws drafted with the best intentions for indigenous peoples are not necessarily properly implemented. The rule of law often has a fragile hold in many parts of Latin America.[135] These problems derive mainly from the inefficiency and corruption of the legal system, and broader problems in establishing a politically accountable government, along with continuing anti-indigenous racism.

3. East and South Asia

A number of indigenous communities are scattered throughout East and South Asia. They tend to have been ignored or persecuted by governments in a region where there has often been little tolerance for the cultural rights of minorities. Consequently, indigenous peoples in much of Asia are still struggling for bare recognition and the most basic of rights, and thus it is somewhat premature to discuss legal reforms for their involvement in environmental decision-making in some countries in this region. Perhaps the most extensive legal protections for indigenous peoples are offered in the less developed countries of the region including Papua New Guinea, the Philippines and the South Pacific states where indigenous collective land tenures are widely recognised.[136] For instance, the Philippines Indigenous Peoples' Rights Act of 1997 establishes procedures for recognition of communal ownership of ancestral land, and about three million hectares are now held by indigenous tribes under these provisions.[137] However,

[133] RR Ortiga, 'Models for Recognizing Indigenous Land Rights in Latin America', *Biodiversity Series No 99* (World Bank, 2004) 21–2.

[134] *Ibid.*

[135] See J Méndez, G O'Donnell and P Pinheiro (eds), *The Rule of Law and the Underprivileged in Latin America* (U Notre Dame Press, 1998).

[136] T van Meijl and F von Benda-Beckmann (eds), *Property Rghts and Economic Development: Land and Natural Resources in Southeast Asia and Oceania* (Kegan Paul, 1999); RG Crocombe (ed), *Land Tenure in the Pacific.* (U South Pacific, 1994).

[137] M Colchester, *Indigenous Peoples and Communal Tenures in Asia*, in *Land Reform* (UN Food and Agricultural Organisation, 2004) 28, 38.

particularly in the case of Indonesia and Malaysia, governments have readily swept aside indigenous land rights which have hindered land resettlement, logging, dams and other 'national development priorities'.[138]

Other experiences have illustrated that mere recognition as distinctive indigenous peoples has been a substantial hurdle to overcome. For instance, Japan's Ainu people, whose territory includes parts of Hokkaido and the Kurile islands, achieved recognition by the government as a distinctive people only in the late 1990s. In 1997 the Hokkaido Former Aborigines Protection Act of 1899, which was designed to 'Japanise' the Ainu by dismantling their traditional system of communal land holdings, was abolished. It was replaced by the Law for the Promotion of the Ainu Culture and Dissemination and Advocacy for the Traditions of the Ainu and the Ainu Culture. It contains the first implicit recognition of an ethnic minority in Japan.[139] However, it offers little more than promotion of research on Ainu culture and support for preservation of some customs and traditions. It does not restore control of traditional lands to the Ainu.

Likewise, Taiwan is only just beginning to come to terms with its indigenous peoples. It established a Council of Indigenous Affairs to advise the government on policies and programmes for the country's 11 identified indigenous tribes. Most of Taiwan's relevant legislation deals with rights of education, language and marriage.[140] Most important for environmental law is Taiwan's Indigenous Peoples Reservation Land Development Management Procedure, which is part of the Mountain Slope Conservation and Utilisation Law.[141] It provides that:

> Indigenous peoples' reservation lands located within the mountain region should be taught [sic] to develop land and obtain cultivation rights, land surface rights, and lease rights. Individuals continuing to operate their cultivation and land surface rights for a period of five years are entitled to acquire gratis ownership of said land, except for land designated for special purposes.[142]

Sometimes indigenous peoples have used the courts to protect their land. In recent years, courts in Cambodia,[143] Malaysia[144] and other Asian countries have ruled in favour of indigenous land claims. But some of these victories have proved pyrrhic. After a Malaysian court ruled in favour of the Iban communities which were seeking the removal of the Borneo Paper and Pulp Company from their

[138] Eg M Colchester, *Pirates, Squatters and Poachers: The Political Ecology of Dispossession of the Native Peoples of Sarawak* (Survival International and INSAN, 1989).

[139] 'Japan and Multiculturalism' (1997) 9 *Asia-Pacific News*, available at www.hurights.or.jp/asia-pacific/no_9/no9_multi.htm.

[140] Eg Status Act for Indigenous Peoples 2001.

[141] Available at www.apc.gov.tw/en/laws/laws_detail_9.aspx.

[142] *Ibid*, s 37.

[143] Cambodia Ministry of Land Management, Urban Planning and Construction, available at www.cdc-crdb.gov.kh/cdc/ministry_landmanagement.htm.

[144] Colchester, above n 137, 37.

lands, the Sarawak state government (reacting to this legal development) passed the Land Surveyors Act 2001, which criminalised land mapping by anyone except licensed surveyors in an effort to hinder the filing of future land claims.[145]

4. Scandinavia

The Sámi people of Scandinavia enjoy some of the most extensive legal rights among indigenous minorities worldwide.[146] Historically, the Scandinavian states viewed the Sámi as nomadic and the lands used by the Sámi as ownerless. 'Immemorial' rights to reindeer herding, hunting and fishing were, however, recognised, and the Norwegian Supreme Court even found in favour of rights of Swedish Sámi to certain Norwegian grazing areas;[147] the Swedish Supreme Court reciprocated in 1981.[148]

Since then, Norway has become the first country to ratify ILO Convention No 169. Norway, Sweden and Finland each have a Sámi parliament comprising individuals elected by and from among the Sámi. These are advisory bodies primarily responsible for the review of policies and proposed legislation of concern to Sámi in each respective country. Norway's Sámi Act 1987 obliges 'state authorities to create the conditions necessary for the Sámi to protect and develop their language, their culture and their society'.[149] Sweden's Sámi Act 1992 mandates the Swedish Sámi parliament to safeguard Sámi interests relating to access and use of land and water resources, particularly for reindeer herding. Finland's Sámi Act 1995 provides for a Sámi homeland of 35,000 square kilometres within which the Sámi have a right to cultural autonomy by virtue of Article 51(a) of the Finnish Constitution.

Nonetheless, some issues about recognition of Sámi land and resource rights remain to be settled.[150] Unsatisfactorily, the Norwegian government still sees Sámi rights to land as largely usufructuary. Consequently, on occasion authorities have granted mining prospecting licences to companies without informing or consulting local Sámi.[151] A similar view of Sámi land rights has prevailed in Sweden, and in 1993 the government opened traditional Sámi hunting grounds to all Swedes,

[145] *Ibid.*

[146] See C Smith, 'The Development of Sami Rights Since 1980' in OT Brantenberg, J Hansen and H Minde (eds), *Becoming Visible: Indigenous Politics and Self-government* (The Centre for Sámi Studies, University of Tromsø, 1995) 65; G Nettheim, G Meyers and D Craig, *Indigenous Peoples and Governance Structures: A Comparative Analysis of Land and Resource Management Rights* (Aboriginal Studies Press, 2002) 209–35.

[147] *Altevatn Case*, L nr 42, nr 8/1966 (1966).

[148] *Taxed Mountain Case* ('Skattefja Ilsma'l'), NJA 1981 s 1 (1981).

[149] The text of the Sámi Act 1987 is set out in (1996) 1 Australian Indigenous Law Reports 286.

[150] L Watters, 'Indigenous Peoples and the Environment: Convergence from a Nordic Perspective' (2002) 20 *UCLA Journal of Environmental Law & Policy* 237.

[151] Nettheim, Meyers and Craig, above n 146, 219.

in the name of equal rights.[152] Finnish authorities have allowed logging and mining on traditional Sámi lands.[153]

5. Canada

Early Canadian case law viewed Indian claims as merely 'personal and usufructuary, dependent upon the goodwill of the Sovereign'.[154] Thus, government legislation prevailed whenever it conflicted with Indian claims to hunt, fish or trap.[155] The Indian Act—the state's principal tool for cultural assimilation—gave indigenous peoples penned in reserves insufficient rights to continue their traditional hunting and fishing. But a legal revolution followed the Supreme Court's 1973 decision in *Calder v British Columbia (AG)*.[156] Some justices held that aboriginal title originated in aboriginal use and occupation of traditional lands, rather than entitlements conferred by the Crown. Following the constitutional amendments of 1982, which provided for the protection of 'existing' aboriginal and treaty-based rights,[157] came the seminal *Sparrow* case of 1990. Here the Supreme Court held that although federal fisheries legislation had long regulated Indian customary fishing, this regulation had not had the effect of exitinguishing those fishing rights and thereby denying them constitutional protection.[158] In the recent *Powley* case, the courts found that the Métis peoples (of mixed Indian and European ancestry) also enjoyed customary rights to hunt wildlife for food like full-status Indians because hunting was historically an 'integral' part of the Métis culture.[159]

But while indigenous rights are constitutionally protected in Canada, they are not absolute. The Supreme Court has held that federal regulations[160] and provincial regulations[161] may restrict aboriginal hunting and fishing rights so long as the regulation rests on 'valid legislative objectives' that are compelling and substantial, and the limitation itself is compatible with the Crown's fiduciary duty to indigenous peoples.[162] An objective aimed at conservation and resource management

[152] L Hannikainen, 'The Status of Minorities, Indigenous Peoples and Immigrant and Refugee Groups in Four Nordic States' (1996) 65 *Nordic Journal of International Law* 1, 35.

[153] Nettheim, Meyers and Craig, above n 146, 229.

[154] *St Catherine's Milling and Lumber Co v The Queen* (1888) 14 App Cas 46 (Privy Council); see generally K McNeil, *Common Law Aboriginal Title* (Oxford UP, 1989).

[155] *R v Sikyea* [1964] SCR 642.

[156] (1973) 34 DLR (3d) 145.

[157] Constitution Act 1982, s 35.

[158] *R v Sparrow* [1990] 1 SCR 1075; see further LI Rotman, 'Defining Parameters: Aboriginal Rights, Treaty Rights, and the *Sparrow* Justificatory Test' (1998) 36 *Alberta L Rev* 149.

[159] *R v Powley* [2003] 2 SCR 207.

[160] *Sparrow*, above n 158.

[161] *R v Côté* [1996] 3 SCR 139.

[162] L Dufraimont, 'From Regulation to Recolonization: Justifiable Infringement of Aboriginal Rights at the Supreme Court of Canada' (2000) 58 *University of Toronto Faculty L Rev* 1.

issues would usually be considered valid. In *Delgamuukw,*[163] Lamer CJ explained how native title could be lawfully infringed by various government policies:

> the development of agriculture, forestry, mining, and hydroelectric power, the general economic development of the interior of British Columbia, protection of the environment or endangered species, the building of infrastructure and the settlement of foreign populations to support those aims, are the kinds of objectives that are consistent with this purpose and, in principle, can justify the infringement of aboriginal title.[164]

Apart from substantive land rights, aboriginal environmental governance also depends on institutional mechanisms that can sustain ongoing resource management. Land title alone is not enough. This is particularly crucial where traditional indigenous institutions for resource management have withered or disappeared. Where this occurs, new self-government structures may provide a means of addressing local environmental care and community welfare.[165]

Perhaps the leading international example of a new process for governance of indigenous lands is Canada's Comprehensive Land Claims Process (CLCP), which has led to over one dozen major agreements since the mid-1970s.[166] Through the CLCP, indigenous nations and the federal government have negotiated complex settlements for financial compensation, co-management of indigenous lands, wildlife management and regional development.[167] Negotiation of the CLCP agreements has often been precipitated by development pressures. The Inuvialuit Agreement of 1984 was negotiated against the backdrop of the discovery of oil and gas deposits in the region.[168] The Nisga'a Agreement of 2003 was shaped in part by disputes over deforestation and British Columbia's lucrative salmon fishery.[169]

The CLCP agreements created institutions for environmental governance that included both indigenous and Canadian government representatives. Quebec's James Bay Agreement of 1975 provided the model for future CLCP agreements.[170]

[163] *Delgamuukw v British Columbia* [1997] 3 SCR 1010.

[164] *Ibid*, para 165.

[165] Indeed aboriginal title arguably implies a right to self-government: K McNeil, *Defining Aboriginal Title in the 90s* (Robarts Centre for Canadian Studies, 1998).

[166] See BJ Richardson, D Craig and B Boer, *Regional Agreements for Indigenous Lands and Cultures in Canada* (Australia National University, 1995); Nettheim, Meyers and Craig, above n 146. The Canadian CLCP however was inspired by the earlier Alaska Native Claims Settlement Act, 1971, though US authorities did not develop this model in the way the Canadians have.

[167] Canada Ministry of Indian and Northern Affairs (MINA), *Comprehensive Claims Policy and Status of Claims* (MINA, 2003).

[168] AJ Black, 'Legal Principles Surrounding the New Canadian and American Arctic Energy Debate' (2002) 23 *Energy LJ* 81, 83.

[169] DE Stokes, 'Modern Treaty Making With First Nations in British Columbia' (2000) 8 *Waikato L Rev* 117, 122.

[170] HA Feit, 'James Bay Cree Self-Governance and Management of Land and Wildlife Under the James Bay and Northern Quebec Agreement' in E Wilmsen (ed), *We Are Here: Social History and Politics of Forager Land Rights* (U California Press, 1989).

The Nunavut Agreement of 1993 contains perhaps the most extensive package of governance institutions, including: a Nunavut Wildlife Management Board; a Nunavut Impact Review Board to screen project proposals and determine whether projects should proceed and monitor projects that do proceed; a Nunavut Planning Commission to establish broad planning policies, objectives and goals for the Settlement Region; a Nunavut Water Board; and a Surface Rights Tribunal.[171] In each institution the government enjoys an overriding obligation to ensure resource conservation and the interests of the general public, but which must be exercised in accordance with basic constitutional principles on aboriginal rights.[172] Thus, in *Kadlak v Nunavut*[173] the court considered the legality of a Minister's decision to overrule a recommendation of the Nunavut Wildlife Management Board to allow traditional hunting of polar bears. The court viewed the decision of the Minister as a prima facie infringement of an aboriginal right that could not be justified under the *Sparrow* test, and the matter was referred to the Minister for his reconsideration.[174]

Perhaps the most empowering CLCP agreement is the recent Nisga'a Final Agreement in British Columbia. It gave the Nisga'a Nation a primary role in the environmental assessment and protection of project proposals on Nisga'a lands, a major distinction from all previous agreements.[175] It provided that 'the Nisga'a Lisims Government may make laws in respect of the environmental assessment of projects on Nisga'a Lands'.[176] While this suggests a move toward indigenous self-government, it is explicitly stated that federal or provincial law will prevail whenever there is a conflict with such a Nisga'a law. However, the Nisga'a Agreement also provides: '[n]o Party should relax its environmental standards in the Nass Area for the purpose of providing an encouragement to the establishment, acquisition, expansion, or retention of an investment'.[177]

6. Australia

Australian governments, by contrast, have been slower to accommodate aboriginal involvement in environmental governance. No treaty of cession was ever

[171] Agreement between the Inuit of the Nunavut Settlement Area and Her Majesty The Queen in Right of Canada, 25 May 1993; see further C Marecic, 'Nunavut Territory: Aboriginal Governing in the Canadian Regime of Governance' in L Watters (ed), *Indigenous Peoples, Environment and Law* (Carolina Academic Press, 2004) 205.

[172] Canada Department of Indian Affairs and Northern Development, *Federal Policy for the Settlement of Native Claims* (Department of Indian Affairs and Northern Development, Mar 1993) 10.

[173] *Kadlak v Nunavut (Minister of Sustainable Development)* [2001] NUCJ 1 (Nunavut CJ).

[174] *Ibid*, para 170.

[175] Nisga'a Final Agreement (Government of Canada, 2000) ch 10, available at www.ainc-inac.gc.ca/pr/agr/nsga/nisdex_e.html.

[176] *Ibid*, para 3.

[177] *Ibid*, para 18.

negotiated, and the Crown regarded Australia as *terra nullius*.[178] Crucially, the High Court's recognition of customary native title in the *Mabo*[179] case of 1992 radically opened the possibility for much more aboriginal participation in or control of resource management than had hitherto been achievable under the statutory land rights regimes.[180] Presently, traditional and non-commercial hunting, food-gathering and ceremonial activities by indigenous persons are protected under several laws such as the Native Title Act 1993 (incorporating and superseding the *Mabo* judgment), and some state- and territory-based land rights legislation such as the Aboriginal Land Rights (Northern Territory) Act 1976.[181] However, the federal Howard government has sought, through amendments to the Native Title Act, to assuage the impact of the *Mabo* judgment and the subsequent *Wik* case[182] on the co-existence of native title and Crown pastoral leases.[183] For instance, it became easier for governments or companies to use native title lands for various purposes contrary to the wishes of the title-holders.[184] The Native Title Act does not allow native title owners to veto mining projects on their land, but merely concedes rights to be consulted and to negotiate with the government and mining company.[185]

A distinctive feature of the Australian approach to indigenous participation in environmental governance is the extensive use of agreements and contractual arrangements between aboriginal organisations, public agencies and developers relating to land and cultural heritage management.[186] These include joint management regimes for national parks, agreements negotiated within Natural Heritage Trust programmes, and Indigenous Land Use Agreements under the Native Title Act. The environmental issues addressed by such mechanisms include endangered species management, ecotourism, fire management and pest control. The federal Environment Protection and Biodiversity Conservation Act 1993 (EPBC Act) allows some aboriginal land councils to manage federal nature reserves where the appropriate land council and the Minister agree, and the reserve is wholly or partly on aboriginal land that is leased to the Director of National Parks. The Indigenous Protected Areas (IPAs) programme, which operates under the Natural Heritage Trust of Australia Act 1997 works with government agencies to develop partnerships and agreements with aboriginal organisations for the co-operative

[178] For an historical overview, see H Reynolds, *Dispossession* (Allen and Unwin, 1989).
[179] *Mabo and ors v Queensland* (No 2) (1992) 175 CLR 1.
[180] See RH Bartlett, *Native Title in Australia* (Butterworths, 2000).
[181] Eg NSW Aboriginal Land Rights Act 1983; Queensland Aboriginal Land Act 1991.
[182] *Wik Peoples v Queensland* (1996) 187 CLR 1.
[183] McHugh, above n 51, 499–500.
[184] Native Title Amendment Act 1998 (Cth).
[185] Native Title Act 1993 (Cth), subdivision P.
[186] See E Young *et al*, *Caring for Country: Aborigines and Land Management* (Australian National Parks and Wildlife Service, 1991); H Jarieth and D Craig, 'Governance Structures for "Country" on and off Native Title Lands' in Nettheim, Meyers and Craig, above n 146.

management of their land and/or sea as a protected area. The Native Title Act 1993 provides for the negotiation of Indigenous Land Use Agreements (ILUAs), by which potential native title claimants can enter into ILUAs concerning territories under claim to address issues relevant to biodiversity conservation and sustainable use.[187]

Most Australian governments have also established various advisory committees, councils and other bodies to enable indigenous communities to present their views on environmental (and other) issues of concern to them.[188] The Torres Strait Fisheries Act 1984 provides for the representation of Torres Strait Islanders on advisory bodies under the fisheries management arrangements established jointly by the federal and Queensland governments for the administration of the Torres Strait region.[189] The EPBC Act provides for an Indigenous Advisory Committee to advise the Minister on the operation of the Act, taking into account the significance of indigenous knowledge of the management of land and the conservation and sustainable use of biodiversity.

The joint management of protected areas is the most significant and sustained example of cross-cultural resource management in Australia. Since 1981, a variety of different models for joint management have been implemented in federal and state parks.[190] The Kakadu and Uluru national parks are often seen as the most comprehensive and successful examples of joint management.[191] Elements of some joint management regimes include an aboriginal majority on the board of park management, aboriginal ownership and lease-back of land to the government conservation agency, and negotiated financial payments to traditional owners. Jointly managed national parks demonstrate the capacity of indigenous Australians to participate in land-use policy and management in an intensive and effective way. It has also led to advances in cross-cultural education, training and the development of new institutions such as joint management boards. Outside this structure, there are numerous examples of less formal partnerships for environmental management. These include the Kowanyama community strategy for joint management of fisheries resources in the Mitchell River delta of Queensland, and the natural and cultural resource management undertaken by the Dhimurru Land Management Aboriginal Corporation in Arnhem Land.[192]

[187] D Craig, 'Native Title and Environmental Planning; Indigenous Land Use Agreements' (2000) 17 *Environmental & Planning LJ* 440.

[188] Nettheim, Meyers and Craig, above n 146, 393.

[189] D Craig, *Aboriginal and Torres Strait Islander Involvement in Bioregional Planning: Requirements and Opportunities under International and National Law and Policy* (Department of Environment, Sport and Territories, 1996).

[190] S Woenne-Green, R Johnston, R Sultan and A Wallis, *Competing Interests: Aboriginal Participation in National Parks and Conservation Reserves in Australia* (Australian Conservation Foundation, 1994).

[191] T DeLacy and B Lawson, 'The Uluru-Kakadu Model: Joint Management of Aboriginal-Owned National Parks in Australia' in S Stevens (ed), *Conservation Through Cultural Survival: Indigenous Peoples and Protected Areas* (Island Press, 1997).

[192] Nettheim, Meyers and Craig, above n 146, 384–5.

7. New Zealand

Another approach, more evident in New Zealand and the United States (US), is the enactment of specific statutory provisions for indigenous involvement in environmental decision-making. A special statutory tribunal, the Waitangi Tribunal, was established in 1975 to investigate and report on claims of breaches of the Treaty, and many of its inquiries have concerned resource management grievances.[193] New Zealand's Resource Management Act (RMA) 1991—the country's principal environmental regulation and planning statute—affirmed as a policy matter of 'national importance' the 'relationship of Maori and their culture and traditions with their ancestral lands, waters, sites',[194] as well as the Maori stewardship principle of 'Kaitiakitanga',[195] to which government decision-makers must have regard when implementing the legislation. The Act has led to local authorities usually consulting with Maori *iwi* (tribal groups) prior to making resource consent decisions.[196] Like the RMA, the Environment Act 1986 also required the Ministry for the Environment to ensure that its decisions took into account the principles of the Treaty of Waitangi.[197]

Apart from treaty-based rights, New Zealand courts have recognised customary rights to fish and other resources in a manner similar to other common law jurisdictions.[198] And as in Canada, negotiated settlements have also been used to address Maori resource claims. The most important environmental settlement was the 1989 and 1992 'Sealords' agreements, by which the Crown agreed to transfer a large proportion of the nation's commercial fisheries quota to a new Treaty of Waitangi Fisheries Commission to manage on behalf of Maori and to provide funding to the Commission to enable it to purchase the Sealords fishing company.[199] In return, Maori agreed that the settlement would discharge and extinguish all commercial fishing rights and interests of Maori.[200] There have been other negotiated settlements for the return of Maori tribal lands, financial compensation and co-management of natural resources, although not as comprehensive as the Canadian examples.[201]

[193] Treaty of Waitangi Act 1975. Among the claims considered by the Tribunal, see eg *Muriwhenua Fishing Report (WAI 22)* (Waitangi Tribunal, 1988).

[194] Resource Management Act 1991, s 6(e).

[195] *Ibid*, s 7(a).

[196] Ministry for the Environment (MfE), *Case Law on Tangata Whenua Consultation* (MfE, 1999).

[197] Preamble and s 17(c); Resource Management Act 1991, s 8.

[198] Eg *Te Weehi v Regional Fisheries Officer* [1986] 1 NZLR 682.

[199] HK Guth, 'Dividing the Catch: Natural Resource Reparations to Indigenous Peoples—Examining the Maori Fisheries Settlement' (2001) 24 *Hawaii L Rev* 179.

[200] The customary taking of seafood for subsistence needs is also recognised and preserved in government fisheries regulations: Fisheries (Amateur Fishing) Regulations, reg 27.

[201] Eg the Tainui and Ngai Tahu settlements: Nettheim, Meyers and Craig, above n 146, 144.

8. United States

Despite great efforts to dismantle Indian tribes and confiscate their territories in the nineteenth and early twentieth centuries, in recent decades Indian tribes in the US have regained land and concomitant self-government powers over their reservations. Indian communities have two primary avenues to achieve control over their lands and natural resources: inherent sovereignty and federal trust responsibility.[202] While the ambit of inherent sovereignty remains unclear, courts have recognised Indian tribes as independent, distinct political entities who retain some sovereign powers not ceded to or taken away by Congress.[203] Thus, tribes enjoy full equitable ownership of timber and mineral resources located on tribal reservations, and can regulate hunting and fishing activities of Indians. The federal trust responsibility has been understood to include the government's duty to protect tribal lands and natural resources.[204] While tribes enjoy their greatest authority over Indians and Indian lands within reservation boundaries, in some situations they may also possess tribal off-reservation fishing, hunting and other environmental rights.[205] Damage to environmental resources is emerging as a feature of some land claims of Indian nations. For instance, a lawsuit filed by the Onondaga Nation in March 2005 for the return of ancestral lands also sought compensation from the New York state government and five corporations named for causing water pollution and other environmental damage to the area.[206]

While there has been some retrenchment away from inherent sovereignty, this has hardly occurred in the area of environmental protection. The federal Environmental Protection Agency (EPA) in 1984 adopted a Federal Indian Policy, which recognised Indian tribal governments as the appropriate sovereign to deal with matters affecting tribal health and welfare. Tribes were viewed as the primary non-federal party in setting environmental standards and managing environmental programmes within reservation boundaries.[207] Since then, numerous federal environmental statutes have authorised delegation of regulatory authority to Indian tribes, including: the Clean Water Act, the Clean Air Act, the Safe Drinking Water Act, the Comprehensive Environmental Response, Compensation and Liability Act, the Federal Insecticide, Fungicide, and Rodenticide Act, the Surface Mining Control and Reclamation Act, and the Resource Conservation and Recovery Act.

202 See RW Johnson, 'Fragile Gains: Two Centuries of Canadian and United States Policy Toward Indians' (1991) 66(July) *Washington L Rev* 643.

203 See *Johnson v M'Intosh* (1832) 21 US (8 Wheat) 543, 572–88.

204 *Worcester v Georgia* (1832) 31 US (6 Pet) 515, 594–97.

205 Nettheim, Meyers and Craig, above n 146, 40.

206 L Matthews, 'Onondaga Nation Sues for Land Rights' (21 Mar 2005), available at www.civilrights.org.

207 WD Ruckelshaus, *EPA Policy for the Administration of Environmental Programs on Indian Reservations* (American Indian Environmental Office, 1984).

To illustrate, in 1987 the Congress amended the Clean Water Act (CWA) to allow the EPA to permit Indian tribes to be 'treated as states' for purposes of establishing water quality standards and issuing permits within reservation borders.[208] But few Indian tribes have received these CWA delegations, owing mainly to a lack of relevant expertise in the tribal governments and the paucity of federal funds to support delegations.[209] Importantly, though, in 2003 the Supreme Court ruled that the Sokaogon Chippewa have the right to regulate water quality on their reservation in northern Wisconsin, and to set water quality standards higher than those promulgated by the Wisconsin Department of Natural Resources.[210] The decision was bitterly fought by the Wisconsin government, which feared that higher water standards would hinder a mining proposal in the vicinity of the reservation.[211]

On the other hand, contemporary Supreme Court decisions have rejected tribal efforts to regulate hunting and fishing on non-Indian fee simple lands within reservation boundaries,[212] or to regulate non-Indian water use within reservations.[213] This limits tribal authorities' ability to provide comprehensive land management schemes in reservations containing substantial non-Indian allotments.

9. Conclusion

There have been legal setbacks for indigenous peoples in all jurisdictions in recent years, as courts became less receptive to or ambivalent about some of their claims. In the US, 'with Chief Justice Rehnquist at the reins, the Supreme Court was backtracking on Indian sovereignty'[214] as evident in cases such as *Nevada v Hicks*[215] and *Rice v Cayetano*.[216] Indian tribal governments have seen their jurisdiction

[208] 33 USC § 1377(e) (2001).

[209] Johnson, above n 202, 704.

[210] *State of Wisconsin v Environmental Protection Agency, et al,* 266 F3d 741 (7th Cir, 2001).

[211] See SM Mandleco, "Surviving a State's Challenge to the EPA's Grant of 'Treatment as State' Status Under the Clean Water Act: One Tribe's Story: State of Wisconsin v. EPA and Sokaogon Chippewa Community" (2002) 8 *Wisconsin Environmental LJ* 197.

[212] *Montana v United States,* 45 US 544, 566 (1981).

[213] *United States v Anderson,* 736 F 2d 1358, 1366 (9th Cir, 1984).

[214] McHugh, above n 51, 330, though there were exceptions to this trend, notably *California v Cabazon Band,* 480 US 202 (1987) (concerning the rights of Indian tribes to operate gaming facilities on Indian reservations).

[215] 533 US 353 (2001). In this case the Supreme Court held that state officers could enter an Indian reservation uninvited to investigate or prosecute an off-reservation violation of state law. It further held that tribal courts are not empowered to hear civil rights cases under federal law because they are not courts of general jurisdiction.

[216] 528 US 495 (2000). Here the Supreme Court struck down the state's Hawaiian-only restriction for voting in elections for a state agency that administered millions of dollars earmarked exclusively for indigenous Hawaiians. The Court ruled that the racial restriction violated the Fifteenth Amendment.

chipped away in recent years, reducing their authority for self-management of their local environments.[217] In Canada, the judiciary has also been somewhat less receptive to aboriginal claims. After the ground-breaking *Sparrow* decision, the Supreme Court retreated somewhat in its judgments in *Van der Peet*[218] and *Pamajewon*.[219] In the former, the Court introduced a controversial test for the existence of an aboriginal right, which was required to have been 'integral to the distinct culture' of the claimant group before contact with Europeans. In the latter, the Court rejected an argument that the indigenous claimants' asserted rights to self-government encompassed the right to regulate on-reserve gambling. And recently, in July 2005, the Supreme Court in the cases of *Marshall* and *Bernard* denied that the Mi'kmaq people held historic treaty rights to log Crown forests without a permit for commercial gain.[220]

In Australia, too, the prospects of a sympathetic judiciary after *Mabo* somewhat evaporated, as evidenced by the majority ruling of the High Court in *Yorta Yorta*[221] that native title required that the claimants prove continuous acknowledgement and observance of traditional laws and customs in relation to land.

Even when courts have supported indigenous claims, such as the crucial decision of the New Zealand Court of Appeal on Maori rights to the foreshore and seabed,[222] governments have intervened to extinguish indigenous rights given sufficient economic and political stakes. Thus, the New Zealand government's controversial Foreshore and Seabed Act 2004 gave ownership of these areas to the state, while allowing Maori to apply for mere 'guardianship' of certain non-strategic areas.

E. Conclusion

In many jurisdictions, the environmental knowledge and practices of indigenous peoples are gradually being recognised as valuable by wider society and incorporated into environmental management regimes. Environmental law requires *effective participation* of indigenous peoples to achieve sustainability. Nature conservation regulation, land tenure laws and intellectual property rights are some of the means by which indigenous livelihoods can be protected and can also prosper.

[217] See D Luckerman, 'Sovereignty, Jurisdiction, and Environmental Primacy on Tribal Lands' (2003) 37 *New England L Rev.* 635

[218] *R v Van der Peet* [1996] 2 SCR 507.

[219] *R v Pamajewon* [1996] 2 SCR 821.

[220] *R v Marshall; R v Bernard* [2005] SCC 43.

[221] *Yorta Yorta Aboriginal Community v Victoria* [2002] HCA 58.

[222] *Ngati Apa v Attorney-General* [2003] 3 NZLR 643.

But enduring measures to safeguard indigenous environmental practices—and thereby their distinctive cultures—are unlikely to be found if policy reforms are framed narrowly in terms of mere usufruct rights to plants and animals. Even full territorial rights may be insufficient. Rather, reforms should be broadened to establish institutional processes that secure indigenous peoples' involvement in environmental decision-making in an integrated and proactive manner consistent with a pluralistic legal regime. This should be accompanied by a shift away from prevailing mono-cultural approaches to resource management to cross-cultural strategies that allow for interaction rather than conflict between indigenous and non-indigenous interests. Initiatives for the co-management of national parks in Australia and negotiation of regional land claims agreements in Canada are examples of promising approaches.

But whatever approach is taken to empower indigenous peoples, it is vital to recognise that their claims to economic and cultural self-determination should not be interpreted as a freedom to engage in unsustainable uses of the environment. The right to self-determination must be understood in the context of common responsibilities for maintaining the health of our ecological systems, which know no jurisdictional boundaries. The significance of Article 10(c) of the Convention on Biological Diversity is pertinent in this regard: the standard is the protection and encouragement of 'customary use of biological resources in accordance with traditional cultural practices that are compatible with conservation or sustainable use requirements'. Indigenous peoples' commitment to ecologically sustainable living is not simply an obligation to assume in return for self-determination: it is, as for all peoples and nations, a precondition for their own future well-being.

The environmental challenge requires governments, communities, indigenous peoples and others to co-operate and employ new institutions that build on indigenous customary laws. While many indigenous peoples provide a model of environmental stewardship or sustainability, various modern environmental problems have arisen in industrial and urban settings for which indigenous traditional knowledge and practice may hold little relevance. At the same time, there are environmental problems for which indigenous communities possess unique expertise. As environmental law brings indigenous and environmental issues closer together, the close link between sustainable development and indigenous self-determination and survival should become more apparent.

Part 3

Economic and Business Dimensions

8

Voluntary Environmental Codes and Sustainability

STEPAN WOOD*

A. Introduction

The past 20 years have witnessed a remarkable worldwide increase in the level of interest in and use of 'voluntary' approaches to environmental protection. Governments, international organisations, private firms, industry associations and environmental non-governmental organisations (ENGOs) have developed or subscribed to a wide variety of voluntary environmental initiatives ranging from firm-specific codes of conduct to negotiated agreements between public authorities and polluters. The purpose of this chapter is to evaluate these initiatives as a form of environmental regulation and draw conclusions about their potential role in environmental law for sustainability.

This line of inquiry invites broad definitions of both 'regulation' and 'law'. While regulation is typically understood to mean authoritative rules promulgated by the state, or more broadly, all forms of state intervention in the economy, we define regulation as all calculated efforts at social control, whether undertaken by state agents or not.[1] Thus regulation includes efforts by polluters at self-regulation, efforts by third parties such as ENGOs to regulate polluters' behaviour, and agreements between polluters and the victims of pollution. Similarly, as legal pluralists have long argued, 'law' is best understood as encompassing not only official legal systems but all systems of rule, formal and informal, official and unofficial, national and transnational, that coexist in social systems.[2] Our inquiry also requires us to

* Professor, Osgoode Hall Law School, York University.

[1] Eg G Majone (ed), *Deregulation or Re-Regulation* (Pinter, 1990); J Braithwaite and P Drahos, *Global Business Regulation* (Cambridge UP, 2000); J Black, 'Regulatory Conversations' (2002) 29 *Journal of Law & Society* 163; J Black, 'Enrolling Actors in Regulatory Systems: Examples from UK Financial Services Regulation' (2003) *Public Law* 63; C Scott, 'Regulation in the Age of Governance: The Rise of the Post-Regulatory State' in J Jordana and D Levi-Faur (eds), *The Politics of Regulation* (Edward Elgar, 2004) 145.

[2] Eg G Teubner (ed), *Global Law Without a State* (Dartmouth, 1997).

reflect upon the meaning of 'sustainability', but we defer this question to the last section, where we examine the possible role of voluntary initiatives in broader legal strategies for sustainability.

In the course of the chapter, we ask seven questions about voluntary codes of conduct for the environment:

—What are they? (Section B)
—Where did they come from? (Section C)
—What forms do they take? (Section D)
—How 'voluntary' are they? (Section E)
—What drives their development and implementation? (Section F)
—How well do they perform? (Section G) And
—What roles can—and should—they play in environmental law for sustainability? (Section H).

B. What are Voluntary Environmental Codes?

We start with questions of terminology and definition. There is disagreement concerning both what to call voluntary environmental rule-making efforts and how to define them. As for terminology, a wide array of terms is used to identify the phenomenon of voluntary environmental rule-making efforts, including voluntary approaches, codes, instruments, programmes or agreements, self-regulation and joint environmental policy making.[3] The choice of terminology should reflect the fact that voluntary rule-making efforts are *normative* in character. They are normative in the dual sense of *prescription* and *standardization*: they prescribe how their addressees should act or the results they should achieve, and they set down standards to regulate conduct consistently over time or across parties.[4] Of the available terms, the word *code*, in its ordinary sense as 'a set of rules on any subject',[5] best captures this normative character.

How, then, should we define this phenomenon? While definitions vary considerably, we define voluntary environmental codes broadly as:

> Commitments undertaken by one or more polluters or resource users, in the absence of an express legal requirement to do so, prescribing norms to regulate their behaviour in relation to their interaction with the environment.

[3] Eg OECD, *Voluntary Approaches for Environmental Policy: An Assessment* (OECD, 1999), 17; P ten Brink, 'Prologue' in P ten Brink (ed) *Voluntary Environmental Agreements: Process, Practice and Future Use* (Greenleaf 2002) 14, 17.

[4] K Webb, 'Understanding the Voluntary Codes Phenomenon' in K Webb (ed), *Voluntary Codes: Private Governance, the Public Interest and Innovation* (Carleton Research Unit for Innovation, Science and Environment 2004) 3, 11.

[5] *Concise Oxford Dictionary* (8th ed, Oxford UP, 1990).

Like almost all definitions of voluntary approaches, this one defines codes as 'voluntary' in the narrow sense that they are not required *de jure*, that is, 'governments do not have to order them to be undertaken'.[6] We will consider the implications of this point in Section E, below. For now we simply note that while voluntary codes are almost always defined in contrast to official regulation, especially of the 'command' variety, in practice the relationship between voluntary codes and official legal systems is very complicated.[7]

Secondly, we reject the common tendency to define voluntary codes as initiatives that require participants to improve their environmental performance 'beyond what the law demands'.[8] This limitation confuses what voluntary codes are with what they should be. That an initiative simply encourages firms to come into compliance with existing laws does not make it less voluntary, and it is arguable whether it makes it less desirable, especially in jurisdictions where the will or capacity to enforce environmental laws is lacking. We therefore include in our definition not just voluntary initiatives that go 'beyond compliance' but those that perform a 'supporting function' in relation to existing legal requirements.[9] Thus voluntary codes might be designed simply to implement targets set by legislation,[10] to bring polluters into compliance with existing legislation,[11] reduce penalties for voluntarily disclosed environmental violations,[12] or offer evidentiary privilege for voluntary environmental audits.[13] Some government-industry agreements go even farther, relaxing existing environmental performance requirements either temporarily or indefinitely for polluters that face difficulty complying with them, as Ontario, Canada's 'programme approvals' do for certain polluters[14] and New Zealand's Negotiated Greenhouse Agreements do for firms

[6] RB Gibson, 'Questions About a Gift Horse' in RB Gibson (ed), *Voluntary Initiatives: The New Politics of Corporate Greening* (Broadview, 1999) 3, 3.

[7] Eg S Wood, 'Environmental Management Systems and Public Authority in Canada: Rethinking Environmental Governance' (2002–03) 10 *Buffalo Environmental Law Journal* 129; K Webb and A Morrison, 'The Law and Voluntary Codes: Examining the 'Tangled Web'" in K Webb, above n 4, 97; E Meidinger, 'Environmental Certification Programs and US Environmental Law: Closer than You May Think' (2001) 31 *Environmental Law Reporter* 10162.

[8] OECD, above n 3, 16; B Paton 'Voluntary Environmental Initiatives and Sustainable Industry' in ten Brink, above n 3, 37; TP Lyon and JW Maxwell "'Voluntary' Approaches to Environmental Regulation" in M Franzini and A Nicita (eds), *Economic Institutions and Environmental Policy* (Ashgate 2002) 75.

[9] ten Brink, 'Prologue', above n 3, 18.

[10] Eg the 1993 Dutch chemical industry covenant (implementing targets derived from the government's National Environmental Policy Plan) and 1994 Danish agreement on recycling of transport packaging (implementing target derived from the 1992 Government Action Plan for Waste and Recycling for the implementation of the EC Packaging and Packaging Waste Directive). European Environment Agency *Environmental Agreements: Environmental Effectiveness* (EEA, 1997) 69–73, 77–79.

[11] Eg 1988 Environmental Protocol between Portuguese Ministries of Environment and Industry and Portuguese pulp and paper association. *Ibid*, 74–77.

[12] Eg US Environmental Protection Agency, *Incentives for Self-Policing: Discovery, Disclosure, Correction and Prevention of Violations*, 65 Fed Reg 19617 (2000).

[13] Eg L Koven, 'The Environmental Self-Audit Evidentiary Privilege' (1998) 45 *UCLA L Rev* 1167.

[14] Ontario Environmental Protection Act, RSO 1990, c. E 19, s 10.

whose international competitiveness would be seriously impaired by complying with legislated energy intensity targets.[15]

Thirdly, while many definitions are limited to voluntary commitments *by business firms*,[16] we define voluntary codes as commitments undertaken by *any polluter or resource user*. This category is in principle unlimited and includes government agencies,[17] universities,[18] environmental non-governmental organisations (ENGOs),[19] landowners[20] and citizens.[21] If we want to take the full measure of voluntary codes as forms of environmental regulation we must consider all varieties of voluntary codes, not just those aimed at business firms.

Finally, our deliberately broad definition is intended to prevent the discussion from devolving into a debate about the relationship between voluntary codes and official state regulation. This common tendency to focus excessively on the 'problem of the state'[22] tends both to oversimplify the role of 'public' authorities in the constitution and exercise of 'private' authority and to eclipse a range of experiments in non-state normative ordering that are worthy of attention as forms of regulation in their own right.[23]

C. Where did Voluntary Codes Come From?

Around the world there are tens of thousands of government-sponsored programs and government-industry negotiated agreements designed to encourage voluntary environmental performance improvement.[24] There are in addition many thousands of voluntary environmental codes developed without direct government involvement, from firm-specific codes of conduct, to general principles

[15] New Zealand Climate Change Office, Negotiated Greenhouse Agreements, www.climatechange.govt.nz/policy-initiatives/nga.html.

[16] Eg United Nations Environment Programme Industry and Environment, *Voluntary Industry Codes of Conduct for the Environment*, Technical Report No. 40 (UNEP IE 1998) 8.

[17] Eg Wood, above n 7 (discussing self-application of voluntary initiatives by public authorities).

[18] Eg Association of University Leaders for a Sustainable Future, *Talloires Declaration* (1990), available at www.ulsf.org/programs_talloires.html.

[19] Eg International Institute for Sustainable Development, *Sustainable Development Report 2003–2004* (IISD 2004), also available at www.iisd.org/about/sdreporting (reporting on IISD's sustainability policies, objectives and targets).

[20] Eg conservation easements and similar voluntary conservation arrangements. See below n 91.

[21] Eg the government of Canada's 'One Tonne Challenge', available at www.climatechange.gc.ca/onetonne.

[22] N Rose and P Miller, 'Political Power Beyond the State' (1992) 43 *British Journal of Sociology* 173.

[23] Eg E Meidinger, 'The New Environmental Law: Forest Certification' (2002–03) 10 *Buffalo Envtl LJ* 211; S Wood, 'Green Revolution or Greenwash? Voluntary Environmental Standards, Public Law and Private Authority in Canada' in Law Commission of Canada (ed) *New Perspectives on the Public–Private Divide* (U British Columbia Press, 2003) 123.

[24] These include, eg, approximately 30,000 government–industry agreements in Japan and more than 300 government–industry agreements in Europe: Paton, above n 8, 37.

for sustainable business, to global certification schemes, all developed with varying degrees of co-operation among firms, industry groups, civil society organisations, professional consultants and academics. Where did this proliferation of voluntary environmental codes come from?

Industry, governments and other actors have experimented with voluntary codes at least since the earliest days of modern environmental regulation. Local governments in Japan, faced with inadequate national environmental legislation, began to negotiate pollution control agreements directly with power companies in the 1960s.[25] Governments in France and Germany first entered environmental agreements with industry in the early 1970s and by the early 1980s 'environmental covenants' were becoming popular in the Dutch-speaking parts of Europe as well.[26] Some of the most famous corporate initiatives for environmental improvement also date from this period, including 3M Corporation's 'Pollution Prevention Pays' programme, launched in 1975, which encourages 3M employees to identify cost-saving opportunities for environmental improvement. The company claims that the programme has eliminated more than 2.2 billion pounds of pollutants and saved it more than US $1 billion in first-year return-on-investment alone.[27]

Voluntary codes really took off starting in the late 1980s. The Netherlands made environmental covenants the centrepiece of its National Environmental Policy Plan in 1989, and by the mid 1990s had concluded more than 100 agreements covering thousands of companies responsible for 90 per cent of the country's industrial pollution.[28] Dutch officials spearheaded European-level interest in voluntary codes, pushing forward the EC's landmark 1992 Fifth Environmental Action Programme.[29] The Programme was widely recognised as heralding a new approach to environmental policy emphasising cooperative policy making, public transparency and 'a reinforcement of the dialogue with industry and the encouragement, in appropriate circumstances, of voluntary agreements and other forms of self-regulation'.[30] While it did not signal a wholesale embrace of voluntary codes at the EU level,[31] it

[25] OECD, *Voluntary Approaches: Two Japanese Cases,* OECD Doc No ENV/EPOC/WPNEP(2002) 12/FINAL (OECD, 2002), also available at www.oecd.org/env/va.

[26] Environmental Law Network International (ed), *Environmental Agreements* (Cameron May 1998) 40–57.

[27] 3M 'Pollution Prevention Pays (3P)', available at www.3m.com.

[28] P Glasbergen, 'Partnership as a Learning Process: Environmental Covenants in the Netherlands' in P Glasbergen (ed), *Co-operative Environmental Governance* (Kluwer, 1998) 133; PE de Jongh and S Captain *Our Common Journey* (Zed 1999); Communication on Environmental Agreements (n 31) 27–28.

[29] EW Orts and K Deketelaere, 'Introduction' in EW Orts and K Deketelaere, *Environmental Contracts* (Kluwer, 2001) 1, 9.

[30] European Commission, *Towards Sustainability: A European Community Programme of Policy and Action in Relation to the Environment and Sustainable Development,* [1993] OJ L/138/5 at 14.

[31] See G van Calster and K Deketelaere, 'The Use of Voluntary Agreements in the European Community's Environmental Policy' in Orts and Deketelaere, above n 29, 199; Communication from the Commission to the Council and European Parliament on Environmental Agreements, COM(96)561 final, 27 Nov 1996.

was followed by rapid growth in the use of voluntary approaches in many Member States.

The US Environmental Protection Agency (EPA) also developed several voluntary programmes in the 1980s, including the 33/50 Program under which participating companies committed to reduce their emissions of seventeen high-priority chemicals by 33 per cent by 1992 and 50 per cent by 1995, over a 1988 baseline.[32] While the programme attracted modest participation and plenty of controversy, it and others like it opened the way for increased use of voluntary programmes in the US, Canada and elsewhere.

At a global level, the Rio Earth Summit of 1992 gave a strong impetus to voluntary codes by emphasising public-private partnerships and the positive role of business in pursuit of sustainable development.[33] UNEP also got into the game, promoting the use of voluntary codes in developing countries.[34]

Industry and ENGO enthusiasm for voluntary codes also blossomed in the late 1980s and early 1990s. The chemical industry's 'Responsible Care' programme, developed in Canada in the late 1980s, heralded a proliferation of sector-based codes. As part of the business contribution to the 1992 Earth Summit, leading industrialists encouraged global business to develop voluntary principles and frameworks for sustainable business.[35] Many ENGOs, for their part, began to reconsider their traditionally adversarial attitudes toward industry and developed voluntary codes either on their own or in collaboration with business, from the CERES Principles (an environmental code for business drafted after the 1989 *Exxon Valdez* spill)[36] to the Forest Stewardship Council (FSC) (a sustainable forestry certification system inaugurated in 1993).[37]

Over a remarkably short period, voluntary codes achieved a remarkable degree of acceptance among governments, business and moderate ENGOs as viable tools for environmental protection. This enthusiasm for and proliferation of voluntary environmental codes were made possible, in part, by the three interwoven and roughly contemporaneous transformations in the character of the state, the environmental crisis, and business, discussed in chapter 1.[38] Widespread criticism of

[32] Eg T Davies and J Mazurek, *Industry Incentives for Environmental Improvement: Evaluation of US Federal Initiatives* (GEMI, 1996).

[33] Agenda 21, Global Programme of Action for Sustainable Development (14 June 1992), in *Report of the United Nations Conference on Environment and Development*, Annex II, UN Doc A/CONF.151/26 (Vol I-III) (12 August 1992), ch 30.

[34] Eg UNEP IE, above n 16.

[35] Eg S Schmidheiny, *Changing Course* (MIT Press, 1992).

[36] Coalition for Environmentally Responsible Economies, *CERES Principles,* available at www.ceres.org (10-point code of environmental conduct developed by coalition of investors, ENGOs and other public interest groups).

[37] See www.fsc.org. The FSC's environmental codes consist of ten principles and 56 criteria for forest stewardship, along with numerous locally-applicable forest stewardship standards (containing detailed indicators and requirements) developed by national or sub-national committees and approved by FSC.

[38] Richardson and Wood, ch 1, this vol.

command regulation and the welfare state led to massive government budget and staff cuts, the dismantling of some environmental regulatory regimes and an increased emphasis on more flexible, cooperative approaches to environmental regulation, including voluntary approaches. Self-regulation and other voluntary approaches figured prominently in many proposals for 'smarter' or more 'responsive' environmental regulation.[39] Many governments relied extensively on voluntary initiatives in response to emerging environmental problems such as climate change and toxic substances.

The changing characterization of the environmental crisis also facilitated the spread of voluntary codes. The rise of the 'sustainable development' agenda, with its faith in the compatibility of economic development and environmental protection, gave a major impetus to the emergence of voluntary codes as a viable form of environmental regulation. The characterization of environmental protection as a 'win-win' proposition for business and society, which was a major component of sustainable development discourse, facilitated the proliferation of voluntary codes by removing one of the most substantial obstacles to their adoption, namely, the assumption that firms will not normally undertake environmental improvement actions voluntarily because environmental improvement is costly and negatively affects their bottom line. As this idea gradually lost ground to the proposition that environmental improvement represents an opportunity to realise cost savings and enhance competitiveness and profitability, a new assumption emerged that most firms have incentives to improve their environmental performance voluntarily because environmental improvement in fact improves their bottom line.[40] The rapid spread of this idea in business and policy circles in the 1990s was crucial to the consolidation of voluntary codes as a credible option.

Finally, the emerging global consensus around the once widely questioned notion of corporate social responsibility ('CSR') provided a further boost to voluntary codes by repositioning industry as part of the solution rather than part of the problem. Business was increasingly seen, in mainstream policy circles at least, as a partner with which to cooperate rather than an adversary to be controlled. Voluntary codes emerged as an effective way to regulate various kinds of environmental problems and reward socially responsible firms.

While these changes were real, we should not overestimate their significance. On one hand, environmental regulation has always been negotiated.[41] Even US environmental law, the paradigm case of unilateral command regulation, has been

[39] Eg N Gunningham and P Grabosky, *Smart Regulation* (Oxford UP, 1998); I Ayres and J Braithwaite, *Responsive Regulation: Transcending the Deregulation Debate* (Oxford UP, 1992).

[40] Eg S Hart, 'A Natural Resource-Based View of the Firm' (1995) 20 *Academy of Management Review* 986; P Shrivastava, 'The Role of the Corporation in Achieving Ecological Sustainability' (1995) 20 *Academy of Management Review* 936.

[41] J Cannon, 'Bargaining, Politics and Law in Environmental Regulation' in Orts and Deketelaere, above n 29, 39.

described as 'a shifting inventory of piecemeal contractual negotiations'.[42] Around the world, environmental regulatory requirements, from emissions standards to pollution taxes, are worked out largely through government-industry negotiations intended to produce rules that will attract voluntary industry compliance. While we may argue whether negotiated rule-making, or 'reg neg' as it is called in the US, should be considered a 'voluntary' approach,[43] government-polluter bargaining is an integral feature of environmental regulation. In most jurisdictions the newfound popularity of voluntary approaches represents a variation on, rather than a radical departure from, well established patterns of rule-making and -enforcement in modern environmental regulation.

On the other hand, the move to voluntary codes may be more rhetorical than real. While an increased emphasis on voluntarism is undeniable at the level of political discourse, and the number of voluntary codes in use has clearly increased, it is not clear that there has been a relative displacement of other regulatory tools in favour of voluntary codes in practice. Paradoxically, the oft-noted movement in recent decades toward deregulation, privatization, market liberalization and public-private partnership has often been accompanied by a substantial increase in the number of regulatory agencies, the volume of official regulation, and the domains of activity subject to official regulation.[44] Whether a real move toward more voluntarism and self-regulation is underway remains to be seen.

D. What Forms do Voluntary Codes Take?

1. A Spectrum of Variation

Voluntary environmental codes take a wide variety of forms and can be classified along many dimensions. Indeed, there are almost as many taxonomies of voluntary codes as there are authors writing about them. It is important to remember that all such taxonomies are over-simplifications of complex social realities, and that codes in fact cover a broad spectrum of variation. One way to conceptualise this spectrum, as Figure 8.1 suggests, is to imagine code development and implementation as occurring in a social space defined by three partially overlapping fields. One field

[42] GC Hazzard and EW Orts, 'Environmental Contracts in the United States' in *Ibid*, 71, 72.

[43] Eg P Thalmann and A Baranzini, 'An Overview of the Economics of Voluntary Approaches in Climate Policies' in A Baranzini and P Thalmann (eds), *Voluntary Approaches in Climate Policy* (Edward Elgar, 2004) 1 (insisting that it is not); Orts and Deketelaere, 'Introduction', above n 29, 12 (suggesting that it is).

[44] J Jordana and D Levi-Faur, 'The Politics of Regulation in the Age of Governance' in Jordana and Levi-Faur, above n 1, 1.

corresponds to polluters,[45] one to public authorities[46] and one to third parties[47] such as local communities and environmental non-governmental organisations (ENGOs). Individual codes might be located anywhere in this social space, varying in terms of the identity of the parties involved and the degree of 'jointness' of decision-making. On this basis we can identify seven generic types of codes:

—polluter codes;
—joint polluter–public authority negotiated arrangements;
—public authority codes;
—joint public authority-third party negotiated arrangements;
—third party codes;
—joint polluter–third party negotiated arrangements; and
—integrated rule making.

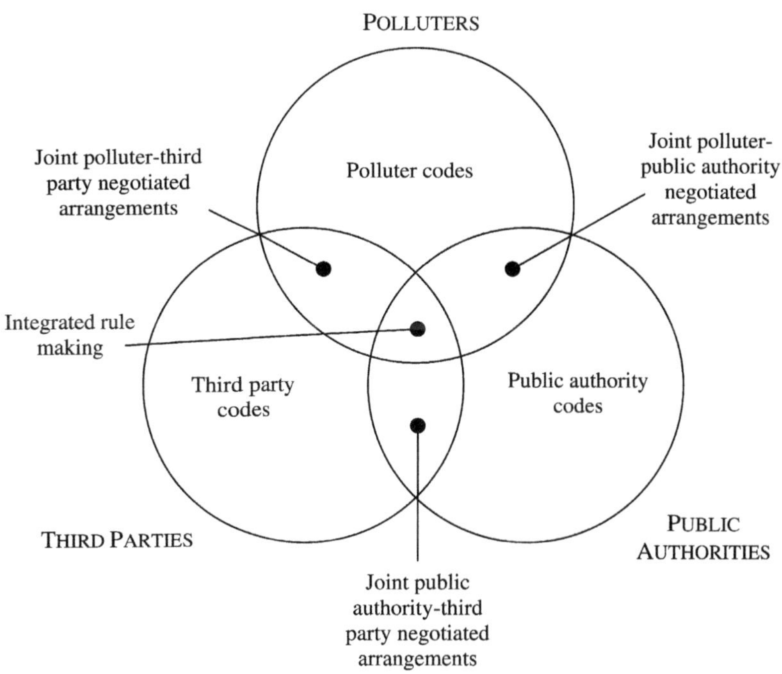

FIGURE 8.1. *The Social Space of Voluntary Environmental Codes*

[45] Hereafter 'polluter' is used as shorthand for 'polluter or resource user'.
[46] Public authorities include local, state/provincial and national government bodies, as well as international governmental organisations such as the European Commission and United Nations.
[47] Third parties are actors independent from both the polluters who implement the codes and public authorities.

(a) Polluter Codes

Polluter codes, also sometimes called unilateral polluter commitments, are self-regulatory codes developed by polluters, organisations representing polluters, or actors with a commercial interest in polluters (eg customers, creditors or insurers), without direct participation by either public authorities or third parties. These codes range from short and general to lengthy and detailed, and their environmental targets range from from highly ambitious to business-as-usual. They may be cross-sectoral (eg the International Chamber of Commerce's 1991 Business Charter for Sustainable Development),[48] sector-specific (eg the chemical industry's Responsible Care[49] and the financial sector's Equator Principles)[50] or firm-specific (eg internal codes adopted by The Body Shop International,[51] The Shell Group[52] and Interface Flooring).[53] While Western European firms have 'led the world in the depth and breadth of unilateral initiatives',[54] firms in other OECD countries are also prominent in this field.[55]

It is misleading to label all polluter codes 'unilateral commitments' because many are, in effect, imposed by one actor upon another. Many industry associations require firms to adhere to an environmental code as a condition of membership[56] and many corporations, especially multinationals, require their suppliers to

[48] See www.iccwbo.org/home/environment/charter.asp. For a somewhat dated list of cross-sectoral environmental codes see UNEP IE, above n 16, 40.

[49] See www.responsiblecare.org (a set of guiding principles and codes of practice first developed in 1985 by the Canadian Chemical Producers' Association after the 1984 Bhopal chemical disaster in India and a much smaller accident at a Dow Chemical facility in Sarnia, Ontario; now embraced by chemical industry associations in 52 countries).

[50] See www.equator-principles.com (a framework for managing environmental and social risks associated with project finance, issued by leading banks in 2003 and currently adopted by 35 banks). For a somewhat dated list of sector-specific environmental codes see UNEP IE, above n 16, 30–39.

[51] For the Body Shop International's environmental commitments see inter alia its Mission Statement, Trading Charter, Core Principles (including 'Protect Our Planet') and Environmental Policy, available at www.thebodyshopinternational.com/web/tbsgl/library.jsp.

[52] For the Shell Group's environmental commitments see inter alia the Shell General Business Principles (to which sustainable development was added in 1997), Health, Safety and Environment Commitment and Policy, and Environmental Minimum Standards. Royal Dutch Shell plc, *Shell General Business Principles* (Shell Intl Ltd, 2005) and *The Shell Report 2004* (Shell Intl Ltd, 2005), available at www.shell.com.

[53] For information on the environmental commitments of Interface, a US-based floor coverings manufacturer and corporate sustainability pioneer, see www.interfacesustainability.com.

[54] Paton, above n 8, 38–39.

[55] For example, in Japan, a voluntary multi-sectoral greenhouse gas emission reduction code developed by the Keidanren (the Japanese Federation of Economic Organisations) is the centrepiece of the government's climate change strategy. *Ibid*, 39.

[56] For example, the Canadian Electrical Association requires its members to have an ISO 14001 or equivalent EMS in place; and the US-based International Council of Cruise Lines announced in 2003 that it would make EMS implementation a mandatory membership condition, in an effort to preempt tougher government regulation and reduce bad publicity around chronic marine pollution.

adhere to codes as a condition of doing business.[57] To capture such situations we may examine codes in terms of 'rule-makers' (actors who develop codes) and 'rule-takers' (actors whose conduct is the target of a code).[58] This distinction is useful for understanding all codes, not just polluter codes. Sometimes one actor is both rule maker and rule taker, as when a firm develops a code for its own conduct, an industry association develops a code jointly with public authorities or third parties, or a government helps to develop a code which it then applies to its own agencies. In other cases an actor is only a rule maker (eg an ENGO or public authority that negotiates an agreement with a polluter to modify the polluter's conduct) or a rule taker (eg a supplier that implements a code required by a customer, or a firm that adopts a code developed by a third party).

(b) Joint Polluter–Public Authority Negotiated Arrangements

Joint polluter–public authority negotiations produce two main kinds of codes: negotiated environmental agreements (NEAs) and broader partnerships. The most common form of joint polluter–public authority code is the NEA. NEAs may involve local, state/provincial, national or international public authorities, on one side, and anything from an individual polluting facility to an entire industry sector, on the other.[59] Most require participating polluters to go 'beyond compliance', either by exceeding existing legal standards or taking action where no legal standards exist. Some are designed to remedy the effects of non-compliance, or to help polluters achieve compliance.[60] NEAs are widely used in both the EU and Japan. While most European NEAs are between national or state governments and industry associations, most of the 30,000 or so Japanese negotiated agreements involve local authorities and single firms.[61] Public authorities in Canada, the US and New Zealand are also making increasing use of negotiated agreements.[62]

57 Some major auto makers and major electronics and semiconductor firms require their suppliers either to implement ISO 14001 or obtain ISO 14001 certification, while some apparel and footwear manufacturers require suppliers to abide by restrictive substances lists prohibiting certain hazardous substances in finished products: K Sissell, 'Autos and Electronics Drive Certification' (2000) 162 *Chemical Week* 42; D Monsma and J Buckley, 'Non-Financial Corporate Performance: the Material Edges of Social and Environmental Disclosure' (2004) 11 *University of Baltimore Journal of Environmental Law* 151.

58 D Szablowski, 'Legitimacy and Regulation in the Global Economy' (PhD dissertation, Osgoode Hall Law School, October 2004), 48.

59 The leading example of an NEA involving a supranational public authority is the 1998 agreement between the European Commission and European car manufacturers relating to automobile emissions of CO_2: van Calster and Deketelaere, above n 31, 228–232.

60 Eg CL Wilson and WL Thomas, 'ASARCO Settlement Attests to Importance of a Sound Environmental Management System' (1998) 12 *Natural Resources & Environment* 290 (discussing US EPA consent decree); Ontario EPA s 10 programme approvals, above n 14.

61 Paton, above n 8, 39.

62 Eg Project XL (US), Environmental Leaders Program (Ontario, Canada). See generally European Environmental Agency, above n 10.

Some polluter–public authority joint arrangements do not fit this simple mould of discrete negotiated agreements, instead creating partnerships covering, for example, the establishment and operation of eco-industrial networks, the development of green technology or the pursuit of 'cleaner production'.[63] Some such arrangements create not just codes but ongoing institutions that develop, apply and interpret codes.

(c) Public Authority Codes

Two main types of voluntary environmental codes are initiated by public authorities: public voluntary programmes and intergovernmental negotiated agreements. Public voluntary programmes are codes developed by public authorities, to which polluters are invited to subscribe on a take-it-or-leave-it basis. They may be aimed either at environmental 'leaders' or 'laggards'.[64] Environmental leadership programmes typically offer recognition and rewards to polluters whose environmental practices and performance significantly exceed what is legally required. The US EPA's National Performance Track, with 368 participating facilities, is a leading example.[65] Programs aimed at 'laggards' typically encourage or reward voluntary environmental compliance audits and voluntary steps to remedy non-compliance, often by relaxing otherwise applicable penalties.[66] Another form of public voluntary programme is the challenge programme, in which public authorities challenge polluters to meet specified environmental performance goals, for instance for greenhouse gases[67] or toxic chemicals.[68] Public voluntary programmes have been the voluntary instrument of choice in the US and Canada but have also been favoured by international organisations such as the European Commission,[69] the UN and its various organs,[70] and the OECD.[71]

[63] Eg UNEP Cleaner Production Network, at www.uneptie.org/pc/cp/network/home.htm; Asian Productivity Organisation Green Productivity Program, at www.apo-tokyo.org/gp/index.htm; MR Chertow, 'Industrial Symbiosis: Literature and Taxonomy' (2000) 25 *Annual Review of Energy & Environment* (discussing eco-industrial network in Kalundborg, Denmark).

[64] N Gunningham and D Sinclair, *Leaders and Laggards: Next-Generation Environmental Regulation* (Greenleaf, 2002).

[65] US EPA, 'National Environmental Performance Track' at www.epa.gov/performancetrack.

[66] Eg JL Jackson, 'Environmental Audit Privilege Laws: Stripping the Public's Right to Know' (2001) 49 *Cleveland State L Rev* 539.

[67] Eg Australian Greenhouse Challenge, at www.greenhouse.gov.au and Voluntary Challenge and Registry (Canada), at www.ghgregistries.ca/challenge (challenging firms to track emissions, set abatement targets and report publicly on performance); and the Canadian government's One Tonne Challenge, above n 21 (challenging Canadian individuals to reduce their greenhouse gas emissions by one tonne).

[68] Eg the US EPA's 33/50 Program and the Canadian government's ARET programme (Accelerated Reduction/Elimination of Toxics).

[69] Eg Regulation (EC) 761/2001 of the European Parliament and of the Council of 19 Mar 2001 Allowing Voluntary Participation by Organisations in a Community Eco-Management and Audit Scheme (EMAS) (2001) OJ L/114/1; Regulation (EC) No 1980/2000 of the European Parliament and of the Council of 17 July 2000 on a Revised Community Eco-label Award Scheme [2000] OJ L/237/1.

[70] Eg UN Global Compact at www.unglobalcompact.org.

[71] Eg *OECD, Guidelines for Multinational Enterprises* (OECD, 2000) (non-binding recommendations for multinational enterprises, to which governments are invited to adhere).

A second, sometimes overlooked, type of public authority code is negotiated agreements among public authorities. Such agreements are found in both unitary and federal states and have been used, for instance, in the Netherlands to address land use and environmental protection[72] and in Canada and Australia to implement international agreements, delegate administration of national law or harmonise national and state/provincial environmental policy.[73] It is also possible to view international environmental agreements generally (treaties, protocols, declarations, resolutions, etc) as voluntary codes, since they are concluded voluntarily by states.[74]

(d) Joint Public Authority–Third Party Negotiated Arrangements

One type of voluntary environmental code that has been ignored almost completely in the existing literature is codes developed jointly by public authorities and third parties, such as ENGOs, without direct involvement by polluters. Such arrangements include eco-labelling schemes developed jointly by government agencies and ENGOs,[75] and private debt-for-nature swaps, in which 'Northern' ENGOs purchase developing countries' sovereign debt in exchange for assurances that the government will conserve more biodiversity, increase funding for conservation projects or protect particular lands.[76]

(e) Third Party Codes

Third party environmental codes are codes developed by third parties, to which polluters are invited to subscribe on a take-it-or-leave-it basis. Some set out detailed, specific requirements[77] while others are fundamental philosophies for

[72] Orts and Deketelaere, 'Introduction', above n 29, 7.

[73] Eg National Strategy for the Conservation of Australia's Biodiversity (1996), available at www.deh.gov.au/biodiversity/publications/strategy/index.html; Canada-Wide Accord on Environmental Harmonization (1998), available at www.ccme.ca/ourwork/environment.html?category_id=25.

[74] They are so treated by some commentators, eg D Leipziger, *The Corporate Responsibility Code Book* (Greenleaf 2003) (including the 1948 Universal Declaration of Human Rights, the 1992 Rio Declaration on Environment and Development and the 1997 OECD Bribery Convention in compendium of corporate codes). See Ellis and wood, this vol, for a discussion of international environmental law.

[75] Eg the TCO eco-labelling scheme for computer displays, developed by a Swedish labour union in collaboration with a leading Swedish ENGO, a Swedish government board and a private auditing firm. As of 2002, the scheme dominated the global market for computer display ecolabels with almost 3,500 certified products. Because computer manufacturers and suppliers were consulted during the development of labelling requirements, this could be classified as an example of integrated rule making (see below); but their participation appears to have been quite limited. PE Boivie, 'A New Trade Union Role in Environmental Agreements' in ten Brink, above n 3, 129.

[76] M Sher, 'Can Lawyers Save the Rainforest? Enforcing the Second Generation of Debt-for-Nature Swaps' (1993) 17 *Harvard Environmental L Rev* 151.

[77] Eg Steering Group of the Global Principles Network, *Principles for Global Corporate Social Responsibility: Bench Marks for Measuring Business Performance* (3rd edn, Steering Group of the Global Principles Network, 2003), also at www.bench-marks.org (hereafter 'Bench Marks').

sustainable business.[78] Many are developed by 'civil society' actors such as environmental and human rights groups,[79] religious groups,[80] universities[81] or eminent individuals,[82] and set demanding performance criteria only a minority of polluters are able or willing to meet in the short run. Others are developed by national or international standardization bodies such as the International Organisation for Standardization (ISO),[83] and tend to stick more closely to prevailing business practices. It is sometimes difficult to distinguish third party codes from polluter codes or joint polluter–third party arrangements, because the polluters who implement them may have substantial influence over their development.[84] This is especially true of standardization bodies such as ISO, in which the interests of standards users (ie business) tend to dominate.[85]

It is important to distinguish between the *development* of codes by third parties and third party *verification of conformity* to codes. There are three main ways to verify conformity: self-verification, where an organisation assesses and declares its own conformity; second-party verification, where conformity is verified by a party with a business interest in the subject organisation (eg a customer or creditor);[86] and third-party verification, where conformity is verified by an independent, objective third party, often resulting in certification. Codes vary widely in the degree to which they encourage or require external verification. There is a trend in recent years toward increased third party verification or certification in both

[78] Eg The Natural Step, at www.naturalstep.org. Organisations claiming to have adopted The Natural Step include IKEA, Home Depot, Nike, McDonalds, Bank of America, DuPont, Starbucks, and various cities and universities. See eg K-H Robèrt, *The Natural Step Story* (New Society 2002).

[79] Eg Collevecchio Declaration on Financial Institutions and Sustainability (Jan 2003), available at www.foe.org/camps/intl/declaration.html (statement by more than 100 ENGOs laying out general principles and specific implementation steps for financial sector firms).

[80] Eg Bench Marks, above n 77 (developed by mostly Christian coalition); Center for Global Ethics, *An Interfaith Declaration: A Code of Ethics on International Business for Christians, Muslims and Jews* (Center for Global Ethics, 1993), reprinted in K McCague and W Cragg (eds), *Compendium of Ethics Codes and Instruments of Corporate Responsibility*, 2005), www.yorku.ca/csr, 9.

[81] Eg Business Ethics Research Project of Reitaku University, *Ethics Compliance Management System Standard ECS2000* (Reitaku Centre for Economic Studies 1999) also at www.ie.reitaku-u.ac.jp/%7Edavis/ html/ecs-eng-main.html.

[82] Eg Rev LH Sullivan, *The Global Sullivan Principles* (1999), also at www.mallenbaker.net/csr/CSRfiles/ gsprinciples.html (broad principles for labour, business ethics and environmental practices written by Rev Leon Sullivan, author of the Sullivan Principles for companies doing business in apartheid South Africa).

[83] Eg *ISO 14001:2004 Environmental Management Systems: Requirements with Guidance for Use* (ISO, 2004) (voluntary standard for environmental management systems; with over 100,000 certified organisations world-wide, one of the most widely implemented voluntary environmental codes).

[84] Eg Sullivan, above n 82 (written with substantial input from several multinational corporations).

[85] Eg N Roht-Arriaza, 'Shifting the Point of Regulation: The International Organisation for Standardization and Global Lawmaking on Trade and the Environment' (1995) 22 *Ecology Law Quarterly* 479.

[86] The Equator Principles, eg, prompt creditors to examine borrowers' observance of the Principles. See Richardson, this vol.

existing and new codes. While this may enhance a code's credibility, it may be prohibitively expensive for many small and medium-sised organisations.[87]

Finally, another complication is that many third party codes (and some public voluntary programmes and public authority–third party codes) are implemented via bilateral agreements between participating polluters and either the code administrator or a third party certification body. Thus rather than being 'purely' third-party or public-authority codes, these arrangements often also involve a mix of polluter–third party or polluter–public authority negotiated agreements.

(f) Joint Polluter–Third Party Negotiated Arrangements

We can distinguish two main kinds of joint arrangements between polluters and third parties: those between polluters and 'pollutees', and those between polluters and other third parties. First, while the interests of those harmed by pollution or resource use are usually represented primarily by elected governments and regulatory agencies, 'pollutees' themselves (eg local residents' groups) and others claiming to speak for them (eg ENGOs) increasingly take it upon themselves to negotiate directly with polluters. Polluter–pollutee codes include industry-community agreements, which are usually relatively localised arrangements affecting a particular site or facility;[88] industry-ENGO agreements, which are often national or worldwide in scope;[89] industry-organised labour 'framework agreements', usually between individual companies and national or international labour unions;[90] and voluntary land or wildlife conservation agreements[91] between private landowners and non-profit groups, such as conservation easements. The latter,

[87] This has led to a search for less expensive, yet still credible, third party 'checks' that are accessible to small organisations. Eg EnviroReady Reports, at www.iso14000registry.com (simplified check of ISO 14001 implementation by accountant).

[88] There are some large-scale examples, eg the Dutch city of Rotterdam's agreement with major upstream polluters of the Rhine river, represented by the German Association of Chemical Industries; but this may be better classified as a public authority–polluter agreement. JM van Dunné (ed), *Environmental Contracts and Covenants* (Institute of Environmental Damages, Erasmus University, 1993) 107–141.

[89] Eg a famous 1990 agreement between the US Environmental Defense Fund and McDonalds which led the firm to eliminate Styrofoam 'clamshell' packaging and adopt a Comprehensive Waste Reduction Action Plan to reduce solid waste in all aspects of its business. Another example is the 1991 New Zealand Forest Accord between large forest companies and conservation and recreation groups, in which the forest companies promised to protect remaining native forests in return for endorsement of plantation forestry as a sustainable option: D Menzies, 'Conflict or Collaboration: The New Zealand Forest Accord' in ten Brink, above n 3, 95.

[90] Such agreements, which typically cover labour, human rights and environmental issues and complement company codes of conduct, are found mainly in companies with strong trade unions and in countries with a tradition of social dialogue, such as those of Scandinavia and Northern Europe. Leipziger, above n 74, 350.

[91] Eg JA Gustanski and RH Squires (eds), *Protecting the Land: Conservation Easements Past, Present, and Future* (Island 2000); A Kwasniak, 'Facilitating Conservation: Private Conservancy Law Reform' (1993) 31 *Alberta L Rev* 607.

while found across the globe, have growing salience in developing countries where public legal frameworks and institutional capacity may be lacking.[92]

Secondly, some codes are the products of co-operation between polluters and third parties who do not purport to speak for those harmed by pollution. Such codes might include consumer contracts for 'green' electricity[93] and some codes developed jointly by polluters, investors and others.[94]

Finally, as with polluter–public authority codes, many codes involving polluter–third party co-operation are not simple negotiated agreements but products of complex institutions in which business, environmental and other interests cooperate to create decision-making structures and develop and apply rules. The leading example is the Forest Stewardship Council (FSC), which sets standards for sustainable forestry and accredits forest certification bodies through a tripartite decision-making structure of industry, environmental and social chambers.[95] Such arrangements often intentionally exclude or minimise public authority involvement, positioning themselves as 'private' alternatives to government policy-making.[96]

(g) Integrated Rule-making

Finally, integrated rule-making occurs when polluters, public authorities and third parties come together to create joint rule-making institutions or develop environmental codes. Official policy-making processes in the advanced industrial democracies, especially as they have evolved in recent years to accommodate public participation alongside industry interests, are probably the best extant examples of integrated rule-making,[97] although what we have in mind here are situations in which public authorities, polluters and third parties come together more or less as equal 'partners' to establish codes or integrated rule-making institutions.[98]

92 Eg A Wolman, 'Review of Conservation Payment Initiatives in Latin America: Conservation Concessions, Conservation Incentive Agreements and Permit Retirement Schemes' (2004) 28 *William & Mary Environmental Law & Policy Review* 859.

93 Eg MJ Kotchen, MR Moore and CF Clark, 'Environmental Contracts between Individuals and Industry: An Analysis of Consumer Preferences for Green Electricity' in Orts and Deketelaere, above n 29, 409.

94 Eg Social Venture Network Standards of Corporate Social Responsibility (Social Venture Network 1999), at www.svn.org (best practice code developed by network of socially responsible entrepreneurs, investors and non-profit organisations). The Global Sullivan Principles, above n 82, arguably fall into this category too, since executives of leading multinationals had substantial input into their content.

95 The FSC's governing organs also balance Northern and Southern representation: Forest Stewardship Council, above n 37. Other leading examples include the Global Reporting Initiative (GRI), at www.globalreporting.org and Marine Stewardship Council (MSC), at www.msc.org.

96 B Cashore, G Auld and D Newsom, *Governing Through Markets* (Yale UP, 2004).

97 Regional land use plans and subregional land and resource management plans concluded under the province of British Columbia's 1992 Provincial Land Use Strategy are good examples: M Mascarenhas, 'Legitimacy, Efficacy and Efficiency: Factors Affecting Public Participation in Environmental Agreements in British Columbia, Canada' in ten Brink, above n 3, 81.

98 Eg a 1998 agreement among the US EPA, Environmental Defense Fund and Chemical Manufacturers' Association for voluntary testing of the environmental, health and safety impacts of 2800 industrial chemicals. A Prakash, 'Responsible Care: An Assessment' (2000) 39 *Business and Society* 183, 203.

Three-way collaboration among industry, government and ENGOs is becoming common in many countries, displacing the closed-door industry-government bargaining that characterised many of the early negotiated environmental agreements. One example found in both developed and developing countries is permit retirement agreements, in which ENGOs pay private individuals or firms to give up their resource rights (grazing, logging, etc), which are then permanently retired by government. Because such arrangements usually require political or administrative reforms and involve the permanent loss of a future income stream for governments and an economic development option for local communities, they require in-depth negotiation and collaboration among ENGOs, rights holders, government officials and local communities.[99]

2. Other Dimensions of Variation

Codes vary along several other dimensions as well, including the following:

(a) Binding vs. Non-binding

Codes may or may not be legally binding on the parties, once entered.[100] Many codes are implemented via legally binding contracts and can be enforced as such; others involve 'gentlemen's agreements' or unilateral commitments and do not create legally recognised rights and obligations.[101] Public authority-polluter negotiated agreements take both forms, depending on constitutional arrangements and the parties' intentions.[102]

(b) Process- vs. Performance-orientation

Codes can be located on a continuum from process-oriented to performance-based.[103] Process-oriented codes address environmental management tools such as EMSs,[104] life cycle analysis (LCA),[105] environmental reports,[106] environmental

99 Wolman, above n 92, 881–884.

100 OECD, above n 3, 19–20; Thalmann and Baranzini, above n 43, 4.

101 J Moffet and F Bregha, 'Non-Regulatory Environmental Measures' in Gibson, above n 6, 15; Meidinger, above n 7.

102 Dutch environmental covenants are generally enforceable against either party, whereas German government–industry pollution agreements are unenforceable 'gentlemen's agreements' and the US EPA insists on a clause indicating that Project XL agreements are not legally binding as contracts. OECD, above n 3; T Caballero, 'Project XL: Making it Legal, Making it Work' (1998) 17 *Stanford Environmental L J* 399.

103 E Meidinger, "'Private' Environmental Regulation, Human Rights, and Community" (1999–2000) 6 *Buffalo Envtl LJ* 132.

104 Eg ISO 14001, above n 83.

105 Eg ISO 14040:1997, *Environmental management – Life cycle assessment – Principles and framework* (ISO, 1997).

106 Eg GRI, above n 95; ISO/DIS 14063 *Environmental management – Environmental communication – Guidelines and examples* (draft international standard, ISO, 2004); The Body Shop International plc, *The Body Shop Values Report 2005*, available at valuesreport.thebodyshop.net.

audits and other environmental self-evaluation tools,[107] design-for-environment guides[108] and eco-labels.[109] Performance-based codes, by contrast, set substantive targets for environmental performance.[110] Most codes combine process and performance elements.

(c) Target- vs. Implementation-based

Many analysts also distinguish between target- and implementation-based codes. In target-based codes, environmental performance targets are set by the parties themselves (eg most German and French negotiated environmental agreements). In implementation-based codes, performance targets are set elsewhere, for instance in legislation, and the code simply addresses implementation of targets (eg most Dutch, Danish, Portuguese and Swedish environmental covenants).[111] Some regimes involve both target- and implementation-based codes.[112]

(d) General vs. Specific

Codes range from general, brief statements of policy and principle[113] to highly specific codes of practice featuring detailed rules, criteria, indicators and targets.[114]

(e) Regulatory Function

Codes may be differentiated from each other and from other regulatory regimes (such as official legal systems) in terms of various regulatory functions such as

[107] Eg H-W Engel and International Network for Environmental Management, *Eco-mapping*, available at www.ecomapping.org; ISO 14031:1999, *Environmental management – Environmental performance evaluation – Guidelines* (ISO 1999).

[108] Eg ISO/TR 14062:2002, *Environmental management – Integrating environmental aspects into product design and development* (ISO, 2002).

[109] Eg ISO 14020:2000, *Environmental labels and declarations – General principles* (ISO 2000); EC Eco-Label Regulation, above n 69. See generally OECD, *Eco-Labelling: Actual Effects of Selected Programmes* (OECD, 1997); US Environmental Protection Agency *Environmental Labeling Issues, Policies and Practices Worldwide* (US EPA, 1998).

[110] Performance targets may be generic (eg to prevent pollution, reduce resource use, conserve biodiversity, maintain ecological integrity or minimise adverse environmental impacts) or specific (eg to reduce emissions of specified greenhouse gases at least 20% below 1990 levels by 2010).

[111] EEA, above n 10; OECD, above n 3, 20–21. The 1994 Swedish agreement on producer responsibility for packaging waste, eg, was an initiative developed by Swedish industry to implement targets set by an official ordinance. Lyon and Maxwell, above n 8, 110–112.

[112] Eg targets may be set in a sector-wide government–industry agreement while implementation details are worked out in facility-specific agreements; or targets may be contained in a third party or governmental certification programme, while implementation is achieved through contracts between participating companies, on one hand, and code administrators or third party auditing firms, on the other.

[113] Eg UN Global Compact, above n 70 (10 concise principles).

[114] Eg Baxter International Inc, 'Environmental, Health and Safety Goals for the Year 2005' reproduced in UNEP IE, above n 16, 18 (Committing *inter alia* to reduce toxic air emissions by 80% in 2005 from 1996 levels).

agenda-setting, rule creation, rule administration, rule enforcement and dispute resolution.[115] There is variation both in how these regulatory functions are carried out in the case of given codes (eg how the idea for a code came onto relevant actors' agendas, how the code was created, how it is administered and how disputes about code implementation are resolved), and which of these regulatory functions given codes seek to regulate (eg does the code prescribe standards for rule creation, administration or adjudication?). While some codes perform just one of these functions,[116] many straddle several.[117] There are even codes about codes, ie, codes for how codes should be developed or what they should contain.[118]

(f) Individual vs. Collective Character

Codes may be individual (applying to just one entity) or collective (applying to a group of potential adherents). The distinction is important mainly because the latter may suffer from free riding and other collective action problems.[119]

(g) Geographic Scope

Codes vary in geographic scope from local to global. While many apply within a particular political jurisdiction (eg local, state/provincial, national or regional),[120] others are defined in terms of the geographic scope of an organisation's activities.[121]

(h) Policy Scope

Finally, codes vary widely in the range of issues they address. Some address environmental protection or pollution prevention generally.[122] Others address environment in the context of a broader agenda for corporate social responsibility.[123] Some address a particular industry sector, such as mining, finance or organic agriculture, while others address particular environmental issue-areas, such as climate

[115] Cf Webb and Morrison, above n 7; M Priest, 'Five Models of Self-Regulation' (1997–98) 29 *Ottawa L Rev* 233, 239.

[116] The GRI and other reporting codes, for instance, set down rules for environmental communications, which is one aspect of rule administration.

[117] ISO 14001, eg, covers agenda-setting (eg creating an environmental policy), rule creation (eg setting environmental objectives and targets) and rule administration (eg resource allocation, operational controls, training, documentation, communication, monitoring and measurement, and auditing).

[118] Eg ISEAL Alliance Code of Good Practice for Setting Social and Environmental Standards, at www.isealalliance.org/programmes; ISO Guide 64:1997, *Guide for the inclusion of environmental aspects in product standards* (ISO 1997).

[119] OECD, above n 3, 19.

[120] Among the many national-level codes, for instance, one finds the Australian Minerals Industry Code for Environmental Management (Australian Minerals Council, 2000).

[121] This may range from a single facility to the worldwide operations of a major multinational company.

[122] Eg ICC Business Charter, above n 48; CERES Principles, above n 36.

[123] Eg Sullivan, above n 82; UN Global Compact, above n 70; Social Accountability International SA 8000, www.sa8000.org; Canadian Business for Social Responsibility (CBSR), *Guidelines for Corporate Social Performance* (CBSR 2001), www.cbsr.ca.

change, energy efficiency, toxic chemicals or packaging waste. Finally, some (eg most of the Dutch environmental covenants) address production processes while others (eg most of the German negotiated agreements) address products.[124]

E. How 'Voluntary' are Voluntary Codes?

What significance should we attach to the modifier 'voluntary' before 'codes'? While the term suggests an autonomous choice made freely, without external pressure, the fact is that voluntary codes are seldom 'voluntary' in this sense. Virtually all voluntary codes are undertaken because the relevant actors have been effectively pressured to act.[125] While voluntary codes are by definition 'voluntary' insofar as their development and implementation are not required by official regulation (see Section B), they may nonetheless be experienced as obligatory or irresistible in practice. As Section F suggests, polluters may feel pressured to undertake voluntary codes to, *inter alia*, defuse a threat of mandatory regulation, realise cost savings, distinguish themselves in a competitive market, ameliorate bad publicity, respond to a consumer boycott, satisfy customer or investor demands, meet industry association membership requirements, maintain social legitimacy or fulfil a perceived ethical obligation.

In some cases implementation of a voluntary code may become a *de facto* requirement for doing business in particular markets, as when the big auto makers began to require all their suppliers to implement EMSs.[126] In other cases implementation of nominally 'voluntary' codes may be made obligatory by express judicial or legislative mandate. Courts have ordered parties to implement voluntary codes, such as the ISO 14001 EMS standard, in sentencing for or settlement of legal charges.[127] Governments have enacted legislation making the development or implementation of 'voluntary' codes mandatory for certain actors, such as Dutch legislation requiring the conclusion of environmental covenants with target industry groups,[128] Canadian provincial legislation requiring gas pipeline companies to implement ISO 14001,[129] or Danish legislation authorising

[124] OECD, above n 3, 58.

[125] RB Gibson, 'Encouraging Voluntary Initiatives for Corporate Greening' (paper presented at UNEP Voluntary Initiatives Workshop, Sep 2000).

[126] Sissell, above n 57.

[127] Eg *R v Prospec Chemicals* (1996) 19 Canadian Envtl L Reports (New Series) 178 (Alberta Provincial Court).

[128] OECD, above n 3, 53.

[129] Pipeline Regulations, N.S. Reg. 66/98, s.19(1) (Nova Scotia); Gas Pipeline Regulation, NB Reg 99–61, s 46 (New Brunswick); Gas Distribution and Marketers' Filing Regulation, NB Reg 99–60, s 7(12) (New Brunswick) (requiring gas pipeline companies to establish an EMS that meets the ISO 14000 standard or equivalent).

the government to impose the terms of government-industry association negotiated agreements on non-participating firms.[130]

In short, the 'voluntary/mandatory' dichotomy does not withstand serious scrutiny. The important question is not whether voluntary codes are really 'voluntary', but what effectively drives the relevant actors to develop and implement them.

F. What Drives the Development and Implementation of Voluntary Codes?

What, then, drives firms, public authorities and third parties ('pollutees' or ENGOs) to develop or implement voluntary environmental codes? For the sake of brevity, we focus here on codes targeting business firms as opposed to other kinds of polluters or resource users. The drivers motivating businesses to undertake voluntary environmental protection action are fairly well known. What has not received so much attention, however, is what drives governments and third parties (especially ENGOs) to embrace voluntary environmental codes for business. Let us consider each of these actors in turn.

1. Drivers for Business

(a) Anticipated Net Benefits

In the absence of compulsory environmental laws, business firms can externalise much of the cost of their pollution and unsustainable resource use onto others. Our starting premise, therefore, is that profit-seeking firms will take voluntary action to improve their environmental impacts only if the expected benefits to the firm equal or exceed the costs.[131] Stated differently, the main driver of voluntary environmental protection action by business firms is the anticipation that such action will produce net economic benefits for the firm.[132] Such benefits include, in roughly descending order of importance:

[130] OECD, above n 3, 117.

[131] C Carraro and F Lévêque, 'Introduction: The Rationale and Potential of Voluntary Approaches' in C Carraro and F Lévêque (eds) *Voluntary Approaches in Environmental Policy* (Kluwer 1999), 1, 5; OECD, above n 3, 25.

[132] A recent global survey indicated that 'economic considerations' (ie net economic benefits) are the most common driver of corporate sustainability initiatives, reported by 74% of surveyed firms: KPMG Global Sustainability Services, *KPMG International Survey of Corporate Responsibility Reporting 2005* (KPMG International, 2005) 18, available at www.kpmg.com/Rut2000_prod/Documents/9/Survey 2005.pdf. See also B Purchase, 'The Political Economy of Voluntary Codes' in Webb, above n 4, 77, 81 ('it is always a commercial benefit that is anticipated').

(i) Cost Savings

Implementing a voluntary environmental code may reduce the costs of inputs (energy, water and raw materials) and waste disposal, lower firms' insurance costs, improve credit ratings, enhance profitability, reduce risk and enhance shareholder value.[133] Such 'no regrets' opportunities are important drivers for voluntary environmental improvement.[134] Government subsidies for code implementation (grants, tax relief, etc) are another cost-saving driver insofar as they reduce the costs of voluntary action for firms.[135]

(ii) Regulatory Gains

Another strong driver is the prospect of avoiding costly official regulation. Implementing a code may reduce the pressure for new regulation, enabling firms to pre-empt or delay the introduction of mandatory legal rules; it may improve relations with public authorities, enabling firms to secure relaxation of existing regulation; and it may promote desired regulation, enabling firms to influence the design of new regulation in line with their preferences.[136] There is considerable evidence that a credible threat of mandatory regulation is among the strongest drivers of voluntary action.[137]

(iii) Higher Revenues

Implementing a code may enable firms to achieve higher revenues than they would have realised without the voluntary action, by securing higher prices or larger market share through product differentiation, or simply by maintaining existing revenues through satisfaction of customer demands that they implement a particular code.[138]

[133] *Ibid*, 88; OECD, above n 3, 27; Carraro and Lévêque, 'Introduction', above n 131, 5.

[134] Thalmann and Baranzini, above n 43, 12.

[135] Subsidies may be particularly strong drivers for small and medium sised enterprises, which may not implement voluntary environmental codes without them and may discontinue implementation of voluntary codes when subsidies cease. European Commission, Enterprise Directorate General, *Public Policy Initiatives to Promote the Uptake of Environmental Management Systems in Small and Medium-Sised Enterprises* (EC, 2004) 40–46. See also RNL Andrews *et al*, 'Environmental Management Systems: History, Theory, and Implementation Research' in C Coglianese and J Nash (eds), *Regulating from the Inside* (Resources for the Future, 2001) 31, 49–50.

[136] OECD, above n 3, 25; Purchase, above n 132, 81; Lyon and Maxwell, above n 8, 86–96. For a summary of empirical evidence for this driver see M Khanna and DT Ramirez, 'Effectiveness of Voluntary Approaches: Implications for Climate Change Mitigation' in Thalmann and Baranzini, above n 43, 31, 46.

[137] Numerous studies indicate that dealing with existing and future regulation is the number one motivation for voluntary environmental improvement action by firms: eg I Henriques and P Sadorsky, 'The Determinants of an Environmentally Responsible Firm: An Empirical Approach' (1995) 30 *Journal of Environment and Management* 381. The 1993 end-of-life vehicles agreement between the French government and auto industry, eg, was prompted largely by the threat of stringent legislation in Germany, accompanied by regulatory rumblings in France and at the European level: Lyon and Maxwell, above n 8, 80–81.

[138] Carraro and Lévêque, 'Introduction', above n 131, 5; OECD, above n 3, 27.

(iv) Reputational Gains

Implementing voluntary environmental codes may enable firms to cultivate a reputation for environmental leadership, gain the confidence and trust of consumers or publics, improve brand image, respond to adverse publicity, and improve relations with NGOs, local communities, workers and labour unions.[139] The potential benefits to the firm include improved asset values (eg trademarks and goodwill) and enhanced ability to recruit and retain talented employees. Some argue that external pressure for legitimacy is a stronger driver for firms than the pursuit of profit.[140] In any case reputational and regulatory drivers often go hand in hand: the chemical industry's Responsible Care initiative, for instance, was developed both to 'regain society's trust' and to limit state intervention 'to a level that is acceptable to the industry.'[141]

(b) Ethics and Legal Compliance

Aside from these benefit–cost considerations, implementation of voluntary environmental codes may be driven in some cases by top managers' ethical commitment to environmental stewardship—it's 'the right thing to do'.[142] In other cases it may be driven by the need to comply with official law. Firms sometimes implement codes either because the law expressly requires it or because they believe that doing so will enable them to fulfil existing legal requirements, whether of private[143] or public law.[144]

(c) Constraints and Disincentives

What might prevent firms from implementing voluntary environmental codes? First, the anticipation of net benefits to the firm not only drives the adoption of codes, it also sets a cap on what we can expect from them.[145] While there is widespread confidence that environmental protection is good for business and that 'win-win' environmental improvement opportunities exist in abundance, we must ask 'what happens when what's good for the environment is not good for the

[139] OECD, above n 3, 27–28; Purchase, above n 132, 81. For a summary of empirical evidence for this driver see Khanna and Ramirez, above n 136, 46–47.

[140] Eg J Meyer and WR Scott (eds), *Organisational Environments: Ritual and Rationality* (Sage 1992).

[141] Lyon and Maxwell, above n 8, 79.

[142] 53% of respondents to a recent global survey reported 'ethical considerations' as a driver for corporate sustainability initiatives: KPMG, above n 132, 18.

[143] For example, voluntary codes may acquire the force of law as judicial standards of 'reasonableness' in negligence or nuisance cases, prompting some firms to implement the codes to avoid the prospect of having their conduct judged against a code they neither helped develop nor adhered to: K Webb, 'Voluntary Initiatives and the Law' in Gibson, above n 6, 32, 40.

[144] For example, some Canadian legal experts believe that implementation of a voluntary EMS will enable firms to demonstrate 'due diligence' if accused of violating environmental regulations: eg D Taylor, 'ISO 14000 and Environmental Regulation' (1999) 9 *Journal of Environmental Law & Practice* 1.

[145] Carraro and Lévêque, 'Introduction', above n 131, 5.

company'?[146] In the absence of compulsory regulation or a credible threat thereof, we can assume that firms will face weak drivers to implement voluntary environmental codes that entail net costs.

Secondly, firms have an incentive to try to capture the benefits of a voluntary code without bearing the corresponding costs.[147] In the case of firm-specific codes this may lead firms to misrepresent their environmental performance or the stringency of their voluntary commitments. In the case of collective codes it leads to free riding and other collective action problems.[148] Because this problem has a major impact on how well voluntary codes perform, we will return to it in the next section.

Thirdly, firm size has a substantial impact on code implementation. For various reasons, smaller firms tend not to feel the drivers discussed above as strongly as large firms, and tend to have less ability (eg money, time and know-how) to respond to them. As a result, larger firms are more likely to adopt voluntary environmental codes.[149]

Finally, we return to law once more. While the desire to comply with or avoid official law can drive firms to implement codes, law can also hinder the development and adoption of voluntary environmental codes. Background legal frameworks such as corporate governance, competition and trade laws may discourage voluntary environmental codes even when other drivers favour their implementation.[150] Many basic corporate governance laws constrain corporate managers from straying far from the goal of profit maximization. Trade and competition laws may erect legal barriers to voluntary codes, for instance by invalidating negotiated agreements that fix surcharges for recycling costs.[151] Finally, environmental laws may prevent public authorities from offering adequate regulatory incentives for voluntary action, such as regulatory flexibility or multi-media integrated targets.[152] In short, voluntary codes exist in a 'tangled web' of law, and it is critical to consider the entire suite of legal motivations and drivers for voluntary codes, including those that fall outside the realm of environmental policy.[153]

[146] SB Banerjee 'Managerial Perceptions of Corporate Environmentalism: Interpretations from industry and Strategic Implications for Organisations' (2001) 38 *Journal of Management Studies* 489, 509.

[147] Carraro and Lévêque, 'Introduction', above n 131, 5.

[148] Eg J Nash, 'Voluntary Codes of Practice: Non-Governmental Institutions for Promoting Environmental Management by Firms' (paper prepared for National Academy of Sciences/National Research Council Workshop on Education, Information and Voluntary Measures in Environmental Protection, Nov 2000).

[149] Lyon and Maxwell, above n 8, 102.

[150] Eg Orts and Deketelaere, 'Introduction', above n 29, 10–11; Meidinger, above n 7; Webb, above n 143; Webb and Morrison, above n 7.

[151] Such situations have materialised in Europe but are also a real possibility in Canada and the US: H Vedder, 'Competition Law and the Use of Environmental Agreements' in Orts and Deketelaere, above n 29, 247.

[152] Eg Davies and Mazurek, above n 32.

[153] Webb and Morrison, above n 7, V Haufler, *A Public Role for the Private Sector: Industry Self-Regulation in a Global Economy* (Carnegie Endowment for International Peace, 2001).

2. Drivers for Public Authorities[154]

Developing, implementing, monitoring and enforcing regulations can be very costly for governments. One reason governments embrace voluntary environmental codes for business is to do something—or be seen to be doing something—to improve industry environmental performance without the cost of official regulation. Many governments welcome voluntary codes as a way to move such costs off-budget. This, combined with disillusionment with conventional command regulation, an aversion to environmental taxes, enthusiasm for more flexible, adaptive or 'reflexive' regulation,[155] a desire for more cooperative relations with business and, in some cases, an ideological commitment to smaller government, drives many governments to promote voluntary approaches to environmental protection. Voluntary codes can supplement existing laws, addressing issues for which there is no regulation or for which existing regulation is inadequate, and transcending jurisdictional boundaries.[156] Finally, governments can use voluntary arrangements with industry or NGOs to enhance their own institutional capacity.[157]

The main disincentive for government support of voluntary codes is the risk of regulatory capture by industry, a situation in which polluters' voluntarily assumed targets reflect nothing more than 'business as usual' while relieving the pressure for mandatory, enforceable regulation.[158]

3. ENGO drivers

Environmental groups' motives for promoting voluntary environmental codes for industry vary from frustration with inadequate and cumbersome official regulatory processes (and a corresponding wish to bypass government and deal with business directly), to enthusiasm for consumer- or market-driven tools for environmental improvement. Either way, ENGO support is driven, and ultimately limited, by voluntary codes' superior ability to deliver improved environmental performance. NGO-led voluntary codes such as the Forest Stewardship Council's sustainable forestry certification scheme enable NGOs to create and operate alternative rule-making systems that are more flexible, agile, environmentally ambitious and effective than many official legal systems. Such codes can act as 'voicing mechanisms' for demand-side interests in the economy, replacing (or supplementing) the blunt

[154] See generally, Purchase, above n 132, 79–80; P ten Brink, 'Part A: Introduction' in ten Brink, above n 3, 30, 32–34; Moffet and Bregha, above n 101, 18.

[155] E Orts, 'Reflexive Environmental Law' (1995) 89 *Northwestern University L Rev* 1227; see Richardson and Wood, ch 1, and Abbot, ch 2, this vol.

[156] Purchase, above n 132, 79; ten Brink, above n 154, 33.

[157] *Ibid*, 32–33.

[158] See OECD, above n 3, 31–35.

technique of consumer boycotts with information-rich, proactive and often highly effective means to enhance public transparency and change corporate behaviour.[159]

The main disincentive for ENGO support is the dual risk of losing their own independence and credibility while conferring legitimacy on environmentally questionable firms or codes.[160] Another disincentive is that participation in a code may entail substantial time and cost without necessarily offering commensurate returns in environmental improvement, a telling consideration when most ENGOs make decisions about where to allocate their scarce resources.[161]

In short, businesses, public authorities and ENGOs all face substantial risks with voluntary codes, but develop and implement them because, for an assortment of reasons, they feel compelled to do so.[162]

G. How Well do Voluntary Codes Perform?

Actors may feel driven to develop and implement voluntary environmental codes, but are the codes they develop and implement effective? There has been relatively little independent empirical analysis of the effectiveness of voluntary environmental codes, due mainly to a lack of reliable monitoring data and consistent reporting,[163] but this is beginning to change.[164] While there are many criteria against which to evaluate codes' performance, we focus here on environmental effectiveness, efficiency, transparency and accountability, and polluter behaviour. The picture that emerges is not encouraging.

1. Environmental Effectiveness

The evidence of voluntary codes' environmental effectiveness is mixed. On one hand, polluters' environmental performance generally improves after they implement voluntary environmental codes.[165] Moreover, when codes are implemented, their environmental targets are usually met or exceeded.[166] Two key questions arise, however: how ambitious are the targets, and would the improvements have occurred anyway?

[159] Webb, above n 4, 17–19.

[160] Ten Brink, above n 154, 35.

[161] *Ibid.*

[162] K Webb, 'Voluntary Codes: Where to From Here' in Webb, above n 4, 379, 380.

[163] EEA, above n 10.

[164] Eg OECD, *Voluntary Approaches for Environmental Policy: Effectiveness, Efficiency and Usage in Policy Mixes* (OECD 2003).

[165] EEA, above n 10.

[166] Khanna and Ramirez, above n 136; OECD, above n 164, 49. There are exceptions, of course (eg ARET, the Government of Canada's public voluntary programme for reduced releases of toxic substances, targeted a 90% reduction in participating firms' releases of persistent and bioaccumulative substances by 2000, but the actual reduction achieved was 61%): *Ibid*, 43.

(a) Ambitiousness of Targets

There is evidence that voluntary environmental targets are lower than externally imposed ones, suggesting that the choice of voluntary codes over regulation or economic instruments may imply less ambitious environmental targets.[167] Reasons include the central role of polluters themselves in goal-setting and the relative exclusion of ENGOs and legislative branches from goal-setting in comparison to conventional regulatory processes. Implementation-based codes, public voluntary programmes and other codes that do not give polluters a central role in environmental target-setting are less susceptible to this problem.[168] The same is true of codes in which 'civil society' interests play a substantial or decisive role. Many such codes set ambitious targets that require greater environmental improvements than would be expected under available alternatives such as polluter–initiated codes, some third party standards or even mandatory legal rules.[169] These codes' environmental effectiveness is constrained mainly by limited implementation. Only the FSC and a few others have achieved widespread market acceptance, and they face fierce competition, often from less demanding, polluter–initiated codes.[170]

(b) Departure from Business as Usual

Secondly, it is frequently unclear whether observed environmental improvements are due to the code or would have occurred anyway in a 'business as usual' (BAU) pattern.[171] On the positive side, some Japanese local authority–company agreements and Danish agreements on industrial energy efficiency appear to have contributed significantly to observed environmental improvements. In these cases the

[167] Eg OECD, above n 3, 25 (German industry's voluntary CO_2 reduction target was significantly lower than the target contemplated by the German government's regulatory programme); van Calster and Deketelaere, above n 31, 230 (European Commission's agreement with the car industry set target for automobile CO_2 emissions of 140g/km by 2008, compared with the EU's own objective of 120g/km by 2010).

[168] OECD, above n 3, 104.

[169] Eg L Gulbrandsen, 'Sustainable Forestry in Sweden: The Effect of Competition Among Private Certification Schemes' (2005) 14 *Journal of Environment & Development* 338 (comparing FSC and Pan-European Forest Certification schemes); Meidinger, above n 103 (comparing FSC and ISO 14001).

[170] The FSC, with approximately 53 million hectares of certified forests and more than 5% of the world timber market, is the most successful sustainable forestry certification scheme by a slight margin, but it faces competition from at least 23 other schemes, enjoys only modest success in developing countries, generally generates no price premium for producers, has attracted criticism from both forest companies for being too demanding and ENGOs for being too lax, and is dogged by ongoing questions about whether a market-driven certification system can ultimately reverse the global advance of deforestation. eg P Pattberg, 'The Forest Stewardship Council: Risk and Potential of Private Forest Governance' (2005) 14 *Journal of Environment & Development* 356.

[171] EEA, above n 10, 83–85. For example, a recent high-profile US study found a correlation between EMS implementation and overall environmental performance improvement but did not investigate whether these improvements were actually attributable to the EMSs. RNL Andrews *et al*, *Environmental Management Systems: Do They Improve Performance?* National Database on Environmental Management Systems Project Final Report (U North Carolina at Chapel Hill, 2003), available at ndems.cas.unc.edu.

voluntary approaches were usually backed by credible threats (eg to block a proposed expansion or impose higher tax).[172] On the other hand, a study of the US EPA's 33/50 programme found that while the target for reduction of releases of specified chemicals was exceeded, only 28 per cent of the reduction could be attributed to the programme.[173] A study of the chemical industry's Responsible Care programme concluded:

> Our data provide no evidence that Responsible Care has positively influenced the rate of improvement among its members. Indeed, we found evidence that members of Responsible Care are improving their relative environmental performance more slowly than non-members.[174]

Studies of German industry's 1995 commitment to reduce CO_2 emissions and energy intensity indicated that it was not even equal to the BAU scenario, even after it was tightened in 1996.[175] Finally, polluters often implement codes to gain recognition for improvements they have already made or decided to make. They may seek to 'cash in' these previous and planned changes, such as closure of a polluting facility or investment in cleaner technology, by having them incorporated in the code's targets.[176] This is made possible partly by pervasive information asymmetries between polluters and regulators.

In short, 'factors other than the given voluntary approach seem to explain the major part of any environmental improvement that has taken place' in most cases.[177] In some cases these problems reflect 'regulatory capture' of rule-making by polluters. While all forms of environmental regulation are at risk of regulatory capture and other failures compromising their environmental effectiveness, voluntary environmental codes may be particularly susceptible.[178]

[172] OECD, above n 164, 50.

[173] M Khanna 'Non-Mandatory Approaches to Environmental Protection' (2001) 15 *Journal of Economic Surveys* 291.

[174] AA King and MJ Lennox, 'Industry Self-Regulation Without Sanctions: The Chemical Industry's Responsible Care Program' (2000) 43 *Academic Management* J 698, 709.

[175] Declaration by German Industry and Trade on Global Warming Prevention (1995, amended 1996). See E Jochem and W Eichhammer, 'Voluntary agreements as an instrument to substitute regulating and economic instruments: Lessons from the German Voluntary agreements on CO_2 Reduction' in Carraro and Lévêque, above n 131, 209; EEA, above n 10, 64–68, OECD, above n 3, 32.

[176] Eg E Brand, 'The Netherlands: Agreement on the Reduction of SO_2 and NOx Emissions from the Power Generation Industry' (paper prepared for NEAPOL project, 2000), available at fetew.rug.ac.be/NEAPOL (a large part of reductions was realised by closing coal-fired plants already slated for closure because of official regulations); OECD, above n 3, 32 (80% of German industry's voluntary target for greenhouse gas abatement had already been achieved when it was announced in 1995); OECD, above n 164, 51–53 (participants in both Canada's ARET programme and the French government's aluminum industry agreement received substantial credit for reductions made before the codes took effect).

[177] *Ibid*, 62.

[178] OECD, above n 3, 31–35.

2. Efficiency

There is little evidence that voluntary codes are economically efficient, whether in terms of target-setting, cost-effectiveness, transaction and operating costs, free-riding or effects on competition.

(a) Efficiency of Targets

First, there is little evidence that codes' environmental targets are set at a level that maximises social welfare,[179] or that welfare maximisation is even code developers' goal when setting targets. This should come as no surprise, since the same is true of other forms of regulation.

(b) Cost-effectiveness

Voluntary codes can, in theory, be cost-effective (ie achieve a given environmental objective at least cost)[180] insofar as they leave the choice of pollution abatement strategy to firms, 'which are most likely to have information about it, and have the incentive to implement the least-cost options.'[181] This is not always borne out in practice, however.[182] Some codes contain mechanisms designed to equalise marginal abatement costs among participants, but the large majority do not, often leaving the allocation of abatement burdens to the participants who almost always allocate them on a basis other than marginal abatement costs. In short, the design of most voluntary codes makes it likely that marginal abatement costs will differ significantly across polluters.[183] Codes may nonetheless be more cost-effective than conventional command regulation, but their advantage in this respect has diminished as more governments move from technology to performance standards, and introduce market-based instruments such as taxes and tradable permit schemes which, if designed properly, are highly cost-effective.[184]

(c) Transaction and Operating Costs

Thirdly, the evidence is equivocal on whether voluntary codes involve lower transaction costs (ie the costs of developing a code) or operating costs than other regulatory options. The main concern is whether the costs of developing and

[179] That is, at the point where the marginal social benefit of further improvement equals the marginal social cost of such improvement.

[180] This occurs when the marginal costs of environmental improvement are equal across all contributors to the problem (versus, eg, all being required to meet the same abatement target).

[181] Carraro and Lévêque, 'Introduction', above n 131, 8.

[182] OECD, above n 3, 108–109.

[183] OECD, above n 164, 66–67.

[184] A Alberini and K Segerson, 'Assessing Voluntary Programs to Improve Environmental Quality' (2002) 22 *Environmental & Resource Economics* 157. On recent innovations in command regulation see Abbot, this vol.

administering a code—or other regulatory instrument—will exceed the value created by the code.[185] We are interested here in both the magnitude of such costs in comparison to policy alternatives, and how these costs are distributed among various actors. It is clear that these costs can be very substantial in absolute terms.[186] Transaction costs (including the costs of identifying relevant participants and negotiating code terms) vary greatly from code to code, and tend to rise with the number of parties involved, the complexity and innovativeness of the code, the volume and complexity of scientific and technical studies needed, the ambiguity of the relation between the code and official legal systems and the lack of a pre-existing institutional framework for code development.[187]

Operating costs (ie the costs of implementing, complying with, administering and enforcing codes) also vary greatly among codes, increasing with the codes' environmental stringency, divergence from prevailing business practices, degree of paperwork and organisational requirements, extent and difficulty of performance monitoring, and emphasis on public consultation or external verification. Even so, operating costs may be lower than for command regulation, partly because codes (especially polluter–led ones) tend to set lower targets, grant more flexibility in meeting them, and place less emphasis (sometimes none at all) on monitoring, verification, enforcement and sanctions.[188]

As to the allocation of transaction and operating costs among various actors, voluntary codes tend to lower public authorities' transaction costs, especially administrative costs. Citizens and governments may thus enjoy an increased supply of public goods (eg environmental standards and quality) without an increased burden on the public purse, although other actors shoulder these transaction costs and may pass some on to consumers.[189] Experience with many codes also indicates that the cost of code development and implementation is often much higher in relative terms for small than large organisations, which works against SME participation, and for non-profit than business organisations, which works against effective participation by NGOs.[190] But this is true of other regulatory instruments, too.

[185] OECD, above n 3, 42.

[186] The annual government budget for administering the Dutch Long-Term Agreements on energy efficiency (covering 600 companies and around 90% of industrial primary energy consumption), for example, was Fl 140m in 1994 (US$70m). OECD, above n 3, 110. The ISO 14001 EMS standard cost millions of dollars to develop, and the initial cost of ISO 14001 implementation and certification can range from $25,000 to over $100,000 per facility. A Kolk, *The Economics of Environmental Management* (Prentice Hall 2000).

[187] Eg OECD, above n 164, 76–80. On the other hand, existing institutions may be hamstrung by past choices and commitments and incapable of the forward thinking required to develop new codes. Prakash, above n 98.

[188] OECD, above n 3, 110.

[189] Prakash, above n 98.

[190] Eg A Blackman and J Mazurek, 'The Cost of Developing Site-Specific Environmental Regulations: Evidence from EPA's Project XL' (2001) 27 *Environmental Management* 109.

(d) Free-Riding

Fourthly, voluntary codes are susceptible to free-riding. Free-riding occurs when actors enjoy the benefits of a code without paying for its costs. This is a particular problem for collective codes, because polluters may be able to reap the benefits of a code (eg reputational gains, avoidance of regulation) without taking any environmental improvement action themselves. The risk of free-riding leads to under-supply of both codes and—more importantly — environmental improvement actions. Certain features increase the opportunities for free-riding, including negotiation of targets with polluters, collective rather than individualised targets, collective consequences for non-attainment, legally unenforceable commitments, inadequate monitoring and lack of serious sanctions for individual firms. The 'German' model of negotiated agreements (NAs) is an example. These agreements:

> not only set collective targets, but also hold industry 'collectively' liable for their implementation. Typically, there is no explicit sanction included in the NA, but in the case of the failure of the agreement, public authority will issue new legislation. This means that in the case of failure firms will be collectively sanctioned, independently of individual pollution abatement efforts. In this framework, the NA provides a collective benefit: avoiding new legislation, without sanctions for individual non-compliance. Therefore, in this setting, free-riding becomes a major concern.[191]

(e) Effects on Competition

Finally, there is little evidence of the effects of voluntary codes on competition, but the number of codes investigated by antitrust authorities is increasing[192] and existing evidence suggests that voluntary codes can have several anti-competitive effects.[193] First, by increasing polluters' costs, codes can lead firms to exit the industry, reducing the number of firms. Secondly, codes may provide a screen for anti-competitive collusion (eg price-fixing).[194] Thirdly, codes can erect barriers to entry for domestic or international competitors.[195] Fourthly, polluters might implement a code unilaterally to signal low abatement costs and influence regulators toward stricter regulation that hurts competitors.[196]

[191] OECD, above n 3, 61.

[192] OECD, above n 3, 112.

[193] See generally Alberini and Segerson, above n 184; Webb and Morrison, above n 7, 155–160.

[194] OECD, above n 3, 112 (European Commission invalidated a uniform environmental surcharge jointly agreed and levied by six Dutch firms to finance implementation of environmental covenant with the Dutch government).

[195] This is a particular concern in developing countries, where many voluntary codes such as EMAS, FSC and ISO 14001 are seen as (potential) non-tariff trade barriers. eg R Krut and H Gleckman, *ISO 14001: A Missed Opportunity for Sustainable Global Industrial Development* (Earthscan 1998).

[196] For example, Du Pont's voluntary acceleration of the phase-out of CFCs and its welcoming of first national, then international regulation of CFCs may have given it an advantage over competitors who were not in a position to introduce alternative products. Lyon and Maxwell, above n 8, 95–96; R Benedick, *Ozone Diplomacy* (Harvard UP, 1991) 30–34.

3. Transparency and accountability

One of the main concerns about voluntary codes is their impact on the transparency and accountability of rule-making, implementation and corporate performance. Expectations for transparency and accountability vary from a simple external check on a polluter's self-declared claims, to democratic deliberation over every aspect of code development and implementation. The main issues in this area are public participation; monitoring, reporting and verification; and sanctions and enforcement. Along with environmental effectiveness, these are widely considered the key determinants of the credibility of voluntary environmental codes.

(a) Public Participation

Voluntary codes' record of fostering public participation in environmental decision making is mixed. Many voluntary codes offer fewer opportunities for public participation in and scrutiny of rule-making and rule-implementation than official policy processes, leading to serious concerns about transparency, accountability and erosion of democratic governance.[197] On the other hand, some codes require participating polluters to institute public consultation mechanisms that go considerably farther than what is required by law, for instance in the form of community advisory processes. Responsible Care, for example, involves both national and facility-level community advisory committees. Other codes go much further, creating rule-making institutions in which civil society interests play a central role (eg the Forest Stewardship Council). The evidence indicates that involvement of ENGOs and community members in code development and implementation improves codes' environmental effectiveness and enhances their credibility with external audiences, usually at relatively modest cost to polluters;[198] but there is also evidence that such involvement is used merely as a public relations exercise in some cases.[199]

(b) Monitoring, Reporting and Verification

Until recently many, and perhaps most voluntary environmental codes made no provision for monitoring or reporting of performance. As the European Environment Agency wrote in 1997, this damages the credibility of codes, denies their accountability and makes it extremely difficult to conduct ex-post evaluations of their effectiveness.[200] In recent years most codes have introduced requirements for self-monitoring and public reporting, and many have introduced

[197] Eg J Gorin, 'Caught Between Action and Inaction: Public Participation Rights in Voluntary Approaches to Environmental Policy' (2005) 24 *Stanford Envtl LJ* 151; EEA, above n 10.
[198] OECD, above n 164, 85.
[199] Prakash, above n 98.
[200] EEA, above n 10.

requirements for external verification. One typical approach is to rely on self-monitoring and -reporting, with independent third-party verification of the methods employed and findings made;[201] another is to allow unverified self-monitoring and -reporting, with external verification of management systems only.[202] As to public reporting of objectives and performance, it is now *de rigeur* in most public voluntary programmes, negotiated environmental agreements and third party codes, with the notable exception of ISO 14001 which requires public disclosure only of the organisation's environmental policy.

The ultimate form of external verification of code implementation is third-party certification. Certification may be awarded to a product (eg certifying the product to meet certain environmental requirements) or an organisation (eg certifying that it has a prescribed environmental management system in place). There is a trend toward more certifications, as existing certification codes expand their market share and other codes introduce certification requirements. A huge industry of auditors, certifiers and accreditation bodies has emerged to serve these expanding certification needs. Certification generally enhances the credibility of an organisation's claims with external audiences and may be the basis for customers or consumers to differentiate among competing firms or products. Certification may not have such effects, however, where it simply verifies that the organisation has certain management tools in place, such as an EMS. One study of US facilities with ISO 14001 EMSs, for instance, found no statistically significant difference in environmental performance, regulatory compliance, or realised benefits and costs between those whose EMSs were and were not third-party certified.[203]

(c) Enforcement and Sanctions

Finally, sanctions and enforcement are critical to a code's credibility. Haufler summarises the key questions in this regard: how are codes enforced, if at all; how credible are they given their general lack of enforcement; and how accountable is business to the wider public when adopting these codes?[204] Most codes contain no explicit sanctions for non-conformity and almost none provide formal mechanisms for enforcement or dispute resolution. This lack of sanctions and enforcement is

[201] Eg EMAS Regulation, above n 69 (initial environmental review, EMS, audit procedure and annual statement of environmental objectives and performance must be approved by an accredited EMAS verifier and the validated statement must be made publicly available).

[202] Eg Responsible Care, above n 49 (US version now requires third-party certification of management system by independent accredited auditing firm, and publication of company-specific performance data, but does not require external verification of self-reported performance data, www.responsiblecare-us.com; Canadian version requires verification of management systems by external team of 2 industry experts, an activist and a community member, but does not require publication of company-specific performance data or external verification of self-reported performance data, at www.ccpa.ca/ResponsibleCare).

[203] Andrews *et al*, above n 171.

[204] Haufler, above n 153, 4.

often identified as one of the key weaknesses of voluntary codes. Where sanctions exist, they usually take the form of withdrawal of privileges (eg decertification or termination of membership), actions for damages, or—in the case of codes involving public authorities—regulatory enforcement actions. But decertifications are rarely made public, industry association members are almost never kicked out, judicial actions to enforce code provisions are rare and regulators almost never take enforcement action when a firm violates the terms of a negotiated agreement.

4. Polluter Behaviour

Finally, the performance of voluntary environmental codes can be assessed in terms of their effects on various aspects of polluter behaviour, including economic performance, legal performance, innovation and so-called 'soft' effects.

(a) Economic Performance

First, there is a substantial body of evidence that implementing voluntary codes improves participating firms' financial performance, either by increasing profits or market value. This has been found across a wide variety of codes, from polluter codes to public voluntary programmes, although the degree of improvement varies widely across codes and polluters and with the degree of environmental improvement actually achieved.[205] For example, paints qualifying for the voluntary German 'Blue Angel' eco-label increased their market share by an amount that was more than could be attributed to the underlying trend toward solvent-free paint even though their prices were higher than non-Blue Angel products.[206] In addition, voluntary codes are typically thought to have a more positive impact on firms' financial bottom lines than command regulation or economic instruments, which are generally seen as imposing deadweight costs.

Experience suggests three lessons about the potential of voluntary codes to deliver improved financial performance. First, there are probably still plenty of win-win opportunities to improve environmental and financial performance simultaneously. Secondly, market pressures alone are inadequate to spur firms to take full advantage of these opportunities, since even after decades of regulation, environmentalist demands and 'green' business ideas, many firms still need to be pushed into profitable environmental initiatives. And thirdly, incremental

[205] Eg G Dowell, S Hart and B Yeung, 'Do Corporate Global Environmental Standards Create or Destroy Market Value?' (2000) 46 *Management Science* 1059; M Khanna and L Damon, 'EPA's Voluntary 33/50 Program: Impact on Toxic Releases and Economic Performance of Firms' (1999) 37 *Journal of Environmental Economics & Management 1*.

[206] J Hemmelskamp and KL Brockmann, 'Environmental Labels: The German "Blue Angel"' (1997) 29(1) *Futures* 67. But see OECD, above n 164, 61 (Nordic 'Swan' eco-label not shown to have significant effect on consumers' brand choices).

environmental gains are likely to become increasingly difficult and costly, so that further environmental improvements will not be attractive enough to be undertaken voluntarily without substantial changes in established market drivers.[207]

(b) Legal Performance

After environmental effectiveness, the most pressing question for public authorities and environmental groups is whether codes improve participating polluters' compliance with legal requirements. This is a critical question for governments considering offering regulatory flexibility to firms with voluntary codes in place. It is also critical question for those hoping that voluntary codes might improve legal compliance in jurisdictions where environmental laws are not adequately enforced. Many voluntary codes commit participants to comply with (or in some cases exceed) the legal requirements in force wherever they operate, but there is not enough evidence yet to indicate how effectively these commitments are observed in practice.

The question of legal compliance arises especially in relation to process-oriented codes such as EMS standards, which put certain management practices in place without prescribing particular environmental performance levels. Some studies have shown a correlation between EMS implementation and improved legal compliance,[208] but most fail to establish whether the improvement would have happened anyway, and there is plentiful evidence of ISO 14001-certified facilities with bad legal compliance records. Potoski and Prakash conjecture that ISO 14001 leads to improved compliance in two ways: first, EMS implementation reduces *unintentional* violations by requiring organisations to systematically address the root causes of non-compliance; and secondly, EMS certification reduces *intentional* violations by having the organisation's EMS audited by a third party.[209] In any case, the jury remains out on whether process-oriented or performance-based voluntary codes lead to improved regulatory compliance.

(c) Stimulation of Innovation

Innovation involves the *development* of new technologies and practices and their *diffusion* among relevant actors. Because most codes do not set very ambitious environmental targets, they do little to stimulate the development of cleaner

[207] RB Gibson, 'Voluntary Initiatives, Regulations, and Beyond' in Gibson, above n 6, 239, 246–247; N Walley and B Whitehead, 'It's Not Easy Being Green' (1994) 72 *Harvard Business Rev* (May-June) 46.

[208] Eg Andrews *et al*, above n 171; M Potoski and A Prakash, 'Green Clubs and Voluntary Governance: ISO 14001 and Firms' Regulatory Compliance' (2005) 49 *American Journal of Political Science* 235.

[209] *Ibid*. The authors fail to above n, however, that ISO 14001 does not actually require certification or that EMS audits are not in fact audits of regulatory compliance.

technologies or innovative practices.[210] On the other hand, many codes facilitate diffusion of existing technologies and practices by increasing awareness of available tools, or creating forums for diffusion of existing technologies between polluters, from third parties (researchers or ENGOs) to polluters or from polluters to public authorities.[211] This may stimulate innovation and decrease its costs by enabling polluters to share information about experiments with abatement technologies.[212] But with the possible exception of some civil society-led initiatives, voluntary codes do not appear very effective at breaking down long-standing barriers to diffusion of innovations from developed to developing economies.

(d) 'Soft' Effects

Numerous analysts conclude that the main benefits of voluntary environmental codes are indirect and unquantifiable but nonetheless substantial. These so-called 'soft' effects include increased awareness of and improved attitudes toward environmental issues; increased generation and sharing of information; enhanced co-operation and trust among polluters, regulators and others; experimentation with new policies and policy development processes; and improvement of corporate environmental management techniques (eg EMSs).[213] In some cases this can create 'collective learning' processes that enable polluters, regulators and (rarely) third parties to combine knowledge and develop new solutions and competencies.[214]

One should not be too sanguine about the significance of these 'soft' effects. Their true extent and their impacts on organisational culture and behaviour are hard to pin down. There is considerable evidence, unfortunately, that many polluters with forward-looking environmental codes in place still lobby governments intensely for public policies that contradict or undermine the commitments they make in voluntary codes and the claims they make in their public environmental

[210] OECD, above n 3, 112. Eg M Rietbergen, M Breukels and K Blok, *Case Studies in the Sectors of Paper and Glass Manufacturing* prepared for Voluntary Agreements—Implementation and Efficiency project, www.akf.dk/VAIE (finding no evidence that the Dutch agreement with the paper and glass manufacturing industry stimulated development of new energy efficient technologies).

[211] OECD, above n 164, 72.

[212] F Aggeri and A Hatchuel, 'A Dynamic Model of Environmental Policies: The Case of Innovation Oriented Voluntary Agreements' in Carraro and Lévêque, above n 131, 151 (discussing the French vehicle end-of-life agreement).

[213] EEA, above n 10, 85; M Storey, G Boyd and J Dowd, 'Voluntary Agreements with Industry' in Carraro and Lévêque, above n 131, 187 (discussing government—industry negotiated agreements for energy efficiency and greenhouse gas abatement in various OECD countries).

[214] Aggeri and Hatchuel, above n 212 (discussing the French vehicle end-of-life agreement); L Price *et al*, 'Voluntary Agreements for Increasing Energy-Efficiency in Industry: Case Study of a Pilot Project with the Steel Industry in Shandong Province, China' (paper prepared for 2003 ACEEE Industrial Summer Study on Energy Efficiency in Industry, May 2003).

reports.[215] There may thus be substantial gaps between what firms say they stand for and how they actually behave.

H. What Roles can—and should—Voluntary Codes Play in Environmental Law for Sustainability?

We arrive, finally, at the most difficult of all the questions posed in this chapter, and the one for which our answers are necessarily the most tentative. First, we need to grapple with the thorny issue of what sustainability means. Then we can begin to sketch out what 'law for sustainability' might entail. Finally, we can consider what role voluntary codes can and should play in environmental law for sustainability. Given the generally disappointing evidence of voluntary codes' performance to date, our basic attitude toward this question is sceptical, but open-minded.

1. Sustainability

Sustainability has emerged as one of the central problems and defining goals of human affairs at the opening of the twenty-first century. It has become a watchword of contemporary business and policy, heard throughout most domains of public discourse. In its most influential formulation, 'sustainable development', it has been embraced as a goal by governments, international organisations, businesses, NGOs and academics around the world. Its successful penetration of political, legal and business discourse is thought to be due in large part to its ambiguity and open-endedness, which enable it to be embraced by a wide variety of actors with radically divergent interests and agendas. This is true, but only to a point. The success of sustainability has more to do with the way its broad potential meaning has been channelled in particular directions that are expedient to political and economic elites.

The idea of sustainability arose first as a warning and a challenge: a warning that industrial growth was increasingly incompatible with human and environmental well-being, and a challenge to bring the former into line with the latter. The success of sustainability as an idea was due mainly to the relative ease with which political and economic elites in the global North and South, helped along by some elite NGOs, were able, first, to transform this warning and challenge into

[215] SustainAbility and WWF-UK, *Influencing Power: Reviewing the Conduct and Content of Corporate Lobbying* (2005), www.corporate-accountability.org/docs/influencingpower.pdf; Prakash, above n 98, 202 (noting that the Chemical Manufacturers' Association has lobbied Congress to remove more than 90% of the chemicals from the Toxics Release Inventory's mandatory reporting list, which appears inconsistent with Responsible Care's commitment to public transparency).

a promise, and second, to define this promise in ways that reinforced their own agendas. First, the challenge of sustainability was redefined as a promise that environmental protection, human fulfilment and economic development are mutually reinforcing. This is not objectionable in itself. Where problems arise, however, and where the key to sustainability's success (or failure, depending on how you look at it) lies, is in the ease with which this promise has been transformed into an excuse to at best tinker marginally with, and at worst intensify, existing patterns of growth, consumption, inequity and ecological degradation.[216] The real danger with sustainability, then, is not its ambiguity, but—like voluntary codes themselves—its susceptibility to being used as a vehicle for the continuation of business as usual.

This is dangerous because business as usual will not do, even if it produces substantial incremental improvements in environmental quality, social equity and human welfare. As Paul Hawken famously observed, 'If every company on the planet were to adopt the best environmental practices of the "leading companies," the world would still be moving toward sure degradation and collapse.'[217] The collective choices we have made in the past century and will make in this century will determine for generations to come whether many billions of humans live intolerable or fulfilling lives, whether we have so soiled, poisoned, degraded and altered our own planetary nest and its life support systems that it becomes hostile to our continued presence, and whether countless species survive at all. Sustainability requires a massive departure from business as usual.

The conceptions of sustainability that have met with the most success in legal, political and business circles—especially the marriage of economic development and environmental protection embodied in mainstream 'sustainable development' theory and practice—are incapable of generating this change. A more promising conception of sustainability is built on two pillars: ecological integrity and social emancipation.

Ecological integrity refers to the restoration, maintenance and enhancement of planetary life support systems (eg clean air, clean water, productive topsoil, climate regulation), ecosystem structures and functions, and biodiversity.[218] It does not imply an absence of human interference in the biosphere, which would be nonsensical, but it does imply dramatically reducing the 'ecological footprints' of individuals and societies in the industrialised, consumption-oriented global North and keeping humanity's overall ecological footprint well within the planet's productive capacity,[219] and redefining poverty and wealth in terms of quality

[216] Eg W Sachs, 'Environment' in W Sachs (ed), *The Development Dictionary: A Guide to Knowledge as Power* (Zed, 1992) 26.

[217] P Hawken, *The Ecology of Commerce* (Harper Collins, 1993) xiii.

[218] Eg D Pimentel, L Westra and RF Noss (eds), *Ecological Integrity: Integrating Environment, Conservation, and Health* (Island Press, 2000).

[219] M Wackernagel and WE Rees, *Our Ecological Footprint: Reducing Human Impact on the Earth* (New Society, 1996); J Venetoulis, D Chazin and C Gaudet, *Ecological Footprint of Nations 2004* (Redefining Progress, 2004).

of life rather than material possessions and money.[220] Drawing a page from the Natural Step book, it implies that the biosphere is not subjected to systematically increasing concentrations of substances extracted from the earth's crust (eg fossil fuels, metals and minerals) or produced by society (eg persistent synthetic chemicals), and that biological resources are not exploited or converted at rates faster than they are replenished (eg over-harvesting of fish or timber, conversion of forest or grassland to agriculture).[221]

Social emancipation refers to freedom from the legal, social, economic and political constraints that keep humans (and by extension nature) in positions of subjugation and oppression.[222] These include violence, social exclusion, economic exploitation, ignorance, poverty, disease, and premature death. Emancipation implies not mere survival, but the flourishing and enfranchisement of those individuals and groups who are effectively excluded from the social contract. On a global scale this means the 'majority world'—the large portion of humanity living with chronic poverty, disease, violence, drought, pollution, or displacement. In advanced liberal democracies it means the inhabitants of 'internal Third Worlds', such as aboriginal peoples, the rural and urban poor, the homeless, and many immigrants. Emancipation, thus understood, has been the goal of democratic politics since the Enlightenment, but it remains far from realisation. In recent decades it seems to be receding farther from our grasp as global and domestic disparities of wealth and well-being have increased rather than shrunk.[223]

We will not get substantially closer to social emancipation or ecological integrity until we sacrifice one of the sacred cows of contemporary politics, law and business, namely the idea that development, prosperity and human happiness depend upon guaranteeing the stability of economic and other expectations. Stability of expectations, on the contrary, is an obstacle to social emancipation and sustainability. For the majority of humanity, expectations follow fairly predictably from experiences and experiences conform fairly grimly to expectations. To strive for emancipation is to strive to increase the discrepancy between experiences and expectations, by confronting and delegitimising the norms, institutions, and practices—among them official law—that guarantee the stability of expectations.[224] Stability of expectations principally favours those who benefit most from current patterns of political organisation and economic development. Political and economic elites—and here we include affluent residents of the privileged global 'North'—currently enjoy relative stability, not just of economic expectations (eg

[220] B Devall, *Simple in Means, Rich in Ends: Practicing Deep Ecology* (Peregrine Smith 1988).

[221] The Natural Step, available at www.naturalstep.org/learn/principles.php.

[222] This discussion is drawn largely from S Clarkson and S Wood, 'Governing Beyond Borders: Law for Canadians in an Era of Globalization' (paper prepared for Law Commission of Canada, Aug 2005).

[223] Eg Richardson, Mgbeoji and Botchway, this vol.

[224] B de Sousa Santos, *Toward a New Legal Common Sense* (Butterworths, 2002) 2.

contracts and private property), but of expectations for good health, clean air and water, prosperity, cheap and plentiful food, and security against arbitrary violence. To extend these benefits to a substantial portion of the global majority will imply destabilising some of the expectations that political and economic elites have come to view as entitlements. Admittedly, such instability is dangerous, both for those struggling to break free of oppression and those clinging to received advantages. But it is also hopeful, especially for those with the least to lose and the most to gain from it.

2. Environmental Law for Sustainability

The contribution of voluntary environmental codes—or any other regulatory instruments, for that matter—to environmental law for sustainability should be evaluated in terms of their potential to advance ecological integrity and social emancipation. This will depend in turn upon their potential for disruption of entrenched patterns of poverty, disease, violence and ecological degradation, and innovative transformation of technologies,[225] institutions,[226] cultures, attitudes and ethics.[227] Experimentation, participatory deliberation, learning and adaptation are among the hallmarks of environmental law for sustainability.[228]

Voluntarism has an ambivalent yet indispensable place in environmental law for sustainability. On one hand, for reasons already discussed, voluntary action by polluters has limited capacity to disrupt business as usual and must, *inter alia*, be backed by credible threats to be effective. On the other hand, as students of politics and law have long known and critics of 'command' regulation have recently reiterated, authorities cannot, ultimately, govern by forcing their wills into the minutiae of governed lives and spaces. Any system of governance relies ultimately on the willingness of subjects to be governed. A system of governance is most effective when governed subjects voluntarily adopt and internalise its norms, values and ambitions as their own, so that they come to govern their own conduct in line with collective goals.[229] This is as true of voluntary codes and environmental law as any other forms of governance.

The question then becomes how to construct a system of environmental governance to maximise the potential for alignment between authorities' ambitions and subjects' decisions—how to enlist governed subjects in their own regulation

[225] Eg Driesen, this vol.

[226] Eg Dovers and Connor, this vol.

[227] Eg Bosselman, this vol.

[228] Eg R Unger, *Democracy Realised: The Progressive Alternative* (Verso, 1998); K Lee, *Compass and Gyroscope: Integrating Science and Politics for the Environment* (Island Press, 1993); Dovers and Connor, this vol.

[229] N Rose, *Powers of Freedom: Reframing Political Thought* (Cambridge, 1999) 50; Rose and Miller, above n 22.

—without falling into the trap of regulatory capture.[230] There can be no uniform answer. There will always be slippage and resistance between authorities' designs and subjects' thoughts and actions, and subjects will act strategically to turn governance efforts to their own ends. In any event, environmental law for sustainability should stimulate critical self-reflection and self-correction by polluters in line with democratically determined goals.[231] Such critical self-reflection not only responds to the need to enlist governed subjects in their own regulation, it also addresses another condition for sustainability, namely learning and adaptation. Learning is something few codes expressly contemplate and almost all need to internalise. As Dovers and Connor point out, it is exceedingly rare in all policy settings.[232]

All of this implies adopting an ambivalent attitude toward both business and the state. Business is both a source of pressure to perpetuate existing unsustainable patterns, and a potential source of innovation. States and state law are in certain respects powerful obstacles to sustainability and in other respects necessary prerequisites for it. Driesen argues, for example, that stringent 'command' regulation may be most effective at spurring the kinds of technological innovation sustainability requires.[233] Santos points out that to struggle for emancipation does not necessarily mean to destabilise existing legal systems. In some cases it may involve defending the legal status quo (eg. campaigning for more effective enforcement of laws on the books), in others struggling for deeper social transformation.[234]

Finally, whereas most experimentation with and attention on codes has focused on mainstream business and policy regimes in advanced industrialised countries, a concern with sustainability invites a focus on developing countries and marginalised populations within the advanced industrialised countries. The central question from the point of view of social emancipation is what contribution codes can make to improving environmental and social conditions for the global majority.

3. The Role of Voluntary Environmental Codes in Law for Sustainability

(a) Designing Environmental Policy

There is by now broad agreement on the elements that should be present for a voluntary code to be a credible and effective instrument for pursuing environmental policy goals.

[230] Eg P Grabosky, 'Using Non-Governmental Resources to Foster Regulatory Compliance' (1995) 8 *Governance* 527.

[231] G Teubner, 'Substantive and Reflexive Elements in Modern Law' (1983) 17 *Law & Society Review* 239; G Teubner, L Farmer and D Murphy (eds), *Environmental Law and Ecological Responsibility: The Concept and Practice of Ecological Self-Organisation* (Wiley, 1994); Orts, above n 155; U Beck, *Risk Society: Towards a New Modernity* (Sage, 1992).

[232] Dovers and Connor, this vol.

[233] Driesen, this vol.

[234] Santos, above n 224, 470.

The list typically includes:

—effective participation by all interested and affected parties in code development and implementation;
—public transparency of code development and implementation, including disclosure of targets and performance;
—clearly articulated roles, rights and responsibilities for all parties involved in code development and implementation;
—clearly specified baseline against which performance will be measured, including characterization of the business-as-usual trend;
—clearly defined environmental performance targets, with interim objectives and measurable indicators;
—encouragement of innovation and flexibility in meeting targets;
—credible and regular monitoring and reporting of both individual and (in the case of collective codes) group performance, with independent verification;
—clearly specified and individualised rewards for good performance and sanctions for nonconformity;
—promotion of informational 'soft' effects through technical assistance, information exchange, diffusion of best practices, etc;
—a credible threat of regulation by public authorities should voluntary action fail; and
—a supportive legal and public policy framework.[235]

These criteria are useful when designing or evaluating voluntary codes in isolation, but most of them offer little guidance when determining whether or how voluntary codes might be employed as elements of a broader 'policy mix.' For years voluntary codes have been employed in conjunction with other regulatory instruments (negotiated agreements with permit schemes, public voluntary programmes with regulatory standards, etc), and all voluntary codes interact in complex ways with official legal systems.[236] Increasing attention is now being devoted to the role and effectiveness of voluntary codes in broader policy mixes.[237]

Sophisticated analyses and prescriptions are beginning to emerge, often building on the burgeoning literature on 'smart' or 'responsive' regulation.[238] These analyses offer a combination of empirical and normative insights into such issues as how self-regulation and other voluntary approaches fit with more coercive regulatory strategies; how to identify and exploit positive synergies among different

[235] Eg OECD, above n 3, 134–135; EC Communication on Environmental Agreements, above n 31; EEA, above n 10; UNEP IE, above n 16; New Directions Group *Criteria and Principles for the Use of Voluntary or Non-Regulatory Initiatives to Achieve Environmental Policy Objectives* (Nov 1997), reproduced in Gibson, above n 6, 230.

[236] Meidinger, above n 7.

[237] Eg OECD 2003, above n 164.

[238] Eg Gunningham and Grabosky, above n 39; Gunningham and Sinclair, above n 64.

instruments and avoid negative ones; how to devise regulatory strategies that are appropriate to the character of environmental problems, the structure of regulated industries and the characteristics of regulated entities (eg SMEs vs large firms); and how to combine mandatory and voluntary initiatives to minimise free-riding and maximise environmental improvement, operational flexibility, public transparency and democratic legitimacy.

These analyses of policy mixes and these rules for successful codes will doubtless contribute to more credible and effective environmental regulation, but we should keep two points in mind. First, even when voluntary codes are designed and used according to these guidelines, they will play at most a modest and supplementary role in environmental law. Most public authorities, ENGOs, academics and perceptive business leaders already recognise this. Secondly, and more importantly, even when these prescriptions for the credible and effective use of voluntary codes are observed, we will still be a long way from environmental law for sustainability. In what follows, we explore in general—and necessarily speculative—terms where voluntary codes fit into the larger challenge of governance for sustainability.[239] The discussion can be boiled down to three points: rethink the drivers, focus on the marginalised, and generate transformative innovation.

(b) Rethink the Drivers

First, forget the threat of regulation. The mere *threat* of regulation is inadequate to spur the changes needed for sustainability. There is almost universal agreement that a credible threat of mandatory regulation if agreement is not reached or the terms of an agreement are not fulfilled is needed to ensure effective voluntary codes.[240] It is also thought that the degree of environmental improvement that can be expected from voluntary action increases with the magnitude of the threat.[241] There is evidence, however, that even a threat of regulation is inadequate, and that actual regulation is needed to drive improved corporate environmental performance. A study of Canadian polluters, for example, concluded that direct government intervention in the form of enforcement action and the promulgation of stringent new regulations—rather than the mere threat of regulation, or spontaneous response to 'green' consumerism—explains the vast majority of improvements in emissions reported in the National Pollutants Release

[239] For other attempts to grapple with this issue see, eg, DVJ Bell, 'Voluntary Codes and the New Sustainability Paradigm' in W Cragg(ed), *Ethics Codes, Corporations and the Challenge of Globalization* (Edward Elgar 2005), 321; Webb, above n 162, 383–398.

[240] Eg ED Elliott *et al*, 'Toward a Theory of Statutory Evolution: The Federalization of Environmental Law' (1985) 1 *Journal of Law, Economics & Organisation* 313; Environmental Law Network International, above n 26, 128.

[241] K Segerson and TJ Miceli, 'Voluntary Approaches to Environmental Protection: The Role of Legislative Threats' in Carraro and Lévêque, above n 131, 105.

Inventory.[242] Moreover, even if regulatory threats can drive voluntary improvements, such improvements are less than would be achieved by mandatory regulation and far less than what would be needed for a transition to sustainability.

The key problem with the threat of regulation as a driver is that, to the extent that voluntary codes are successful in achieving environmental or social goals, they tend to undermine the motivations for their own success. It is difficult to maintain a credible threat of regulation in the face of evidence that business is improving its performance without regulatory compulsion.[243] The threat of regulation is bound to dissipate over time, removing the impetus for effective voluntary action. It takes actual regulation, whether in the form of mandatory standards, economic instruments or some combination of both, to provide an effective ongoing impetus for action in the medium to long term.

The threat of regulation is also self-defeating in another way. Along with explicit sanctions in the voluntary code itself, the threat of regulation is thought to be critical to solving the problems of free-riding and public credibility. But the evidence indicates that the more credible these threats, the less likely polluters will participate in a code.[244] Polluters, especially environmental 'leaders' who already comply with or exceed existing legal requirements and are motivated to improve their performance further, do not want to join voluntary codes that entail a serious risk of public humiliation, brand damage, regulatory crackdown or other costs if they slip up. Neither do they want to invest in developing and implementing a code without some assurance that regulators will refrain from introducing new regulation in return for the voluntary action. The threat of credible sanctions, including regulation, tends to frighten away the very actors the code is trying to attract. The seeds of a code's success thus become the reasons for its failure.

This brings us to the second point about drivers. Forget about the market—or at least forget about relying on 'green' consumerism and similar devices to drive markets toward sustainability. Market-driven governance is incapable of getting us where we need to go. Even if new opportunities for profitable environmental improvements continue to emerge with increasing resource scarcity and changing technology, and even if the market for 'green' or 'socially responsible' goods and services continues to expand rapidly, the effects on the global economy will be marginal. Polluters will ultimately be driven toward sustainability 'not by the

[242] W Antweiler and K Harrison, 'Toxic Release Inventories and Green Consumerism: Empirical Evidence from Canada' (2003) 36 *Canadian Journal of Economics* 495; W Antweiler, 'How Effective Is Green Regulatory Threat?' (2003) 93 *American Economics Review* 436.

[243] Gibson, above n 207, 244–245.

[244] This is the experience, for instance, with the province of Ontario's Environmental Leaders programme (which specifies genuine sanctions for non-attainment and reserves the government's right to introduce mandatory regulation at any time) and Denmark's Environmental Protection Act (which allows the government to make negotiated agreements legally binding on non-participating firms). Eg OECD, above n 3, 117 (discussing the Danish example).

promise of gain but by the grind of obligation', and this 'grind', according to Gibson,

> is not just friction from regulatory enforcers, but the sum total of aggravations from the combination of government authorities, financiers and insurers, neighbours, peers, non-governmental watchdogs, employees, customers, suppliers, and perhaps even investors.... The governance system that will begin to make this work ... is one that strengthens both the promise of gain and the aggravating significance of all those who demand environmentally responsible behaviour.[245]

Finally, we should focus not just on the drivers of voluntary action but the causes of unsustainable patterns of production, consumption, wealth, poverty, domination and exclusion. We could have substantially more impact on environmental and social quality by eliminating subsidies to the oil and gas industries than by tweaking the rewards and threats for voluntary action. Along with eliminating environmentally and socially destructive subsidies, we could turn our attention to ecological tax reform (eg taxing environmental 'bads' such as raw materials, waste and pollution rather than 'goods' such as labour, investment and profit), environmental accounting (fully incorporating ecological costs and benefits into both corporate and national accounting), new ways of measuring prosperity (eg rejecting GDP growth as the key measure of progress) and new ways of understanding poverty (eg bursting the 'poverty' myth which has fuelled the development industry for the last half century).

(c) Focus on the Marginalised

Secondly, we must shift our attention to the global majority. Whatever environmental and social progress is made in the mainly affluent societies of the global North will soon be overshadowed by events in China, India, Indonesia, Brazil and the rest of the developing world. Developing countries have received relatively little attention in debates about environmental policy generally and voluntary codes in particular, even though a great deal of experimentation with voluntary codes is occurring in the developing world.[246] As to marginalised communities in advanced industrialised countries, they have received even less attention in the voluntary codes literature, and when they do, the emphasis tends to be on applying externally developed codes to these communities rather than indigenous development of new approaches.[247]

The focus of governance for sustainability must be on empowering the marginalised: not just by turning the four billion people living on less than $2 a day into consumers, as ideas like Prahalad's 'fortune at the bottom of the pyramid' would

[245] Gibson, above n 207, 251–252.

[246] Eg ten Brink, above n 3, 156–205.

[247] Eg P Evers, 'ISO 14001 and the American Indian Reservation' in R Hillary (ed), *Environmental Management Systems and Cleaner Production* (Wiley, 1997) 173.

suggest,[248] but by stimulating disruptive, pro-poor economic and social development. Such stimulation should be aimed not at multinational firms and other large enterprises, but at sustainability activists and social entrepreneurs both within and outside marginalised communities. Some 'Northern' NGOs have already begun to pursue such opportunities in partnership with NGOs and pro-poor entrepreneurs in the South, and these emerging initiatives may provide fertile ground for the emergence of new codes for sustainability. Pro-poor, disruptive development strategies will also depend upon recognising and reinvigorating the great wealth of knowledge, inventiveness, social institutions and capacities that sustained most of these societies through millennia and continue to operate when not repressed by states, international organisations and global capitalism. Without invigorating the capacities within civil society to develop and implement indigenous norms for individual and corporate conduct, no infusion of money, goods or services will lead to emancipation.

The focus, in other words, should be on 'bottom up' initiatives to enhance the capacity of marginalised groups to develop codes for their own use or in negotiation with other actors such as governments, international organisations, multinational corporations and foreign NGOs. In both developing and developed countries, efforts should be made to ensure that environmental and social interests are well organised in NGOs and political parties, so that they can be effective advocates for grassroots movements and watchdogs of both government and industry.[249] Emphasis should also be placed on strengthening transnational networks of grassroots movements and NGOs, especially within the global South. But, unlike the homogenising tendencies of the 1960s Law and Development movement and many contemporary development institutions, the emphasis must be on local autonomy, specificity, diversity and experimentation. Codes and other governance arrangements cannot be transposed wholesale from one situation to another. These are some of the prerequisites for effective development and use of voluntary codes to advance the cause of emancipation.

Empowering the marginalised will also require 'top down' strategies, aimed mainly at controlling the destructive potential of global capital. This may mean, ultimately, enforceable international standards for corporate conduct; enhanced home state responsibility for the conduct of multinational corporations; increased legal and institutional capacity in developing countries to regulate business and environment; effective access to home state courts for foreign victims of corporate misconduct; legal controls on the rapid movement of capital in global financial markets; and reconsideration of the legal rules of international trade that give capital a host of rights without commensurate obligations. All of these initia-

[248] CK Prahalad, *Fortune at the Bottom of the Pyramid* (Pearson Education 2005); S Hart *Capitalism and the Crossroads: The Unlimited Business Opportunities in Solving the World's Most Difficult Problems* (Pearson Education 2005).

[249] Carraro and Lévêque, 'Introduction', above n 131, 10.

tives would emphasise mandatory, enforceable rules. While some voluntary codes may set constructive examples,[250] they are more likely to present obstacles. Indeed, voluntary codes such as the OECD Guidelines for Multinational Enterprises were originally developed as part of an effort to forestall the development of a mandatory UN Code of Conduct for Transnational Corporations. The effort was successful and the threat of mandatory regulation was averted, giving way instead to a series of less demanding voluntary codes culminating in the UN Global Compact.

There is a strong temptation to treat voluntary codes as a substitute for effectively enforced environmental and human rights laws in developing countries, given the lack of adequate laws or enforcement in many such jurisdictions and the lack of effective regulation of transnational business, but this temptation must be resisted. The priority should be on creating those legal frameworks, with voluntary codes playing a supporting role.

(d) Generate Transformative Innovation

Finally, governance for sustainability requires a focus on codes and other regulatory initiatives that are capable of generating transformative, not just incremental, innovation. This includes not just technological innovation but innovation in governance institutions and practices, and this will be our focus here.

The main significance of contemporary voluntary codes is, as Webb argues, that they may be examples of 'breakthrough rule innovation.'[251] Certain voluntary codes create new rule-making institutions involving novel forms of collaboration among civil society, polluters and public authorities. These new institutions enrich and vitalise societal norm development and implementation, and incubate new policy approaches. They operate as innovative voicing mechanisms, giving new and more subtle influence to demand side interests in the economy (ie consumers, environmentalists) and providing leverage to influence actors and conduct well beyond the parties directly involved.[252] Finally, they are increasingly being used to address problems associated with new technologies and to address the way products are produced rather than product characteristics themselves.[253]

Codes developed mainly by civil society actors appear to offer the most promise on this front. Unfortunately, it is also these codes that struggle the most to achieve acceptance by polluters. Certain third party codes that set out broad ethical and scientific frameworks for sustainable business, such as the Natural Step, may also be promising since—if they are implemented—they may foster fundamental reorientation rather than incremental change in a particular firm, jurisdiction or sector.

[250] Eg the UN Draft Norms on the Responsibilities of Transnational Corporations and other Business Enterprises on Human Rights, Un Doc E/CN.4/Sub.2/2003/12/Rev.2 (26 Aug 2003).

[251] Webb, above n 4, 16.

[252] *Ibid*, 16–20.

[253] Webb, above n 162, 379.

I. Conclusion

The challenge of environmental law for sustainability is to advance ecological integrity and social emancipation. We should evaluate the role of voluntary environmental codes in law for sustainability, whether such law is official or unofficial, state or non-state, in terms of its potential to disrupt unsustainable patterns and practices, empower the marginalised, generate transformative technological and institutional innovation, and stimulate self-reflection, self-correction and collective learning.

Voluntary environmental codes, as we have known them hitherto, have only a modest contribution to make to the improvement of existing systems for environmental regulation, and an even smaller one to this broader challenge of law for sustainability. We should continue to refine and improve their design, operation and use in regulatory mixes. But in the meantime we should begin to lay the groundwork for more disruptive, emancipatory alternatives in which the voluntary action of autonomous subjects plays a different, but still significant role as both a source and outcome of the 'cumulative aggravations' that must increasingly be brought to bear on entrenched political and economic elites. It will take different kinds of knowledge, different kinds of institutions, different kinds of collaboration, different kinds of voluntary codes and new kinds of law to meet this bigger challenge.

9

Economic Instruments for Sustainable Development

DAVID DRIESEN*

A. Introduction

This chapter primarily addresses the means of environmental protection, as distinguished from its goals. Most writing about the question of means posits a dichotomy between 'command and control' regulation and economic incentive programmes, such as emissions trading and eco-taxes. This dichotomy, however, may distort our understanding of both traditional regulation and alternatives to it.

Because economic theory shows that 'economic incentive' programmes are more cost effective than traditional regulation, one might assume that economic incentive programmes offer a superior method for achieving sustainable development. This chapter questions that assumption. It argues that achieving sustainable development requires an emphasis on transformative technological innovation and that traditional economic incentive programmes do not work as well in this regard as commonly assumed.

This topic has taken on great importance as the use of economic instruments has spread worldwide. Their growing popularity has sometimes had little to do with the technical merits of competing approaches. Rather, governments skeptical of the efficacy of government intervention, such as the Thatcher government in Britain and the Reagan and George W Bush administrations in the United States (US), have tended to embrace a deregulatory philosophy that relies on the 'free market' to solve many social problems.[1] Those sharing this perspective have found 'market-based' approaches to environmental protection attractive.[2] These market-based

* Angela R Cooney Professor at Syracuse University College of Law.

[1] See generally H Stretton, *Public Goods, Public Enterprise, Public Choice: Theoretical Foundations of the Contemporary Attack on Government* (St Martin's Press, 1994); PM Jackson and CM Price, *Privatisation and Deregulation: A Review of the Issues* (Longman, 1994).

[2] See RB Stewart, 'Models for Environmental regulation: Central Planning versus Market-based Approaches' (1992) 19(3) *Boston College Envtl Affairs L Rev* 547; FE Anderson *et al*, *Environmental Improvement through Economic Incentives* (Johns Hopkins UP, 1977).

approaches have also proven congenial to many governments not as committed to free market ideology, such as those in Europe seeking a 'third way' alternative to the welfare state and laissez-faire.[3] They may view economic incentive approaches as moderating the excesses of command and control regulation, without giving in to a laissez-faire ideology.

The goal of this chapter, however, is not a thorough description of the political economy of instrument choice. Rather, it is to provide an introduction to the variety of instruments that have been labelled 'economic instruments' and to contribute to the assessment of their value to sustainable development. The chapter will begin with a review of traditional regulation, with some emphasis on correcting the misimpressions that the term 'command and control' creates. It will then review the nature of economic incentive programmes and the traditional theory behind them. The third part will explain the importance of technological innovation to sustainable development. The final part will question the traditional view that emissions trading programmes help much with technological transformation and suggest ways of encouraging a pattern of sustainable development through the design of instruments aimed at encouraging innovation.

B. Traditional Regulation[4]

The term command and control regulation suggests that regulators employing traditional regulation usually proceed by telling polluters how they must reduce pollution.[5] In fact, however, regulators very often set performance standards that limit the amount of pollution allowed, but do not dictate compliance techniques.[6] A good example of a performance standard comes from the New Source Performance Standard for coal-fired power plants that Professors Ackerman and Stewart addressed in their book, *Clean Coal/Dirty Air*,[7] a leading critique of 'command and control' regulation. While Professors Ackerman and Stewart claim that this standard required 'forced scrubbing', (ie, the use of coal scrubbers), the regulation itself required operators of power plants to meet a target for

[3] T Giddens, *The Third Way and its Critics* (Polity Press, 2000).

[4] See also Abbot, this vol.

[5] D Keeth, 'The California Climate Law: A State's Cutting-Edge Efforts to Achieve Clean Air' (2003) 30 *Ecology Law Quarterly* 715, 720 (characterising 'command and control' regulation as regulations where the government mandates particular technologies); DM Driesen, 'Is Emissions Trading an Economic Incentive Programme? Replacing the Command and Control Economic Incentive Dichotomy' (1998) 55 *Washington & Lee L Rev* 289, 290–1.

[6] Driesen, above n 5, 297–8.

[7] BA Ackerman and WT Hassler, *Clean Coal/Dirty Air: Or How the Clean Air Act Became a Multibillion-Dollar Bailout for High-Sulfur Coal Producers and What Should be Done About it* (Yale UP, 1981).

pounds of pollution per million BTUs or, in the alternative, a percentage reduction requirement.[8] The Court of Appeals that reviewed this regulation stated that 'given the current state of technology' this standard would require scrubbing.[9] But this statement implies that owners of coal-burning power plants could employ any new technology that came along, if it met the performance standard. Indeed, the regulation nowhere states that it requires scrubbing. Such performance standards have been common under the air and water pollution control laws of many countries and under the Convention on Long-Range Transboundary Air Pollution.[10]

Sometimes, however, setting a performance standard is not possible, because measurement of the pollution a facility releases is technically impracticable. In such a case, regulators often set 'work practice' standards that dictate the use of a technique known to reduce pollution, in lieu of requiring compliance with a performance standard.

An example is the regulation of asbestos emissions during building demolition.[11] Since destruction of buildings containing asbestos sends fibres hither and yon, one cannot measure the amount of asbestos emanating from a building undergoing demolition. Accordingly, when the US Environmental Protection Agency (EPA) regulated asbestos emissions in building demolitions, it did so by requiring a set of practices, such as wetting down the building, known to reduce emissions.[12] These command and control regulations are acts of desperation, denying regulated entities flexibility only because it is impossible to verify compliance with the more flexible regulatory instrument—the performance standard.

Whether the regulator establishes a performance standard or a work practice standard, the regulator must make decisions about how stringent the regulation will be—decisions about whether to require a great reduction in pollution or just a small reduction. Statutory criteria usually guide these administrative goal-setting decisions. Many statutes employ some kind of technology-based criteria. These imply that an administrative agency will establish the level of stringency that technologies are capable of achieving.[13] While writers often use the term 'command and control' regulation as a synonym for technology-based regulation, most technology-based regulation consists of performance standards, not technology-dictating work practice standards. Moreover, one can use technological capability to determine a regulation's goals and use emissions trading or pollution

[8] *Sierra Club v Costle*, 657 F 2d 298, 312 (DC Cir, 1981).

[9] *Ibid*, 316.

[10] Convention on Long-Range Transboundary Air Pollution 1979, 18 ILM 1442.

[11] C Twight, 'Regulation of Asbestos: The Microanalytics of Government Failure' (1990) 10 *Policy Studies Review* 9.

[12] *Adamo Wrecking Co v US*, 434 US 275, 277, 294–5 (1978).

[13] DM Driesen, 'Distributing the Costs of Environmental, Health and Safety Protection: The Feasibility Principle, Cost-Benefit Analysis, and Regulatory Reform' (2004) 32 *Boston College Environmental Affairs L Rev* 1.

taxes as the means of achieving those goals. In other words, technology-based emissions trading programmes and tax programmes are possible. So, one should not equate technology-based regulation with particular regulatory instruments. To avoid confusion, this chapter will use the term 'traditional regulation' to refer to both performance standards and work practice standards, rather than the term command and control regulation.

Traditional regulation, especially technology-based traditional regulation, has produced significant reductions in pollution in many countries. The US, for example, has developed technology-based federal standards for point sources of water pollution, which has, by most accounts, led to great reductions in pollution.[14] Although most analysts treat traditional regulations as the opposite of an economic incentive programme, a traditional regulation creates a significant economic incentive to reduce pollution.[15] Governments usually levy substantial fines on violators of traditional regulatory limits. Polluters conform to the limits, in part, to avoid these fines. Despite traditional regulation's success in reducing pollution, scholars have criticised traditional regulation on numerous grounds.

First of all, traditional regulation frequently makes inefficient use of private sector compliance expenditures.[16] Because facilities have uneven control costs, uniform standards for an industry category require relatively large compliance expenditures from some facilities, while requiring relatively small expenditures from others.[17] In theory, it is possible to get the same industry-wide reduction that a uniform standard demands at lower cost by demanding more reductions from facilities with low control costs and fewer reductions from facilities with higher control costs. The difficulty of acquiring good marginal control cost information for individual facilities, however, can limit a regulator's ability to engage in efficient fine-tuning of this nature.

While this cost effectiveness critique has merit, a seemingly related critique, claiming that traditional regulation is often excessively stringent, has also sometimes been cited in the US as a reason to prefer economic instruments. This argument usually rests on the proposition that command and control regulation often requires cost grossly disproportionate to benefit.[18] Recent work by Professors Heinzerling and Parker raises serious issues about the data underlying this critique.[19] The more

[14] WL Andreen, 'Water Quality Today—Has the Clean Water Act Been a Success?' (2004) 55 *Alabama L Rev* 537.

[15] JT Preston, 'Technology Innovation and Environmental Progress' in MR Chertow and DC Esty (eds), *Thinking Ecologically: The Next Generation of Environmental Policy* (Yale UP, 1997) 136, 148.

[16] RB Stewart 'Economic, Environment, and the Limits of Legal Control' (1985) 9 *Harvard Environmental L Rev* 1, 7.

[17] RW Hahn and RN Stavins, 'Incentive-Based Environmental Regulation: A New Era for an Old Idea?' (1991) 18 *Ecology Law Quarterly* 1, 3.

[18] See NO Keohane RL Revesz and RN Stavins, 'The Choice of Regulatory Instruments in Environmental Policy' (1998) 22(2) *Harvard Environmental L Rev* 313.

[19] RW Parker, 'Grading the Government' (2003) 70 *University of Chicago L Rev* 1345; L Heinzerling 'Regulatory Costs of Mythic Proportions' (1998) 107 *Yale LJ* 1981.

important point, for purposes of understanding the instrument choice debate, is that this argument may have little to do with instrument choice. The argument that a problem of excessively stringent regulation provides evidence of the need to use economic instruments seems to confuse means and ends. If a traditional regulation is desirable as a means of environmental protection, then a conclusion that environmental regulation is too strict could be met by relaxing the standards, not necessarily by changing the means of environmental protection. Moreover, since economic instruments have the potential to reduce compliance cost, cost effectiveness arguments favour them whether or not current regulations are excessively stringent. This stringency claim is more properly directed to a debate about the proper criterion for determining the goals of environmental regulation, and has less relevance to a debate about the means. And most proponents of this view lavish most of their energy on calls for more use of cost-benefit analysis to determine the goals of environmental regulations.[20]

Conversely, some environmentalists criticise trading programmes as efforts to subvert the achievement of environmental goals.[21] While this can be a fair criticism of the design of particular trading programmes, it should not be taken as a criticism of the concept of emissions trading itself.

Traditional regulation has been criticised for its failure to simulate innovation.[22] In fact, a dearth of post-compliance studies makes it difficult to know precisely how effective traditional regulation has been in stimulating innovation. There are a number of cases, however, where traditional regulation has stimulated significant innovation.[23] For example, some companies responded to the US Occupational Safety and Health Administration's regulation of vinyl chloride by employing a proprietary 'stripping process' or by employing other innovations.[24] These measures not only lowered vinyl chloride exposure but also improved vinyl chloride resin production. Manufacturers responded to regulation of occupational exposure to cotton dust through modernisation of equipment needed anyway

[20] Eg CR Sunstein, *The Cost-Benefit State: The Future of Regulatory Protection* (American Bar Association, 2002); CR Sunstein, *Risk and Reason: Safety, Law, and the Environment* (Cambridge UP, 2002); RW Hahn, *Reviving Regulatory Reform: A Global Perspective* (AEI-Brookings Joint Center for Regulatory Studies, 2000).

[21] OECD, *Implementing Domestic Tradeable Permits: Recent Developments and Future Challenges* (OECD, 2002).

[22] MH Levin and BS Elman, 'The Case for Environmental Incentives' (1990) 7(Jan/Feb) *Environmental Forum* 7, 8–9.

[23] K Strasser, 'Cleaner Technology, Pollution Prevention, and Environmental Regulation' (1997) 9 *Fordham Environmental LJ* 1, 32 (innovation sometimes results from emission and discharge limits); eg US Congress Office of Technology Assessment, *Gauging Control Technology and Regulatory Impacts in Occupational Safety and Health—An Appraisal of OSHA's Analytical Approach* (US Government Printing Office, 1995) 64; NA Ashford and GR Heaton Jr, 'Regulation and Technological Innovation in the Chemical Industry' (1983) 46 *Law & Contemporary Problems* 109, 139–40; NA Ashford, C Ayers and RF Stone, 'Using Regulation to Change the Market for Innovation' (1985) 9 *Harvard Environmental L Rev* 419, 440–1.

[24] US Congress, above n 23, 89; also Ashford *et al*, above n 23, 419–66.

to compete internationally.[25] Most metal foundries responded to regulation limiting workplace formaldehyde, not through the ventilation and enclosure approach expected by the regulator, but through development of low-formaldehyde resins.[26] While most established smelters responded to sulphur dioxide limits with a conventional approach, copper mining firms developed a new and cleaner process to assist their entry into the smelting business.[27] And operators of chloralkali plants responded to EPA regulation of mercury with some process innovations.[28]

Innovation tends to occur when regulators demand significant reductions through performance standards, thereby creating incentives for polluters to innovate to escape potentially high control costs. A good example involves decisions to phase out ozone depleting substances. While the Montreal Protocol[29] authorised some trading of compliance obligations, in practice most countries relied on a strict traditional regulatory approach, a phase out of ozone depleting substances, to achieve the Protocol's goals. Even when countries authorised trading, little or no trading occurred. The Montreal Protocol set off a wave of innovations as companies sought substitutes for the substances being phased out.[30]

Polluters have an economic incentive to use the flexibility performance standards offer, if they can meet the standard through innovations that provide less costly, but adequate, compliance methods. Nevertheless, some writers have suggested that technology-based performance standards discourage technological innovation, even when they allow it as a matter of law. Professor Stewart, for example, has argued that technology-based standards may provide an incentive to choose the technologies that regulators evaluated in setting a performance standard, in order easily to persuade the regulator of compliance.[31] Yet, this incentive may be less powerful than the incentive to innovate to escape high compliance costs. Polluters should have little difficulty in persuading regulators of their compliance when they can readily monitor pollution to show that their alternative technology does produce emissions meeting the performance standard. Similarly, when they choose to eliminate a pollutant from their production process to avoid costly regulation, they will have no difficulty at all persuading the government of compliance.

Thirdly, writers have criticised traditional regulation for slow plodding progress. They have associated traditional regulation with litigiousness and intensive lobbying.[32] This criticism accurately describes a central problem with

[25] US Congress, above n 23, 90.

[26] *Ibid*, 95.

[27] Strasser, above n 23, 28–29.

[28] Ashford, *et al*, above n 23, 437.

[29] Protocol on Substances That Deplete the Ozone Layer 1987, 26 ILM 1550.

[30] ER DeSombre, 'The Experience of the Montreal Protocol: Particularly Remarkable, and Remarkably Particular (2000) 19 *UCLA Journal of Environmental Law & Policy* 49.

[31] RB Stewart, 'Regulation, Innovation, and Administrative Law: A Conceptual Framework' (1981) 69 *California L Rev* 1256, 1269.

[32] See Stewart, above n 31; Ackerman and Hassler, above n 7.

traditional regulation in the US. But it raises questions about whether this problem stems from the selection of regulatory means, or from the culture of 'adversarial legalism' that prevails in the US.[33] Also, it is far from obvious that a move to economic instruments necessarily leads to a significant reduction in lobbying and litigation. President Clinton's effort to introduce a domestic carbon dioxide (CO_2) tax, the sort of economic incentive measure economists favour, stimulated a firestorm of lobbying that defeated the measure.[34] And polluters have lobbied and litigated to seek to weaken the design of emissions trading programmes, not just traditional regulation.[35] It is possible that the selection of less costly and more flexible instruments might offer some potential to reduce opposition to regulation. But we need more empirical and theoretical work on this question.

C. Types of Economic Instruments with Examples

Scholars usually use the term 'economic incentive programmes' or the synonym, 'market-based instruments', to refer to a wide variety of alternatives to traditional regulation.[36] This usage reflects convention, rather than a clear analysis of the differences between traditional regulation and the alternatives. For traditional regulatory programmes provide an economic incentive to clean up; they threaten polluters with fines for failing to comply with standards, as noted previously. Traditional regulation also creates a market for pollution control ideas and equipment, since it requires polluters to clean up. Regulations can raise the price of goods associated with large amounts of pollution, and therefore encourage consumers to substitute less polluting goods or reduce consumption, thereby further reducing emissions.

Even though all forms of regulation provide economic incentives to reduce pollution, scholars generally agree about what instruments the term 'economic

[33] N Gunningham and P Grabosky, *Smart Regulation: Designing Environmental Policy* (Clarendon Press, 1998) 6.

[34] See M Kriz, 'A Green Tax?' (1993) 25 (June) *National Journal* 917.

[35] Eg, *Appalachian Power Co v EPA*, 249 F 3d 1032, 1036–40 (DC Cir, 2001) (recounting the litigious history of a trading programme for regional nitrogen oxide emission reductions); *Texas Municipal Power Agency v EPA*, 89 F 3d 858, 861 (DC Cir, 1996) (litigating claim for additional emission allowances); *Indianapolis Power and Light Co v EPA*, 58 F 3d 643, 647 (DC Cir, 1995) (same); *Madison Gas and Electric Co v EPA* 25 F 3d 5246 (7th Cir, 1994) (same); *Monongahela Power Co v Reilly*, 980 F 2d 272, 272–4 (4th Cir, 1992) (same).

[36] Eg T Panayotou, *Instruments of Change: Motivating and Financing Sustainable Development* (Earthscan, 1998); J Rietbergen-McCraken and H Abaza, *Economic Instruments for Environmental Management: A Worldwide Compendium of Case Studies* (Earthscan, 2000); C Jeanrenaud, 'Economic Instruments for Environmental Policy' in C Jeanrenaud (ed), *Environmental Policy Between Regulation and the Market* (Springer Verlag, 1997) 3; OECD, *Economic Instruments for Pollution Control and Natural Resources Management in OECD Countries: A Survey* (OECD, 1999).

incentive programmes refers to, even if the term has no rigorous definition. And they use the term to refer to alternatives to traditional regulation. Scholars have also employed varying typologies to classify the many economic instruments used around the world. It might prove useful to distinguish between price-based instruments, quantity-based instruments and informational-based instruments.[37]

1. Price-based Instruments

Price-based instruments fall into three basic categories, those offering negative incentives, positive incentives or mixed incentives.[38] Negative incentives basically tax environmental destruction, thereby encouraging better environmental practice as a means of lessening the tax. Positive incentives enable those improving their environmental practices to earn money for doing so. Mixed incentives combine negative and positive incentives.

A pollution tax provides the quintessential example of a negative price instrument. Such taxes can induce pollution clean-up, if the cost of clean-up is less than the marginal tax rate. On the other hand, if the tax rate is less than the marginal cost of clean up, one can expect the polluter to pay the pollution tax, rather than to clean up. France's taxes on effluent, where the government charges a fee for each unit of water pollution discharged, exemplify pollution taxes.[39] Korea taxes sulphur emissions, whilst Sweden, Norway, Denmark and the Czech Republic tax the sulphur content of fuel, which correlates rather directly with sulphur emissions.[40]

The literature sometimes uses the broader term 'eco-taxes' to refer to a wide variety of negative price incentives, including not just direct pollution taxes, but also less direct taxes that aim to provide incentives for environmental protection. For example, Singapore charges high taxes on automobiles, fees for entry into the city and charges for driving during rush hour to discourage both congestion and the associated air pollution from cars.[41] None of these taxes constitutes a pollution tax, because they do not vary directly with the amount of pollution. But all of them encourage pollution reductions, because they discourage driving, which produces emissions. Almost all OECD countries levy some sort of tax on the purchase or use of vehicles,

37 KR Richards, 'The Instrument Choice Game: When do Environmental Taxes Win?' in J Milne, K Deketelaere, L Kreiser and H Ashiabor (eds), *Critical Issues in Environmental Taxation: International and Comparative Perspectives* (Richmond Law and Tax, 2003) 66 (distinguishing between price-based and quantity-based emission limits).

38 The general rationale for using price-based mechanisms in environmental policy is outlined in OECD, *Taxation and the Environment* (OECD, 1993); OECD, *Improving the Environment through Reducing Subsidies* (OECD, 1998).

39 RN Stavins (ed), *Economics of the Environment: Selective Readings* (Norton, 2000) 437–38.

40 OECD, *Environmentally Related Taxes in OECD Countries: Issues and Strategies* (OECD, 2001) 66–67.

41 LH Lye, 'Environmental Taxation in the Regulation of Traffic and the Control of Vehicular Pollution in Singapore' in Milne *et al*, above n 37, 387–405.

although none is as environmentally effective as Singapore's. European countries, especially the United Kingdom, Norway and the Netherlands, impose rather high gasoline taxes, which may induce motorists to forego trips or use mass transit.[42]

Direct pollution taxes have been used sparingly around the world. Pollution taxes appear to enjoy more support in Europe than in the US, which seems to have an aversion to taxation generally. Most developed countries tax pollution indirectly through energy taxes, such as the gasoline tax, which produces the lion's share of revenue from pollution-related taxation in OECD countries.[43] These taxes tend to be much higher in Europe than in the US.[44]

While this chapter will give eco-taxes more extended treatment below, other negative price-based instruments exist. Commentators frequently mention liability as an economic instrument, because those potentially subject to liability for environmentally destructive activities may alter their conduct to avoid liability. The US Comprehensive Environmental Response, Compensation, and Liability Act (CERCLA)[45] offers a frequently mentioned example. The CERCLA programme addresses the problem of abandoned toxic waste sites.[46] Because the party dumping waste often either has become insolvent or cannot be identified, this law makes a wide variety of parties having some association with a toxic waste site potentially liable for the clean-up costs.[47] While this programme has been criticised for sparking very time consuming litigation seeking to apportion the liability among those potentially responsible for disposal sites left behind by past dumpers, it has provided a powerful disincentive for others to dump waste.[48] Companies desperately want to avoid being caught up in CERCLA's liability net, so the liability provides a strong incentive to make sure that future wastes are eliminated or properly disposed of.

Liability can prove effective, but often provides too little certainty to motivate conduct change. For example, common law nuisance claims require proof that a

[42] See P Ekins, 'European Environmental Taxes and Charges: Recent Experience, Issues and Trends' (1999) 31 *Ecological Economics* 39.

[43] OECD, above n 40, 55. For a detailed review of many environmental taxes and a discussion of theoretical issues, see Milne *et al,* above n 37.

[44] *Ibid,* 57.

[45] 42 USC ss 9601–9675.

[46] JM Organ, 'Superfund and the Settlement Decision: Reflections on the Relationship Between Equity and Efficiency' (1994) 62 *George Washington L Rev* 1043, 1046.

[47] 42 USC s 9607(a).

[48] RL Steinzor and LE Greer, 'In Defense of the Superfund Liability Scheme: Matching the Diagnosis and the Cure' (1997) 27 *Environmental Law Reporter* 10286, 10290 (explaining that CERCLA provides incentives to avoid dumping hazardous waste); G Van Cleve, 'Would the Superfund Response Cost Allocation Procedures Considered by the 103d Congress Reduce Transaction Costs?' (1995) 25 *Environmental Law Reporter* 10134, 10134; JP Acton and LS Dixon, *Superfund and Transaction Costs: The Experiences of Insurers and Very Large Industrial Firms* (Rand Institute for Civil Justice, 1992); WN Hedeman, JZ Cannon and DM Friedland, 'Superfund Transaction Costs: A Critical Perspective on the Superfund Liability Scheme' (1991) 21 *Environmental Law Reporter* 10413, 10426 (criticising CERCLA's generation of transaction costs).

single polluter has interfered with the use or enjoyment of property. The difficulty of proving such a link in societies where multiple pollution sources combine to create health and environmental problems has often rendered nuisance law ineffective.[49] Indeed, the ineffectiveness of the common law liability regime led to the promulgation of modern environmental statutes.

In the wake of the US withdrawal from the Kyoto Protocol, New York's attorney general has spearheaded a suit to force reductions of CO_2 emissions from large power plants under a common law nuisance theory.[50] It remains to be seen whether the common law regime can prove an effective substitute for missing administrative action in this context.

Subsidies provide the most obvious example of a positive price incentive. Subsidies are moneys granted by government to reduce the private costs of specified goods, services or behaviour. They take many forms including grants, favourable loan terms, tax concessions and assumption of liability. They can provide incentives for environmentally beneficial behaviour, compensating those persons who perform environmental services of benefit to society.[51] Many governments, for example, subsidise clean renewable energy to some degree.[52] But subsidies often go to the companies that can lobby most effectively, which are often 'dirty' existing industries, rather than to companies employing the most environmentally beneficial approaches. In the US, for example, subsidies for environmentally dubious clean coal technology exceed the subsidies for renewable energy, and Germany has been criticised for subsidising coal.[53] If one counts tax exemptions, the US provides greater subsidies for older dirty energy than for newer cleaner energy. Subsidies can also encourage over-production. Both Europe and the US provide significant subsidies for agriculture, which may encourage greater use of pesticides and over-use of water, thereby contributing to associated water quality and supply problems.[54] On the other hand, governments tailor some

[49] On the limitations of common law torts as means of environmental protection, see J Lowry and R Edmunds (eds), *Environmental Protection and the Common Law* (Hart Publishing, 2000). A good example is the British case of *Cambridge Water Co v Eastern Counties Leather plc* [1994] 1 All ER 53.

[50] Press Release, Office of New York State Attorney General Eliot Spitzer, 'States, Cities, Environmental Groups Sue Bush Administration on Global Warming, Challenge EPA's Refusal to Reduce Greenhouse Gas Pollution' (23 Oct 2003).

[51] See F Cairncross, 'Natural Resource Management and Subsidies' in F Cairncross (ed), *Green Inc. A Guide to Business and the Environment* (Earthscan, 1995) 74; R Gale, S Barg and A Gillies (eds), *Green Budget Reform: An International Casebook of Leading Practices* (Earthscan, 1995).

[52] Eg BJ Richardson and KL Chanwai, 'The UK's Climate Change Levy: Is It Working?' (2003) 15(1) *Journal of Environmental Law* 39 (discussing UK government grants for clean energy and energy efficiency investments, financed from climate change levy revenues).

[53] N Myers and J Kent, *Perverse Subsidies* (International Institute for Sustainable Development, 1998).

[54] M Cardwell, 'Common Agricultural Policy Quotas and the Environment' (1997) 45 *Drake L Rev* 71; OECD, *Water Subsidies and the Environment* (OECD, 1997).

agricultural subsidies, such as soil conservation incentives, toward environmentally desirable ends.[55]

Some economic instruments combine positive and negative incentives. Deposit-refund systems are a frequently mentioned example. Many governments obligate sellers of beverages to collect a deposit from consumers associated with the cost of collecting bottles. This deposit funds a refund paid to a person when she returns the empty bottle for recycling.[56] It is doubtful that the negative incentive created by the deposit reduces waste, since the added cost is probably too small to affect beverage consumption.[57] But even small refunds provide a surprisingly powerful incentive to reduce litter, encouraging the unemployed, for example, to search for discarded bottles which they can redeem as a source of income. Denmark has created one of the most effective deposit-refund programmes in the world, in part, because it combines this economic instrument with a command and control regulation banning the use of aluminium beverage cans.[58] Another example of mixed negative and positive price incentives is the United Kingdom's landfill charge, which reduces the volume of waste and helps funds environmental restoration of former dump sites.[59]

2. Tradeable Environmental Rights

Tradeable environmental rights, or environmental benefits trading, offer the best example of a quantity-based economic incentive measure, as opposed to a price-based measure.[60] Quantity-based measures differ from price-based incentives in a fundamental way. With price-based instruments, government sets the price creating incentives to reduce. This government action leaves the private sector free to decide what quantity of pollution reduction to offer in response. By contrast, when government enacts a quantity-based instrument, such as an environmental benefit trading programme, the government, not the private sector, determines the requisite quantity of emission reductions. The private sector retains some control over the price through its ability to choose techniques to meet the quantitative limit.

[55] In the US, positive environmental subsidies have been introduced to encourage sustainable agriculture though the Conservation Reserve Programme, implemented under the Food Security Act 1985, Pub L No 99–198, 99 Stat 1504.

[56] F Ackerman, *Why Do We Recycle? Markets, Values, and Public Policy* (Island Press, 1997) 126.

[57] Generally *ibid*, 131–3.

[58] *Ibid*, 137–8.

[59] BJ Richardson, "Economic Instruments in EU Environmental Law Reform: Is the UK Government 'Sending the Right Signals'" (2002) 3 *European Journal of Law Reform* 427, 437.

[60] For an introduction to the vast literature, see eg TH Tietenberg, *Emissions Trading: An Exercise in Reforming Pollution Policy* (Resources for the Future, 1985); CL Kling, 'Environmental Benefits from Marketable Discharge Permits or an Ecological vs Economical Perspective on Marketable Permits' (1997) 11(1) *Ecological Economics* 57.

A performance standard, like a trading programme, constitutes a quantity-based instrument. But trading programmes differ from traditional performance standards in that governments authorise polluters (for example) to forego compliance with the government limit, if they purchase credits from some other polluter that has made 'extra' reductions, ie, reductions beyond those otherwise required. Thus, these programmes create markets in the trade of pollution reduction credits.

The same trading concept, however, applies to programmes addressing environmental problems other than pollution. Governments have applied trading approaches to land use problems. New York City employed a trading approach to the preservation of landmark buildings long before any government had applied this approach to pollution.[61] When it restricted development that would involve destruction of landmark buildings, it sometimes offered developers a right to build elsewhere in the city. These transferable development rights programmes have spread and offer a way of ameliorating the hardship of tight restrictions on development in especially sensitive locations.[62] And the US federal government has encouraged its states to use 'wetlands mitigation' banking. Under this approach developers may destroy otherwise protected wetlands, if they purchase credits created by developers enhancing wetlands, which have been 'banked'.

Many governments around the world have used transferable quotas to regulate fishing.[63] They limit the total allowable catch, but allow fishers to catch more than their individual quota by purchasing quota from other fishers. A recent review found that 24 of the 37 transferable quota programmes experienced declines in the fish stocks after implementing the programme.[64] These setbacks reflected failures to set sufficiently conservative limits and enforcement failures.[65] While tradeable quota programmes make enforcement more complex than in non-tradable quota systems, verification of compliance with non-tradable quotas has also proven difficult.[66] One might argue that a ban on especially destructive technologies, such as driftnets, might better address fisheries problems, since the tradeable quota system does not effectively address the issue of by-catch (the incidental destruction of species not targeted by the programme), and governments can more easily monitor fishing equipment than catches.

[61] JJ Costonis, 'The Chicago Plan: Incentive Zoning and the Preservation of Urban Landmarks' (1972) 85 *Harvard L Rev* 574, 576.

[62] JC Juergensmeyer, JC Nicholas and BD Leebrick, 'Transferable Development Rights and Alternatives After *Suitum*' (1998) 30 *Urban Lawyer* 441.

[63] See generally A Rieser, 'Prescriptions for the Commons: Environmental Scholarship and the Fishing Quotas Debate' (1999) 23 *Harvard Environmental L Rev* 393, 410 (discussing their use in the US); R Arnason and H Gissurarson (eds), *Individual Transferrable Quotas in Theory and Practice* (U Iceland Press, 1999).

[64] OECD, *Tradeable Permits: Policy Evaluation, Design, and Reform* (OECD, 2004) 24; also OECD, *Towards Sustainable Fisheries: Economic Aspects of the Management of Living Marine Resources* (OECD, 1997).

[65] *Ibid*, 24.

[66] See generally DS Ardia, 'Does The Emporer Have No Clothes? Enforcement of International Laws Protecting the Marine Environment' (1998) 19 *Michigan Journal of Environmental Law* 497.

Governments have also occasionally used trading to address water, solid waste disposal and agricultural issues. The Dutch have introduced a nutrient quota system to limit phosphates flowing into rivers as a result of animal production.[67] Since it is not possible to measure the pollution directly, the government assigned each type of animal an assumed phosphate contribution amount, based on estimates of manure excretion.[68] Quotas limit phosphate pollution by limiting the number of animals, and farmers may sell quotas, which they frequently do when they go out of business. Trades have not reached great volumes, but the limits on animals have modestly contributed to reductions of nutrient loadings.[69]

Australia has created a trading system for water use rights.[70] Such a system tends to improve the economic efficiency of water use, but should have negative effects on the environment. The reason for this is simple. When a user has a right to more water than she can use, the water may remain in the river, where it supports instream flow and associated ecological values, such as sustaining fisheries and avoiding excessive salinity (at least until the water is used further downstream). If water rights can be sold, however, surplus water will be reallocated to some economic use, rather than being allowed to support environmental ones. Australia's programme so far has produced too few trades to have a large environmental impact, but analysts expect negative impacts on salinity.[71] Therefore, this programme has created the need for additional regulations to head off the negative environmental impacts the trading programme should produce.[72]

In the pollution control field, there have been several applications of tradeable emission allowances in the US, which are discussed in greater detail later in this chapter.[73] The most substantial example is the acid rain abatement programmeme, introduced by the 1990 amendments to the federal Clean Air Act.[74] It caps sulphur dioxide emissions from the power sector and allows participating power suppliers to trade their pollution allowances in a national market.[75] California's Regional Clean Air Incentives Market (RECLAIM) was introduced in 1994 to reduce levels of nitrogen oxides and sulphur oxides in the Los Angeles airshed.[76]

[67] OECD, above n 64, 99.
[68] *Ibid,* 102.
[69] *Ibid,* 112–14.
[70] *Ibid,* 135–53; M Bond and D Farrier, 'Transferable Water Allocations—Property Right or Shimmering Mirage' (1996) 13 *Environmental & Planning LJ* 213.
[71] OECD, above n 64, 146.
[72] *Ibid.*
[73] Section D, below.
[74] Pub L No 101–549, 104 Stat 2399, Pub L No 104–316, 1001 Stat 3838. See generally CC Park, *Acid Rain: Rhetoric and Reality* (Methuen, 1987).
[75] R Rico, 'The U.S. Allowance Trading System for Sulphur Dioxide: An Update on Market Experience' (1995) 5 *Environmental & Resource Economics* 115.
[76] See V Foster and RW Hahn, 'Designing More Efficient Markets: Lessons from Los Angeles Smog Control' (1995) 38 *Journal of Law & Economics* 19.

A number of states have also implemented effluent trading regimes to reduce water pollution, such as Wisconsin's Fox River programme.[77]

European interest in marketable permits has focused on greenhouse gas emissions. Denmark was the first European country to legislate a limited trading system for CO_2 quotas among the country's largest electricity producers.[78] In April of 2001, Great Britain piloted a system of negotiable, transferable emission permits as an adjunct to the government's new climate change levy.[79] In 2005, most of the remaining members of the European Union submitted emission trading programmes to the European Commission pursuant to an EU Directive on trading.[80]

3. Informational Policy Instruments

Most scholarly treatments of economic incentive measures include information-based programmes, not just price and quantity instruments, as examples of 'economic incentive' programmes.[81] Right-to-know programmes in numerous OECD countries require polluters to report the amount of pollution emitted in various media. The data are published in pollutant release and transfer registers such as the US's Toxics Release Inventory. There is evidence that these programmes have induced some heavy polluters to reduce their emissions.[82] In any event, it is not obvious that these programmes rely upon economic incentives. If polluters choosing to clean up are responding to fears that consumers may cease to buy their products or investors may decline to purchase shares in reaction to unfavourable data about their pollution levels, then it would be accurate to say that information-based approaches create an economic incentive for clean-up. On the other hand, if the clean-up reflects a more generalised concern with reputation or a desire to behave ethically, then the incentive might be thought of as moral or reputational, rather than purely economic.

Voluntary environmental certification systems provide another example of an information-based programme. Sustainable forestry or fisheries management programmes and environmental management systems seek to encourage more

[77] Michigan Department of Environmental Quality 'Water Quality Trading Programme', available at: www.deq.state.mi.us/swq/trading/Statesum.htm.

[78] Act No 376 of 2 June 1999. See OECD, above n 21, 74, 79–81.

[79] UK Department of the Environment, Transport and the Regions, 'Business and Climate Change', available at: www.environment.detr.gov.uk/climateoffice/10.htm.

[80] Directive 2003/87/EC of the European Parliament and of the Council of 13 Oct 2003 establishing a scheme for greenhouse gas emission allowance trading within the Community and amending Council Directive 96/61/EC [2003] OJ L/275/32.

[81] See generally DA Kysar, 'Preferences for Processes: The Process/Product Distinction and the Regulation of Consumer Choice' (2004) 118 *Harvard L Rev* 525; DC Esty, 'Environmental Protection in the Information Age' (2004) 79 *NYU L Rev* 115.

[82] BC Karkainnen, 'Information as Environmental Regulation: TRI and Performance Benchmarking, Precursor to a New Paradigm?' (2001) 89 *Georgetown L Rev* 257.

sustainable conduct by companies through private certification processes, which both spread information to companies about how to improve environmental management and provide information about environmental performance (or at least management systems) to consumers and suppliers.[83] These programmes may provide economic incentives to clean up to the extent that firms fear that consumers and suppliers may reduce purchases if environmental performance proves unsatisfactory.

Sometimes simply the provision of information to companies can bring about environmental improvements. Environmental management systems can encourage private companies to seek out information about profitable pollution prevention opportunities.[84] Voluntary government programmes can also aid in encouraging at least those environmental improvements that have no net cost. For example, energy efficiency improvements often pay for themselves over time. Once companies have adequate information about the cost savings, they often make these improvements voluntarily. In the US, the federal Environmental Protection Agency's 'Green Lights' programme has encouraged more efficient use of energy in commercial spaces.[85] The effectiveness of these programmes often depends on the adequacy of budgetary support to hire staff to spread the information.

Another example of an information programme comes from eco-labelling. Several European countries have required extensive labelling to reveal the environmental attributes of competing products. The European Union has legislated the most comprehensive eco-label scheme in the world, covering both products and services, though participation in the scheme is voluntary.[86] Eco-labels provide incentives for companies to conduct themselves in ways that earn labels that will allow them to attract customers. Proposition 65, a ballot initiative passed in California, offers an example of a particularly powerful application of the information-based approach.[87] This law requires companies to warn consumers when their products contain carcinogens. Concerns about the effects of this labelling on their sales and/or reputation led many companies to reformulate products, rather than label them in an alarming manner. This led, for example, to settlement of a court suit enforcing the labelling requirement with an agreement to cease manufacturing

[83] Leading examples include the Forest Stewardship Council, the Marine Stewardship Council, the ISO 14001 environmental management system standard and the EU's voluntary Eco-Management and Audit Scheme. Eg EE Meidinger, 'The New Environmental Law: Forest Management Systems' (2003) 10 *Buffalo Environmental LJ* 211; EE Meidinger 'Private Environmental Regulation, Human Rights, and Community' (2000) 7 *Buffalo Environmental LJ* 123.

[84] See J Voorhees, 'Global Environmental Solutions: Management Systems and Synchronicity' (1999) 28 *Stetson L Rev* 1155.

[85] US Environmental Protection Agency, *EPA Green Lights Program* (Environmental Protection Agency, 1993).

[86] Council Regulation 1980/2000 of 17 July 2000 on a revised Community eco-label award scheme [2000] OJ L/237/1.

[87] C Rechtschaffen, 'The Warning Game: Evaluating Warnings Under Proposition 65' (1996) 23 *Ecology Law Quarterly* 303.

lead pipe, which contributes to lead in drinking water, a significant public health concern.[88]

In spite of the value of labelling approaches, they pose some tricky issues. Limits exist to how much information consumers can process.[89] A tension exists between giving comprehensive reliable information that would fully inform consumers' environmental choices and the simplicity required to make it realistic to expect consumers to pay attention to the information. Yet, in an era in which market-based approaches and scepticism of government tend to dominate, a model of environmental protection that relies, at least to some degree, upon consumer sovereignty as a means of environmental protection has great appeal.[90]

No typology perfectly captures all instruments. For example, Germany has required producers to take back the packaging that comes with their products or otherwise provide for its proper recycling.[91] One can call this a command and control regulation, because it mandates a particular form of conduct and imposes performance standards, in the form of requirements for what percentage of material must be recycled.[92] But one might treat it as an economic incentive measure, because it creates an incentive to reduce the amount of packaging used. It is not obvious that this novel measure fits into any of the types above. But the distinction between price, quantity and information instruments does provide a useful tool for classifying and thinking about many instruments, including some that defy ready classification.

While the German law has required some adjustment over time and proven controversial, it calls attention to the importance of careful analysis of how incentives operate. Often, enthusiasm for free markets, especially among ideological governments, has led to a failure to carefully analyse precisely how the incentives offered by both traditional regulation and economic instruments operate. Belief in economic instruments as a panacea sometimes can cut short careful detailed analysis. The German recycling law rests on recognition that an approach to waste treatment that places the responsibility for disposal on local governments (the predominant approach) provides no incentives for producers to reduce the generation of wasteful packaging that ends up creating a disposal problem. By putting the responsibility for recycling on the producer, the German approach does create some incentives to reduce unnecessary packaging material. Whether one considers this a command and control regulation or an economic incentive programme is less important than the recognition that careful analysis of how incentives operate aids the design of all sorts of instruments.

88 C Rechtschaffen, 'The Lead Poisoning Challenge: An Approach for California and Other States' (1997) 21 *Harvard Enrvironmental L Rev* 387.

89 PS Menell 'Structuring a Market-Oriented Eco-Information Approach' (1995) 54 *Maryland L Rev* 1435.

90 See generally Kysar, above n 81.

91 Ackerman, above n 56, 107.

92 *Ibid.*

Another example of a mixed instrument comes from the British approach to climate change. This programme combines emissions trading, a quantitative instrument, with a positive price incentive, a subsidy.[93] Under this programme, British firms can receive public subsidies if they agree to greenhouse gas emission reductions. This approach raises questions about departing from the polluter pays principle. Traditional regulation, pollution taxes and trading generally conform to this principle, but pollution abatement subsidies, ie, positive price incentives, do not.

D. Analysis of the Merits of Economic Instruments

Economists frequently recommend pollution taxes and emissions trading as 'economic incentive' measures capable of reducing pollution more cost effectively than traditional regulation.[94] Environmental benefit trading (including emissions trading) has assumed enormous prominence, becoming a common approach to fisheries management throughout the world, central to international negotiations on climate change, and ubiquitous for all sorts of environmental problems in the US. Direct pollution taxes, while less widespread, serve as the primary focus of economic analysis and policy prescription. And the analytical framework for pollution taxes aids analysis of indirect taxes aimed at pollution, which are more widespread in Europe than trading programmes. Accordingly, this discussion of the theory of economic incentives will focus primarily upon pollution taxes and trading.

1. Pollution Taxes

Economists generally prefer pollution taxes above all competing instruments.[95] A pollution tax can reduce pollution more cost effectively than traditional regulation. In theory, polluters with marginal pollution control costs less than the tax rate will respond to a pollution tax by reducing pollution to avoid some of the tax.[96] Polluters with marginal pollution control cost exceeding the tax rate will prefer paying the tax to reducing pollution.[97] Hence, a pollution tax can induce cost effective pollution reduction by encouraging greater reductions from facilities with low marginal control costs and fewer reductions from facilities with high

[93] OECD, above n 21, 19.

[94] Eg R Stavins, 'Experience with Market-Based Environmental Policy Instruments' in K Maler and J Vincent (eds), *Handbook of Environmental Economics* (Elsevier, 2003) 355, 359.

[95] For analysis of taxes versus tradeable rights, see CW Howe, 'Taxes Versus Tradable Discharge Permits: A Review in the Light of the U.S. and European Experience' (1994) 4(2) *Environmental & Resource Economics* 151.

[96] OECD, above n 40, 22.

[97] *Ibid.*

marginal control costs than a traditional regulation stimulating the same quantity of net reductions would.[98]

In practice, though, many governments design eco-taxes in a cost ineffective manner.[99] Instead of applying a uniform tax rate to all polluters emitting the target pollutant, governments often apply varying rates to different polluters and exempt the highest polluting products and firms from taxes outright.[100] Governments can, however, realise cost effectiveness benefits by designing more uniform taxes.

When consumers pay eco-taxes, they may respond by decreasing their purchases of goods with prices augmented by the amount of the tax.[101] They may either decrease consumption or choose to substitute less polluting goods.[102] Unfortunately, a lack of data and a dearth of ex post studies have left us without good estimates of the influence of existing taxes on pollution in many cases.[103] Available estimates, however, suggest that pollution taxes can prove effective. A Swedish ex post study found that taxes related to CO_2 emissions produced a 19 per cent drop in emissions between 1987 and 1994.[104] A Norwegian study found that carbon-related taxes reduced stationary source combustion emissions by 21 per cent from 1991 to 1995, but reduced household vehicle emissions by only 2 to 3 per cent.[105] Much of the industrial reduction in CO_2 emissions involved switching fuels, ie, substituting natural gas for coal.[106] Swedish taxes on nitrogen oxide and sulphur emissions have likewise contributed to significant declines in these emissions.[107]

Proponents of pollution taxes argue that they offer a 'double dividend'. Since many countries employ an income tax, a shift in the tax burden from income to pollution involves taxing 'bads'—ie, pollution—instead of 'goods'—ie, jobs. This gives rise to the double dividend hypothesis, the claim that pollution taxes will encourage job growth (or some other economic benefit) as well as a better environment.[108] This claim has proven controversial among economists. Whether or not the double dividend hypothesis proves correct, an increase in pollution taxes does provide an opportunity either to reduce other taxes or to increase government services. Indeed, pollution taxes can fund environmental improvement (as in the French effluent fee example).

98 *Ibid.*
99 OECD, above n 40, 126.
100 *Ibid.*
101 *Ibid,* 99.
102 *Ibid,* 23.
103 *Ibid.*
104 *Ibid,* 109.
105 *Ibid.*
106 *Ibid.*
107 *Ibid,* 106–7.
108 This argument has been advanced most prominently in the debate regarding 'ecological tax reforms', reforms which aim comprehensively to overhaul the taxation and fiscal system rather than just focus on ad hoc environmental taxes: see further T O'Riordan (ed), *Ecotaxation* (Earthscan, 1997); T Barker, 'Taxing Pollution Instead of Employment' (1993) 6(1) *Energy & Environment* 1.

Indirect taxes can provide imperfect incentives for pollution reduction. Taxes on gasoline usage may do little to encourage changes in emission rates through reformulation of gasoline or installation of pollution control devices on cars. But they may encourage consumers to use cars less, thereby reducing emissions. Also, if energy taxes focus on polluting fuels only, they can create incentives to switch to less polluting fuels. The European Union's recent proposal to replace vehicle taxes with carbon related taxes may reflect some recognition of the limits of indirect eco-taxation.

Even direct pollution taxes can fail to perform properly if exemptions create perverse incentives. Denmark, France, Italy, the Netherlands, Norway, New Zealand and Sweden have introduced levies touted as carbon taxes.[109] These taxes apply to fossil fuels but vary with CO_2 content to some extent.[110] The lack of consistent correlation with CO_2 content stems from various exemptions and rebates serving non-environmental objectives, such as fair distribution of income and competitiveness.[111] Thus, for example, several of these carbon taxes exempt energy used in the generation of distribution of electricity, aviation fuel, and energy used in commercial fishing.[112] Exemptions can undermine either direct or indirect taxation's incentives greatly to reduce pollution.[113]

Still pollution taxes raise some tricky issues. For one thing, they may prove regressive. For example, taxes on energy or on pollution highly correlated with energy use can adversely affect the poor, since the poor spend more of their money on energy than the rich.[114] On the other hand, some non-pollution taxes are also regressive. For these reasons, many proponents of pollution taxes favour pollution taxes over other taxes that disproportionately affect the poor, or propose some adjustment to compensate for the regressivity of pollution taxes. These concerns have led most of continental Europe to impose relatively light taxes on home heating oil and the US, the United Kingdom, Canada and New Zealand to impose no such tax at all.[115]

Also, pollution taxes' environmental goals conflict, to some degree, with fiscal goals.[116] Governments imposing taxes usually hope to maximise revenue collection and minimise tax avoidance. Yet, pollution taxes will have their maximum environmental effect if they stimulate widespread tax avoidance, through pollution reduction. Perhaps an escalation of tax rates over time could help address this problem.

[109] *Ibid*, 55; Richardson and Chanwai, above n 52; Anon, 'New Zealand Sets Carbon Tax Rate', 2 *Carbon Finance*, May 2005, 12.

[110] OECD, above n 40, 56.

[111] *Ibid*, 55.

[112] *Ibid.*

[113] Stavins, above n 94, 355, 363–72.

[114] See C Larrue, 'The Political (Un)feasibility of Environmental Economic Instruments' in B Dente (ed), *Environmental Policy in Search of New Instruments* (Kluwer, 1995) 37.

[115] OECD, above n 40, 57.

[116] OECD, *Environmental Taxes and Green Tax Reform* (OECD, 1997) 30.

2. Emissions Trading

Environmental benefit trading can also reduce pollution in a cost effective manner.[117] Historically, the most prominent trading programmes have involved air pollution, and these will be the focus of the following discussion. But the trading concept applies equally to trading of other environmental benefits, such as effluent reductions, land conservation and fishing quotas.

An emissions trading programme begins with a regulator developing a performance standard for a group of regulated facilities, just as in a traditional regulation. This means that emissions trading, like command and control regulation, requires difficult government decisions about the stringency of regulation. It does not involve a spontaneous magical market.[118] Thus, for example, California's RECLAIM programme, which allowed for trades of air pollution reductions, led to an emissions increase in its early years for the simple reason that California set the cap for emissions above then current levels.[119] Government officials may either sell or give out emission allowances. In either case, the decision about how many allowances to give out or sell involves the same sort of decision that governments make when they set a performance standard.

In a trading programme, however, polluters need not comply with the performance standard if they pay another polluter who has 'over-complied', ie, reduced pollution (or the fish catch, or other environmental metric) below the required level. This trading of obligations should improve the cost effectiveness of environmental protection.[120] Polluters with relatively low marginal control costs will tend to make extra emission reductions in order to sell some of the surplus to other polluters. Polluters with high marginal control costs will tend to avoid local pollution control in favour of purchasing credits from facility owners enjoying relatively law marginal control costs. The trading programme accomplishes the same sort of redistribution of control obligations that a pollution tax accomplishes, shifting reductions from facilities with high marginal control cost to facilities with lowest marginal compliance cost. This shift makes emissions trading more cost effective than a traditional uniform standard.

While most accounts of emissions trading attribute the idea to the Canadian economist JH Dales,[121] the US has been the foremost champion of the trading approach. Vigorous US advocacy of the trading approach's value led to its inclusion as the principal compliance mechanism in the Kyoto Protocol to the Framework Convention on Climate Change,[122] the principal international

[117] JH Dales, *Pollution, Property, and Prices* (U Toronto Press, 1968) 92–100.

[118] DM Driesen, 'Markets are Not Magic' (Nov/Dec 2003) 20 *Envtl Forum* 19.

[119] OECD, above n 64, 48.

[120] See RA Devlin and RQ Grafton, 'Marketable Emission Permits: Efficiency, Profitability and Substitutability' (1996) 29 *Canadian Journal of Economics* 260.

[121] Dales, above n 117,

[122] (1998) 37 ILM 22; (1992) 31 ILM 849.

agreement addressing global climate change. While emissions trading has enjoyed a somewhat chequered history in the US, it has become a dominant approach there and increasingly influential internationally.[123]

The US began experimenting with trading under the 1977 Amendments to the Clean Air Act.[124] The US Environmental Protection Agency (EPA) authorised states to substitute plant-wide standards for pollution source specific standards. Because many plants contained multiple pollution sources, this allowed trading limits among different sources within a plant. Because this sort of intra-facility trading treats a plant as if a bubble enclosed it, US air pollution experts often refer to these limited trading programmes as 'bubble' programmes.[125]

It is widely known that these bubbles saved polluters millions of dollars.[126] But these cost savings often came from emissions fraud of various kinds, where plants claimed to make fresh reductions when they had not made any or convinced regulators to accept past measures as a substitute for fresh further progress.[127] These programmes were an economic success, but an environmental failure in many cases.

An early experiment in more widespread trading, ie, trading between facilities and not just within them, involved water pollution discharges into Wisconsin's Fox River.[128] This experiment, however, produced only one trade.[129] While economists generally considered this a failure attributable to a thin market, the lack of trades involves a loss of cost savings. If the reductions planned for occurred, the programme succeeded environmentally. It just did not differ significantly from what a traditional regulation would achieve.

In 1990, however, Congress enacted a well-designed emissions trading programme to reduce sulphur dioxide, a pollutant causing 'acid rain', which produced

[123] Driesen, above n 5, 291–2 (giving some examples of how extensive reliance upon trading has become); Stavins, above n 94, 392 (noting the increasingly frequent use of tradeable permit systems in the US).

[124] W Griffin, 'The EPA's Emissions Trading Policy: A Clouded Past, But a Bright Future' (1992) 20 *Northern Kentucky L Rev* 207, 218–33.

[125] I use the term 'bubble' to refer to a variety of approaches that involve the bubble concept. This includes netting and offset programmes under the Clean Air Act. See TH Tietenberg, 'Economic Instruments for Environmental Regulation' (1995) 6 *Oxford Review of Economic Policy* 17 (defining the bubble more narrowly and explaining offsets and netting).

[126] WJ Baumol and WE Oates, *The Theory of Environmental Policy* (2nd edn, Cambridge UP, 1988) 171–2; RW Hahn and GL Hester, 'Where Did All the Markets Go? An Analysis of EPA's Emissions Trading Program' (1989) 6 *Yale Journal of Regulation* 109, 128; AB Jaffe and RN Stavins, 'Dynamic Incentives for Environmental Regulations: The Effects of Alternative Policy Instruments on Technology Diffusion' (1995) 29 *Journal of Environmental Economics & Management* S–43, S–43–44.

[127] California Air Resources Board and US EPA, *Phase Three Rule Effectiveness Study of the Aerospace Coating Industry* (EPA, 1990) 4 (finding that almost all aerospace facilities under a bubble are not complying with regulatory limits); D Doniger, 'The Dark Side of the Bubble' (July 1985) 4 *Environmental Forum* 33, 34–5; RA Liroff, *Reforming Air Pollution Regulation: The Toil and Trouble of EPA's Bubble* (Conservation Foundation, 1986) 62–67, 80–91 (providing examples of bubbles used to avoid pollution reduction requirements).

[128] Michigan Department of Environmental Quality, above n 77.

[129] OECD, above n 21, 29.

serious ecological harms.[130] This programme, unlike most bubble programmes, featured continuous emissions monitoring, a cap on the mass of emissions, and clear, game-proof rules. This enhanced design produced the first major success with emissions trading, a great decline in emissions and significant cost savings coming from redistribution of reductions, rather than emissions fraud.

Citing the acid rain programme's success, the US successfully urged the international community to make trading central to the Kyoto Protocol, notwithstanding the very different context provided by an international agreement on climate change.[131] Thus, the Kyoto Protocol anticipates international trading of credits, which creates fresh problems of international co-ordination not present in a merely national emissions trading programme.[132] While the principal greenhouse gas, CO_2, can be reliably monitored, other gases subject to the protocol present some of the same monitoring problems that infected the bubble programmes (which applied to difficult to monitor volatile organic compounds).[133] Also, the Protocol as elaborated in subsequent agreements contemplates some credits for programmes that do not reduce emissions, but rather improve the capacity of land to sequester CO_2. This raises a host of methodological and monitoring issues.

Notwithstanding President George W Bush's decision not to ratify the Kyoto Protocol, Europe has continued down the international emissions trading path suggested by the US. Meanwhile, the US copied attributes of the failed bubble programmes at least as often as it copied key features of the successful acid rain programme in creating new pollution control programmes. For example, the US has heavily promoted wetlands mitigation banking, which involves allowing otherwise illegal development on some land in exchange for wetland enhancement and restoration activities elsewhere.[134] These restoration and enhancement projects have rarely succeeded. So, this wetlands trading programme, like the bubble programme, has saved money without always delivering comparable value. Many states have continued to authorise trading of pollutants that cannot be properly monitored through 'open market' trading programmes that the federal EPA has encouraged.[135]

[130] Park, above n 74.

[131] DM Driesen, 'Free Lunch or Cheap Fix? The Emissions Trading Idea and the Climate Change Convention' (1998) 26 *Boston College Environmental Affairs L Rev* 1, 27.

[132] DM Driesen, 'Choosing Environmental Instruments in Transnational Legal Context' (2000) 27 *Ecology Law Quarterly* 1.

[133] OECD, above n 40, 119–20.

[134] See RC Gardner, 'Banking on Entrepreneurs: Wetlands, Mitigation, Banking and Takings' (1996) 81 *Iowa L Rev* 527 (for a very thorough review of this programme).

[135] These programmes do not cap the mass of emissions, but instead encourage generation of credits in anticipation of regulatory limits driving demand for them. See RE Ayres, 'Developing a Market in Emissions Credits Incrementally: An "Open Market" Paradigm for Market-Based Pollution Control' (1994) 25 *Environmental Reporter* 1522, 1525.

These programmes have also produced embarrassing failures, thus emulating the bubble programmes.[136]

Trading frequently poses equitable issues that limit its utility. For example, California's RECLAIM programme, an emissions trading programme, authorised facilities releasing toxic chemicals in low income communities of colour to forego reductions reducing high local cancer risks in exchange for reductions from similar pollutants from vehicles driven throughout the Los Angeles metropolitan area.[137] Even if these vehicle reductions were well monitored, the problem of foregoing reductions in a community of colour with relatively high exposure to cancer-causing pollution would pose an environmental justice issue. A closely related issue involves what Professors Salzman and Ruhl call the 'currency' of emissions trading.[138] Most trading regulations use a fairly simple unit to measure credits and debits, such as the amount of a pollutant emitted from a facility or the number of acres of wetlands restored. But these metrics do not guarantee that the public gets full value when a trade occurs. For example, a trade allowing destruction of 10 acres of wetlands in exchange for restoration of 10 acres elsewhere might allow the destruction of a parcel with enormous ecological or flood control value in exchange for a restoration of a wetland with relatively little environmental value.

The acid rain programme gained acceptance, because it seemed to pose few of these equitable and equivalence issues. Acid rain comes from atmospheric loadings of sulphur dioxide (and other pollutants) across a large region, so that the geography of reductions is not nearly as important as the total quantity reduced. Even so, Congress included a provision allowing a local deposition standard to be set, if the acid rain programme produced hot spots of acid rain.[139] Europe had used a similar 'critical loads' concept in implementing the Convention on Long Range Transboundary Air Pollution.[140] Thus, if the geography of reductions failed to ameliorate the acidification of a particular ecosystem, scientists would calculate how much deposition should decline to address the environmental problem and government officials would derive appropriate geographically specific emission reductions from that calculation. As it happens, the programme produced significant reductions from Midwestern power plants that have a large impact upon New York's Adirondack Park (a state protected reserve that has been a major focus

[136] Eg, US Environmental Protection Agency, 'Approval and Promulgation of Air Quality Implementation Plans; New Jersey; Open Market Emissions Trading Programme' (18 Oct 2002) 67 *Federal Register* 64347 (announcing EPA decision not to proceed with processing New Jersey SIP revisions, because New Jersey had found such serious problems in its emissions trading programme that it was planning to abandon it).

[137] RT Drury *et al*, 'Pollution Trading and Environmental Injustice: Los Angeles' Failed Experiment in Air Quality Policy' (1999) 9 *Duke Environmental Law & Policy Forum* 231, 251–5.

[138] J Salzman and JB Ruhl, 'Currencies and the Commodification of Environmental Law' (2000) 53 *Stanford L Rev* 607.

[139] LB Parker *et al*, 'Clean Air Act Allowance Trading' (1991) 21 *Environmental L* 2021.

[140] (1979) 18 ILM 1442.

of potential concerns about hot spots), so a deposition standard proved unnecessary. Greenhouse gases also seem to pose few difficulties for emissions trading in terms of equity and equivalence issues, as it does not seem that the geography of reductions matters much, at least for purposes of addressing climate change itself (some collateral benefits of reducing greenhouse gases have local consequences).

In short, trading programmes have a good record in saving money. Their record in meeting environmental and equitable objectives has been decidedly mixed. It is not hard to see why. A well designed programme for pollutants that can be well monitored and pose only minor geographic issues can work well, but trading works badly when applied to pollutants that cannot be well monitored, when rules do not carefully preclude gaming, or when simple metrics do not produce environmentally reliable and equitable trades.

While a casual review of the literature might lead to the impression that emissions trading offers a viable alternative to command and control regulation, it cannot substitute for true command and control regulation dictating compliance techniques. Regulators resort to true command and control regulation precisely in the situation where trading cannot work well, when good monitoring is impracticable. In that situation, direct pollution taxes do not work properly either. The acid rain experience shows, however, that a well designed trading programme can sometimes offer a viable alternative to a performance standard.

E. Innovation and Sustainable Development

1. Instrument Choice for Innovation: Taxes, Trading and Traditional Regulation

While writers sometimes use the term 'sustainable development' as a synonym for environmental protection, most have in mind a substantial change in the pattern of development. While the sort of change envisaged has many elements, a vision of significant technological change lies at the heart of sustainable development. A brief analysis of the problem of climate change can show why this is so.

Currently, the industrial world employs a development pattern heavily dependent upon burning fossil fuel. This pattern of development has contributed to a warming of the Earth's average surface temperature. As population and consumption increase, fossil fuel consumption will tend to grow.[141] This implies rising CO_2 emissions, which will increase the warming. Scientists associate this warming with rising sea levels inundating coastal areas, more droughts in areas where hunger is

[141] DM Driesen, *The Economic Dynamics of Environmental Law* (MIT Press, 2003) 9.

already widespread and a spread of infectious diseases.[142] This suggests that current patterns of development premised on increased use of fossil fuels are not sustainable. If this is correct, then sustainable development requires development of technologies that can lessen unsustainable dependence on increased use of fossil fuels, which are not renewable resources. Choosing instruments for sustainable development therefore implies choosing instruments most likely to encourage progress toward a sustainable technological base.

The track record of emissions trading programmes and traditional regulation as instruments to stimulate innovation is both mixed and incomplete (because of a dearth of post-compliance studies of many regulations, especially in the US)[143]. Both types of programmes have often encouraged increased diffusion of conventional technologies, rather than significant advances in the development of technology. Some writers have claimed that the acid rain programme has encouraged technological innovation.[144] Most utilities complied with the acid rain trading programme by employing scrubbers or switching to low sulphur coal. While many writers have referred to these approaches as innovations, they constitute the best understood conventional approaches to reduction of sulphur dioxide emissions from utilities. While scrubbers usually are quite conventional, some scrubber designs deployed under the acid rain programme have received patents, so utilities may have produced some innovation under this programme.[145] The most thorough review of the history of technological change in sulphur dioxide control to date, however, 'does not support' the conclusion that trading provides superior innovation incentives.[146] Similarly, the economist David Popp concludes that fewer scrubber designs received patents under the acid rain programme than under the prior new source performance standards.[147] But, he claims, the acid rain produced more scrubber designs improving control efficiency under the acid rain programme.[148] This suggests that trading reduces the frequency of innovation,

[142] Intergovernmental Panel on Climate Change, *Climate Change, 2001: Issues, Impacts, Adaptation, and Vulnerability: Summary for Policy Makers* (Cambridge UP, 2001) ch 3.5, 4.7.

[143] DM Driesen, 'Does Emissions Trading Encourage Innovation?' (Jan 2003) 33 *Environmental Law Reporter* 10094, 10103–5 (reviewing the empirical literature); AB Jaffe *et al*, 'Environmental Policy and Technological Change' (2002) 22 *Environmental & Resource Economics* 41, 55.

[144] Eg B Swift, 'Command without Control: Why Cap-and-Trade Should Replace Rate Standards for Regional Pollutants' (Mar 2001) 31 *Environmental Law Reporter* 10330, 10331, 10338; B Swift, 'The Acid Rain Test' (May–June 1997) 14 *Environmental Forum* 17 (describing fuel switching and use of scrubbers as 'innovations' from the acid rain programme).

[145] D Popp, 'Pollution Control Innovations and the Clean Air Act of 1990' (2003) 22 *Journal of Policy Analysis & Management* 641. For a detailed discussion of the technologies employed in the acid rain programme, see DM Driesen, 'Does Emissions Trading Encourage Innovation?' (2003) 33 *Environmental Law Reporter* 10094, 10105; generally AD Ellerman *et al*, *Markets for Clean Air: The US Acid Rain Programme* (Cambridge UP, 2000).

[146] M Taylor, E Rubin and D Hounshell, 'Regulation as the Mother of Invention: The Case of SO_2 Control' (2005) 27 *Law & Policy* 348, 370.

[147] Popp, above n 145, 62.

[148] *Ibid.*

but may change the type of innovation. While one can find examples of stringent traditional regulation encouraging significant innovation, often traditional regulation also encourages conventional approaches, like scrubbers.

The literature recognises that the question whether emissions trading encourages significant innovation is more complicated theoretically than the question whether it is cost effective.[149] Many writers supporting the view that trading encourages innovation point to its ability to encourage polluters to go 'beyond compliance' in order to have credits to sell into the market. But as the economist David Malueg pointed out a number of years ago, this analysis focuses only on the incentives facing facilities with relatively low marginal control costs.[150] Facilities with relatively high marginal control cost increase emissions above otherwise required levels in trading programmes. Trading programmes create less impetus for owners of these high cost facilities to innovate than an identically designed performance standard (where trading is not allowed) would create. Hence, trading provides inferior innovation incentives for half the market and superior innovation incentives for the other half, relative to a comparably designed traditional regulation. The difficult question is whether the net incentives provided by a trading programme for all sources encourage more innovation than would occur in a comparably designed non-trading programme.

Economists have recently begun to recognise that a tension might exist between the traditional goal of efficiency and the goal of encouraging significant technological change.[151] Economists often employ the 'induced innovation' hypothesis—the hypothesis that high costs induce innovations to avoid them—in analyzing innovation in free markets.[152] But in the past they have usually ignored this hypothesis in analyzing emissions trading's effect upon innovation. Since emissions trading lowers the cost of routine compliance, the induced innovation hypothesis suggests that emissions trading lowers incentives for innovation relative to a traditional regulation with the same emission limits.

[149] Eg JF Bruneau, 'A Above n on Permits, Standards, and Technological Innovation' (2004) 48 *Journal of Environmental Economics & Management* 1192; JP Montero, 'Permits, Standards, and Technology Innovation' (2002) 44 *Journal of Environmental Economics & Management* 23; JP Montero, 'Market Structure and Environmental Innovation' (2002) 5 *Journal of Applied Economics* 293 (trading, taxes, or traditional regulation can best encourage research and development when firms' products are strategic substitutes); DA Malueg, 'Emissions Credit Trading and the Incentive to Adopt New Pollution Abatement Technology' (1987) 16 *Journal of Environmental Economics & Management* 52; WA Magat, 'Pollution Control and Technological Advance: A Dynamic Model of the Firm' (1978) 5 *Journal of Environmental Economics & Management* 95.

[150] Malueg, above n 149, 29; D Wallace, *Environmental Policy and Industrial Innovation: Strategies in Europe, the USA, and Japan* (Royal Institute of International Affairs, 1995) 20 (explaining that Malueg's more sophisticated model casts doubt on the claim that emissions trading spurs innovation).

[151] KE Rosendahl, 'Cost-Effective Environmental Policy: Implications of Induced Technological Change' (2004) 48(3) *Journal of Environmental Economics & Management* 1099 (questioning 'fully flexible implementation of the Kyoto Protocol' because of potential spillover effects from technological innovation).

[152] Eg RG Newell *et al*, 'The Induced Innovation Hypothesis and Energy-Saving Technological Change' (1999) 114 *Quarterly Journal of Economics* 941.

Emissions trading surely discourages relatively expensive innovation. Without trading, high cost facilities have an incentive to create innovations that cost less than their marginal cost of pollution control. Under trading, no need exists to seek out these relatively costly innovations. High cost facilities will purchase credits from low marginal cost facilities instead.

This may not greatly trouble those who value highly emission trading's capacity to lower the cost of achieving any given short-term goal. But high cost innovation may have special value for sustainable development. While some incremental changes may occur through low cost innovation, developing technologies powerful enough to supplant coal-fired power and gasoline-burning car engines may require substantial investment. This investment may prove extremely valuable in the long run, even if the short-term costs are high. Substituting a renewable technology for a fossil fuel-based approach can simultaneously reduce a whole raft of pollutants and thereby produce a panoply of environmental benefits. These potential benefits include reduced climate change impacts, less urban smog, less acidic aquatic ecosystems, fish with lower mercury levels, fewer oil spills and water free from pollution from oil, mining and drilling. Also, while significant innovations usually require significant outlays to deploy in their earlier years, as their use becomes more common, costs often drop. For this reason, an investment in today's expensive new technology may ultimately lead to cheaper ways of meeting human needs for energy.

Emission trading creates an incentive to choose the technology capable of meeting the trading programme's performance standard with the lowest short-term cost. There is no reason to assume that this choice will coincide with the cheapest long-term dollar cost or the greatest long term environmental benefit.

Pollution taxes have a greater potential to promote innovation than either emissions trading (at least when permits are given away, rather than sold) or traditional regulation. Both emissions trading and performance standards produce incentives only to attain the standards government sets, rather than to go further. While trading does provide incentives for low cost sources to produce some 'extra' credits, it does so only to the extent that high cost sources need credits to meet their limits. Once the high cost sources have purchased enough credits to attain their limits, no further incentive to go beyond compliance exists. Pollution taxes, however, provide a continuous incentive for polluters to deploy innovations costing less than the marginal tax rate. Nevertheless, a recent OECD report notes that in spite of a fairly long history of environmental taxation in OECD countries, we have 'scant information' on technological development in response to eco-taxes.[153]

Any instrument can provide good incentives to innovate if government makes tough decisions. If it sets high pollution tax rates or strict performance standards

[153] OECD, above n 40, 112.

for either traditional regulation or emissions trading, then routine compliance options can become unattractive and polluters will tend to innovate. In practice, however, government often faces significant pressures not to set tough standards.

Other design elements can influence innovation rates as well. For example, regulators have a choice between writing standards that limit the *rate* of emissions and writing standards that limit the *total mass* of emissions. Rate-based standards limit the emissions per unit of output. For example, utility regulations often limit the pounds of pollutant per kilowatt hour of electricity. Since these standards limit only emission rates, increased output under these standards can increase pollution. By contrast, regulators have sometimes written standards limiting the total mass of pollutants allowed from a unit. Under this sort of standard, regulated parties must reduce the emissions rate if they wish to increase output, because the standard limits the total mass of emissions allowed. Standards that limit the total mass of emissions, rather than just the rate of emissions per unit of output, provide better innovation incentives than rate-based standards. While most writers on economic incentives associate rate-based standards with command and control regulation and mass-based limits with emissions trading (largely because the frequently studied acid rain programme uses mass-based limits), in reality, regulators have sometimes written rate-based emissions trading programmes and mass-based traditional regulations. The question whether to use mass-based or rate-based limits constitutes a design question that writers of traditional or trading programmes should confront.

The pressures on government to limit the stringency of standards and other practical impediments can limit the use of mass-based limits in trading programmes, notwithstanding their effectiveness in stimulating innovation. For example, averaging programmes for vehicles have usually involved rate-based limits,[154] because limiting the mass of vehicle emissions would require limits upon driving. The Austrian Ecopoints programme indirectly limits the mass of emissions through driving restrictions, and its history illustrates the political difficulty of such an approach. Austria became concerned about rising emissions and noise caused by increased European truck traffic across it territory, especially in the Brenner valley. The European Commission addressed this problem through an 'Ecopoint' programme that limits the nitrogen oxides per kilowatt hour for large trucks.[155] The European Commission distributes allowances based on 1991 traffic shares.[156] Because the allowable Ecopoints decrease over time, this approach should favour both improved nitrous oxide reduction technology and limits on driving trucks. In order to make sure that this programme reduced noise as well as emissions, it provided for a decrease in total distributed Ecopoints

[154] OECD, above n 21, 16.
[155] *Ibid.*
[156] *Ibid.*

should the number of transit trips increase by more than 8 per cent over 1991 levels.[157] In 1999 when transit trips increased sufficiently to trigger the reduction in Ecopoints, a dispute erupted between Austria and other EU members which had to be resolved by the European Commission and the European Court of Justice.[158] While this programme indirectly limits mass, it does not provide tradeable allowances,[159] which illustrates that the form of limits is separable from the issue of whether a regulatory programme allows trading or not.

2. Innovation through other Policy Instruments

Because trading programmes, taxes and traditional regulation have limited ability to stimulate innovation, regulators around the world have sometimes relied upon other instruments to stimulate innovation. For example, several European countries and US states have used 'renewable portfolio' standards to encourage use of renewable energy.[160] These standards require utilities to rely upon renewable energy sources for a specified percentage of output or require large-scale purchasers of electricity to buy a specified percentage of renewable energy.[161] This sort of command and control regulation suggests a recognition that a simple requirement to use more progressive technology may produce innovation more reliably than to seek to stimulate technological change indirectly through performance standards, emissions trading or pollution taxes.

Recently, however, several countries and states have begun implementing tradeable renewable energy certificates.[162] Such systems combine government technological mandates, albeit a mandate to use a range of technologies rather than one favoured technology, with the flexibility of trading to reduce the compliance cost.

The international regime governing ozone depleting substances used perhaps the most effective innovation simulating approach, simply banning a traditional obnoxious technology, in this case, the use of ozone depleting substances.[163] This can stimulate innovation, since users of banned substances and their suppliers feel an economic imperative to come up with substitutes. Other examples include Great Britain's phase-down of coal and the US phase-out of certain pesticides.

[157] *Ibid,* 157.

[158] *Ibid,* 157–8.

[159] *Ibid,* 155 (describing this as a cap but not trade programme).

[160] KS Golden, 'Senate Bill 1078: The Renewable Portfolio Standard: California Asserts its Leadership' (2003) 30 *Ecology Law Quarterly* 693, 701, 704 (listing states within the US that have adopted renewable portfolio standards, California's legislature considered but rejected a credit trading system to allow trading of the obligation to incorporate a fixed percentage of renewable energy into production plans); RL Ottinger and R Williams, 'Renewable Energy Sources for Development' (2002) 32 *Environmental Law* 331, 349–50 (discussing countries with renewable portfolio standards).

[161] OECD, above n 21, 16 (in most cases, obligations for renewable energy are 'formulated as minimum shares of renewable energy sources in total electricity output').

[162] *Ibid,* 105–36.

[163] Montreal Protocol on Substances that Deplete the Ozone Layer (1989) 26 ILM 1550.

It is open to debate whether such standards are a distinct form of regulation. A ban or phase-out can be viewed simply as a stringent performance standard, requiring zero emissions of a particular substance. But unlike a zero-emission standard, a ban does not simply prohibit emissions, it prohibits the manufacture, sale or use of the substance altogether. A ban might alternatively be considered a work practice standard. While many work practice standards tell regulated entities what to do, a ban or phase-out tells regulated entities what *not* to do.[164] Thus, a ban on ozone depleting chemicals widely used as solvents and refrigerants does not command any particular approach to refrigeration or degreasing. It leaves the field wide open to innovation.

Liability rules, if sufficiently onerous, can also stimulate innovation.[165] After the US government failed to enact a phase-out of asbestos, tort liability bankrupted asbestos manufacturers and forced the development of substitutes. But onerous liability has come under attack in the US and has never commanded much support in other countries. Also, problems of proof limit its capacity to stimulate environmental innovation.

Information regimes can sometimes stimulate innovation. For example, right-to-know laws requiring US chemical companies to report toxic releases appear to have led to pollution prevention within the industry.[166] California's Proposition 65 requiring labelling of carcinogens led to citizen suits settled by supplanting lead pipe with technologies posing less risk to human health.[167]

Pollution taxes can stimulate innovation more effectively when the proceeds pay for innovation.[168] The idea of using negative economic incentives to fund positive economic incentives can provide the clue to designing better instruments for sustainable development. For example, New Zealand sold fishing permits and dedicated some of the proceedings to paying some fishermen to retire, thus reducing overall pressures to allow too much fish to be taken.[169] California and other state legislatures have considered a 'feebate' proposal.[170] This proposal would

[164] If work practice standards are defined to include product standards, bans and phase-outs can be considered a relatively common form of work practice standard. Product standards have been used to prohibit or require the phase-out of such products or components as brominated fire retardants, ozone depleting substances, pesticides, silicone breast implants and lead in gasoline.

[165] See S Shavell, 'Liability for Harm Versus Regulation of Safety' (1984) 13 *Journal of Legal Studies* 357; P Wetterstein (ed), *Harm to the Environment: The Right to Compensation and the Assessment of Damages* (Clarendon Press, 1997).

[166] Emergency Planning and Community Right-to-Know Act, 1986, 42 USC §§ 11001–11050.

[167] California Office of Environmental Health Hazard Assessment, 'Proposition 65', available at www.oehha.org/prop65/background/p65plain.html.

[168] MS Anderson, *Governance by Green Taxes: Making Pollution Prevention Pay* (Manchester UP, 1994).

[169] See RO Boyd and CM Dewees, 'Putting Theory into Practice: Individual Transferable Quotas in New Zealand's Fisheries' (1992) 5 *Society & Natural Resources* 5.

[170] D Ingram, 'Emissions Panel Looks at "Feebate" Proposals' (17 Dec 1994) *Winston-Salem Journal*, available at www.journalnow.com/servlet/Satellite?pagename=WSJ%2FMGArticle%2FWSJ_BasicArticle&c=MGArticle&cid=1031779730489.

impose a fee upon purchasers of high emission vehicles, the proceeds of which would provide a rebate to customers who purchased low emission vehicles. Such an approach could significantly influence the incentives facing manufacturers, encouraging them to compete to produce cleaner vehicles in order to sell to customers who have extra money in their pockets (through the rebate).

One could build on this model to emulate competitive free market dynamics using an 'environmental competition statute'. This statute would require high polluting firms in an industry to reimburse their competitors who pay for the environmental improvements that allow them to achieve lower pollution levels and pay them a preset premium on top of that. Such an approach could create a race to become the cleanest facility, a race fuelled by incentives similar to those existing in competitive markets. Firms that innovate and achieve superior levels of pollution control would stand to profit and firms that failed to achieve superior levels would pay. Competitive markets tend to encourage innovation because of fear and greed. Firms' greed encourages innovation in hopes of grabbing market share from competitors. Firms' fear of losing market share to more innovative competitors encourages innovation. The environmental competition statute creates similar incentives, with the transfer payment from high to low polluting firms functioning much like a shift in market share. Such an approach would require an anti-collusion rule, otherwise regulated firms might agree not to compete to limit emissions, thereby incapacitating an environmental competition statute. Absent such collusion, a properly designed environmental competition statute may stimulate a race to the top.

Government research and development offers a very different approach to innovation. While the current era tends to de-emphasise the value of government in leading innovation, government has often brought together leading scientists to meet major technical challenges such as the development of atomic power, the internet, and the fuel cell. So, it might provide a fruitful approach to solving technical challenges in the environmental area. On the other hand, government research can be misdirected if special interest influence predominates, as the example of US government programmes aimed at 'clean coal' illustrate. But little incentive exists to deploy environmentally beneficial technologies in private markets without government in some way creating a demand for the technologies' use. All instruments of environmental regulation, even much maligned command and control regulation, create some incentives to use environmental technology that free markets do not provide.

All of this points to the need for a more imaginative search for approaches capable of stimulating transformative innovation, such as the environmental competition statute described above. Secondly, it calls attention to the importance, not just of selection of instruments, but of design considerations, such as decisions about stringency, in stimulating innovation. Thirdly, it should lead to more judicious use of emissions trading, instead of a glib assumption that trading offers some kind of panacea for sustainable development. Fourthly, it reminds us that traditional regulation, if designed to stimulate innovation, can prove effective in paving the way toward sustainable development.

F. Conclusion

Economic instruments have become an increasingly important environmental policy tool in many jurisdictions over the past 30 years. Pollution taxes, tradeable emission allowances and other economic instruments can enable society to achieve the same environmental goals of traditional regulation at a lower cost, or superior environmental outcomes at the same cost. In other words, they have the potential to increase the efficiency of environmental protection. But instrument choice for sustainable development requires a conscious decision to make transformative innovation a priority, rather than just assume that such innovation will emerge as a by-product of the use of the most cost effective instruments. That decision should lead to more imaginative use of economic incentives, careful attention to design issues for all instruments, targeted use of traditional regulatory approaches and perhaps government research (in some countries) to provide a technical basis for a technological transformation towards sustainability.

10

Sustainable Finance: Environmental Law and Financial Institutions

BENJAMIN J. RICHARDSON*

A. Introduction

The development of economic instruments and reliance on business self-regulation, as discussed in the previous chapters, are not the only aspects of the renaissance of market institutions and methods in environmental governance. Another is the promotion of ethical investment and sustainable financing in capital markets. Interest in financial institutions as a means of sustainable development has arisen from debates regarding the seeming ineffectiveness of traditional environmental policy instruments.[1] Environmental law regimes world-wide have suffered from a serious deficiency: targeting the companies that extract, consume and pollute, but rarely targeting their financial sponsors, such as banks, pension trusts and mutual funds.[2] Because the financial services sector is where 'wholesale' decisions regarding future development arise, it is also where future pressures on the environment begin. Thus, the reform of investment, banking and insurance services to promote greater sensitivity to environmental concerns offers a way to reduce the incidence of unsustainable developments. While financiers profit from such development, and have the means to influence it, there has been little policy intervention until recently.

This chapter explores how to create legal frameworks to encourage environmentally sustainable finance among commercial financiers. The primary focus is private banks, mutual funds and similar commercial entities, rather than public

* Professor, Osgoode Hall Law School, York University.

[1] K Bosselmann and BJ Richardson, 'Introduction: New Challenges for Environmental Law and Policy' in K Bosselmann and BJ Richardson (eds), *Environmental Justice and Market Mechanisms* (Kluwer, 1998) 1, 1–4; N Gunningham and P Grabosky, *Smart Regulation. Designing Environmental Policy* (Clarendon Press, 1998).

[2] *See* M Jeucken, *Sustainable Finance and Banking: The Financial Sector and the Future of the Planet* (Earthscan, 2001).

financial and development institutions such as export credit agencies or multilateral development banks. Private financiers hold the lion's share of financial resources in capital markets, and hence have a greater ability to influence corporate developments. The environmental effects of their financing have also been somewhat neglected in the extant literature, which has tended to focus on World Bank lending and other public development financing.[3] This chapter also largely ignores the role of insurers in their capacity as risk managers, as this topic involves activities and policy issues that differ from the role of financial institutions as providers of development finance.[4]

Thus, the chapter focuses on explaining the environmental significance of financial institutions. It investigates a suite of recent reforms adopted in Britain, Australia, Germany and elsewhere to promote ethical investment, and it considers further additional reforms that are probably necessary. The basic argument is that the current reforms, comprising mainly incentive and informational policy tools, are useful but insufficient. This is because they do not provide a sufficient counter-weight to other institutional and legal characteristics of capital markets that adversely affect the capacity and willingness of financiers to be environmentally sensitive.

If sustainable development is understood to imply, among other things, maintenance of natural and human-made capital for posterity, the role of capital markets must be recognised as pivotal to this goal.[5] Financial markets generally provide capital with the objective that it should grow. While there is obviously a difference between financial capital (ie, economic assets and income) and the broader concept of capital in sustainable development (ie, natural resources and ecosystem integrity), financial capital is relevant to the environment—financial investments in project developments and technological innovation invariably have environmental effects of some form, and failure to respect ecological constraints can undermine development and influence financial returns.

The relationship between financial markets, investors and sustainable development is problematic. There is evidence that financial markets do not allocate capital efficiently, and that unsustainable, speculative bubbles suck in financial resources while inefficient under-investment arises at other times or in other sectors.[6] Such capital flows may trigger undesirable social and environmental effects

[3] The role of international economic institutions is explored further in ch 12, this vol.

[4] See BJ Richardson, 'Mandating Environmental Liability Insurance' (2002) 12(2) *Duke Environmental Law & Policy Forum* 293.

[5] RW England, 'Natural Capital and the Theory of Economic Growth' (2000) 34 *Ecological Economics* 425; S Schmidheiny and F Zorraquin, *Financing Change: The Financial Community, Eco-Efficiency and Sustainable Development* (MIT Press, 1996). While some writers insist that sustainability should not allow substitution of human for natural capital, capital markets still play a critical role in this 'strong' version of sustainability by influencing whether and at what rate natural capital stocks are exploited.

[6] D Baker and A Fung, 'Collateral Damage: Do Pension Fund Investments Hurt Workers?' in A Fung, T Hebb and J Rogers (eds), *Working Capital: The Power of Labor's Pensions* (Cornell UP, 2001) 13.

arising from company and project investment choices. Examples of the adverse environmental effects of financial institutions include speculative investments in real estate projects that blight urban landscapes, the financing of pesticides in farming, and loans and investments in companies uninterested in pollution control.

So far, few governments have been prepared to acknowledge these connections between commercial finance and environmental quality. In the European Union (EU), the notion that environmental regulation should be a 'shared responsibility' with financial institutions was first formally acknowledged in the European Commission's *Fifth Environment Action Programme* (1992–2000). The Commission envisaged a role for private financial entities in environmental policy, when it declared that 'financial institutions which assume the risk of companies and plants can exercise considerable influence—in some cases control—over investment and management decisions which could be brought to play for the benefit of the environment'.[7] Financial institutions would appear to be generically relevant to environmental management in several ways: as providers of capital, they supply the resources for development initiatives; as stakeholders, such as shareholders and lenders, they exercise influence over corporate management; and, as valuers, they price risks and predict the income of companies. Only recently have scholars and commentators begun to study earnestly the potential of financiers in environmental governance.[8]

B. Enlisting Financiers in Support of Sustainable Development: Some Policy Challenges

Many factors will influence the prospects for successfully harnessing financial institutions as a means of environmental governance. First, we need to understand how the discourse on 'ethical' investment and lending has been defined by regulators, financiers and other stakeholders, and what the implications of this discourse are for the struggle over how to govern business in the interest of environmental sustainability. Environmentally responsible investment can be effected in several ways, most commonly through 'ethical screening', involving the inclusion or exclusion of shares in investment portfolios on environmental grounds,

[7] European Commission (EC), *Fifth Environment Action Programme. Towards Sustainability: A European Community Programme of Policy and Action in Relation to the Environment and Sustainable Development* (EC, 1992) 27.

[8] See eg Delphi International and Ecological GmbH, *The Role of Financial Institutions in Achieving Sustainable Development* (Delphi International, 1997); BJ Richardson, *Environmental Regulation through Financial Organisations* (Kluwer, 2002); M Haigh and J Hazelton 'Financial Markets: A Tool for Social Responsibility?' (2004) 52(1) *Journal of Business Ethics* 59.

and shareholder activism to change corporate policy and practice.[9] There is, unfortunately, no authoritative definition of 'ethical investment'. Commentators have highlighted the dangers posed by this lacuna.[10] Ethical environmental financing can be defined in terms of its substantive content (eg, rules or guidelines regarding approved types of industries and developments), or in terms of procedural requirements (eg, positing mechanisms for assessing the environmental impacts of investment and lending decisions). These issues have yet to be addressed by most policy reformers. The failure to do so may lead to certain environmental and social perspectives (eg, occupational safety, consumer protection and ecological integrity) being marginalised or excluded in discourses about ethical investment.[11] There is some standardisation occurring through the work of ethical investment lobby and research institutions, and the criteria applied by the ethical investment stock market indices that have emerged in North America and Europe.

In the EU, there are at least some 250 specialist ethical investment funds, taking account of ecological and social concerns, up from a mere 50 such funds in the early 1990s.[12] The founding of several indices to track ethical investments points to the growing popularity of this sector. Leading ethical investment indices include the Dow Jones Sustainability Group Index and the UK's Financial Times Stock Exchange's 'ethical index'. Yet, the total size of ethical investment funds is still tiny compared to the market capitalisation of companies in which they invest; in the UK, ethical investment in September 2001 comprised a mere 3.5 per cent share of the investment market, compared to 13 per cent in the US.[13] But, encouragingly, the growth of ethical investments in recent years has tended to exceed that of other types of investments.

A second policy challenge is to determine whether commercial financiers should be subject to direct environmental regulation, like many manufacturing companies are, or managed indirectly through incentive-based and informational policy instruments. Existing theory and empirical evidence suggest the latter approach is often more appropriate for all kinds of firms, from industrial polluters to financial service providers. Many legal theorists suggest that effective regulation in complex,

[9] R Sparkes, *The Ethical Investor* (Harper Collins, 1995) 1–18; see also R Sparkes, *Socially Responsible Investment: A Global Revolution* (John Wiley and Sons, 2002).

[10] MS Knowl, 'Ethical Screening in Modern Financial Markets: The Conflicting Claims Underlying Socially Responsible Investment' (2002) 57 *Business Lawyer* 681; C Mackenzie, 'The Choice of Criteria in Ethical Investment' (1998) 7(2) *Business Ethics* 81; MS Schwartz, 'The "Ethics" of Ethical Investing' (2003) 43(3) *Journal of Business Ethics* 195.

[11] On the construction of environmental discourses, see MA Hajer, *The Politics of Environmental Discourse* (Clarendon Press, 1995); D Salskov-Iversen, HK Hansen and S Bislev, 'Governmentality, Globalisation and Local Practice: Transformations of a Hegemonic Discourse' (2000) 25 *Alternatives: Social Transformation & Humane Governance* 183.

[12] Sustainable Development Research International Group, *Green, Social and Ethical Funds in Europe in 2001* (SDRIG, 2002) 7.

[13] Cerulli Associates, 'The Cerulli Edge—Global Edition' (Sept 2001), available at: www.cerulli.com.

modern economies often requires the adoption of flexible, collaborative mechanisms, in which traditional governmental functions are shared with or devolved to private interests.[14] Instead of direct government regulation, they argue that effective policy-making requires a process of 'governance', harnessing a combination of rules, incentives and informational mechanisms by which the state seeks to steer and co-ordinate, or collaborate with, the non-government sector.[15] Thus, governance theorists describe 'negotiated relationships' between public and private actors,[16] or shared 'regulatory spaces' inhabited by strategic government and market institutions.[17] 'Roundtable' policy dialogues among key stakeholders, such as trade unions, industry associations and government authorities, illustrate these styles of governance. Financial organisations such as banks and pension funds are germane to such analyses, for they are gate-keepers to the economy, supplying development loans for small businesses, equity capital for large public companies, or insurance coverage for companies engaged in environmentally risky activities.

The ability to harness financial organisations as a means of environmental governance depends on the policy instruments available. Banks and other financial service providers are commercial entities interested in profitability, rather than pursuing ethically laudable objectives per se. They are not usually, if at all, in the business of subsidising good environmental practices. But direct regulatory commands on financiers would likely be politically controversial, and thus vulnerable to implementation failure. There are several reasons why informational, incentive and liability tools should be emphasised. Reflexive law theorists such as Teubner argue that because of the disaggregation of modern societies into relatively discrete subsystems, such as the market, with their own codes and norms, regulation is more likely to succeed when it deploys less invasive mechanisms that serve to *stimulate* desired behaviour within market actors, producing an enhanced sensitivity to public policy objectives and a readiness to reflect on and adjust organisational policies and procedures accordingly.[18] Corporate environmental reporting has reflexive properties, facilitating investors' and other stakeholders' scrutiny of the environmental behaviour of firms, and thereby promoting reflection and change within reporting firms. Economic instruments such as pollution taxes and tradeable emission permits also have reflexive properties, as they can explicitly convey in the language of market systems the price of engaging in environmentally exploitative activities.[19]

[14] See M Rein, 'The Social Structure of Institutions: Neither Public nor Private' in SB Kamerman and AJ Kahn (eds), *Privatisation and the Welfare State* (Princeton UP, 1989); JQ Wilson, *The Politics of Regulation* (Basic Books, 1980); I Ayres and J Braithwaite, *Responsive Regulation* (Oxford UP, 1992).

[15] G Stoker, 'Governance as Theory' (1998) 155 *International Social Sciences* J 17; P Grabosky, 'Using Non-Governmental Resources to Foster Regulatory Compliance' (1995) 8 *Governance* 527.

[16] J Freeman, 'The Private Role in Public Governance' (2000) 75 *NYU L Rev* 543.

[17] L Hancher and M Moran, 'Organising Regulatory Space' in L Hancher and M Moran (eds), *Capitalism, Culture and Economic Regulation* (Clarendon Press, 1989).

[18] G Teubner, 'Substantive and Reflexive Elements in Modern Law' (1983) 17 *Law & Society Review* 239.

[19] EW Orts, 'Reflexive Environmental Law' (1995) 89(4) *Northwestern University L Rev* 1227.

Reflexive environmental regulation may be enhanced where private financiers are harnessed into the chain of regulatory controls. Financial organisations are decision-making communities, potentially providing spaces for reflection, learning and experimentation with environmental management. Banks and insurers for instance can provide organisational spaces for assessing and pricing environmental risks and advising clients on risk management. Financiers can also be vehicles for 'legal' communication, transmitting information about correct corporate environmental behaviour. Jessop suggests that organisations straddling the boundaries of different social subsystems are potentially well placed to 'enhance mutual understanding' and 'play a role in linking sub-systems'.[20] Financiers hold strategic, intermediate positions between the state and market for channelling environmental norms to industry. Overall, the aim of government regulation here should primarily be to make corporate *environmental* performance relevant to financial institutions' evaluation of corporate *economic* performance. Without such a synergy, shared environmental governance will likely be resisted by financial organisations as a set of extraneous, imposed requirements.

Incorporating financial markets into the environmental governance matrix poses some special challenges and potential problems for the state. Dangers span from policy incoherence if the state is unable strategically to direct decision-making, to complete policy failures if private institutions capture and distort regulatory programmes. Rhodes warns that without effective systems of democratic supervision, governance networks may become less accountable if decisions are largely removed from the traditional governmental apparatus.[21] Because of the risk that shared environmental governance may generate confusion among regulatees and the broader community as to where final authority and policy responsibility lies, it is essential that chains of regulatory control are readily traceable to the primary government authorities. Careful design of monitoring and oversight mechanisms is needed to ensure the state is able to track and verify implementation of policy goals and ensure governance systems are democratically nourished, and authoritative intervention reserved where private sector motivation or expertise are lacking.[22]

Another major challenge for policy-makers is to understand how differences in the legal and institutional characteristics of financiers (eg, between pension funds and mutual funds) have influenced their capacity or willingness to respond to environmental causes. For example, how can policy measures to promote ethical investment be reconciled with the traditional fiduciary duties of investment trustees that restrict policies that put morality before profit? Reflexive legal theory posits that the internal, institutional structure of business corporations and other entities influences their

[20] B Jessop, *State Theory: Putting the Capitalist State in its Place* (Polity Press, 1990) 329.

[21] RAW Rhodes, *Understanding Governance: Policy Networks, Governance, Reflexivity and Accountability* (Open UP, 1997) 54.

[22] Grabosky, above n 15, 544.

sensitivity to external regulation.[23] Part of that structure is these fiduciary rules, though their impact differs depending on the type of financial institution. Salient differences exist between pension funds and mutual funds or, more generally, between investors and lenders, that influence their sensitivity to environmental policy. It is also crucial to consider the pervasive role of fund managers[24] and contrast that with beneficiary members of pension and mutual funds in investor governance.[25] Furthermore, the institutional character of financial institutions is shaped by the increasing integration of financial markets and institutions, evident, for example, by the emergence of financial conglomerates and the globalisation of financial operations. The increasing transnationalisation of financial services has affected the prospects for national-level environmental financing and its regulation. In virtually any OECD country, a big proportion of development capital is foreign sourced, which poses jurisdictional problems for national regulators.

We thus need to assess changes in the nature and extent of ethical financing for environmental causes in different countries in light of their legal and policy reforms, and to understand the motivations for and the conditions that enabled such reforms. There are differences across countries and business sectors that foster or inhibit governments from bringing financial entities into the environmental policy framework. For example, to mobilise institutional investors as a vehicle for corporate environmental responsibility arguably depends on the existence of extensive equity markets dominated by pension funds and other large investors. Individual, unrelated shareholders are much less able to co-ordinate pressure on companies. In the EU, only the UK, Switzerland and the Netherlands strongly feature such conditions. Opportunities for shareholder activism to promote corporate responsibility also differ between Anglo-American and continental European corporate governance systems.[26] In Germany and Japan, banks play a relatively more assertive role in corporate financing, and so environmental regulatory strategies to mobilise financial service providers in these jurisdictions would need to focus on lenders.

Government regulation and differences in the institutional characteristics of financiers are not the only variables that explain the state of environmental financing. The US is reported to have the highest levels of ethical investment, though it has not adopted the ethical investment reforms found in Western Europe.[27] Thus, in defining the contribution of law, we need to identify other factors that have a bearing on

[23] N Luhmann, *The Differentiation of Society* (Columbia UP, 1982); G Teubner, *Law as an Autopoietic System* (Blackwell, 1994).

[24] See A Harmes, *Unseen Power: How Mutual Funds Threaten the Political and Economic Wealth of Naions* (Stoddart, 2001).

[25] See F Kodar, *Corporate Law, Pension Law and the Transformative Potential of Pension Fund Investment Activism* (LLM Thesis, Osgoode Hall Law School, 2002).

[26] See B Nörk, 'Institutional Investors and their Implications for Financial Markets in Germany' in OECD (ed), *Institutional Investors in the New Financial Landscape* (OECD, 1998) 179.

[27] Social Investment Forum (SIO), *2001 Report on Socially Responsible Investing Trends in the United States* (SIO, 2000).

the status of environmental financing, such as the impact of non-government lobby groups and stock exchange ethical indices.[28] Ethical investment is growing in Australia and the US, partly because of the presence of mature lobby groups for ethical investment in these jurisdictions, namely Australia's Ethical Investment Association and the US Social Investment Forum. Another important driver of reform is the existence of supranational institutions and policies with an interest in this subject. Some European developments have occurred against the backdrop of EU policy in the Fifth Environment Action Programme. Globally, an emerging catalyst to boost the profile of environmental issues in global financial markets is the United Nations Environment Programme (UNEP), which in 1992 launched a Financial Institutions Initiative wherein banks and other financial entities pledge themselves to specified sustainable development practices.[29] In 2003, a new set of environmental principles known as the 'Equator Principles' emerged.[30] Drafted under the auspices of the International Finance Corporation, the Equator Principles had been ratified by 30 banks by June 2005.[31] The principles provide a framework which commits signatory banks to develop individual policies, procedures and practices to ensure that projects are assessed and carried out according to specific social and environmental considerations.

A further critical concern is how differences in the character of environmental issues (eg, climate change, agricultural pollution, biodiversity conservation) have influenced the response of financiers. Why is ethical investment more likely to focus on some environmental issues, but not others? It is critical to consider how variations in the nature of environmental problems can affect the response of financiers. Are specialist policy instruments required for each type of environmental challenge, or are generic approaches tolerable? And does the complexity of some environmental problems, such as climate change perhaps, point to a certain class of environmental problems requiring more state intervention? Dealing with global warming undoubtedly requires co-operation from the financial sector, particularly massive investment in renewable energy supplies and energy efficiency technologies.[32] States can make such financing more likely by creating or restructuring markets. For example, the Kyoto Protocol[33] introduces some economic mechanisms (eg, emissions quota trading and the clean development mechanism) that create

[28] See C Scott, 'Regulation in the Age of Governance: The Rise of the (Post-) Regulatory State' in D Levi-Faur and J Jordana (eds), *The Politics of Regulation* (Edward Elgar, 2004).

[29] UNEP, *Statement by Banks on Environment and Sustainable Development* (Advisory Committee on Banking and the Environment, 1992).

[30] The text of the principles is available at www.equator-principles.com.

[31] For analysis of implementation of the principles, see Freshfields Bruckhaus Deringer, *Banking on Responsibility* (Freshfields Bruckhaus Deringer, July 2005).

[32] See M Grubb and R Vigotti, *Renewable Energy Strategies for Europe: Vol. II: Electricity Systems and Primary Electricity Sources* (Royal Institute of Economic Affairs, 1997); J Zarnikau, 'Consumer Demand for "Green Power" and Energy Efficiency' (2003) 31(15) *Energy Policy* 1661.

[33] (1998) 37 ILM 22.

new market opportunities for environmental financing,[34] and national schemes are already operating in Denmark and the UK.[35]

Regardless of the environmental cause, there are probably always some fundamental limitations to commercial financiers' ability to address a wide range of environmental management concerns. There are extensive writings on the environmental blind-spots of markets, which include their undervaluation of ecological properties, failure to internalise third-party environmental costs, the discounting of future environmental costs and benefits,[36] and an inability to address the problem of scale, or aggregate resource use within biosphere limits.[37] Decentralised financial markets can hardly co-ordinate society towards specific environmental policy goals without government direction. Also, concerns about privacy of clients' information prevent financial institutions from offering the same public participation and informational transparency that are an integral part of current environmental policy regimes. Economic analyses can best help to determine the cost of achieving particular ecological standards, but it is less relevant to understanding the substantive merits of environmental goals, which should arise principally from participatory policy-making. Owing to lack of appropriate expertise and management competence, financial service providers also cannot discharge many of the specialist functions of modern environmental agencies in government. Thus, while there should be a place for making financiers use their financial leverage to make corporate management and policy more mindful of natural resource use and pollution concerns, it is inconceivable that banks could operate national parks or undertake municipal planning functions.

Finally, we need to consider whether and how governments should become more involved in capital allocation in order to promote sustainable finance where commercial financiers fail. Some scholars have advocated the socialisation of the process of capital investment as a way to promote sustainable, democratic development.[38] One way this can be achieved is through harnessing the resources of state pension funds. There have already been reforms to *public* pension schemes in New Zealand and Sweden that mandate ethical investment.[39] Another possibility is for

[34] K Halsnaes, 'Market Potential for Kyoto Mechanisms. Estimation of Global Market Potential for Co-operative Greenhouse Gas Emission Reduction Policies' (2002) 30(1) *Energy Policy* 13; J Janssen, 'Implementing the Kyoto Mechanisms: Potential Contributions by Banks and Insurance Companies' (2000) 25(4) *Geneva Papers on Risk and Insurance* 602.

[35] See BJ Richardson, 'Climate Law and Economic Policy Instruments: A New Field of Environmental Law' (2004) 12(1) *Environmental Liability* 1.

[36] See R Costanza *et al, An Introduction to Ecological Economics* (St Lucie Press, 1997).

[37] H Daly, 'Allocation, Distribution and Scale: Towards an Economics that is Efficient, Just and Sustainable' (1992) 6 *Ecological Economics* 185.

[38] T Ghilarducci, *Labour's Capital: The Economics and Politics of Private Pensions* (MIT Press, 1992); R Unger, *Democracy Realised: The Progressive Alternative* (Verso, 1998); R Blackburn, 'The New Collectivism: Pension Reform, Grey Capitalism and Complex Socialism' (1999) 233 *New Left Review* 3.

[39] New Zealand Superannuation Act 2001; Trejde AP-fonden, *Third Swedish National Pension Fund Annual Report 2002* (Trejde AP-fonden, 2002) 6.

the state to co-finance development with commercial financiers, and use its leverage to ensure that social and environmental goals are addressed by them. While financial market deregulation theory sees economic inefficiencies arising in state involvement in capital allocation,[40] recent literature highlights constructive roles states can play in promoting investment in environmental improvement projects.[41]

Another domain for state involvement is international co-operation to regulate financial markets. Technological advances and the deregulation of capital markets in Western economies have greatly accelerated the geographical mobility of capital in its search for the most lucrative investments.[42] The globalisation of banking, insurance and investment services reduces the power of states individually to regulate financial institutions.[43] Domestic regulatory moves that threaten economic interests can prompt the migration of financial resources to jurisdictions perceived as offering a more benign regulatory milieu. National regulators may also face capacity and information deficits when attempting to supervise enterprises engaged in complex trans-border commerce. International agreements and institutions are thus necessary to prevent environmentally enlightened financial service providers from suffering competitive disadvantages in their transnational business. Apart from in the EU, the existing international regulatory mechanisms in this sector are largely at an embryonic stage of development.[44]

C. The Growth of Institutional Investment and Its Impact on Sustainable Development

Large institutional investors dominate many capital markets through their vast financial holdings.[45] The investment community has a diverse membership, including public and private pension funds, mutual funds, life insurance companies, university foundations and funds managed by banks. A distinction can be made between *institutional* investors, involving, for example, the investment

[40] See ES Shaw, *Financial Deepening in Economic Development* (Oxford UP, 1975); G Yago, 'Financial Repression and the Capital Crunch Recession: Political and Regulatory Barriers to Growth Economics' in BS Zycher and C Lewis (eds), *Economic Policy, Financial Markets, and Economic Growth* (Westview Press, 1993) 81.

[41] Eg, Staniskis and Z. Stasiskiene, 'Promotion of Cleaner Production Investments: International Experience' (2003) 11 *Journal of Cleaner Production* 619.

[42] A Walter, *World Power and World Money* (Harvester Wheatsheaf, 1993) 202–4.

[43] J Braithwaite and P Drahos, *Global Business Regulation* (Cambridge UP, 2000) 7–8.

[44] See European Commission, *Institutional Arrangements for the Regulation and Supervision of the Financial Sector* (EC Internal Market Directorate General, 2000).

[45] J Rada and A Trisoglio, 'Capital Markets and Sustainable Development' (1992) 27(3/4) *Columbia Journal of World Business* 42; CK Brancato, 'The Pivotal Role of Institutions in Capital Markets' in AW Sametz and JL Bicksler (eds), *Institutional Investing: Challenges and Responsibilities of the 21st* Century (Business One Irwin, 1991).

actions of pension funds using their beneficiaries' pooled monies, and *retail* investments, where individuals directly contribute to a mutual fund that specialises in investing in certain market segments. In both cases, however, a specific investment institution is managing investments on behalf of others. In recent decades, institutional savings have mushroomed as ageing Western societies make greater private provision for retirement to compensate for declining state welfare benefits. Investment institutions are popular, because as financial intermediaries, they can reduce financial risk by pooling and diversifying assets, and lowering the transaction costs of contracting and information processing.[46] Within the OECD group, insurance companies are the largest investors, followed by pension funds.[47] Both invest heavily in corporate equities, real estate and bonds. Apart from commercial investors, there is also an assortment of communal financial entities, such as credit unions, building societies, industrial and provident associations and public charities, which can make an important contribution to social investment and community regeneration.[48]

Some commentators stress the potential benign influence of investors. In *The Rise of Fiduciary Capitalism,* Hawley and Williams proclaim the institutional investor as a voice for promoting corporate social and environmental responsibility.[49] This is because institutional investors are supposedly 'universal owners', holding a broad portfolio of stocks, and possessing an interest in the health and long-term sustainability of the entire economy rather than only the profitability of individual businesses. As fiduciaries, long-term investors and majority share owners, Hawley and Williams argue that institutional investors are not overly concerned with short-term returns on investment but, rather, favour long-term performance to meet the needs of their present and future beneficiaries. Similarly, Monks, in his book, *The New Global Investor,* argues that the universal or 'global investor', 'is likely to make good decisions for the long-term of society, because it can afford in most cases to take a long-term view, and a diversified view'.[50] Hawley and Williams believe that universal owner status gives institutional investors an interest in a broad array of public policy governance issues beyond traditional macroeconomic ones. They reason, 'a universal owner that really wants to maximise the shareholder value of its portfolio would need to develop public policy-like positions and monitor regulatory developments and legislation on a number of key issues to the economy as a whole'.[51]

[46] BS Black, 'Agents Watching Agents: The Promise of Institutional Investor Voice' (1992) 39 *UCLA L Rev* 813.
[47] Organisation for Economic Co-operation and Development (OECD), *Institutional Investors: Statistical Yearbook 1998* (OECD, 1999).
[48] See A Hudson, *The Law on Investment Entities* (Sweet and Maxwell, 2000) 259–94.
[49] JP Hawley and AT Williams, *The Rise of Fiduciary Capitalism* (U Pennsylvania Press, 2000).
[50] RAG Monks, *The New Global Investors* (Capstone Publishing, 2001) 105.
[51] Hawley and Williams, above n 49, 170.

Certainly, the growth of institutional investment funds has pooled mammoth resources capable of exerting significant leverage over corporate environmental activities. And there are many tangible reasons why the environment might be of interest to institutional investors. Pension funds and life insurance companies in particular have long-term financial liabilities, providing a structural incentive for long-lasting, sustainable investment. In North America, there is growing empirical evidence of a correlation between share price movements and corporate environmental performance.[52] Good environmental achievements are increasingly seen as an indication of business health, while poor environmental performance may lead to adverse company publicity or, worse, costly pollution liabilities. Further, fund managers have fiduciary responsibilities in trust law and statute to take an active interest in corporate governance.[53] Ethical screening can appeal to investors because it reinforces notions of socially responsible governance. Good environmental and social performance is sometimes interpreted as a proxy for a financially well-managed company. Poor environmental performance that threatens enterprise profitability can be a basis for intervention in corporate management or the switching of investments. But there are also countervailing barriers to more environmentally sensitive investment practices, including: inadequate information about corporate environmental performance; and the absence of appropriate taxes on environmental resource use and pollution, which can thereby make it difficult to measure environmental performance in financially relevant terms. There are also structural barriers in corporate governance systems that can impede ethical shareholder activism, such as the primacy of the profit motive in the fiduciary responsibilities of corporate managers and directors to shareholders, and the limited liability of corporate shareholders themselves, which can shield them from full responsibility for their businesses' social and environmental harms.

D. Environmental Reform of Financial Services Regulation

The starting point for reform of capital markets is to ensure that sustainable development policy considerations are embedded in the legislative envelope governing financial regulators. Among the environmental provisions that could be usefully

[52] Eg P Lanoie, B Laplante and M Roy, 'Can Capital Markets Create Incentives for Pollution Control?' (1998) 26 *Ecological Economics* 31; D Cormier, M Magnan and B Morard, 'The Impact of Corporate Pollution on Market Valuation: Some Empirical Evidence' (1993) 8 *Ecological Economics* 135.

[53] E Tasch and S Viederman, 'New Concepts of Fiduciary Responsibility' in F Capra and G Pauli (eds), *Steering Business Toward Sustainability* (United Nations UP, 1995) 125.

included in financial regulators' responsibilities would be obligations to set guidelines on what constitutes 'ethical' investment, restrictions on environmentally risky investments, obligations of financiers to conduct environmental assessments of proposed investments, and various environmental auditing and reporting stipulations. These requirements could be grafted into the licensing provisions that authorise the establishment and operation of investment and lending institutions.

While sustainable development principles commonly feature in environmental laws around the world, no jurisdiction in the world has yet incorporated sustainability precepts into its financial markets legislation. There have been attempts, though. During the preparation of the UK's Financial Services and Market Act 2000, which created the Financial Services Authority (FSA) as a single regulator for the financial services industry, the UK Social Investment Forum argued before the House of Commons Environmental Audit Committee that there had been no environmental appraisal of the Bill. The Forum unsuccessfully requested inclusion of a reference to sustainable development in the Authority's mandate; for example, to require that it promote best practice in environmental risk management and to encourage the provision of environmental investment and environmental lending products.[54]

Environmental policy has also failed to be included in EU financial services regulation to date. The EC's 2003 Directive on the Activities and Supervision of Institutions for Occupational Retirement Provision[55] omits any environmental disclosure provisions, even though an amendment to the Directive was earlier unsuccessfully advanced in the European Parliament to provide an obligation to consider 'ethical and socially responsible investment principles' in the requirements for disclosure of investment policies.[56] Elsewhere, fortunately, amendments to the EU's Eco-Management and Audit Scheme[57] and the Eco-Label Regulation[58] have allowed for their extension to financial services, thereby enabling investment and other financial service products to be more readily assessed and compared in terms of their environmental credentials.[59]

[54] UK Social Investment Forum, 'UK Social Investment Forum tells MPs of need to include environment in framework for financial services regulator', Press Release, 19 April 1999. Later, the Department for Environment and the Corporation of London issued their so-called *London Principles of Sustainable Finance*, which advocate some soft measures to improve the consideration of the environmental dimensions of financial market activities: *Financing the Future. The London Principles: The Role of UK Financial Services in Sustainable Development* (DEFRA, 2002).

[55] Directive 2003/41/EC [2003] OJ L/235/10.

[56] Art 12(1), European Parliament Committee on Economic and Monetary Affairs, *Draft Report on the Proposal for a European Parliament and Council Directive on the Activities of Institutions for Occupational Retirement Provision* (8 May 2001), PE 295.986/AM/48-134, 52.

[57] Council Regulation 761/2001 of the European Parliament and of the Council of 19 Mar 2001 allowing voluntary participation by organisations in a Community eco-management and audit scheme [2001] OJ L/114/1.

[58] Council Regulation 1980/2000 of the European Parliament and of the Council of 17 July 2000 on a revised Community Eco-label Award Scheme [2000] OJ L/237/1.

[59] For analysis, see B J Richardson, 'Implications of Recent Changes to the EMAS and Eco-label Regulations for the Financial Services Sector' (2002) 14(2) *Environmental Law & Management* 131.

Company law and prudential investment standards rules in many countries can also constrain ethical-minded investor activism. Because of legal constraints on concentrated ownership, fiduciary obligations that require extensive diversification to minimise risk and a strong preference for liquidity, institutional investment agents have tended to seek portfolios comprising fragmented holdings across a plethora of companies.[60] This can reduce the influence of an investor or discourage activism because the stakes may be considered too small given the size of the institution's equity holdings. However, the regulatory trend in Western states has been for securities watchdogs progressively to liberalise rules restricting shareholder proposals from management's proxy statement and other company law obstacles to shareholder activism.[61]

Concerning national banking regulation, there has also been little consideration by authorities of environmental policy. Because of their responsibilities as repositories for people's savings, banks are subject to prudential regulation to meet investor-protection and consumer service standards, through capital adequacy and liquidity requirements.[62] The harnessing of banks to facilitate policy goals is not unprecedented in public policy design; the contractual relationship between financial institutions and their customers has long been regulated to facilitate public policy goals.[63] Money laundering controls, requiring financial institutions to report suspicious transactions, illustrate governments' ability to harness banks as co-regulators in furtherance of policy objectives. Because of their expertise and access to relevant information, financial institutions are at the forefront of efforts to control fraud. Such controls, however, are more easily reconciled with the financial priorities of banks than amorphous environmental concerns. Banks are certainly in a position to demand detailed environmental information concerning the development projects they fund. Banks can request information from borrowers as part of loan approval contracts, which gives them an advantage over investors in corporate shares, which must rely on publicly reported information. However, banks' incentives to gather such environmental information are often lacking. And it may not be desirable or even possible for financiers to make detailed analyses of social and ecological impacts or to evaluate the acceptability of such impacts.

Reforming the financial services sector to make it more responsive to environmental and social concerns must also address the legal and market context of specific financial institutions. The financial services sector is institutionally heterogeneous. Despite market liberalisation reforms that have encouraged convergence and assimilation of financial services, financial organisations retain

[60] W Lee, 'Modern Portfolio Theory and the Investment of Pension Funds' in P Finn (ed), *Equity and Commercial Relationships* (Law Book Company, 1987) 303.

[61] See eg recent changes to Australia's Company Law Review Act 1998 (Cth); and Canada's 2001 amendments to the Business Corporations Act 1985, SC 2001, c 14.

[62] R Lastra, *Central Banking and Banking Regulation* (Financial Markets Group, 1996).

[63] R Cranston, *Principles of Banking Law* (Clarendon Press, 1997) 153.

distinctive institutional characteristics shaped by their legal structure and obligations, the nature of their financial services provided and the influence of market forces involved. Consequently, financiers may respond differently, and sometimes less effectively, to the same environmental reforms. This can be illustrated by looking at pension funds, mutual funds and banks.

E. Pension Funds

Occupational pension funds established by companies and public authorities are unique in that they are established to pay benefits upon their members' retirement.[64] In Anglo-American legal systems, the consequential fiduciary obligations on fund trustees to maximise members' financial returns can hamper ethical investment. There are several cases in the UK and US where the relationship between ethical investment and pension fund trustees' fiduciary responsibilities was considered.[65] In Britain, notions of fiduciary responsibility were interpreted in *Cowan v Scargill*,[66] *Martin v City of Edinburgh District Council*[67] and *Bishop of Oxford v Church Commissioners for England*[68] as constraining pension fund trustees from embracing ethical criteria in investment policy.[69] This is because the best interests of trust beneficiaries have generally been considered to be their *financial* interests.[70] Though, in *Church Commissioners for England*, Nicholls V-C accepted that there were at least two exceptions to the duty to maximise financial returns: namely, where the aims of the charity and the objects of investment would conflict and, secondly, where particular investments would detract from the charity's work, the trustees must weigh the extent of financial loss from offended supporters and the financial risk from exclusion.[71] From the US case law, in *Board of Trustees of Employee Retirement System of the City of Baltimore v Mayor and City Councillors of Baltimore*,[72] a state court found that a city ordinance requiring a municipal authority pension fund to disinvest from companies engaged in business in South Africa did not cause trustees to violate their

[64] On the development and role of pensions, see R Blackburn, *Banking on Death. Or, Investing in Life: The History and Future of Pensions* (Verso, 2002).

[65] JD Hutchinson and CG Cole, 'Legal Standards Governing Investment of Pension Assets for Social and Political Goals' (1980) 128 *University of Pennsylvania L Rev* 1340; D Hayton, 'English Fiduciary Standards and Trust Law' (1999) 32 *Vanderbilt Journal of Transnational Law* 555.

[66] [1985] 1 Ch 270; [1984] 2 All ER 750.

[67] [1988] SLT 329.

[68] [1992] 1 WLR 1241; [1993] 2 All ER 300.

[69] For analysis, see JH Farrar and JK Maxton, 'Social Investment and Pension Scheme Trusts' (1986) 102 *LQR* 32.

[70] On the roots of trusts, see A Hudson, *Principles of Equity and Trusts* (Cavendish Publishing, 1999).

[71] Above n 68, at 304 (All ER).

[72] 562 A 2d 720 (CA Mld, 1989).

prudential investment duties, so long as the cost of investing according to social responsibility precepts was *de minimis*, as was considered in this case. These precedents do not apply in the continental European legal systems where, instead of prudential standards, 'quantitative' regulation of investment portfolios is typically applied, such as restrictions on the volume of funds that can be devoted to particular classes of investment including foreign securities, real estate and loans.[73]

In some jurisdictions, there has also been limited statutory reform to clarify investment fiduciary duties and the scope for ethical investment. In Canada, the provincial governments in Manitoba and Ontario legislated to improve the prospects for ethical investment. Following recommendations from the Manitoba Law Reform Commission, in 1995 the province's Trustee Act[74] was amended expressly to permit trustees to consider non-financial criteria in developing investment policies.[75] Ontario enacted in 1988 the South African Trust Investments Act[76] to permit a trustee to divest or to reject investments in companies doing business in apartheid South Africa without infringing his or her duty despite the effect on investment proceeds.

Since 2000, more substantial reforms have been adopted in Western Europe and Australia directed towards legislative requirements for pension trustees and their agents to take account of the environmental effects of their investment decisions, or at least to report publicly on their policies, if any, in this respect.[77] The UK was the first country to take a step in this direction when, in July 1999, the government issued a regulation under the Pensions Act 1995 requiring occupational pension fund trustees to disclose their policies on socially responsible investment and on the exercise of shareholder rights, including voting rights.[78] A similar requirement was imposed on local government pension funds.[79] Legislation requiring pension fund managers to disclose or explain how they have taken into account environmental, social or ethical considerations in their investment policies has since arisen in France,[80] Germany,[81] Belgium[82] and Italy.[83] In Australia, the Financial Services

[73] However, asset type investment restrictions are diminishing, as is evident eg in the UCITS amendment Directive 2001/108/EC [2002] OJ L/41/20.

[74] Trustee Act SM (Statutes of Manitoba) 1995, s 79.1.

[75] Manitoba Law Reform Commission, *Ethical Investment by Trustees* (Manitoba Law Reform Commission, 1993) 32.

[76] RSO 1990, c S 16.

[77] B.J Richardson, 'Pensions Law Reform and Environmental Policy: A New Role for Institutional Investors?' (2002) 3 *Journal of International Financial Markets: Law & Regulation* 159.

[78] Enacted pursuant to Pensions Act 1995, s 35(3)(f): Occupational Pension Schemes (Investment, and Assignment, Forfeiture, Bankruptcy etc.) Amendment Regulations 1999, SI 1999 No 1849, cl 2(4).

[79] Local Government Pension Scheme (Management and Investment of Funds) (Amendment) Regulations 1999, SI 2000 No 2552.

[80] *Projet de loi sur l'épargne salariale*, 7 Feb 2001, No 2001-152, art 2; *Projet de loi portant diverses dispositions d'ordre social, éducatif et culturel*, 28 June 2001, Ch V*bis*, art L.135–8.

[81] *Betriebliche Altersvorsorge*, art 10, *Änderung des Versicherungsaufsichtsgesetzes.*

[82] Law for Pension Funds, ch VIII, arts 42 and 47, cited in Council of Europe, Social Cohesion Development Division, *Examples of Economic Solidarity Supporting Regulations in the Member States of the Council of Europe and of the European Union* (Council of Europe, 2004).

[83] Reported in 'Pension Reform Bill Approved', *European Social Investment Forum Newsletter,* Sept 2004 .

Reform Act 2001 applied an ethical disclosure obligation to a wider range of investment products than found in the European examples, covering pensions, managed investment products and investment life insurance products.[84] But some governments have rejected this type of reform. The Canadian government in September 2002 rebuffed an opposition Private Member's Bill, modelled on the UK law.[85] It is important to recognise that all of these reforms require only disclosure of, rather than actual adoption of, ethical investment practices.

None of these ethical investment reforms statutorily define ethical investment, and all only superficially address the problem of monitoring compliance. Recent surveys of the effect of the UK reforms suggest that, while there has been a significant increase in adoption of ethical investment policies by pension funds, the quality and implementation of such policies has been quite variable.[86] A rise in ethical investment funds has also been reported in France.[87] In coming years, it will be critically important to undertake extensive empirical research to assess the impact of these ethical investment reforms. If they do not work, authorities may need to consider more direct forms of intervention into capital markets to compel environmental financing. By the end of 2002, explicit socially responsible investment amounted to only 2.1 per cent of European pension fund equity holdings.[88]

A neglected aspect of pension fund reform is their internal governance. There has been a long-standing debate on the question of democratisation of pension fund governance to give worker beneficiaries more say in how their monies are invested.[89] Through worker influence over pension fund investments, there could be a shift away from short-term profit focus to long-term real investment. Some labour movement activists are attempting to acquire greater representation on pension fund boards of trustees either through joint or sole trusteeship, or to establish advisory boards to these bodies. In Canada, for example, Quebec pension legislation establishes mechanisms for employee representation on pension management boards.[90] But contrary to the optimism expressed by Peter Drucker in his book, *Unseen Revolution: How Pension Fund Socialism Came to America*,[91] the reality is that pension plan beneficiaries generally do not control or direct the corporations in which their pension monies were invested.[92] The question of how

[84] See BJ Richardson, 'Ethical Investment and the Commonwealth's Financial Services Reform Act 2001' (2002) 2 *National Environmental L Rev* 47.

[85] Bill C–394, An Act to amend the Pension Benefits Standards Act 1985.

[86] D Coles and D Green, *Do UK Pension Funds Invest Responsibly?* (JustPensions, July 2002) 1.

[87] European Social Investment Forum (ESIF), *Socially Responsible Investment Among European Institutional Investors: 2003 Report* (ESIF, 2003) 48.

[88] *Ibid*, 14.

[89] Kodar, above n 25, 57.

[90] Supplemental Pension Plans Act SQ 2001, c R–15.1.

[91] (Harper and Row, 1976).

[92] J Rifkin. and R Barber, *The North Will Rise Again: Pensions, Politics and Power in the 1980s* (Beacon Press, 1978).

the governance of pension funds and other investment entities should be democratised, and the connections between democratic governance and sustainable development, is an important research issue that must be addressed in future environmental reforms of this segment of the financial markets.

F. Mutual Funds

Mutual funds are one of the most popular investment vehicles, and have been used heavily by insurance companies for investing their premium income. Whereas the pension sector has faced the problem of reconciling ethical investment with trustees' fiduciary responsibilities, mutual funds have been able largely to avoid this conundrum. This is because the mutual fund form, catering to both retail and institutional investors, can be adapted to pursue a variety of desired investment goals.[93] Of course, when pursuing an ethical investment policy, a mutual fund must exercise care to achieve the optimal financial returns within the parameters of its stated policy. So, where a mutual fund advertises an ethically responsible investing policy, fiduciary and contractual obligations arise in that the fund must practise what it preaches. Dedicated ethical investment funds usually require much more than mere compliance with environmental law as a criterion for inclusion in an investment portfolio. For example, Canada's Ethical Funds demand that businesses adopt 'an effective environmental management system', and demonstrate 'a level of commitment to disclosure of environmental practices including compliance record'.[94]

Although national regulation of the mutual fund industry does not generally distinguish between ethical mutual funds and traditional mutual funds, some commentators have suggested that investment regulation should make a distinction because the distinct investment agenda of ethical funds gives rise to specific expectations from investors.[95] It is no longer a case of crudely maximising financial returns, but applying a policy of ethical screens and, if necessary, engaging in shareholder activism. Through shareholder activism, ethical mutual funds (along with other institutional investors) can be an instrument for environmental governance, applying pressure to corporate management to make policy changes that affect the environment.

Consequently, regulation should aim to improve the objectivity and transparency of ethical funds' investment policies, and should require disclosure by

[93] Hudson above n 48, 191–252.

[94] Ethical Funds available at www.ethicalfunds.com/do_the_right_thing/sri/ethical_principles_criteria/environmental.asp.

[95] G Djurasovic, 'The Regulation of Socially Responsible Mutual Funds' (1997) 22 *Journal of Corporation Law* 257.

mutual funds of how they exercise their shareholder rights. Of particular importance is how funds vote their shareholdings. In addition to selecting and trading corporate stocks, mutual fund managers vote millions of shares on behalf of the fund investors. This process, known as proxy voting, can keep mutual fund clients in the dark about how their fund is voting on a particular issue, or whether their mutual fund manager voted at all. Mutual fund managers typically vote according to the recommendations in the proxy circular.[96] Ideally, however, fund managers should vote according to proxy voting guidelines issued by their mutual fund company. Typically, in most jurisdictions there is no requirement in mutual fund regulations for funds to disclose proxy-voting practice or to ensure shares are voted in any particular way. Consequently, ethical mutual funds may not be adequately applying their stake in corporations to improve the environmental performance of their investments. Significantly, in April 2003 the US Securities and Exchange Commission adopted a rule for Disclosure of Proxy Voting Policies and Proxy Voting Records by Registered Management Investment Companies, to require registered management investment companies to disclose how they vote proxies relating to portfolio securities they hold.[97] Elsewhere, some mutual funds are voluntarily disclosing their voting guidelines and voting activity, but this is not occurring systematically.[98]

Although some see mutual funds as the preferred vehicle for ethical financing, the mutual fund sector generally is not a natural ally of sustainable investment.[99] Pension fund investment is probably more compatible with sustainability. Pension funds tend, on average, to hold shares for longer periods than mutual funds because of their longer term financial liabilities.[100] Because portfolio turnover ratios are lower in pension funds than among other institutional investors, pension fund managers also have more opportunity for engaging in shareholder activism. Furthermore, unlike the mutual fund industry, pension funds are not competitive. Their focus on performance is one of ensuring returns adequate to meet anticipated liabilities, not to attract investors. Mutual funds do compete to attract investors, and this competition leads to an emphasis on profit gains and market share, rather than long-term returns. Furthermore, owing to their competitive nature, mutual funds are much less likely than pension funds to be shareholder activists.[101] This is

[96] JG MacIntosh, 'Institutional Shareholders and Corporate Governance in Canada' (1996) 26 *Canadian Business LJ* 145, 160.

[97] Securities and Exchange Commission, *Final Rule: Disclosure of Proxy Voting Policies and Proxy Voting Records by Registered Management Investment Companies* (SEC, 14 Apr 2003).

[98] S Heinrich, 'Ethical Funds Comes Clean on Voting Policies', *Financial Post* (6 July 2000) D4.

[99] See especially the critique made by Harmes, above n 24.

[100] Public and union pension funds display this characteristic more than private pension plans: MO'Connor, 'Labor's Role in the Shareholder Revolution' in *Working Capital,* above n 6, 67, 69.

[101] E Becker and P McVeigh, 'Social Funds in the United States: Their History, Financial Performance, and Social Impacts' in *Working Capital,* above n 6, 44, 64 (referring to very low levels of shareholder resolutions sponsored by US ethical mutual funds).

because efforts by mutual funds to increase corporate value through shareholder activism will benefit all shareholders and may thus benefit rival funds. However, it must be noted that the distinction between mutual and pension fund investment styles can sometimes be blurred, given that some pension funds invest through mutual funds rather than craft their own investment portfolios.[102]

G. Banks and Debt Finance

In contrast to institutional investors whose relevance to environmental financing arises through their involvement in equity markets, banks are important for providing project finance for specific developments and for funding small, unlisted companies. Banks are financial intermediaries for the receipt of deposits from members and redistribution of such deposits as loans and investments for development and consumption purposes. For banks world-wide, the environment is becoming a stronger concern for several reasons.[103] First, there is the prospect of direct lender liability where a bank becomes responsible for the environmental liabilities of its clients, such as liability to clean up contaminated land.[104] Secondly, environmental problems can generate indirect credit risks for lenders where a borrower experiences financial hardship, such as incurring an onerous pollution fine. Thirdly, there is a reputational risk for banks when they associate with environmentally controversial developments or firms.

A few banks have gone beyond these forms of 'defensive' banking, involving the avoidance of obvious environmental problems, to a strategy of conscious promotion of sustainable development. This can be achieved through the offering of differential interest rates to reflect borrowers' environmental performance and the provision of advisory services to clients to integrate financial and environmental risk management.[105] Notable environmentally conscious banks include UmweltBank (Germany), Triodos Bank (The Netherlands), Citizens' Bank (Canada) and the Co-operative Bank (UK). In the home loan and building finance markets, some lenders are offering 'green mortgages' as a way of meeting consumer demand for environmentally friendly, energy-efficient houses. The lending schemes offer borrowers higher credit ratios and, sometimes, lower

[102] World Bank, *Private Capital Flows to Developing Countries: The Road to Financial Integration* (Oxford UP, 1997) 129.

[103] BJ Richardson, 'Environmental Liability and Banks: Recent European Developments' (2000) 17(10) *Journal of International Banking Law* 289, 290.

[104] S Rose-Ackerman, 'Environmental Liability Law' in TH Tietenberg (ed), *Innovation in Environmental Policy* (Ashgate, 1992) 243; JJ Norton, RM Auerback and JM Gaba, *Environmental Liability for Banks* (LLP, 1995).

[105] See JJ Bouma, M Jeucken and L Klinkers (eds), *Sustainable Banking: The Greening of Finance* (Greenleaf Publishing, 2001).

interest rates.[106] But, as with ethical investment funds, green mortgages are a niche segment of the financial markets currently addressed by only a few institutions, and the incentives for more general practices in the banking sector in this area seem to be lacking.

Interest by private banks in environmental matters has also been shaped by reforms to the provision of public development finance. Since the 1980s, there have been extensive changes to the operations of the multilateral development banks (MDBs), which have adopted environmental procedures and standards to govern development project loans and other forms of financial assistance.[107] The European Bank of Reconstruction and Development has gone the furthest in this respect, and it is the only MDB with a specific environmental mandate in its charter.[108] Multilateral development bank environmental lending standards can provide benchmarks for private banks interested in environmental issues.[109] Of course, many private banks have not been inspired by the MDB reforms or other reasons to consider the environment, because of differences in their loan portfolio, clientele and other aspects of the financial markets they work in, and differences in the regulatory structures by which they are governed. Thus, for many lenders, policy measures to promote greater environmental consciousness will likely remain inconsequential until the underlying environmental costs and benefits of economic activities are appropriately priced through eco-taxes and similar economic instruments. But the effect of the latter mechanisms (discussed later in this chapter) can be enhanced when coupled with other policy interventions.

The challenge for policy reformers is to identify areas of banking operations in which environmental policy concerns can be made relevant and can be feasibly embedded into governance regimes. In contrast to equity investors, commercial banks face some unique challenges and opportunities when addressing environmental concerns. Unlike pension or mutual funds, which must rely on publicly reported information to assess the environmental performance of companies, banks have the advantage that they can obtain additional information about environmental risk and other aspects of a borrower's environmental performance through contractual techniques as part of loan administration procedures. Banks could use this information as part of credit appraisal systems. This may require the development of some internal professional competencies in relevant environmental management techniques or the contracting-in or sharing of such competencies for smaller financial institutions. Environmental appraisal by financial

[106] See eg S Brady, 'Fannie Mae/NAHB Launch Effort to Develop "Green" Mortgages' (1999) 6 *Professional Builder* 1.

[107] World Bank, *Mainstreaming the Environment: The World Bank Group and the Environment* (World Bank, 1995).

[108] Art 21(vii) requires the Bank to 'promote in the full range of its activities environmentally sound and sustainable development': *Agreement establishing the European Bank for Reconstruction and Development* [1990] OJ L/372/ 34.

[109] Bank of America, *1999 Environmental Progress Report* (Bank of America, 2000) 17.

institutions probably could not be a substitute for government environmental impact assessment systems, owing to limitations in banks' access to environmental expertise and the possibly reduced opportunities for public participation in such processes, but it could operate as a point of initial screening and assist in improving project design before submission to planning permission authorities.

Another difference between investors and lenders in their responses to corporate environmental performance stems from liability rules. Whereas investment shareholders are largely protected by rules of limited company liability from the environmental liabilities of their investee companies, lenders face liability risks if they become too closely involved in their borrowers' business or take possession of loan security.[110] Through appropriately directed liability legislation, governments could promote environmentally responsible lending in the banking sector. Increased lender liability may eventually lead to a reduction in the number of environmentally damaging activities that are financed and thereby eliminate industries and businesses associated with environmental problems in the market.

Environmental lender liability has become a grievance in various industrial economies because of legislative changes or judicial precedents.[111] The potential environmental liability of lenders arises from the definitions of 'owner', 'operator', 'permits' or 'causes' commonly found in pollution control legislation. A wide interpretation of such words may implicate lenders despite the fact that they had no direct role in causing the contamination. A lender could incur liability by being the potential owner of a contaminated property through the right to realise the security previously offered by the project borrower; and providing guarantees for firms with potential or actual environmental liability (eg, firms handling hazardous wastes).

The most persuasive evidence of the effect of government intervention into financial markets comes from the US, where the behaviour of banks was profoundly influenced by the implementation of the Comprehensive Environmental Response, Compensation and Liability Act 1980, which may make a lender vicariously liable for contaminated site remediation.[112] According to a survey by the American Bankers' Association, 62 per cent of community commercial banks had rejected loan applications or potential borrowers because of the possibility of environmental liability, and 45 per cent had withdrawn from lending in known

[110] Richardson, above n 103.

[111] JD Lipton, 'Project Financing and the Environment: Lender Liability for Environmental Damage in Australia' (1996) 11 *Journal of Banking Law* 7; MH Ogilvie, 'Enter at Your Own Risk: Environmental Lender Liability in Canada', *Journal of Business Law,* Jan 1996, 94; JY Levy, 'Landlord and Lender Liability for Hazardous Waste Clean-up: A Review of the Evolving Canadian and American Case Law' (1992) 20(2) *Canadian Business LJ* 269.

[112] Pub L No 96–510, 94 Stat 2767 (11 Dec 1980) (codified at 42 USC §§ 9601–9675); DR Berz, 'Lender Liability under CERCLA: In Search of a New Deep Pocket' [1991] *Banking Law Journal*: 108; J Norton, 'Lender Liability in the United States' in R Cranston (ed), *Banks, Liability and Risk* (LLP, 1995) 358–9.

hazardous sectors because of similar concerns.[113] Perversely, however, reduced investment in brownfield sites has sometimes encouraged urban and industrial expansion into untouched greenfields.[114] The US experience has been followed with interest in Europe, where the European Commission's new environmental liability Directive avoids specifically attaching liability to financial sponsors, but leaves open the possibility of lender liability where banks exercise operational control over polluting facilities or sites.[115]

More research is needed into devising the optimal liability regime—one that provides appropriate incentives for banks to avoid funding environmentally damaging developments, but without stifling potentially socially valuable investments. For instance, while the retroactive nature of some environmental liability regimes may enhance environmental compensation goals, there is little deterrence achieved by penalising organisations for unforeseeable, non-negligent contamination caused by long ago, historic activities.[116] This situation can be compounded by joint and several liability rules, whereby each liable party can be required to pay the total cost of damage, not just the share for which it was responsible. They are a mechanism for mutual regulation, encouraging each party to contract only with other reputable parties, and creating strong incentives for parties to monitor each other's behaviour.[117] Joint and several liability rules are at odds with the polluter pays principle because they encourage the channelling of liability to the deepest pockets—such as financial lenders—rather than the actual or primary contributor of environmental harm.[118] Joint and several liability can cause 'over-deterrence' by deep pocket parties, and 'under-deterrence' by less solvent parties who may believe that no environmental claims will be brought against them.[119] To allow deep pocket parties to recover contributions from joint tortfeasors generates additional transaction costs and is of little

[113] Cited in P Blackman, 'Part II of the Environment Act and the Amendments to the Environmental Protection Act 1990' (IBC Conference on the Environment Act, 1995). Following extensive lobbying by banks, in 1996 the US Congress amended CERCLA to reduce lenders' exposure to environmental liabilities: see Asset Conservation, Lender Liability and Deposit Insurance Protection Act of 1996 (HR 3610, Title II, Subtitle E, §§ 2501–4).

[114] L Morelli, 'Cleaning Up Superfund: The State of Superfund Reauthorisation' (1998) 6(2) *Environmental Liability* 27, 32.

[115] Parliament and Council Directive 2004/35/EC of 21 Apr 2004 on environmental liability with regard to the prevention and remedying of environmental damage, [2004] OJ L/143/56.

[116] JJ Lyons, 'Deep Pockets and CERCLA: Should Superfund Liability Be Abolished?' (1986) 6 *Stanford Environmental LJ* 271, 301.

[117] G Teubner, 'The Invisible Cupola: From Causal to Collective Attribution in Ecological Liability' (1994) 16(2) *Cardozo L Rev* 429, 430.

[118] TH Tietenberg, 'Indivisible Toxic Torts: The Economics of Joint and Several Liability' (1989) 65(4) *Land Economics* 305.

[119] MJ Gergen, 'The Failed Promise of the "Polluter Pays" Principle: An Economic Analysis of Landowner Liability for Hazardous Waste' (1994) 69 *NYU L Rev* 624, 674.

value if the joint tortfeasors are insolvent. Current economic theory suggests 'partial' lender liability for borrowers' environmental harms is the most appropriate compromise.[120]

Even if a lender is shielded from direct environmental liability, its borrower's financial difficulties caused by an environmental problem might still be reason for concern. Insolvency law can have a bearing on this situation. Conflicts can arise between the claims of creditor banks and any outstanding environmental expenses owed by a bankrupt firm, such as costs associated with a regulator's clean-up order.[121] The traditional norm in bankruptcy codes is that priority is given to the claims of secured creditors such as bank lenders. In the absence of court determinations to the contrary, this can result in environmental debts being unpaid and so displaced onto society. Interestingly, Canadian and British courts have concluded that environmental remediation and related expenses should sometimes take priority over the distribution of assets to the bankrupt company's creditors.[122] In the notable *Panamericana* case, the appointed receiver-manager was directed by the Alberta Court of Appeal to implement the environmental authority's order to clean up oil wells in accordance with provincial environmental regulations, despite the corporate licensee's bankruptcy and even though the expense of protecting the wells meant less money for distribution to creditors.[123] In the British case of *Environment Agency v Clark (Administrator of Rhondda Waste Disposal Ltd)*,[124] the Court of Appeal displaced the interests of creditors by granting leave under the Insolvency Act 1986[125] to allow criminal prosecution of serious pollution offences against a company under administration.

H. Public Institutions in Capital Allocation

The deficiencies of commercial financiers in promoting sustainable development probably require that states become more involved in capital allocation for some environmental causes. Public institutions—states and supranational institutions—should be most actively involved in environmental policy in dealing with strategic, long-term environmental problems, as well as environmental problems

[120] R Pitchford, 'How Liable Should a Lender Be? The Case of Judgement-proof Firms and Environmental Risk' (1995) 85 *American Economic Rev* 1171.

[121] See DL Baker, 'Bankruptcy—The Last Environmental Loophole?' (1993) 34 *South Texas L Rev* 131; JD Barnett, 'Conflict Between Bankruptcy and Environmental Law and Policy: The Courts are Still Out' (1991) 1 *Environmental Finance* 191.

[122] See eg *Canada Trust v Bulora Corporation* (1981) 34 CBR (NS) 152 (Ont CA); *Panamericano De Bienesy Servicos v Northern Badger Oil & Gas Ltd* (1992) 8 CBR (3d) 31 (Alta CA); *Environment Agency v Stout* [1999] *Environmental Reports* 407.

[123] *Ibid*, 52 per Laycraft CJ.

[124] CA, 10 Feb 2000.

[125] S 10(1)(c).

that are transnational in scale. Climate change is such an example. The promotion of sustainable development, particularly for strategic global environmental problems, goes far beyond policy tools that require the inclusion of environmental externalities in investment asset costs, reporting on environmental risks and the like. In this terrain, a much deeper set of environmental and public health issues become relevant—eg, social decisions about natural resource use, and the trade-off between precaution and risk aversion.

Regarding development financing at a supranational level, there is already a sizeable literature on the role and impacts of international economic institutions.[126] These include the World Bank and its sister MDBs, the International Monetary Fund and the World Trade Organisation. In addition to the conditions attached to project-based development loans, these institutions may influence the general economic policy of borrower countries through the use of conditional structural adjustment and sector policy loans.[127] Their activities have been interpreted as geared to the efficient dispensation of money to recipient countries and, more broadly, enshrining a particular set of capitalist economic relations and the absorption of developing countries into the OECD-dominated world economy. Although often portrayed as politically neutral, in reality the MDBs and the IMF have tended to function as surrogates for the wealthiest nations that dominate their primary decision-making forums.[128] Since the 1980s, the international economic institutions have experienced increasing public pressures to modernise their financial policies to accommodate ecological and social concerns. Although some reforms have been made to their operations (eg, EIAs of project financing proposals), more systematic reform is probably needed.[129]

For the state crudely to direct where private financiers allocate capital in order to defend social and environmental causes would simply be a political disaster, and it would likely engender major economic inefficiencies, given that regulators typically lack the required information and expertise. However, through national pension schemes, governments could to some extent enhance public control over capital allocation.[130] The Swedish and New Zealand national pension schemes, for instance, have recently been amended to enable authorities better to direct the funds towards socially and environmentally investments.[131] A new Swedish law

[126] See further Z Plater, 'Multilateral Development Banks, Environmental Diseconomies, and International Reform Pressures: The Example of Third World Dam-Building Projects' (1989) 9(2) *Boston College Third World LJ* 169; S Hansen, 'Macroeconomic Policies and Sustainable Development in the Third World' (1990) 2(4) *Journal of International Development* 533.

[127] See J Warford and Z Partow, 'Evolution of the World Bank's Environmental Policy' (1989) 26(Dec) *Finance & Development* 5.

[128] R Swedberg 'The Doctrine of Economic Neutrality of the IMF and the World Bank' (1986) 23(Dec) *Journal of Peace & Research* 377.

[129] BM Rich, 'The "Greening" of the Development Banks: Rhetoric and Reality' (1989) 19(2) *Ecologist* 44.

[130] See R Unger, *Democracy Realised: The Progressive Alternative* (Verso, 1998).

[131] See J Myles and P Pierson, 'The Comparative Political Economy of Pension Reform' in P Pierson (ed), *The New Politics of the Welfare State* (Oxford UP, 2001) 305.

that came into effect in December 2000 stipulates that the national pension funds 'must take environmental and ethical considerations into account without relinquishing the overall goal of a high return on capital'.[132] In the case of New Zealand, the Superannuation Act 2001 specifies in section 61(d) that a 'statement of investment policies, standards, and procedures must cover (but is not limited to) . . . ethical investment, including policies, standards, or procedures for avoiding prejudice to New Zealand's reputation as a responsible member of the world community'.[133] It is too soon to determine the effects of the Swedish and New Zealand reforms, and future research is needed to compare the extent of ethical financing between the public and private pension sectors.

In addition to harnessing the resources of public pension funds, governments could become more involved in capital allocation through co-financing schemes with the private sector. Partnerships between public and private financial institutions can offer benefits for the financing of environmentally sound development. Neither public finance nor private capital alone is sufficient to provide appropriate levels of environmental finance. Public financial resources are too small and private financiers are too risk-averse.[134] A synergy could arise, however, by using public funds to complement private investment in environmental projects by reducing initial barriers and implementation costs.[135] Environmentally conditioned public finance on preferential terms could have a role in bridging the cost gap between what private financiers are prepared to commit and what is necessary to undertake climate change friendly developments. Climate change mitigation projects in particular have characteristics that can be unattractive to private investment, given the lack of financial resources in developing countries coupled with the current uncertainty surrounding the viability of new greenhouse gas emission (GHG) controls and the market disadvantages of experimental renewable energy technologies. The high initial project costs, risks and externality of GHG reductions make it difficult for private investors to predict and capture benefits from financing such projects.

The MDBs increasingly use co-financing arrangements when lending to developing countries. They are using networks of financial intermediaries in host borrower countries, to channel finance through equity, debt and other forms of financing to companies and projects in beneficiary countries. The World Bank Group is taking a lead role among multilateral development banks in establishing seed trust funds for co-financing climate change mitigation projects in developing

[132] Quoted in Trejde AP-fonden, above n 39, 6

[133] New Zealand Superannuation Act 2001.

[134] See H French, *Investing in the Future: Harnessing Private Capital Flows for Environmentally Sustainable Development* (Worldwatch Institute, 1998).

[135] See OECD, 'The Growing Importance of Co-Financing in Funding Development Projects', *OECD Observer*, July 1982, 31.

countries and the economies in transition.[136] The World Bank has established a variety of financial mechanisms to address climate change mitigation activities, comprising the Prototype Carbon Fund,[137] Community Development Carbon Fund,[138] Renewable Energy Efficiency Fund and the BioCarbon Fund.[139]

Co-financing for sustainable energy is also an important dimension of the European Bank for Reconstruction and Development's (EBRD) lending policies. One of the cited reasons for the lack of clean energy investment in Eastern Europe since the communist collapse is the unavailability of commercial loans on long terms and affordable interest rates.[140] The EBRD financial assistance is guided by its 2001 Energy Operations Policy, which encompasses energy conversion, transportation, distribution and consumption.[141] For example, the EBRD reached an agreement in 1995 with the Hungarian Ministry for Environment and the European Commission to establish an 'environmental credit line', which by the end of 1999 had resulted in the funding of 16 projects worth €13 million, with the majority of funds issued by the EBRD.[142] In 2000, the EBRD and the Franco-Belgian banking group Dexia launched a new private equity fund aimed at reducing energy consumption and GHG emissions in Central and Eastern Europe. The €150 million Dexia-FondElec Energy Efficiency and Emission Reduction Fund (EEER) have a number of power companies as investors.[143] By investing in equity, the Bank can provide specific risk guarantees for regulatory, political, credit and certain performance risks that mainstream lenders and investors in energy projects are not able to manage. The EBRD may also provide financial guarantees to enable commercial lenders to offer more generous terms through lower margins, longer grace periods and longer maturities to enable long-term energy investment projects.[144]

These public sector initiatives will not solve the underlying weaknesses in capital markets. They can help address bottlenecks that arise for specific environmental problems, such as promotion of renewable energy. But they should be seen as a supplementary strategy to the main goal of changing the institutional and legal barriers to more environmentally sensitive financing by private institutions. The following section concludes with consideration of additional necessary reforms.

[136] World Bank Carbon Finance, available at www.CarbonFinance.org.
[137] See www.prototypecarbonfund.org/splash.html.
[138] See www.communitycarbonfund.org.
[139] See www.biocarbonfund.org.
[140] EBRD, *Energy Operations Policy* (EBRD, 2001) 8.
[141] See EBRD at www.ebrd.com/about/policies/sector/energy/energy.pdf.
[142] EBRD, 'Budapest Bank Environment Credit Line', *Environments in Transition,* Spring 2000, 8–9.
[143] S Labatt and RR White, *Environmental Finance: A Guide to Environmental Risk Assessment and Financial Products* (John Wiley and Sons, 2002) 86.
[144] EBRD, *Energy Operations Policy* (EBRD, 2001) 28–9.

I. Further Reforms for Improving Financiers' Environmental Performance

Although it can be seen from previous sections of this chapter that the heterogeneity of financial service providers requires various institutional-specific reforms, there are also some common regulatory themes. Liability rules, economic incentives, fiduciary responsibilities and informational policy instruments, while all requiring adaptation to specific financial institution contexts, need to be applied throughout financial markets to create a stronger foundation for sustainable investment. Harnessing financiers as a driver for sustainability requires complementary reforms to provide stronger financial incentives, provision of more and clearer environmental information, and more effective means of leverage in corporate affairs. These policy instruments can support a reflexive style of environmental governance that can help reorient the protocols and norms of financial markets.

As a priority, governments should introduce a wider array of economic instruments, in particular pollution taxes and tradeable emission schemes, so that the financial costs or benefits of corporate environmental behaviour are made more transparent and relevant to the calculations of commercial financiers.[145] Asset prices and company valuations need to reflect environmental performance if sustainable financing is to have an objective basis. Eco-taxes directly affect company balance sheets, and financial institutions should support polluter pays charges since, as low-energy users, they would not be heavily penalised by new charges. With tradeable permits, companies that are able to generate cost savings through trade in pollution permits could become more attractive investment opportunities for financial organisations. Creating new markets for environmental goods could significantly augment ethical financing. The UK government's recent Climate Change Levy and Emissions Trading Scheme are in this respect welcome initiatives, but more extensive use of economic instruments as a means of environmental policy in many other countries is lacking.[146] Until equity and debt prices reflect environmental performance, then environmental investment and lending will remain somewhat arbitrary in determining which businesses are to be favoured or disavowed.

Economic instruments should also be applied directly to environmentally friendly investments to create tax advantages for such practices. In 1995 the Dutch

[145] On economic instruments, see TH Tietenberg, 'Economic Instruments for Environmental Regulation' (1990) 6 *Oxford Review Economic Policy* 17; RB Stewart, 'Economic Incentives for Environmental Protection' in RL Revesz *et al* (eds), *Environmental Law, the Economy and Sustainable Development* (Cambridge UP, 2000) 171.

[146] BJ Richardson and KL Chanwai, 'Taxing and Trading in Corporate Energy Activities: Pioneering UK Reforms to Address Climate Change' (2003) 14 *International Company & Commercial L Rev* 18.

government introduced a green investment scheme that allows banks to offer depositors funds the interest and dividends of which are exempt from personal taxation. To qualify, the dedicated green fund must invest at least 70 per cent of its assets in environmentally friendly projects. Projects currently certified by government regulators as acceptable in this respect include renewable energy, organic agriculture and environmental technology.[147] As a result of this initiative, several Dutch banks moved to set up their own green investment funds. The funds have been heavily subscribed to and, because of the large volume of funds consequently generated, finance has been available to project proponents on very competitive terms. The attractive interest rates can induce investment in projects formerly perceived as risky with limited return.[148] Although this unique reform may be explained by the fact that the Netherlands is a country with a relatively high level of environmental awareness and a strong tradition of environmental law innovation, other countries might now follow suit, given emerging evidence that the Dutch green investment schemes is succeeding to promote sustainable development projects.[149]

A second topic for reform is corporate environmental reporting. To require companies to report regularly on their environmental activities and impacts can help generate reliable and comprehensive information regarding corporate environmental performance for financiers. Reliable information is crucial to the proper functioning of capital markets, improving accurate pricing of securities and so enabling the market to allocate capital efficiently.[150] Without material information, investment decisions are likely to be distorted. Disclosure of environmental information that reflects corporate assets and liabilities can help inform consumers and investors about a firm's level of resource use, emissions and other environmental impacts.[151] Not only does such information feed the ethical concerns of investors, but it also affects the market value of an enterprise by disclosing liabilities and other factors that can affect earnings and profitability.

Traditional corporate reporting statements have not adequately captured the financial consequences of a company's environmental management. Corporate accounting has been associated with myopic, profit-centred performance measurement.[152] However, disclosure is a central tenet of emerging voluntary standards

[147] Netherlands Agency for Energy and the Environment (Novem), *Financing Energy and Environmental Technology: The Dutch Way* (Novem 1997).

[148] Jeucken, above n 2, 92–94.

[149] T van Bellegem *et al*, *Green Investment Funds: Organic Farming* (OECD, 1997).

[150] JB Baskin and PJ Miranti Jr, *A History of Corporate Finance* (Cambridge UP, 1997) 322.

[151] See A von Ahsen, C Lange and M Pianowski, 'Corporate Environmental Reporting: Survey and Empirical Evidence' (2004) 3(1) *International Journal of the Environment & Sustainable Development* 5; G Harte, L Lewis and D Owen, 'Ethical Investment and the Corporate Reporting Function' (1991) 12 *Critical Perspectives on Accounting* 227.

[152] D Owen (ed), *Green Reporting: Accountancy and the Challenge of the Nineties* (Chapman and Hall, 1992).

such as the CERES Principles and the Global Reporting Initiative.[153] Traditionally, only in the US were environmental reporting requirements well integrated into mainstream company law through the regulations of the Securities and Exchange Commission (SEC).[154] One reason why the SEC (set up in the 1930s) has gone further in corporate disclosure requirements than other jurisdictions is that US policy-makers have long traced the causes of the Great Depression to the failure to establish adequate regulations to ensure investors and other stakeholders have adequate information regarding corporate performance. Environmental reporting requirements are most likely to succeed when regulators provide detailed guidance on reporting criteria and ensure that reports reflect an enterprise's full range of operations, including relationships with subsidiaries and franchisees that may otherwise be exploited by the parent company to disguise its overall environmental impacts.

In Europe, corporate reporting is currently one of the dominant environmental policy concerns. Among EU states, mandatory environmental reporting has been instituted in various forms in France, the Netherlands, Sweden, Denmark, and very recently also proposed in the UK.[155] The European Commission's *Communication on Corporate Social Responsibility* refers to the desirability of adopting corporate environmental reporting standards.[156] Already, the EU's Eco-management and Audit Scheme (EMAS) Regulation and Eco-label Regulation, both voluntary schemes for businesses, have been amended to encompass financial institutions and products. The need to open the EMAS Regulation to the financial sector has been acknowledged for several years, as the site-based focus of the original 1993 EMAS Regulation made it unsuitable for capturing the environmental effects of the clients of banks and other financial entities.[157] The EMAS Regulation was revised in March 2001 to extend the scheme to all sectors of economic activity and to shift the focus to company operations, as a whole, rather than their specific industrial sites.[158] There is also more emphasis on 'indirect environmental aspects', defined as including 'capital investments, granting loans and insurance services'.[159] In addition, the 1992 Eco-label Regulation was amended in 2000 to redefine

[153] JA Smith, 'The CERES Principles: A Voluntary Code for Corporate Environmental Responsibility' (1993) 18 *Yale Journal of International Law* 307.

[154] EIAG Geltman, 'Disclosure of Contingent Environmental Liabilities by Public Companies under the Federal Securities Laws' (1992) 16 *Harvard Environmental L Rev* 129, 144.

[155] KMPG, *International Survey of Environmental Reporting* (KPMG, 1999) 8; in relation to the new UK developments, see Department of Trade and Industry, *Draft Regulations on the Operating and Financial Review and Directors' Report: A Consultative Document* (Department of Trade and Industry, May 2004).

[156] EC Commission, *Communication from the Commission concerning Corporate Social Responsibility: A Business Contribution to Sustainable Development,* COM(2002)347 final (July 2002) 14–15.

[157] EC Directorate-General XI – Environment, *Workshop on Sustainable Development—Challenge for the Financial Sector* (EC, 1998) 12.

[158] Council Regulation 761/2001/EC, above n 57.

[159] EMAS Regulation, Annex, cl 6.3(b).

'products' to include 'any goods and services', thus implementing earlier European proposals to expand the Eco-label scheme to the financial services sector.[160] This change will allow banking and investment products to be more readily assessed and compared in terms of their environmental credentials, and this should facilitate marketing and reward innovation. These EU innovations point to a style of shared environmental governance that relies on voluntary approaches and market incentives for corporate participation, such as an improved environmental profile among environmentally conscious consumers and productivity gains through reduced waste and resource consumption.

Thirdly, reforms should be made to systems of corporate governance to enable or direct shareholders to be more active in corporate decision-making. Most EU ethical funds use a screening approach, which tends to reduce their influence on corporate environmental practice. As Miller suggests, 'the main arguments against [ethical investment] are that: one cannot hope to change the ways of a major institution simply by buying or selling its shares'.[161] Shareholder proposals sponsored by institutional investors are a key means by which institutions can influence company policy.[162] In some jurisdictions, significant barriers to shareholder activism persist, such as investor portfolio diversification obligations and proxy context rules. The Enron scandal has highlighted the potential huge damage that malfunctioning corporate governance can inflict on pension savings. Various reforms are possible, although the subject raises thorny economic and political concerns. In theory, financial regulators could require investment institutions to register their share votes, so as to encourage institutions to formulate and express a view on all issues put to a vote at shareholders' meetings. Another possibility is the appointment of minority independent directors to corporate boards, nominated by institutional investor groups rather than enterprise management.[163] Beyond measures to stimulate accountability and shareholder involvement, there is the persistent question whether corporate liability should be broadened so as to discourage environmentally risky activities.[164] Thus, in principle, imposing liability on institutional shareholding investors for the environmental impacts of their portfolio companies could promote environmentally responsible investment because of the lower liability risks offered by green companies.

[160] Council Regulation 1980/2000, above n 58.

[161] A Miller, *Socially Responsible Investment: The Financial Impact of Screened Investment in the 1990s* (Financial Times Business Information, 1991) 7.

[162] See D Del Guercio and J Hawkins, 'The Motivation and Impact of Pension Fund Activism' (1999) 52 *Journal of Financial Economics* 293.

[163] RJ Gilson and R Kraakman, 'Reinventing the Outside Director: An Agenda for Institutional Investors' (1991) 43 *Stanford L Rev* 863, 870.

[164] On this debate, see FH Easterbrook and DR Fischel, 'Limited Liability and the Corporation' (1985) 52 *University of Chicago L Rev* 89.

J. Conclusions

This chapter has explored one of the new frontiers of environmental law reform. It has shown that, because of commercial financiers' gate-keeping role within the economy, they should be incorporated into the networks of environmental governance. But it is clear that beyond the desire to avoid the traditional kinds of environmental liabilities, the incentives for financial institutions to address the environment systematically currently are often lacking. To date, generally only negative environmental performance has concerned financial markets, if at all, and there is a paucity of appreciation of how a company's environmental management can be a reliable indicator of good business management. Intervention by governments will therefore be necessary to facilitate the integration of environmental concerns into financial markets.

In reforming financial markets, government incentive measures (eg, tax concessions) rather than regulatory commands are likely to be more acceptable and more efficiently implemented. Regulatory measures to facilitate information disclosure on environmental liabilities and ethical investment practices can help to allow institutions and customers to judge environmental performance. Governments, of course, must also subject their own economic institutions and financial reforms to strategic environmental appraisal and public scrutiny. Environmental policy-makers will not achieve sustainable development unless they understand and address the principal economic forces that shape the arenas within which they operate.

Part 4

International and Comparative Perspectives

11

International Environmental Law

JAYE ELLIS* AND STEPAN WOOD**

A. Introduction

1. Introduction

In 1985, the British Antarctic Survey discovered that the stratospheric ozone layer over Antarctica had thinned. This discovery confirmed the link between emissions of certain substances such as chlorofluorocarbons (CFCs) and damage to the ozone layer, and brought home to politicians and members of the public the startling fact that humans are capable of changing the earth's ecosystem in fundamental and potentially permanent ways. By this time, a consensus had already emerged that environmental degradation is a global issue that requires co-operation among states, but this discovery lent urgency to the project of developing new rules and institutions at the international level for the protection of the environment.

The emergence of international environmental law as a distinct legal field is generally dated to the 1972 United Nations (UN) Conference on the Human Environment, held in Stockholm.[1] This conference is credited with cementing the place of global environmental protection on the international agenda, and with launching the development of a separate body of international law focused on the environment. Of course, issues that we would today consider environmental were addressed at the international level prior to Stockholm as well. Prominent examples include conservation of fauna and flora,[2] control of

* Professor, Faculty of Law, McGill University. I would like to thank Caroline Leduc and Jared Will for their invaluable research and editing assistance. The financial support of the Social Sciences and Humanities Research Council of Canada is also gratefully acknowledged.

** Professor, Osgoode Hall Law School, York University.

[1] For a discussion of the history of international environmental law, see P Sands, *Principles of International Environmental Law* (2d edn, Cambridge UP, 2003) 25 ff; and generally J DiMento, *The Global Environment and International Law* (U Texas Press, 2003).

[2] See London Convention Concerning the Preservation of Wild Animals, Birds and Fish in Africa 1900, 94 BFSP 715; London Convention Relative to the Preservation of Fauna and Flora in their Natural State 1933, 17 LNTS 241; International Convention for the Regulation of Whaling 1946, 161 UNTS 62. See *Behring Sea Fur Seals Arbitration* (1898) 1 Moores Int'l Arbitration Awards 755, for an

nuclear energy[3] and transboundary air pollution.[4] The contribution of Stockholm was rather to solidify an emerging consensus that these and related issues should be treated as phenomena belonging to a distinct category of *environmental* issues, and that these issues should be addressed at the international level through international co-operation. Stockholm also acted as a catalyst for the development of a separate body of international environmental law and policy.[5]

This chapter begins with a general discussion of the context in which international environmental law operates: the global nature of environmental degradation; the phenomenon of globalisation; and the anarchical nature of international society. We then move on to a discussion of international environmental law specifically. Rather than seek to introduce the reader to the whole range of international environmental treaties, conventions and other legal instruments, attention has been focused on a series of overarching themes in international law. We will begin with a fundamental but surprisingly difficult question: is it illegal under international law to cause transboundary environmental degradation?

2. Interdependence and Globalisation

Environmental protection is an international or global issue due to the biophysical reality that supersedes the political division of the globe into sovereign states and areas beyond state jurisdiction. Ecosystems are interrelated in profound and complex ways. Due to these interrelationships, environmental impacts can have widespread repercussions across vast distances and over long periods of time. As a result, no state acting alone can hope either to protect the environment within its own territory or to account for the global impacts of activities carried out on its territory.

The interdependence of states and other international actors is a major theme in discussions of the broader phenomenon of globalisation. This much-used and much-contested term refers at its core to forces of integration among economies around the world, leading, many would argue, to the creation of a global economy that is beyond the control of individual states. The role of the state in international society has changed dramatically, with some commentators arguing that

early example of international conservation litigation, and CPR Romano, 'The Behring Sea Fur Seals Dispute (Great Britain v. USA)' in CPR Romano, *The Peaceful Settlement of International Environmental Disputes* (Kluwer, 2000) 133, for a discussion of the case.

[3] Vienna Convention on Civil Liability for Nuclear Damage, 21 May 1963, 1063 UNTS 265; Treaty Banning Nuclear Weapon Tests in the Atmosphere, in Outer Space and Under Water 1963, 480 UNTS 45.

[4] *Trail Smelter Arbitration, United States v Canada* (1931–1941) 3 RIAA 1905; (1939) 33 AJIL 182; (1941) 35 AJIL 716.

[5] T Sullivan, 'The Stockholm Conference: A Step Toward Global Environmental Co-operation and Involvement' (1972) 6 *Indiana L Rev* 267.

the state is becoming increasingly irrelevant in the face of international economic forces. One of the implications of this from the point of view of the environment is that states may be losing their ability to establish and implement environmental policies.[6]

Some of the environmentally harmful phenomena associated with globalisation include the shifting of environmentally damaging processes to states with lax environmental standards or lax enforcement of existing standards, or both. Governments are seen to be in competition with one another to offer hospitable conditions for investment, promoting a race to the bottom in environmental standards. It is feared that as global economic actors become more powerful there will be increasing pressure on states and international organisations to place profit and economic growth ahead of other social values, including environmental protection.[7]

The challenge posed by ecosystem interdependence, globalisation and related phenomena may be understood as a challenge of governance. There is no *government* at the international level consisting of centralised structures for the promulgation, implementation and enforcement of laws and policies, but there are *governance structures* that serve these ends. These structures are organised in a decentralised, horizontal fashion; as a result, they function in very different ways from similar structures found within states. Scholars both of global environmental protection and of economic globalisation often come to similar conclusions regarding international governance structures, namely that if the scope and scale of the problems with which these scholars are concerned are too great for individual states acting alone, international governance structures must be strengthened and exploited more effectively. In the next section, we will consider how one such structure, namely international law, operates under conditions of anarchy, or decentralisation.

3. Co-operation in an Anarchical System

Anarchy is defined by the absence of central authority, such as a central government. It is often argued that a central governmental structure is necessary for the achievement of common goals, and that co-operation in an anarchical system will

6 APJ Mol, 'The Globalization of Side Effects' in A Mol (ed), *Globalization and Environmental Reform: The Ecological Modernization of the Global Economy* (MIT Press, 2001) 71; RC Paehlke, *Democracy's Dilemma: Environment, Social Equity and the Global Economy* (MIT Press, 2003).

7 See J Mander, 'Intrinsic Negative Effects of Economic Globalization on the Environment' in JG Speth (ed), *Worlds Apart: Globalization and the Environment* (Island Press, 2003) 109; V Shiva, 'The Myths of Globalization Exposed: Advancing Toward Living Democracy' in JG Speth (ed), *Worlds Apart: Globalization and the Environment* (Island Press, 2003) 141; A Scott, 'Globalization: Social Process or Political Rhetoric?' in A Scott (ed), *The Limits of Globalization: Cases and Arguments* (Routledge, 1997) 1.

be fragile, shallow and ultimately short-lived.[8] Such arguments often rest on the assumption that actors have to be forced to set aside their short-term interests and join in co-operative ventures. A centralised governmental structure, with legal authority to enact binding rules and enforce them with threats of punishment, is often seen as a necessary condition for co-operation.

Garrett Hardin's famous scenario of the tragedy of the commons[9] provides one perspective on obstacles to co-operation.[10] In Hardin's scenario, a number of herdsmen graze their flocks of sheep on a common field. All the herdsmen know that the field can sustain only a certain number of sheep, and that if they all increase the size of their flocks beyond a certain number, the carrying capacity of the field will be exceeded and all the sheep will eventually starve. However, if a number of herdsmen decide to restrict the size of their flocks and others do not, any benefits resulting from this restraint will be equally felt by all, but will delay rather than prevent catastrophe. Those who choose restraint will fail to achieve the goal of sustainable exploitation of the commons, and they will be in a worse position than those who choose to increase the size of their flocks and—temporarily—reap the resulting profits. Hardin describes this scenario as tragic because the herdsmen are compelled to act in a way they know to be against their long-term interest.

If we apply the reasoning implicit in these scenarios to the international sphere, we observe that co-operation among states can be extremely risky. Even if a number of states agree to co-operate, all are aware that each could defect at any moment, leaving the rest to pay the costs of co-operation while the defectors continue to reap the benefits of independent, unconstrained behaviour. Yet co-operation is observed to occur between states. This observation has led many commentators to return to the models and re-examine the assumptions that underlie them in an attempt to explain those cases in which the obstacles to co-operation appear to have been overcome.

One important observation, made in a ground-breaking study by Robert Axelrod,[11] is that the 'herdsmen' do not make decisions about whether or not to exercise restraint—whether to co-operate or defect—in a one-off fashion. On the contrary, they share the commons over a long period of time and have many opportunities to decide what course of action to adopt. Hardin was well aware of this, but what he failed to account for is that the herdsmen will have opportunities

[8] Eg W Ophuls, 'Leviathan or Oblivion?' in HE Daly (ed), *Toward a Steady-State Economy* (WH Freeman, 1973); G Hardin, *Exploring New Ethics for Survival* (Viking Press, 1972).

[9] G Hardin, 'The Tragedy of the Commons' (1968) 162 *Science* 1243; see also G Hardin and J Baden (eds), *Managing the Commons* (WH Freeman, 1977).

[10] Other useful perspectives include the 'prisoner's dilemma', the game of 'chicken' and various other models derived from game theory, collective action theory or common-pool resource theory: eg M Olson, *The Logic of Collective Action* (Harvard UP, 1965); E Ostrom, *Governing the Commons* (Cambridge UP, 1990).

[11] R Axelrod, *The Evolution of Co-operation* (Basic Books, 1984).

to reward or punish one another's behaviour, as well as further opportunities to adjust their behaviour in light of these rewards and punishments. The fact that the herdsmen will continue to encounter one another and will face the possibility of rewards and punishments for their behaviour is referred to as the 'shadow of the future'.[12]

A further element must be added to Hardin's tragedy scenario, namely the fact that the herdsmen interact in a variety of settings. The herdsmen are not just economic actors, but also social and political actors who live in the same community, share certain of the same values, and live the same way of life. They thus have myriad opportunities for developing shared understandings about appropriate and efficient uses of their common resource and fair apportionment of that resource amongst themselves. Once they have established these shared understandings, they are well-equipped to create rules about the use of the commons.[13]

Thomas Risse has drawn attention to this missing dimension of scenarios such as the tragedy of the commons by noting that, in such scenarios, the players do not speak to one another.[14] Yet actors in the real world communicate all the time. This is as true for herdsmen as it is for states. Foreign ministries issue communiqués; government representatives engage in negotiations; journalists report on the statements of world leaders and diplomats. Should this just be regarded as 'cheap talk', in other words, an inaccurate and potentially deceptive representation of what international actors think and plan to do? What is the significance of communication in international affairs?

4. International law as a Discursive Process

Let us try to extract some implications of this general discussion for the development of a robust and effective body of international environmental law. First, we may wish to recall what we have in mind when we think of international law. In particular, what are the implications of the decentralised nature of international law?

If we take one famous definition of law, namely that it is the command of a sovereign backed by the threat or use of force,[15] we encounter immediate difficulties. There is no sovereign in international law; rather, there is a multitude of equal sovereign states not subject to any higher legal authority. Furthermore, many of the rules of international law are not commands, but rather statements of purpose and objectives, or texts that create procedures or institutions. Finally, although it is possible to impose sanctions on states that violate the law, there are many provisions, particularly in international environmental law, for which no sanction is

[12] *Ibid.*

[13] Ostrom, above n 10.

[14] T Risse, 'Let's Argue! Communicative Action in World Politics' (2000) 54 *International Organization* 1.

[15] J Austin, *The Province of Jurisprudence Determined* (Ashgate/Dartmouth, 1998) 18.

provided. And of course there is no sovereign with centralised authority to identify violations and impose sanctions.

Thus, the notion of law as a series of sovereign commands backed by force does not describe international law at all well. We might be tempted to conclude, as many have done, that international law is not really law. However, the above definition of law does not provide an accurate description of domestic systems of law either. In particular, it does not tell us much about vital bodies of domestic law addressing contract, administrative law and constitutional law, to name a few. Therefore, we need to consider alternate approaches.

One such approach focuses on law as built upon shared understandings of the world, the nature of the actors that populate it, their relationships to one another, and the various avenues available to them to pursue their goals and to interact with each other. More specifically, the shared understandings on which law relies focus on a series of processes for developing, presenting and responding to arguments.[16]

If we return to our richer account of Hardin's herdsmen, we see that one option open to them is to reach agreement on the best way to manage their common resource. We know that they are capable of doing so because they have obviously engaged in this exercise in the past: they already know what the common is, roughly where its boundaries lie, what use can be made of it and who is entitled to have access to it. These questions may have been settled by a series of ad hoc decisions, but it is much more likely that the herdsmen are already operating under a set of formal and informal, explicit and implicit rules, including rules about how rules are to be made, interpreted, applied and enforced. Thus, they simply need to take this process one step further, by establishing rules regulating the size of each flock.

The first task that the herdsmen face is reaching consensus about the existence and nature of the problem of over-exploitation. Some herdsmen may simply deny that the resource is being exploited unsustainably; others may acknowledge that the common is under pressure but may disagree amongst themselves about the number of sheep that the common can support. Thus, a prerequisite to making up rules to protect the commons is a process in which information is gathered and exchanged and arguments presented, critiqued and countered. Once consensus on these preliminary issues is achieved, the herdsmen will need to begin the difficult process of agreeing on a set of principles to govern the fair distribution of the resource. Should account be taken of how large each herdsman's flock was prior to the start of negotiations? If so, what time frame should be referred to? Is it relevant that some herdsmen are wealthy enough to increase their flock while others are not? Should special allowance be made to herdsmen with large families to support or other types of financial burdens? Should there be some mechanism

[16] J Brunnée and S Toope, 'International Law and Constructivism: Elements of an Interactional Theory of International Law' (2000) 39 *Columbia Journal of Transnational Law* 19.

whereby herdsmen can trade their right to graze sheep to other herdsmen in exchange for a benefit? This task is likely to be made simpler by the fact that the herdsmen have already reached some general agreement on similar distributional issues; they may share a certain conception of what is fair and appropriate. They will be able to use these background understandings to frame their arguments about the most appropriate response to the current problem. Indeed, they may already have devised procedures for presenting arguments and making decisions on changes to their commons regime, and they will be able to use these procedures to reach agreement on the issue of overgrazing.

Of course, states are very different from our medieval herdsmen. Herdsmen are individuals; states are collections of individuals that are often very poorly represented by their governments. These herdsmen share a mode of life and, in all probability, a worldview; states have very different histories and current positions in international society, and hold a diverse range of interests, preferences and values. The herdsmen are facing a relatively limited set of issues, while states have to deal with a vast and complex array of questions and problems. Nevertheless, we may draw some important analogies between herdsmen in the common and states in international society with respect to the manner in which these two groups of actors make use of rules and procedures to understand their respective worlds, to interact with one another and to address common problems.

In the remainder of this chapter we will focus on rules, processes and mechanisms adopted by states to promote global environmental protection. In particular, we shall see that these rules, processes and mechanisms were formulated with a decentralised system of sovereign actors in mind: emphasis is placed on negotiation and consultation; the diversity of values and interests of those actors is accounted for in various ways; solutions cannot be imposed from above. Nevertheless, we observe the emergence of a rich and complex network of shared understandings about the nature of the problem and pathways to solutions. International environmental law provides states, at the very least, with a common vocabulary and a set of structures within which to pursue solutions to environmental problems.

B. International Environmental Law

1. Emergence of Environment as an International Issue: The Role of General Rules of Public International law

(a) Transboundary Environmental Harm

We will begin our exploration of international environmental law with a discussion of the general rules of public international law that were used to address environmental problems before a specialised body of international law existed to address them. These early attempts to resolve environmental problems using the basic framework of international law remain relevant even now that specialised environmental rules have emerged. The manner in which these specialised rules have developed owes a great deal to what was learned from early cases.

One of the most famous of these early international environmental cases was the *Trail Smelter* arbitration between the United States (US) and Canada.[17] The dispute arose as a result of fumes and ash emitted by a smelter in Canada and deposited on US territory. The smelter was found to have caused damage in the US, and Canada was ordered to institute pollution control measures and to pay compensation. In reaching this ruling, the arbitral panel stated:

> [N]o State has the right to use or permit the use of its territory in such a manner as to cause injury by fumes in or to the territory of another or the properties or persons therein, when the case is of serious consequence and the injury is established by clear and convincing evidence.[18]

This *dictum* has become one of the most oft-cited texts in international environmental law. It appears on its face to offer solid legal foundation for the proposition that states have an obligation to prevent transboundary environmental harm, and has generally been taken to do so. As such, it constitutes one of the cornerstones of international environmental law.

However, international environmental jurists do not agree on the meaning to attribute to this ruling or on its importance to international environmental law today. There are a number of problems both with the panel's reasoning and with its conclusion. In the first place, it is doubtful that the ruling stands for the proposition that a state will be responsible for transboundary environmental harm caused by a private individual on its territory, unless it can be shown that the source state has violated an international obligation by allowing the harm to arise.[19] Secondly, although the *dictum* quoted above appears to lay down a blanket prohibition on transboundary environmental harm, this has never been reflected in either international environmental law or the behaviour of states. Instead, a certain degree of tolerance of environmental harm is recognised.[20] Thirdly, in many cases it will be an insurmountable task to prove 'by clear and convincing evidence' the source of pollution and/or a causal link to harm in another jurisdiction.[21] What, if any, lessons can we draw from *Trail Smelter*?

[17] *Trail Smelter Arbitration, above* n 4.

[18] *Ibid.*

[19] See X Hanqin, *Transboundary Damage in International Law* (Cambridge UP, 2003) 145–51.

[20] Most obviously, for instance, in relation to fossil fuel emissions and climate change: UN Framework Convention on Climate Change (UNFCCC) 1992, 31 ILM 851.

[21] Hanqin, above n 19, 178.

The first question we must ask is whether transboundary environmental harm itself constitutes a breach of international law. Until a specialised body of international environmental law began to emerge in the 1970s, the answer to this question had to be sought in general rules of public international law, so that is where we begin our exploration.

(b) Territorial Integrity

Flows of pollutants across a border can be understood to violate a state's territorial integrity and in some instances the source state will be responsible for this violation in international law. The basic idea is that serious environmental harm, such as that caused by emissions from a metal smelter, can be conceptualised as a violation of the right of every sovereign state to territorial integrity. Since a state has sovereignty over its territory, incursions by another state—in these cases, in the form of serious environmental impacts—may be actionable at international law.[22]

Territorial integrity is not now and never was an absolute right; states, like individuals, must accommodate themselves to the fact of living in society, in close proximity with other members of that society. Territorial integrity is tempered by another principle, good neighbourliness.

(c) Good neighbourliness

The principle of good neighbourliness is a corollary to territorial integrity. Good neighbourliness reminds states that, on many occasions, it is inappropriate to simply stand on one's rights. As discussed above, states are increasingly seen as interdependent and mutually vulnerable; the impacts of events and activities within a state will almost never be constrained to its territory. In light of this reality, one cannot insist on absolute territorial integrity—on the right to be free of any and all transboundary impacts. Conversely, states cannot rely on this fact of mutual vulnerability freely to cause impacts to their neighbours. Good neighbourliness stands for the proposition that, even when one is acting within one's rights, one is obligated to take into account the rights and interests of one's neighbours.[23] The right of a state to exploit natural resources on its territory does not trump another state's right to protect itself against serious environmental harm. Nor does the latter right trump the former.[24]

[22] See the discussion on customary international law in PW Birnie and AE Boyle, *International Law and the Environment* (2nd edn, Oxford UP, 2002) 104 ff.

[23] VP Nanda and GW Pring, *International Environmental Law and Policy for the 21st* Century (Transnational Publishers, 2003) 19.

[24] See PN Okowa, *State Responsibility for Transboundary Air Pollution in International Law* (Oxford UP, 2000); H Blomeyer-Bartenstein, 'Due Diligence' (1992) 10 *European Public Law*. 138; and RP Mazzeschi, 'The Due Diligence Rule and the Nature of the International Responsibility of States' (1992) *German Yearbook of International Law* 9.

Because the principle of good neighbourliness does not tell states *how* the balance between their respective interests is to be struck, but rather *that* such a balance must be struck, states are compelled to reach agreement on the proper interpretation and application of this principle in a particular set of circumstances. What counts as a violation of this principle will vary depending on the interests and priorities of states. For example, in a context in which two neighbouring states are pursuing aggressively programmes of economic development, transboundary pollution may be considered a cost of doing business and therefore an inconvenience that each is required to tolerate. Thus, only when the level of environmental degradation reaches a point at which economic development is threatened—through severe harm to natural resources such as fresh water, forests or farmland, for example—will the states come to understand the transfrontier pollution as harming their sovereign rights.

States and other actors will not inevitably regard high levels of industrial pollution as a natural and acceptable side-effect of economic growth and development, however. As we have seen, one of the major contributions of the Stockholm Conference was to promote a shift in thinking about transfrontier pollution and other forms of international environmental degradation. States, prompted by a range of actors such as members of the scientific community, non-governmental organisations (NGOs), and intergovernmental organisations (IGOs), have been gradually moving towards a reconceptualisation of environmental degradation. This does not necessarily mean that a state invoking the good neighbourliness principle to argue that transboundary pollution is unacceptable and must be halted or reduced will invariably succeed in its claim. What it does mean, however, is that such an argument will be understood today as a potentially valid legal claim and must, as such, be taken seriously. As a consensus about the importance of global environmental protection emerges, source states are no longer able to respond to such claims by simply asserting their sovereign rights to pursue economic development on their territory.

Even if territorial integrity is violated by transboundary pollution in a manner that cannot be reconciled with the principle of good neighbourliness, this will not automatically mean that a state will be responsible for a violation of international law. A further set of conditions must be met, which are contained in the rules governing the responsibility of states.

(d) State Responsibility

The rules of state responsibility place an important limitation on the applicability of territorial integrity to transboundary environmental damage.[25] These rules

[25] The rules of state responsibility are unwritten, customary rules. The most prominent effort to codify these rules is the International Law Commission's (ILC) non-binding but highly influential *Draft Articles on the Responsibility of States for Internationally Wrongful Acts, Report of the ILC* (ILC, 2000). Many of the ILC's rules are acknowledged to have the status of customary international law.

require, first and foremost, that the state itself has violated an international obligation.[26] The difficulty is that in many cases of environmental damage, the person responsible is a private individual. Unless we can find some means of linking the act of the private individual with the state—of *attributing* the individual's act to the state—the state will not be responsible.[27]

In the *Trail Smelter* case, Canada had chosen to accept liability in the event that the arbitral panel found that the fumes had caused damage to US territory. The tribunal nevertheless sought to deal with this issue by referring to an eminent publicist, Eagleton, on the issue of state responsibility.[28] However, the tribunal misconstrued the point that Eagleton was trying to make in the quoted passage.[29] In short, the tribunal never explained the basis of state responsibility for transboundary damage caused by a private actor. This was not a serious problem in the instant case, since Canada had already accepted responsibility. However, this lacuna does have important implications for the application of the tribunal's rule to other situations.

If the individual actually responsible for the pollution cannot be linked to the state, we must determine whether the state has independently breached some international legal obligation. One of the most promising obligations in this respect is the obligation to exercise due diligence to prevent the interests of other states from being harmed as a result of activities on one's territory. This principle is found in the judgment of the International Court of Justice in the *Corfu*

[26] Art 2 of the *Draft Articles* reads: 'There is an internationally wrongful act of a State when conduct consisting of an act or omission: (a) Is attributable to the State under international law: and (b) Constitutes a breach of an international obligation of the State'. (But note that there may also be international liability for non-wrongful acts, such as Convention on International Liability for Damage Caused by Space Objects 1972, 24 UST 2389).

[27] The *Draft Articles* contain a number of provisions that help us to determine when the state, rather than a private individual, can be said to have acted. For present purposes, the most important of these provisions is Art 4, which states that: '[t]he conduct of any State organ shall be considered an act of that State under international law'. See especially EB Weiss, 'The ILC's State Responsibility Articles: Invoking State Responsibility in the Twenty-First Century' (2002) 96 *AJIL* 798. See also J Crawford (ed), *The International Law Commission's Articles on State Responsibility: Introduction, Text and Commentaries* (Cambridge UP, 2002).

[28] *Trail Smelter Arbitration*, above n 4, 713, citing C Eagleton, *The Responsibility of States in International Law* (New York UP, 1928).

[29] The tribunal cited the following passage from Eagleton: 'A State owes at all times a duty to protect other States against injurious acts by individuals from within its jurisdiction'. *ibid*, 80. However, in the text cited, which is drawn from a section on the responsibility of states for harm caused to foreign nationals, Eagleton goes on to state:

> But while the responsibility of a state is fundamentally based upon the control which it exercises within its borders, it does not follow that the state may be held responsible for any injury occurring therein. The law of nations does not make the state a guarantor of life and property. It is answerable, under international law, only for those injuries which are internationally illegal in character, and which can be fastened upon the state itself. . . . [T]he responsibility of the state is to be ascertained from the duties of control within its territorial limits and over its agents laid down for it by positive international law . . . . (*ibid* 8–9).

Channel case,[30] in which it was held that a state has a duty to warn another state that mines are to be found in its territorial waters, thus posing a danger to shipping. This duty arises due to the state's knowledge that the mines are present, even if the state did not itself lay the mines. In an environmental context, an obligation of due diligence might mean that a state must adopt environmental laws and policies and ensure that they are implemented and enforced. Thus, if a factory emits pollutants that travel through the air and cause harm to a neighbouring state, the state of origin has an obligation to impose environmental standards to eliminate or reduce harm caused to its neighbours. This does not make the state directly responsible for the act of the individual polluter; rather, the state becomes responsible for its own breach, namely its failure to live up to its obligation of due diligence.[31]

The obligation of due diligence is, however, rather vague. It tells states that they must take some measures to prevent pollution, but it does not state what these measures are. Thus, it may be more effective to conclude international conventions that spell out in detail the measures that states are to take with respect to particular environmental problems. If a state fails to take such measures, it is in breach of its international obligations and potentially responsible at international law, even if the failure did not result in any actual transboundary damage.

The adoption of international conventions that identify environmental protection measures that states are obligated to implement also addresses a further difficulty with the application of rules of state responsibility to environmental law.[32] Although incidents such as massive chemical leaks, the breakup of oil tankers at sea, and accidents in nuclear facilities cause significant damage and suffering and attract a good deal of attention, a major part of environmental damage is caused by much less spectacular, more routine events and activities that occur continually over long periods of time, such as emissions from industry or vehicles. The principle of due diligence tells us that states should take action to reduce or eliminate these incremental sources of environmental harm, but it does not tell us when the limits of tolerance are reached. How are the rights of one state to pursue various activities on its territory to be balanced against that state's obligation not to cause environmental harm to its neighbours? Once again, the adoption of

[30] *Corfu Channel Case* [1949] ICJ Rep 4 (Merits), in which the Court concluded that a general principle existed which imposed an obligation on states 'not to allow [knowingly] its territory to be used for acts contrary to the rights of other States.' The word 'knowingly' appears in brackets because it did not appear in the official French version of the Court's decision.

[31] But note that 'due diligence' is not the exclusive standard and that international law does contemplate strict (or absolute) liability in some situations of environmental harm, eg. nuclear accidents, space objects, civil liability for marine oil spills: see further Hanqin, above n 19, 305–12. States have adopted conventions dealing with such special hazards, and these are special conventional regimes not based on the general rules of state liability.

[32] See U Beyerlin and T Marauhn, *Law-Making and Law-Enforcement in International Environmental Law after the 1992 Rio Conference* (Max Planck Institute for Comparative Public Law and International Law, 1997); Sands, above n 1, ch 4.

issue-specific conventions that impose specific environmental obligations on states may help us to address this issue.

Taking action before an international court or tribunal against a state that has breached its international environmental obligations remains a possibility, but it very rarely happens in practice. Instead, states have developed a wide range of procedures and mechanisms for resolving environmental disputes. The most important of these is and remains negotiation between states. In addition, in recent years, international conventions have provided for the creation of specialised bodies responsible for supervising and promoting the compliance of states with their obligations under the conventions.[33] As a result of these developments, the issue of state responsibility has receded into the background.

By the 1970s, these general rules of public international law had begun to be supplemented by a specialised, discrete body of international law concerned specifically with environmental protection. Let us now consider how this specialised body of rules applies to our question whether transboundary environmental degradation is illegal under international law.

2. Principles of International Environmental Law

(a) Introduction

We begin our discussion of modern international environmental law with Principle 21 of the Stockholm Declaration, the most famous element of the main document to come out of the 1972 Conference on the Human Environment. We then consider nine other basic principles of international environmental law: prevention, equitable balancing of interests, precaution, common concern of humankind, common but differentiated obligations, co-operation, prior notice and consultation, prior informed consent and environmental impact assessments.[34] Together these principles form a basic network of obligations that compel states to turn their attention to environmental protection and to other states'

[33] The most important innovations are to be found in the Protocol on Substances that Deplete the Ozone Layer 1987, 26 ILM 1541; and the Protocol to the Framework Convention on Climate Change 1997, 37 ILM 22 (Kyoto Protocol): see M Koskenniemi, 'Peaceful Settlement of Environmental Disputes' (1991) 60 *Nordic Journal of Internationl Law* 73, 81–2; J Werksman, 'Compliance and Transition: Russia's Non-Compliance Tests the Ozone Regime' (1996) 56 *Zeitschrift für ausländisches öffentliches Recht und Völkerrecht (ZaöRV)* 750; J Brunnée, 'The Kyoto Protocol: Testing Ground for Compliance Theories?' (2003) 63 *Zaö RV* 255.

[34] This list is far from exhaustive. Other principles that arguably form part of international environmental law include public participation (including public access to environmental information, public participation in environmental decision-making, and public access to judicial remedies in environmental matters; see Sands, above n 1, 852 ff.), a human right to a healthy environment (see Sands, above n 1, 291 ff; D Shelton, 'Human Rights, Environmental Rights, and the Right to Environment' (1991) 28 *Stanford Journal of International Law* 103), and the polluter pays principle (eg Rio Declaration on Environment and Development 1992, 31 ILM 874, Principle 16).

interests in the environment in the course of their domestic and international affairs.[35] Many of these principles are closely interrelated with the broader concept of 'sustainable development', considered in the concluding part of this section.

The principles discussed below are applicable in a number of environmental sectors.[36] By examining a selection of the most ubiquitous and influential principles, readers will gain a broad understanding of the structure of international environmental law.[37] None of the principles at issue specifies precisely what environmental standards a state must attain or exactly when the environmental impacts of its activities will be considered illegal. As principles, they are phrased in language too general to accomplish these goals; part of their vocation is rather to help states develop more specific rules to govern their behaviour as it affects the environment. These principles also help states in their political negotiations with one another as they try to decide how to distribute the costs of protecting the environment and how to control and manage exploitation of environmental resources.

Providing guidance to states in the formulation of rules and in the making of individual decisions constitutes an important task of environmental principles. However, these principles play another, more fundamental role, namely to shape states' understandings of their own and one another's activities and interests. As we will see below, the Stockholm Conference and Declaration were of great importance in putting global environmental protection on the international agenda. The Declaration represents a consensus on the importance of environmental protection to all states and the need for each state to address the issue within its own jurisdiction and in its relations with other states. The principles to be considered below provide international actors, including but not limited to states, with a vocabulary that enables them to understand environmental degradation in terms relevant to international politics and law, and to phrase their arguments and claims about environmental protection in language that will be readily comprehensible to their counterparts. The principles thus encapsulate shared understandings about, for example, what counts as harm or damage, as a plausible argument, or as a valid political or legal claim.

With this in mind, we can turn to the key principles that make up the architecture of international environmental law.

[35] Many of these principles emerged as 'soft law' and only in recent years have been codified into substantive international treaties: PM Dupuy, 'Soft Law and the International Law of the Environment' (1991) 12 *Michigan Journal of International Law* 420.

[36] See R Wolfrum, 'Purposes and Principles of International Environmental Law' (1990) 33 *German Yearbook of International Law* 308.

[37] See generally PM Haas and J Sundgren, 'Evolving International Environmental Law, Changing Practices of National Sovereignty' in N Choucri (ed), *Global Accord: Environmental Challenges and International Responses* (MIT Press, 1993); E Brown Weiss (ed), *Environmental Change and International Law: New Challenges and Dimensions* (United Nations UP, 1992).

(b) Principle 21

Principle 21 of the Stockholm Declaration stands alongside the *dictum* from the *Trail Smelter* arbitral award, quoted earlier, as one of the foundational texts of international environmental law. It declares that:

> States have, in accordance with the Charter of the United Nations and the principles of international law, the sovereign right to exploit their own resources pursuant to their own environmental policies, and the responsibility to ensure that activities within their jurisdiction or control do not cause damage to the environment of other States or of areas beyond the limits of national jurisdiction.[38]

This principle bears more than a passing resemblance to the *Trail Smelter* dictum: indeed, that decision is generally regarded as a major source of inspiration for Principle 21.

By speaking of both rights and responsibilities, Principle 21 encapsulates a tension at the heart of international environmental law. On one hand, it recognises states' sovereign right to exploit their own resources as they see fit. Such recognition was considered indispensable by many national governments at Stockholm, especially those of developing countries that had recently emerged from colonialism and had as their top priorities poverty alleviation, economic development and a more equitable international economic order. On the other hand, Principle 21 clearly aims at the creation of a specifically environmental obligation to prevent harm to the environment of other states or areas beyond state jurisdiction.

Serious questions remain as to the best interpretation to give to this famous text.[39] One possible interpretation is that the principle contains an absolute prohibition on environmental damage beyond the borders of a state. This would be at odds with the principles of state responsibility, due diligence and good neighbourliness, but as new rules of law develop it often happens that existing rules come to be interpreted more narrowly or are even left behind.

The general rules of public international law considered above would permit or tolerate certain types of environmental damage in certain circumstances. For example, it may be that the state had no knowledge of the damaging activity, or perhaps it had taken all reasonable measures to prevent damage but had been unable to eliminate environmental impacts entirely; in this way, the obligation of due diligence would have been fulfilled. Or the damage might not meet the standard identified in the *Trail Smelter* arbitration in that it did not entail 'serious consequences'. The principle of good neighbourliness suggests that not all transboundary harm will qualify as a violation of international obligations; part of the obligation of good neighbourliness involves tolerating impacts up to a certain extent. In such cases,

[38] *Stockholm Declaration* (Report of the United Nations Conference on the Human Environment, Stockholm, 5–16 June 1972 (UN publication No E.73.IIA14 and corrigendum), ch I).

[39] See Sands, above n 1, 186ff.

does the state from whose territory the damage originated have any obligation to the affected state? Taken at face value, Principle 21 seems to suggest that it would. However, if we step back and look at the body of international environmental law as it has evolved since Stockholm, we may have reason to doubt this. On one hand, states do not behave as though they believe that any and all transboundary environmental harm constitutes a violation of international obligations. They do not appear to feel obligated to halt all sources of environmental degradation that have transboundary impacts; furthermore, they often tolerate pollutants or other sources of environmental harm originating in other states and affecting their territory. Secondly, international conventions on global and regional environmental protection call for the control, limitation and reduction of various sources of environmental degradation rather than their elimination, even in cases where those sources have transboundary environmental impacts.[40] In some instances, international conventions impose bans on the production, use or emission of certain substances, with or without exceptions,[41] but the fact that the scope of these conventions is limited to certain classes of substances is telling.

To summarise, then, it would appear that Principle 21 has not supplanted existing rules of public international law. The growing concern with global environmental degradation has certainly had a significant impact on the interpretation of these general principles, as we saw above in the discussion of good neighbourliness. However, it would appear that states have not yet reached a consensus on the need to prohibit all forms of transboundary environmental degradation. This is no doubt due in part to the fact that they do not have the means to meet such an obligation.

(c) Equitable balancing of interests

The principle of equitable balancing of interests has its origins in international law governing transboundary watercourses. Initially, this principle focused on striking a balance between the uses that different riparian states make of a transboundary watercourse. However, it has evolved to encompass a wide range of environmental obligations as well and appears in many contexts throughout international environmental law.[42] It is reflected in Principle 21's juxtaposition of

[40] See Art 2(2)(a), Convention on the Protection and Use of Transboundary Watercourses and International Lakes 1992, 1936 UNTS 33207, which creates an obligation of due diligence by requiring states to 'take all appropriate measures to prevent, control and reduce pollution of waters causing or likely to cause transboundary impact'. The Protocol on Further Reduction of Sulphur Emissions 1994, 1480 UNTS 25247, to the Convention on Long-Range Transboundary Air Pollution 1979, 1302 UNTS 21623 provides, at Arts 3 and 2 respectively, that parties are to control and reduce emissions, but no obligation to eliminate them is established. The Montréal Protocol (above n 33) provides for the regulation and gradual elimination of certain substances, while the Kyoto Protocol (above n 33) requires states to make a modest reduction in their greenhouse gas emissions.

[41] See Stockholm Convention on Persistent Organic Pollutants 2001, 40 ILM 532.

[42] Eg R Zacklin and L Caflisch (eds), *The Legal Regime of International Rivers and Lakes* (Kluwer, 1981); Sands, above n 1, 199–208; M Fitzmaurice and M Szuniewicz (eds), *Exploitation of Natural Resources in the 21st Century* (Kluwer, 2003).

the obligation to prevent transboundary environmental damage with the right of states to exploit their own resources pursuant to their own environmental policies.[43] It is found in the principle of 'equitable utilisation', which is one of the fundamental tenets of the law governing international watercourses.[44]

A further example is provided by the International Law Commission's Draft Articles on Prevention of Transboundary Harm from Hazardous Activities.[45] These Articles deal with activities that are not prohibited at international law but that pose certain risks beyond the borders of the state in which they take place. Potentially affected states would not necessarily have the right to halt hazardous activities undertaken by their neighbours, but the Draft Articles recognise a right on the part of affected states to be informed and consulted. A list of factors to be taken into consideration in the equitable balancing of interests is provided,[46] but the Draft Articles do not seek to tell states exactly what they can and cannot do. This must be determined on a case-by-case basis in light of this list of relevant factors.

This may seem like a disappointing result. Rules on equitable balancing of interests such as those contained in the texts mentioned above do not automatically provide solutions to transboundary environmental problems. However, provisions such as these do make several contributions. First, they make it clear that states whose interests may be harmed by activities or events in other states have a right to be informed and to be at the negotiating table. Secondly, they establish that the interests of potentially affected states must be taken into consideration. Thus, the bargaining power of potentially affected states is increased. Thirdly, they place a wide range of environmental concerns squarely on the agenda, setting the stage for mutually beneficial linkages and trade-offs across issue areas.[47] Thus, in the context of transboundary watercourses, it is not enough for the riparian states to agree on apportionment between them of shared water resources. They must also consider the ecosystem of which the watercourse is a part, along with a range of other environmental and ecological issues.[48] Fourthly, vague standards like

[43] Stockholm Declaration, above n 38. Principle 2 of the Rio Declaration is virtually identical to Principle 21, but refers to 'environmental *and developmental* policies' (emphasis added): *Report of the United Nations Conference on Environment and Development*, GAOR, UN Doc A/CONF.151/26 Vol I (1992).

[44] Convention on the Law of the Non-navigational Uses of International Watercourses 1997, 36 ILM 719, Arts 5–6; A Schwabach, 'The United Nations Convention on the Law of Non-navigational Uses of International Watercourses, Customary International Law, and the The interests of Developing Upper Riparians' (1998) 33 *Texas International Law Journal* 257.

[45] *Draft Articles on Prevention of Transboundary Harm from Hazardous Activities*, GAOR, A/56/10.

[46] *Ibid*, Art 10. Factors listed include the degree of risk; the availability of means of preventing harm; the socio-economic importance of the proposed activity; and the willingness of the state of origin and the potentially affected state to contribute to the costs of prevention.

[47] Eg L Susskind, *Environmental Diplomacy* (Oxford UP, 1994) 82–98.

[48] Convention on Non-Navigable Uses of Transboundary Watercourses, above n 44, Art 7 and Part IV.

'equitable utilisation', unlike specific entitlements, require parties to negotiate and renegotiate their mutual rights and obligations over time, encouraging the creation of mechanisms for ongoing decision-making, intensifying mutual interaction, lengthening the 'shadow of the future' and increasing the prospects for co-operative outcomes.[49]

A further, more general comment is in order regarding the central role of equitable balancing of interests in international environmental law. Many—indeed, most—environmental dilemmas raise highly ambiguous and difficult issues. To appreciate the difficult choices that must often be made among competing priorities, one need only consider the dilemma facing many developing countries in which economic growth is a question of basic health and survival, not a matter of increasing an already high standard of living. In such circumstances, many investments in environmental protection may seem impossible luxuries. Having said this, we must also acknowledge that the decentralised nature of international society, along with the relatively underdeveloped state of international environmental law and policy, play a role here as well. States, even when they recognise the benefits of co-operation to solve international environmental problems, are very reluctant to constrain themselves by accepting clearly defined limits on the activities they can undertake on their territories. Because there is no central authority to carry out the weighing and balancing in the name of states, states themselves must be brought, often slowly and painfully, to agree on environmental protection measures.

Given that there are no 'right' answers to many issues of environmental protection and that different actors in international society approach the issue from different points of view, international law cannot simply impose a solution. Substantive environmental protection obligations must be agreed upon, which involve a good deal of bargaining and, almost inevitably, compromise. In addition, issues such as management of shared watercourses pose truly difficult distributional issues.[50] The states involved have to determine not only which of them is entitled to make what use of the watercourse and to what extent, but also how different types of uses by different actors within riparian states are to be apportioned. In addition, at least in the modern law of watercourses, we must consider not only the uses that humans on both sides of the border make of the water but also the way in which the watercourse fits into a broader ecosystem. Even in a domestic system, where there may be a high level of agreement on values and priorities among interests, and where there is a central authority capable of identifying and imposing a solution, such issues are not easy to resolve. And we can expect

[49] Eg E Benvenisti, 'Collective Action in the Utilization of Shared Freshwater: The Challenges of International Water Resources Law' (1996) 90 *AJIL* 384; Axelrod, above n 11.

[50] JW Dellapenna, 'Treaties as Instruments for Managing Internationally-Shared Water Resources: Restricted Sovereignty vs Community of Property' (1994) 26 *Case Western Reserve Journal of International Law* 27.

such difficulties to intensify as demand for and conflicts over water multiply during this century.[51] Therefore, we should not expect any legal rule to tell us what the solution to such problems is. The best legal rule in the circumstances may well be a rule that helps us to identify the parameters within which a decision is to be made, the factors to be taken into consideration and the process to be followed. Arguably, this is precisely what we have in rules that incorporate the principle of equitable balancing of interests.

(d) Prevention

The principle of prevention calls on states to take anticipatory action to prevent damage to the environment before it occurs by avoiding, prohibiting or controlling activities that threaten such damage.[52] This principle is reflected in, but also goes somewhat farther than, Principle 21's admonition to states to ensure that activities within their jurisdiction do not cause harm to the environment of other states. As evidence of the principle, legal experts point to myriad treaties and declarations in which states have committed to take action to prevent specified environmental harms.[53] Because the principle may require a state to take measures to prevent harm to its *own,* not just other states', environment, its legal status is controversial especially among developing countries.

(e) Precaution

The obligation of prevention is a cornerstone of international environmental law,[54] but it is difficult to apply where there is uncertainty about the existence, nature or extent of an environmental risk. For example, in the early days of the ozone protection and climate change regimes, there remained scientific uncertainty as to the cause–effect relationship between emissions of certain substances and impacts on the ozone layer and climate change, respectively. Further uncertainty reigned regarding the implications for the environment of these impacts. Today, policy-makers are seeking to grapple with uncertainty over the risks posed by genetically modified organisms. The precautionary principle was developed to help law-and policy-makers reach decisions in cases such as these where scientists are uncertain as to the potential environmental impacts of a given substance or activity.

[51] RE Just and S Netanyahu (eds), *Conflict and Co-operation on Trans-Boundary Water Resources* (Kluwer, 1998).

[52] N de Sadeleer, *Environmental Principles: From Political Slogans to Legal Principles* (Oxford UP, 2002) ch 2.

[53] Eg Convention on the Transboundary Effects of Industrial Accidents 1992, 31 ILM 1330, Art 3; Consolidated Version of the Treaty of the European Union [1997] OJ C/340/1 Art 174; World Charter for Nature 1982, 27 ILM 455, Arts 12–13.

[54] See D Freestone and E Hey, *The Precautionary Principle in International Law: The Challenge of Implementation* (Kluwer, 1996); A Trouwborst, *Evolution and Status of the Precautionary Principle in International Law* (Kluwer, 2002).

Perhaps the most well-known and widely-accepted version of the precautionary principle is found in Principle 15 of the Rio Declaration:[55]

> Where there are threats of serious or irreversible damage, lack of full scientific certainty shall not be used as a reason for postponing cost-effective measures to prevent environmental degradation.[56]

Note that this principle does not specify what states are to do; it simply tells them that they cannot use scientific uncertainty as a reason or excuse for inaction.

A simple way to distinguish prevention and precaution, at least in principle, is to consider the nature of risk and uncertainty.[57] Prevention is concerned with risk, that is, with phenomena and activities that we know to be associated with certain kinds of environmental harm. Obligations of prevention are owed even in cases where it is not certain that environmental harm could be caused by a given activity, but where we know enough to be aware that there is a risk of such harm and that, in light of this known risk, prevention is in order. Precaution, on the other hand, applies to those cases where a good deal less is known about the possible environmental impacts of an activity. There may be some indication that a risk might be present, but too little is known about the relevant cause–effect linkages to identify that risk with any certainty. This is the terrain of the precautionary principle.

The precautionary principle is more than simple common sense of a 'better safe than sorry' variety, since the implementation of environmental measures imposes a wide range of costs, and must somehow be justified to those who bear the costs. If a good deal is known about an environmental risk, the case for preventive measures will often be relatively easy to make. However, asking members of a community to forego benefits in order to avoid the possible realisation of a risk that may or may not be present and is of unknown magnitude is much more difficult. The precautionary principle helps actors to accept the logic of such arguments by reminding them of the limits of our knowledge and of the very real dangers of ignoring indications of potential risk.

Despite a growing consensus among governments and commentators that the precautionary principle forms a part of international environmental law, its definition, operational meaning and legal status remain highly controversial.[58] Some

[55] Above n 34. The Rio Declaration was adopted at the 1992 Earth Summit on Environment and Development held in Rio de Janeiro, Brazil. It will be considered in greater detail below.

[56] Other prominent statements of the principle include UNFCCC, above n 20, Art 3(3); UN Agreement for the Implementation of the Provisions of the UNCLOS of 10 Dec 1982 relating to the Conservation and Management of Straddling Fish Stocks and Highly Migratory Fish Stocks 1995, 34 ILM 1542, Art 6.

[57] See Fisher, ch. 4, this vol, for more detailed discussion of risk, uncertainty and the precautionary principle.

[58] S Boutillon, 'The Precautionary Principle: Development of an International Standard' (2002) 23 *Michigan Journal of International Law* 429.

major states, notably the US, deny that it has attained the status of a principle of international law.[59] Debates continue over how to define the principle, including the magnitude of risk and degree of scientific certainty needed to trigger its application, and whether precautionary action should be subject to the constraints of cost-effectiveness or governments' capabilities.[60]

When we consider in more depth how the precautionary principle operates, we encounter more difficulties. The question of how to operationalise the principle remains highly controversial, including whether and in what circumstances precaution implies changes to risk management techniques, environmental impact assessment procedures, public notice and consultation mechanisms and environmental regulatory instruments (eg, command regulations, taxes and liability rules), whether it implies a shift in the weight accorded to technocratic expertise and local or traditional knowledge in decision-making, and whether it implies shifting the onus onto the proponent of an activity or substance to prove that it is safe.[61] As noted above, the principle does not tell decision-makers that they must take action, or what kind of action they must take, or under what conditions environmental measures must be contemplated. Indeed, a close look at Principle 15 and many other texts expressing the precautionary principle reveals that it does not impose any positive obligations at all.[62] Like the principle of equitable balancing of interests, it is—perhaps frustratingly—open-ended.

If we wish to identify the impact, actual and potential, of the precautionary principle, we must turn our attention away from the substance of decisions that are made in light of it and towards the manner in which those decisions are made. Precaution represents a conceptual shift away from the concept of assimilative capacity, that is, the notion that the environment has a certain capacity to assimilate environmental impacts and that science can tell us when those limits are about to be exceeded. Precaution reminds us that we know very little about the impact of human activities on ecosystems—indeed, that we know precious little about the functioning of ecosystems at all. Secondly, precaution reflects a realisation that science cannot answer questions such as 'What is a safe level of emissions?' or 'How many tonnes of fish can safely be harvested in a year?' Science can certainly provide us with invaluable information on the impact of emissions on

[59] S Lafranchi, 'Surveying the Precautionary Principle's Ongoing Global Development: The Evolution of an Emergent Environmental Management Tool' (2005) 32 *Boston College Environmental Affairs L Rev* 679.

[60] See JB Weiner, 'Whose Precaution After All? A Comment on the Comparison and Evolution of Risk Regulatory Systems' (1997) *Duke Journal of Comparative & International Law* 207.

[61] On these policy challenges, see J Morris, *Rethinking Risk and the Precautionary Principle* (Oxford UP, 2000); T O'Riordan and J Cameron (eds), *Interpreting the Precautionary Principle* (Cameron May, 1994); J Tickner, *Putting Precaution into Practice: Implementing the Precautionary Principle* (Lowell, 2002).

[62] C Henry and M Henry, *Formalization and Application of the Precautionary Principle* (Institut de Recherches Économiques et Sociales, 2002) 3.

humans and ecosystems or the response of fish stocks to particular harvesting levels, to name a few examples. However, even if scientific knowledge were complete, perfect and infallible, the answer to the question 'How much environmental degradation is safe?' is in fact a political, rather than a scientific, matter. The question should in fact read: 'How much environmental degradation is a given society willing to tolerate, given a range of factors including the social, economic and other benefits flowing from activities having an environmental impact, the social, economic and other costs of available environmental protection measures, and the limits of our knowledge?' Thus, the question can be answered only through a partnership between scientists and decision-makers and—if democratic principles are to be respected—interested and concerned members of the public.

(f) Common Concern of Humankind

The principle of common concern of humankind has its origins in the regulation of deep seabed mining on the high seas. The high seas are *res communis*, meaning that they belong to all states collectively and none can be excluded from enjoyment of their resources. Among the resources of the high seas are the mineral resources of the deep seabed. However, the expense and technological sophistication required to carry out deep seabed mining make it impossible for any but the wealthiest states to contemplate exploitation of this resource. If these resources are legally available to all, they will almost certainly be exhausted or severely depleted by the time developing states have the wherewithal to exploit them. Therefore, during the protracted UN law of the sea negotiations in the 1970s, developing countries, led by Malta, proposed that these resources be declared the 'common heritage of mankind', meaning that their exploitation would be permitted only on the condition that the benefits of such exploitation would be distributed among all states.[63] This principle was incorporated into the 1982 UN Law of the Sea Convention (UNCLOS), which envisaged an elaborate international regime for the control, exploitation and sharing of the benefits of deep seabed resources.[64] These provisions were so objectionable to the American government and petroleum industry that the US refused to ratify the Convention until it succeeded in negotiating significant changes to what it considered the most offensive parts of the deep seabed regime.[65]

Although common heritage was not initially aimed at environmental protection, its relevance to environmental resources soon became apparent. Because of

[63] K Steinacker, *The Legal Principle of the Common Heritage of Mankind and Deep Sea-Bed Mining Outside the UN Convention on the Law of the Sea* (Broschiert, 1985); R Wolfrum, 'The Principle of the Common Heritage of Mankind' (1983) 43 *ZaöRV* 312; R St-John Macdonald, 'The Common Heritage of Mankind' in U Beyerlin *et al* (eds), *Recht zwischen Umbruch und Bewahrung: Völkerrecht, Europarecht, Staatsrecht: Festschrift für Rudolf Bernhard* (Springer, 1995) 153.

[64] (1982) 21 ILM 1261, Art 136.

[65] Council on Ocean Law, 'US Will Sign Modification Agreement', *Oceans Policy News* June 1994, 1. The Convention eventually entered into force in 1994.

the interrelatedness of ecosystems, damage to certain resources would have potentially serious consequences around the globe. Thus, it was argued, mainly by 'Northern' environmentalists and governments, that certain environmental resources such as the atmosphere, tropical rainforests or biodiversity should be regarded as the common heritage of humanity. This time it was primarily developing countries that objected, fearing an assertion of external control over resources within their sovereign territories. In some cases an uneasy compromise was struck to designate resources as being of common '*concern*' to all humankind, arguably a less intrusive standard than 'common heritage' but still implying some international protection.[66] This principle has been applied expressly to protection of the global climate[67] and biodiversity,[68] and has been influential in the Antarctic treaty system.[69]

There is an important difference between common heritage and common concern.[70] The former has been applied to resources or areas lying beyond state jurisdiction, such as the deep seabed. However, huge quantities of important environmental resources are located within the borders of states. Furthermore, activities taking place on the territory of states can cause harm to common resources such as the atmosphere. The principle of common concern serves to highlight the global importance of certain national resources and activities. It reminds states that, even though a given activity, such as forestry, takes place within their borders and concerns resources over which they have sovereign jurisdiction, they must take into consideration interests that surpass the national interest. The resources in question are not transformed into internationalised resources, as 'common heritage' is typically understood to imply. States maintain jurisdiction. However, the idea behind the principle is that a wider set of interests be taken into account when decisions affecting these resources are made at the state level.

Whereas common heritage was proposed by developing countries to ensure equitable access to resources, common concern has often been invoked by states of the global 'North' to impose obligations on the global 'South', as in the case of biodiversity. Transnational pharmaceutical companies, almost all based in the North, are among the principal actors interested in the biological resources of the South. Northern states proposed designating biological resources as a 'common concern', partly to ensure their pharmaceutical industries' access to these resources. Many Southern states resisted these proposals, asserting their exclusive

66 EM Borgese, 'The Common Heritage of Mankind: from Non-Living to Living Resources and Beyond' in N Ando *et al* (eds), *Liber Amicorum Judge Shigeru Oda* (Kluwer, 1992) ii 1313.

67 UNFCCC, above n 20.

68 Convention on Biological Diversity (1992) 31 ILM 818.

69 See eg C Joyner, *Governing the Frozen Commons: The Antarctic Regime and Environmental Protection* (U South Carolina Press, 1998) 230ff.; Z Keyuan, 'The Common Heritage of Mankind and the Antarctic Treaty System' [1991] *Netherlands International Law Review* 173.

70 F Biermann, 'Common Concern of Humankind: The Emergence of a New Concept of International Law' (1996) 34 *Archiv des Völkerrechts* 426.

sovereign rights over these resources.[71] This raises two sets of concerns: interest in preserving biodiversity may not be as altruistic as the phrase 'common concern' suggests; and biodiversity preservation may result in the imposition of burdens on the South whose benefits accrue in large measure to the North.

The financial interests at stake in the issue of biodiversity protection remind us of the relevance of the broader globalisation debate to the issue of environmental protection. While the pharmaceutical value of biodiversity serves as a powerful argument in favour of its protection, it also signals the unequal nature of mutual vulnerabilities that transform environmental protection from a local to a global concern. On one level, we are all united in our fundamental interest in protecting the earth's ecosystem, but on another level, we must be attentive to the distributional aspects of global environmental protection. Economic interests play a significant role in determining what issues make it onto the international agenda and how they are dealt with; therefore, we must carefully consider how the costs and benefits of both environmental degradation *and* environmental protection are distributed on a global scale.

The issue of access by pharmaceutical and agricultural companies to biodiversity also reminds us how complex issues of environmental protection can be.[72] As suggested above, controversies regarding environmental protection do not always result from tensions between pro- and anti-environmental groups. Pharmaceutical companies stand to benefit from biodiversity protection, because they stand to profit from exploiting biological resources; furthermore, a wide range of actors, including local communities in which biological resources are harvested and societies in which certain types of disease are endemic, may stand to benefit from the activities of the pharmaceutical companies. Clearly some conditions must be placed on access by these companies to biological resources, but it seems equally clear that denying access to resources is not the answer. Precisely how this access should be governed is a difficult issue that will require for its resolution the input of a wide variety of actors with very different perspectives and interests and very different levels of political and economic clout.[73]

(g) Common but Differentiated Responsibility

The principle of common but differentiated responsibility acknowledges that while environmental protection is a common responsibility of all states, developed

[71] Eg the campaign led by Ethiopia's Tewolde Egziabher, director of Ethiopia's Environmental Protection Authority: 'GMO Import Ban Caught in Crossfire', *New Scientist,* 10 Sept 2003.

[72] See L Glowka, *Determining Access to Genetic Resources and Ensuring Benefit Sharing: Legal And Institutional Considerations for States Providing Genetic Resources* (IUCN, 1995).

[73] See eg Convention on Biological Diversity, above n 68, Art 15; LA Firestone, 'You Say Yes, I Say No: Defining Community Prior Informed Consent under the Convention on Biological Diversity' (2003) 16 *Georgetown International Environmental L Rev* 171; E Longacre, 'Advancing Science while Protecting Developing Countries from Exploitation of their Resources and Knowledge' (2003) 13 *Fordham Intellectual Property Media & Entertainment LJ* 963.

countries bear a special responsibility in view of their historic contribution to environmental degradation, the continuing pressures they place on the global environment and the technologies and financial resources at their disposal.[74] The principle was first implemented in the 1987 Montreal Protocol on Substances that Deplete the Ozone Layer. All parties to this protocol accept obligations to reduce and gradually phase out production and consumption of listed substances. However, the Protocol distinguishes between developed and developing countries, and gives the latter a 10-year delay in their phase-out timetable. In addition, they are to receive financial and technological assistance from developed countries in realising their phase-out goals.[75]

The Kyoto Protocol of 1997 took a more controversial approach.[76] It invokes the principle of common but differentiated obligations, but in this case developing countries have no targets for the reduction of greenhouse gas emissions. Developed countries agree to reduce their greenhouse gas emissions to an average of 5 per cent below 1990 levels by 2008–2012, but this obligation does not apply to developing countries. The latter have general obligations under the Protocol and the Framework Convention on Climate Change to gather data and provide various types of information, as well as to take a range of initiatives such as developing emissions reductions policies to meet the goals of the regime. For the time being, however, they have not accepted binding targets. This has become a sore point for some states including the US, which raised it as a reason for refusing to ratify the Protocol.[77] Even without US participation, the Protocol came into force in February 2005. Nonetheless its approach to common but differentiated responsibilities is bound to be severely tested, since it seems clear that many developed countries will not meet their own targets (at least not through actual domestic emission reductions) and that, unless major developing countries such as China, India and Brazil, take on emission reduction targets of their own, their increasing emissions are likely soon to dwarf any reductions achieved by the developed countries.[78]

The principle of common but differentiated responsibilities is likely to remain a central bone of contention in international environmental law. On the one hand, it is likely to remain the price demanded by many developing countries for their participation in multilateral environmental agreements. Without serious commitment, followed by genuine action, by developed countries to 'make the

[74] Rio Declaration, above n 34, Principle 7; see especially P Cullet, *Differential Treatment in International Environmental Law* (Ashgate Publishing, 2003).

[75] Montreal Protocol, above n 33, Art 5.

[76] Kyoto Protocol, above n 33.

[77] DE Sanger, 'Bush Will Continue to Oppose Kyoto Pact on Global Warming' *New York Times*, 6 Nov 2001.

[78] J Hepeng, 'China is Second Biggest Greenhouse Emitter' (24 Nov 2004) Science and Development Networks available at www.scidev.net/news/index.ctm?fuseaction=readnews&itemid=1761&language=/; A Bugge, 'Amazon Burning Makes Brazil a Leading Polluter', Reuters, 8 Dec 2004.

first move' on global environmental problems, developing countries are unlikely to agree to substantial action themselves. On the other hand, as developing countries' proportional contribution to these problems increases, complaints of unfairness and an 'uneven playing field' are likely to increase in the North and to be exploited by certain Northern governments to justify inaction on environmental problems.

(h) Co-operation

Co-operation is a venerable obligation with deep roots in public international law. Given the decentralised nature of the international legal system, this is not surprising. There being no international government, states must themselves determine how conflicts and tensions over issues such as shared resources are to be resolved. Since solutions to interstate problems cannot be imposed on states by some higher authority, the most effective way of resolving these problems is through negotiations toward a consensus. Therefore, the obligation to co-operate —to share information, to consult with other interested states, to negotiate openly and in good faith, to name just a few basic elements of this obligation—has always been of fundamental importance in international law.[79]

Co-operation is of particular relevance in the environmental context given the interdependence of ecosystems and therefore of states.[80] If individual states wish to pursue environmental protection goals within their borders, they must at some point co-operate with other states. In some cases this co-operation could take the fairly modest form of agreeing to adopt similar environmental standards, thus reducing sources of transboundary environmental harm.[81] In other cases, however, the complexity of the environmental problem may require the creation at the international level of elaborate regulatory machinery to identify sources of environmental harm, monitor environmental quality, permit the adoption and continuing modification of environmental protection measures, ensure the flow of information across borders, and many other activities.[82]

Co-operative mechanisms for environmental protection will generally be more complex if the states involved are not similarly situated: for example, if one is more vulnerable to the environmental impacts of another, if their levels of contribution to the problem differ or if they have varying degrees of capacity to respond to the environmental threat. In these cases, it will not be sufficient simply to establish a certain level of environmental protection that all states involved

[79] *Report of the Expert Group Meeting on Identification of Principles of International Law for Sustainable Development* (UN Commission on Sustainable Development, 1996) paras 110–3.

[80] See Sands, above n 1, 249 ff.

[81] Eg UNCLOS, above n 64, Arts 145, 194(1), 207–212, concerning marine pollution.

[82] This has occurred to the greatest extent under the auspices of the EU, whose members have agreed to numerous environmental directives and compliance systems: see M Lee, *EU Environmental Law: Challenges, Change and Decision-making* (Hart Publishing, 2005).

in the co-operative effort agree to implement. Mechanisms for capacity-building, transfers of technology or financial assistance may be necessary, for example.

Globalisation provides both additional arguments for the importance of co-operation and further challenges to its realisation. As noted above, one of the arguments commonly made by globalisation theorists is that the state, previously considered to be the most important actor—according to some, the only important actor—in international society, may be in the process of being eclipsed by powerful economic actors such as transnational corporations or disembodied economic phenomena such as international markets. Under such conditions, states may feel compelled to work with one another, for example through international organisations and institutions, to counter these threats to their influence.

Thus far we have been discussing the importance of political co-operation, or perhaps the political importance of co-operation. In addition to these themes, we also need to focus on co-operation as a set of international *legal* obligations. At its most basic level, the legal obligation to co-operate requires states to enter into communications with one another in a good faith attempt to resolve or forestall conflicts between them.[83] The obligation to co-operate generally entails an obligation to engage in negotiations in good faith, but does not require states to reach an agreement.[84]

A number of obligations may flow from the basic obligation to co-operate in particular situations. For example, if states are in possession of information relevant to the negotiations, they may be obligated to divulge it; alternatively, they may face an obligation to carry out research in order to gather appropriate information. If plans are in the works that may affect the interests of other states, an obligation to inform potentially affected states will generally be present. In such cases, there may also be an obligation to take the interests of potentially affected states into account in developing and implementing plans. Each of these aspects of the general obligation to co-operate will now be considered in turn.

(i) Prior Notice and Consultation

Prior notice and consultation[85] are of particular relevance in the context of transboundary environmental impacts, such as transboundary pollution or exploitation of a transboundary river.[86] As we have seen, states accept that some transboundary environmental impact must be tolerated; however, the exact limits of this tolerance cannot be identified in the abstract.

[83] *Report of the Expert Group Meeting on Identification of Principles of International Law for Sustainable Development*, above n 79, 112.

[84] *Ibid*, 112–3.

[85] Sands, above n 1, 838 ff.

[86] Benvenisti, above n 49; SC McCaffrey, 'An Assessment of the Work of the International Law Commission' (1996) 36 *Natural Resources Journal* 297; Schwabach, above n 44.

Duties of prior notice and consultation have been present in rules governing the use of transboundary watercourses for decades.[87] In that context, when states intend to conduct works on a transboundary river, such as hydroelectric dams or irrigation projects that are likely to affect the interests of other states in the river basin, they have an obligation to inform those states of the project and to consult with them to find ways to minimise impacts on their interests.[88] This obligation does not grant neighbouring states a right of veto over the project, or the right to require modifications, but it does imply the need for negotiations in good faith and co-operation to arrive at an appropriate solution.[89] The principle of prior notice and consultation is now widely applied in cases where activities in one state are likely to affect the interests of neighbours.[90]

(j) Environmental Impact Assessment

In cases where activities taking place in one state may have impacts beyond its borders, one of the first requirements is to gather as much information as possible on potential impacts and means of mitigating them. One well-recognised way of collecting such information is to perform an environmental impact assessment (EIA) prior to undertaking a project.[91] As its name suggests, an EIA is a scientific study in which the potential environmental effects of a given project are identified, and ways of mitigating these effects are considered.[92] Some commentators argue that there is a general customary duty to conduct EIAs of projects with potential transboundary impacts, while others argue that such a duty exists only where specifically contemplated by an international convention.[93] The most prominent such convention is the Espoo Convention, which requires its signatories to conduct EIAs of projects with transboundary implications.[94] Obligations to conduct EIAs are found in various other conventions and texts as well, including the Draft Articles on Transboundary Harm[95] and the Protocol on Environmental Protection to the Antarctic Treaty.[96] The obligation to conduct an EIA is normally supplemented by an obligation to share information about environmental impacts with potentially

[87] See *Lake Lanoux Arbitration* (*France v Spain*) (1957) 12 RIAA 281, 24 ILR 101; C Romano, 'The *Lake Lanoux* Dispute (*Spain v France*)' in CPR Romano, *The Peaceful Settlement of International Environmental Disputes* (Kluwer, 2000) 219.

[88] *Report of the Expert Group*, above n 79, 117–20.

[89] *Ibid*, 112–13.

[90] Convention on the Protection and Use of Transboundary Watercourses and International Lakes, above n 40, Arts 11 and 12; *Draft Articles*, above n 25, Arts 8 and 9.

[91] JH Knox, 'The Myth and Reality of Transboundary Environmental Impact Assessment' (2002) 96 *AJIL* 291.

[92] See, this vol, Abbot, and Richardson and Razzaque.

[93] *Report of the Expert Group*, above n 79, 114–6; Knox, above n 91.

[94] Convention on Environmental Impact Assessment in Transboundary Context (Espoo), 25 Feb 1991, 30 ILM 802.

[95] Above n 45, Art 7.

[96] (1991) 30 ILM 1455, Art 8.

affected states.[97] In this manner, when states begin to negotiate, they have sufficient information at their disposal to conduct negotiations in an informed manner. As with prior notice and consultation, however, the obligation to conduct and disseminate the results of an EIA does not imply an obligation to halt the project or to carry out major modifications at the request of potentially affected states. Once again, states are expected to negotiate in good faith and to co-operate to find an appropriate solution.[98]

(k) Prior Informed Consent

The principle of prior informed consent differs in important respects from the principle of prior notice and consultation. In the first place, under prior informed consent, the affected state does have the chance of refusing to consent to the activity in question. In the second place, prior informed consent applies in a narrower set of circumstances, notably those involving hazardous activities or substances.

Prior informed consent arose in the context of transboundary movements of hazardous waste[99] in response to concerns about the practice of shipping hazardous waste to countries that lacked proper facilities for handling and disposal of such waste, and which were often not made aware of the nature of the waste and the dangers that it posed.[100] The main response of the international community to this problem was to negotiate treaties requiring exporting countries to obtain the prior informed consent of the importing country.[101] Exporting countries are required to provide extensive information on the nature of the substance being exported and to obtain the consent of the importing country before the waste is exported. This principle is based on an assumption that states are in the best position to determine for themselves whether or not they have the capacity to receive the substance in question and, furthermore, whether it is in their interest to do so. It appears to have the virtue of respecting sovereignty and independence while at the same time providing recipient states with the means to protect their own interests.

[97] Eg Espoo Convention, above n 94, Arts 3 and 4.

[98] *Ibid*, Art 5.

[99] Eg Basel Convention on the Control of Transboundary Movements of Hazardous Wastes and Their Disposal 1989, 28 ILM 657, Art 6; Bamako Convention on the Ban of the Import into Africa and the Control of Transboundary Movement and Management of Hazardous Wastes Within Africa 1991, 30 ILM 775. Prior informed consent has also been applied in the context of trade in hazardous chemicals. The leading convention on this subject is the Rotterdam Convention on the Prior Informed Consent for Certain Hazardous Chemicals and Pesticides in International Trade 1998, 38 ILM 1. For a critical appraisal of this convention, see RW Emory Jr, 'Trade and the Environment: Probing the Protections in the Rotterdam Convention on Prior Informed Consent' [2000] *Colorado Journal of International Environmental Law & Policy* 47.

[100] See examples discussed in J LaDou, 'Deadly Migration: Hazardous Industries' Flight to the Third World' (1991) 94 (July) *Technology Rev* 46; R Lu 'West Africa: the Industrial World's Dumping Grounds' (1989) 11(summer) *Harvard International Rev* 57.

[101] Basel Convention, above n 99, Art 6.

Prior informed consent is one of the centrepieces of the Basel Convention.[102] Under this convention, parties must establish a competent authority to receive information on hazardous waste transport and to issue, where appropriate, the necessary permission.[103] Parties wishing to export waste must submit specified information to the competent authority in the state of import, which will then grant permission for the import, with or without conditions, or deny such permission.[104] A party may ban imports of hazardous waste and provide notification of such a ban to the other parties, in which case export to those parties is prohibited.[105]

The logic of prior informed consent as applied in the context of hazardous waste appears to have broken down, in particular as it imposes a significant burden on developing countries. It is difficult for developed countries, let alone developing countries, to prevent the illegal importation of substances from narcotics to hazardous waste. The burden of ensuring that the various provisions of the Basel Convention are being respected falls disproportionately on developing countries, with the result that compliance is far from satisfactory. As a result, developing countries began working towards the adoption of an outright ban on exports of hazardous waste from developed to developing countries.

At a meeting of the Third Conference of the Parties to the Basel Convention in 1995 developing countries appeared to accomplish their goal. An immediate ban on the export of hazardous wastes for final disposal from developed to developing countries was adopted, along with a ban, by the end of 1997, on the export of hazardous materials destined for recycling or recovery operations.[106] However, the ban has not yet entered into force, due to resistance from a number of developed countries. Moreover, it does not even begin to address the more pressing problem of eliminating the massive stockpiles of toxic waste in developing countries, especially in Africa.[107]

Prior informed consent also features prominently in debates over genetically modified organisms (GMOs).[108] One of the features of the GMO debate is a lack of consensus regarding the actual and potential costs of GMOs, and more particularly regarding the weighing of those costs against benefits. It is not surprising that different societies have different levels of risk aversion, and that they will

[102] *Ibid.* See generally K Kummer, *International Management of Hazardous Wastes: The Basel Convention and Related Legal Rules* (Clarendon Press, 1995); M Bradford, 'The United States, China and the Basel Convention on the Transboundary Movements of Hazardous Wastes and their Disposal' (1997) 8 *Fordham Environmental LJ* 305.

[103] Basel Convention, above n 99, Art 5.

[104] *Ibid*, Art 6.

[105] *Ibid*, Art 4(1)(b).

[106] Decisions Adopted by the Third Meeting of the Conference of the Parties to the Basel Convention, Geneva 18–22 Sept 1995, UNEP/CHW.3/35, Decision III.1.

[107] The international 'Africa Stockpiles Programme' was established by various stakeholders to co-ordinate strategies to reduce toxic waste dumps in the region: see www.africastockpiles.org.

[108] Cartagena Protocol on Biosafety 2000, 39 ILM 1027.

identify risks differently. In such a context, it becomes virtually impossible to reach an international consensus on prohibitions or strict controls on GMOs, and international law has no choice but to demonstrate a certain level of tolerance for different opinions and approaches. In an interdependent world, states with a high level of aversion to the risks and threats posed by GMOs seek the help of international law in protecting themselves from this risk. In this context, prior informed consent has a potentially valuable role to play. It leaves to individual states to decide whether or not to allow importation of GMOs, while at the same time providing them with access to information that will help them make this decision.

3. Sustainable Development

(a) Emergence of the Concept of Sustainable Development

It is possible to view all the legal principles discussed in the previous section as elements of a wider, over-arching principle that emerged in the closing years of the twentieth century as a new global policy goal: 'sustainable development' (or 'sustainability'). Sustainable development was famously defined in the 1987 Brundtland Report, *Our Common Future*, as 'development that meets the needs of the present without compromising the ability of future generations to meet their own needs'.[109] Sustainability is typically understood to entail the simultaneous pursuit of three policy goals that are often seen as competing with each other: environmental protection, economic development and social equity. Thus, sustainable development goes well beyond the scope of international environmental law, embracing the fields of international trade and economic law and policy, as well as human rights and social and economic development. At its most basic level, it is grounded in a recognition that the perspectives of developed and developing countries on environmental protection differ in important respects.[110] These differences are due to many factors, which can be loosely categorised as follows.

In the first place, the types of environmental problems experienced in developing countries, the impacts that they have and their apparent root causes are dramatically different from those in developed countries. Many of the environmental problems experienced in industrialised countries are the result of high levels of economic development and affluence, such as industrial pollution and over-consumption. In developing countries, pressure on the environment is often caused by poverty that forces individuals and communities to put unsustainable pressure

[109] World Commission on Environment and Development, *Our Common Future* (Oxford UP, 1987) 43.

[110] See TE Campbell, 'The Political Meaning of Stockholm: Third World Participation in the Environmental Conference Process' (1975) 8 *Stanford Journal of International Studies* 138; AK Biswas, 'Environment and Law: A Perspective from Developing Countries' in RJ Dupuy (ed), *L'avenir du droit international de l'environnement, Colloque de L'Académie de La Haye* (Seijthoff, 1985) 389.

on already marginalised resources. Issues such as access to potable water and degradation of agricultural soils rank high on the list of environmental problems in developing countries.

Secondly, developed countries have the financial and administrative resources and capacity to study and seek to resolve environmental problems by, for example, conducting research, developing new processes and technologies, and establishing laws, policies and institutional structures for environmental protection. These resources are often lacking in developing countries, and environmental protection may seem like a luxury compared to provision for basic needs.

Thirdly, the historic contribution to current global levels of environmental degradation by developed countries is vastly greater than that of developing countries, and the current impacts on the environment caused by developed countries continue to overwhelm those caused by developing countries. Fourthly, developed countries have benefited immensely from these environmentally damaging activities, benefits that manifest themselves in the form of strong economies and high standards of living.

Developing countries made their perspectives on environmental protection known even before the 1972 Stockholm Conference,[111] and these perspectives were acknowledged both in the lead-up to the Conference[112] and in the Stockholm Declaration itself.[113] It was the 1987 Brundtland Report, however, which brought the term 'sustainable development' into public discourse and provided an early articulation of the sustainable development agenda. Sustainable development became a crucial theme at the Rio Summit on Environment and Development, held in Rio de Janeiro, Brazil, in 1992. The choice of a city in the developing world as the host city for the Summit was no accident; organisers sought to send a clear message that concerns of developing countries would receive full attention.

The Rio Summit produced two documents that immediately became the central texts of sustainable development: the Rio Declaration, a pithy statement representing a global consensus on the core principles of sustainable development; and Agenda 21, a detailed 800-page action plan for achieving sustainable development.

[111] Eg 'Permanent Sovereignty over Natural Resources', UN General Assembly Resolution 1803 (XVII) of 14 Dec 1962 (permanent state sovereignty over natural resources).

[112] A series of regional seminars was held prior to the Stockholm Conference, and knowledge gained on environmental problems in developing countries was published in the Founex Report on Environment and Development (1971), reproduced in (1972) 586 *International Conciliation.* See U Beyerlin, 'The Concept of Sustainable Development' in R Wolfrum (ed) *Enforcing Environmental Standards: Economic Mechanisms as Viable Means?* (Springer, 1996) 95.

[113] Stockholm Declaration, above n 38, especially Principles 8–12 (accelerated development and favourable terms of trade are the best recipe for environmental protection in developing countries, environmental policies should not hamper economic development, developed countries should provide technical and financial resources to enable environmental protection in developing countries, and environmental standards suitable for the advanced countries may be inappropriate and too costly for developing countries).

The consensus achieved at Rio was fragile, ambiguous and based on delicate political compromises, but it was an important consensus nonetheless.[114]

While the meaning of sustainable development has been controversial and ambiguous from the start, many legal experts agree that it embraces four basic elements:

1. the idea that the needs of present and future generations must be taken into account;
2. the need to ensure that renewable and non-renewable resources are conserved and not exhausted;
3. the requirement that access to and use of natural resources must take equitable account of the needs of all peoples, and
4. recognition that issues of environment and development must be treated in an integrated manner.[115]

(b) Needs: Humans at the Centre

The first element in the international legal discourse of sustainable development is the concept of needs. Sustainable development implies, first and foremost, a concern with satisfaction of human needs: the need, especially, for poverty eradication and social and economic development in developing countries. According to Principle 1 of the Rio Declaration, '[h]uman beings are at the centre of concerns for sustainable development. They are entitled to a healthy and productive life in harmony with nature.' This statement is controversial because it appears to privilege an anthropocentric vision, placing human concerns and interests ahead of those of environmental protection. Many commentators in the South, conversely, were concerned that environmental protection was more important in the North than the well-being of populations in developing countries.[116]

The need for economic development, particularly in the South, is one of the foundational themes of sustainable development. Developing countries did not want to be forced to forego economic development in the interests of global environmental protection; nor did they wish to accept a global environmental agenda built around environmental concerns of wealthy industrialised countries. In response, Rio's Principle 3 refers to a right to development, Principle 5 identifies poverty eradication 'as an indispensable requirement for sustainable development',

[114] A Boyle and D Freestone, 'Introduction' in A Boyle and D Freestone (eds), *International Law and Sustainable Development* (Oxford UP, 1999) 3–4.

[115] Foundation for International Environmental Law and Development (FIELD), *Report of a Consultation on Sustainable Development: The Challenge to International Law* (FIELD, 1993); P Sands, 'Introduction' in P Sands (ed), *Greening International Law* (Earthscan, 1993); S Wood, 'Sustainability in International Law' in EOLSS, *Encyclopedia of Life Support Systems* (EOLSS Publishers, 2004), available at www.eolss.net.

[116] See further on the Rio Declaration, FK Boon 'The Rio Declaration and its Influence on International Environmental Law' (1992) *Singapore Journal of Legal Studies* 347.

and Principle 6 calls for 'special priority' to be given to the needs of developing countries, underlining the link between global environmental protection and international development.

The need for economic development is often presented as a need for economic *growth*, and 'sustainable development' as entailing sustainable (or sustained) economic growth, not just for developing countries but for developed countries as well.[117] The Brundtland Report, for instance, calls for rapid economic growth in developing countries,[118] and the Rio Declaration calls for 'a supportive and open international economic system that would lead to economic growth and sustainable development in all countries, to better address the problems of environmental degradation'.[119]

(c) Limits: Resource Conservation

A second major element in the international legal discourse of sustainability is respect for the limits of the environment and natural resources. This is typically taken to imply rational conservation of natural resources, a proposition that has featured prominently in international environmental law since its earliest days and is reflected in the contemporary notion of 'sustainable utilisation' of natural resources.[120] The theme of limits also refers to the ultimate limits of planetary life support systems. The Brundtland Report, for example, warns against endangering earth's natural life support systems and acknowledges 'ultimate limits' to economic growth, although it characterises these primarily as social and technological rather than ecological.[121]

(d) Equity: Intra- and Intergenerational Fairness

A third element of the discourse of sustainable development is equity in the distribution of the benefits and burdens of environmental protection and economic development. There is broad agreement that this includes at least two kinds of equity: 'intragenerational' and 'intergenerational'.[122] Intragenerational equity refers to equity among states and people(s) in existence now; intergenerational equity refers to equity between present and future generations of humans.

In international legal discourse, the main concern of intragenerational equity is equity among *states*, or 'international' equity, especially between developing and

[117] Eg UNFCCC, above n 20, Preamble and Arts 3(5), 4(2); UN Convention to Combat Desertification in Those Countries Experiencing Serious Drought and/or Desertification, Particularly in Africa 1994, 33 ILM 1328, Preamble; Resolution on an Agenda for Development, UNGA Res 51/240 of 20 June 1997, paras 1, 43.

[118] Brundtland Report, above n 109.

[119] Above n 34, Principle 12.

[120] *Report of the Expert Group Meeting*, above n 79, paras 57–63.

[121] Brundtland Report, above n 109.

[122] I Voinovic, 'Intergenerational and Intragenerational Equity Requirements for Sustainability' (1995) 22(3) *Environmental Conservation* 223.

developed states. At a minimum international equity means that the use of resources or the environment by one state should take into account the needs and interest of other states, an idea that is reflected in numerous principles of international environmental law including good neighbourliness, equitable balancing of interests, equitable utilisation, prior notice and consultation and prior informed consent.[123] A specific concern with equity between developing and developed countries is reflected in legal principles such as common but differentiated responsibilities and common heritage (or concern),[124] in calls for a more open and equitable international economic system, elimination of barriers to developing country exports, debt reduction and elimination of unsustainable patterns of production and consumption in the developed countries.[125] It is also reflected in calls for capacity-building and transfer of technology or financial resources to developing countries.[126]

Intragenerational equity can also be understood in terms of equity among people, rather than states. Sustainable development, in this sense, is concerned with redressing inequities both within and between countries. This conception of equity recognises that women, the poor, minorities and indigenous peoples often bear a disproportionately large share of the burdens of environmental degradation and enjoy a disproportionately small share of the benefits of economic growth. This conception of equity is controversial insofar as it may imply international interference in national affairs, but it is reflected in international legal principles of gender equity, a human right to a healthy environment, public participation, access to information, access to justice, poverty eradication and indigenous rights.[127]

One aspect of the discourse of equity that has attracted broad consensus among international lawyers is the proposition that sustainability rests on a commitment to respect the needs of future generations, ie, a commitment to intergenerational equity.[128] The principle of intergenerational equity calls upon states to take into account the long-term environmental effects of their present policies, in order to ensure that future generations will have access to environmental

[123] See GF Maggio, 'Inter/Intra-generational Equity: Current Applications under International Law for Promoting the Sustainable Development of Natural Resources' (1997) 4 *Buffalo Environmental L Rev* 161.

[124] D French 'Developing States and International Environmental Law: The Importance of Differentiated Obligations' (2000) 49 *I C LQ* 34; K Baslar, *The Concept of Common Heritage of Mankind in International Law* (Brill Academic Publishers, 1998).

[125] Eg Rio Declaration, above n 34, Principles 8, 12.

[126] UN Development Programme (UNDP), *Capacity 21: A Programme in Support of Agenda 21* (UNDP, 1993); UN Commission on Sustainable Development (CSD), *Transfer of Environmentally Sound Technology, Co-operation and Capacity-Building: Report of the Secretary-General*, (UNCSD, 1994).

[127] Eg Rio Declaration, above n 34, Principles 5, 10, 20, 22, 23; Agenda 21, above n 126, ch 3, 26, 34, 36, 40.

[128] See EB Weiss, *In Fairness to Future Generations* (Transnational Publishers, 1989).

resources adequate to meet their needs and permit their flourishing. While this idea is found, in various forms, in a large number of international environmental instruments covering a wide range of subject matters and spanning many years,[129] its exact meaning and implications for sustainability remain controversial.

All of these forms of equity, whether intra- or intergenerational, concern equity among humans. While there have been frequent proposals to address inequities between humans and non-humans throughout the history of international environmental law,[130] none has gained the widespread support of governments, with the possible exception of the non-binding 1982 World Charter for Nature, a UN General Assembly resolution which declared that 'every form of life is unique, warranting respect regardless of its worth to man'.[131]

Finally, as discussed earlier, the concept of equity addresses rights and obligations in general, flexible terms, leaving their precise extent and implications to be worked out in particular circumstances, and drawing the concerned actors together in a reiterative cycle of negotiation. While the issues addressed under the rubric of equity are among the most intractable problems facing the international community—poverty, inequality, funding, technology transfer, etc, the open-textured quality of equitable principles may help to ensure, at least, that the relevant actors continue to strive for co-operative outcomes.

(f) Integration: Uniting Environment and Development

The fourth basic element of sustainable development discourse is the proposition that environmental protection should not be considered independently of economic development issues. This idea is encapsulated in Principle 4 of the Rio Declaration, which states that '[i]n order to achieve sustainable development, environmental protection shall constitute an integral part of the development process and cannot be considered in isolation from it'. That environmental protection and economic development can be integrated in decision-making processes and that both can be achieved simultaneously is an article of faith in sustainable development discourse.[132] The idea of integration has featured in international environmental discourse since at least the Stockholm Conference,[133] and is operationalised in numerous procedural arrangements such as EIA, sustainable development

[129] Eg International Convention for the Regulation of Whaling 1946, 161 UNTS 72, Preamble; UNFCCC, above n 20, Art 3(1); Convention on the Protection and Use of Transboundary Watercourses and International Lakes, above n 40, Art 2(5)(c).

[130] See A Gillespie, *International Environmental Law, Policy, and Ethics* (Oxford UP, 1998).

[131] Above n 33, Preamble.

[132] Eg S Schmidheiny, *Changing Course: A Global Business Perspective on Development and the Environment* (MIT Press, 1992); M Hajer, *The Politics of Environmental Discourse* (Clarendon Press, 1995); J Elkington, *Cannibals With Forks: The Triple Bottom Line of 21st Century Business* (New Society, 1998).

[133] Above n 38, Principle 13.

criteria and indicators, obligations to notify or consult with other states, and schemes for gathering and disseminating environmental information.[134]

The principle of integration draws attention to the links between the global economy and the problems of poverty and environmental degradation in the South. The problems of environmental degradation and the difficulties that countries of the South have in regulating and controlling such degradation cannot be considered in isolation from transnational flows of capital and manufactured goods. Furthermore, the environmental and economic policies of both states and international agencies, including economic and financial agencies such as the World Bank and World Trade Organisation, are among the issues that must be considered in order to address the issue of global environmental protection and promotion of sustainable development.[135] The principle of integration signals the 'mainstreaming' of environment concerns into national and international law- and policy-making.[136] It calls for environmental concerns to be incorporated in economic and development institutions rather than being confined to specialised environmental institutions such as the UN Environment Programme or national environment ministries. Under the banner of sustainable development, environmental issues have become routine concerns of international economic, social and development institutions. Integration thus marks both a major victory for environmental concerns in international legal discourse and the possible start of their demise as an autonomous body of law.[137]

(g) Whither Sustainable Development?

What are the prospects, then, for sustainable development as a new 'meta-principle' of international environmental law, or international law more generally? The term 'sustainable development' has generated a great deal of international legal and policy activity, but it has not been embraced by ordinary citizens and grass-roots social movements the way some other ideas, such as human rights or environmental protection, have. The 10-year anniversary of the Rio Summit, held in Johannesburg in 2002, was marked more by reckoning of failures and scaling back of expectations than by renewed enthusiasm for the goal of sustainable development.[138] This may reflect more the magnitude of the challenge of sustainable development than its failure as a political and legal objective. In any event we can

[134] NA Robinson, 'Legal Structures and Sustainable Development: Comparative Environmental Law Perspectives on Legal Regimes for Sustainable Development' (1998) 3 *Widener Law Symposium Journal* 247.

[135] See MC Cordonier Segger and A Khalfan, *Sustainable Development Law: Principles, Practices and Prospects* (Oxford UP, 2004); A Boyle and D Freestone (eds), *International Law and Sustainable Development: Past Achievements and Future Challenges* (Oxford UP, 1999); Sands, above n 1, 252 ff.

[136] Wood, above n 115.

[137] *Ibid.*

[138] K Ruffing, 'Johannesburg Summit: Success or Failure?' *OECD Observer*, Oct 2002.

expect the meaning and role of sustainable development to continue to preoccupy international environmental lawyers for decades to come.

C. Conclusion

International environmental law is a dynamic and growing field, characterised by a high degree of experimentation, but its development is often frustratingly slow: in the face of an international scientific consensus on the dangers to the global atmosphere of greenhouse gas emissions, for example, the response of states has been to agree to emissions reductions that are generally acknowledged to be inadequate.[139] Furthermore, the state with the highest emissions on the planet, the US, refuses to ratify the document, and developing countries, many with growing economies and ever-increasing greenhouse gas emissions, have no binding emission reduction targets.[140] On the other hand, texts such as the Kyoto Protocol represent significant progress. It is remarkable that only 30 years after states first reached a consensus on the global nature of environmental protection and the need to develop a body of international legal rules to address problems of environmental degradation, a group of states responsible for the majority of developed country CO_2 emissions have ratified an international agreement that imposes emissions reductions on them and exposes them to the possibility of sanctions handed down by an international body in the case of non-compliance.[141]

One of the major challenges facing international environmental law today is the need to integrate the myriad legal norms for environmental protection, and to integrate environmental rules with rules governing international trade and finance, protection of intellectual property, human rights and other areas. As international environmental rules come to penetrate more and more spheres of activity, the possibility of collision among various environmental rules, and between environmental and other rules, is increased. Furthermore, environmental goals cannot be achieved on the basis of a strictly environmental agenda: since all areas of human endeavour have environmental implications, environmental considerations need to be woven into law- and policy-making in virtually all fields. This, in essence, is the challenge of international law-making for sustainability.

[139] PD Cameron and D Zillman (eds), *Kyoto: From Principles to Practice* (Kluwer, 2002).

[140] N Matsuo, 'Analysis of the U.S.'s New Climate Initiative: The Attitude of the Bush Administration Towards Climate Change' (2002) 3(1) *International Review of Environmental Strategies* 177.

[141] Kyoto Protocol, above n 33. For figures on ratifications and shares of emissions, see UNFCCC secretariat, at http://unfccc.int.

12

International Trade Law and the Environment

OREN PEREZ*

A. Introduction

The global society has experienced an extensive process of economic integration over the last decade.[1] This process was reflected both in an unprecedented increase in cross-border economic and financial transactions, and in a parallel empowerment of global economic institutions, such as the World Trade Organisation ('WTO'), the International Monetary Fund (IMF), the World Bank and the International Chamber of Commerce (ICC).[2] The possible adverse effects of this far-reaching process of economic integration—in the environmental and other domains—have been the subject of wide-ranging and highly intense public debate, evident both in street protests in major economic meetings (eg, at the WTO conference in Seattle, 1998) and in the popular media and scholarly journals. This chapter carefully assesses this conflict, decoding the social frictions underlying it, and exploring the impact of trade liberalisation on the prospects for sustainable development. The chapter explores these themes in one critical institutional domain: the WTO.

This chapter is organised into eight sections. The next section provides a brief introduction to the multiple legal systems and transnational institutions that

* Professor, Bar Ilan University, Israel.

[1] R Went, 'Economic Globalization Plus Cosmopolitanism?' (2004) 11 *Review of International Political Economics* 337.

[2] The literature on trade law and other international economic institutions, and their social and environmental effects, is vast. See especially G Teubner (ed), *Global Law Without a State* (Dartmouth, 1997); BR Copeland and MS Taylor, *Trade and the Environment: Theory and Evidence* (Princeton, UP, 2003); D Esty, 'Bridging the Trade–Environment Divide' (2001) 15(3) *Journal of Economics Perspectives* 113; B Hoekman and M Kostecki, *The Political Economy of the World Trading System: The WTO and Beyond* (Oxford UP, 2001); R Howse and M Trebilcock, 'The Fair Trade—Free Trade Debate: Trade, Labor, and the Environment' (1996) 16 *International Review of Law & Economics* 61; J Jackson, *The World Trading System: Law and Policy of International Economic Relations* (MIT Press, 1997); A Quereshi, *International Economic Law* (Sweet and Maxwell, 1999).

together constitute the field of 'international trade law'—itself part of the broader realm of international economic law. The process of global economic integration is driven and facilitated by this complex legal network; the tendency of some of the observers of this process to associate it solely with the WTO is, I will argue, wrong. Section C explores the various frictions which together constitute the 'trade and environment' conflict. It also discusses the place of the concept of sustainable development within this debate. Section D starts with a general question: what role can the law play in resolving this conflict? It focuses on the potential synergies between the trade and environment realms, and on the possible role of law in enabling their actual realisation. The section explains this idea, setting it against the various frictions discussed in the previous section. The next four sections focus on a concrete institution—the WTO. They analyse the legal manifestations of this conflict within the boundaries of the WTO, exploring how the frictions and synergies between the trade and environment realms are reflected in the law of the WTO (highlighting the role of the idea of sustainable development in the WTO jurisprudence). Sections F and G draw some general conclusions and make some tentative proposals for reform. The chapter concludes with a brief analysis of the Doha negotiations framework on the 'trade and environment' question.

B. Global Economic Integration and Legal Pluralism

In thinking about the legal network underlying the process of global economic integration one needs, first, to make sense of this term. Following Rodrik, I will define this process as denoting a movement towards a world in which markets for goods, services and factors of production are perfectly integrated.[3] In this chapter I am focusing prominently on the market for goods. The move towards a more integrated global economy can be attributed to two main processes, which can be traced back to the twentieth century.[4] First, far-reaching technological progress, especially in the fields of transportation and telecommunication, has helped to create an integrated global economy. The second factor has been the creation of multiple legal systems that support and facilitate transnational trade.

Understanding the critical role of law in the facilitation of global trade requires us to take a step back and to consider the costs that are imposed on cross-border interactions by legal and political discontinuities. These costs or trade barriers include classic trade-related measures, such as tariffs, quotas and export and

[3] D Rodrik, 'How Far Will International Economic Integration Go?' (2000) 14 *Journal of Economic Perspectives* 177, 178.

[4] Despite the far-reaching integrative processes, which have taken place over the last decade, the world is still far from being a fully integrated economy. See the discussion in Went, above n 1, and Rodrik, above n 3.

import licensing requirements, indirect impediments such as dissimilar technical, health and environmental standards (what are called in the trade-law jargon 'non-tariff barriers'), and the strategic use of distorting economic policies (eg, subsidies and anti-dumping measures). But there is another sense in which the discontinuity between national legal systems creates impediments to trade. The fact that cross-border transactions may be subject to disparate national rules and competing jurisdictions subjects transnational deals to extra risks, relating primarily to problems of conflicting doctrinal constructions (eg, in private law and corporate law) and questions of contract enforcement.

Over the last 50 years the global society has developed multiple legal frameworks in an effort to reduce the transaction costs associated with transnational commerce.[5] These systems have varied structures. Some of them such as the WTO and regional trade agreements, are treaty-based, while some have private origins (such as the systems of technical standardisation and standard business contracts). The General Agreement on Tariffs and Trade (GATT),[6] established in 1947, and replaced by the WTO in 1995,[7] occupies a central place in this network. The GATT's main contribution was a gradual reduction of tariffs and quotas, prominently on industrial products.[8] The WTO extended the GATT agenda in several respects. First, its rule-book does not cover just trade in goods, but deals with other fields such as trade in services and intellectual property rights. Second, the WTO targets, through several, specifically tailored instruments,[9] non-tariffs barriers such as food standards and health and safety standards.

However, despite its undeniable importance, the WTO is only one element of the complex 'international trade law' network. Some of these systems deal with issues that are also dealt with by the WTO. Among these are regional trade treaties, such as the European Union (EU) and Mercusor of South America and multiple bilateral trade agreements, generating together a complex labyrinth of trade rules.[10]

[5] The examples below refer prominently to trade law. There are further examples relating to other aspects of global economic integration, such as the various systems of law that facilitate the work of the global financial system: see further Quereshi, above n 2; Jackson, above n 2.

[6] (1947) 755 UNTS 194. The text of the GATT's original agreement, as amended through the years, was incorporated into the WTO framework through the GATT 1994.

[7] Agreement Establishing the World Trade Organization, 15 April 1994, Uruguay Round of Multilateral Trade Negotiations: Legal Instruments Embodying the Results of the Uruguay Round (GATT Secretariat 1994), in World Trade Organisation, *The Legal Texts—The Results of the Uruguay Round of Multilateral Trade Negotiations* (Cambridge UK, 1999).

[8] Consecutive GATT negotiating rounds reduced the average tariff rate on industrial goods from 40% in 1945 to near 6% in 1978. The Uruguay Round, which led to the establishment of the WTO, reduced average industrial tariffs to 4%. See, USDA, 'Agriculture in the WTO,' *International Agriculture and Trade Reports* (WRS-98-4, Dec 1998) 6.

[9] Prominently, the Agreement on the Application of Sanitary and Phytosanitary Measures, Marrakesh, 15 Apr 1994 and the Agreement on Technical Barriers to Trade, Marrakesh, 15 Apr 1994, both in World Trade Organisation above n 7.

[10] See WTO, *Regionalism and the World Trading System* (WTO, 1995); World Bank, *Trade Blocs* (Oxford UP, 2000).

The issue of technical standards is governed by various global organisations such as the International Organization for Standardisation and the Codex Alimentarius Commission, with varying levels of state involvement.[11] Other systems deal with the problem of disparate rule structures and contract enforcement. Thus, various systems provide universal normative frameworks, governing various aspects of cross-border transactions. Paradigmatic examples are the International Chamber of Commerce, 'Uniform Customs and Practices for Documentary Credits—1994' ('UCP 500'), which governs the field of international letters of credit,[12] and FIDIC's standard construction contracts.[13] The Lex Mercatoria or Law Merchant is another source of universal rules governing transnational commerce. Other legal instruments target the problem of jurisdictional discontinuity. The two main instruments in this context are the New York Convention on the Recognition and Enforcement of Foreign Arbitral Awards, 1958,[14] and the recent Hague Convention on Choice of Court Agreements of 2005.[15] Both of these treaties seek to reduce the risks of opportunistic behaviour in transnational deals by providing mechanisms for global enforcement. This is achieved through the establishment of rules for the recognition and enforcement of arbitral awards and foreign court judgments (both treaties focus, primarily, on business-to-business agreements).

C. Frictions Between International Trade and Environmental Protection

The trade and environment conflict is realised, simultaneously, in multiple legal domains. Studying the legal aspect of this conflict requires, therefore, a multi-facet examination, exploring how it is mirrored and reconstructed in any of the distinct sub-domains of the global trade law network. This chapter focuses only on the WTO, thus providing only a partial picture of the legal realisation of this conflict.[16] However, the ideas developed here can be applied to other institutional domains, such as the North American Free Trade Agreement (NAFTA).[17] To facilitate the legal analysis of the trade–environment dilemma, we need to look first at the underlying nature of this conflict.

[11] See further, Wood, this vol.

[12] Most of the standard forms international letters of credit ('LC') issued by banks include a provision that the LC is governed by the UCP.

[13] FIDIC stands for the International Federation of Consulting Engineers. It produces several standard contracts for big construction projects.

[14] 330 UNTS 38.

[15] Available at www.hcch.net/index_en.php?act=conventions.text&cid=98%20.

[16] I explored the manifestations and policy consequences of the trade–environment conflict in other institutional domains elsewhere: O Perez, *Ecological Sensitivity and Global Legal Pluralism: Rethinking the Trade and Environment Conflict* (Hart Publishing, 2004).

[17] (1993) 32 ILM 289.

1. The Adverse Effects of Global Economic Integration: An Economic Perspective

Over the last decade or longer environmentalists and 'anti-globalisers' have criticised the move toward a more open global economy (led by the GATT and the WTO), arguing that this process has adverse ecological impacts which are being ignored by the global business community, and are undermining the prospects for sustainable development.[18] One of the more common responses to this criticism was the claim that trade liberalisation, by promoting global efficiency, is in effect beneficial to the environment. Thus a WTO report from 1999 argued that free trade can both help to generate the resources developing countries 'need to protect the environment and work towards sustainable development', and contribute to 'improved allocation and more efficient use of resources'.[19] This argument pictures the trade and environment conflict as an imaginary construct. I will argue that this characterisation of the trade–environment conflict is too simplistic, and that the friction between trade and environmental concerns represents a real and systemic dilemma, which cannot be ignored and requires creative institutional response. In support of this argument I will briefly review the recent economic research that considered the trade–environment question.[20] While this research does not provide a conclusive answer to the trade–environment dilemma, it points out, first, that this dilemma constitutes a real theoretical possibility. Second, while the results of the empirical studies are mixed, they nonetheless provide sufficient grounds for concern with respect to the environmental impacts of trade liberalisation (especially if one interprets these studies using a precautionary perspective).

The trade–environment problem can be examined through several perspectives. The first perspective looks at the way in which international trade influences the *domestic environment* of the trading parties; the second examines the way in which trade affects *transboundary ecological problems*.[21] The third perspective

[18] See Friends of the Earth (FoE), "Fools Gold . . ."—the General Agreement on Tariffs and Trade and the Threat of Unsustainable Development' (FoE, 1992); WWF's Trade and Investment Programme website, at: www.panda.org/about_wwf/what_we_do/policy/ trade_and_investment, and H Daly, 'From Adjustment to Sustainable Development: The Obstacle of Free Trade' (1992) 15 *Loyola LA International & Comparative LJ* 33.

[19] WTO, *Trade and the Environment in the GATT/WTO, Background Note by the WTO Secretariat for the High Level Symposium on Trade and Environment* (WTO, 15 March 1999) 7.

[20] For more detailed surveys see: SB Brunnermeier and A Levinson, 'Examining the Evidence on Environmental Regulations and Industry Location' (2004) 13 *Journal of Environmental & Development* 6; BR Copeland and MS Taylor, 'Trade, Growth, and the Environment' (2004) 42 *Journal of Economic* Literature 7; DI Stern, 'The Rise and Fall of the Environmental Kuznets Curve' (2004) 32 *World Development* 1419.

[21] Transboundary pollution can arise in two ways. First, it may represent the incidental result of industrial processes. The emissions of country A's power plants may affect—through acid rain for example—people in country B. Secondly, transboundary pollution can be the result of trade in hazardous products.

examines the link between transnational trade and *'global ecological resources'* (eg, the ozone layer, fish stocks, etc). These issues underpin many of the debates about the achievement of sustainable development.

The economic literature has tackled the question of the environmental impact of trade liberalisation by distinguishing between four causal effects.[22] The *scale* effect measures the ecological impact of the expansion in the scale of production, which is likely to occur with the transition to an open trading regime. *Ceteris paribus*, the scale effect is likely to prove damaging to the environment: if production and/or consumption of a product is polluting, an expansion in the global output of that product is likely to lead to greater environmental degradation. The *composition* effect examines the change in the composition of industry, which is triggered by the process of trade liberalisation, as countries *specialise* in sectors in which they enjoy a comparative advantage. Whether the ecological impact of this change is positive or negative depends on the nature of the specialisation (ie, whether it is geared toward more or less pollution-intensive sectors).

The *technological* effect examines how the technological changes, associated with the process of trade liberalisation, could influence the environment. It is usually assumed that these technological changes should, overall, be beneficial to the environment, whether through the introduction of cleaner production methods or through improved waste treatment methods. This hypothesis is supported by two different arguments. First, open economies should have greater access to foreign 'environmental' technologies. Secondly, the transition to an open market regime should lead to an increase in individual income, which, in turn, should generate a greater demand for 'environmental goods', such as clean air and uncontaminated water (generating steeper demand for 'clean technology'). Finally, the *regulatory effect* examines the way in which trade liberalisation affects local environmental standards. In this context one can distinguish between two conflicting trends. On the one hand, the anticipated increase in average income, as well as more extensive exposure to foreign regulatory methods, is likely to lead to increase in the demand for environmental control, pushing the government to adopt stricter environmental regulations. On the other hand, the 'race to the bottom' hypothesis suggests that free trade may induce a process by which countries will lower their environmental standards in order to gain competitive advantage.[23]

[22] Grossman and Krueger were probably the first to use this analytical framework in their study of the environmental impact of NAFTA: GM Grossman and AB Krueger, 'Environmental Impacts of a North American Free Trade Agreement' in PM Garber (ed), *The Mexico–U.S. Free Trade Agreement* (MIT Press, 1993) 14–15.

[23] See Daly above n 18, 36–7. Some of the economic literature treats the regulatory and technological effects as one effect. While this joint treatment makes some sense, because both effects depend to some extent on income, it may obscure the fact that pro-environmental technological change does not depend just on income-driven regulatory change, but also on non-regulatory processes.

Since each of these different effects can generate distinct environmental impacts all of them must be taken into account simultaneously. Resolving the trade–environment dilemma requires, then, an empirical evaluation, which would be sensitive to the way in which these varied effects interact in the unique context of a country/region and the ecological variable in question. So what does the economic research tell us? The picture generated by these studies is mixed. Cole and others examined the environmental impact of the Uruguay Round in terms of five air pollutants for a number countries/regions.[24] They concluded that 'trade liberalization may result in some degree of environmental damage, particularly in the developing regions, as a result of increased emissions of local air pollutants and perhaps globally for carbon dioxide emissions'.[25] Their findings regarding carbon emissions were confirmed in subsequent studies.[26]

However, other writers reached different conclusions (albeit examining the impact of trade on other types of pollution). Antweiler and others examined the impact of a policy of 'openness' on *sulphur dioxide concentrations*, relying on data from the Global Environment Monitoring Project.[27] Their estimates of scale and technique elasticities indicate that 'if openness to international markets raises both output and income by 1%, pollution concentrations fall by approximately 1%'.[28] Freer trade, according to Antweiler, is good for the environment.[29]

Several other studies examined the effect of trade liberalisation on specific countries, particularly in the developing regions. Overall, their findings indicate that a transition toward a more open global trading regime causes some environmental damage in the developing world.[30] Because the regulatory establishment in developing countries is generally weaker and the local industry is (on average) more pollution intensive, the economic expansion that follows the move toward a

[24] MA Cole *et al*, 'Trade Liberalisation and the Environment: the Case of the Uruguay Round' (1998) 21 *The World Economy* 337.

[25] *Ibid*, 347.

[26] See L Adkins and R Garbaccio, 'The Effects of the Proposed FTAA on Global Carbon Emissions: A General Equilibrium, Analysis' *Second World Congress of Environmental and Resource Economics* (Monterey, June 2002), available at http://weber.ucsd.edu/~carsonvs/papers/853.PDF; S Managi, 'Trade Liberalization and the Environment: Carbon Dioxide for 1960–1999' (2004) 17 *Economic Bulletin* 1.

[27] W Antweiler *et al*, *Is Free Trade Good For the Environment* (National Bureau of Economic Research August 1998).

[28] *Ibid*, 41.

[29] Ferrantino and Linkins reach similar conclusions with respect to the impact of trade liberalization on global toxic industrial emissions: MJ Ferrantinoand and LA Linkins, 'The Effect of Global Trade Liberalization on Toxic Emissions in Industry' (1999) 135(1) *Review of World Economics* 128.

[30] These findings should not be interpreted as giving support to the 'pollution haven' hypothesis. They reflect mostly changes in the local economy, such as changes in the make-up of the local industry, and increasing domestic demand for various pollution-intensive goods, and not the results of flight of polluting industries into developing countries. The reason there has not been such flight is probably due to the fact that those industries with the largest pollution abatement costs, and hence the largest motivation to relocate, also happen to be the least geographically mobile: J Ederington *et al*, *Footloose and Pollution Free* (National Bureau of Economic Research 2003) 13–14. See further, Copeland and Taylor, above n 20, 35, 48.

more open trading regime is more likely to increase the level of pollution.[31] Further, trade liberalisation may also have unexpected impacts. Thus, for example, a study of the environmental impacts of NAFTA showed how an increase in American exports of maize into Mexico had adverse ecological effects in both markets.[32] In the US the new export opportunities have provided additional support to unsustainable, mass-production, agricultural practices. In Mexico the liberalisation of the maize market led to a loss of bio-diversity both through out-migration of farmers with traditional knowledge and through the displacement of local corn varieties with other crops or with commercial hybrid seeds.[33]

The theoretical and empirical insights included in this expanding body of literature provide sufficient grounds for concern regarding the environmental effects of trade liberalisation and its consequences for sustainable development. This body of research demonstrates that there is a solid theoretical and empirical basis for the green critique.[34] If trade liberalisation can indeed be harmful to the environment there is good reason to spend resources in devising proper policy responses that could counteract it.

2. Discursive Cleavages

But it is wrong to view the trade–environment conflict just through the prism of the adverse tangible effects of trade-induced economic growth. It is also a crossroads of complex and conflicting discursive structures. Like the broader sustainable development discourse, the trade–environment debate is not governed by a single discursive system (with common and well-defined criteria for reaching understanding), but is, rather, the playground of multiple discourses and ideologies. Making the differences between these conflicting discourses more transparent is a necessary step in the attempt to alleviate the social frictions associated with the trade and environment conflict.

One way by which the rich discursive horizon which underlies the trade–environment conversation can be exposed is by looking at it through the lens of a distinct

[31] See D Wheeler, 'Beyond Pollution Havens' (2002) 2 *Global Environmental Politics* 1, 6; S Dessus and M Bussolo, 'Is There a Trade-off Between Trade Liberalization and Pollution Abatement: A Computable General Equilibrium Assessment Applied to Costa Rica' (1998) 20 *Journal of Policy Modelling* 11; J Beghin *et al*, 'Trade Integration, Environmental Degradation, and Public Health in Chile: Assessing the Linkages' (2002) 7 *Environment & Development Economics* 45.

[32] A Nadal and TA Wise, *The Environmental Costs of Agricultural Trade Liberalization: Mexico-U.S Maize Trade Under NAFTA* (Working Group on Development and Environment in the Americas, 2004).

[33] *Ibid*, 20.

[34] The current literature is limited in two important ways. First, it focuses on a limited number of pollutants. Second, it does not provide, in most cases, a complete cost-benefit analysis of the trade–environment problem (comparing the social costs of trade-induced environmental degradation, with the social benefits of free trade). These limitations reflect both the deep scarcity of environmental data and the difficulties in translating environmental data into monetary terms. Drawing policy conclusions from the available studies is therefore somewhat speculative, reflecting the intuitions and world-view of the observer.

problematic: the relationship between *society* and *nature*. The traditional construction of the *nature/society* duality insisted that nature could be of value—whether intrinsic or instrumental—only to the extent that it is of value to humans.[35] One of the major achievements of the modern 'environmental' movement has been to call the validity of this traditional conceptualisation into question. However, as the discussion below demonstrates, this common challenge has not produced a singular understanding of the nature/society duality (a common *environmental rationality*). Instead, it has created an assemblage of different visions, which produces competing interpretations of the trade–environment conflict.

Consider, first, the view of 'deep ecology'. The deep ecologists argue that the *nature/society* duality should be understood in terms of a new *transcendent, non-anthropocentric ethics*. The answer to the current ecological crisis lies, according to this view, in a different conception of nature, which gives nature a 'social role beyond being a means for human well-being'.[36] This trend of thought sees the major problem of modern society in the idea of 'domination' of nature, which informs all our political and economic institutions. In practical terms, the deep ecologists call for a complete withdrawal from the industrial system and the adoption of a pre-capitalist way of life.[37] For them, 'social asceticism' constitutes the only route by which the belief in the intrinsic value of nature can be given fulleffect.

Other ecological and moral thinkers reject the foregoing challenge to the long-established Kantian, anthropocentric morality. What we need, they argue, is simply to take more seriously the idea that what is 'good-for-man' depends on what is good for 'nature'. The ecological challenge is constructed, therefore, not as a demand for alternative 'ethics', but as a locus of *pragmatic dilemmas*: how to utilise (or exploit) nature more responsibly. This pragmatic vision provides the basis for a range of interpretations. Some (economic conservatives) take this view to mean that there is no need for a fundamental change in the basic *ethos* of modern society, with its strong reliance on technology and free-market structures, and its endless appetite for growth. In the eyes of neo-classical economics and conservative mercantilists the trade–environment conflict is a 'false dilemma': trade liberalisation cannot be harmful to the environment because it leads to more efficient use of resources and helps in generating the resources needed to protect the environment.[38] Other economic observers take a more sceptical view of the power of the 'market', and believe in the need to develop a more 'enlightened', or ecologically-sensitive, economic thought, which will be able to deal with the various maladies (eg, market failures, externalities) of the current economic system.[39]

[35] This point of view is the heritage of the Enlightenment tradition; see J Whitebook, 'The Problem of Nature in Habermas' (1979) 40 *Telos* 41.

[36] K Eder, *The Social Construction of Nature: A Sociology of Ecological Enlightenment* (Sage, 1996) 207.

[37] See eg A Naess, 'The Shallow and the Deep, Long-Range Ecology Movement: A Summary' (1983) 16 *Inquiry* 95.

[38] See WTO, above n 19, 7.

[39] See eg the various contributions in JM van den Bergh (ed), *Handbook of Environmental and Resource Economics* (Edward Elgar, 1999).

Yet, for others, the current ecological crisis is, in fact, a reflection of a deeper *political crisis*: our multiple environmental problems are seen as the inevitable result of, on the one hand, the failure of the political institutions of the modern democratic state to create mechanisms for fair deliberation, which could give voice to the *different constituents* of the polity (from marginal human communities to non-humans[40]). From this perspective ('eco-politics') the solution to the trade–environment conflict lies in the creation of a new political order.

These various visions of the nature/society dichotomy provide a different portrait of the trade–environment conflict. Thus, for those who accept the Kantian framework, the debate focuses on the *value* of free trade and the institutional framework that supports it *for humanity*. Trade liberalisation and the various institutions supporting it can be criticised only if it is shown that they are not sufficiently attentive to the environmental impact of international commerce, to the extent that it also has adverse impacts on the lives of human beings.

The idea of sustainable development, as it was interpreted in environmental economics, offers a model for balancing between the benefits of trade liberalisation and its adverse ecological impacts.[41] For non-Kantian observers such as deep ecologists and eco-socialists, the economic world view, and its vision of sustainability, does not form an acceptable solution to the trade–environment conflict because it leaves *unchallenged* the *basic paradigms* and *social structures* that dominate the contemporary society. Accepting this 'starting point' will bar any discussion of the radical reforms that these non-anthropocentric viewpoints call for.[42] For these non-Kantian observers, the trade–environment conversation is seen as an opening to a broader debate about the structure of human society and its relationship with the natural (non-human) environment.

3. The Role of International Trade Law

What is the place of law in this disputed discursive landscape? From the perspective of deep ecology, international trade law may be useful only to the extent that it can contribute to its own destruction, opening the door for a completely different governance structure—a new global political order. Merely introducing

[40] See eg B Latour, 'To Modernise or to Ecologise? That is the Question' in N Castree and B Willems-Braun (eds), *Remaking Reality: Nature at the Millenium* (Routledge, 1998); M Gadgil and R Guha, *Ecology and Equity: the Use and Abuse of Nature in Contemporary India* (Penguin, 1995) 118–20.

[41] Modern environmental economics defines a sustainable path as one that is both efficient and non-decreasing in utility over time: see RL Revesz and RN Stavins, *Environmental Law and Public Policy* (Resources for the Future May 2004) 6.

[42] For a different vision of sustainability, closer to the view of deep ecology, see: Daly, above n 18. For Daly sustainable development means 'living within environmental constraints of absorptive and regenerative capacities': *ibid*, 41. This understanding of sustainability is based on the idea of keeping the eco-system carrying capacity—rather than utility—intact. See, further H Daly 'Sustainable Development: Definitions, Principles, Policies' Invited Address (World Bank, 30 Apr 2002) 1–2, available at http://info.worldbank.org/etools/VoD/PresentationView.asp? PID=5530/EID=269.

changes to the current system (eg, 'greening' the WTO) will not suffice, because this system is structurally 'corrupt'. However, from the perspective of both eco-politics and environmental economics, law presents an interesting playground. Law has long-lasting expertise in representing and giving life to non-speaking objects—from firms (corporate law) to the dead (inheritance law). As such, it can provide a forum in which nature can be given voice, and actively participate in a dialogue with humans. Law, in other words, can create the institutional setting necessary for multi-party conversation, leading to actual deals. The policy challenge lies in designing institutional mechanisms that could realise this potential. From the perspective of environmental economics, law offers a mechanism for transforming its models and guidelines for balancing trade and environment interests into normative prescriptions.

A further unique feature of law is its capacity to resolve disputes between competing world-views without making a clear ideological commitment. This capacity is valuable both because of the deep cleavages between the distinct schools of thought associated with the trade–environment conflict, and because neither of them provides a definite algorithm for resolving this conflict. One of the major mechanisms through which the law performs this 'neutral' arbitration function is by using fluid concepts, which can acquire different meanings depending on context, timing and external pressures.[43] In our context, it is the concept of sustainable development—with its deep vagueness and malleability—which provides the law with the discursive freedom necessary to develop these transient bridges. International trade law can build, in that context, on the ways in which this idea is invoked in other domains.[44]

My foregoing observations were driven by an interest in the possible contribution of international trade law to the resolution of the trade–environment conflict, considered from different perspectives. But in analysing the ecological sensitivity of international trade law one can also adopt a more detached perspective, focusing not on how different systems of trade/economic law can be utilised to resolve this conflict, but on decoding the institutional and historical idiosyncrasies that determine the approach of these systems to ecological concerns.

D. From Friction to Synergy: Can Trade Institutions Promote Environmental Cooperation?

The idea of regime-linkage, which builds on insights from modern environmental and institutional economics, provides an interesting response to the

[43] See O Perez, 'The Institutionalization of Inconsistency: From Fluid Concepts to Random Walk' in O Perez and G Teubner (eds), *Paradoxes and Inconsistencies in Law* (Hart Publishing, 2006).

[44] See eg Rio Declaration on Environment and Development 1992, 31 ILM 874; UN Conference on Environment and Development (UNCED), *Agenda 21: Earth's Action Plan* (UNCED, 1992).

trade–environment conflict. Law has an important role to play in the process of putting this idea into effect. What is interesting in the idea of regime-linkage is that it not only provides a mechanism for comparing between trade and environmental interests, by acknowledging the economic value of global ecological assets (through the use of economic valuation techniques), but also is able to translate this insight into concrete institutional proposals. However, as argued below, this idea also suffers from certain blind spots.

The argument for linkage is based on two key insights regarding the difficulties of resolving transnational environmental dilemmas.[45] First, it is difficult to provide collective solutions to transnational ecological dilemmas because of their inherent *public-good* characteristic. In negotiating solutions to problems such as climate change some countries may prefer to free-ride. That is, countries may prefer to profit from the public good—stable climate—without paying the associated costs, relying instead on the joint efforts of other countries. This is possible because the ecological benefits associated with these agreements are not excludable.[46] This feature of environmental negotiations goes a long way toward explaining the weakness of transnational environmental institutions. In a world without a central authority free-riding cannot be deterred through hierarchical control. A further difficulty concerns the asymmetries among countries, with respect to both their moral preferences regarding ecological and economic issues and the way in which their economies may be affected by different ecological problems (and the associated policy responses).

Trade law and trade institutions can play a positive role in resolving these difficulties through the mechanism of linkage. There are three major paths through which linkage can assist in resolving part of the aforementioned difficulties. First, linkage can resolve the problem of reaching an international agreement in a world without a central authority by allowing countries to use the surplus enforcement power that may be available in one policy domain to discipline co-operation in other domains.[47] Linkage provides a method for aggregating available enforcement power, allowing for its more efficient allocation to additional policy domains. Second, issue linkage may be used to resolve the problem of free-riding also by linking the negotiations on a regional or global public good to negotiations on

[45] The idea of linkage has less to say about the possible role of trade measures in resolving purely local problems. For a discussion of that issue see Parts E and F and Perez, above n 16, chs 3 and 4.

[46] I Kaul *et al*, 'Defining Global Public Goods' in I Kaul *et al* (eds), *Global Public Goods* (Oxford UP, 1999) 2.

[47] I use the idea of surplus enforcement power in two ways. First, it can reflect disparities in institutional capacities (eg, denoting the extra powers of the WTO dispute settlement system). Second, it can also be used in a game-theoretic way, which considers this notion in the context of infinitely repeated Prisoner's Dilemma interaction. Surplus enforcement power is defined in terms of disparities between domains with respect to the difference between the *expected losses* from punishment (in reply to defection) and the *expected gains* from one-off defection (free-riding), as they occur in each domain. See generally G Spagnolo, 'Issue Linkage, Delegation, and International Policy Cooperation', CEPR Working Paper, 2001.

another issue which has the characteristic of a club good (that is a good whose benefits are provided only to club members, and thus cannot be reaped by free-riders). Paradigmatic examples of international clubs are the European Union, NAFTA and the WTO. The intuition behind this proposal is that the incentives to free-ride on the non-excludable benefits of the global public good can be offset by the incentives to appropriate the excludable benefits of the club good.[48]

Finally, issue linkage can resolve the problem of asymmetric preferences and varied geo-economic conditions, by allowing countries to link together issues in which they have dissimilar interests. Institutional linkage operates in this context as an indirect form of side payment. If co-operation on an individual issue benefits country A but hurts B (or is simply not of interest to B), then linkage allows country A to compensate B by offering co-operation on a different issue that benefits B. The mechanism of linkage uses the mechanism of free exchange to bridge between different world-views regarding the social and moral value of ecological resources. The use of linkage as a form of side payment when there are asymmetric benefits across countries is especially important in the context of the relations between Northern and Southern countries.[49]

The idea of linkage, and the various institutional mechanisms associated with it, provides a possible road map for bridging between the trade and environmental domains. However, setting the linkage modules explored above against the discursive frictions that were discussed in the previous section raises several questions, which must be considered. One difficulty emerges from the fact that all the forms of linkage explored above depend on the idea that nature, or environmental damage, can be commodified or monetised. Thus, for example, the idea that linkage could facilitate barter between trade concessions and environmental commitments is based on the assumption that the value of these exchanged commitments can be calculated and compared using common monetary values.

The assumption that a monetary value can be assigned to all aspects of the natural environment is problematic in several senses.[50] First, there is a tension between this assumption and the visions of deep ecology and political ecology. While this framework gives nature a voice in the trade universe, this voice is filtered by economic calculations, which are embedded in an anthropocentric world-view. The radical thesis of these two ecological world-views—that nature should be viewed

[48] For a study of this aspect of the linkage question see B Buchner *et al*, 'Back to Kyoto? Us Participation and the Linkage between R&D and Climate Cooperation', CESifo Working Paper Series No 688, 2002.

[49] This possible role of treaty-linkage is explored, eg, by L Abrego *et al*, 'Trade and Environment: Bargaining Outcomes from Linked Negotiations' (2001) 9 *Review of International Economics* 414. See also H Sigman, 'Does Trade Promote Environmental Coordination? Pollution in International Rivers' (2004) 3 *Contributions to Economic Analysis & Policy Sciences* 1.

[50] Although there has been significant progress on the question of valuing nature and translating environmental damage into monetary terms. See eg SC Farber *et al*, 'Economic and Ecological Concepts for Valuing Ecosystem Services' (2002) 41 *Ecological Economics* 375.

as an equal member of the global moral and political community—is therefore left unchallenged. But the idea of linkage is also problematic from the perspective of classical mercantilism because the kind of exchange it calls for—between tangible trade concessions and ecological commitments whose economic value is uncertain and even speculative—is seen as artificial and problematic. A further problem concerns the possibility that the institutional mechanisms responsible for implementing the idea of linkage will be captured by narrow political forces, and be used to promote particularistic (rather than collective) interests.

The idea that there could be synergic linkage between trade and sustainable development can be found in several international instruments. Thus, for example, the 1992 Rio Declaration on Environment and Development urges states to 'promote a supportive and international economic system that would lead to economic growth and sustainable development in all countries, to better address the problems of environmental degradation'.[51] Similarly, Agenda 21, adopted at the 1992 Earth Summit, states that the 'international community should provide a supportive international climate for achieving environment and development goals' by, among other things, 'promoting sustainable development through trade liberalization' and 'making trade and environment mutually supportive'.[52] In the same spirit, when the GATT was amended in 1994 and the WTO established, sustainable development was incorporated into the WTO's objectives.[53] However, none of these instruments offers a detailed institutional plan for realising the idea of linkage, nor do they offer a satisfactory response to the foregoing concerns.

While the notion of linkage constitutes a compelling idea, implementing it requires deeper analysis of the various issues noted above. At this point it should be useful to turn our gaze to a concrete institutional setting. The following sections offer a detailed analysis of the response of the WTO legal system to the trade–environment challenge, exploring it in view of the frictions and synergies, outlined in the foregoing sections.

E. The State of Play: The Approach of Wto Law to the Trade-Environment Conflict

1. Introduction

The WTO regime, involving about 150 member nations, actually comprises a number of discrete trade agreements dealing with trade in services, agricultural products, financial measures, intellectual property rights and much more. But a

[51] Above n 44, Principle 12
[52] *Ibid*, 2, section 2.3.
[53] Preamble, Agreement Establishing the World Trade Organization, 15 Apr 1994, above n 7.

number of fundamental principles and rules run throughout these agreements, evolving from the original GATT of 1947.[54] At the core of the GATT–WTO system are two non-discrimination principles: the most-favoured nation (MFN), established in Article I of the GATT, and the national treatment principle, established in Article III. Article I, the most favoured nation clause, requires WTO Members to grant to the products of other Members treatment no less favourable than that accorded to the products of any other country. The MFN principle extends to customs, duties and rules connected with importation and exportation. Article III, the National Treatment principle, stipulates that once goods have entered a market, they must be treated no less favourably than equivalent domestically produced goods (in terms, for example, of local taxes and rules regulating the selling and distribution of goods). Article XI addresses the elimination of quantitative restrictions introduced by countries on the importation or exportation of products. It prohibits such restrictions with the objective of encouraging countries to convert them into tariffs, a more transparent and less trade-distorting instrument.

The 'General Exceptions' provision of the GATT, Article XX, comprises various conditional exceptions to the GATT obligations, including Articles I, III and XI. Article XX's sub-sections (b) and (g) provide a framework for deliberating both *inward-oriented* and *extra-territorial* trade–environment conflicts. The relevant provisions state:

> Subject to the requirement that such measures are not applied in a manner which would constitute a means of arbitrary or unjustifiable discrimination between countries where the same conditions prevail, or a disguised restriction on international trade, nothing in this Agreement shall be construed to prevent the adoption or enforcement by any contracting party of measures:. . .
>
> (b) necessary to protect human, animal or plant life or health;
>
> . . .
>
> (g) relating to the conservation of exhaustible natural resources if such measures are made effective in conjunction with restrictions on domestic production or consumption"
>
> . . .

The burden of establishing that an Article XX exception applies is placed upon the party asserting it as a defence.

The WTO regime includes a system of compulsory binding dispute settlement.[55] Where disputes cannot be resolved by consultation and negotiation, they

[54] See generally Jackson, above n 2.

[55] WTO Understanding on Rules and Procedures Governing the Settlement of Disputes, 1994, in World Trade Organisation, above n 7.

are adjudicated upon by dispute settlement panels and appealed to an Appellate Body. In the event of a party's non-compliance with a panel or Appellate Body ruling, it can be subjected to sanctions in the form of compensation and suspension of trade concessions.[56]

The establishment of the WTO has changed the structure of the legal deliberation of trade–environment disputes because of the creation of a new regime, regulating the field of non-tariff barriers. The adoption of the Agreement on the Application of Sanitary and Phytosanitary Measures and the Agreement on Technical Barriers to Trade meant that most of the *inward oriented* cases, which under the GATT were considered under Article XX(b), are now considered through the prism of these two agreements.[57] These agreements raise new kinds of questions, mainly because they impose broader restrictions on the regulative capacities of WTO Members (by imposing new obligations such as risk assessment). Because of limits of space, this chapter considers only the jurisprudence of the GATT/WTO with respect to Article XX.[58]

Principally, two types of trade–environment conflicts arise within the WTO system. The first type involves environmentally motivated trade measures, which are *inward-oriented*; that is, governmental measures whose objective is the protection of a domestic ecological unit or the health and safety of the local population. The second type of conflict is characterised by an *extra-territorial* motivation. These conflicts are triggered by trade measures whose objective lies outside the territory of the regulating state; the target of such measures can be an ecological asset that is located within the borders of another state but has a global significance (eg, the Brazilian tropical forests), a common access resource (eg, the high seas) or a migratory species (eg, sea turtles). The term '*outward-oriented*' is used to describe this type of conflict.

These two types of disputes produce quite different legal dilemmas. The disputes involving inward-oriented measures raise the question of the freedom of WTO members to determine the environmental regime that will persist within their borders.[59] The key question in this context is to what extent the WTO limits this freedom. '*Outward-oriented*' disputes raise a different question: the freedom of WTO members to respond with trade measures to environmental policies of their trading partners, which they find problematic—even if these policies are otherwise consistent with WTO rules. These trade measures are usually triggered by a production externality, taking place outside the borders of the importing

[56] See M Bütler and H. Hauser, 'The WTO Dispute Settlement System: First Assessment from an Economic Perspective' (2000) 16 *Journal of Law Economics & Organization* 503.

[57] But not all cases. See eg *European Communities—Measures Affecting the Prohibition of Asbestos and Asbestos-Containing Products*, WT/DS135, 18 Sept 2000 (Appellate Body Report) ('*EC–Asbestos*').

[58] For a discussion of the SPS and TBT Agreements, and their role in the trade-environment conflict, see Perez, above n 16, ch 4.

[59] Inward-oriented measures involve both *production standards* (eg, emission controls) and standards relating to *consumption* (eg, recycling laws or regulations controlling the sale and distribution of products).

country—eg, incidental killing of dolphins or production practices that endanger the ozone layer. The focus of these disputes, then, is on the adverse ecological aspects of the *production method* of the imported product.[60] The main question raised by these cases is the consistency of such indirect interference in the way in which foreign products are produced with the rules of the WTO (and previously the GATT). Since outward-oriented measures cannot influence directly the production processes which take place abroad; they are based on trade restrictions that influence local consumption choices.

The resolution of these disputes within the WTO can become more complex if the disputed trade measure is authorised by an external regime such as a Multilateral Environmental Agreements (MEA). An increasing number of MEAs use trade mechanisms to achieve their objectives.[61] In certain MEAs, such as the Basel Convention,[62] trade measures serve to discourage or prohibit the transfer from one nation to the other of hazardous waste. Like the Basel Convention, the Convention on International Trade in Endangered Species (CITES)[63] also sanctions the use of trade measures to achieve its objectives. The CITES aims to ensure that the international trade in specimens of species of wild fauna and flora does not threaten the conservation status of the species concerned. Thus, trade in certain species is prohibited or carefully regulated. Other MEAs use a variety of trade and economic measures to encourage states to become parties to the agreement. The Montreal Protocol[64] and the Kyoto Protocol,[65] dealing with ozone depleting chemicals and fossil fuels respectively, use trade measures in this way. The relationship between trade restrictions in MEAs and the rules of the WTO is still unresolved. It has been on the WTO negotiation agenda since the Fourth Ministerial Conference, held at Doha, Qatar, in 2001. This question is considered again in the sections below.

2. The Ground-breaking Decisions of the Appellate Body in the Shrimp Case

(a) Background and general observations

The WTO–GATT trade and environment jurisprudence has a long history, stretching back to the early 1990s. Two early disputes—the US–Mexico *Tuna—Dolphin*

60 Theoretically these disputes can also arise in the context of concerns over the adverse effects (still, strictly foreign) of the consumption or end-of-life treatment of certain products (eg, the possible global impact of the disposal of hazardous waste in the Amazonian forests).

61 L Schalatek (ed), *Trade and Environment, the WTO, and MEAs: Facets of a Complex Relationship* (Heinrich Böll Foundation, 2001), available at www.boell.org/docs/WTO-MEA.pdf.

62 Convention on the Control of Transboundary Movements of Hazardous Wastes and their Disposal (Basel Convention) 1988, 28 ILM 657.

63 Convention on International Trade in Endangered Species of Wild Fauna and Flora 1973, 993 UNTS 243.

64 Protocol on Substances That Deplete the Ozone Layer 1987, 26 ILM 1550.

65 Protocol to the Framework Convention on Climate Change 1997, (1998) 37 ILM 22.

dispute,[66] and the U.S–Thailand dispute regarding the *Importation of and Internal Taxes on Cigarettes*[67]—have become the symbol of the trade system's inattentiveness to environmental values. The *Tuna—Dolphin* dispute was triggered by a US programme, which sought to reduce the number of dolphins that were killed as an incidental result of fishing of yellowfin tuna using purse-seine nets (mainly in the Eastern Tropical Pacific Ocean). In order to convince other countries to adopt fishing techniques which were less harmful to dolphins the US government introduced a *ban* on the importation of fish caught with fishing technology that resulted in the incidental killing of dolphins. Two GATT panels which heard this case ruled that the US regulations were inconsistent with the rules of the GATT. The US measure being a direct import prohibition, was seen as inconsistent with Article XI(1) prohibition against quantitative restrictions. The panels also ruled that the US measure did not qualify for the protection of Article XX (for reasons clarified below).[68] This ruling was interpreted as a general prohibition on the introduction of trade measures targeting the process and production methods ('PPMs') of imported products.

The *Thai—Cigarettes* case focused on certain Thai measures that limited the ability of foreign cigarettes producers (mostly US companies) to penetrate the Thai tobacco market. The Thai authorities invoked Article XX(b), arguing that these measures had a positive public health impact, because of the contracting effect they had on the tobacco market (and on cigarette consumption). The Panel rejected this argument, ruling that the Thai measures were inconsistent with GATT's Article XI(1),[69] and did not qualify for the defence of Article XX. The Panel noted that while measures designed to reduce the consumption of cigarettes fell within the scope of Article XX(b), because smoking constituted a serious risk to human health, the Thai measures did not meet the 'necessity' condition of Article XX(b) and, as such, could not enjoy its protection. The Panel noted that the Thai authorities could have used alternative policy measures, such as labelling, disclosure requirements, restrictions on advertisement and taxes, which, in its view, were as efficient (in terms of Thailand public-health objectives) as the measures under dispute, and were not inconsistent with the GATT. Both rulings reflected deep insensitivity to the adverse ecological and social aspects of

[66] *United States—Restrictions On Imports of Tuna ('Tuna I') (*1991) 30 ILM 1594; and *United States—Restrictions On Imports of Tuna ('Tuna II')* (1994), 33 ILM 839.

[67] *Thailand—Restrictions on Importation of and Internal Taxes on Cigarettes* (*'Thai—Cigarettes'*), GATT Doc DS10/R - 37S/200, 7 Nov 1990.

[68] The Panels also rejected the US attempt to justify the measures under Art III, as legitimate border tax adjustment. For a more detailed discussion of the Tuna–Dolphin cases, see Perez, above n 16, 60–65.

[69] Para 67 of the Panel's decision.

trade liberalisation, and disregard of the synergies between the trade and environmental domains.[70]

The Appellate Body's two decisions in the *Shrimp—Turtles* dispute[71] have broken new ground, by breaking the mould of the GATT's mercantilist culture.[72] The *Shrimp* decisions offer a broader and more responsive reading of the WTO mandate, relying, among other things, on the inclusion of the concept of sustainable development in the WTO Agreement.[73] These decisions—which reflect a clear exercise of judicial autonomy—signal a stronger institutional willingness to incorporate ecological considerations into the legal universe of the WTO. However, this willingness remains bounded by the heritage of the GATT and is still facing substantial opposition both within the organisation and beyond.

The *Shrimp* dispute was triggered by an import ban that was introduced by the US authorities on the importation of shrimp which were harvested in a way that endangered the lives of sea turtles. The US regulations required exporting countries to adopt, as a condition for obtaining an export certificate, a conservatory programme including a requirement to use ecologically friendly fishing technology (ie, Turtle Excluder Devices or 'TEDs'), supported by credible enforcement system.[74] The Appellate Body concluded that the US import ban on shrimp was not consistent with GATT Article XI, being a quantitative restriction on trade, and could not be justified under Article XX.[75] The second *Shrimp* ruling was triggered by a complaint by Malaysia accusing the US of failing properly to implement the recommendations of the Appellate Body. This complaint was deliberated according to the

[70] Thus, the *Tuna* Panels did not recognise the difficulties of negotiating international environmental agreements, and the role that the GATT can play in overcoming them. The *Thai—Cigarettes* Panel down-played the health risks associated with the liberalisation of the cigarettes marker, demonstrating a too optimistic belief in the capacities of national regulatory bodies. Consequent studies showed that the market share of US cigarettes increased dramatically in countries that have opened their markets following US pressure, and, further, that *per capita* cigarette consumption was 10% higher than it would have been absent liberalisation; see FJ Chaloupka and A Laixuthai, *US Trade Policy and Cigarette Smoking in Asia* (National Bureau of Economic Research April 1996).

[71] *United States—Import Prohibition of Certain Shrimp and Shrimp Products*, WT/DS58/R, 12 May 1998 (Panel Report), WT/DS58/AB/R, 12 Oct 1998 (Appellate Body Report); *United States—Import Prohibition of Certain Shrimp and Shrimp Products—Recourse to Article 21.5 by Malaysia*, WT/DS58/RW, 15 June 2001 (Panel Report), WT/DS58/AB/RW, 22 Oct 2001 (Appellate Body Report), henceforth, the *first* and *second Shrimp* reports/rulings.

[72] With its obsession with market access and narrow understanding of welfare. See, further P Krugman, 'What Should Trade Negotiators Negotiate About?' (1997) 35 *Journal of Economics Literature* 113, 114; Perez, above n 16, 51–3.

[73] The preamble to the WTO Agreement states that the organisation of the trade relations between WTO Members should allow 'for the optimal use of the world's resources in accordance with the objective of sustainable development, seeking both to protect and preserve the environment and to enhance the means for doing so in a manner consistent with their respective needs and concerns at different levels of economic development'.

[74] 1996 Guidelines, 17344, 61 Fed Reg 17342, 19 Apr 1996. In order to simplify the presentation, some of the details of the US programme were omitted.

[75] First *Shrimp* Report, above n 71, paras 187–188.

procedure set out in Article 21(5) of the Dispute Resolution Understanding.[76] The complaint challenged the measures that were taken by the US to implement the Appellate Body decision, focusing, in particular, on the Revised Guidelines, which were issued by the US in July 1999.[77] The Appellate Body rejected the Malaysian complaint and upheld the Panel's finding that the US's revised regulatory framework was being applied in a manner that met the requirements of Article XX.[78]

In the first *Shrimp* ruling the Appellate Body reconstructed the normative hierarchy of the WTO by creating parity between the environmental exceptions included in Article XX and the substantive obligations of the GATT (eg, Articles I and III).[79] The Appellate Body rejected the Panel's attempt to reintroduce to the WTO legal system, through the interpretation of the introductory section of Article XX—the chapeau, a pro-trade preference (in the spirit of the *Tuna—Dolphin* decisions). The Panel ruled that measures (such as unilateral trade embargos) which undermine the WTO multilateral trading system must be regarded as not within the scope of measures permitted under the chapeau of Article XX,[80] a formulation similar to the one used by the *Tuna* Panels.[81] The Appellate Body disagreed. It noted that the interpretation of the chapeau should *not* be governed by the narrow goal of maintaining the multilateral trading system, emphasising the importance of the idea of sustainable development in that context.[82] The main goal of the chapeau, the Appellate Body stated, is to prevent the abuse of the exceptions of Article XX;[83] it is, in fact, 'one expression of the principle of *good faith*'.[84] The chapeau reflects the necessity to strike a balance between these competing rights.[85] The Appellate Body emphasised in this context that a failure to comply with one of the general obligations of the GATT cannot, in itself, prevent a Member from invoking Article XX successfully, because such interpretation would deprive Article XX of any practical meaning, denying the idea that Article XX environmental exceptions have an independent value.[86] The

[76] Under Art 21.5 a panel is called to review the measures taken to implement the Panels or Appellate Body rulings. Second *Shrimp* Report (Appellate Body), above n 71, at para 2.

[77] Revised Guidelines for the Implementation of Section 609 of Public Law 101–162 Relating to the Protection of Sea Turtles in Shrimp Trawl Fishing Operations (the 'Revised Guidelines'), US Department of State, 64 Federal Register no 130, 8 July 1999, Public Notice 3086, 36946.

[78] Second *Shrimp* Report, above n 71, paras 153–54.

[79] See also *United States—Standards for Reformulated and Conventional Gasoline*, WT/DS2/AB/R, 29 Apr 1996 (Appellate Body Report) ('Reformulated Gasoline'), 17–18.

[80] First *Shrimp* Report, above n 71, paras 7.44 and 7.49.

[81] See *United States—Restrictions On Imports of Tuna ('Tuna I')*, (1991) 30 ILM 159, para 5.27; *United States—Restrictions On Imports of Tuna ('Tuna II')*, (1994) 33 ILM 839, para 5.26, and First *Shrimp* Report, above n 71, paras 7.46.

[82] First *Shrimp* Report, above n 71, paras 116 and 155. The Appellate Body made a similar comment with respect to the interpretation of Art XX(g), at paras 129–31.

[83] *Ibid*, para 151.

[84] *Ibid*, para 158.

[85] *Ibid*, paras 156, 159.

[86] *Ibid*, para 150.

Appellate Body's general ruling was embedded in a new framework for interpreting Article XX, based on a two-tiered model.[87] According to this model, to be accorded the protection of Article XX a measure must not only come under one of the particular exceptions listed in Article XX; it must also satisfy the requirements imposed by the opening clause of Article XX—the chapeau.[88]

(b) Article XX(b) and XX(g)

The Appellate Body accepted the US provisional claim under Article XX(g), finding that the US scheme satisfied Article XX(g)'s three conditions. The *first condition* requires that the measure in dispute shall target 'exhaustible natural resources'; sea turtles, the Appellate Body noted, meet this condition.[89] The *second element* of Article XX(g)—'relating to the conservation of exhaustible natural resources'—is a causal condition, focusing on the relationship between the disputed measure and the policy goal it purports to serve. The Appellate Body examined whether the US scheme is 'reasonably related to the ends', that is, to the goal of conserving sea turtles.[90] Despite the fact that the US measures sought to prevent the incidental take of sea turtles *indirectly*, through the imposition of an import ban the Appellate Body found that the US scheme satisfied this requirement. The Appellate Body found that the requirement to use TEDs by commercial shrimp trawling vessels was 'directly connected with the policy of conservation of sea turtles', relying on the experts' testimony regarding the efficacy of TEDs in protecting sea turtles.[91] The *third element* of Article XX(g), is an *'even-handedness'* requirement, according to which the disputed measure should be 'made effective in conjunction with restrictions on domestic production or consumption'. Since the requirement to use ecologically friendly fishing technology applied to US shrimp trawlers, as well as to foreign vessels, the Appellate Body decided that US measure satisfied this requirement.[92]

The *Shrimp* ruling did not discuss Article XX(b), which provides provisional protection to measures 'necessary to protect human, animal or plant life or health'. The core of this provision—the necessity condition—was interpreted in *EC—Asbestos* as requiring the defendant to demonstrate, first, that there is no alternative measure which it could reasonably be expected to employ and which is not inconsistent with other GATT provision, and, secondly, in those cases where a measure consistent with other GATT provisions is not reasonably available, that it has chosen, among the measures reasonably available to it, that which entails the least degree of inconsistency with other GATT provisions.[93] In *EC—Asbestos* the

[87] *Ibid*, para 118.
[88] See *Reformulated Gasoline* decision, above n 79, 22.
[89] First *Shrimp* Report, above n 71, paras 127–134.
[90] First *Shrimp* Report, above n 71, paras 141.
[91] *Ibid*, para 140.
[92] *Ibid*, paras 143, 145.
[93] *EC-Asbestos*, above n 57, para 171.

Appellate Body showed willingness to relax the causal standard of Article XX(b) by noting that, in evaluating the element of necessity, a panel can also take into consideration the importance of the common interests or values protected by the disputed trade measure, and that "the more vital or important [the] common interests or values pursued, the easier it would be to accept as 'necessary' measures designed to achieve those ends".[94] By creating a link between the 'pursued value' of the measure and the 'necessity' condition, this ruling extends the judicial discretion in making Article XX(b) causal determinations.

(c) The Interpretation of the Chapeau in the Shrimp Ruling

After concluding that the US regulatory scheme satisfied the requirements of Article XX(g), the Appellate Body considered whether the US scheme, as it was applied in practice, met the requirements of the Article XX chapeau. The Appellate Body found that it did not. It noted, first, that while the US scheme permitted a degree of flexibility with respect to the determination of comparability between the exporting countries' policies and those of the US, this flexibility has been effectively eliminated. In implementing the 1996 Guidelines the US officials required the exporting countries to adopt essentially the same regulatory programme as that in force within the US, *disregarding* the possibility that different conditions may occur in those countries.[95] The Appellate Body further noted the 'failure of the United States to engage the appellees, as well as other Members exporting shrimp to the United States, in serious, across-the-board negotiations with the objective of concluding bilateral or multilateral agreements for the protection and conservation of sea turtles, before enforcing the import prohibition against the shrimp exports of those other Members'.[96] Finally, the Appellate Body noted that in applying its regulatory scheme the US has discriminated among various countries desiring certification.[97]

The US administration implemented the Appellate Body recommendations in new Guidelines which were issued in 1999, and by making further attempts to negotiate an international environmental agreement. A renewed attempt to challenge the US regulatory scheme was rejected by the Appellate Body in subsequent proceedings.

[94] *Ibid*, para 172.
[95] First *Shrimp* Report, above n 71, para 164.
[96] *Ibid*, para 166.
[97] The Appellate Body noted that 'far greater efforts to transfer that technology successfully were made to certain exporting countries—basically the fourteen wider Caribbean/western Atlantic countries—than to other exporting countries, including the appellees' (*ibid*, para 175).

2. Implications of the *Shrimp* Case for Extending the Linkage between the WTO and the Environmental Realm

The Appellate Body's innovative reading of Article XX reflects a deep recognition of the linkage between the trade and environmental domains, and a willingness to give this linkage a legal effect. In the second *Shrimp* ruling, the Appellate Body accepted as legitimate the imposition of an effective embargo by the US against certain shrimp producing countries (mainly from East Asia), as a mean to pressurise these countries to join a multilateral effort to promote the conservation of sea-turtles. By that, the Appellate Body has recognised the seminal role that trade measures can play in securing participation in and compliance with multilateral environmental agreements, acknowledging that the conclusion of multilateral environmental agreements may be thwarted by 'free-riding', and that the threat of trade sanctions may be necessary in order to deter such behaviour.

The Appellate Body laid down several conditions, which must be satisfied by a trade measure if it is to receive the protection of Article XX (which I call the *good faith protocol* of Article XX). The conditions consist of the following obligations: a requirement to *explore* the possibility of solving the environmental problem through a multilateral agreement rather than unilaterally; the measure in question should be applied in a transparent, flexible and even-handed manner—a *'due process' requirement*; any provision of technical assistance should be pursued on a *non-discriminatory basis*; and, finally, an obligation to consider the *incremental costs* that the environmental programme may generate, both for the domestic manufacturers and for the foreign exporters as a result of the measure.[98]

It is important to point out, however, the differences between the *Shrimp* ruling, and the economics-inspired models of linkage discussed above. The two forms of linkage which are relevant to our discussion involve, first, the utilisation of the greater enforcement capacities of one regime to facilitate co-operation in another regime and, second, conditioning the access to one regime, with 'club-good' features, with a requirement to contribute to the production of a public good that is the subject of another regime. The Appellate Body's decision is much more modest in what it authorises. It merely allows one country to suspend some of the trade concessions that it has previously negotiated with another country. Despite the narrow scope of the Appellate Body's decision, the rationale of its decision can be used to justify broader actions, which are closer in their structure to those envisaged in the theoretical literature.

To identify these possible extensions we need to understand the *ratio decidendi* of the *Shrimp* case. The *Shrimp* ruling dealt with a relatively narrow environmental

[98] The first three requirements are based on the decisions of the Appellate Body in the *Shrimp* case above n 71. The last obligation is based on the Appellate Body decision in the *Reformulated Gasoline* case, above n 79, at 28. For a more detailed exposition of this argument, see Perez, above n 16, 82.

dilemma—the conservation of an endangered migratory species,[99] and focused on the difficulties of forging a new Multilateral Environmental Agreement (MEA). It was triggered by a unilateral trade measure which was initiated by the US without formal legal backing from an international legal authority (eg, from an MEA).[100] One possible extension questions the applicability of the *Shrimp* ruling to cases involving *pure global public goods*, such as problems relating to the atmosphere. This extension seems to follow naturally from the case reasoning.[101] A second possible direction concerns extending the *Shrimp* ruling to a *group of countries acting together*. Such extension seems consistent with the logic of the decision (as long as these countries satisfy, collectively, the 'good-faith' protocol depicted above). This possible extension may be very important in real life, because, given the current asymmetries that characterise the global economy, pressurising big players such as the US or the EU to collaborate on some environmental cause, can happen, if at all, only through the concerted action of several countries.

A further question involves the extension of the *Shrimp* ruling from the *negotiation* phase to the *post-contractual* phase. While the free-riding problematic is most visible at the *pre-contractual* phase, similar difficulties can arise after the conclusion of an MEA, both with respect to non-signatories that free-ride on the efforts of contributing parties, and with respect to members that fail to comply with the provisions of the MEA. This scenario raises the question of the legality of a trade measure that was initiated in order to force non-signatories to join the agreement or in order to force a non-complying party to fulfil its commitments. Such measures may be authorised by the MEA or reflect a private initiative.[102] Whether such measures can be justified under the *Shrimp* ruling may be open to debate.[103] On the one hand, if it is legitimate to use a unilateral trade measure in order to secure participation in a multilateral effort to resolve a global ecological problem (the *Shrimp* case), it is hard to see why it should not be legitimate to invoke this tool in order to secure participation in or compliance with the provisions of an existing agreement. On the other hand, one can argue that once an agreement has entered into force, its parties should abide by its provisions, including those governing the issues of compliance and dispute resolution. Thus, if the trade measures in dispute were not authorised by the MEA, they can be

[99] See para 133 of the first *Shrimp* ruling, above n 71.

[100] Such as the Convention on the Conservation of Migratory Species of Wild Animals (Bonn Convention) 1979, 19 ILM 15.

[101] Possible difficulties may arise in the case of global public goods, such as tropical forests which are located in the territory of one nation. This case involves deeper tension between the collective interests of the global community and the sovereignty of the nation hosting the global public good.

[102] States may use a variety of trade measures to pressurise their trading partners. These include, in addition to trade embargos, eco-tariffs, countervailing measures and green subsidies.

[103] The following discussion resonates, of course, with the more general question regarding the relationship between the WTO and MEAs; see further section H below.

interpreted as an act of 'bad faith', denying the acting state(s) from the protection of Article XX.[104]

Overall the *Shrimp* ruling seems to open the door to a partial usage of trade measures in order to facilitate co-operation in the environmental realm. Note that all of the extensions discussed above continue to assume that the WTO does not authorise directly the use of trade measures to facilitate co-operation or compliance in environmental matters. Rather, the validation provided by the WTO is indirect, channelled through the environmental exemptions of Article XX. This means that the WTO leaves to the parties the task of structuring the sanctioning measures (in contrast to the very active role of the WTO judicial bodies in authorising sanctions in the case of trade disputes).

F. Synergy and Friction Reconsidered: The Institutional Challenge Within the WTO

Linking trade and environmental regimes can have positive synergic effects. However, as explained in section D, implementing the idea of linkage in a society that is divided in its stance toward nature is fraught with difficulties. There are primarily three institutional challenges facing the linkage programme. First, the idea of linkage requires the development of a single metric which will enable one to compare and balance between the projected costs and benefits of the trade and environmental regimes—otherwise it will not be possible to uncover any potential synergy. Second, to the extent that the environmental regime at stake targets a regional/global public good, there must be a consensus about the universal value of that good. Finally, the linkage thesis, as I previously described it, also disregards the local institutional barriers and transaction costs that are likely to accompany the actual linking process.

These various difficulties also influence the legal world. To understand how they could influence the legal deliberation of trade–environment disputes let me consider some concrete example. The principal forms of linkage that are currently recognised by WTO law are: Article XX enforcement actions (following the *Shrimp* ruling), incentive measures (under the Generalised System of Preferences ('GSP')),[105] and

[104] According to this view there is no conflict between the rules of the WTO and trade measures used and authorised by certain MEAs, such as the Basel Convention and CITES.

[105] The GSP provides preferential market access to developing countries; it reflects the non-homogenous efforts of developed countries to provide preferential tariffs and other privileges to developing countries, in response to Art XXXVI(3) of the GATT. Some of these schemes, such as the EU's GSP programme, require the beneficiary countries to meet certain environmental requirements as a condition for receiving preferential treatment. See S Charnovitz, 'Internet Roundtable: The Appellate Body's GSP Decision' (2004) 3 *World Trade Review* 239; Appellate Body decision: *European Communities: Conditions for the Granting of Tariff Preferences to Developing Countries,* WT/DS246/AB/R, 7 Apr 2004.

very restricted institutional co-operation (eg, limited observer status to certain MEAs). Consider, for example, the idea of using Article XX to authorise enforcement action. In deliberating the consistency of such measures with Article XX, WTO tribunals are likely to face serious difficulties, which were not given sufficient consideration in the *Shrimp—Turtle* rulings. Deciding on the legality of trade-based enforcement action would require the WTO tribunals to apply the good-faith protocol, which was developed by the Appellate Body as a guide for interpreting the chapeau. This protocol requires a state, before introducing a unilateral trade measure, to *explore* the possibility of responding to the environmental risk in question through international agreement.

The law of the WTO does not however, contain evaluative criteria that could allow its tribunals to determine whether the Member using a trade measure has made a good-faith effort to negotiate an MEA with the countries targeted by the trade measure. The ultimate failure of such negotiations may be the result of conflicting moral preferences with respect to the value of the ecological asset that was the subject of the dispute.[106] In some cases this philosophical dispute may be (legally) resolved by looking into the existing body of international environmental law. Thus, for example, in the *Shrimp—Turtle* dispute, the thesis that sea turtles are worth preserving was supported by their classification as endangered species in CITES.[107] But this move can provide only a partial solution because international environmental law is prominently treaty-based, and the membership of MEAs is far from universal. And, of course, some negotiations may focus on issues that are not covered by existing agreements.[108]

The negotiations may also fail because the parties may have different views with respect to the economic value of the ecological asset, preventing the conclusion of eco-financial barters. To give a concrete example, imagine that Malaysia had agreed to join a multilateral effort to protect sea turtles, but required certain financial compensation, which would help it to fund the environmental technology needed to protect sea turtles. This demand could reflect differences between Malaysia and the US concerning their environmental preferences and national economic wealth. Suppose, next, that a certain package, which was proposed by the US, was rejected by Malaysia. According to what criteria should a WTO Panel evaluate the fairness of this proposed deal?

But linking trade and environmental regimes does not involve just complex cultural and ideological discords. It may also involve substantial transaction costs. In the case of the WTO, the main costs involve the increasing cognitive,

[106] And not a result of bad faith of either party. Compare, for example, the wide gaps in the approach to nature of Jainism in India and the English Animal Welfare Movement, and the views of Judaism and Christianity.

[107] See the first *Shrimp* ruling, above n 71 para 132.

[108] Thus, for example, in *ibid*, both the US and some of the complainants (Malaysia and Thailand) were not parties to the Bonn Convention.

decisional and political burdens that cross-regime linkage is likely to impose on the administrative and judicial branches of the WTO. These branches will now have to face the challenge of administering two domains (think, for example, of the complexity of determining a breach of the obligations under the Kyoto Protocol, given the multiple options through which parties can offset their emissions, using carbon sinks, joint projects and emissions trading). These increasing burdens could severely erode the operational efficacy of these branches, with all the adverse effects such erosion may have on the functioning of the WTO and linked regime.

H. Toward a Possible Resolution

The trade–environment dilemma is complex. It is embedded in a deeply conflicted discursive landscape, consisting of highly opposing visions regarding the relationship between nature and society. These difficulties are exacerbated by deep informational scarcities, and scientific uncertainties, as to the environmental problems facing humanity, and the complex relationship between economic development and ecological degradation.[109] In these circumstances, achieving a conclusive solution to the trade and environment conflict is not only difficult, but highly improbable. Nonetheless, it is possible to draw few policy conclusions from the foregoing discussion.

First, recognising that trade liberalisation is likely to have adverse ecological impacts means that both the global community as a whole and nation states in their independent capacity must develop strong environmental institutions, which could counteract these effects. These institutions face two key challenges: first, developing a better understanding of the environmental risks facing humanity, and the complex causal relations between economic growth and ecological degradation; and, second, designing and maintaining a regulatory network which could cope with the externalities generated by short-sighted economic development. This argument should not, however, be interpreted as allowing trade law to be indifferent to environmental concerns. The argument, frequently made by the trade community, that the trade and environmental domains should be kept separate[110] is highly misleading. It is misleading because it disregards the enduring weakness of environmental institutions (both locally, especially in

[109] Although there has been significant progress on these issues. See eg the work of the Intergovernmental Panel on Climate Change, at www.ipcc.ch.

[110] See 'Third World Intellectuals and NGOs Statement Against Linkage', a letter circulated on the Internet, and signed by several prominent economists including J Bhagwati, at www2.bc.edu/~anderson/twin-sal12.pdf

developing countries, and globally), reflecting the persistent failure of human society to deal with the ecological repercussions of economic progress.[111]

The key question, however, is how should the trade universe react to or implement this call for ecological responsibility. At a very general level this argument calls on the law to develop *ecological sensitivities*. But it is possible to point to a few more concrete actions. First, because ecological damage can be irreversible (eg, loss of bio-diversity), it is crucial to assess the possible ecological impacts of trade decisions at an early stage, before the actual decisions are made. Developing mechanisms that will enable such assessment is highly important, and there has been some progress in this direction.[112] Second, trade institutions should take into account the current asymmetry between the trade and environmental spheres. The weakness of environmental institutions—at both the local and global levels—may necessitates using trade measures (even if these are indeed second-best instruments). Finally, trade institutions should support the development of linkage modules, which could exploit the various synergies between the trade and environment domains. This idea was tentatively endorsed by the Appellate Body in the *Shrimp* decision and by other international instruments.[113]

Incorporating the foregoing proposals into the law of the WTO may require radical changes, which are likely to be deeply controversial. Neither economics nor environmental philosophy offers a precise algorithm for balancing between trade and environmental objectives that can be crystallised into the WTO rule-book. It is also unrealistic to expect the Appellate Body to lead this process of ecological sensitisation independently through a creative reading of Article XX. Such a move could generate intense opposition, both because of its incompatibility with the mercantilist culture that still influences the WTO, and because it is likely to be interpreted as an illegitimate intrusion into state sovereignty. The idea of sustainable development, which is mentioned in the preamble to the WTO Agreement, cannot provide a satisfactory anchor for such juridical-led reform,

[111] For a discussion of the weakness of transnational environmental institutions see J Whalley and B Zissimos, 'An Internalisation-based World Environmental Organisation' (2002) 25 *World Economy* 619, 620.

[112] Both the US and the EU engage in environmental review of trade agreements. In the US, the United States Trade Representative ('USTR'), following Executive Order 13141 (1999) regarding Environmental Review of Trade Agreement, published several environmental reviews of bilateral trade agreements (see www.ustr.gov/Trade_Agreements/Bilateral/Section_Index.html). The European Commission developed a methodology for Sustainability Impact Assessment ('SIA'), which was applied to the Doha Agenda, and to the EU negotiations with Mercusor/Chile (see http://europa.eu.int/comm/trade/sia/studies.htm). In considering these mechanisms, the key question is to what extent they influence the structure of the ensuing trade instrument. The global community was not able so far to develop more comprehensive mechanisms of environmental reviews. UNEP has done some work in this area (which has had, however, little influence on the WTO). See UNEP, *Reference Manual for the Integrated Assessment of Trade-Related Policies* (UNEP, 2001), and at www.unep.ch/etu/etp/acts/manpols/urlrmia.htm.

[113] Eg, in the Rio Declaration, above n 44, and Agenda 21, above n 44, see above text to nn 50–52.

since its meaning and possible applications are still the subject of deep controversies.[114] At this point, it might make more sense, therefore, to leave intact the substantive rules of the WTO (eg, Article XX), focusing instead on reforming the institutional setting in which trade–environment disputes are deliberated. This could create the necessary conditions for a gradual transformation of the WTO rule-book.

In terms of possible institutional changes, a key step in this context should be the expansion of the organisational setting in which the trade and environment question is deliberated within the WTO (in the context of both negotiations and disputes). This should take place through the creation of deeper organisational ties between the WTO and environmental organisations, such as the United Nations Environment Programme (UNEP) and MEAs Secretariats. These changes should create a setting in which the various groups involved in this conflict could converse, and reach certain understandings (even if only local and tentative) on some of difficult dilemmas noted above. Extending the organisational relations between the two regimes can both improve the problem-solving capacities of the emerging (augmented) regime and increase its legitimacy. Broader institutional ties between the regimes could also extend the capacity of the WTO judicial and executive branches to cope with the more extensive decisional and cognitive burdens that are likely to be generated by taking more seriously the ecological impacts of trade.

The real challenge lies in developing specific institutional modules which would realise this vision. One option would be to give environmental organisations a more active role in the governance of the WTO. This role should transcend the notion of observer, which is currently discussed in the WTO. It could include, for example, giving UNEP and key MEAs' secretariats full member rights at the WTO Trade and Environment Committee and other relevant committees, and a seat at the Appellate Body in cases that involve environmental issues. Article XV(2) of the GATT, which requires the Contracting Parties to consult with the IMF in cases that involve 'problems concerning monetary reserves, balances of payments or foreign exchange arrangements, could provide a possible blueprint for the incorporation of UNEP in the WTO decision-making apparatus.

H. The Road Ahead

There are strong grounds for concern with respect to the ecological effects of trade liberalisation. The *Shrimp* decision reflects an important first step toward establishing a more responsive trade regime, which will be sensitive to non-trade concerns. It is clear, though, that this embryonic step will not suffice. Extending the responsiveness of the WTO to ecological concerns and realising the potential for

[114] Daly, above n 18.

synergic linkage between the WTO and the environmental realm can take place only in an extended institutional space. A broader institutional network has a better chance of coping with the deep discursive frictions that characterise the trade–environment conflict, and the extensive administrative burdens associated with implementing the idea of linkage.[115]

Unfortunately—at least from the perspective of the environmental community—the bold vision of the *Shrimp* ruling has failed so far to make an impact on the WTO negotiation agenda. The environmental part of the Doha negotiation framework, introduced in the 2001 Doha Declaration,[116] is very modest in the targets it sets out, and even on these very limited targets there are still wide disagreements. There are three major items in the environmental part of the Doha declaration. The *first* item refers to the relationship between existing WTO rules and specific trade obligations set out in MEAs.[117] The negotiations on this item sought to clarify the relationship and possible tension between trade measures taken under MEAs and WTO rules. The question whether the WTO excessive enforcement capacities could be used to enforce the various environmental obligations set out in these agreements was not part of the Doha negotiation framework. The *second* item focuses on establishing procedures for regular information exchange between MEA Secretariats and the relevant WTO committees, and on granting observer status to certain MEAs.[118] More radical ideas, such as granting UNEP (or leading MEA Secretariats) a formal voice in the decision-making process within the WTO, are not part of the negotiation agenda. No agreement has been reached so far on any of these items.[119] The only item, on which there seems to be a growing consensus is the negotiations on the reduction of tariff and non-tariff barriers to environmental goods and services.[120] However, the range of products that are due to benefit from the projected reductions is limited.[121]

[115] For a similar critique, emphasising the lack of co-operation between the trade and environmental arms of the NAFTA agreement, see RA Sanchez, 'Governance, Trade, and the Environment in the Context of NAFTA' (2002) 45 *American Behavioral Scientist* 1369, 1388.

[116] Negotiated in the Fourth WTO Ministerial Conference, held at Doha, Qatar, in 2001. See further www.wto.org/english/tratop_e/dda_e/dda_e.htm.

[117] *Ibid*, Art 31(i).

[118] *Ibid*, Art 31(ii).

[119] For a detailed description of the status of the negotiations prior to the Sixth Ministerial Conference in Hong Kong (Dec 2005), see the Committee on Trade and Environment special session's report to the Trade Negotiations Committee, TN/TE/12, 20 July 2005.

[120] Doha Declaration, above n 117, Art 31(iii).

[121] While the negotiations are still going on as this chapter is being written, the focus, so far, has been on end-use products and services (see the paper by New Zealand, TN/TE/W/6, and the recent Secretariat report, TN/TE/R/11). The main beneficiaries of the proposed cut would be the developed countries—the main exporters of green technology and services. A broader definition of 'green' goods, which would also have embraced products made through 'green' production methods, including, for example, organic agricultural products and sustainable forest products, could have had a greater ecological impact and would have enabled developing countries to reap some of the economic benefits of these cuts (for a tentative move in this direction see, the EU proposal, TN/TE/W/47).

The deep frictions underlying the trade and environment conflict ensure that this conflict will continue to be the subject of wide-ranging debate. While it is possible to imagine various 'middle grounds', which can provide partial solutions to this conflict, such solutions continue to face deep challenges. The frequent use of 'green' rhetoric by political and economic leaders (manifested, for example, in the frequent invocation of the notion of 'sustainability') is, in that sense, misleading because it masks the deep cultural and ideological gaps that continue to divide the global society with respect to the relationship between society and nature. These gaps, which are embedded in a cosmopolitan society that is increasingly controlled by financial drives, and indulgent consumerist culture,[122] will continue it seems, to block substantial progress in resolving this conflict.

[122] See L Cohen, *A Consumers' Republic: The Politics of Mass Consumption* (Alfred A Knopf, 2003).

13

Environmental Law in Post-colonial Societies: Aspirations, Achievements and Limitations

BENJAMIN J. RICHARDSON,* IKECHI MGBEOJI**
AND FRANCIS BOTCHWAY***

A. Introduction: From Colonialism to Post-colonialism

Nations differ in their aspirations and achievements concerning environmental law and policy. The starkest differences exist between the industrialised Western nations and their former colonies in the developing world.[1] While the discourse of sustainable development has been embraced by nearly all governments worldwide, its relevance to and implementation in post-colonial societies remain problematic.[2]

* Professor, Osgoode Hall Law School, York University.
** Professor, Osgoode Hall Law School, York University.
*** Reader, University of Hull Law School.

[1] Good overviews of environmental law and policy in the developing world include: N Islam *et al* (eds), *Environmental Law in Developing Countries: Selected Issues* (IUCN, 2002); AM Halvorssen, *Equality among Unequals in International Environmental Law: Differential Treatment for Developing Countries* (Westview Press, 1999); B Chaytor and R Gray (eds), *International Environmental Law and Policy in Africa* (Springer, 2003); A Thomas, S Carr and D Humphreys (eds), *Environmental Policies and NGO Influence: Land Degradation and Sustainable Resource Management in Sub-Saharan Africa* (Routledge, 2001); MAM Salih and S Tedla (eds), *Environmental Planning, Policies and Politics in Eastern and Southern Africa* (St Martin's Press, 1999); JT Roberts and ND Thanos, *Trouble in Paradise: Globalization and Environmental Crises in Latin America* (Routeldge, 2003); GJ MacDonald, DL Neilson, MA Stern (eds), *Latin American Environmental Policy in International Perspective* (Westview Press, 1996); NP Peritoire, *Third World Environmentalism: Case Studies from the Global South* (UP Florida, 1999); B Boer, R Ramsay and DR Rothwell, *International Environmental Law in the Asia Pacific* (Kluwer, 1998); R Mushkat *International Environmental Law and Asian Values: Legal Norms and Cultural Influences* (UBC Press, 2004); AJ Bolla and TL McDorman (eds), *Comparative Asian Environmental Law Anthology* (Carolina Academic Press, 1999).

[2] AD Hecht, 'The Triad of Sustainable Development: Promoting Sustainable Development in Developing Countries' (1999) 8(2) *Journal of Environmental & Development* 111.

This chapter canvasses the aspirations, achievements and limitations of environmental governance in post-colonial countries. It does not probe in detail the experiences of any particular jurisdictions. Rather, it explores sustainable development policies and environmental law reforms and their set-backs through the lenses of several overarching themes. These are: the environmental regulatory challenges in the most rapidly industrialising economies (predominantly in East Asia); the tension between nature conservation and local communities' social and economic needs; and regulation of transnational corporate activity in developing countries. Before canvassing these themes, the next section outlines the key challenges for building effective environmental law in post-colonial societies. Ultimately, the chapter aims to explain why developing countries have struggled to develop effective environmental law, and what kind of reforms could turn things around.

The difficulties of post-colonial states in building effective systems of environmental governance reflect many causes, including structural weaknesses and normative flaws in international environmental law and its sustainability discourse,[3] the inequities of the global economy especially the international trade and financial systems,[4] the legacies of colonial rule, as well as various institutional and political factors endogenous to post-colonial societies.[5] The combination of unsustainable resource consumption by industrialised nations (and their companies), and the chronic conditions of poverty in the developing world, has created in post-colonial societies some of the planet's severest ecological and social problems.[6]

'Post-colonial states' are those that arose in the decolonised countries of Africa, Asia, Latin America and Oceania. These states are also commonly referred to as 'developing countries', 'less developed countries' or 'industrialising states'.[7] However labelled, they are not a homogenous group. There is immense variety and difference among the more than 130 states conveniently characterised as members of the Third World.[8] East Asia's industrialising tigers, for instance, are faced with ecological problems and governance challenges that differ markedly from the poorest agricultural economies of Sub-Saharan Africa. But what marks these nations as an identifiable group is their shared history of colonisation and

[3] For its historical roots, see D Kelly *et al, The Economic Superpowers and the Environment* (WH Freeman, 1976); and Chaytor and Gray, above n 1, for a recent perspective.

[4] S Mallaby, *The World's Banker: A Story of Failed States, Financial Crises, and Poverty of Nations* (Penguin, 2004).

[5] AH af Ornas and MA Mohamed Salih (eds), *Ecology and Politics: Environmental Stress and Security in Africa* (Scandinavian Institute of African Studies, 1989).

[6] C Zheng-Kang, 'Equity, Special Considerations, and the Third World' (1990) 1 Colorado J Intl Envtl L 57. Commission for Africa, *Our Common Interest: Report of the Commission for Africa* (Penguin Books, 2005).

[7] It should be borne in mind that the category of post-colonial states cannot always be equated with developing countries. Some countries such as China in the 19th century did not fall under direct colonial rule, although they suffered indirectly.

[8] W Langley, 'The Third World: Towards A Definition' (1981) 2 *Boston College Third World LJ* 1.

subordination to the geo-political interests of the advanced capitalist economies. Part of that shared history is the legacy of colonial resource management policies. When colonies obtained 'flag' independence, the environment they inherited was already severely damaged from years of exploitation by colonial administrations.

Today, post-colonial societies face new but equally serious threats. Trade liberalisation, foreign debt burdens, transnational corporate investments and International Monetary Fund structural adjustment programmes are elements of a global economic system that can undermine socially just and ecologically sound development for post-colonial societies. Even the remedial discourse of sustainable development seems to be mired in these inequities. Although several principles of sustainability address the plight of the most disadvantaged nations—eg, the concepts of 'intragenerational equity' and 'common but differentiated responsibilities'[9]—the sustainable development discourse has tended to reflect Western institutions and interests.[10] Thus, explains Geisinger:

> Sustainable development is not just a reflection of Western ideology, but a force for defining environmental problems in Western terms. The ecocratic discourse that has developed around the principle of sustainable development serves to further marginalize any conception of environment that does not fit into the Western framework. Its implementation assumes the ability of science to develop technologies to limit environmental damage while ensuring material growth. Such a scheme has no place for other conceptions of the human/nature relationship.[11]

Properly to evaluate the prospects for competent environmental governance in post-colonial states, one must consider the character of the colonial state and its environmental laws. The capacity of post-colonial states to internalise and enforce environmental norms is still affected by the legacy of the colonial administrative apparatus. Colonial authorities were not uninterested in the environment, and occasionally passed regulations on rivers, mining and wildlife to facilitate their orderly exploitation and management.[12] Colonial states, by definition and practice, were designed to serve economic and political ends that were often at odds with the long-term interests of the colonised. Power tended to be centralised in the colonial capital and exercised insensitively without the participation of

[9] DB Magraw, 'Legal Treatment of Developing Countries: Differential, Contextual, and Absolute Norms' (1990) 1 *Colorado Journal of International Environmental Law & Policy* 69; EB Weiss, 'In Fairness to Future Generations and Sustainable Development' (1992) 8 *American University Journal of International Law & Policy* 19.

[10] Compare Ellis and Wood, this vol. But see S Lele, 'Sustainable Development: A Critical Review' (1991) 19 *World Development* 607.

[11] A Geisinger, 'Sustainable Development and the Domination of Nature: Spreading the Seed of the Western Ideology of Nature' (1999–2000) 27 *Boston College Enivironmental Affairs L Rev* 68.

[12] Eg, in the then West African Gold Coast: Concessions Ordinance was passed in 1900, the Ordinance for the Preservation of Wild Animals, Birds and Fish in 1901, Rivers Ordinance in 1907, Mosquitoes Ordinance in 1911 and Forest Ordinance in 1927: see F Botchway, *Environmental Law in Ghana* (Kluwer, 2004) 27–9.

colonial subjects.[13] In this schema, natural resources were managed principally to serve imperial markets, while colonial administrations propagated new discourses and practices for the utilitarian and instrumental management of nature.[14]

In their preoccupation with economic exploitation of the colonies' bounty, colonial powers created few institutional structures for good governance. The institutions of 'indirect rule' established in the British colonies, which combined British-style local government with tribal authority, were perhaps a rare exception.[15] As Mgbeoji observed, 'in many cases the colonial bureaucracy was designed as a mechanism to facilitate the economic exploitation of natives and their resources in such tasks as mining, logging of forests, and the production of raw materials for the cosmopolitan imperial cities'.[16] The legacy today has been a continuation of inappropriate centralised government decision-making and frequent reliance on cumbersome, authoritarian modes of regulation, which together tend to disenfranchise local communities closest to nature.[17] Post-colonial scholars thus wish to remind us that the accession of post-colonialism was 'prematurely celebratory',[18] as significant political and economic disequilibria remain, not merely between the West and developing countries, but within post-colonial societies.[19]

B. Building Blocks for Envirnmental Law

1. Emergence of Environmental Law in Colonial and Post-colonial States

There is no shortage of environmental laws in the developing world. Apart from 'failed states' such as Afghanistan and Somalia where there is little semblance of effective government, most nations have marshalled a seemingly impressive array of environmental legislation. As with developed nations, there have been certain common steps in the historical evolution of their environmental regulatory regimes.

[13] JS Wunsch and D Olowu (eds), *The Failure of the Centralized State: Institutions and Self-Governance in Africa* (Westview Press, 1990).

[14] RH Grove, *Green Imperialism: Colonial Expansion, Tropical Island Edens, and the Origins of Environmentalism 1600–1860* (Cambridge UP, 1995); AP Kameri-Mbote and P Cullett, 'Law, Colonialism and Environmental Management in Africa' (1997) 6 *Review of European Community and International Environmental Law* 23.

[15] HF Morris and JS Read (eds), *Indirect Rule and the Search for Justice* (Clarendon Press, 1972).

[16] I Mgbeoji, *Collective Insecurity* (UBC Press, 2003) 33.

[17] D Rothchild and N Chazan (eds), *The Precarious Balance: State and Society in Africa* (Westview Press, 1988); CY Thomas, *The Rise of the Authoritarian State in Peripheral Societies* (Monthly Review Press, 1984).

[18] A McClintock, *Imperial Leather* (Taylor and Francis Books, 1995) 12–13.

[19] See generally A Memmi, *The Colonizer and the Colonized* (Beacon Press, 1991); G Rajan and R Mohanram (eds), *Postcolonial Discourse and Changing Cultural Contexts* (Greenwood Press, 1995).

During the early years of post-colonialism, newly independent governments ushered in constitutional reforms that saw the elevation of economic policy matters into constitutional legal discourse. This emanated from a desire to nationalise the 'commanding heights of the economy' and achieve economic independence.[20] These constitutional provisions often had significant environmental implications. For example, the Mexican constitution of 1936 vested all natural resource exploitation in state-owned companies.[21] Such provisions did not change the ethos of environmental practice associated with the colonial economy. If anything, they supported the degradation of the environment in a self-righteous justification of the need for accelerated development of the post-colonial economy.

On the other hand, there were other aspects of the independence constitutions that indirectly provided avenues for environmental protection and management. These were predominantly the fundamental human rights and due process administrative procedures that the constitutions mandated.[22] Judicial review by courts in the developing world has proven in some instances to offer a valuable check on administrative actions that threaten the environment,[23] such as the Philippines Supreme Court decision in *Oposa*[24] and the Indian Supreme Court decision in *Mehta*.[25]

In the aftermath of the Cold War, much more rigorous and direct efforts were made to incorporate environmental provisions in the new constitutions. The new constitutional provisions fall into three categories: preambular statements, directive principles of state policy and basic environmental rights or duties for citizens.[26] There have been doubts about the status and effect of constitutional provisions, especially the preambles. The Nigerian constitution provides that 'the state shall protect and improve the environment and safeguard the water, air and land, forest and wildlife of Nigeria'.[27] Most experts consider such statements to be standards of attainment but not justiciable nor enforceable. However, constitutional principles incorporated into legislation can be made justiciable.[28]

While constitutional principles can serve to express long-term political commitment, they clearly cannot alone provide an adequate framework for effective

[20] N Schrijver, *Sovereignty Over Natural Resources: Balancing Rights and Duties* (Cambridge UP, 1997).

[21] See A Chua, 'The Privatization—Nationalization Cycle: The Link Between Markets and Ethnicity in Developing Countries' (1995) 95 *Columbia L Rev* 223, 232.

[22] See generally A Boyle and M Anderson (eds), *Human Rights Approaches to Environmental Protection. Jan Hancock, Environmental Human Rights* (Clarendon Press, 2003).

[23] J Widener, *Building the Rule of Law: Francis Nyalali and the Road to Judicial Independence in Africa* (WH Norton, 2001).

[24] *Minors Oposa v Secretary of the Department of Environment and Natural Resources* (1994) 33 ILM 173 (Sup Ct).

[25] *MC Mehta v Union of India* [1997] AIR SC 734.

[26] C Bruch, W Coker and C Van Arsdale, 'Constitutional Environmental Law: Giving Force to Fundamental Principles in Africa' (2001) 26 *Columbia Journal of Environmental Law* 131.

[27] Constitution of the Federal Republic of Nigeria 1999, s 20: see EE. Okon, 'The Environmental Perspective in the 1999 Nigerian Constitution' (2003) 5 *Environmental L Rev* 256.

[28] See the Nigerian Sup Ct judgment (in particular Uwaifo JSC's opinion) in *AG of Ondo State v AG of the Federation & ors* (1982) 13 NSCC.567.

environmental governance. Government legislation is also necessary. Like the legal regimes of many Western states, early post-colonial environmental legislation tended to be organised around particular economic activities, and the environmental goals were neither clearly visible nor appreciated by the populace. The legislation was also piecemeal, dealing with specific environmental media—eg, forestry, water, marine resources, and air quality.[29]

Recent decades have been marked by more comprehensive legislative effort constructed in the consciousness of environmental management and advancement. Most post-colonial states have enacted national environmental framework legislation, providing for land use planning, environmental impact assessment and pollution control. Thus, for example, Pakistan has the Environmental Protection Ordinance 1983, Egypt the Environmental Protection Law 1994, Uganda adopted the National Environment Act 1994 and Brazil has the National Environment Policy Law 1981.[30] These national environmental statutes tend to concentrate decision-making among central government authorities, and rely heavily on command-and-control regulation.[31] Thus, India has the Ministry of Environment and Forests, Chile has the National Commission for the Environment, and Nigeria established the Federal Environmental Protection Agency.

In recent years, references to 'sustainable development' have increasingly surfaced in these statutory regimes.[32] With the assistance of international institutions such as the World Conservation Union (IUCN) and the United Nations Environment Programme (UNEP), post-colonial states have been embellishing their environmental laws in the language of sustainability. Thus, Vietnam's Law on Environmental Protection 1993 declares its goal as 'serving the cause of sustainable development of the country',[33] and Zambia's Environmental Protection and Pollution Control 1990 gives the national Environment Council the duty to 'identify, promote and advise on projects which further or are likely to further . . . sustainable development'.[34]

This plethora of environmental laws in the developing world masks a variety of structural weaknesses in the capacity of their legal systems to promote sustainable development. Unlike examples from some developed nations, such as New Zealand's Resource Management Act 1990,[35] most post-colonial legislation hardly provide the policy tools to implement sustainability. Its more material concepts,

[29] BJ Richardson, 'Environmental Law in Postcolonial Societies: Straddling the Local—Global Institutional Spectrum' (2000) 11(1) *Colorado Journal of International Environmental Law & Policy* 1, 22.

[30] For these and more examples, see ED McCutcheon, 'Think Globally, (En)Act Locally: Promoting Effective National Environmental Regulatory Infrastructure in Developing Nations' (1998) 31 *Cornell International LJ* 395.

[31] See U Desai (ed), *Ecological Policy and Politics in Developing Countries* (SUNY Press, 1998).

[32] SO Subedi, 'Incorporation of the Principle of Sustainable Development into the Development Policies of the Asian Countries' (2002) 32 *Environmental Policy & Law L* 85; Hecht, above n 2.

[33] Preamble, available at www.vietnamlaws.com.

[34] S 6(2)(m), Cap 204 of the Laws of Zambia.

[35] See Bosselmann, ch 5, this vol.

such as the precautionary principle and environmental risk management or internalisation of environmental costs through environmental taxation, are barely acknowledged. Yet, for some post-colonial states, especially the rapidly industrialising and urbanising countries of East Asia, these should be highly relevant policy concerns. On the other hand, for some other nations, especially those in sub-Saharan Africa, different policy concerns, such as land tenure, the position of women and agricultural trade, tend to have a greater bearing on the state of environmental management. Environmental law in this region often fails to address these structural constraints to ecologically sound and socially just development. To the extent that the sustainable development discourse and its reforms fail to be tailored to the specific needs of different types of post-colonial societies, it will remain largely a framework devised by and for Western institutions and interests.

2. Good Governance and the Rule of Law

Part of the problem with current environmental law reforms is that they are not sufficiently supported by policies and administrative or other implementation institutions.[36] Hence, there has been growing talk about the need for 'capacity-building' in developing countries.[37] Mayda observes that new environmental legislation is of questionable value unless 'accompanied by a substantial increase in each nation's capability for policy development, institutional structures, administrative competence, and ability to train management, monitoring and enforcement personnel'.[38] Unfortunately, these elements are not always present. For instance, according to the Asian Development Bank's recent *Asian Environment Outlook*, 'the root cause of the poor state of the environment in the region was a failure of policy and of institutions'.[39]

Certainly, new or better environmental laws are not enough. Governments must also have an administrative system with the capacity and the motivation to implement and enforce regulations.[40] Legal reform must include mechanisms for public participation, access to information and judicial review. Unfortunately, there has been a tendency for governments to 'relegate the consideration of legal and institutional arrangements to artificially isolated chambers, destined for sequential consideration once the necessary policy document has been developed'.[41] Not

[36] On policy and institutional frameworks, see Dovers and Connor, ch 1, this vol.

[37] OJ Ebohon *et al*, 'Institutional Deficiencies and Capacity Building Constraints: The Dilemma for Environmentally Sustainable Development in Africa' (1997) 4(3) *International Journal of Sustainable Development & World Ecology* 204.

[38] J Mayda, 'Environmental Legislation in Developing Countries: Some Parameters and Constraints' (1985) 12 *Ecology Law Quarterly* 997, 998.

[39] Asian Development Bank (ADB), *Asian Environment Outlook* (ADB, 2002) p. xv.

[40] WL Andreen, 'Environmental Law and International Assistance: The Challenge of Strengthening Environmental Law in the Developing World' (2000) 25 *Columbia Journal of Environmental Law* 17, 26.

[41] *Ibid*, 28.

uncommonly, environmental legislation in post-colonial states has been a dead letter because of insufficient skilled personnel, lack of administrative and technical support, and meagre financial resources.[42] Concomitantly, there has been a tendency to ignore the potential contributions of non-governmental organisations (NGOs), local communities, and businesses and trade unions as a means of environmental governance.

Thus, many commentators argue that environmental law will hardly promote sustainable development unless anchored to wider reforms to promote good governance and the rule of law.[43] While this is part of the picture, the danger is that we can lose sight of the fundamental political and economic constraints to such reform. In other words, there can be confusion between the symptoms and causes of failed environmental governance. Law acquires its meaning and performs its social functions through processes of implementation and enforcement, without which it has little life in any given society. While some countries have made substantial progress in addressing these encumbrances, there has been a tendency for some states naïvely to import foreign precedents incompatible with local institutional and social conditions.[44] Thus, as Wang warns, 'law becomes effective by social forces and pressures interested in and working for its implementation. Without a proper institutional setting, the law will remain a fig-leaf, pretending action without changing social reality'.[45]

The failure of the 'Law and Development' movement of the 1960s and 1970s—a programme for legal technical assistance and reform to developing countries, as part of Western development aid programmes—shattered the naïve belief that if laws are reformed and legal institutions strengthened, nothing can restrain the 'rule of law's' triumph.[46] The law and development movement has re-emerged in a new guise recently, through the 'New Public Management' and 'Good Governance' prescriptions recited by the international development assistance community.[47] Thus, corruption, lack of transparency and accountability in administration, and cumbersome and outdated decision-making processes, are targeted as the principal villains to be reformed.

[42] Richardson, above n 29, 26–7.

[43] See B Boer, 'Institutionalising Ecologically Sustainable Development: The Roles of National, State, and Local Governments in Translating Grand Strategy into Action' (1995) 31 *Willamette L Rev* 307.

[44] P Legrand, 'The Impossibility of Legal Transplants' (1997) 4 *Maastricht Journal of European & Comparative Law* 111, 119.

[45] Y Wang, *Chinese Legal Reform: The Case of Foreign Investment Law* (Routledge, 2002)28.

[46] DM Trubek and M Galanter, 'Scholars in Self-Estrangement: Some Reflections on the Crisis in Law and Development' (1974) 4 *Wisconsin L Rev* 1062.

[47] J Demmers *et al* (eds), *Good Governance in the Era of Global Neoliberalism* (Routledge, 2004). For a trenchant Third World critique, see J Gathii, 'The Limits of the New International Rule of Law on Good Governance' in EK Quashigah and OC Okafor (eds), *Legitimate Governance in Africa* (Kluwer, 1999) 207; A Anghie, *et al* (eds), *The Third World and International Order: Law, Politics and Globalization* (Martinus Nijhoff, 2003).

Law reform can wrongly presuppose that certain societies do not have a 'rule of law' and are characterised by anarchy and disorder, and must therefore be restructured. But a society whose members are guided by, and comply with, traditional norms of behaviour rather than a state-supported edifice of codes and rules is clearly not one devoid of law. Many indigenous and local communities in post-colonial societies retain customary environmental management traditions that provide norms and sanctions that can complement government environmental law.[48] Successful law reform in so-called 'transitional countries' therefore at a minimum requires appropriate incentives and organisations that take account of the local culture and the past constraints that shaped the existing legal system.[49]

3. International Institutions and Co-operation

Many commentators believe that the prospects for effective environmental governance hinge not so much on endogenous conditions in post-colonial societies but on exogenous ones, especially the structure of the global economy and international environmental co-operation. During the 1960s and 1970s, theories of dependency and underdevelopment figured prominently in explanations of the environmental and economic dilemmas of the developing world. Like their colonial antecedents, post-colonial economies were seen as tied to the markets of the former colonial masters.[50] The privileged position of international capital under such conditions constrained the environmental policy options for post-colonial states. During the 1980s, the deteriorating terms of trade and the ballooning foreign debts of the Third World led critics to broaden the responsibility for the failure to achieve sustainable development to the general structure of the global economy.[51] Many commentators believe that 'the present economic system is grotesquely unsustainable and for all practical purposes it is impossible for a sustainable world to emerge and be maintained via the workings of an unconfined, undirected market system',[52] in which post-colonial states are besieged on all fronts. This global market order is underpinned by the Bretton Woods institutions of the World Bank, the International Monetary Fund and the General Agreement

[48] See D Bromley, *Environment and Economy: Property Rights and Public Policy* (Basil Blackwell, 1991).

[49] PH Brietzke, 'The Politics of Legal Reform' (2004) 3 *Washington University Global Studies L Rev* 1, 25.

[50] AG Frank, *Capitalism and Underdevelopment in Latin America* (Monthly Review Press, 1957); S Amir, *Unequal Development: An Essay on the Social Formations of Peripheral Capitalism* (Monthly Review Press, 1976).

[51] G Carvalho, 'Sustainable Development: Is it Achievable Within the Existing International Political Economy Context?' (2001) 9 *Sustainable Development* 61.

[52] R Douthwhite, 'Is it Possible to Build a Sustainable World?' in R Munck and D O'Hearn (eds), *Critical Development Theory: Contributions to a New Paradigm* (Zed Books, 1999); S Kuznet, 'Economic Growth and Income Inequality' (1955) 54(1) *American Economic Rev* 1. But see P Aghion *et al*, 'Inequality and Economic Growth: The Perspective of the New Growth Theories' (1999) 37: 4 *Journal of Economic Literature* 1615;

on Tariffs and Trade (now absorbed into the World Trade Organisation).[53] For instance, the lending policies of the World Bank and its sister multilateral development banks have been condemned for favouring large-scale, environmentally intrusive projects such as dams and highways which devastate community livelihoods.[54] The World Bank, however, has implemented a range of reforms to promote more attention to the environmental dimensions of projects it finances,[55] and it has created an independent Inspection Panel to monitor compliance with its environmental and human rights policies.[56] In recent years, the so-called anti-globalisation movement has focused attention on the need for international debt relief for the poorest countries and a shift away from 'free trade' to 'fair trade' policies to help economic producers in developing countries.[57]

A second set of concerns relates to the effectiveness of current mechanisms to promote international environmental co-operation. Certainly, few doubt that international environmental treaties, organisations and assistance are necessary to assist post-colonial societies to develop sustainability. Many lack the financial resources, technical expertise and management systems to devise and implement environmental laws and policies. However, international environmental institutions arguably do not adequately address these shortcomings, and do not provide a sufficient counterweight to the egregious effects of the global economy. For example the World Heritage Convention[58] and the Ramsar Wetlands Convention[59] problematically emphasise nature conservation rather than local sustainable use and management of resources that communities often crucially depend on.[60] The financial resources they make available, with the World Heritage fund and the Ramsar fund, are too meagre to make a difference.

Encouragingly, there are some international environmental institutions attentive to the need for local environmental governance and community empowerment.

[53] R Swedberg, 'The Doctrine of Economic Neutrality of the IMF and World Bank' (1986) 23 *J Peace Research* 377; H Wachtel, *The Money Mandarins: The Making of a Supranational Economic Order* (Pantheon, 1986).

[54] B Rich, *Mortgaging the Earth: The World Bank, Environmental Impoverishment and the Crisis of Development* (Beacon Press, 1995).

[55] R Wade, 'Greening the Bank: The Struggle Over the Environment, 1970–1995' in D Kapur, J Lewis and R Webb (eds), *The World Bank: Its First Half Century* (Brookings Institution Press, 1997) ii, 611.

[56] R Bisell, 'Current Development: Recent Practice of the Inspection Panel of the World Bank' (1997) 91 *AJIL* 741.

[57] B Hoekman and M Kostecki, *The Political Economy of the World Trading System: The WTO and Beyond* (Oxford UP, 2001); R Nader (ed), *The Case Against Free Trade, GATT, NAFTA and the Globalization of Corporate Power* (Earth Island Press, 1993); J Stiglitz, *Globalization and Its Discontents* (Norton, 2002); JB Gelinas, *Freedom From Debt; The Reappropriation of Development through Financial Self-Reliance* (Zed Books, 1998).

[58] Convention concerning the Protection of the World Cultural and Natural Heritage 1972, 11 ILM 1358.

[59] Convention on Wetlands of International Importance 1971, 996 UNTS 245.

[60] See generally M Bowman and C Redgwell (eds), *International Law and the Conservation of Biological Diversity* (Kluwer, 1996).

For example, the 1992 Earth Summit's Agenda 21 plan contained extensive prescriptions for strengthening local government, NGOs and indigenous peoples.[61] The emerging principle of 'common but differentiated responsibility' in international environmental law expresses the idea that the West has greater responsibilities to address global environmental problems because of its larger contribution to such problems and its superior financial and technological resources to address them.[62] Some international treaties are also shifting their prescriptions away from inappropriate top-down bureaucratic and scientific solutions, in favour of local government, land tenure and other institutions often essential for sustainable, community livelihoods. Thus, the 1994 Desertification Convention sees the solutions to desertification of lands as including programmes to combat local poverty, give secure property rights to farmers and enhance local self-government.[63] Emerging international legal standards for indigenous peoples also emphasise land rights and self-government as the building blocks for sustainable natural resources management.[64]

Some treaties also include provisions for environmental technology exchange and financial assistance. For example, China owes its success in reducing ozone-depleting chemicals principally to the financial and technological support it received pursuant to the Montreal Protocol.[65] The Kyoto Protocol[66] will likely become more influential, mainly due to its dedicated funds[67] to help developing countries abate greenhouse gas emissions through technology transfer for energy efficiency and by land use and waste management changes.[68] The Kyoto Protocol's Clean Development Mechanism can also support investments in non-fossil energy projects in developing countries.[69] Other important financial mechanisms include the Global Environment Facility, which disburses grants for high profile environmental projects,[70] and the debt-for-nature swaps, which reduce a government's

[61] UN Conference on Environment and Development (UNCED), *Agenda 21: Programme of Action for Sustainable Development* (UNCED, 1992) chs 26–28.

[62] Halvorssen, above n 1; see also Ellis and Wood, this vol.

[63] Convention to Combat Desertification in Those Countries Experiencing Serious Drought and/or Desertification 1994, 33 ILM 1328.

[64] SJ Anaya, 'Divergent Discourses about International Law, Indigenous Peoples, and Rights Over Lands and Natural Resources: Toward a Realist Trend' (2005) 16(2) *Colorado Journal of International Environmental Law & Policy* 237.

[65] Montreal Protocol on Substances that Deplete the Ozone Layer 1987, 26 ILM 1550.

[66] Kyoto Protocol to the Framework Convention on Climate Change 1997, 37 ILM 22.

[67] Namely, the Special Climate Change Fund, Least Developed Countries Fund and Kyoto Protocol Adaptation Fund.

[68] See European Commission (EC), *Summary of Key Elements of the Bonn Agreement on Climate Change* (Directorate-General XI—Environment, 23 July 2001).

[69] Kyoto Protocol, above n 66, Art 12(3)(b). The CDM allows industrial countries to invest in projects in non-Annex I parties and to use the 'certified emissions reductions' that derive from the projects towards compliance with their Protocol commitments.

[70] Instrument for the Establishment of the Restructured Global Environment Facility 1994, 33 ILM 1273.

foreign debt burden in exchange for additional financial resources for environmental initiatives.[71]

Regional intergovernmental co-operation can also be a useful means of modernisation of environmental laws and policies. In theory, an advantage of regional collaboration is that it is sometimes easier for states to reach agreement on environmental policy at the regional plane where there is less diversity of social and economic characteristics among the participating parties than would be found at a broader, global scale. Presently, regional agreements dealing with marine pollution and fisheries management are the most advanced instruments developed for regional environmental problems. Several regional conventions in these fields have been drafted specifically for many parts of Africa, the South Pacific, Asia and Latin America.[72] Regional environmental co-operation has also been advanced through institutions as diverse as the South Pacific Regional Environmental Programme (SPREP) and Association of South-East Asian Nations (ASEAN).[73] But despite the growth of regional environmental regimes in the Third World, there is as yet no compelling evidence that such an approach promotes sustainable development better than global institutions.

C. Evictions from Eden

Nature Parks Versus People

Having surveyed general developments in environmental governance affecting post-colonial societies, we now consider some of the more specific challenges facing developing countries. The first is the long-standing 'parks vs people' debate. The colonial confrontation was not only a political conquest but also the imposition of alien environmental norms, values and institutions. In contrast to indigenous environmental management norms and practices oriented to conservation and sustainable use,[74] the imported colonial development model emphasised large-scale, commercial exploitation of all useable natural resources. But authorities chose to set aside some natural areas as game reserves and parks, though again their purpose would primarily be to serve the recreational and scientific

[71] RT Deacon and P Murphy, 'The Structure of an Environmental Transaction: The Debt-For-Nature Swap' (1997) 73(Feb) *Land Economics* 1.

[72] See eg C Giraud-Kinley, 'The Effectiveness of International Law: Sustainable Development in the South Pacific Region' (1999) 12 *Georgetown International Environmental L Rev* 125; M Holley, 'Sustainable Development in Central America: Translating Regional Accords into Domestic Enforcement' (1998) 25 *Ecology Law Quarterly* 89.

[73] D Craig, K Kheng-Lian and NA Robinson (eds), *Capacity Building for Environmental Law in the Asian and Pacific Region: Approaches and Resources* (Asian Development Bank, 2002) 289–351.

[74] See generally D Brokensha *et al* (eds), *Indigenous Knowledge Systems and Development* (UP America, 1980).

interests of the colonisers, not the local people displaced to make way for such estates.[75]

Colonial development policies thus separated 'nature' and 'humankind', treating the former largely as a resource to be managed instrumentally in service of the latter. Colonial economic progress was conceived of and pursued as a linear process in which the 'civilised' and 'developed' nations were at the forefront, while the 'backward peoples' of the Third World brought up the rear.[76] By equating urban lifestyle with the highest state of civilisation and forest dwelling with savagery, early resource management law legitimised the forcible eviction and removal of forest-dwelling peoples from their habitats.[77]

National parks are not the only areas where local peoples have been displaced. More importantly, colonialism thrived on the most extensive land grab in human history, and one that gave rise to some of the worst environmental disasters in history.[78] The imported European concepts of property differed from those of traditional societies of the colonised world. In his evidence before the West African Lands Commission in 1908, Chief Elesi Odogbolu, a traditional chief of the Yorubas of West Africa, expounded the traditional conception of land ownership among the Yorubas thus: 'I conceive that land belongs to a vast family of which many are dead, few are living and countless members are unborn'.[79]

In many jurisdictions, land rights were pivotal to nationalist struggles for independence, yet such struggles did not necessarily lead to a restoration of traditional land tenure systems.[80] In Kenya, for instance, European settler lands were often not redistributed to their former traditional custodians, but were privatised and distributed to those allied to the new post-colonial political elites.[81] In Uganda and Zimbabwe, the post-colonial governments preferred to nationalise tribal and European-held lands in the name of nation-building.[82] Today, most traditional common property resources in Africa have been either privatised or nationalised—in either case, local communities remain disenfranchised from land management.

[75] JM MacKenzie, *The Empire of Nature: Hunting, Conservation and British Imperialism* (Manchester UP, 1988).

[76] V Tucher, 'The Myth of Development: A Critique of Eurocentric Discourse' in R Munck and D O'Hearn (eds), *Critical Development Theory: Contributions to a New Paradigm* (Zed Books, 1999) 8; M Lindley, *The Acquisition and Government of Backward Territory in International Law* (Longmans, 1926).

[77] C Geisler, 'A New Kind of Trouble: Evictions in Eden' (2003) 55(175) *Intl Social Science Journal* 69.

[78] SW Awry, 'Tenure Policy Toward Common Property Natural Resources in Sub-Saharan Africa' (1990) 30(2) *Natural Resources Policy* 403; CK Meek, *Land Law and Custom in the Colonies* (Frank Cass, 1968).

[79] West African Lands Commission (WALC), *Report* (WALC, 1908)183, para 1048.

[80] S Moyo (ed), *Reclaiming the Land: The Resurgence of Rural Movements in Africa, Asia and Latin America* (Zed Books, 2005).

[81] D Porter *et al*, *Development in Practice: Paved with Good Intentions* (Routledge, 1991)29.

[82] Richardson, above n 29, 34–35.

The contemporary 'bush meat' crisis in Africa and the staggering loss of biodiversity from the breakdown in traditional community resource management[83] disguise the fact that biodiversity has evolved in the region, not in spite of human habitation, but because of it.[84] There is ample evidence that many local communities have indigenous norms and practices governing human interaction and co-existence with wildlife and other manifestations of nature.[85] The key challenge now is to mobilise the accumulated traditional knowledge systems and practices in contemporary environmental governance.[86] This is unlikely without the restoration of vibrant community-level common property regimes and effective and participatory local government.[87] Inequities in access to land have been linked to deforestation and environmental mismanagement as landless peasants invade ecologically sensitive areas such as erosion-prone hillsides or thin-soiled rainforests.[88] Myers for instance has traced the relationship between agricultural colonisation of the Amazon and poverty, population growth and maldistribution of land in rural communities.[89] Government policies that marginalise traditional community institutions and customary laws further contribute to the breakdown of community livelihoods.[90]

The creation of nature parks in post-colonial states has often been done pursuant to international environmental agreements acceded to by post-colonial states. The problem is not the creation of nature parks per se, but the chronic and disastrous lack of local participation in the decision as to where the nature parks are to be located and how local communities may interact with the parks.[91]

[83] MI Bakarr *et al*, *Hunting and Bushmeat Utilization in the African Rain Forest: Perspectives Toward a Blueprint for Conservation Action* (Conservation International, 2001).

[84] D Wood, 'Conservation and Agriculture: The Need for a New International Network of Biodiversity and Development Institutes to Resolve Conflict' in AF Krattiger *et al* (eds), *Widening Perspectives on Biodiversity* (Natraj Publishers, 1994) 425.

[85] P England, 'Tree Planting, Sustainable Development and the Roles of Law in Bongo, North East Ghana' (1995) 39(2) *Journal African Law* 138; J Labuschagne and C Boonzaaier, 'African Perception and Legal Rules Concerning Nature' (1998) 5 *South African Journal of International Environmental Law & Policy* 58; SK Date-Bah, 'Rights of Indigenous Peoples in Relations to Natural Resources Development: An African Perspective' (1998) 16 *Journal Energy & Natural Resources Law* 389.

[86] Richardson, above n 29.

[87] *Ibid*, 31–61.

[88] EP Eckholm, *The Dispossessed of the Earth: Land Reform and Sustainable Development* (Worldwatch Institute, 1979); P Utting, *Trees, People and Power. Social Dimensions of Deforestation and Forest Protection in Central America* (Earthscan, 1993).

[89] N Myers, 'The World's Forests: Problems and Potentials' (1996) 23 *Environmental Conservation* 156.

[90] For an important IUCN case study on northern Pakistan, see A Bilal, H Haque and P Moore, *Customary Laws: Governing Natural Resource Management in the Northern Areas* (IUCN Law Programme, 2003).

[91] R Neumann, 'Primitive Ideas: Protected Area Buffer Zones and the Politics of Land in Africa' (1997) 28 *Development & Change* 559; RA Schroeder, 'Geographies of Environmental Intervention in Africa' (1999) 23 *Progress in Human Geography* 359; K Brandon, KH Redford, and SF Sanderson (eds), *Parks in Peril: People, Politics, and Protected Areas.* (Island Press, 1998); J Cordell, 'Boundaries and Bloodlines: Tenure of Indigenous Homelands and Protected Areas' in E Kemf (ed), *Indigenous Peoples and Protected Areas. The Law of Mother Earth* (Earthscan, 1993) 61.

Treaties such as the Convention on the Conservation of Migratory Species of Wild Animals[92] oblige states parties to preserve and/or restore the habitats of these species, but without concomitant obligations to take into account the social and economic needs of local communities which might be affected by implementation of the convention. Similarly, the emphasis on parks over people is implicit in the 1973 Convention on International Trade in Endangered Species of Wild Fauna and Flora (CITES).[93] It governs international trade in endangered species, and/or in their products and derivatives through a system of import/export permits. Though its focus has been to control trade in species rather than to conserve their habitats,[94] CITES has helped to reverse the decline in African elephant populations through a process that includes the creation of nature parks and the eviction of natives from areas hitherto shared with elephants and other wildlife. Perhaps as a sign of this success, the elephant populations of the southern African states grew to a point where those countries were allowed under the CITES arrangements to resume the cull and trade in their herds.[95]

Notwithstanding some successes recorded by CITES and other nature conservation treaties, an enduring criticism is that international legal instruments that emphasise wildlife 'preservation' in post-colonial societies ignore or understate the grinding poverty among many local communities. They fail to take into account the political and economic conditions that foster poverty, hardship and community breakdown that often fuel unsustainable exploitation of biodiversity evident in the bushmeat crisis.[96]

The 1992 Convention on Biological Diversity (CBD)[97] perhaps offers a more appropriate legal framework for addressing these issues.[98] Ratified by most developing nations, the CBD requires parties to develop national strategies for the conservation and sustainable use of biodiversity and to integrate those with development planning. Parties are required to establish protected areas to conserve biodiversity, regulate and manage resources for the same purpose, and ensure that

[92] 1979, 19 ILM 11.

[93] 1973, 993 UNTS 243. There were 49 African parties and 31 South/Meso American parties to this Convention as of July 2005.

[94] For critical reviews of the Convention's influence on the conservation of biological resources, see J Hutton and B Dickson (eds), *Endangered Species—Threatened Convention: The Past, Present and Future of CITES* (Earthscan, 2000).

[95] For a concise discussion of the political economy of getting to this point, see M Kidd and M Cowling, 'CITES and the African Elephant' in Chaytor and Gray, above n 1, 49.

[96] L Gray and W Moseley, 'A Geographical Perspective on Poverty-Environment Interactions' (2005) 171(1) *Geographical Journal* 9.

[97] 31 ILM 818.

[98] See generally D Bodansky, 'International Law and the Protection of Biological Diversity' (1995) 28 *Vanderbilt Journal of Transnational Law* 623; R Panjabi, 'International Law and the Preservation of Species: An Analysis of the Convention on Biological Diversity Signed at the Rio Earth Summit in 1992' (1993) 11 *Dickinson Journal of International Law* 187.

areas adjacent to protected zones are also managed sustainably.[99] The CBD recognises the contributions local communities can make to such efforts, reflected most prominently in Article 8(j), which provides that each party must:

> respect, preserve and maintain knowledge, innovations and practices of indigenous and local communities embodying traditional life-styles relevant for the conservation and sustainable use of biological diversity and promote their wider application with the approval and involvement of the holders of such knowledge, innovations and practices and encourage the equitable sharing of the benefits arising from the utilisation of such knowledge, innovations and practices.[100]

Furthermore, the CBD obliges developed nations and foreign companies to transfer financial resources and technologies to assist developing countries to implement the Convention.[101] Sustainable utilisation of biodiversity, such as for the development of new biotechnologies, is *expected* to be for the mutual benefit of all parties, not a mechanism for developing countries or local communities to surrender intellectual property rights over their genetic resources to the interests of capital.

The challenge to post-colonial states, therefore, is to regulate access to their genetic resources with specific regard to non-nationals.[102] This is important for at least two reasons. First, the balance of rights and interests between the industrialised and developing states on this matter is skewed in favour of the former on account of the global regulatory regimes on trade, patents and related matters.[103] In particular, these regimes do not accommodate traditional knowledge,[104] yet traditional knowledge is the indispensable intangible component of the composite treasure of post-colonial states' biological resources and access to it must thus be negotiated under the CBD.[105]

[99] On the development of *national biodiversity strategies and action plans*, and their achievements, see P Herkenrath, 'The Implementation of the Convention on Biological Diversity—A Non-Government Perspective Ten Years On' (2002) 11 *Review of European Community & International Environmental Law* 29.

[100] Above n 97, and see also Arts 5–10, 15–19. A similar emphasis on the environmental rights or needs of local and indigenous peoples is evident in the Desertification Convention, above n 63. See further LP Breckenridge 'Protection of Biological and Cultural Diversity: Emerging Recognition of Local Communities Rights in Ecosystems Under International Law' (1992) 59 *Tennessee L Rev* 735.

[101] G Duncan, 'Common But Differentiated Responsibilities: The Implications of Principle Seven and the Duty to Cooperate in the Implementation of the Convention on Biological Diversity' (2002) 16 *Ocean Yearbook* 75.

[102] See further LA Firestone, 'You Say Yes, I Say No: Defining Community Prior Informed Consent under the Convention on Biological Diversity' (2003) 16 *Georgetown International Environmental L Rev* 171.

[103] J Ntambirweki, 'Biotechnology and International Law Within the North-South Context' (2001) 14 *Transnational Lawyer* 103; A Adewopo, 'The Global Intellectual Property System and Sub-Saharan Africa: A Prognostic Reflection' (2002) 33 *University of Toledo L Rev* 749; JFB Atibasay, 'The International Legal Regime for Biotechnology Patenting: An Appraisal from the Standpoint of Developing Countries' (2001) 31 *Revue Générale de Droit* 291.

[104] L Godshall, 'Making Space for Indigenous Intellectual Property Rights Under Current International Environmental Law' (2003) 15 *Georgetown International Environmental L Rev* 497.

[105] R Coombe, 'The Recognition of Indigenous Peoples and Community Traditional Knowledge in International Law' (2002) 14 *St Thomas L Rev* 275.

The second and more urgent reason is that continuing efforts to implement the CBD in the developing world are often embedded within a problematic, broader environmental law framework. Though these laws and plans are increasingly informed by principles of modern international environmental law, they are not sufficiently moored away from their colonial law principles and regulatory antecedents. Nor are the requisite financial and technical resources in place to implement the CBD.[106] Yet, in many post-colonial states where national legislation exists to regulate these matters, their broadness, vagueness or outmodedness keep them out of step with the obligations and benefits of the CBD.[107]

Certainly, some developing countries are belatedly seeking to decentralise decision-making and give local peoples a greater voice in environmental management. Uganda, for instance, shows that decentralisation of decision-making and active participation by local communities in environmental governance yield positive results.[108] Uganda's National Environment Act 1994 introduced provisions for public participation through local and district environment committees.[109] Its Wildlife Statute 1996 repealed the colonial-era National Parks Act and the Game (Preservation and Control) Act. The Wildlife Statute introduced the concept of benefit sharing with the local communities surrounding wildlife conservation areas.[110] The Uganda Wildlife Authority (UWA) must pay 20 per cent of park entry fees collected to the local government responsible for the area adjacent to the park. Further, the traditional rights of occupation and resource use of individuals in conservation areas are recognised.[111] Participation of local communities in wildlife management is guaranteed by a requirement that one-third of the UWA Board members should be representatives of local communities.[112] The relevant Minister must also consult the affected local community before a new wildlife conservation area is designated. This reform has been complemented by reforms to local government (Local Government Act 1995) and property rights (Land Act 1998) that have restored some customary land rights and local control over resource management. For example, the Land Act enables individuals to obtain certificates of customary ownership, and for holders of customary tenure, who

[106] P Kameri-Mbote and P Cullet, 'Biological Diversity Management in Africa: Legal and Policy Perspectives in the Run-up to WSSD' (2002) 11 *Review of European Community & International Environmental Law* 38.

[107] AG Oludayo, 'The Convention of Biological Diversity, Access to and Exploitation of Genetic Resources and the Land Tenure System in Nigeria' (1999) 11 *African Journal of International Law* 86; G Nnona, 'Choice of Law in International Contracts for the Transfer of Technology: Critique of the Nigerian Approach' (2000) 44 *Journal of African Law* 78.

[108] J Ntambirweki and E Dribidu, *The Legal and Policy Instruments for Sustainable Management of Resources in Uganda* (Scandinavian Seminar College, 1999); BJ Richardson, 'Environmental Management in Uganda: The Importance of Property Law and Local Government in Wetlands Conservation' (1993) 37 *Journal of African Law* 109.

[109] S 4.

[110] S 70A.

[111] S 20.

[112] Sched 1.

wish to use land as a group, to establish common land associations to manage and protect their interests in the communal land.[113]

The Ugandan example exemplifies a shift from authoritarian state control of the environment to a paradigm of community-focused sustainability.[114] If ownership of land in post-colonial states were vested in members of the community rather than nationalised or privatised, local communities would be better placed to manage their environments well.[115] Decisions on how best to utilise natural resources of a given community must take into consideration the social, political and cultural realities of the local peoples affected.[116]

However, while local input is usually a necessary condition for sustainable use, it is insufficient in itself. This is evident in those countries where traditional community institutions survived the colonial period largely intact. In Western Samoa, for example, the maintenance of customary land tenure systems and strong tribal authorities has not prevented significant conversion of indigenous forest to agriculture.[117] These conversions have arisen to meet the increasing population and concomitant growth in economic demand. Paulson suggests that 'one of the unfortunate consequences of viewing indigenous forest peoples simply as victims of political economic marginalisation and exploitation is that the equally real challenges which these groups face in controlling . . . their own increasing demands on their resources tend to get neglected'.[118] Consequently, environmental reform must also address mechanisms by which local communities can collaborate with management institutions at other levels of economic policy-making and development planning. These institutions include those that shape the global economy, trade and other fundamental causes of environmental pressure in post-colonial societies.

D. Environmental Regulation in Rapidly Industrialising Economies

The economies, environmental challenges and legal regimes of post-colonial states are not homogenous. The experiences of East Asia's industrialising 'tigers' in

[113] R Mwebaza, 'How to Integrate Statutory and Customary Tenure: The Uganda Case', Paper presented at *Land Rights and Sustainable Development in Sub-Saharan Africa* (Drylands Programme Issue Paper No 83, International Institute for Environment and Development, Feb 1999).

[114] R Goodland, 'Sourcebook: Policy Options for the World Bank Group in Extractive Industries', *Independent Extractive Review for International Finance Corporation and the World Bank Group,* 26 July 2004, 9.

[115] PE Oshio, 'Indigenous Land Tenure and Nationalization of Land in Nigeria' (1990) 43 *Boston College Third World LJ* 43.

[116] K Lawal, *Ecology and Culture: Reflections on Environmental Law and Policy in Sub-Sahara Africa* (Nigeria Law Centre, 1998) 31.

[117] DD Paulson, 'Understanding Tropical Deforestation: The Case of Western Samoa' (1994) 21 *Environmental Conservation* 326, 329.

[118] *Ibid,* 330.

these respects differ in particular from those in Africa or Latin America where tensions between biodiversity conservation and local communities have been a dominant concern. East Asia's bullish economic growth in the post-World War II period has wrought massive ecological change and stress.[119] It has been estimated that while it took the West some 400 years to achieve a tenfold increase in *per capita* income, South Korea and Taiwan bolted to the same gain in merely 50 years.[120] A ubiquitous philosophy in East Asia has been to 'grow first, clean up later'. Air and water pollution engulfs many of its cities, posing inter alia serious public health risks.[121] Rapid urbanisation and industrialisation have engendered environmental problems that require legal and policy responses quite different from those found in other developing countries. The apotheosis of this economic transformation is the special economic zones (SEZs). In China, South Korea, Thailand and other industrialising hotspots in the region,[122] special areas have been designated to lure foreign investment and export production through favourable investment and trade conditions, and often exemption from certain kinds of regulation.[123]

Ostensibly, most East Asian states have amassed considerable environmental laws and policies, often borrowing from Western precedents.[124] Many states have opted for the seeming simplicity and convenience of central environmental administration, so as to bring coherence and co-ordination to policy-making.[125] Legislation often takes the form of command-and-control regulation with wide discretionary powers given to administrators.[126] This, however, can create inappropriate scales for environmental management and an institutional vacuum at local levels of governance. This institutional centripetalism is reflected in governments' preferences for national environmental strategies, national environmental agencies and other policy centralising mechanisms. Examples of national framework statutes include China's Environmental Protection Law 1979, Malaysia's Environmental Quality Act 1974, Thailand's Enhancement and Conservation of National Environmental Quality Act 1992 and Taiwan's Basic Environmental Act 2002. Further, some states have incorporated environmental protection clauses into their national constitutions as an expression of their commitment. To illustrate, the South Korean constitution was amended in 1980 to provide its citizens with the right to live in a healthy and clean environment.[127] Nonetheless, these

[119] See MC Howard (ed), *Asia's Environmental Crisis* (Westview, 1993).

[120] M Dowling, 'Industrialization in Asia: A Tale of Two Regions' (1997) 8 *Journal of Asian Economics* 295, 295.

[121] UN Economic and Social Commission for Asia and the Pacific (ESCAP) *State of the Environment in Asia and the Pacific* (ESCAP, 2000) 124–5.

[122] Others include Taiwan and Malaysia, and recently the Philippines and Vietnam.

[123] DA Rondinelli, 'Export Processing Zones and Economic Development in Asia' (1987) 46 *American Journal of Economics & Society* 89.

[124] See B Boer, R Ramsay and DR Rothwell, *International Environmental Law in the Asia Pacific* (Kluwer, 1998).

[125] Richardson, above n 29, 21–26.

[126] See generally Thomas, above n 17.

[127] South Korean Constitution, Art 35, available at www.oefre.unibe.ch/law/icl/ks00000_.html.

constitutional provisions often lack the legal significance found in Western examples. For example, the Supreme Court of Korea has construed the environmental protection provision of its constitution as not self-executing.[128] Most East Asian states have national environmental management agencies, which operate in conjunction with line ministries dealing with water, minerals and other natural resources.[129] All nations in the region have also adopted national environmental policies and plans, though their regulatory impact has been highly variable. At best, they serve to indicate long-term political commitment and, at worst, are mere public relations exercises.

Even China, the region's greatest industrialising behemoth, boasts a laudable array of environmental laws, policies and institutions—comparable to that of many Western countries.[130] Earlier, Mao Tse-tung's reign was described as a 'war against nature',[131] where Mao's grandiose aspirations led to ecologically destructive projects such as the Sanmenxia dam on the Yellow River.[132] While the gigantic Three Gorges dam reveals that the 'Think Big' mentality persists among contemporary Chinese leaders,[133] environmental issues are being acknowledged in other contexts. A raft of new environmental laws has been promulgated or revised, notably the Environmental Impact Assessment Law 2002 and the amendments to the Air Pollution Prevention and Control Law 2000, overseen by the State Environmental Protection Administration.

What factors have shaped environmental law reform in East Asia? Rising economic prosperity and democratic reform appear to have been relevant factors. Economic prosperity is said to boost the prospects for sustainable development. Kuznets' theory predicts a correlation between a society's standard of living and its rising concern for the environment.[134] This is because pollution damage supposedly receives a higher priority after rising wealth has financed basic investments in public health and education, and because wealthier societies have more resources to devote to environmental protection.[135] There is insufficient empirical research to verify these hypotheses in relation to East Asia. The growth of an

[128] Eg Dae-bup-won [DBW] [Sup Ct] 94 ma 2218 (23 May 1995) (S Korea); DBW 95 da 23378 (15 Sept 1995) (S. Korea); DBW 96 da 56153 (22 July 1997) (S Korea).

[129] BJ Richardson, 'Is East Asia Industrializing Too Quickly? Environmental Regulation in Its Special Economic Zones' (2005) 22 *UCLA Pacific Basin LJ* 150.

[130] H Zhang and RJ Ferris Jr, 'Shaping an Environmental Protection Regime for the New Century: Environmental Law and Policy in the People's Republic of China' (1998) 6 *Asian Journal of Environment Management* 35.

[131] J Shapiro, *Mao's War Against Nature: Politics and Environment in Revolutionary China* (Cambridge UP, 2001).

[132] *Ibid*, 23.

[133] RL. Edmonds, 'Recent Developments and Prospects for the Sanxia (Three Gorges) Dam' in T Cannon (ed), *China's Economic Growth: The Impact on Regions, Migration and the Environment* (St Martin's Press, 2000) 161, 165.

[134] S Kuznets, 'Economic Growth and Income Inequality' (1955) 45 *American Economic Rev* 1.

[135] *Ibid;* YS Lee and A So (eds), *Asia's Environmental Movements: Comparative Perspectives* (ME Sharpe, 1999).

urban consumer society in the region, however, appears to be generating a host of environmental problems that many governments have yet to address[136]—with the notable exception of Singapore, whose city state government is renowned for its authoritarian control of waste and pollution where even individuals can be fined for merely chewing bubble gum in public.[137]

Democracy is arguably a relevant ingredient for reform in some contexts, because it allows for the articulation of public concerns and social pressures for policy reform. The authors of a study on *Civil Society and the Future of Environmental Governance in Asia* argue that the 'growth and effectiveness of [Asian] civil society—and the process of democratisation that nourish [sic] it—are likely to be the most significant force in the emergence and implementation of [a new paradigm of sustainable development in Asia]'.[138] The corporatism and clientelism that have marked state–society relations in East Asia during the post-war period are increasingly being challenged by democratic and civil societal movements.[139] During the 1990s, Taiwan and Korea embraced Western liberal-democratic reforms to strengthen their rule of law, including constitutional and parliamentary reforms and the promotion of more effective administrative and judicial structures.[140] South Korea's and Taiwan's democratisation reforms have fuelled various environmental activist movements, which in turn have contributed to the strengthening of environmental laws.[141] As a result of environmental degradation from South Korea's 'poisoned prosperity', some people began reassessing their leaders' 'faster and faster' motto.[142] Taiwan has also experienced popular protests against pollution, particularly nuclear energy programmes.[143] But other states in the region have been slower to reform, such as Thailand and Indonesia where 'money politics' and periodic interference from the military have hampered better environmental governance.[144] But democratisation alone appears to be insufficient to pro-

[136] D Connor, *Managing the Environment with Rapid Industrialization: Lessons from the East Asian Experience* (OECD, 1994).

[137] LL Heng, 'Singapore's New Environmental Law: The Environmental Pollution Control Act, *1999*' [2000] *Singapore Journal of Legal Studies* 1.

[138] L Zarsky and S Tay, 'Civil Society and the Future of Environmental Governance in Asia' in D Angel and M Rock (eds), *Asia's Clean Revolution: Industry Growth and the Environment* (Greenleaf Publishing, 2001) ch 6, abstract.

[139] KE Brodsgaard and S Young, 'Introduction: State Capacity in East Asia' in KE Brodsgaard and S Young (eds), *State Capacity in East Asia: Japan, Taiwan, China and Vietnam* (Oxford UP, 2001) 6.

[140] S Cooney, 'The Effects of Rule of Law Principles in Taiwan' in R Peerenboom (ed), *Asian Discourses of Rule of Law* (RoutledgeCurzon, 2004) 417.

[141] Lee and So, above n 135.

[142] See generally N Eder, *Poisoned Prosperity: Development, Modernization and the Environment in South Korea* (ME Sharpe, 1996); S Kim, 'Democratization and Environmentalism: South Korea and Taiwan in Comparative Perspective' (2000) 35 *J Asian & African Studies* 287.

[143] Eg K Bradsher, 'Nuclear Dump Disrupts a Peaceful Taiwan Island', *New York Times*, 30 June 2002, 3; JH Lim and SY Tang, 'Democratization and Environmental Policy-Making in Korea' (2002) 15 *Governance* 561, 568–73.

[144] *See* CA Samudavanija and S Paribatra, 'Thailand: Liberalization Without Democracy' in JW Morely (ed), Driven by Growth: Political Change in the Asia-Pacific Region (ME Sharpe, 1993) 119;

duce major shifts in environmental policy, as the situation of the Philippines shows.[145] Conversely, high living standards can produce strong environmental laws even in the absence of vibrant civil society, as exemplified by Singapore's soft-authoritarian democracy.

Despite its achievements, East Asia's extensive body of environmental law is somewhat misleading. Their governments' success in environmental law and policy *formation* has not been matched by policy *implementation*. Persistent weaknesses in their underlying legal institutions have hampered environmental reforms. One basic problem is that legislation is often poorly drafted, framed in very general and exhortational terms, with undefined terminology, legislative gaps and inconsistent provisions.[146] Sometimes environmental legislation seems more akin to policy guidance than legal rules. For example, China's Environmental Protection Law 1989 vaguely proclaims that local governments are 'responsible for the quality of the environment within their own administrative regions'.[147] Vague provisions can pose problems in the context of legislative sanctions.

Indeed, enforcement is the weakest link in East Asia's environmental law regimes. In 1994, Lester Ross wryly commented, 'for many years, China's environmental authorities have been like a muzzled dog: plenty of bark but little bite'.[148] Occasionally, major administrative enforcement crackdowns are launched with considerable fanfare.[149] But sustained enforcement seems unlikely, given the personal relationships that flourish between regulators and industry.[150] Speaking of China, Hills and Man suggest that because of 'a cultural predisposition to harmony and consensus-building . . . heavy-handed imposition of environmental regulations is typically avoided, unless an edict is delivered from the upper echelons of the Government'.[151] So far, the courts in East Asia have been used mostly as a last resort; policies and regulations serve as guidance, and disputes are settled largely through negotiation and bargaining outside the court system.[152] A few significant public interest environmental cases have been litigated in recent years in the

DL. Tookey, 'Southeast Asian Environmentalism at its Crossroads: Learning Lessons from Thailand's Eclectic Approach to Environmental Law and Policy' (1999) 11 *Georgetown International Environmental L Rev* 307, 330–2.

145 MS Feliciano, *Environmental Law in the Philippines* (Institute of International Legal Studies, University of the Philippines, 1992).

146 P Crone, 'China's Legal Structure' in C Hunter *et al* (eds), *A Guide to the Legal System of the PRC* (Asia Law and Practice, 1997) 1, 1.

147 Art 16.

148 L Ross, 'The Next Wave of Environmental Legislation' (1994) 21 *China Business Rev* 30, 30.

149 See eg 'China Punishes 12,000 Firms for Environmental Offences', *Xinhua News Agency*, 21 Nov 2003.

150 P Hills and CS Man, 'Environmental Regulation and the Industrial Sector in China: The Role of Informal Relationships in Policy Implementation' (1998) 7 *Business Strategy & Environment* 53.

151 *Ibid*, 61.

152 BJ Sinkule and L Ortolano, *Implementing Environmental Policy in China* (Praeger, 1995)27.

region, notably in Malaysia and the Philippines.[153] Other states such as Vietnam and Indonesia lack an effective and independent judiciary willing and able to entertain such cases.[154]

Industrialisation and market transformation will remain an indelible feature of East Asia's economic policy for some time. But the region's long-term economic modernisation will ultimately not be sustainable unless its economic policy is wedded to stronger environmental regulation. The challenge is to reform environmental law and policy to take account of East Asian circumstances without accommodating them so completely as to surrender all possibilities of improvement. A model of 'ecological modernisation' reform could offer major advantages to the more advanced economies of East Asia. Ecological modernisation promises a healthy synergy between economic development and environmental protection when economies and technologies are 'modernised' to allow for more efficient and less wasteful production.[155] Modernisation can occur through corporate environmental management systems and the application of advanced, clean technologies, encouraged through policy instruments such as pollution taxes and corporate environmental reporting obligations. Although criticised by some environmentalists as a compromise that alleviates, rather than solves, the environmental crisis, the advantages of ecological modernisation would appear to outweigh its disadvantages, especially for economies rapidly industrialising.[156] The ecological modernisation model was the basis of Japan's successful response to air pollution in the 1970s, and the clean-up of West Germany's industrial and energy sectors after the acid rain-induced forest death in the 1980s.[157]

So far, command and control regulation in Asia's industrialising economies is gradually being supplemented by a mosaic of environmental governance mechanisms, spanning market incentives, business self-regulation, management system-based approaches, voluntary reporting schemes and audit requirements designed to increase the transparency and accountability of industry and regulators.[158] One such innovation is China's Clean Production Promotion Law (CPPL) 2002. It shifts China's environmental regulatory focus from traditional end-of-pipe controls to the products and processes from which pollution originates, by requiring

[153] See M Raman, 'The Malaysian High Court Decision Concerning the Bakun Hydro-Electric Dam Project' (1997) 2 *Asia Pacific Journal of Environmental Law* 93; DB Gatmaytan, 'The Illusion of Intergenerational Equity: Oposa v. Factoran as Pyrrhic Victory' (2003) 15 *Georgetown International Environmental L Rev* 457.

[154] C Warren and K Elston, *The Politics of Environmental Regulation in Indonesia* (U Western Australia Press, 1994) 12.

[155] P Christoff, 'Ecological Modernization, Ecological Modernities' (1996) 5 *Environmental Politics* 476.

[156] R Welford and P Hills, 'Ecological Modernisation, Environmental Policy and Innovation: Priorities for the Asia-Pacific Region' (2003) 2 *International Environment & Sustainable Development* 324.

[157] See SC Young and J van der Straaten, *The Emergence of Ecological Modernisation: Integrating the Environment and the Economy?* (Routledge, 2001); OECD, *Environmental Policies in Japan* (OECD, 1977).

[158] Richardson, above n 129

enterprises to recycle specified products and packaging, and it encourages some preferential measures for those who adopt the clean production model, such as preferential loans or tax cuts. Another sign of ecological modernisation reform is environmental taxation. Air pollution charges have been levied in South Korea and China; and water effluent treatment charges exacted in Thailand, Hong Kong and China; and water consumption charges exacted in virtually all countries.[159] But these initiatives are just the beginnings, and systematic reform in these directions has yet to transpire in Asia's industrialising economies.

E. Transnational Corporations and the Environment

A third seminal theme in the experiences of post-colonial states and environmental law concerns the activities of transnational corporations (TNCs). Many environmental problems in the developing world (and indeed in other regions) are closely associated with the activities of TNCs. Some TNCs wield economic resources that dwarf the size of the developing country economies that host them. While TNCs are predominantly from OECD countries, increasingly firms from emerging economies such as South Korea and Taiwan are investing internationally.[160] The growing transnational character of business has intensified concerns about the social and environmental impacts of large companies and the adequacy of their regulation.[161] A succession of catastrophes, such as the chemical spill at Bhopal, India, and the oil industry's devastation of Nigeria's Niger Delta, as well as the dumping of toxic waste in West Africa and mega-mining projects such as at Ok Tedi in Papua New Guinea, are some of the more sensational hazards of foreign investment.[162] Such investment has also been unfavourably associated with 'dangerous working conditions, child labour and the violent repression of dissent'.[163]

The environmental effects of TNC investment can be divided primarily into scale effects (expansion of economic output), structural effects (reallocation of

[159] Asian Development Bank, above n 39, ch 11; OECD, *Economic Instruments for Environmental Management in Developing Countries* (OECD, 1993).

[160] HF French, 'When Foreign Investors Pay for Development' (1997) 10 *World Watch* 8.

[161] See N Hood and S Young (eds), *The Globalization of Multinational Enterprise Activity and Economic Development* (St Martin's Press, 2000); HM Kim, *Globalization of International Financial Markets: Causes and Consequences* (Ashgate, 1999).

[162] See PR Kleindorfer and HC Kunreuther (eds), *Insuring and Managing Hazardous Risks: From Seveso to Bhopal and Beyond* (Springer, 1987); A Ekpu, 'Environmental Impact of Oil on Water: A Comparative Overview of the Law and Policy in the United States and Nigeria' (1995–97) 24–25 *Denver Journal of International Law & Policy* 64; L Starke (ed), *Breaking New Ground: Mining, Minerals, and Sustainable Development. The Report of the MMSD Project* (Earthscan, 2002); S Holwick, 'Transnational Corporate Behavior and its Disparate and Unjust Effects on the Indigenous Cultures and the Environment of Developing Nations: Jota v. Texaco, a Case Study' (2000) 11(1) *Colorado Journal of International Environmental Law & Policy* 183.

[163] French, above n 160, 10.

production and consumption) and technological effects (technology innovation and diffusion).[164] In general, the former two effects tend to be negative, while the technology effects are anticipated to be positive.[165] Foreign investment may exacerbate the inadequacies of local environmental regulation by increasing the scale of production and consumption.[166] Even if increased foreign investment leads to local environmental improvements through the infusion of cleaner technologies, these benefits may be offset on an international scale if production of pollution-intensive products is simply shifted to other countries.

It can be difficult for governments to regulate TNCs, especially their environmental behaviour. A report by the UN Centre on Transnational Corporations explained that this difficulty arose 'due to transnational corporate flexibility, mobility, leverage, communication and control gaps, secrecy, non-transparency, limited accountability, [and] divided loyalties'.[167] More specifically, the environmental impacts of TNCs are seen by some commentators as primarily a result of inter-jurisdictional competition for economic investment. Their theories predict that competition between nations for economic investment affects regulatory behaviour by leading to a 'race to the bottom', 'regulatory chill' or a 'pollution haven'.[168] The gist of the argument is that stringent environmental standards in industrial countries push businesses to relocate operations to developing countries, where standards are relatively weaker, which results in financial savings. Concomitantly, post-colonial states, in their drive to join the ranks of developed countries, prefer to endure environmental abuse as a trade-off for rapid industrial development.[169] This generates a 'race to the bottom' as governments compete to lower environmental and social regulation to attract investment. Even if there is no race, competitive concerns may still affect environmental decision-making in host countries by causing a 'regulatory chill'.[170] This arises where states refrain from stricter environmental controls for fear of alienating existing or potential foreign investors.[171]

[164] T Jones, 'Trade and Investment: Selected Links to Domestic Environmental Policy', paper presented at the International Conference on Globalization and National Environmental Policy, Sept 2003, 6.

[165] *Ibid.*

[166] *See* A Markandya, 'Overview and Lessons Learnt' in V Jha *et al* (eds), *Reconciling Trade and the Environment: Lessons from Case Studies in Developing Countries* (Edward Elgar, 1999) 1.

[167] UN Centre on Transnational Corporations (UNCTC), *Environmental Aspects of the Activities of Transnational Corporations* (UNCTC, 1985).

[168] For an overview of these debates, see H Nordstrom and S Vaughan, *Trade and Environment* (World Trade Organisation, 1999).

[169] G Handl, 'Environmental Protection and Development in Third World Countries: Common Responsibility-Common Destiny' (1998) 20 *NYU Journal of International Law & Policy* 603.

[170] DC Esty and D Geradin, 'Environmental Protection and International Competitiveness' (1998) 32 *J World Trade* 5; HJ Leonard, 'Confronting Industrial Pollution in Rapidly Industrializing Countries: Myths, Pitfalls, and Opportunities' (1995) 12 *Ecology Law Quarterly* 779.

[171] Nordstrom and Vaughan, above n 168.

Despite numerous empirical studies and individual examples on this subject, there are no conclusive data on whether foreign investment is overall beneficial or harmful to the environment.[172] The majority of studies suggest that the evidence of a race to the bottom or pollution haven is uncommon, though it seems more likely to arise in poor developing countries and rapidly industrialising regions.[173] Countering the pollution haven theory, there are examples where TNC investment has stimulated improvements to the host country's environmental regulations. Wheeler, for instance, found improvements in air quality in the major cities of the US, China, Brazil and Mexico during the 1990s, the latter three representing the top three shares of foreign direct investment for developing countries during this period.[174] Some research suggests that investors rarely give environmental costs a high priority in their decision-making on investment locations.[175] Environmental compliance costs are more likely to influence the choice of location of a *new* production facility than the relocation of an *existing* facility. The availability of cheap labour, raw materials, existing infrastructure, taxes, transportation costs and market size is usually higher priority for corporate managers in both situations.[176]

On the other hand, some evidence suggests that governments have eased their environmental regulations to entice investment. For instance, some Japanese companies relocated to their poorer South-east Asian neighbours apparently to take advantage of more lenient environmental controls.[177] Mexico's *maquiladora* border region is often seen as proof of industrial flight and pollution haven.[178] Low pollution abatement costs due to lax environmental regulation appear to have been a determinant for drawing foreign investment to this industrial development region bordering the US.[179] Evidence of business relocation was seen in

[172] See eg DC Esty, 'Private Sector Foreign Investment and the Environment' (1995) 4 *Review of European Community & International Environmental Law* 99; E Neumayer, *Greening Trade and Investment* (Earthscan, 2001).

[173] See eg G Porter, 'Trade Competition and Pollution Standards: "Race to the Bottom" or "Stuck at the Bottom"?' (1999) 8 *Journal of Environment & Development* 133; M Mani and D Wheeler, 'In Search of Pollution Havens? Dirty Industry in the World Economy, 1960–1995' (1998) 7 *Journal of Environment & Development* 215; Esty and Geradin, above n 170.

[174] D Wheeler, 'Racing to the Bottom? Foreign Investment and Air Pollution in Developing Countries' (2001) 10 *Journal of Environment & Development* 225, 227–31.

[175] L Zarsky, 'Havens, Halos and Spaghetti: Untangling the Evidence about FDI and the Environment' in OECD (ed), *Foreign Direct Investment and the Environment* (OECD, 1999) 47.

[176] Esty and Geradin, above n 170.

[177] See O Cameron, 'Japan and Southeast Asia's Environment' in MJG Parnwell and RL Bryant (eds), *Environmental Change in Southeast Asia* (Routledge, 1996) 67; AJ Ferreria *et al*, 'Investments and TNCs in the Philippines: Towards Balanced Local and Regional Development' (1997) 14 *Regional Development Dialogue* 67, 78.

[178] *See* EJ Williams, 'The Maquiladora Industry and Environmental Degradation in the United States–Mexico Borderlands' (1996) 27 *St Mary's LJ* 765; DC Esty and BS Gentry, 'Foreign Investment, Globalisation and the Environment' in OECD (ed), *Globalisation and the Environment: Preliminary Perspectives* (OECD, 1997)141, 161.

[179] DJ Molina, 'A Comment on Whether Maquiladoras are in Mexico for Low Wages or to Avoid Pollution Abatement Costs' (1993) 2 *Journal of Environment & Development* 221.

the chemical industry where investment in Mexico ballooned over 20-fold from 1982–1990, following a tightening of environmental regulations in the US.[180] Leonard, however, sees the Mexican situation as more a product of regulatory chill than a race to the bottom, as the environmental regime in the *maquiladora* region area has apparently always been quite easy on industry.[181]

The experience of East Asia's special economic zones (SEZs) is an important example that helps clarify the relationship between environmental regulation and TNCs. The SEZs are specific areas designated by governments for foreign investment and export-oriented industrialisation, to which are conceded favourable investment and trade conditions, and reduced red tape.[182] Taiwan and South Korea established Asia's first SEZs in the mid-1960s and the model soon spread. China has since engineered the most comprehensive SEZs in the region.[183]

Given their strategic economic significance, one might expect environmental regulation in the SEZs, and particularly in relation to TNC investors, to be relatively lenient compared to non-SEZ areas or domestic businesses. Certainly, there are some notorious instances where authorities have waived environmental rules to avoid jeopardising foreign investment deals.[184] An OECD environmental performance review of China noted 'foreign firms promoted imports of outdated technologies and polluting or toxic substances, taking advantage of the lower (or more flexible) environmental standards in China'.[185] And pollution conditions in East Asia's SEZs have attracted some vituperative criticism from observers.[186]

Environmental regulations developed for Asia's SEZs vary, however, in the extent to which they accommodate TNCs. South Korea's Act on Designation and Operation of Free Economic Zones 2002 provides that, when selecting potential sites, the Free Economic Zone Committee must take into account 'securing the environmentally sound and sustainable development'.[187] Further, the plan for each zone must include a 'programme for environmental preservation'.[188] But, controversially, the Korean legislation permits the authorities to reduce or waive

[180] J Clapp, 'Foreign Direct Investment in Hazardous Industries in Developing Countries: Rethinking the Debate' (1998) 7 *Environmental Policy* 92, 99.

[181] Leonard, above n 170.

[182] Among the extensive literature on the history and economics of East Asia's SEZs, see JA Mathews, 'High Technology Industrialization in East Asia' (1996) 3 *Journal of Industry Studies* 1; Rondinelli, above n 123; KY Wong and D Chu, 'Export Processing Zones and Special Economic Zones as Generators of Economic Development: The Asian Experience' (1984) 66B *Geograkiska Annaler* 1; KV Vuoristo, 'The Special Economic Zones and Regions in Southeast Asia' (1994) 106(2) *Terra* 96.

[183] GT Crane, *The Political Economy of China's Special Economic Zones* (ME Sharpe, 1990).

[184] Eg, from China: see C Wing-Hung Lo and P Kwong-To Yip, 'Environmental Impact Assessment Regulation in Hong Kong and Shanghai: A Cross-city Analysis' (1999) 42 *Journal of Environmental Planning & Management* 355, 366.

[185] OECD, *Environmental Priorities for China's Sustainable Development* (OECD, 2001) 28.

[186] Eg F Tester, 'Existential Landscape: China and the Modern Superstore' (1995) 16 *New City Magazine* 41.

[187] Art 5(5).

[188] Art 6(11).

any applicable pollution levies and other environmental charges where they consider this necessary 'for smoothly carrying out the development project of any free economic zone'.[189] In another example, the Philippines' Special Economic Zone Act 1995 provides that the Philippine SEZ Authority 'in coordination with the appropriate agencies, shall take concrete and appropriate steps and enact the proper measures for the protection of the local environment'.[190] The legislation unfortunately gives no hint as to what constitutes 'concrete and appropriate steps'.

China has the most extensive SEZ environmental regulations in Asia. Its Provisional Regulations on Environment Control for Economic Zones Open to Foreigners 1986 state the aim: 'to prevent and control environmental pollution and ecological damage, to ensure the health of human beings, to protect and create a sound investment environment and to promote economic and social development'.[191] These regulations require SEZ authorities to include environmental protection measures in their development plans;[192] to conduct environmental assessments of development proposals;[193] and to prohibit new projects that pose specified serious harms.[194] Local authorities are permitted to introduce supplementary environmental controls, which may be stricter than baseline provincial or national standards.[195] These local SEZ regulations typically encompass land use planning, provision of urban amenities, pollution licensing and waste disposal.[196] Poor legislative drafting, reflected by vague or unworkable provisions, plagues many local regulations however.[197]

Some research suggests that environmental conditions in Asia's SEZs are no worse than other areas of their economies, and indeed may be superior owing to the greater availability of pollution control technologies from foreign investors, as well as the more systematic land use planning of the zones.[198] This phenomenon is known as the 'pollution halo' effect, which posits that host country environmental standards are improved as a result of TNC investment imports of advanced, cleaner technologies and corporate environmental management systems.[199]

[189] Art 15(2).
[190] S 33.
[191] Art 1.
[192] Art 3.
[193] Art 4.
[194] *Ibid.*
[195] Art 5.
[196] Eg Q Du and J Davis, 'Local Enactment of Urban Environmental Management Law: The Case of Shenzhen City, China' (2001) 6 *Asia Pacific Journal of Environmental Law* 79.
[197] Richardson, above n 129.
[198] World Bank, *Export Processing Zones* (World Bank, 1992); G Sivalingam, *The Economic and Social Impact of Export Processing Zones: The Case of Malaysia,* ILO Working Paper no 66 1994; Asian Development Bank, above n 39, 31; Richardson, above n 129.
[199] Zarsky, above n 175; and T Tsai, *Corporate Environmentalism in China and Taiwan* (Palgrave Macmillan, 2002).

It also appears doubtful that TNCs are regulated relatively leniently compared to their domestic counterparts. It is worth pausing to look again at China, which has attracted more foreign investment than any developing country. Ostensibly, Chinese environmental law applies equally to all entities, whether a TNC, state-owned enterprise (SOE) or a domestic private company.[200] The procedures governing approval of foreign investments seek to 'encourage' projects that use renewable resources or new pollution control technology, and to 'prohibit' or 'restrict' projects that inter alia seriously pollute the environment or endanger human health.[201] Furthermore, in practice foreign investment projects 'are almost always monitored at the national level . . . because of the widely acknowledged fact that local regulators may be overly sensitive to the need to attract outside investment'.[202]

Existing research suggests that TNCs' investment in China are regulated more stringently than domestic firms' investment. Klee and Thomas argue that, 'because many Chinese officials consider international companies to have more resources and more experience in meeting pollution-control requirements, they often expect them to be in full and immediate compliance with the requirements'.[203] Sims found that authorities are much more likely to collect environmental fines from foreign companies 'that are believed to have deep pockets', than from SOEs, which are often at the margins of solvency.[204] Huang suggests that the foreign investor enterprise–government relations are typically at 'more arm's length' than equivalent relations between regulators and domestic enterprises.[205] Concomitantly, foreign enterprises are also less likely to be immersed in local political networks (*guanxi*), which can impede impartial enforcement of the law.[206]

Whereas the letter of the law is more likely to be applied to foreign entities, a pragmatic and tolerant approach is often displayed towards local enterprises.[207] Enforcement action against SOEs is less likely than against foreign enterprises because SOEs function as more than mere factories. Because they provide important local social services to workers and their families, such as housing and health care,[208] many SOEs are allowed to continue operations despite grave

[200] See generally Y Huang, 'One Country, Two Systems: Foreign-Invested Enterprises and Domestic Firms in China' (2003) 14 *China Economic Rev* 404; GO White, 'Enter the Dragon: Foreign Direct Investment Laws and Policies in the PRC' (2003) 29 *North Carolina Journal of International Law & Commercial Regulation* 35.

[201] Wang, above n 45. Listed in State Environmental Protection Administration, available at www.zhb.gov.cn/english/chanel-3/chanel-3-end-2.php3?chanel=3&column=2.

[202] Zhang and Ferris, above n 130, 50.

[203] JE Klee and FC Thomas, 'An Evolving Environmental Framework' (1997) 24 *China Business Rev* 34, 39.

[204] H Sims, 'One-fifth of the Sky: China's Environmental Stewardship' (1999) 27 *World Development* 1227, 1241.

[205] Huang, above n 200, 410.

[206] *Ibid*, 409.

[207] U Steger *et al*, *Greening Chinese Business* (Greenleaf Publishing, 2003) 25.

[208] X Ma and L Ortolano, *Environmental Regulation in China: Institutions, Enforcement and Compliance* (Rowman and Littlefiled, 2000) 145.

pollution.[209] These polluting SOEs, argue Klee and Thomas, 'frequently lack the capital to invest in clean technologies to meet the requirements of environmental regulation and, thus, receive deferential application, if any, of environmental requirements'.[210]

While the East Asian experience suggests that we should eschew sweeping criticisms of TNCs and their environmental regulation, there is nonetheless plenty of evidence from other jurisdictions to give cause for concern.[211] Arguably, some international co-operation and regulation of TNCs would seem necessary.[212] The right of states to regulate TNCs operating within their jurisdiction is explicitly recognised in international law.[213] But, as shown above, the national exercise of such prerogatives is another matter. The UN has pursued proposals for international regulation of TNCs without much success. In 1972, the UN Economic and Social Council established the Commission on Transnational Corporations for the purpose of formulating a Code of Conduct on Transnational Corporations. The draft Code it prepared in 1984 was eventually abandoned for lack of government support.[214]

Among other initiatives, the OECD also prepared in 1976 (and revised in 2000) a set of non-binding Guidelines for Multinational Enterprises, but these are aimed specifically at improving the climate for investment and restricting discrimination against TNCs.[215] In recent years, more effort has gone into creating a more liberal environment for TNC investment, for example through the North American Free Trade Agreement's provisions for investor protection,[216] the aborted Multilateral Agreement on Investment,[217] the proposed Free Trade Area of the Americas[218] and numerous bilateral investment treaties.

The corporate sector itself has advanced policies and procedures for corporate social and environmental responsibility. Environmental issues have become more included in businesses' decision-making, through new markets for environmental technologies and subscription to relevant corporate environmental systems and

[209] JG Taylor and Q Xie, 'Wuhan: Policies for the Management and Improvement of a Polluted City' in Cannon, above n 133, 143.

[210] Klee and Thomas, above n 203.

[211] M Flahery, *Multinational Corporations and the Environment: A Survey of Global Practices*. (Center for Environmental Management, Tufts University, 1990); DL Levy, 'The Environmental Practices and Performance of Transnational Corporations' (1995) 4(1) *Transnational Corporations* 44.

[212] RJ Fowler, 'International Environmental Standards for Transnational Corporations' (1995) 25(1) *Envtl L* 1.

[213] UN Charter of Economic Rights and Duties of States 1974, 14 ILM 251, Art 2(2).

[214] (1984) 23 ILM 626. But recently the UN revived work on developing standards to govern TNCs. In 2003 it released its draft UN Norms on the Responsibilities of Transnational Corporations and other Business Enteprises with Regard to Human Rights: UN Doc E/CN.4/Sub.2/2003/12/Rev.2 (2003)

[215] OECD, *The OECD Declaration and Decisions on International Investment and Multinational Enterprises: Basic Texts* (OECD, Nov 2000) 5–6.

[216] (1993), 32 ILM 289, ch 11.

[217] OECD, *The MAI Negotiating Text* (OECD, 1998); for a critique, see M Berlow and T Clarke, *The MAI: A Charter for Corporate Rule* (Lorimer Publications, 1997).

[218] See www.ftaa-alca.org.

codes of conduct.[219] The Business Council of Sustainable Development and the International Chamber of Commerce have promoted initiatives in these areas.[220] A flourishing corporate social responsibility movement has already arisen among some companies predominantly in developed nations.[221] It has been structured in part around corporate environmental management systems, such as the International Standard Organisation (ISO) 14000 series.[222] Some TNCs see advantages from taking the environment more seriously, including access to green consumer markets, material savings from greater energy efficiencies, as well as helping them to pre-empt unwanted external environmental regulation.[223]

F. Conclusion

This chapter has canvassed some of the salient environmental law developments, setbacks and possible future directions of reform in post-colonial states. Since the end of colonial rule, many developing countries have pioneered extensive environmental laws and policies. Many such initiatives are now framed around concepts of sustainable development. But their implementation has often lagged, and environmental conditions in much of the developing world are worsening to crisis proportions.

There is no single blueprint for more effective environmental governance in these countries for many reasons: they differ in their economic structures and resources, colonial histories, and legal traditions, among many other factors. This chapter has highlighted major differences between East Asia's industrialising economies and the poorest countries of Sub-Saharan Africa. Consequently, it would be naïve to draw simple conclusions about what sustainable development means for the developing world's, evolving environmental legal systems. If anything, the developing countries experience adds further evidence to the arguments made elsewhere in this book that sustainability is essentially a fluid concept in which basic principles and standards are contestable. So far, many post-colonial states have problematically relied on imported foreign precepts of sustainable development. Sustainability's most promising institutionalisation perhaps resides in those countries that realise that policies that address social justice, poverty, fair trade are likely to be the strongest foundations for good environmental governance.

[219] See HS Brown *et al*, *Corporate Environmentalism in a Global Economy: Societal Values in International Technology Transfer* (Greenwood Press, 1998); B Gentry, 'Foreign Direct Investment and the Environment: Bone or Bane?' in OECD, *Foreign Direct Investment and the Environment* (OECD, 1999)21; see further Wood, this vol.

[220] CO Holliday Jr *et al*, *Walking the Talk: The Business Case for Sustainable Development* (Greenleaf Publishing, 2002).

[221] D Crowther and L Rayman-Bacchus (eds), *Perspectives on Corporate Social Responsibility* (Ashgate, 2004).

[222] R Hillary (ed), *ISO 14001: Case Studies and Practical Experience* (Greenleaf Publishing, 2000).

[223] For detailed consideration of these 'voluntary' approaches see Wood, this vol.

Index

www.ingramcontent.com/pod-product-compliance
Ingram Content Group UK Ltd.
Pitfield, Milton Keynes, MK11 3LW, UK
UKHW020202290926
15471UKWH00005B/1021

9 781841 135441